ISBN 978-0-484-21176-5
PIBN 10015142

EX-PRESIDENT J. C. FRASIER, Bloomfield, Iowa.

Served as director of the Iowa State Agricultural Society, from January 1894, until December 1900, when he was elected vice-president of the Iowa Department of Agriculture. He served two years as vice-president being elected president of the department in Debember of 1901, serving one year 1902.

THE

Iowa Year Book of Agriculture

3.

ISSUED BY THE IOWA DEPARTMENT OF AGRICULTURE.

CONTAINING

EXTRACTS OF NEW ROAD LAW, ETC.; REPORT OF THE STATE FARMERS INSTITUTE FOR THE YEAR 1902; STATE AGRICULTURAL CONVENTION FOR THE YEAR 1902; MEETING OF THE STATE BOARD OF AGRICULTURE; REPORT OF MEETING OF STATE FAIR MANAGERS;

WITH

EXTRACTS FROM THE REPORTS OF THE STATE DAIRY COMMISSIONER; STATE DAIRY ASSOCIATION; IOWA AGRICULTURAL EXPERIMENT STATION; IOWA WEATHER AND CROP SERVICE; IMPROVED STOCK BREEDERS' ASSOCIATION; IOWA SWINE BREEDERS' ASSOCIATION;

ALSO

PAPERS READ AT COUNTY FARMERS' INSTITUTES; REPORTS OF LOCAL COUNTY AND DISTRICT FAIRS; STATISTICS AND OTHER THINGS OF INTEREST.

EDITED BY

J. C. SIMPSON,

SECRETARY STATE BOARD OF AGRICULTURE.

DES MOINES:
B. MURPHY, STATE PRINTER.
1903.

Rev. W. M. Beardshear, deceased, late president of the Iowa State College of Agriculture and Mechanic Arts.

STATE BOARD OF AGRICULTURE.

LETTER OF INTRODUCTION.

OFFICE OF
THE STATE BOARD OF AGRICULTURE,
CAPITOL BUILDING,
DES MOINES, IOWA. February 2, 1903.

To THE MEMBERS OF THE STATE BOARD OF AGRICULTURE—

GENTLEMEN—In compliance with Chapter Fifty-Eight, Acts of the Twenty-Eighth General Assembly, creating a Department of Agriculture, and Section Ten of said Chapter providing for the publication of THE IOWA YEAR BOOK OF AGRICULTURE, by the Secretary, I have the honor to transmit herewith the third annual "Iowa Year Book of Agriculture," for the year 1902.

JOHN C. SIMPSON,
SECRETARY STATE BOARD OF AGRICULTURE.

PART I.

·

ROADS.

ROAD LAW IN IOWA.

The enactment of the Anderson road law (which becomes operative on the first Monday in April of this year) and several other bills which were enacted by the Twenty-ninth General Assembly, has greatly changed the system of collecting and expending the property road tax in this state, and we have received numerous inquiries, from parties in this and other states, for information concerning the law as it now exists.

We are of the opinion that the changes which have been made in our road laws will meet with general favor, when they are once in operation and understood, and that they will result in great improvement in our public roads.

Believing there is a general desire for information on this subject, we have had compiled the laws relative to levying, collecting and expending the road tax in this state, as they will exist after the sixth day of next April when the new law becomes operative, which, by permission of the Executive Council of the State of Iowa, we give herein.

J. C. SIMPSON,
Secretary State Board of Agriculture.

TITLE VIII—OF WORKING ROADS.

CHAPTER 2. CODE OF 1897.

Section 1528. POWERS AND DUTIES OF TRUSTEES. The township trustees of each township shall meet on the first Monday in April, or as soon thereafter as the assessment book is received by the township clerk, and on the first Monday in November, in each year. At the April meeting said trustees shall determine:

1. The rate of property tax to be levied for the succeeding year for roads, bridges, guideboards, plows, scrapers, tools and machinery adapted to the construction and repair of roads, and for the payment of any indebtedness previously incurred for road purposes, and levy the same, which shall not be less than one nor more than four mills on the dollar on the amount of the township assessment for that year, which, when collected, shall be expended under the direction and order of the township trustees;

2. The amount that will be allowed for a day's labor done by a man, and by a man and team, on the road. To certify to the board of supervisors the desire for an additional road tax, of not to exceed one mill, to be levied in whole or in part by the board of supervisors as hereinafter provided. At the November meeting, they shall settle with the township clerk and supervisors of roads.

Section 1529. GENERAL TOWNSHIP FUND—CLERK TO GIVE BOND—CUSTODY OF IMPLEMENTS. The trustees shall set apart such portion of the tax provided in the preceding section as may be necessary for the purpose of purchasing the tools and machinery and paying for the guideboards mentioned therein, and the same shall constitute a general township fund; and they shall require the township clerk to give bond in such sum as they think proper, conditioned as the bonds of the county officers, which bond, and the sureties thereon, shall be approved by them. Said clerk shall have charge of and properly preserve and keep in repair such tools, implements and machinery as may be purchased, and may determine at what time the supervisors of the several road districts may have the use of the same or any part thereof, and he shall be responsible for the safe keeping of the same when not in the custody of some one of the supervisors, and shall receive such compensation as they shall provide to be paid out of such fund.

Section 1530. COUNTY ROAD FUND—HOW LEVIED AND PAID OUT. The board of supervisors of each county shall, at the time of levying taxes for other purposes, levy a tax of not more than one mill on the dollar of the assessed value of the taxable property in

its county, including all taxable property in cities and incorporated
towns, which shall be collected at the same time and in the same manner as other taxes, and be known as the county road fund, and paid
out only on the order of the board for work done on the roads of the
county in such places as it shall determine; but so much of the county
road fund as arises from property within any city or incorporated town
shall be expended on the roads or streets within such city or town, or
on the roads adjacent thereto, under the direction of the city or town
council; and the county treasurer shall receive the same compensation
for collecting this tax as he does for collecting corporation taxes.
Money so collected shall not be transferable to any other fund nor used
for any other purpose. The board of supervisors shall levy such an
additional sum for the benefit of such townships as shall have certified
a desire for such additional levy, as provided for in section fifteen hundred and twenty-eight of this chapter; but the amount for the general
township fund and the county road fund shall not exceed in any year
five mills on the dollar.

Section 1531. EXPENDITURE. It shall, at the regular meeting in
April, determine from the auditor's and treasurer's books the amount
of money collected and credited to said road tax fund. It shall also
determine the manner in which said tax shall be expended, whether by
contract or otherwise.

Section 1532. CONSOLIDATION OF TOWNSHIP INTO ONE ROAD
DISTRICT. The board of township trustees of each civil township in
this state, at its regular meeting in April, 1903, shall consolidate said
township into one road district, and all road funds belonging to the road
districts of said township shall at once become a general township road
fund, out of which all claims for work done or material furnished for
road purposes prior to the change, and unsettled, shall be paid.

Note.—This section makes the one road district plan mandatory.

Section 1533. DUTY OF TRUSTEES. Where the one road district
plan is adopted, the board of township trustees shall order and direct
the expenditure of the road funds and labor belonging or owing to the
township; may let, by contract, to the lowest responsible, competent
bidder, any part or all of the work on the roads for the current year, or
may appoint a township superintendent of roads, to oversee, subject to
the direction of the board, all or any part of the work, but it shall not
incur an indebtedness for such purposes unless the same has been or
shall at the time be provided for by an authorized levy; and shall order
the township road tax for the succeeding year paid in money and collected by the county treasurer as other taxes. It shall cause both the
property and poll road tax to be equitably and judiciously expended for
road purposes in the entire road district; shall cause at least seventy-
five per cent. of the township road tax locally assessed to be thus expended
by the fifteenth day of July in each year; shall cause the noxious weeds
growing in the roads to be cut twice a year, when necessary, and at such
times as to prevent their seeding, and it may allow any land owner a

reasonable compensation for the destruction thereof, when growing in the roads abutting upon his land. If a superintendent of roads is employed, it shall fix the term of office, which shall not exceed one year, and the compensation, which shall not exceed three dollars a day; and no contract shall be made without reserving the right of the board to dispense with his services at its pleasure.

Section 1534. QUALIFICATION OF OFFICERS. The trustees shall require the township clerk, contractor and superintendent, contemplated in this plan, each to qualify as other township officers, and to execute a bond with approved sureties for twice the amount of money likely to come into their hands, respectively.

Section 1535. DAY'S WORK. Eight hours' service for a man, or man and team, shall be required for a day's work; but except on extraordinary occasions no person shall be required to go more than three miles from his place of residence to work, and, for the purposes of the one road district plan, the residence of a man with a family shall be construed to be where his family resides, and for a single man, it shall be at the place where he is at work.

Section 1536. CONTRACTORS AND SUPERINTENDENTS. The powers, duties and accountability imposed on road supervisors, so far as may be, under the one road district plan, shall apply to contractors, superintendents and assistants.

Section 1537. TOWNSHIP SYSTEM TAKES EFFECT. In all cases where the one road district plan for the township shall have been adopted, it shall be competent for the township trustees to designate when the same shall take effect as to the working of the roads.

Section 1538. COMPENSATION OF TRUSTEES, TREASURER AND CLERK. The trustees shall receive the same compensation per day for time necessarily spent in looking after the roads as thy do for other township business; the county treasurer shall receive the same per cent for collecting the road taxes here contemplated that he does for collecting corporation taxes; and the township clerk shall receive two per cent of all the money thus coming into his hands and by him paid out for road purposes.

Section 1539. FURNISH PLAT. The township clerk shall furnish each road supevisor a copy of so much of the map or plat furnished him by the county auditor as relates to the roads in his district, and from time to time shall mark thereon the changes in or additions to such roads as the same are certified to him by the auditor, which map or plat shall be transferred by him to his successor in office.

Section 1540. TAX LIST—LEVY OF PROPERTY ROAD TAX FOR 1903—DELINQUENT ROAD TAX FOR 1903. He shall within four weeks after the trustees have levied the property road tax for the succeeding year, certify said levy to the county auditor, who shall enter it upon the tax books for collection by the county treasurer as other taxes. And he shall, not later than the fifteenth day of April, make out and deliver to the superintendent of roads a list of all persons required to pay road poll tax under the provisions of this act. To enable him to make out such list, the assessor shall furnish the clerk of said township, before the first day of April of each year, a complete copy of the assessment lists of said township for that year, which shall be the basis of such poll tax list. Provided, that the property road tax for the year 1903, shall be levied as heretofore, that it shall be paid in cash and shall be collected by the superintendent of roads appointed by the trustees or the township clerk, as the board of trustees shall determine and direct. Provided, further, that all delinquent road tax for the year 1903, shall be certified to the county auditor by the clerk of each township, for collection as provided by section one thousand five hundred and forty-two (1542) of the code, as amended by this act.

Note.—Section 1528 provides that, at the regular meeting on the first Monday in April (1903), the board of township trustees shall determine the rate of property road tax to be levied for the succeeding year (1904), which section 1540 provides the township clerk shall certify to the county auditor, who shall enter it upon the tax books for collection by the county treasurer as other taxes. Section 1540 also provides, that the property road tax for the year 1903, shall be levied as heretofore (on the first Monday in April), that it shall be paid in cash and be collected by the superintendent of roads or the township clerk. Therefore, at the regular meeting in *April, 1903*, the trustees are required to levy the property road tax for both 1903 and 1904.

Section 1542. DELINQUENT TAX CERTIFIED. He shall on or before the second Monday of November of each year, make out a certified list of all property, including lands, town lots, personal property and property otherwise assessed, including assessments by the executive council on which the road tax has not been paid in full, and the amount of the tax charged on each separate assessment or parcel of said property, designating the district in which the same is situated and transmit the same to the county auditor, who shall enter the amount of tax on the lists the same as other taxes, and deliver the same to the county treasurer, charging him therewith which shall be collected in the same manner as county taxes are collected. In case the township clerk shall fail or neglect to make such return, he shall forfeit and pay to the township for road purposes a sum equal to the amount of tax on said property, which may be collected by an action on his bond.

Section 1543. TAXES PAID TO CLERK. The county treasurer shall, on the last Monday in April and October of each year, pay to the township clerk all the road taxes belonging to his township which are at such time in his hands, taking the duplicate receipts of such clerk therefor, one of which shall be delivered by the treasurer to the trustees on or before the first Monday in May and November in each year.

Section 1544. ROAD TAXES APPORTIONED. The county auditor shall provide a column in the tax lists, in which shall be shown the road district to which the road taxes belong, and the treasurer, when he pays the same to the several township clerks, shall furnish each a statement, showing the district or districts to which the money belongs, and the amount to each.

Section 1545. SUPERINTENDENT—QUALIFICATION. Each road superintendent or contractor shall give bond in such sum and with such security as the township clerk may require (but in no case shall a township trustee sign such bond as surety), conditioned that he will faithfully and impartially perform all the duties required of him, and devote all moneys that may come into his hands by virtue of his office according to law.

Section 1547. POSTING TAX LIST. The road supervisor shall, within ten days after receiving the tax list, post up in three conspicuous places within his district written notices of the amount assessed to each taxpayer in said district.

Section 1548. HOW TAX EXPENDED. The road supervisor shall cause all road taxes collected by him to be expended for road purposes on or before the first day of November of that year, seventy-five per cent. of which shall be expended before the fifteenth day of July, except the portion set apart for a general township fund, which shall be by him paid over to the township clerk from time to time as collected, and his receipt taken therefor.

Section 1549. IN EACH DISTRICT. The money tax levied upon the property in each district, except that portion set apart as a general township fund, whether collected by the road supervisor or county treasurer, shall be expended for road purposes in that district only.

Section 1550. WHO TO PERFORM LABOR. The road supervisor shall require all able bodied male residents of his district, between the ages of twenty-one and forty-five, to perform two days' labor upon the roads, between the first days of April and September of each year.

Section 1551. NOTICE OF TIME AND PLACE—RECEIPTS. The road supervisor shall give at least three days' notice of the day or days and place to work the roads to all persons subject to work thereon, or who are charged with a road tax within his district, and all persons so notified must meet him at such time and place, with such tools, implements and teams as he may direct, and labor diligently under his direction for eight hours each day; and for such two days' labor the supervisor shall give to him a certificate, which shall be evidence that he has performed such labor on the public roads, and exempt him from performing labor in payment of road poll tax in that or any other road district for the same year.

Section 1552. PENALTY FOR FAILURE TO ATTEND OR WORK. Each person liable to perform labor on the roads as poll tax, who fails to attend, either in person or by satisfactory substitute, at the time and place directed, with the tools, implements or teams required, having had three days' notice thereof, or, appearing, shall spend his time in idleness, or disobey the road supervisor, or fail to furnish him, within five days thereafter, some satisfactory excuse for not attending, shall forfeit and pay him the sum of three dollars for each day's delinquency; and in case of failure to pay such forfeit within ten days, he shall recover the same by action in his name as supervisor, and no property or wages belonging to such person shall be exempt from execution therefor. Such action shall be before any justice of the peace in the proper township. The money, when collected, shall be expended on the public roads.

Section 1554. REPORT. The superintendent of the township shall report to the township clerk on the first Monday in April and November of each year, which report shall embrace the following items:

1. The names of all persons in his district required to perform labor on the public road, and the amount performed by each;

2. The names of all persons against whom actions have been brought, and the amount collected of each;

3. The names of all persons who have paid their property road tax in labor, and the amount paid by each;

4. The amount of all money coming into his hands by virtue of his office and from what sources;

5. The manner in which moneys coming into his hands have been expended, and the amount, if any, in his possession;

6. The number of days he has been employed in the discharge of his duty;

7. The condition of the roads in his district, and such other items and suggestions as he may wish to make, which report shall be signed and sworn to by him, and filed by the township clerk in his office.

Section 1555. TAX COLLECTED AND CERTIFIED. If it appears from such report that any person has failed to perform the two days' labor required, or any part thereof, and that the road supervisor has neglected to collect the amount of money required to be paid in case of such failure, the clerk shall add the amount required to be paid to such person's property tax and certify the same to the auditor, who shall enter it on the proper tax list, and the treasurer shall collect the same.

Section 1556. SHADE TREES—TIMBER—DRAINAGE. The road supervisor shall not cut down or injure any tree growing by the wayside which does not obstruct the road, or which stands in front of any town lot, inclosure or cultivated field, or any ground reserved for any public use, and shall not enter upon any lands for the purpose of taking timber therefrom without first receiving permission from the owner or owners of said lands, nor destroy or injure the ingress or egress to any property, or turn the natural drainage of surface water to the injury of adjoining owners; but it shall be the duty of the supervisor to use strict diligence in draining the surface water from the public road in its natural channel, and to this end he may enter upon the adjoining lands for the purpose of removing obstructions from such natural channel that impede the flow of such water.

Section 1557. LIABILITY FOR UNSAFE BRIDGE OR HIGHWAY. When notified in writing that any bridge or portion of the public road is unsafe, the road supervisor shall be liable for all damages resulting therefrom, after allowing a reasonable time for repairing the same. If there is in his district any bridge erected or maintained by the county, he shall, on receiving written notice of its unsafe condition, obstruct the passage thereon, and notify at least one member of the board of supervisors, in writing, of its condition. If he fails to obstruct and notify, he shall be liable for all damages growing out of the unsafe condition thereof, occurring after the time he is so notified, and while he neglects to obstruct such passage. Any person who shall remove such obstruction shall be liable for all damages occurring to any person resulting therefrom, but nothing herein contained shall be construed to relieve the county from liability for the defects of said bridge.

Section 1558. EXTRAORDINARY REPAIRS. For making such repairs as are required in the preceding section, the road supervisor may call out any or all of the able bodied men of the district in which they are to be made, but not more than two days at one time without their consent, and persons so called out shall be entitled to receive a certificate from him of the number of days' labor performed, which shall be received in payment for road tax for that or any succeeding year, at the rate per day established for that year.

Section 1559. PENALTY. Any able bodied man, duly summoned, who fails to appear and labor by himself or substitute, or send satisfactory excuse therefor, or pay the value thereof in money before an action is brought, shall forfeit and pay ten dollars, to be recovered in an action in the name of the road supervisor, and for the use of the road fund of the district.

Section 1560. OBSTRUCTIONS REMOVED. The road supervisor shall remove all obstructions in the roads, but must not throw down or remove fences which do not directly obstruct travel, until notice in writing, not exceeding six months, has been given to the owner or agent of the land inclosed in part by such fence.

Section 1561. CONDITION—GUIDE BOARDS. The road supervisor shall keep the roads in as good condition as the funds at his disposal will permit, and shall place guide boards at such crossroads and at the forks of the roads in his district, which shall be made out of good timber, well painted and lettered, and placed upon good substantial hard wood posts, to be set four feet in, and at least eight feet above ground.

Section 1562. CANADA THISTLE—WRITTEN NOTICE. The road supervisor, when notified in writing that any Canada thistles or any other variety of thistles are growing upon the lands or lots within his district shall cause a written notice to be served on the owner, agent, or lessee of such lands or lots, if found within the county, notifying him to destroy said thistles within ten days from the service of said notice, and in case the same are not destroyed within such time, or if such owner, agent or lessee is not found within the county, then the road supervisor shall cause the same to be destroyed, and make return in writing to the board of supervisors of his county, with a bill for his expenses or charges therefor, which in no case, shall exceed two dollars per day for such services, which shall be audited and allowed by said board and paid from the county fund, and the amount so paid shall be entered up and levied against the lands or lots on which said thistles have been destroyed, and collected by the county treasurer the same as other taxes, and returned to the county fund.

Section 1562-a.—WEEDS—DUTY OF ROAD SUPERINTENDENT. It shall be the duty of road supervisors to cause to be cut, near the surface, all weeds on the public roads in their respective districts between the fifteenth day of July and the fifteenth day of August of each year. But nothing herein shall prevent the land owner from harvesting the grass grown upon the roads along his land in proper season.

Section 1563. RUSSIAN THISTLE—NOTICE. No owner or occupant of any land or lots, or corporation or association of persons owning, occupying or controlling land as right of way, depot grounds or other purposes, or public officer in charge of any street or road, shall allow to grow to maturity thereon the Russian thistle or salt wort (*salsoli kali*, variety *tragus*). It shall be the duty of every person or corporation so owning, occupying or controlling lands, lots or other real property, or any road supervisor or other public officer having charge of any street or road, to cut, burn or otherwise entirely destroy such thistles growing on such premises, right of way, road or street, before the same shall bloom or come to maturity; and any person, corporation or public officer neglecting to destroy all such thistles as aforesaid, after receiving notice in writing of their presence, shall be deemed guilty of a misdemeanor and be punished accordingly. It shall be the duty of any person knowing of the presence of Russian thistles upon any premises, lands, lots, streets, roads or elsewhere, at any time after the first day of July, to give notice immediately to any member of the board of trustees of the township in which thistles are growing; or if within a city or town, then to give notice to the mayor, recorder or clerk thereof; who shall immediately give notice in writing to the owner, occupant, or person or corporation in possession or control thereof; and if not destroyed by such owner or occupant or person in possession in proper time to prevent maturity, cause their total destruction, the costs thereof, together with the costs of serving notice, to be paid out of the county funds upon the certificate of the township trustees or the council, as the case may be, which board shall cause the sum so paid to be levied as a special tax against the premises upon which the thistles are growing, and against the person or corporation owning or occupying the same; which amount shall be collected by the county treasurer as other taxes, and paid into the county fund. Where township trustees have received notice, as aforesaid, of the presence of such thistles upon lands owned by the United States or this state, it shall be their duty to cause their destruction, and the costs thereof, upon proper certificate of the amount, shall be paid out of the county fund.

Section 1564. INFORMATION—BULLETIN. A bulletin shall be prepared by the professor of agriculture of the agricultural college, briefly describing by words and cuts the Russian thistle, with the best known means of staying its progress and effecting its extermination, which shall be printed by the state printer at public expense, from time to time, in such numbers as the secretary of state and said professor of agriculture may direct to supply the demand. A sum of money sufficient to pay for the cost of printing and making suitable plates for illustrating said bulletin is hereby appropriated from any funds in the state treasury not otherwise appropriated.

Section 1565. DISTRIBUTION. The secretary of state shall furnish to the agricultural college such number of said bulletins as it may desire to circulate, and also to county auditors, on their requisition, such number as may be necessary to supply all township and town or city officers with copies, and a sufficient number to supply all farmers desiring the same.

Section 1566. SETTLEMENT WITH SUPERVISOR. The road supervisor shall, on the first Monday in November, meet the township trustees, at which time there shall be a settlement of their accounts connected with the road fund, and after payment the trustees may order such distribution of the fund remaining in the hands of the township clerk as may be expedient for road purposes, which shall be paid out as ordered by them.

Section 1566-a. ITEMIZED ACCOUNT—DUTY OF TRUSTEES. That the trustees of each township shall take (make) and file with the board of supervisors on or before the first Monday in each year a full and itemized account verified by the township clerk showing each item of expenditures and receipts of all moneys received and disbursed during the preceding year for road purposes in said township, which report shall remain on file with the county auditor, and a copy thereof shall be published in the published report of the proceedings of the January session of the board of supervisors.

Section 1566-b. MEANING OF "ROAD SUPERVISOR." That wherever the term "road supervisor" appears in the code and amendments thereto it shall be held so far as applicable to mean the superintendent or contractor.

Section 1567-b. ACTS IN CONFLICT. That all acts and parts of acts in conflict with the provisions of this act, are hereby repealed.

Note.—The above section is a part of Chapter 53, Acts of the Twenty-ninth General Assembly, and has special reference to any act or part of an act in conflict with the intent of that particular law.

Section 1568. NEGLECT OF DUTY—PENALTY. A supervisor failing to perform the duties required of him by this chapter shall forfeit and pay, for the use of the road fund of his district, the sum of ten dollars, to be collected by an action by the township clerk in his name.

Section 1569. TURNING TO RIGHT. Persons on horseback or vehicles meeting each other on the public roads shall give one-half of the same, turning to the right. A failure in this regard shall make the delinquent liable for all damages resulting therefrom, together with a fine not exceeding five dollars, which fine shall be devoted to the repair of the roads in the district where the violation occurred but no prosecution shall be instituted except on complaint of the person wronged.

Section 1570. TRIMMING HEDGES. Owners of osage orange, willow or any other hedge fence along the public road, unless the same shall be used as a windbreak for orchards or feed lots, shall keep the same trimmed, by cutting back within five feet of the ground at least once in every two years, when so ordered by the trustees of their respective townships, and burn or remove the trimmings so cut from the road.

Upon a failure to comply with the foregoing provision the road supervisor shall immediately serve notice in writing upon the owner of the hedge to trim the same, and if he fails to do so for sixty days thereafter, such supervisor shall cause the same to be done at a cost not exceeding forty cents per rod, which shall be paid out of the road fund, and make return thereof to the township clerk, who shall, in certifying the lands upon which the road tax has not been paid, include the lands along which the hedge has been trimmed, together with the amount paid therefor, which shall be collected by the county treasurer in the manner other county taxes are collected.

Where the one district system is adopted as provided in this chapter, it shall be the duty of the township trustees to enforce the foregoing provisions.

Section 1571. STEAM ENGINES ON ROADS—PENALTY. Whenever any engine driven in whole or in part by steam power is being propelled upon a public road, or is upon the same, the whistle thereof shall not be blown, and those having it in charge shall stop it one hundred yards distant from any person or persons with horses or other stock in or upon the same, and at a greater distance away if they exhibit fear on account thereof, until they shall have passed it, and a competent person shall be kept one hundred yards in advance of such engine to assist in any emergency arising from frightened animals, and to prevent accidents. In crossing any bridge or culvert in the public road, or plank street crossing in any city or town, four sound, strong planks not less than twelve feet long, each one foot wide and two inches thick, shall be used, by placing and keeping continuously two of them under the wheels. A failure to comply with either of the provisions of this section shall be a misdemeanor, punishable by imprisonment in the county jail not more than thirty days, or by a fine of not more than $100, and, in addition, all damages sustained may be recovered in a civil action against the violator, and in no case shall the county be liable for damages occurring to any engine or separator.

EARTH ROADS.

ELDRIDGE—UNITED STATES DEPARTMENT OF AGRICULTURE BULLETIN.

INTRODUCTION.

Drainage is the key to success in making earth roads, and constant watchfulness is the sure means of keeping them up after they are once well made. Water is destructive to any road, especially to a dirt road therefore, drainage that will at once carry away rainfall or melting snow is absolutely necessary. Again, little breaks in the road may be made by rain or by a heavy load at any time, and if not repaired immediately will grow into mud holes, especially in the winter, and these mud holes easily and rapidly develop into an almost impassable mire. But frequent inspection and a little work will keep the road in good condition and with less cost than under ordinary methods. With good drainage established in building the road and frequent inspection to keep the drainage efficient and to mend promptly small injuries to the surface, the earth roads of the United States could be maintained in a much higher state of usefulness than at present, and at considerably lower cost.

The aim in making a road is to establish the easiest, shortest and most economical line of travel. It is therefore desirable that roads should be firm, smooth, comparatively level, and fit for use at all seasons of the year; that they should be properly located so that their grades shall be such that loaded vehicles may be drawn over them without great loss of energy; that they should be properly constructed, the roadbed graded, shaped and rolled; and that they should be surfaced with the best available material suited to their needs.

It is to be hoped that all the heavy traffic roads in the United States can be macadamized, graveled, or otherwise improved in the not distant future; but owing to the absence in many places of rock, gravel, or other hard and durable substances with which to build good roads, and by reason of the excessive cost of such roads where suitable material is scarce, the majority of our public highways will of necessity be composed of earth for many years to come. It is fortunate, therefore, that under favorable conditions of traffic, moisture, and maintenance the earth road is the most elastic and most satisfactory for pleasure and for light traffic. The condition of the common roads in this country, especially in the Middle West, is so deplorable at certain seasons of the year as to operate as a complete embargo on marketing farm products. It therefore behooves every interested citizen to know something about the location, drainage, construction and maintenance of the earth road, and it will be the object to present in this paper the fundamental principles of earth-road construction and maintenance and to furnish instruction and advice to the road builders whose facilities are limited and who are so often supplied with only inferior materials.

LOCATION.

The grade is a most important factor in the location of any kind of road, and a common error in the laying out of roads is made in the endeavor to secure routes covering the shortest distance between fixed po.nts. For this purpose the road is often made to go over a hill instead of around it. To illustrate the folly of this practice, it will be observed that the bail of a bucket is no longer when held in a vertical position than in a horizontal. Just so the road halfway around the hill or the valley is sometimes no longer than the road over the hill or through the valley. The difference in the length even between a straight road and one that is slightly curved is less than many suppose. For instance if a road between two points 10 miles apart were made to curve so that the eye could see no farther than a quarter of a mile of it at once, its length would exceed that of a perfectly straight road between the same points by only 150 yards. Furthermore, graceful and natural curves conforming to the lay of the land add beauty to the landscape and enhance the value of the property.

ERRORS AND THEIR CORRECTION.

One of the chief difficulties with the average country road through the United States is the steep grade. Many of the steeper ones are too long to be reduced by cutting or filling on the present lines, and if this should be done it would cost more, oftentimes, than a change of location. Many of our roads were originally laid out without any attention being given to general topography, natural drainage, or road materials. In most cases they followed the settlers' path from cabin to cabin, or ran along the boundary lines of farms regardless of grades and direction. Most of them remain today where they were located years ago and where a very large expense of energy and material have been wasted in trying to travel and haul loads over them, and in endeavoring to improve their deplorable condition. It is a great error as well as poor economy to continne to follow these primitive paths with our public highways. A more advisable course would be to employ a civil engineer to change their location as was done recently at Knoxville, Tenn. (Fig. 1.)

Another and perhaps greater error in location is made in the West by continuing to lay out roads on section lines. These sections are all square, with sides running north, south, east and west. The principal reason for this practice seems to be the desire to have the roads follow the boundary lines of farms, townships and counties. A person wishing to cross the country in any direction must follow a series of rectangular zigzags, sometimes crosing and recrossing hills and valleys which would be avoided if the roads were located without reference to farm or county lines. This would often take much more of one farm than another, but the inequality of burden could be adjusted by a money payment for the excess.

Fɪɢ. 1.—The road from Knoxville to the Experiment Station farm formerly went up one steep hill A Y, and down another, Y Z. The relocated road, A to C, is comparatively level and much shorter.

In the prairie State of Iowa, for example, where roads are not as steep as in many other states, there is a greater number of roads having steep grades, and on an average the grades are steeper, than are found in the mountainous republic of Switzerland. A great saving could be effected by relocating many of them.

In Maryland the old stage coach road running from Washington to Baltimore makes almost a "bee line," regardless of hills or valleys. The grades in places are as steep as 10 or 12 per cent,*where by skirting the hills the road might have been made almost level, or by running it less abruptly up the hills which had to be ascended the grades might have been reduced to 3 or 4 per cent.

DISADVANTAGES OF HEAVY GRADE.

Straight roads are best, other things being equal, but in hilly countries straightness should always be sacrificed to reduce grades. Hilly roads often become covered with ice or slippery soil, making them very difficult to ascend with loaded vehicles, as well as dangerous to descend. Water rushes down them during rainy weather at such a rate as to wash

*Per cent of grade means so many feet up, vertically, in 100 feet horizontal. A 10 per cent grade, for instance, means a rise of 10 feet for each 100 feet of horizontal distance traveled. There being 5,280 feet in a mile a 1 per cent grade means a rise of 52 8 feet in that distance. A 10 per cent grade means a rise of 528 feet, and a 12 per cent grade means a rise of 634.6 feet to the mile.

great gaps along their sides or to carry the surface material away. As the grade increases in steepness either the load has to be diminished in proportion or additional horsepower used.

Accurate tests have shown that a horse which can pull on a level road 1,000 pounds, on a rise of—

    1 foot in 100 feet can draw only ....900 pounds.
    1 foot in 50 feet can draw only............... 810 pounds.
    1 foot in 44 feet can draw only............... 750 pounds.
    1 foot in 40 feet can draw only............... 720 pounds.
    1 foot in 30 feet can draw only............... 640 pounds.
    1 foot in 25 feet can draw only ....540 pounds.
    1 foot in 24 feet can draw only............... 500 pounds.
    1 foot in 20 feet can draw only............... 400 pounds.
    1 foot in 10 feet can draw only............... 250 pounds.

It will therefore be observed that when the grades are 1 foot in 44 feet a horse can draw only three-fourths as much as he can on a level. Where the grade is 1 foot in 24 he can draw one-half as much, and on a grade of 1 foot in 10 he is able to draw only one-fourth as much as on a level road. The difficulty as well as the cost of hauling is therefore necessarily increased in proportion to the roughness of the surface or steepness of the grade.

LIMIT OF GRADE ALLOWABLE.

The proper grade for any particular road must be determined by the conditions and requirements existing on that road. The ideal grade is, of course, a level, but as the level road can seldom be obtained in rolling countries, it is well to know the steepest allowable grades for ordinary travel.

It has been found by experiment that a horse can, for a short time, double his usual exertion. From the above table we find that a horse can draw only about one-half as much on a 4 per cent grade as he can on a level road. As he can double his exertion for a short time, he can pull twice as much more and the slope or grade which would force him to draw that proportion would therefore be a 4 per cent grade. On this slope, however, he would be compelled to double his ordinary exertion to draw a full load, and this will therefore be the maximum grade if full loads are to be hauled. Most road builders prefer 3 per cent grades to those of 4 per cent where they can be secured without additional expense, but in some places it is necessary, for various reasons, to increase the grades to 5 per cent. With the exception of mountainous regions, where steeper grades are often unavoidable, the aim should be, on all public highways which are traveled by heavily loaded vehicles, to keep the grade down to 3 or 4 per cent and never to let it exceed 5 per cent.

QUESTIONS OF MATERIAL AND EXPOSURE.

If the road must be constructed out of the materials over which it passes, it is often possible to select a route where the soil is better adapted for the purpose than that found where first located. For instance, soils adjacent to the beds of streams or in morasses and swamps, being close and pervious, are very difficult to surface and subdrain, but routes over such ground can often be avoided by locating the road upon higher ground, where the natural drainage is better.

Another consideration in choosing the line of travel is that roads on slopes having a southern or western exposure can be much more satisfactorily and economically maintained than those located on eastern or northern slopes.

DRAINAGE.

Water is the most destructive agent to a road, and yet if a few simple principles are followed it can be easily dealt with. Earth is more susceptible to the action of water and more easily dissolved and moved by it than any other road material, and for this reason too much attention can hardly be given to the drainage of roads. Drainage alone will often change a bad road into a good one, while, on the other hand, the best road may quickly go to ruin for lack of drainage.

Most country roads are too flat on top to shed water; indeed, a great many of them are not only flat but concave, the center being the lowest part; in other words, their crowns are inverted. The sides of the roads are often square shoulders (Fig. 2) which obstruct the water on its pas-

FIG. 2.—Improper cross section contrasted with proper cross section.

sage to the side drains, and as a result the water lies on the surface until it is absorbed by the material or evaporated by the sun. It is often allowed to stand in the traveled way until the material softens and yields to the impact of the horses' feet and the action of the wheels of the vehicles; the holes and ruts rapidly increase in number and size; wagon after wagon sinks deeper and deeper, until the road becomes utterly bad. (Fig. 3.)

The importance of drainage has been emphasized in the statement that the "three prime essentials to good roads are, first, drainage; second, better drainage; third, the best drainage possible." On open or pervious soils, surface drainage, in connection with heavy rolling, is usually quite satisfactory, provided the slope is good and the traffic is not too heavy; but for the close, impervious, alluvial and clayey soils subdrainage is sometimes necessary. With heavy traffic, narrow tires and long-continued rains, freezes and thaws, the surface of any dirt road is liable to be completely destroyed, and in this case the only remedy is a consolidated mass or crust of gravel or broken stone, forming a roof to keep out and carry off the water. This, of course, constitutes "the best drainage possible."

SURFACE DRAINAGE.

STEEP SLOPES.—On ground with good natural underdrainage, as on hillsides, surface ditches are sufficient to carry off surface water from rain or snow. In order to prevent washouts on steep slopes, however, it sometimes becomes necessary to construct water breaks; that is,

FIG. 3 —Poorly crowned and badly drained roadbed.

broad, shallow ditches so arranged as to catch the surface water and carry it each way into the side ditches. Unfortunately, some road builders have an idea that the only way to prevent hills, long and short, from washing, is to heap upon them a large number of those ditches known in different sections of the country as "thank-you-ma'ams," "breaks," or "hummocks," and the number they sometimes squeeze in upon a single hill is astonishing. Such ditches retard traffic to a certain extent, and often result in overturning vehicles; consequently they should never be used until all other means have failed to cause the water to flow into the side channels. They should never be allowed to cross the entire width of the road diagonally, but should be constructed in the shape of the letter V, with the point uphill. This arrangement permits teams following the middle of the road to cross them squarely and thus avoid the danger of overturning. These ditches should not be deeper than is absolutely necessary to throw the water off the surface, and the part in the center should be the shallowest.

SHAPE OF CROSS SECTION ON HILLS.—Where a road is con-
structed on a hill, the slope from the center to the sides should be slightly steeper than on the level. The reason for this is that every wheel
track on an inclined roadway becomes a channel for carrying down the
water, and unless the curvature is sufficient these tracks are quickly
deepened into water courses which cut into and sometimes destroy the
best surface. (Fig. 4.) The slope must be sufficient to lead the water

FIG. 4.—Poorly crowned earth road on steep hillside.

quickly into the side ditches instead of allowing it to flow down the middle of the road, but should not be so steep that water will rush off the
surface so quickly as to wash away berms or shoulders. The cross section, consisting of two plane surfaces sloping uniformly from the center
to the sides, is perhaps a little better for a steep grade than the ciren-
lar form because of the danger of overturning, which would necessarily
be increased if the circular or elliptical cross section were used. Water
should never be permitted to flow long distances or to collect in puddles
by the roadside, for it soon sinks into the adjacent soil and softens the
foundation of the road. Open drains should not be allowed to become

deep and dangerous from neglect of proper outlets. Careful attention should be given to the regularity of the grade and fall of the side ditches.

PROTECTION FROM "GULLYING."—Where the road is built on a steep grade some provision should be made to prevent the washing of the gutters into deep gullies. This can be done by paving the bottoms and sides of the gutters with bricks or field stones. In order to make the flow as small as possible in side ditches it is often advisable to construct frequent outlets into the adjacent fields or streams, or, if possible, to lay underground pipes or blind drains with screened openings into side ditches at frequent intervals. The size of side ditches should depend upon the amount of water they are expected to carry. If possible they should be located at least 3 feet from the edge of the traveled roadway.

CONSTRUCTION OF SIDE DITCHES.—All side ditches should have a gradual fall of at least half a foot in every 100 feet. Their sides, particularly those sloping toward the roadway, should be broad and flaring, so as to prevent accidents as well as the caving in of their banks. Their bottoms should be wide enough to carry the largest amount of water that is likely to flow through them at any one time. Sometimes the only ditches necessary to carry off the surface water are those made with the road machine. The blade of the machine may be set at any desired angle, and when drawn along by horses or by a traction engine cuts into the surface and spreads the earth uniformly over the traveled way. (Fig. 5.)

FIG. 5.—Road machine at work on earth road.

CROSS DRAINS.

NEED OF QUICK DRAINAGE.—To drain a road surface properly, water should be gotten rid of before it gains force or headway or has time to damage the road. It is just as economical, and far more practical, for the road builder to put in four or five 12-inch culverts at such points as may be found necessary in a mile of roadway as it is to carry water along the higher side of the road a mile or more and be compelled to deliver it in a 24-inch culvert.

LAYING CULVERT PIPES.—In the laying of culvert pipes or box drains the upper end or intake should be kept sufficiently high to insure a proper flow of the water. The excavations for culvert pipes should be straight and of uniform grade, so as to provide a regular, even fall from the upper to the lower side of the road. Earth should be carefully tamped around such pipes and they should be placed at sufficient depth to prevent their being broken by the traffic. In order to protect pipe culverts from damage when discharging water under full pressure it is desirable that the joints be cemented and that the ends of the culvert be protected with masonry. (Fig. 6.) Under no circumstances should a

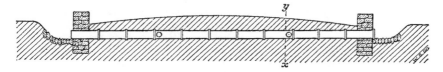

FIG 6.—Culvert pipe with ends protected by masonry.

ridge over the culvert pipe be allowed; for it not only endangers the life of the culvert, but is a menace to traffic.

SIZE OF CULVERT PIPES.—In determining the size of the culvert pipe it is necessary to consider the area to be drained as well as the maximum rainfall. One inch of rainfall per hour gives about 22,600 gallons of water for each acre, and it is probably true that only about one-half of this amount ordinarily reaches the culvert within the same hour. This fact should also be considered in determining the size of pipe or culvert required. The following table shows the capacity of round vitrified clay pipes ordinarily used for culverts:

SIZES OF DRAINPIPE REQUIRED FOR CULVERTS IN PROPORTION TO CAPACITY AND FALL.

DIAMETER.	3-inch fall per 100 feet.	6-inch fall per 100 feet.	9-inch fall per 100 feet.
	Gallons per minute.	*Gallons per minute.*	*Gallons per minute.*
6 inches	129	183	224
8 inches	265	375	460
9 inches.....	355	503	617
10 inches..........	463	655	803
12 inches.......	730	1,033	1,273
15 inches..............	1,282	1,818	2,224
18 inches.............	2,022	2,860	3,508
24 inches	4,152	5,871	7,202

It will be seen from the above table that as the fall increases the capacity of the pipe is increased in proportion. Observing this principle, it is often possible to decrease the size of the pipe and by so doing decrease the cost of culverts. For instance, a 24-inch culvert pipe with a fall of only 1 inch in 100 feet has a capacity of about 2,300 gallons per minute, while a pipe of only half that size, when given a fall of 3 feet to the 100, has a capacity of about 2,500 gallons per minute. Fall is therefore a very important factor in disposing of water.

CONCRETE DRAINS AND CULVERTS.

Culvert or bridge construction forms a very important branch of highway improvement. Large sums are often appropriated for this actual improvement of the road. It would be impossible, in the space allowed here, to include many details in reference to bridge work, but it is so very important that it can not be passed by without comment.

Wooden bridges and culverts wear, warp and decay so rapidly under the action of rain, sunshine, frost and traffic that their usefulness is very short, and their maintenance consequently very expensive. Wherever the expenditure will justify, and the materials can be had, it is much more economical in the long run to use sewer pipe, home made or manufactured concrete pipe, or stone, brick or concrete arches to carry the water under the road. These materials are much more durable than timber, and if protected from frost and traffic they can be considered permanent.

Molds for making concrete pipe can be constructed of spring steel and can be secured at a foundry for a few dollars. They are composed of an inner and outer casing resumbling a stovepipe, and should be about 2½ feet in length, the inner one being less in diameter, so as to leave a space between the two of from 3 to 5 inches. The diameter of the pipe may be regulated as necessity may require. These molds are set on end on a solid base, with the smaller mold inside. The concrete is then mixed, having a proportion of about one part Portland cement to five parts of clean gravel, and while one person shovels it into the mold another rams it down with an iron rammer until the casing is full. The clamps are then loosened and the pipe left to dry, after which it can be placed in position.

The construction of concrete, brick and stone arches is equally simple. A false work of common boards can be erected in the shape of the arch desired, a perfect semicircle being preferred. If concrete is to be used this arch should be constructed of smooth-planed boards closely boarded up against the work as it progresses. The concrete can then be mixed in the proper proportions and rammed well into position until moisture appears on the surface. The false work for concrete arches should be substantial and should be left in position for ten days or two weeks. Enough earth should be placed on the top of concrete arches, culverts and drains to protect them from the wheels of vehicles.

SUBDRAINAGE.

WET LANDS.—Where a road runs through low, wet lands, or over retentive or clayey soils, surface drainage is not all that is required. In cold climates, where if water is allowed to remain in the substructure and form a deep frozen crust, the surface is heaved up by frost and destroyed by the wheels of vehicles on thawing. If the subsoil is kept dry, frost has nothing to act upon, and to this end subdrainage is essential. It is undoubtedly true that many of our worst roads could be improved by subdrains as to yield benefits to their users many times greater in value than the cost of the drains themselves. Subdraining earth roads is neither expensive nor difficult, but, like all other kinds of road work, it takes good judgment.

Hundreds of miles of our roads are located on low level lands and on springy soils, and thousands of miles in the prairie states are for many weeks in the year wet and well-nigh impassable. (Fig. 7.) Such

FIG. 7.—Western road that could be made tolerable by drainage.

roads may be greatly benefited by subdrainage. When wet weather or perennial springs exist in the soil under the road, they should be tapped by blind drains of stone or brick or clay pipe (Fig. 8), leading diagonally

FIG. 8.—Cross sections showing construction of subdrain.

to the side ditches. Where sidehill roads are springy, deep open ditches on the higher sides will often suffice, otherwise subdrainage must be resorted to.

REMEDY FOR FREEZING.—When water is permitted to remain in the foundation of a road through the winter, it freezes, expands and loosens the soil. One hundred volumes of water make, when frozen, 109 volumes of ice. When the warm spring weather comes, this ice melts, and, as there is no place for the water to go, the ruts in the springy soil become deeper and deeper until wagons often sink to their hubs and horses flounder laboriously through the resulting slough. (Fig. 9.) **The**

FIG. 9.— Poorly drained earth road.

remedy, therefore, is to get rid of the water in the foundation of **the** road, and get rid of it before it has time to soften the substructure or freeze. For this purpose it is advisable to construct horizontal drains under the roadway, which should empty into the open drains or the natural water courses at frequent intervals. (Fig. 10.) If the road sur-

FIG 10 —Cross sectio of underdrained road. If lower outlets can be secured subdrains may be placed as at *a* and *b*, or directly under side ditches.

face is composed of retentive soils, such as fine clay, there should be two or three drains; but if the soil is open or pervious, and if two drains are considered too expensive, one drain in the center of the traveled way (Fig. 11) will often be found to suffice.

DEPTH AND FALL OF SUBDRAINS.—The depth to which drains should be laid will depend upon the character of the soil as well as the depth of the frost line. These drains can be placed parallel with the surface of the road in rolling countries, provided they have a fall of not less than three-tenths of a foot to each 100 feet. Outlets into side ditches, or preferably into the adjacent fields or streams, should be provided as

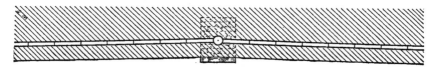

FIG. 11.—Longitudinal section at "*x y*," on figure 7, showing discharge of subdrain into culvert pipe.

often as practicable. The size of the drains will depend upon the distance between outlets as well as the grade of the ditch. Ordinarily if the distance is 500 feet or less, 3-inch pipe will answer. If the distance is greater than that, the size of the tile should be increased about 1 inch in diameter for every 400 feet in length.

In the prairie states, where the roads are practically level, it is sometimes advisable, to construct blind ditches of vitrified clay tiles, into which the contents of the subdrains above mentioned can be discharged. (Fig. 12.) Water can be carried a long distance in well-laid

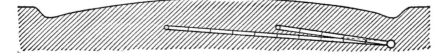

FIG. 12.—Cross section of underdrained level road, showing method of discharging subdrains into a larger and lower pipe.

pipes with but little fall. Six or 8-inch pipes can be placed alongside the road, with a fall of 1 inch to the 100 feet, *if carefully laid*, with the discharge in a river or stream. Such drains can be run several miles with the fall mentioned, and their size increased, if necessary, as they approach the place of discharge. The level road can then be drained by giving the subdrains a fall of about 3 inches to each 100 feet. The upper end of these drains can be from 12 to 18 inches below the surface, and the lower end, where the discharge is made into the large pipe, can be 3 or 4 feet below the surface. The operation can then be repeated until the entire surface is underdrained. (Fig. 13.)

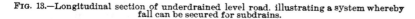

FIG. 13.—Longitudinal section of underdrained level road. illustrating a system whereby fall can be secured for subdrains.

LAYING OF SUBDRAINS.—The greatest care should be exercised in the laying of subdrains. They should be carefully graded and should have a continuous and even fall throughout their entire length. But it requires no special engineering skill or expensive instruments to lay

:an ordinary tile drain. Any intelligent farmer with a home-made level ·(Fig. 14) can do the work sufficiently well. If drains are not laid with

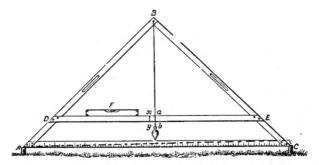

FIG. 14.—Grade level of light planed boards, made accurately as shown. To establish a 5 per cent grade, for example, bring the instrument to a level along the line of the drain by use of spirit level F; mark center $a b$; then raise the updrain end through a distance one-twentieth of the length of the base line A C. The plumb line will cross the board D E in some line away from the center, $a b$. Mark this crossing as $x y$. The same grade can then be found at any point in the drain by leveling till plumb line crosses at $a b$, and then raising the updrain end till the plumb line crosses again at $x y$. A uniform grade can thus be maintained.

:great care, low points are liable to form where the mud and sand will ·collect and reduce the flow, and finally choke the drains altogether. ·(Fig. 15.) After the drains have been carefully laid, the ditch should

FIG. 15.—Poorly laid drain tile.

then be half filled with rough, broken stones, or if no stones are available, with broken brickbats, coarse sand, gravel, cinders or some other imperishable material. A little hay, sod or brush packed around the tile ·to prevent silt from washing in and clogging the drains will be useful. ·The ditch can then be tamped full of firm earth. Care should be exer·cised in keeping the drains open and unobstructed at outlets. Under·drains are useless unless outlets are provided; for if the outlet is ob·structed, the water is kept standing in the drains until it soaks and ·softens the foundation.

CONSTRUCTION.

PROPER CROSS SECTION.

The wearing surface of a road must be, in effect, a roof; that is, the ·section in the middle must be the highest part, and the traveled road·way should be made, by consolidation, as impervious to water as possible, so that the rainfall or melting snow will flow freely and quickly into the gutters alongside. Probably the best shape for the cross section of the earth road is an arc of a circle with a gradual fall from the center to the sides of about 1 in 20, after the surface has been thoroughly rolled or compacted by traffic. (Fig. 12.) Such a surface can be constructed and repaired with the road machine, and a roller can be used upon it to good advantage. When the surface is not kept smooth and compact the crown should be a little steeper than 1 in 20, but should under no circumstances exceed 1 in 12. If the crown is too great, the traffic will follow the middle of the road, and this will result in making ruts and ridges which retard the prompt shedding of the water into the side ditches. Too much crown is as detrimental as too little.

CLEARING THE ROADWAY.

Where new roads are to be built, all stumps, roots, vegetable matter, rocks, etc., should be removed from the surface and the holes should be filled in with suitable material, carefully and thoroughly tamped. In forming a permanent embankment no perishable material should be used. If suitable material is discovered in the subgrade, it should be removed and replaced with good material which should be tamped or rolled until smooth and compact. As stated above, the longitudinal grade should be kept down to 3 or 4 per cent if possible and should, under no circumstances, except in mountainous regions, exceed 5 per cent; while that from the center to the sides should be maintained at about 5 per cent. After the roadbed has been brought to the required grade and crown, a roller should be secured and used in consolidating the material. All ruts or depressions discovered during the rolling should be leveled off and rerolled. (Fig. 16.)

WIDTH AND ELEVATION.

The width of the traveled way will depend upon the requirements of traffic. Sometimes 12 feet will suffice, but 18, 24 and 40 feet are the usual widths for the various classes of country traffic. Where the road is likely to be improved with brick, stone or gravel, sufficient width should be provided for a hard road for winter use and a space alongside for summer use. The right of way should be much wider than the traveled way, in order to provide for widening when traffic requires it.

In level countries where the natural drainage is poor it is very desirable that roads should be elevated above the subgrade or surrounding ground. For this purpose the required material may be secured by widening the side excavations or from cuttings on the line of the roadway by means of road machines, elevating graders, or modern dumping wagons. When the earth is brought up to the desired level it should be thoroughly mixed by harrowing, then trimmed with a road machine, and finally rolled with a road roller, the weight of which should be gradually increased by ballast as the rolling progresses. During the rolling the surface should be sprinkled with water if the character of the soil requires such aid for its proper consolidation. The crown of the roadway should be carefully maintained during the rolling by the addition of earth as needed.

FIG. 16.—Properly crowned and well-drained earth road. Note slope from center to sides. Road was worked with road machine and horse roller in March; photograph taken June 1, about 48 hours after long, hard rain.

TREATMENT OF CLAY ROADS.

On clay roads a thin layer of sand, gravel or ashes will prevent the sticking of clay to the roller or to the wheels of vehicles. Clay soils as a rule absorb water quite freely and soften when saturated, but water does not pass through them readily. When used alone clay is the least desirable of all road materials, but roads composed of clay may be treated with sand or small gravel from which a comparatively hard and compact mass is formed, which is nearly impervious to water. Material of this character found in the natural state commonly known as "hardpan" makes, when properly applied, a very solid and durable road. In soil composed of a mixture of sand, gravel and clay, all that is necessary to make a good road is to crown the surface, keep the ruts and holes filled, and the ditches open and free.

TREATMENT OF SAND ROADS.

While clay alone never makes a good road, except in dry weather, sand alone never makes a good road except in wet. The more the drainage of a sand road is improved the more deplorable becomes its condition. Nothing will ruin one quicker than to dig a ditch on each side and drain all the water away. The best way, therefore, to make such a road firm is to keep it constantly damp. This can be done by planting shade trees along its sides to prevent the evaporation of water, or by growing upon the surface of such sand roads a thick turf, preferably Bermuda grass. Roads running through loose sand may be improved by mixing clay with the sand and slightly crowning the surface.

For the temporary improvement of earth or sand roads, any strong, fibrous substance, especially if it holds moisture, such as refuse of sugar-cane or sorghum, and even common straw, flax, swamp grass or pine needles will be useful. Spent tan bark is sometimes beneficial and wood fiber in any form is excellent. Enough sand or earth should be thrown over such roads to keep them damp and to protect them from catching fire.

IMPORTANCE OF ROLLING.

Earth is composed of small, irregular fragments which touch each other at points, leaving voids between. When the earth is broken up and pulverized these voids are almost equal in volume to the solid particles, and as a result the earth will absorb almost an equal volume of water. In the building or maintaining of earth roads it is, therefore, very desirable that these small, irregular particles be pressed and packed into as small a space as possible, in order that surplus water may not pass in and destroy the stability of the road. To this end rolling is very beneficial. The work of maintaining dirt roads will be much increased by lack of care in properly rolling the surface. (Fig. 17.)

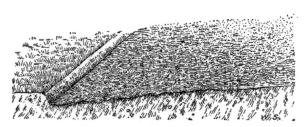

FIG. 17.—Section of unrolled earth road showing a loose, soft surface.

After the material has been placed on the surface, it should not be left for traffic to consolidate or for rains to wash off into the ditches, but should be carefully surfaced and then rolled. If loose earth is left in the middle of a road, the narrow-tire wheels will cut it and knead it into uneven ridges and ruts, which hold water, and this ultimately results, if in the winter season, in a sticky, muddy surface, and in dry weather in covering the surface with dust. If, however, the surface be crowned with a road machine and properly rolled with a heavy roller (Fig. 18), it can usually be made sufficiently firm and smooth (Fig. 19) to sustain the traffic without deep rutting and to resist, in a large measure, the penetrating action of the water. Such work should be done while the soil is in a plastic state, when it will pack. The rolling not only consolidates the small particles of earth and leaves less space for water, but puts the road in proper shape for travel immediately. If there is anything more trying on man or beast than traveling over an unimproved

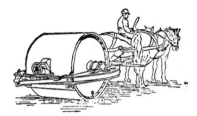

FIG. 18.—Reversible road roller.

road, it must be to travel over one which has just been worked by the slipshod methods followed in many places.

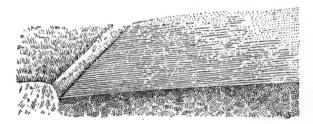

FIG. 19.—Section of properly rolled earth road, showing a firm, smooth surface

MAINTENANCE AND REPAIRS. FILLING HOLES AND RUTS.

With earth roads there is a pronounced tendency to rut, and when ruts begin to appear on the surface, great care should be used in selecting new materials with which they should be immediately filled. Every hole or rut in the roadway if not tamped full of some good material, like that of which the road is constructed, will become filled with water and will be made deeper and wider by each passing vehicle. A hole which could have been filled with a shovelful of material will soon need a cartful. The rut or hole to be repaired should be cleared of dust, mud or water and just sufficient good fresh earth placed in it to be even with the surrounding surface after having been thoroughly consolidated with the pounder. Sod should not be placed on the surface, neither should the surface be ruined by throwing upon it the worn-out material from the gutters alongside. Ruts and holes should not be filled with stone nor gravel unles a considerable section is to be so treated; for if such material is dumped into the holes or ruts, it does not wear uniformly with the rest of the road, but produces lumps and ridges and in many cases results in making two holes for every one repaired.

USE OF ROAD MACHINES IN MAKING REPAIRS.

Reversible road machines are often used in drawing the material out of ditches to the center of the roadway, which is left there to be washed

again into the ditches by the first heavy rain. A far more satisfactory
method, when the roadway is sufficiently high, and where a heavy roller
cannot be had, is to trim the shoulders and ridges off and smooth the
surface with the machine. This work should begin in the center of the
road, and the loose dirt should be gradually pushed to the ditches and
finally shoved off the roadway or deposited where it will not be washed

FIG. 20.—Road surface under weight of heavy block of stone supported on wide tires.

back into the ditches by rain. Where this method is followed, a smooth,
firm surface is immediately secured, and such a surface will resist the
action of rain, frost, and narrow tires much longer than one composed
of loose and worn-out material thrown up from the ditches.

In making extensive repairs, plows or scoops should never be used,
for such implements break up the compact surface which age and traffic
have made tolerable. Earth roads can be rapidly repaired by a judicious use of road machines and road rollers. The road machine places
the material where it is most needed and the roller compacts and keeps
it there. These two labor-saving machines are just as effectual and
necessary in modern road work as the mower, self-binder, and thrasher
are in modern farm work. Road machines and rollers are the modern
inventions necessary to satisfactory and economical earth-road construction and repair. Two good men with two teams can build or repair
more road in one day with a roller and road machine than many times
that number can with picks, shovels, scoops, and plows, and do it more
uniformly and more thoroughly.

USE OF WIDE TIRES AND SIMILAR MEANS.

One of the best ways to prevent the formation of ruts and to keep earth roads in repair is by the use of wide tires on all wagons carrying heavy burdens. (Fig. 20). In most foreign countries they not only use from 4 to 6 inch tires on market wagons but on many of the four-wheel freight wagons, in addition to wide tires, the rear axles are made 14 inches longer than the front ones, so that the hind wheels will not track and form ruts. Water and narrow tires aid one another in destroying the roads, while on the other hand wide tires are road-makers. They roll and harden the surface, and every loaded wagon becomes, in effect, a road roller. The difference between the action of a narrow tire and a wide one is about the same as the difference between a crowbar and a tamper; the one tears up and the other packs down. By using wide tires on heavy wagons the cost of keeping roads in repair would be greatly reduced. The introduction in recent years of wide metal tires which can be placed on the wheels of any narrow-tired vehicle at a nominal cost, has removed a very serious objection to the proposed substitution of broad tires for the narrow ones now in use. The formation of deep ruts has been prevented on some of the toll roads of Pennsylvania by lengthening the doubletrees on wagons and by hitching the horsees so that they will walk directly in front of the wheels, a device worthy of consideration.

REGULAR, PROMPT, SYSTEMATIC ATTENTION.

VALUE OF FREQUENT INSPECTION.—Earth roads should be repaired particularly in the spring and fall of the year, but the mistake of letting them take care of themselves during the balance of the year should not be made. The greatest need of the common road in this country is daily or weekly care. A road receiving daily attention will require no extensive repairs, and, instead of becoming worse, will gradually improve. It is minute and frequent homeopathic treatment that the earth road needs. It is obviously not within the scope of this paper to discuss the relative merits of the statute-labor, cash-tax, and contract systems of building and maintaining roads, but it will be remarked in passing that so long as the farmers continue to "work" the roads in a shiftless manner and whenever it best suits their convenience, so long will they have bad roads.

It has been stated that England and France are justly noted for their excellent roads, and both have the labor-tax system, and that, therefore, it is possible to have good roads under the labor-tax system. This statement, although partially true, is not conclusive argument in favor of the way in which Americans "work out" their road tax in most of the states.

It makes little difference what system they have in Europe or what system we have in this country—the matter of greatest importance in road maintenance is constant attention. All the important French and English roads receive daily attention and are always maintained in an excellent manner, but our application of the statute-labor system too often results in promoting rather than in diminishing the defects which should be overcome. If the great railroads of the country were to practice the methods ordinarily used in maintaining our public highways they would probably be compelled to go into the hands of receivers before many months.

SUCCESS IN VERMONT.—It would, therefore, seem wise for us to adopt a modified form of the system which has been so successful in England, France and other European countries and which has been recently introduced in the State of Vermont; that is, of dividing the roads into certain lengths and alloting each length to a section man, caretaker, or farmer. Every one is familiar with this system as applied to railway maintenance, and it is a matter worthy of note that in Vermont the general results from its application are "that much better roads are secured at less expense, and the tax rate for highways has been reduced each year as the roads grow better and as we learn to maintain them free from damage at less cost."*

Our most important country roads could be divided into sections or beats varying in length from 1 to 5 miles, according to the importance of the road and the condition of its surface. A good road man, who lives on the section or beat, should be placed in charge, and it should be his duty to devote a few hours each week to the filling of small ruts or holes and to protecting the road from damage by running water. If the road is a very important one, and if the funds will permit, such a care-taker should, by all means, be employed the year round. There is always plenty of work to do in keeping roads clean, free from loose stones and rubbish; in cutting weeds and cleaning drains and side ditches. In fact, the care-taker should be on the road, rain or shine, and particularly in wet weather, in order to find the uneven places in the road as well as to note the existing defects in surface and subdrainage. On account of the great efficiency and economy of this plan it is becoming general in the State of Vermont, and it has made the roads of France and other European countries famous. It is the application of the old adage, "A stitch in time saves nine."

CONCLUSION.

The methods of earth road construction and maintenance given above are those generally practiced by the most successful road builders. They are simple and in the main inexpensive. They are based entirely on a thorough system of drainage, and if applied with common sense and judgment, according to the particular needs of each locality, better roads are sure to follow. While the earth road, under favorable traffic and climatic conditions, can be made excellent and satisfactory in every way, yet it must be borne in mind that the earth road is essentially a light-traffic road. When the traffic of a road increases beyond a certain point it becomes necessary to supply new material to take the place of a large

*J. O. Sanford, state highway commissioner of Vermont.

amount abraded by traffic and carried off by the wind and rain, or the way will soon wear down to such an extent that drainage will become a very difficult problem. As the traffic of most roads increases slowly, the adjacent earth can first be used for repairs, then gravel or crushed stone. These, however, are problems to be solved by those familiar with the local conditions and should be regulated by the requirements of traffic, the availability of material, and the cost of necessary repairs. The large majority of roads for some time to come will require only earth for their construction, and for this reason it is essential to the prosperity of each community that the earth road be properly cared for.

4

PART II.

STATE FARMERS' INSTITUTE.

AGRICULTURAL CONVENTION—PROCEEDINGS OF THE STATE BOARD.

UNDER THE AUSPICES OF THE IOWA DEPARTMENT OF AGRICULTURE.

DES MOINES, IOWA, December 9, 1902.

The annual sesson of the Iowa State Farmers' Institute was held in the rooms of the Agricultural Department at the capitol building, on Tuesday, December 9, 1902. In the absence of President J. C. Frasier, Vice-President W. W. Morrow presided and called the meeting to order at ten o'clock a. m., as per the published program.

The chairman announced the first paper on the program, "How to maintain the fertility of the soil upon a farm devoted to grain raising," which was read by its author, Mr. Henry Parsons, Rockwell City, Iowa, as follows:

HOW TO MAINTAIN THE FERTILITY OF THE SOIL UPON A FARM DEVOTED TO GRAIN RAISING.

Henry Parsons, Rockwell City, Iowa.

This question is of vital importance to the farmer of Northwestern Iowa, it being a country naturally adapted to the growing of grain, and the high price of land making it unprofitable to use it for grazing.

On many farms there is much land that overflows, or is too rough to plow, which must be used for pasture and meadow. This makes it necessary to grow grain continually upon that part which is adapted to grain farming. The West being able to supply us with cattle and sheep cheaper than we can raise them to which we may feed our grain.

And the increasing demand for corn for manufacturing purposes makes the growing of corn profitable.

The question has arisen in my mind; is there no way by which we may take a crop of grain from the ground every year and retain the fertility of the soil as we received it from the hand of nature.

With these thoughts I began to look about to see in what way nature supplied the soil with fertility. I noticed she made use of all dead vegetation. The conclusion I drew was there is enough vegetation left from every crop after the grain has been taken away, if properly saved and returned to the ground, to retain its fertility.

But how to apply this coarse manure, save the stubble and corn stalks, and get a full crop the same year it was put on the ground has been the source of much grief to me. I found that if I plowed under coarse manure and a dry season followed, there was danger of shutting off the supply of water from below, thereby injuring the crop for that year, and to scatter it on top of the ground after it was plowed made it almost impossible to tend a crop of corn.

I once had a field of oats that was lodged so bad I could not get them with a binder, so I turned a bunch of hogs on them, expecting to burn it off after the hogs had eaten the oats. The hogs rooted the ground up and mixed the straw with the soil. I did not burn it, but plowed it the next spring and planted it in corn. The summer was rather dry, but that field had just as good corn as any in the neighborhood. I have noticed that on low flat ground that has a heavy stubble the plow will not scour, but only push through the ground leaving the stubble in rows; that it did not make any difference how dry the season was the heavy stubble did not seem to shut off the supply of moisture from the subsoil. So I came to the conclusion that undecomposed vegetable matter of any kind plowed under did not necessarily shut off the available water stored below, providing it did not make a complete blanket under the furrow.

It has been my plan for a number of years to disc the ground before plowing. By so doing the undecomposed vegetable matter is mixed up with the soil in such a way that it does not break the water connection between the furrow and the under soil.

The spring of 1901 I covered 10 acres with very coarse manure and treated the ground as I have mentioned. This piece of ground was quite high and sloped to the southwest. When the hot winds in July came this 10 acres was the only part of a field of 90 acres that did not have white or dead tassels in it. The corn was a darker color and grew about one and a half feet higher than that that was not manured, and yielded 15 bushels more corn per acre.

It is claimed by some that it is better to well rot all barnyard accumulations before returning it to the soil. My experience has taught me that manure spread upon the field as fast as made, will cover more ground, and will enrich it more than manure that has lain in the barn yard until it was thoroughly decomposed.

There should be kept upon every farm enough live stock to consume all of the roughness that would otherwise go to waste, thereby converting it into money and at the same time increasing its value as a fertilizer.

When sowing spring grain one should estimate the number of acres that can cover that year with barnyard manure, and on what connot be covered with manure, sow clover seed with the grain; giving the clover seed the same covering as the grain. After the grain is harvested do not pasture the clover but give it a chance to grow. The following spring plow that part of the field first on which the manure was spread, leaving the part on which the clover was sown as long as possible before plowing. In this way all the land sown to small grain would be fertilized each year. There can be as much loss of fertility from the way the ground is handled as there is used by the crop. This year has given us some very good examples. Last March and April were very dry and windy months. The ground that had been plowed the fall before blew very badly. Along the edge of some of these fields the dust drifted two feet deep. In some places where the cornstalks had been raked and burned the oats and wheat was blown out so badly there was scarcely half a stand. Where the dust settled on meadow land the grass grew much heavier, which goes to show there must have been a loss to the land from whence it blew.

In June the season changed from very dry to very wet, and now these same fields that blew the worst in the dry weather washed the worst in wet weather. How are these losses to be overcome?

First. I noticed that spring plowing blew scarcely any, and fall plowing that was disced and left ridged did not blow much.

Second. Land that had its cornstalks and stubble burned every year and had not been manured any, blew and washed out a great deal worse than land that had not been burned over and had been kept well fertilized. I have therefore come to the conclusion that it is better to burn nothing, but leave all rubbish on the ground to decay. Plow only in the fall when it is necessary to kill weeds that live over winter, and that as soon after harvest as possible. Never plow over five inches deep or when the ground is muddy. Keep land well drained. Sow clover' every spring with the small grain. All hay and fodder raised on the farm should be fed on the farm. Keep all stock well bedded and haul manure to field as fast as made. Where these principles have been carried out the land has increased rather than diminished in fertility.

CHAIRMAN: This paper, gentlemen, is now open for discussion, and we will be pleased to hear from any of you. Mr. Calderwood, we would like to hear from you.

MR. CALDERWOOD: Mr. Chairman, I believe that I do not care to say anything. I would prefer to hear from some of these older farmers.

CHAIRMAN: Mr. Packard, we would like to hear from you.

MR. PACKARD: Mr. Chairman, I agree, so far as my observations have gone, substantially with all that was said in the paper. In the matter of fall plowing I think that the general opinion is that where the ground is so situated as not to be subject to any wash through the winter, fall plowing is favorable; but where, by any possibility, from the slope there can be a wash as the ground is thawed and frozen during the winter, there is a substantial loss of fertility as the result of fall plowing, and the ground and the crops would be better if the plowing was done in the spring.

I have never before heard of the matter of discing before plowing, to mix the earth with the rubbish. I cannot say as to that, but the thought strikes me that it might be a good plan to get the rubbish and dirt somewhat mixed before it is turned under the furrow. I am not prepared to say as to that but am willing to accept his observations in regard to the matter, and it seems to me a good idea in the end. It will help to get the rubbish under and introduce what the soil wants in the way of humin, which I think is the best thing with regard to it.

J. R. WALLER: Mr. Chairman, in regard to fall plowing, my experience has been this, that by plowing in the fall you plow under a great deal of green vegitation, a great many weeds, which you kill.

My experience has been that it pays to plant the ground I plow in the fall, as far as practicable and as soon as practicable—even in August—I sow the ground to rye, thereby securing fall pasturage of the very best quality, on which I turn my stock all winter and in fact up into the following June. Last year I was away from home, down in North Carolina, and my wife did not turn the stock off as early as I would have done, but she turned them off in June, thinking the crop was probably ruined; but nevertheless I harvested thirty-five bushels of rye to the acre off that crop, notwithstanding that there was at least one-third of it that we could not get on account of its being down.

I have taken the same character of land and plowed it this fall, sowing it to rye. I sowed last spring to clover as soon as the snow was gone sufficiently, sowed it on the ground and harrowed, and

I got a stand right on that rye ground, so that I have a magnificent field of clover on that and if I want to plow it under I have all the humus I need, and thereby keep my land clean.

My experience is that with the character of fall cultivation I have referred to, if the ground is anyway clean, if I plow the rye under I have got a good manure turned under. But where I do not sow clover or use rye, I take my fall plowing and pulverize thoroughly before planting corn, so that it is like a garden. I believe that almost as much is acomplished by this cultivation before planting corn as there is by cultivation afterwards. By so doing I find that my ground is like a garden bed, and that the seed germinates quickly and thrives better.

Another thing; I believe that there is as much trouble with corn in planting too early as in planting too late. I would not plant corn the first day of May under any consideration. I would rather have corn, one year after another, planted the first day of June than on the first day of May, because I believe that the first day of May is out of season.

S. B. PACKARD: I would like to ask the gentleman a question. What objections have you to planting in May providing the conditions are right?

MR. WALLER: My experience has been this: that when corn is planted the first of May the ground, as a general thing, is not warm enough. The climatic situation is not such as to make rapid germination and growth. When the ground gets thoroughly warm and you have it thoroughly worked up, it is in such condition that your corn germinates quickly and when it comes up it has a more rapid growth, has a dark green color and does not get stunted, nor turn yellow by cold nights.

CHAIRMAN: Are there any further remarks by any one? If not, we will proceed with the program. The next paper is "How to Secure a Perfect Stand of Corn" by W. W. Morrow.

HOW TO OBTAIN A PERFECT STAND OF CORN.

W. W. Morrow, Afton, Iowa.

To obtain a perfect stand of corn requires a perfect seed bed and reliable seed. If fall plowing is desired the stubble fields should be plowed early—clover and timothy sod as late in the fall 'as possible. The depth to depend upon the character of the soil.

Spring plowing should be as near planting time as possible. If the ground should be damp the harrow should follow the plow. If the ground is in good condition, the harrowing should be postponed until ready to plant. In that case the harrow will kill the young weeds and also create a dust mulch, which is desirable.

In fall plowing a disk or pulverizer should be used. The same may be used in the spring plowing, if the season is wet, followed by the harrow prior to planting.

Early planting is desirable, but in no case should corn be planted until the ground is in proper condition.

In order to obtain your seed corn, the first thing to do is to get the kind of corn you wish to raise—the variety that will best mature in your latitude. Remember, however, that a small ripe ear is preferable to a large one that will not mature in your locality. To insure good seed, corn should be gathered some time in Sepetember, by going through the best part of your field and selecting ears of uniform size and length. Sufficient husks should be left on the ears to tie together and the corn should be placed in a dry place and left until the following spring, when it should be taken down and shelled off both ends sufficiently to insure an even size of grains which will enable the planter to drop an equal number of grains in a hill, three grains in a hill being sufficient of such seed. Under ordinary conditions corn should be planted two and one-half inches deep. The harrow should follow the planter. This will leave the ground in good condition and give you a perfect stand of corn.

The matter of seed corn is one in which every farmer and stock feeder should be interested. When we take into consideration the facts that the principal grain used in the production of beef, pork and mutton is corn, and that Iowa produces more pounds of meat than any other state, you will agree with me that the members of this Institute, also the members of the State Department of Agriculture should encourage all honest efforts to secure the best possible corn for seed.

CHAIRMAN: I would like to hear from any of the gentlemen present. I see Prof. Holden is here. I would like to hear from him.

PROF. P. G. HOLDEN: Mr. Chairman, I agree with the President in the main, and especially in regard to the one point that he brought out so emphatically, viz.; the importance of selecting ears of uniform size until we have insured an even-sized grain. If there is any one thing more than another that would conduce to the production of four or five or six bushels to the acre increase in Iowa next year, it would be the procuring of even-sized grains, because we must depend upon the planter to plant these and it is entirely mechanical. Last year in selecting the seed for a little over 7,000 acres of ground at the Funk Bros. Farm, Blooming-ton, Ill., we separated the corn and shelled it by ears; each ear was one by itself. That corn was then laid on a table and, a man who had been trained, examined it, and if there was anything wrong with the grains or the shape was not right, the whole ear was thrown out, for we found that the strength of the corn is peculiar to the ear and not to the grain. For example, if there is four or five grains that—you take four or five grains and test them and find them defective, you can be sure the whole ear is weak, and if you plant rows, an ear in each row and you will see the difference. Even though it may have been in a wet, low place, the strong ears will come up all right, while the weak right by the side on the same ground would suffer. So we threw out the whole ear.

We found by taking different planters and putting this corn in and testing them by sorting and kept sorting until we would plant 19 out of 20 hills three grains. Of course with some of the plant-ers we had to drill in a place or two, but we tried to get the ker-nels uniform with the result that we got over ten bushels to the acre more than was ever produced before, and I attribute it more than any one thing to the fact that grains were of uniform size, It takes some time to do this, but it pays. It costs just as much to cultivate the ground for seed not thus selected and when you get through you will certainly be surprised to see how greatly they count.

In regard to the question discussed before, I was interested in it considerably. The matter of discing the ground before plow-ing. For two years I had charge of the growing of about 3,000 acres of seed corn and through some accident we discovered that the ground disced before plowing would retain the moisture long-er and finally we went ahead and made several tests, in which we tested, I suppose, with the disc about five or six hundred acres out of 3,000, and in every case the disced ground went through the dry weather better than the plowed land.

Mr. R. T. St. John: Mr. Chairman: I am much interested in your paper, and greatly interested in what Prof. Holden has told us in regard to securing a good stand of corn and the importance of good seed. All I know about seed corn is from practical knowledge on my farm; and I know this, that I have made the same mistakes in northern Iowa, for the first time, that a great many of our people in our part of the state have made, and that is, trying to raise too large corn. I know some of my neighbors raised good, big, nice corn and I thought I would raise some and improve a little on the size of it in my county, and I discarded my corn that I had been raising, that had been adapted to this soil, and I made the mistake of my life. Some of it is sound and the rest of it is cheap and soft. But I took the precaution to go back to the old plan used when I was a boy, of going into the field and selecting my seed corn and tying it up and drying it—putting it in a good sunny place and letting it be dried thoroughly. I took the precaution not to gather that corn where there were barren stalks. Some say it is in the soil; some say it is in fertilizing the polen that is the cause of these things. Let it be as it may, I think it would be a good thing in selecting the corn to avoid doing so around those barren stalks; and, as has been said here in the discussion, select even kernels, well-formed ears and those which are the most mature, and this year has been a grand one to experiment on that, and I believe that next year I can say to this convention I will make no mistake; I will have a good stand of corn. It is true that if we miss a good stand, we miss a great part of the product of the farm. So that matter of having good seed corn is a very important one.

Mr. Waller: Mr. Chairman: This question of seed corn is one that is paramount to anything else, and I might say, everything else in the state of Iowa, because it is virtually our crop. And while I endorse almost everything the gentlman said on this, I do thing that sometimes we are mistaken. Now, I might say it has been my misfortune to plant a large variety of corn this year. I planted the Iowa Silver Mine which you all know is a large white corn. Some may say plant yellow corn, which is much earlier, whereas my yellow corn was sounder and more fully matured, but much smaller variety, and I didn't get much more than half as much corn or feed per acre. Nevertheless, my immatured crop both in fodder and corn was greater and was worth more acre for acre. I don't think I lost anything by so doing. While our Silver Mine corn for the last four years has ripened well, this year it did not get ripe and I guess this will hold good throughout the whole state.

In regard to the time to plant corn, I believe the great trouble is that we ask of our soil more than it is in condition to bear. I believe that is one cause of the trouble of our having barren stalks. Now, I have made a study of that to a considerable extent. This last fall Mr. Wallace, through Wallaces' Farmer, sent out papers containing questions to be answered by people throughout the state. For the farmers to go through the cornfield and count the barren stalks. I noticed his report when it came in was that there was twenty-five to thirty-five per cent of barren stalks throughout the state reported on. That caused me to go into my field. I counted 200 stalks in a row. In the first 200 stalks I counted only one barren stalk. I then went six rods further and counted 200 stalks in that row and found three barren stalks. I went another six rods and counted 200 stalks and found three barren stalk, so out of 800 stalks I counted in the row I only had seven barren stalks of corn. That set me to thinking as to what might be the reason for this; that while others found from 25 to 35 per cent, I found less than one per cent. I will tell you what the reason was: This land of mine had been thoroughly manured both with horse and cattle manure for the last ten years; has been thoroughly covered with not less than twenty loads per acre every three years. Consequently, the elements were to be found in the soil for germinating, growing and producing and perfecting a stalk of corn in every hill, and, mnd you, these hills had from three to four stalks in every hill, and where there would be less than three stalks in a hill there were two ears to the hill. Consequently, I came to the conclusion that these people that had such a per cent of barren stalks did not put sufficient elements in the soil to make a stalk produce for the amount of seed planted; that if they had enriched their ground more and put the elements in the soil for producing that amount, every stalk would have an ear on it.

Now last season I spent all the season up to July in Virginia and North Carolina, and I was studying the farm conditions down there. I went into the cornfields and saw that they were doing there. They told me that they fertilized their soil in order to produce the largest crops possible, and I universally found this fact: they planted their corn six feet apart in rows with only one stalk in a hill and, mind you, they have no barren stalks at all They have from three to five ears on almost every stalk of corn. I wrote this up for Mr. Trigg's Register. One man just over the line, but joining North Carolina, drew $1,000.00 in premiums on corn where he produced 254 bushels and three pecks per acre. He did this, notwithstanding the fact that he only planted one stalk in a hill and six feet apart. Another man told me he planted but one stalk in a hill and he raised 152 bushels of corn to the acre and he drew $150.00 on it. He told me that this coming year he intended to plant his corn five feet apart and he thought he would raise over 200 bushels to the acre. And I believe it is the elements in the soil. If you put your manures or necessary fertilizers in the soil to raise the corn properly and force it, you will have no barren stalks in your hill; that it is owing to the barrenness of your soil in comparison to the amount of seed planted.

I was talking to a gardener at Charles City, who was engaged in raising cauliflower. He said to me, "Mr. Waller, did you ever know a man in the United States to raise cauliflower seed?" I answered it was a thing I was not informed with reference to. He said, "you can't find a man in the United States that can raise cauliflower seed," He said "I have succeeded in doing it." I said, "How do you account for that?" He said, "I have a piece of sandy land inside of the limits of Charles City, and I have fertilized it so thoroughly,—I have forced it to such an extent that I can raise cauliflower seed." I am not informed on that subject, but he told me that was a fact, and I leave it to you.

I had some corn from thirty miles southwest of Savannah, known as the "Maryland, White." I planted that at Charles City and it ripened well and it produced very well, and two or three stalks per hill. The corn raised there is generally white. It is not what we call large corn, but a medium sized corn and every single ear of corn raised in that country is equal to the very best seed corn we have here that we can pick out for our seed corn.

MR. WALLACE: Mr. Chairman: It would not be hardly best to let the statement made by Mr. Waller go without explanation. The percentage of barren stalks, as has been reported by the paper, is correct, but it was so unusual that we asked the parties to make another count, and owing to that, it reduced the amount —I do not remember just the amount—but my recollection is that the percentage was a little over ten per cent on the second count, in which great care was taken to have it accurate.

MR. D. B. NIMS: Mr. Chairman: I would like to hear something in regard to maintaining the standard of corn. I have not had in a great many years trouble in starting corn, but when it comes to forming the ear I lack a great deal of having a full stand of corn, a great many times having only two or two and a quarter ears to the hill. Two to two and a quarter is about as much as I have been able to succeed in getting. It is not because of the weakness of the seed, but is because after it has got up to 16 or 18 inches in height it dies off. I think that is largely the cause of producing the barren stalk. In years like this while I have not gone through and counted, I think in one field that we husked we would not find one-half of one per cent barren stalks; in fact, we do not find any; but in looking through the field we occasionally found a weak stalk that had no ear, with either a sucker or one stalk alongside, which overshadowed and prevented it succeeding. If some will tell me how to prevent the destruction of the stand, we will have no trouble in procuring the starting off.

THE CHAIRMAN: Professor Holden, can you not answer the gentleman's quetion?

PROFESSOR HOLDEN: Mr. Chairman: He has certainly suggested a very important question, and one I know causes all of us a good many heartaches when we see our harvesting going to pieces; when, instead of having three to three and a quarter ears on an average, we have two. On two hundred and fifty acres out in our fields, we found that during the season just before it began to show the joints, the stalks were very tender, and a heavy wind would break off a great deal of the corn, and that in certain rows the stalks were vigorous, and none of them in the whole eighty rods were broken, and in another right by the side of it there would probably be a third or a quarter of them broken off. And another thing, we found in some of those rows, there was a great difference in the strength of the kernels; the grain was uniform throughout the ear. It is not always so. Sometimes we find one or two kernels very weak, that were started behind the others and remained behind all the year, and were overshadowed; and there is where the barren stalks come in. And the thing that appeals to us most in our work seems to be the need of strong, vigorous, even corn-branch.

I would have been very glad to have had some suggestions myself. But I can say this; that the only thing is for us to take these and experiment with them and help them over, as we are here. It seems to me it would aid more than any other one thing in this corn matter (and we all know that corn lies at the very foundation of our prosperity, as well as the success of every industry in this state), if we could have an appropriation sufficient to carry on experiments throughout the state. Now, as the gentlemen said, corn that has given excellent results in the southern districts will not give best results in the northern part of the state. In Illinois we found about one hundred miles made a great difference in the adaptability of corn, and we ought to co-operate with these men to know what variety is going to give the best results in any particular district. Men in portions of Illinios have year after year gone on raising corn that yielded 50 per cent of what might be raised, and yet, they supposed they had the greatest corn in the whole state. But a great change has come over the condition of things there owing to this study that has been given to the corn question and those varieties that are yielding so small a percentage, just like the condition of trying to make a big animal out of the Jersey and the Hereford. We do not want a variety in the

Courtesy of Wallaces' Farmer.

Wheat on the farm of Wallaces' Farmer, in Warren county, Iowa.   Grain is from Imported Russian seed.

that lies at the foundation of all our prosperity and that nobody has given attention to these things. I wish we had the data that has been gathered at the agricultural college since September, in regard to corn. We have sent out a thousand letters asking for the variety of corn, and a great majority of answers that have come in give, "corn, without any name; corn, without any particular variety; mixed corn"; showing that there has been no attention paid to these things. I know from my experience in Illinois that two-thirds or three-quarters of the people are just growing corn; that is all; just as though they had picked up a dog, no difference what he was, while they wanted a Shepherd dog, and find out it is nothing but a pug-nosed dog. Very great improvement could be made. Where we now grow thirty to fifty bushels to the acre it is just as possible for every farmer to grow forty-five to sixty with the soil that we have. This year on these farms where this corn was selected, as I have before said, on this seven thousand acres, there is fifteen hundred acres of it growing over one hundred bushels to the acre. Think of it. It would amount to a great deal of corn; one hundred and fifty thousand bushels every year; and you know what that means to grow.

CHAIRMAN: The next on the program is a paper by H. C. Wallace, entitled, "Winter Wheat Growing in Iowa."

WINTER WHEAT GROWING IN IOWA.

H. C. Wallace, Associate Editor Wallaces' Farmer, Des Moines, Iowa.

It is most difficult to secure with any degree of satisfaction reliable statistics covering the production of winter wheat in Iowa during the past twenty-five years. The government reports do not separate the winter wheat from the spring. The only figures available are those beginning with the year 1892, and collected by the State Agricultural Society, and the accuracy of these figures, for several years at least, is open to serious question. However, they are the only figures we have and we must use them for what they are worth. According to the best available statistics, the acreage of winter wheat in Iowa for the year 1892 was 235,000 acres. It decreased steadily but slowly until the year 1898, when there were 191,451 acres. The next winter was a most disastrous one on the winter wheat crop and in 1899 but 27,427 acres were harvested. In the neighborhood of 200,000 acres were grown annually up to that time, this winter proved a permanent backset to this crop, for in 1900 but 76,080 acres were harvested, and in 1901 but 49,068 and in 1902 but 48,449. The highest yield of the decade was 19 bushels per acre, in 1895. In 1901 the average yield was 17.6 bushels and in 1892, 17 bushels. The yield for 1902 has not yet been reported, but will probably be heavy. The average for the ten years is 15.6 bushels per acre.

If the acreage of winter wheat in Iowa is anywhere near correctly reported in the figures above quoted, and if it has decreased as steadily and as materially as they seem to indicate, it is pertinent to ask, why? While a small grain crop may not be an absolute necessity to the Iowa farmer, it is a practical necessity. Successful farming in Iowa or in any other state or country makes it imperative that crops be rotated for the double purpose of conserving and restoring fertility and to keep the land in good mechanical tilth. The clovers and grasses are vital in such a rotation in this state, and the study of the best nurse crops for them is an important one. What will be the result of tentative experiments with new leguminous plants, it is too early yet to know, but at the present time clover is the one legume upon which the Iowa farmer can depend to restore to the soil the fertility which he can remove with other crops. Clover he must have, for the double purpose of forming a balanced ration for his growing stock and dairy cows, and to draw upon the air for the nitrogen, the most important element in plant nutrition. The question of securing a stand of clover has become a most serious one throughout the state, and in considering the claims of any small grain crop to recognition, its value as a nurse crop for the young clover must be given much weight.

Assuming that the clover will be sown with a nurse crop, as it is in this state in ninety-nine cases out of every hundred, success in securing an even and thrifty stand will depend largely upon: First, getting it in early and covered properly; second, giving it a sufficiency of sunlight; third, getting the nurse crop off the ground before the hot days of July. Winter wheat enables these requirements to be fulfilled as well or better than does any other small grain crop. First, it is sown in the fall, and the clover can be sown at any time during the fall, winter or spring, at pleasure, preferably on the last snow in the spring. It can be harrowed in, if thought desirable, without injury (usually with positive benefit) to the wheat, if the ground be not too wet. Second, the wheat, if drilled in north and south as it should be, gives the sunlight opportunity to reach the young clover plant nicely. Third, the wheat is harvested early, and as it stands up well the clover suffers little injury by the change from shade to sunshine. As compared with oats, winter wheat is very much superior as a nurse crop. The oats cannot be sowed until the ground is fit to work in the spring, and as a result the clover is not sowed for from one to three weeks later than with wheat. It not infrequently happens that it is not properly covered, owing to frequent spring rains between the time the oats is sowed and the clover, and even when covered sufficiently to germinate, the field is often left rough for a meadow because of the impossibility of getting onto it with a harrow. The oats makes a denser shade than the wheat, thereby increasing the danger of smothering the clover; it is much more likely to lodge, especially on our rich land, and it matures later, thereby increasing very much the danger of the tender plants being killed by the hot sun.

The absolute necessity of a rotation which includes the clovers makes it important to consider the value of a small grain crop in the light of its adaptability as a nurse crop, and measured by this standard winter wheat, in that part of Iowa where it can be successfully grown, is very much superior to oats. But throwing this out of consideration altogether, it is difficult to understand why we are growing so much oats and so little winter wheat. In the year 1901, according to the figures found in the annual report of the United States Department of Agriculture, Iowa grew 4,104,180 acres of oats, the average yield per acre being 25.4 bushels and the average value per acre being $10.73. The average value per acre of our winter wheat the same year was $10.56. For the ten years beginning with 1892, the average yield of winter wheat was 15.6 bushels per acre; the average price on the farm December 1st of each year was 56.8 cents and the average value per acre, $8.86. The average yield of oats for the same period was 31 bushels; the average price on the farm December 1st, 21.8 cents and the average value per acre, $6.75, a difference in favor of winter wheat of $2.11 per acre. For the same period of ten years, the average value per acre of the corn grown in Iowa is given by the same authority as $8.01 per acre, and the average value of rye as $6.88 per acre. In other words, the gross value per acre of the winter wheat crop of Iowa for a period of ten years exceeds the value per acre of the corn crop by 85 cents, of the oats crop by $2.11 and of the rye crop by $1.98. In the light of these figures it is rather difficult to understand why, with its almost 9,000,000 acres of corn, over 4,000,000 acres of oats and over 76,000 acres of rye, Iowa grows so little winter wheat. It is true that winter wheat may be said not to be adapted to the entire state. It can, however, be safely grown in all that part south of the North-Western railroad and in some of that section north of it. It does best in the very part of the state where oats is most unsatisfactory.

To grow a good crop of winter wheat requires a more careful preparation of the seed bed than for oats. The ideal seed bed for wheat is firm below and mellow above. The corn field, so far as the condition of the soil is concerned, furnishes a seed bed that can hardly be improved. The continual working of the field through the season compacts the lower soil while leaving the upper two or three inches loose and mellow. The corn field offers the ideal seed bed ready made, and as this is where clover is usually wanted, it is the place for the winter wheat field. This makes it necessary that the corn be cut and shocked, a practice already established on most well managed, average sized farms in this state. The wheat should be drilled in, using a disk drill in preference to any other and either drilling closely around each shock or moving the shocks. A careful driver will put the wheat within one to three inches of the bottom of the shock. I have found it better to cross the rows; that is, to drill opposite the way the corn is laid by, rather than run with them. There are two reasons for this: one, because when drill-

ing with the rows the drill riding the row will put in the wheat too deep
while the drills next to it on either side are likely to put in it too shallow, and the other because drilling crosswise will knock out more corn
stubs, and leave the land more level, as well as covering the wheat more
uniformly. For the benefit of the young clover, the drills should run
north and south to give as free entrance as possible to the sunlight; and
therefore, if it is intended to sow wheat in the cornfield the corn should
be laid by east and west. In 1889 I raised one crop of winter wheat by
drilling in standing corn with a hoe drill, the hoes set on arms which
could be spread or contracted as necessary, in the same manner as the
one-horse garden cultivator of today. This drill was pulled by one horse
between the rows of standing corn. It is not a satisfactory way, although
I think an excellent crop could be raised if the corn stands up well.
If the corn is down much, more of it will be broken and wasted and
the wheat stand will not be even. With the hoe drill, it would be difficult to secure a very even stand if there is much foxtail in the field.
The stalks would have to be thoroughly harrowed the next spring.

On the farm owned by Wallaces' Farmer, 7 miles south of Des
Moines, we raised this season over 1,100 bushels of winter wheat on
about 27.5 acres, one field of 7 acres averaging 43 bushels to the acre
and another of 20.05 acres averaging 40 bushels. As much of this sold
for seed at $1.00 and $1.50 per bushel, it would not be fair to take our
returns per acre as a basis for averaging figures; but taking the average market price of say 50 cents per bushel, which is full low enough,
these fields yielded us over $20.00 per acre. The financial statement
would be as follows:

<pre>
    40 bushels of wheat, at 50 cents per bushel.... $20.00
    Seed, 1¼ bushels, at $1.00 per bushel..........$1.25
    Labor of man and team, drilling.............. .40
    Harvesting 1.75
    Cost of threshing, about 3.60   7.00
                                                          _____
    Net profit per acre $13.00
</pre>

This statement does not include the cost of harrowing the field in
the spring for the purpose of covering the clover seed, for that does not
properly belong to the cost of raising the wheat crop. The figures given
are not actual. The seed of the 7-acre field was imported from Russia
last season, and cost us say something over $2.50 per bushel. Our re-
turns per acre from this field were considerably over $20.00, but the fig-
ures I give are representative and will apply in an average year and to
the average farm. The first part of this season was very favorable, but
from harvest time on it was most unfavorable. There were probably
one or two acres of the larger field that we were not able to cut at all
on account of the wet weather. And the yield on all of it was several
bushels less than it would have been under favorable conditions.

In April we sowed the clover seed. It should have been sowed earlier
but we could not secure the seed we wanted in time. The ground was
very dry when the clover was sowed, and as there was no chance of its

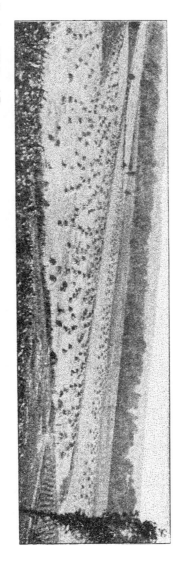

Courtesy of Wallaces' Farmer.

Wheat grown on the farm of Wallaces' Farmer, in Warren county, Iowa. This wheat is grown from regular Turkish Red seed.

germinating unless covered, we determined to run over the field with a Hallock weeder. The wheat at this time was several inches high and looking very nice. The ground was so dry and hard, however, that the weeder was ineffective, and at what seemed to be a risk of injuring the wheat, we put on the heaviest steel harrow on the farm and went over the field thoroughly. As a result, the clover seed sprouted with the first shower and the wheat seemed to have been helped, rather than injured, by the harrowing. The clover made a splendid growth; so much, in fact, that, contrary to our original plans, we expect to turn most of it under for corn this coming spring. This is mammoth clover. The season was, of course, favorable for clover. Such a yield cannot be expected every year, but with proper attention to preparing the seed and putting in the crop, I am confident that a good farmer on a good piece of land can make an average wheat yield of 25 bushels per acre for a period of ten years, and that he will find it as profitable a crop, one year with another, as any staple crop he grows.

Where the wheat is sown on fall plowing instead of in the cornfield, the ground should be plowed early and carefully and well harrowed repeatedly, until the furrow slice is thoroughly settled down and compacted. This is absolutely necessary for two reasons: First, to establish capillary connection with the subsoil, and second, to eliminate the air spaces and thus lessen the danger of the wheat winter killing. The object should be to get the field in as nearly as possible the same mechanical condition as the September cornfield. This will take work and time, but the wheat grower will be well repaid for both. If he is not willing to go to the pains necessary to secure a good seed bed, he should not attempt to grow winter wheat on summer or fall plowing. When the season for sowing arrives, and the seed bed has been well prepared, the wheat should be drilled in as in the cornfield. The disk drill leaves the ground in what might be called small ridges. Let the field alone, as the drill leaves it, as these irregularities in the ground help hold the snow.

The cost of growing a crop of wheat on plowed ground will be considerably more than in the cornfield. The logical place of wheat in the rotation, is following corn and in the cornfield is the place to sow it.

I have spoken of the importance of drilling wheat. Too much emphasis cannot be laid upon this. The drill puts in the seed at an even depth, covers it all so that it is ready to grow as soon as there is sufficient moisture and enables it to make a well developed root system before cold weather sets in. One or two successful wheat growers, with whom I am acquainted, this year tried drilling the field both ways, using half the necessary amount of seed each way. They report such a plan to be very satisfactory, the advantage being that it makes more thorough use of the land. Whether there would be sufficient advantage in this, to justify the extra expense, I do not know. It would have one disadvantage, that of shading the clover more than when drilled but one way.

As for varieties, the Turkish red has been grown in this state for 15 years and seems to be as hardy as any variety could possibly be. It is probable that we will find one or two other varieties that will prove hardy, but the Turkish red can be depended upon. The seed I spoke of as having been imported from Russia last season, came from the original home of the Turkish red and is the same variety. It has, I think, some advantage over our Turkish red, as modified by Iowa conditions for 15 years. It grows closer to the ground, spreading out over the surface in the fall, instead of growing upright, and it stools better. After it has been grown here for a number of years, it will probably develop the same characteristics as the Turkish red we have been growing. It has a longer head and I think, other conditions being equal, will yield several bushels per acre more.

There is no staple crop that the up-to-date Iowa farmer, on his own land, can afford to grow year after year, for the money value of that crop alone. The claims of every crop for his consideration must be based, not alone on its value, but on its adaptability to fit into the rotation and do its part in the general farm economy. Measured ьy this standard, winter wheat has strong claims for consideration at the hands of every farmer in northeastern Iowa, and in that part oι the state lying south of the Chicago & North-Western Railroad. I believe that it may be grown successfully farther north than is now supposed. Briefly summed up, these claims are:

The small cost of putting in the crop.

Its superior value as a nurse crop for clover.

Its profitable yield per acre as compared with our other staple crops.

To these claims must be added its value as food for animals, when the market price is too low to justify selling it. Experiments have demonstrated it to be worth pound for pound, about as much as corn for fattening cattle and hogs, while for growing animals it is worth more, because of its muscle making constituents.

Taking winter wheat at its just valuation, the farmers in the part of Iowa before mentioned, will certainly consult their own interests by reducing their oats acreage, which yields less net profit than any other crop they grow, and substituting winter wheat. They will not lose as much wheat by winter killing, if they stick to known hardy varieties, as they will oats by going down before harvest, and whereas they can grow oats successfully only on their poorer land, they will find with wheat, the richer the land, the greater their returns.

CHAIRMAN: This paper is now open for discussion, gentlemen.

MR. JOHN FOX: Mr. Chairman: This question of raising winter wheat is one of locality. My location is the north half of Dallas county; soil, black prairie loam. From nine to ten years ago my neighbors beagan to raise Russian wheat; had one or two heavy crops; during a dry fall or dry winter it failed to germinate or perished; not from winter killing, but from drouth in winter, and it became so uncertain that very few are growing it now. However, there were some very large crops of it grown. At that time we were not drilling much; but those that did drill had the same trouble; found trouble in getting it started in the fall of the year. There have been several occasions when it would lie in the ground and not germinate until spring. I have known of seventeen bushels to the acre, winter wheat, that when spring opened showed scarcely a sign of life.

Mr. Trigg: Mr. Chairman: It is a matter of history that when Iowa quit raising wheat she commenced to prosper. In 1878 the farmers of the state were bankrupt as the result of wheat raising. Now, while wheat may be raised to fairly good advantage in the southern tiers of counties of the state, here a few spots and there a few spots, it is not profitable when taken up generally. It is my idea that any crop raised in the state should be convertible into some other form for market. A bushel of corn that sells on the market for twenty-five cents is easily convertible into fifty cents, one year with another, by any man who will feed it as it may be fed. Our state is a great stock and dairy state, and we never should lose sight of that fact. The only recommendation in the paper that I would indorse is the fact that winter wheat is a god nurse crop. In any event, rye will do just as well. Then how can we compete with this northern country on wheat? The record shows that in the territories of Manitoba they have raised 19.95 bushels of wheat per acre for an average of ten years. Just think of it; a record we cannot approximate into nearly nine bushels. So I honestly think that the best thing farmers can do is to let wheat raising alone and raise corn, hogs, cattle and nice fat, healthy boys and girls.

Chairman: The next on the program will be a paper entitled "Points to be Considered in the Economic Production of Beef," by W. J. Kennedy.

POINTS TO BE CONSIDERED IN THE ECONOMIC PRODUCTION OF BEEF.

W. J. Kennedy, Ames, Iowa.

A prominent statistician, in a recent report, has very clearly shown that the greatest gain in wealth, education and population in this country has taken place in those states where farming and the production of first-class live stock are being carried on together. This has been amply illustrated throughout the corn belt states and in this respect we as Iowa people may well be proud of the fact that our state stands first and foremost of them all. When comparisons are made in almost every instance Iowa is used as an illustration of what live stock, when properly bred and cared for, can do for the farmer.

Notwithstanding the fact that we are in the very front rank, we still have a great deal to learn regarding the production of the various kinds of meat producing animals. High priced farm lands and strenuous competition from many sources are daily making the profitable production of meat a more difficult problem. Things are very much different to what they used to be when land was worth from twenty to forty dollars per acre and corn could be purchased for twenty cents per bushel. In order that we may successfully meet these changed conditions which have been brought about by the marked advances in the value of farm property our former methods may have to undergo some modification. Not that the stock men who bred and fed animals during the last two decades were ignorant men and did not understand their business. They, as a class, were just as intelligent and solved the problems which confronted them in a much better way than most of our men are doing today. Old time methods which can be successfully applied under present conditions must not be replaced by new and untried theories. Before adopting any method, new or old, we should consider very carefully as to what the outcome will be; as to where we will land should we follow the same. In this connection I am reminded of an epitaph which is to be found in a cemetery in old Virginia which reads as follows:

> "Remember, man, as you pass by,
> As you are now, so once was I;
> As I am now, so you must be;
> Prepare for death and follow me."

The Virginia epitaph, however, has received an addition in the following couplet which has been written below the original in a clear, old-fashioned hand:

> "To follow you is not my intent,
> Until I know which way you went."

Just so in the live stock business; before following the methods of those who have been successful we must be sure of what the outcome will be under the present conditions.

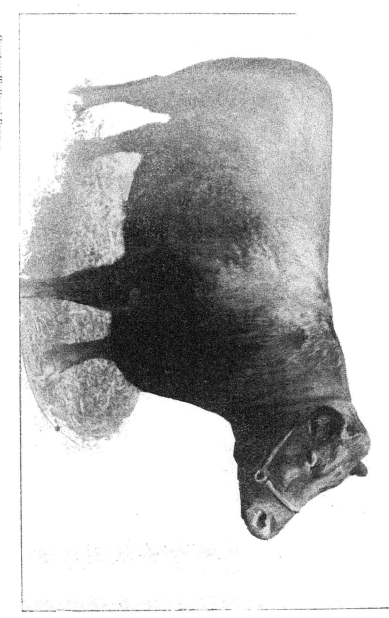

Courtesy Wallaces' Farmer.

Grade Aberdeen-Angus Steer Shamrock, champion steer at International Live Stock Exposition, 1902.   Age 38 months; weight, 1,805 pounds!

It is not my intention to dwell on the production of live stock in general as I have been asked to discuss a few features pertaining to the economical production of beef. In the past no branch of live stock, save the fat hog, has been so generally handled throughout this state as has beef cattle. Iowa's natural conditions have been most favorable and have done much towards making her the greatest breeding and feeding center of the central west. Her virgin soil was so well adapted to the production of corn and the growth of blue grass pasture, the two things which, when combined, have no equal for economical production of beef of the very best quality. Then she is situated between the range territory, where so many cattle are grown, and the leading cattle market of the world. These conditions have been of untold value to the Iowa farmer. Notwithstanding these advantages, in many sections of this state farmers who formerly reared and fed cattle for the market are no longer engaged in the business. They claim that with land selling in the neighborhood of one hundred dollars per acre that it is too valuable to carry stock on. When land was cheap they reared their own cattle, when land advanced in price to fifty or sixty dollars per acre they changed their business and became cattle feeders, but now, since land has made such marked advances in value, they are compelled to go out of the business. We are glad to note, however, that we have a great many very successful beef producers. Men who reared cattle when land was cheap, when land advanced and who are still successfully and profitably rearing and finishing cattle which, when consigned to market, always command the very top prices.

We have had and are likely to have for some time to come two classes of men engaged in the beef cattle business. The first class, which at one time was much the larger of the two, might be called the "beef grower." He reared his own calves, fed and finished them for the market. To the second class belong that now large number who might be termed "cattle feeders." They do not pretend to rear their own cattle as during a part of the year they have no cattle whatever on the farm. They buy their feeders from the ranges or from the small farmer who rears a few calves each year.

One of the most vital problems which many a farmer has to solve at the present day is where he should classify. Will he be a beef grower or a cattle feeder? At the present day and under existing conditions there is room for both. Where good judgment and common sense business methods are applied a man can make a success of either method. Both methods have their advantages and disadvantages. The man who rears his own cattle can control the quality of the animals he feeds. On the other hand he must force them from the day they are dropped until ready for the butcher if he hopes to realize a profit on our present high priced lands. He has a herd of breeding cows to feed and care for the year round. Can he afford to keep and feed a cow for the calf alone? It takes a good calf to bring twenty-five or thirty dollars at weaning time, while at the present prices of feed stuffs it will cost at least thirty dollars per year to feed a cow. This looks like a losing proposition and it surely is on high priced land. This leads up to the question of milking cows, something which the average man does not take kindly to, but a question which sooner or later he will be obliged to solve. In England this question has been solved. Over there the first requisite of a beef cow is that she be a fair milker. A cow that will not give a liberal flow of milk is condemned. At the Iowa Experiment Station we have cows of more than one of the recognized beef breeds which, in addition to possessing the desired beef form, have produced from three to four hundred pounds of butter per year. We have also found that when the milk is separated while warm and fed directly to the calves that, by addition of some flax seed meal, oat meal, or corn meal to the skim milk, practically as good calves can be reared as when whole milk has been fed. The butter fat, when separated from the milk, netted us from fifty to eighty dollars per cow. Calves from these cows, fed on skim milk and the adjuncts mentioned, have been marketed at twenty-six months of age when they weighed over fourteen hundred pounds.

When land reaches the one hundred dollar mark it requires careful farming and stockraising to return a paying profit on the investment. But the Iowa farmer must not abandon stock raising, else his land will surely deteriorate in value. In many of the eastern states when land advanced in value the owners considered it too valuable for stock raising, thus in many instances they went out of the business. What has been the result? There is but one outcome to any such practice, which is wornout farms, which, in many instances, have been deserted. They have been taught a valuable lesson, one which the farmer of the Central West should not have to learn through experience. Successful farming cannot be carried on continuously without live stock. Commercial fertilizers may apparently answer the purpose for a short time, but soil fertility can only be maintained in one way and that is by stock farming. In England stock farming is the mainstay of the farmer and land is worth twice as much as it is here. In the island of Jersey land rents around twenty dollars per acre, still live stock, especially dairy farming, is their main occupation. If Iowa farm lands are to maintain their present values, and they surely will, it will be because the farmers will adhere to the live stock business. In this respect no line of live stock is better adapted to our conditions than beef cattle when produced from *dual purpose* cows. The cow that will net her owner forty dollars or upwards for the butter fat sold and at the same time produce a calf which can be marketed at the age of two and a half years weighing in the neighborhood of fifteen hundred pounds. Such a method is practicable and when adopted by the Iowa farmer he will not consider land too valuable even at one hundred and fifty dollars per acre for the economical production of beef.

We have at the present time a great many men who are cattle feeders. This method has some advantages and many disadvantages. There seems to be a great many uncertainties about this kind of work. The cattle feeder must, first of all, buy his cattle right else he cannot hope to realize a profit. It is very difficult to get animals of good quality.

This is due largely to the fact that the men who breed the cattle have been accustomed to receiving a certain price for animals of the various ages with little or no discrimination so far as quality is concerned. All two-year-olds brought about the same price, thus there was not much encouragement for the breeder who spent money in securing valuable sires. We are glad to note a decided change in favor of the man who breeds good cattle. The feeders are acting wisely when they are willing to recognize good blood and quality by paying more for the same. It is certainly most gratifying to receive a letter from a commission merchant stating that he is about to receive a bunch of cattle from a certain ranch where nothing but the best of pure bred sires have been used for a certain period of years. Range cattle are no longer being sold as just "range stuff." They are being graded and sold on their merits. When this policy is universally adopted the results will be far reaching. It will mean better markets for our surplus bulls, better feeders for the corn belt farmer to put in his feed lot and last and most important of all, a much better market through which the farmer may dispose of his corn crop.

Success in any line of work is largely governed by the methods pursued at the beginning. This is especially true in the production of beef. There is no other one feature of the business quite so important as to have the right kind of an animal. An animal possessing the desired form combined with plenty of quality. Bear in mind that width of back, loin and hindquarters are indispensable in the good steer. The three factors which determine the selling price of the steer on any of our leading markets are *percentage;* that is, per cent. of dressed weight to live weight; *quality,* that is, a thick covering of good flesh over back and loin; and *proportion,* which means as much weight as possible in the back, loin and hindquarters where the high priced cuts are to be found.

Having secured the right kind of an animal the next and most essential point is how to secure the greatest gain in weight at the very lowest cost. When feed stuffs were low in price and labor was high the feeder acted wisely when he economized labor at the expense of feed. With corn ranging from forty to fifty cents per bushel he can no longer follow such methods. It is now a question of economizing in feed. The feeder must get more pounds of gain from a bushel of corn than he has ever done in the past. In this respect there is a great need for investigations pertaining to the advisability or nonadvisability of feeding lighter grain rations. If fifteen or eighteen pounds of corn per steer per day will give as good results as twenty-five and thirty pounds of the same, it certainly would be much more economical for the feeder to adopt such methods. Feeding experiments conducted at the Minnesota Station and at the Ontario Agricultural College with light, medium and heavy meal rations for fattening steers have shown the medium and light rations to be much more economical than the heavy rations. In these experiments, however, the gains calculated were those made by the cattle alone, as there were no hogs to utilize that part which the steer did not assimilate. With our present methods of feeding we are simply at the mercy of the hog and the ravages which afflict him. If cholera attacks the hog and wipes him out, about twenty-five per cent. of our high priced corn is wasted except from a fertility standpoint. This is a question which every farmer should study carefully. How can he make beef without the hog to consume the waste feed? Not that we have any objections to the dog, for he certainly is the farmers' best friend, but we must be prepared for emergencies. We must feed cattle oftentimes when we have no hogs. We must study more carefully the process of digestion of feed stuffs. When we see from twenty to thirty per cent. of the corn which a steer is made to consume passing through the digestive system it is a sure indication that there is something wrong. We are either feeding the animal more that it can assimilate or its digestive system is out of condition. In most instances the trouble is due to a deranged digestive system caused by over feeding. This leads up to another point which is the mixing of grain and roughage together which is, in our estimation, the ideal way of feeding cattle.

When the grain is fed separately from the roughage it is greedily swallowed and passes into the third and fourth stomachs of the animal, thus escaping mastication and the action of the saliva of the mouth, which has the power of converting starch into sugar which is digestible. By mixing the grain with the roughage it will be remasticated, thus much more thoroughly digested than when each is fed separately. This method of feeding involves the cutting of roughage, a step which most farmers are not prepared to take as yet, but one which they can well afford to be thinking about as in the near future it will be practiced by the most successful cattle feeders.

Another question which is worthy of our attention is the silo. The silo, while a new thing in Iowa, is by no means an experiment. It has been thoroughly tested in the eastern states and Canada and when once tried it speaks for itself. It is now considered to be indispensable on the dairy farm, and while it has not been, as yet, very generally used in the production of beef, the results as reported to date are most encouraging. The silo is by all odds the cheapest medium through which we can obtain succulent feed for our stock during the winter months.

In recapitulation I may say that the successful farmer of the future will be the man who combines the production of first-class live stock with his farming operations, who keeps beef cows for the double purpose of producing butter and calves intended for the block, who gets nearly as many pounds of gain from sixteen pounds of corn as the average feeder of today gets from twenty-five pounds when fed to cattle. Who combines his grain with the roughage fed to his animals thereby securing more complete digestion of the same, and who stores his corn stalks in the silo that they may be converted into beef and dairy products instead of being burned in the fields.

CHAIRMAN: We have a few minutes before noon and would like to hear from any gentleman present.

Courtesy of Wallaces' Farmer:
Rear view of champion steer Shamrock.

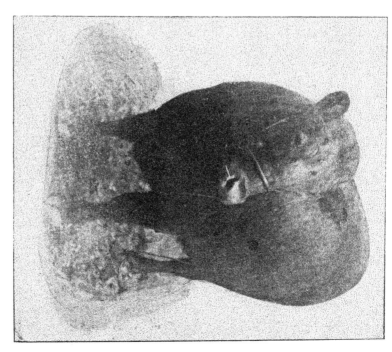

Courtesy of Wallaces' Farmer:
Front and side view of champion steer Shamrock.

MR. TRIGG: Do I understand you to say, Mr. Kennedy, in your paper, that the feeding of silage to beef animals was a success?

PROFESSOR KENNEDY: So far very few results have been reported but the reports show results to have been successful. It is a new thing and has not been reported on extensively.

MEMBER: Is the ration limited? Supposing the average ration of a dairy animal is thirty pounds, how much would you feed this beef animal?

PROFESSOR KENNEDY: Feed about twenty-five or thirty pounds. The best way would be to feed a ration of silage and hay and grain. The silage furnishing the succulent part of the ration. I have seen a great many farmers feeding silage to fat cattle. They were not conducting feed experiments, but were pleased with results. It is a new thing, yet all the light we have on the subject shows it is a good thing.

MR. BARNEY: Mr. Chairman, with regard to the results of feeding cattle silage, I want to say that Professor Kennedy is absolutely right in that respect. I have in the last five years used a hand separator and nothing else. I bought the separator five years ago and I think I have raised better calves in the last five years than I did when I fed them a good portion of new milk and the balance of the milk as it came from the creamery. The milk fed warm on the farm, I think, with oil meal or with a little corn meal is fully equal to letting the calf run with the cow. In fact I have just as good results as I ever had letting the calf run with the cow.

MR. TRIGG: Probably there are a good many young fellows here in the audience who were raised on the bottle, yet, there is no doubt but they have got as good a start as the fellows raised the other way.

MR. FOX: There is one question I would like to ask, whether an animal in a cold climate should have silage? Has it a tendency to make the animal more tender?

PROFFESSOR KENNEDY: Not necessarily so. I have heard a great many people ask about the balanced ration. Now, I will say in the cattle feeding business as in any other line of business, common sense is the best guide. In feeding we should try to imitate manure and feed a ration of a succulent nature; by so doing we will keep the animal's digestive system in a good condition. Now, some folks have trouble feeding cotton seed meal. We had trouble last winter in our cattle feeding experiment at Odebolt, in feeding cotton seed meal to cattle. Cotton seed is different from oil meal. Oil meal aids digestion and when fed to dairy cows makes butter fat soft. Cotton seed, on the contrary, has a tendency to constipate the animal and when fed to the dairy animal makes butter hard in texture. I think the real trouble does not come from poison of the cotton seed but it is a matter of indigestion. I know men who have fed cotton seed meal with silage and got the best of results from the combined ration. Silage is easily digested and keeps the system in good shape; not that silage is a feed in itself. It is not. You have to feed something else with it. It is one of the things which we should have.

Mr. Fox: It is not out of prejudice that I ask the question. A friend of mine years ago, living on a farm adjoining my own, fed his cattle somewhat as I have indicated and I frequently observed the difference between his cattle and mine. I think his cattle were better than mine which were fed on dry feed. They were more tender when they were turned out in the weather from the barn; did not seem so vigorous; and I came to the conclusion that for cattle that were fed and turned out doors, silage was not just the thing. However, I think inside of the barn where proper ventilation is had, perhaps it is a cheaper feed, and I am not prepared to say it is not better than any other way.

Professor Kennedy: You will find if you keep cattle in a warm barn and turn them out they will hump their backs; but you can feed cattle silage out in open lots and you will not notice any very marked difference. It is not due to the difference in feeding.

Professor Holden: Mr. Chairman, this feeding experiment of which Professor Kennedy has spoken, I happen to know considerable about. They were fed on a farm, twenty-five in each bunch, and 3.73 fed corn and silo, made good gains and as much increase in beef as 5.20 of their corn fed stock. And in regard to the question just asked, it was very noticeable to all of us that the twenty-five animals fed at the same ranch and under the same conditions, were somewhat more tender than those fed corn fodder. The animals fed silage were tender but the gains were much greater in the silage fed animals than those fed fodder.

PROFESSOR KENNEDY: I have seen them fed in the open lots and there was no appreciable difference.

MEMBER: Well, don't we all want tender beef, anyhow?

CHAIRMAN: We have a few minutes before adjournment and while we have heard a great deal about the prize steer, Shamrock, I would like to have Professor Kennedy tell us how he was fed.

PROFESSOR KENNEDY: In regard to the steer Shamrock, I might say that steer was purchased two years ago by the college. There was an impression throughout the country and a few years ago a great many people here in Iowa had the idea that anything kept at the Agricultural College was something to laugh at; that men at the Agricultural College could not do anything along feeding lines. Now, when the Agricultural College gets out and feeds in competition with the practical feeders and wins over them, all things present a much different aspect and the criticism is the other way. Shamrock was purchased two years ago by Professor Curtiss at Tipton, Iowa, at five cents a pound. He was taken in with a bunch of steers; he had a good frame, which was about the only commendable thing about him. Took him to the college and developed him, and showed him last year in Chicago, where he won second prize. He was taken home and carried on till this year, when he was first in class and grand champion over all breeds of all ages.

Now, in regard to feeding. We fed him a balanced ration, as nearly as we could. He was fed nothing but what any farmer could feed. Last summer fed him corn, oats, barley, bran and oil meal.

Now, I want to say—sometimes in feeding an animal for a show ring after he is ripe and you carry him along a little farther, he is liable to get somewhat soft. This calls for a change of feed, something to firm him up. Shamrock had to be fed so as to firm him up.

Iowa had the grand champion carload lot of steers at Chicago, owned by Chas. Escher. The grand champion herd of fat cattle over all breeds came from Iowa. They were fed at the college, and the grand champion steer over all came from Iowa, and all of these are from the Iowa State College. His mother was seven-eighths Angus and his sire was a pure bred Angus bull. He was very nearly a full-blood.

MR. TRIGG: The reason I asked the question is because it was reported he was a pure bred steer.

PROFESSOR KENNEDY: His mother was seven-eighths and sire pure bred Angus. When we speak of beef cattle we speak of the beef type; and I think in that respect it is not necessary to have pure bred, but that the pure bred must be back of it all. I do not believe in every man handling pure bred cattle, but I believe every man should use a pure bred sire. The trouble is, most people want females! and I have noticed that at these stock shows— they will give a big prize for females; whereas, on every farm in Iowa we should have pure-bred bulls.

MR. TRIGG: Will you be kind enough to emphasize the fact of pure-bred sires, because we have a great many big men who think that $35.00 is too much to pay for a bull.

PROFESSOR KENNEDY: Three hundred dollars is not too much to pay for a good bull to be used on a herd of good grade cows. Every man should use a pure bred bull. I do not believe every man should go into the pure-bred breeding business.

MR. TRIGG: How much did Shamrock weigh?

PROFESSOR KENNEDY: He weighed 1,805 pounds.

AFTERNOON SESSION.

Meeting called to order by Vice-President Morrow.

The first on the program is a paper entitled "Forage Crops in Iowa," by James Atkinson of Des Moines.

FORAGE CROPS IN IOWA.

James Atkinson, Des Moines.

There are many indications which lead us to believe that farmers of Iowa employ wasteful methods in their feeding operations. For the practice of feeding half a bushel of corn per day to a steer there is no reasonable justification. Experiments in England, Canada and the United States, together with the experiences of a few feeders that may be found in every state, demonstrate that results equally as good may be obtained by feeding half this quantity of grain, combined with good roughage. As the land increases in value more animals must be kept on a given area if the holding of land is to continue to be a good investment. The cost of fitting an animal for the block must be lowered, and if this is done advantage must be taken of the fact that the steer is a ruminating animal, and because of this is able to convert a large amount of rough feed, as well as grain, into meat. Therefore, what I have to say about forage crops is based on the assumption that these are grown for feeding purposes and not to be marketed directly.

Our greatest forage crop is corn. What we need most of all is to be taught how to handle the forage part of this crop economically. In spite of the fact that 40 per cent of the nutrients of the corn plant is contained in the leaves and stems, we find that millions of acres of corn stover are annually wasted in this state. There is little need for the introduction of new crops until this standard fodder of the state is utilized to its fullest extent. Just how this is to be done depends upon circumstances, and although it is somewhat outside the province of this paper, I will say that the shredder is one step in advance of the old-time methods of handling the corn crop. However, there are instances where it would not be advisable to shred. It will seldom pay, for example, to shred part of the crop and allow part to stand in the field until it is worthless, for the reason that shredding is only done when it is necessary to increase the feeding value of the fodder grown on the farm. The same argument may be advanced in behalf of the silo. There is no question but what the food from a given acreage will go farther if converted into ensilage than if fed in any other form, and yet so long as part of the fodder is wasted there is little need for incurring the expense of building a silo and storing the corn.

The costly experience of the past season, due to the injury to the corn fodder by frost, suggests the wisdom of making some advances in our present methods of handling the corn crop. Where the crop is converted into ensilage it is possible to cut and store it even before the grain has reached the glazed condition, the same being to some extent true where the shredder is used extensively. In fact where large areas of corn are handled in this way it is absolutely necessary to begin harvesting early in the season. If there is a little shrinkage of the grain after cutting the feeding value of the fodder will be all the greater, providing, of course, that the grain has passed the milk condition. By shredding the fodder or storing it in the silo one is relieved of a large amount of disagreeable labor during the feeding period. Not only is the labor disagreeable, but it involves no little expense to employ sufficient help when fodder is drawn from the field daily. With silos located in the immediate vicinity of feed yards or stacks of shredded fodder located similarly, one man can accomplish much more than if the fodder is drawn from the field daily.

Sorghum is a comparatively new crop in the state, and yet it is meeting with favor in many quarters. Even where corn fodder is well cared for there are those who grow sorghum for the purpose of adding variety to their roughage. There are few crops that will give a greater yield of fodder per acre than sorghum, while there is no crop that is more palatable. Sorghum is a gross feeder and for the best results should be grown on land that is fairly rich. A clover meadow plowed in the fall or spring will make a splendid seed bed for this crop. It is a southern plant and should never be seeded until the soil has become warm. It should not be sown before the twentieth of May, and even this date is early when the season is cold and backward. If sown when the soil is cold the seed may germinate but the plants take on a yellow appearance and growth becomes stunted. Few crops require more careful preparation of the seed bed. If, for example, a clover sod is plowed in the spring it should afterwards be well worked down with disc and harrow, and so much the better if the roller can be pressed into service. This makes a firm, fine seed bed and consequently presents ideal conditions for covering the seed uniformly.

There are a number of methods of planting the seed. Where a grain drill is not available at least two bushels of seed should be used per acre. Unless the soil is more than ordinarily wet the seed should be covered with a disk, when it is sown broadcast, the harrow not being sufficient to insure a perfect covering. Where a drill is available one of two methods may be employed in the manner of sowing the seed. Some prefer to sow from eighty to 120 pounds per acre. In other instances a number of spouts in the drill are stopped up leaving the rows thirty to forty inches apart. In this case the feed is thrown wide open so that the seed is sown very thickly in the row. Even when this is done, however, only a small quantity of seed is required, six or eight quarts being enough for one acre. When sorghum is sown in this manner it is usually cut with the binder, so that the expense of harvesting is much less than where it is sown thickly, necessitating harvesting with the mower. On poor land, even where the crop is sown thickly, it is sometimes possible to harvest with the ordinary binder, but as a rule on our richer soils the fodder grows so rank as to render this method impracticable.

As to the manner of curing sorghum, there is considerable difference in the methods employed by those who grow this crop. When it can be handled with a corn binder or even an ordinary binder it may be shocked up immediately and left to cure out in the shock. Where the crop is so heavy that it must be cut with the mower it is generally advisable to allow the fodder to dry out for a few days previous to shocking. I am well aware of the fact that a great many persons shock it up at once in the green condition, but the objection to this practice is that it makes the handling of the sorghum somewhat expensive owing to the great weight of the green sorghum. A twenty-five ton crop of green fodder will be reduced in weight to seven or eight tons in the course of ten days, providing the weather is favorable. Drying may be hastened by stirring the sorghum with a hay tedder. By curing in this way one gets rid of handling a large quantity of water. After drying, the fodder can be placed in shocks of 500 or 600 pounds weight and allowed to remain there until it is thoroughly cured. During the winter it may be drawn to the mow or stack or may be left in the field and hauled directly to the feed yards when required.

Sorghum fodder is well adapted for all kinds of stock. Cattle prefer it to corn fodder, and indeed if it is properly cured they will leave good hay for the sorghum. I have known horses to do exceedingly well during the winter, while sheep eat it with great relish and put it to good use. It makes excellent food for brood sows, more especially if the seed is not sown thickly so that the stems are somewhat large.

Before leaving the subject of sorghum I should like to say that it is practicable to sow it after a cereal crop is removed. I have in mind one instance where a barley crop was removed and sorghum sown about the middle of July. This was cut the last day of September and gave a yield of seven tons of cured fodder per acre. As to the value of sorghum as a pasture crop there is considerable difference of opinion. It is true that there are instances where animals seem to have been suddenly poisoned when turned onto green sorghum. More especially has this been the case where attempts were made to pasture the second growth. Just what the cause is in such cases is not definitely known, but it is generally believed that if greater caution were used in turning animals onto pasture of this character that there would be little or no trouble. Thousands and tens of thousands of animals are pastured on first, second and third growth sorghum in surrounding states, and for one person who has experienced a loss it is possible to find hundreds who have nothing but praise to offer for this crop when it is used for pasture. Animals should never be turned onto green sorghum when they are hungry, nor should they at any time be changed from dry feed to green sorghum. If they are allowed to fill themselves with clover or some succulent grass before being turned on the sorghum the danger is practically eliminated.

Kaffir corn in some respects is quite similar to sorghum, but so far as my experience goes it is scarcely so well adapted to Iowa conditions as the sorghum. It does not give such large yields, while it is not so palatable to stock. There are those, of course, who are growing it with profit. It is usually sown thickly at the rate of from eighty to one hundred pounds of seed per acre, and is harvested in the same way as sorghum. There is usually more waste in feeding out this crop on account of the fact that the stems are not palatable and are left uneaten. The crop is drouth-resisting in character, and on this account it is sure to produce a liberal amount of forage no matter how dry the season may be.

The characteristics of millet are so well known that it is scarcely necessary to dwell on them here. There is a place for millet on the farm, providing one knows how to handle it. As it is ordinarily handled it is not a very satisfactory crop, the mistake being in not cutting it in time. If the seed is allowed to harden the leaves and stems become fibrous and when this takes place there is always a disappointment in feeding

6

it. When cutting is not done at the proper time there is also a shelling out of the seed on the ground, and this insures a crop of annual weeds next year. Millet should be cut while the seed is in the milk condition, and it should be cured with as little exposure as possible. So much the better if it can be put in shocks soon after cutting, as this helps to keep the leaves and stems soft and also retains the aroma. When cured in this way millet hay may be fed to all kinds of stock with impunity, providing a little judgment is used in the feeding. It is never advisable to feed millet hay exclusively to farm animals. An experiment is reported by the North Dakota Station in which horses were fed millet hay alone for roughage. The effect was to produce an increased action of the kidneys, causing lameness and swelling of the joints, as well as producing general unthriftiness. Because of this injurious effect upon animals it does not follow that the crop should be discarded altogether, but rather that more judgment is necessary in feeding it to animals. One feed of millet hay per day is sufficient for work horses, while all farm animals will thrive much better if other forms of roughage are fed in conjunction with millet.

While alfalfa is usually classed more as a hay crop than forage, yet the enormous yield of this crop when it is grown under favorable conditions, leads me to put it in this category at this time. The area seeded to alfalfa in Iowa is exceedingly small, although hundreds of attempts are annually made to get the crop established. Under our conditions the crop should be seeded early in the spring on a well prepared seed bed, without a nurse crop. A drill should be used in sowing the seed, ten pounds being sown in one direction and a similar quantity in the opposite direction. This insures a uniform covering of the seed and a good stand. As a rule it is necessary to cut back the weed growth once or twice during the first season. It does not seem to injure the alfalfa even if the leaves and stems are also cut back somewhat closely. If conditions are at all favorable the crop should produce two or three cuttings the second year, but ordinarily one cannot expect a crop the first year. My experience has been that alfalfa takes on a sickly appearance in the spring of the second year and it is then soon affected with leaf spot disease, to which it succumbs. The inspection of a number of alfalfa fields recently, however, in the state, convinced me that our soil is lacking the organism that lives on the alfalfa roots. To the fields referred to, these organisms had been introduced by making an application of soil from the alfalfa fields of Nebraska. Shortly after the organisms are introduced in this way the alfalfa takes on a healthy appearance, and it is not unusual when these are present to obtain four cuttings a year. The fields referred to produced twelve tons of cured hay per acre. My idea in speaking of alfalfa is not based on the belief that our farmers are suddenly going into alfalfa growing, but I simply want to call attention to the fact that our failures in the past undoubtedly have been due to the fact that our soils have not been properly inoculated. This may be done chiefly by the introduction of small quantities of soil, and if we do reach that point where alfalfa can be grown successfully it will solve one of the most difficult problems, that is now presented to the Iowa farmer, namely, that of getting a stand of clover. There is need for some plant of this character in our rotations in order to make additions to the nitrogen supply in the soil. Red clover frequently fails because the nurse crop smothers it out, while it is not sufficiently strong to resist weed growth when it is sown without a nurse crop. Even when it comes through the first summer there is considerable danger that it will be winter killed. Alfalfa, on the other hand, is a much deeper rooting plant and when once established sends its roots beyond the region where frost can do harm. The ordinary drouth such as we are apt to have in Iowa has little or no injurious effect on the alfalfa plant, owing to the fact that it obtains its moisture supply from the lower soil and subsoil.

The last plant about which I wish to speak is very different in its characteristics from any of those that have been mentioned, it being impossible to cure it in any way so as to make hay. I refer to rape. An exceedingly small area of the state is devoted to this crop at the present time, but where it is grown there are few crops that are more highly spoken of. Rape must be used primarily for pasture. It may be sown almost any time after spring opens until the middle of August. Bare feed lots may be made to produce enormous crops of rape, it being only necessary to scatter over the surface four or five pounds of rape seed per acre early in the spring and run a disc over the surface. Where whole fields are devoted to this crop the soil is generally well worked down and the rape sown either in rows or broadcast. If sown in rows these should be placed from twenty-six to thirty inches apart, and two or three pounds of seed should be sown per acre. When the crop is put in in this manner it affords an opportunity for cleaning the land by the use of the one-horse cultivator. It is also practicable to sow one or two pounds of rape seed per acre along with cereals. In this case the crop comes on and furnishes fall pasture after the cereal crop is removed. In South Dakota and Minnesota thousands of sheep are annually fed off of rape when put in after this manner. Rape makes almost a perfect food for sheep, lambs or hogs, and hogs indeed may be used to advantage as a fall pasture for steers. There is just a little danger that bloating will be induced when animals are first turned on, but if a little care is exercised this may be prevented. It has been ascertained that animals pasturing on rape will make better gains if they have access to a pasture. It cannot be fed with impunity to milk cows, owing to the fact that it is apt to taint the dairy products. Rape may be pastured at almost any period of its growth, although it is generally advisable to allow it to make considerable top before pasturing it extensively. We have many times seen instances where this crop proved very disappointing, owing to the fact that it was too heavily pastured during the early part of its growth. If it is left alone for six or seven weeks after germination there will in all probability be considerable top, and this means that there will be a strong root growth. After this period the crop will generally grow fast enough to keep pace with the pasturing, providing of course that the number of animals are not too great for the area, as the leaves and stems grow very rapidly after the root has become thoroughly established. It might also be said that when one leaf is eaten off two appear in its place.

CHAIRMAN: We would be glad to hear from any one on this question. If there is no one who desires to discuss the paper, we will proceed to the next, which is a paper entitled "The Louisiana Exposition, 1904," by J. H. Trewin, member of the Iowa Commission, Cedar Rapids, Iowa. (The author not being present, the paper was read by Mr. F. R. Conaway.)

MR. CONAWAY: Mr. Chairman and Gentlemen of the Convention: I am very sorry that Senator Trewin cannot be present this afternoon. I have just received a letter from him, stating that owing to some very important cases in court, he could not be here, and asking me to read his paper, which I will proceed to do.

LOUISIANA PURCHASE EXPOSITION, 1904.

J. H. Trewin, Cedar Rapids, Iowa.

The hardy, adventuresome and determined American pioneers, who at the close of the Revolution invaded and commenced to subdue the wilderness to the east of the Mississippi, brought about an event in the history of our country second only in importance to the gaining of independence. By the treaty of 1773 the American and British had stipulated that "the navigation of the River Mississippi from its source to the ocean shall forever remain free and open to the subjects of Great Britain and the citizens of the United States." But Spain controlling both sides of the lower Mississippi denied free navigation of that river to the western Americans, while the latter considered it their "God given highway to the sea and to civilization." Trade restrictions were imposed by Spain, vessels and cargoes were confiscated and crews imprisoned. The inhabitants became enraged and threatened invasion and the forcible establishment of their right of free navigation of the river.

In June, 1775, Washington wrote of the situation: "The emigration to the waters of the Mississippi is astonishingly great and chiefly of a description of people who are not very subordinate to the law and constitution of the state they go from. Whether the prohibition of the Spaniards is just or unjust, politic or impolitic it will be with difficulty that the people of this class can be restrained in the enjoyment of natural advantages."

Washington, Livingston, Hamilton, Jefferson and other early statesmen and patriots recognized the necessity of an open river, but the nation was too weak to do more than anxiously wait the rapidly changing conditions in European affairs. Hamilton said in 1799, "I have long been in the habit of considering the acquisition of the Floridas and Louisiana as essential to the permanency of the Union." His far seeing eye discerned the probabilities in all the country west of the Mississippi to the Pacific, but Jefferson and Madison urged on by the persistent demands of the people for free navigation were willing to accept the river as the western boundary of the republic. April 20, 1803, a week after the great treaty had been agreed upon and ten days before it was signed, Secretary of State Madison wrote to Monroe, then in Paris, "certain it is that the hearts and hopes of the western people are strongly fixed on the Mississippi for the future boundary." Meanwhile the people directly interested continued to demand their rights as defined by the treaty 1783, and Robert R. Livingston of undying fame as a diplomatist, patriot and statesman, never ceased in his untiring efforts in their behalf at the court of France, and though only authorized to negotiate for the portion east of the river when the capricious first consul offered it to him, he purchased the entire territory. It was the wisest and most audacious act ever done by an American ambassador, and its vast consequences can never be measured. Without it, the British would probably have acquired the territory as a result of the Napoleonic wars and the United States would now, if in existence as a nation, be bounded on the west by the Mississippi with a British colony on the other side.

The differences as to the admission of new states might not have arisen; we might never have known of the Missouri Compromise and poor bleeding Kansas; we might even have escaped the horrors of civil war, but we should not have achieved greatness as a nation.

The consequences of the acquisition of Louisiana are so stupendous and have exerted such an enormous influence over our destiny as a nation that it is most fitting a great commemorative world's fair should be held in the largest city of the region and upon the banks of the mighty river whose free navigation gave rise to the controversy so happily ended by Livingston's unauthorized treaty. Difficulties arose after the treaty was signed. Jefferson always a strict constructionist of the constitution doubted the right to acquire territory without an amendment, and even proposed one, but the demands and necessities of the people swept away all his doubts and objections and the treaty was ratified—our national domain was doubled, a precedent set for future acquisitions of territory, and permanent foundation for our greatness laid. This territory, comprising practically thirteen magnificent states and two territories, has three times the population and many times the wealth of the entire United States at the time of the acquisition. It now teems with a population of over seventeen millions of intelligent, prosperous people, and with its vast areas and resources yet undeveloped is capable of supporting in comfort many millions more. Besides this, its possession made possible the acquisition of the great northwest and Texas and California.

The centennial of this great event will be celebrated in a world's fair twice the size of any other ever attempted in any country. Its success is assured by ample funds. The entire cost will be about forty millions of dollars. It will in every respect be an international exposition and under its agressive and able management be worthy of the event commemorated.

The grounds and buildings are laid out in a larger scale than ever before attempted, covering more than 1,200 acres, and will be surpassingly beautiful.

The exhibits, display and attractions like the event commemorated will be a departure from all precedent. Here will be gathered the most marvelous productions of the mighty brain and brawn of this wonderful age. A distinctive feature is the prizes offered for a great air ship competition.

The national government and all the states of the Union and all the territories and dependencies will be represented—all the nations of earth will take part in friendly interchange of ideas and in the competitions. It will probably be the last opportunity for adults to see a world's fair in this country. St. Louis furnishes great advantages as a place to hold such a fair; she has the largest railroad station in the world; twenty-four railroads will carry millions of visitors to the fair and lines of palatial steamboats on the Father of Waters will take many more who desire to travel more leisurely, and a view of the beautiful scenery on the upper river which rivals that of the Hudson.

What part shall Iowa take in this great enterprise? Within her boundaries are fifty-five thousand square miles of the choicest land of the entire purchase, and two and a quarter millions of as intelligent and progressive people as can be found anywhere. They possess ample means and abundant resources with and from which to make exhibits. A just state pride should induce every citizen to encourage a proper showing for Iowa. We are first in education, agriculture, stock raising, butter producing and in many other things we are too modest to mention. Let us maintain supremacy in these and win it in others. Let no line be neglected—there is room and opportunity for all. Our manufacturing interests should be exploited, and the advantages afforded in Iowa cities and towns for the increase and enlargement of these industries made apparent. We should show the world the excellence of our public and private schools, colleges, universities, churches and other institutions and that as an abiding place, Iowa has no superior on earth, and thus invite good people to come and help us develop our almost limitless resources and share our prosperity and our many other blessings.

CHAIRMAN: Are there any remarks on this paper? If not we will listen to the paper entitled "The silo for the Iowa farmer," by W. B. Barney of Hampton, Iowa.

THE SILO FOR THE IOWA FARMER.

—

W. B. Barney, Hampton, Iowa.

Centuries ago, on the British Isle, our forefathers learned that a greater number of their herds and flocks would withstand the rigor of the winter season by the cutting and making of their grasses into hay for winter feed than could be maintained by letting their kine run at large over the fields as had been their custom.

We all know that twenty years ago a very small per cent of our corn was cut up and that about one-half of this, the most valuable crop we have in Iowa, was wasted.

With land at $60 to $100 per acre, the question now arises as to what is the best means of saving, storing and utilizing this crop.

I built my first silo in 1895. It was oblong and not deep enough. In the use of this I found there was no feed as cheap as ensilage, if the loss was not too great by spoiling. I concluded to try again, and visited the dairy districts of Wisconsin, where silos are about as numerous as corncribs in Iowa. I found these were nearly all round; and, after getting all the pointers possible, I made my old one over into a barn below, bran and feed room above, and built a new one circular in form. The dimensions are as follows: Diameter, 25 feet; depth, 35 feet. I am wintering 125 head of Holstein Friesians. The matter of size and capacity of silo must be regulated by the amount of feed required, and size of herd. As the feeding is done from the top, arrange the size of your silo to take off from one to two inches per day.

The location of my silo is at the side of barn—about six feet from same—with a building connecting it with barn. The foundation is of good stone, 6 feet high, 18 inches thick. Two feet of this wall is above ground; four feet in the ground; the excavation being twenty-eight feet in diameter. The stone is laid in Louisville cement. The bottom is in clay, well tamped, and covered with two inches of grout, and a good coat of Portland cement put on bottom and sides up to woodwork. The wall at top in inside is flat for the width of six inches, the building being put on flush with inside of wall. The foot width of wall to outside slopes about two inches, and is covered with Portland cement. The sill is formed by cutting 2x6 in three feet lengths, hewing or sawing to radius of the building, laying on two layers of these, break joints, spike together. For studding I used 2x4, fourteen feet, lapped eighteen inches, and spiked together to get proper height. Set on sill one foot apart from center to center, toe nailed at bottom. In ordering studding get them sized. The plate at top is same as sill at the bottom. The studding where doors come should be double. Four doors are used for taking out silage. They are two and one-half feet wide by three and one-half feet high. I used 2x4s cut to circle on inside, laid on top of each other to fill the space in place of doors and in filling lay tarred paper against these on the inside. The silage will hold it there, if you will put in a few carpet tacks to hold in place while filling. Inside lining use No. 1 dressed fencing resawed or split and sized. By ordering the fencing resawed quite a saving will be made, as this charge is about $1.00 or $1.50 per thousand. In putting this on, rip first board to get a three-inch piece so as to break joints, spring to circle of studding, nail on with 8d nails. Carry up for a ways, then put on a layer of three-ply Giant P. & B. acid and water proof paper. This is much better than common tarred paper. After this, put on another layer of lumber, then paint the inside with coal tar. I know some do not advise this, but my experience shows me that it is a preservative.

For outside, use one layer of some sheeting as used inside, one coat of building paper cover with white pine. C siding rabbeted. In putting on both in and outer lining and siding, break joints as often as possible by starting on alternate studs. All these boards act as hoops and this is where the round silo gets its strength and why it is better than any other kind. If silo is less than twenty feet in diameter the layer of half-inch stuff under siding may be dispensed with. Use conical shingle roof, with good ventilator, the diameter of which schould be at least one-fifth that of the silo. A dormer window should be put in roof above plate for filling. Do not cut away the top plate to get this window in, as the plate helps brace the top. I use window sash for the upper half of this to let in light. The lower part is a door hinged at the top. The opening, including door and window, is about two feet, eight inches, by five feet.

Rats are very fond of silage, and this is the reason the bottom should be cemented and the foundation come above the ground afoot or more.

I am aware that some stave silos have been found fairly satisfactory; but on account of the shrinkage in drying out in the spring the hoops get loose and the wind is apt to rack or blow them down.

One of the important things is to get the silo as deep as possible in proportion to the diameter. The deeper the silo the greater the pressure and the smaller the feeding surface exposed. A silo twenty feet in diameter and twenty-two feet deep will hold about one hundred and seven tons. If you will add ten feet to the depth you about double its capacity, or have two hundred and four tons. My silo will hold three hundred and fifty tons and cost to build in 1901, $550.

The silage keeps perfectly. There is practically no loss. What shall we put in our silo? Where corn can be grown as abundantly as in Iowa, we believe it the best crop for ensilage, though clover, sorghum, millet and other plants have been tried with good success.

TIME OF FILING.

I have found best results from taking corn when ears are as nearly matured as possible and yet have at least half of the leaves green. I use corn harvester and haul direct from field to cutter. My cutter is 16-inch with 45-foot elevator. For power we use a six horse power gasoline engine. The distance to field, and the conditions are so varied about different places as to make it impossible to tell just how many hands can be profitably employed.

If your silo is twenty feet or more in diameter, put two of your trustiest men in the silo, to see that the corn is evenly and well spread, and tamped. General tamping of the whole surface is important; but much the larger amount of labor should be expended around the sides, as the friction against the walls prevents its settling.

If corn gets a little dry or has been frosted, as was the case this year, use water. In filling, I used twenty-five pails of water at noon and twenty-five at night. When I had finished, I put on six or eight barrels. Three or four inches on top is all the ensilage that spoiled.

Courtesy of Wallaces' Farmer.

Silo on farm of W. B. Barney, Hampton, Iowa.

One of the greatest objections offered to the silo is the work of filling. This is often more imaginary than real, and may be done largely by help about the farm.

I think slow filling preferable to too much haste, but the silo, as a rule, should not stand longer than two days between successive fillings.

Hauling shocked corn from the field in winter is not a very desirable job, and the unavoidable waste is too great. If it is to be shredded and fed in that form, it might as well be cut a little earlier and put in the silo, where it is practically all saved. We like the common variety of corn, though B. & W. ensilage has proven quite satisfactory. Whether planted in the regular way or to be cultivated only one way it is best to plant somewhat thicker than for ear corn.

As to the value of ensilage as a feed for dairy cows, or young stock, it is, in my opinion, hard to overestimate it. For the economical production of milk, there is nothing its equal. The silo is, we believe, the best safeguard against summer drouth. It is very difficult to have a soiling crop ready to feed when pasture fails, as this varies from year to year. H. B. Gurler, who milks 250 cows, always saves one of his silos and has it ready to open up at any time. Last year we put a good deal of corn in our silo that would have been of little value for other purposes on account of dry weather. This year a silo was a good thing on account of early frost. I have tried beets and mangels, but much prefer ensilage.

I am often asked how many acres of corn is required to fill my silo of 350 tons. An average year thirty acres will do this. I consider this equal to 175 tons of mixed clover and timothy hay. I would like to ask how many acres of land are required to produce this amount of hay an average year.

I have never used ensilage for beef making other than to feed it to old or barren cows. It has, with me, proven an excellent feed for this purpose.

The Illinois Experimental Station is now conducting an experiment with two lots of steers that will be of great value. The following data is taken from their bulletin:

Fifty steers were taken in 1901 at eight months old, and divided into two lots. The corn from 5.33 acres of land was put into a silo, while the corn from a like acreage was cut and shocked. One lot was fed ensilage with two pounds of oats and four pounds mixed clover and timothy hay; the other lot shock corn with a like amount of hay and oats. Pigs were put with each lot. The result shows May 5, 1902—the number of pounds of meat (beef and pork) per acre—are as follows:

Where ensilage and oats and hay were fed, 385.35 pounds of meat were produced per acre.

Where shock corn, oats and hay were fed, 337.91 pounds of meat were produced per acre.

As the amount of hay and oats fed to the two lots were practically the same, it is reasonable to suppose that this difference of 47.45 pounds of meat produced per acre was due to the different form in which the corn plant was fed. This showing would indicate that it is possible to make 47.45 pounds more of meat from an acre of corn put in a silo than fed out of the shock. In case of the silage fed steers 97.69 per cent of the meat produced was beef, and 2.31 per cent pork. The shock corn fed steers 84.22 per cent of the meat produced was beef and 15.78 per cent pork. This would show that in case of hog cholera on the farm, beef may be produced by the use of silage with but a small loss. That in the use of shock corn the hog is a most important factor, and that a loss of nearly 16 per cent of the meat produced would accrue from its elimination.

We understand that the experiment with these steers will be continued until both lots are finished for market. The result will be awaited with a good deal of interest and should be of great value.

In conclusion, I will say that I have found my silo one of the very best investments on my farm, and I think the silo for the Iowa dairy farmer—like the hand or farm separator—almost a necessity. For the economical production of beef on the ordinary farm, where the steer is grown from the calf, I believe it is to come into general use.

THE IMPROVEMENT OF SEED CORN.

P. G. Holden, Ames, Iowa.

The season of 1902 was characterized by two factors which made the maturing of seed corn a very difficult problem. A wet season followed by an early frost, rendered much of the corn soft and unfit for planting. Probably never before in the great Central West has the farmer so often asked himself "what shall I do to obtain good seed corn?"

IMPORTANCE OF USING HOME-GROWN SEED.

No doubt it will be necessary for many to secure corn for planting other than that which was grown on their own farms. And in this connection great care should be exercised.

Remembering that plants are very susceptible to their environments we cannot fail to recognize the damage of importing seed for the entire crop. If corn is imported from the southern part of the corn belt where a long season is shorter there is a tendency for the corn to produce a large growth of stalks and to partially or wholly fail to mature. The same danger exists in changing seed corn from east to west although not to so great a degree.

With land at present prices the corn grower throughout the central west cannot afford to incur such risk. The farmers should plant the major portion of their corn land with seed grown on their own farms or at least in their own locality, so that reliable returns will be insured.

It is well known that most of the seed corn put on the market by seedsmen was bought of farmers in crib lots, shelled, screened and sacked for sale, little or no attention being paid to the selection, in fact it is generally handled with the scoop shovel and is known as the "scoop shovel method of selection."

The chances are that the farmer has in his own crib better corn than that which he purchases from seedsmen at four or five times the market price. And then he runs the additional risk that it will not mature in his locality.

TRY WELL-BRED VARIETIES ON A SMALL SCALE.

The result of much careful work shows us that the corn plant can be bred up and the desirable qualities fixed, so that they will be reproduced in the succeeding crops. Some careful breeders have spent many years giving attention to this point and the result of their work is shown in the good qualities possessed by many of the standard varieties. Corn growers ought to take advantage of this valuable work and secure seed to plant an acre or so. In many cases there may be considerable immaturity in the first year's crop, yet only those ears which mature most perfectly should be selected for the following crop. If this plan of selection is repeated, year after year, corn is grown which is well adapted to the latitude and conditions in which it is raised. In this way the farmer will be able to get the improved variety which has become acclimated and the danger of loss from immaturity will be overcome to a very large degree, while the desirable qualities, the result of years of breeding, will be retained.

PURCHASE SEED CORN ONLY IN THE EAR.

In securing seed the factor of the greatest importance is the purchase of that corn which will give the largest yield per acre and of the best quality. The acre is the unit in corn production and therefore that seed is best which gives the largest yield per acre. Hence the important question for the farmer who must purchase seed corn this year, is not one of cost but of quality. It will prove far more profitable to pay three or four dollars for a bushel of seed corn which will germinate well, and insure an even stand and a large yield than to accept an inferior grade, although the first cost be exceedingly low.

These two rows of kernels were taken from two different ears. Judging from outward appearances of the ears, little or no difference in their values could be discovered. The ears from which these two rows of kernels were taken were almost exactly the same size, yet ear No. 2 weighed 16 per cent more than ear No. 1, and shelled out 20½ per cent more corn than ear No. 1. Ear No. 1 is not only very much poorer in feeding value than No. 2, but has a much lower vitality and gives a weaker plant.

It is very important that the tips of the kernels—the portion next to the cob—should be full and plump so that there is no space between the kernels down near the cob. In selecting our seed corn, it is important that we should do more than look at the ears; we must study the kernels.

Purchasing seed corn in the ear offers the farmer the surest and safest way to secure seed which will prove satisfactory. When the corn is in the ear the farmer can see just what he has. If, after a critical examination, he is confident that the corn is unsatisfactory he can reject it and return it at once. This plan will enable him to secure corn from another source or use his own seed which in fact may be superior to that which has been shipped to him. He will not lose a year in discovering that he has an undesirable type of corn as the kind of ears from which the seed is taken will determine the kind of ears that will be reproduced.

Corn in the ear also is the surest protection of the farmer against the unscrupulous practices of some of our seedsmen. The seedsman cannot improve the corn by shelling it so there is no good excuse for him to refuse to ship in the ear.

IMPORTANCE OF UNIFORMITY IN SIZE AND SHAPE OF KERNELS.

Of far-reaching importance is the value of a uniform stand of corn as without a good stand we cannot hope for the best results. During the past season the Agronomy Department of the Iowa Agricultural College gathered considerable data concerning the number of missing and barren stalks with the idea of finding, if possible, the cause of the low yield of about thirty-two bushels per acre for a period of years.

Upwards of 1,000 requests were sent out to farmers in different parts of the state asking them to count one hundred hills several places in their cornfields and determine accurately the per cent of missing hills and barren stalks.

The results of these counts show an average of 5.6 per cent of missing hills, which means over 1-20 producing absolutely nothing. Of the 278.59 stalks in the one hundred hills, 7 per cent were barren, yielding fodder, but no grain. These counts do not take into account the still greater number of hills which contain but one stalk, and as a consequence are producing less than one-half of what they should produce.

When we remember that nine and one-half millions of acres are devoted to the raising of corn in Iowa we can appreciate the serious loss that such irregularity causes.

Illustration No. 1.

Regular kernels.	Irregular kernels.		Regular.	Irregular.
I.	II.		I.	II.
	Ears.	c		Kernels.

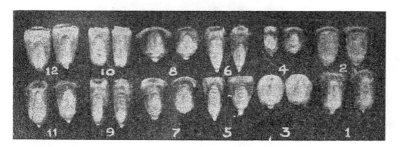

C.—Shows good and bad forms of kernels. The pairs of kernels 1, 2, 11 and 12 show the best forms in the order named, while Nos. 4, 5, 6, 7 and 8 show the poorest forms in the order named. Pair No. 1 are the best, since they are full and plump at the tips next to the cob and have large germs. Both of these points are important as they indicate strong vitality and feeding value. On the other hand, pairs Nos. 5, 6 and 7 are especially weak, with low feeding value and small per cent of corn to cob.

It will also be observed that these kernels are far from uniform in size and shape (compare with No. 4, and Nos. 2 and 6) and hence no planter will drop an even number per hill. (See table of tests.) When we realize that all of these kernels were taken from ears that appeared to be good ears, when examined from the standpoint of the ear alone, we can readily appreciate the importance of paying more attention to the study of the kernels of corn in our seed ears.

P

4   3   2   1

P.—In selecting seed corn ears 2 and 3 should be discarded as no planter will drop a uniform number of these kernels per hill.

Ears 1 and 4 have kernels of uniform size and shape, and when the butts and tips were shelled off the planter dropped three kernels to a hill 93 to 95 times out of every hundred tests while ear No. 3 tested 74-3's. 19-2's. 6-1's and 1-4's.

In the above illustrations C and P we see a condition which often exists in corn that has been selected for planting. Ear Number One shows rows that are straight with kernels that are uniform in size, and if we set our planter to drop any definite number of these kernels we can be sure the rate of dropping will be regular. Ear Number Two, though it is well filled with kernels and so far as feeding purposes are concerned would be very satisfactory, yet when we consider the size and shape of the kernels in relation to our planter we see the utter impossibility of getting the corn at all regularly.

IOWA DEPARTMENT OF AGRICULTURE.

The corn grower can do much to better this condition of affairs by carefully picking over his corn until all the ears show kernels of uniform size and shape. A careful study of the conditions which tends to an' uneven stand reveals that the cause is due largely to the lack of uniformity in the size and shape of the seed planted.

Illustration No. II.

Ears with kernels that are

| Large. | Small. | | Deep. | Shallow. |
| I. | II. | | III. | IV. |

B

| 3 | 2 | 1 |

B.—The kernels on earn No. 1 are nearly the same depth from tip to butt, while the kernels on ear No. 2 grow rapidly shorter towards the tip. The kernels on ear No. 3 are small, shallow and flinty, little larger than grains of pop corn and will run through the planter about like wheat. When these three ears were shelled together and tested in the planter there was a range of all the way from two to seven kernels per hill.

Q

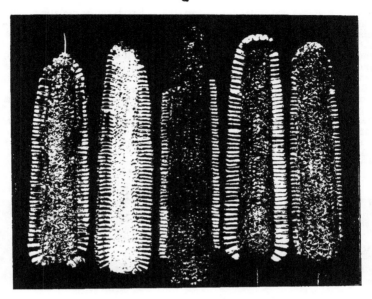

5   4   3   2   1

Q.—Ears Nos. 5 and 2 illustrate ears of corn with good strong kernels of medium depth. Ears Nos. 1 and 3 illustrate very shallow kernels, and if the kernels from these four ears are mixed, it is impossible to get them planted evenly.

Ear No. 4 shows space at the cob which indicates weak vitality, low percentage of corn to cob and low feeding value, the valuable portion of the kernel not being filled out. When examined externally these ears all appeared equally good, and this shows the importance of removing several kernels when selecting seed corn.

Illustration No. 2, B and Q, shows another feature which tends very much to an uneven stand. In each ear the rows are straight and the kernels of uniform size. However, when the grains from these two ears are placed in the planter box together, the possibility of getting a uniform drop is all removed. The same difficulty will be experienced when we attempt to plant ears of shallow grains with those having deep grains. To secure the best results ears should be selected that have kernels of uniform size and shape. By discarding the butt and tip kernels much of the trouble caused by lack of uniform size will be removed, the kernels on these parts being of various shapes and sizes.

SEED CORN SHOULD BE TESTED.

In order to secure a good stand and vigorous growth it is essential that the seed should be of strong vitality. Therefore all seed corn should be thoroughly tested.

Cigar Box and folder.

One of the simplest methods of testing seed corn and one which requires very little attention is shown in illustration No. III. Moisten some ordinary newspaper or cloth and fold it as shown in the folder above. Use several thicknesses, so that considerable moisture will be held; care being taken to soak the paper thoroughly. Then place the kernels to be tested on the folder and fold the sides down. It is advisable that duplicate tests be made by using several folders. Place some moistened paper in the bottom of the box, also a few thicknesses on top, so that sufficient moisture will be insured. Then tie the lid down, so as to prevent evaporation. Set the box in an ordinary living room and the heat will be sufficient for germination. If 94 per cent of the kernels send out strong sprouts within four or five days the corn will be safe for planting. Increasing the number of kernels to the hill does not compensate for low vitality. There may be a good many kernels germinate which when planted with those of strong vitality will send up a stalk which acts as a weed in occupying room and using plant food and moisture. Therefore in making a germination test we should note the evenness with which all kernels germinate.

Illustration No. III.

1   2

Illustrates one of the most convenient methods of testing the vitality of seed corn.
Figure No. 1 shows the box in which are placed three folders containing samples of corn to be tested.
Figure No. 2 shows a folder ready to put in box after the edges have been folded down over the corn. Any box will answer the purpose, although the cigar box represented in the cut, or a wooden one like it, is preferable.
The folders should be thoroughly moistened before placing the corn in them. Put four or five thicknesses of moistened paper in the bottom of the box and as many more over the samples to prevent drying out. Then shut the cover and wrap string around the box to hold the cover down to prevent the corn from drying out, and set away in the sitting room or some place where the temperature does not fall below 55 degrees. The best folders are made by taking five or six thicknesses of newspaper and cutting in strips about five or ten inches and folding as shown in the cut. The only precaution necessary is to be sure that the folders are thoroughly moistened before placing the corn in them for testing. In two or three days it will be well to examine the corn and if the folders are getting dry, they should be moistened by sprinkling water over them in the box. At the end of five days, the samples should be taken out and examined carefully. Every kernel that has not at this time sent out vigorous root and stem sprouts should be counted unfit for seed. The corn ought to test not less than 94 per cent to 95 per cent. This method has the advantage of requiring very little attention and makes it possible to see whether the kernels are making a uniform and vigorous germination, which is very important. Kernels which make a slow, feeble germination are not fit to plant.

SORTING SEED CORN.

Seed being an important factor in determining the yield of the crop, care ought to be exercised in its selection and preparation. The method of selecting and preparing corn for planting may be outlined as follows:

Make a preliminary test of the vitality of the corn from which the seed is to be selected. This can best be done by selecting from the pile say fifty to one hundred ears and removing two or three kernels from each ear and testing them. If the germination test shows 94 per cent or above the seed will be in good condition. This point determined, the corn should be selected with regard to getting a uniform stand. Place the ears in a row where the light is good and, carrying in the hand two ears which represent most nearly the desired type and possess the desirable qualities, remove all those ears which show objectionable features in the general appearance. They may be too short or too long, the butts and tips may not be covered, kernels may be too wide or too narrow, to thick or too thin, blocky, irregular in size or mixed.

From the remaining twenty-five or thirty ears remove two kernels from each and place them germ side up in front of the ear, so that they

4   3   2   1

Showing different types of corn. In selecting seed corn, it is important that all the ears be as nearly as possible of the same type. Ears Nos. 3 and 4 are very good ones, but they should not be planted with Nos. 1 and 2 as they are fifteen days later in maturing than the latter. In order o secure the best pollenization it is important that all the stalks should shoot and silk at about the same time. The very early and very late stalks are usually barren or partly so, owing to lack of pollen at these times. It is also difficult to secure an even stand with corn of different ty es, as the kernels are almost certain to be of different types and shapes, making it impossible for a planter to drop them evenly.

7

can be easily seen. We are now in a position to examine the ears more critically. All ears with very large or small kernels should be thrown out, no matter how perfect they are in other respects. The same is true of all ears with very short or long narrow grains and the irregular butt and tip kernels should be shelled off. It is also essential that we look for kernels of a good shape and with large germs which are neither colored, stained or wrinkled, kernels that are free from chaff and of good color.

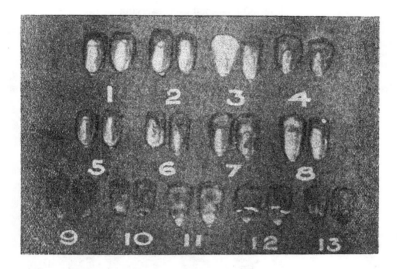

Pairs of kernels numbers 1, 2, 5 and 6 show good, deep, well-filled germs, thus indicating strong vitality and good feeding value. Numbers 3, 4 and 7 show short germs and this indicates weak vitality and low feeding value. No. 8 shows wrinkled germs indicating immaturity and weakened vitality. No. 13 shows chaff adhering indicating lack of maturity. No. 12 shows broken outer covering and undesirable state of the cuticle. No. 10 shows darkened end and is generally unhealthy, and of low vitality. No. 9 shows good backs of kernels.

The color and size of the cob should be noted: A white cob in white corn and a red cob in yellow corn. A small cob is desirable, as it is usually associated with a deep kernel and it also contains less moisture, and so long as moisture is in the cob it will be impossible to dry the kernel sufficiently to prevent harm from frost.

The ears finally chosen should have kernels of uniform size and shape; the kernels to taper slightly, but be well filled down at the tip.

Then each ear should be shelled by itself, so that it can be examined more closely before it goes in with the rest of the corn. Place the kernels on a screen or seive and by hand picking sort out all irregular, broken or injured kernels and those with stained, discolored or wrinkled kernels. After this process the corn is ready to be introduced to the planter. Set the planter up on blocks in some conveient place and with the corn in the planter box turn the wheel at about the rate it would

move when planting. About a peck of the corn should be taken at a time
and the test should be to get a regular number of kernels for each drop

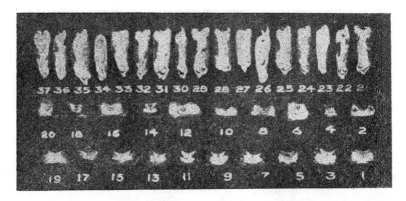

Cross-sections of kernels showing depth of germ and the white floury or starchy
portion lying just below the germ. The kernels in the lower row have better germs than
those in the upper row. Nos. 17, 15, 13 and 11 are among the best, while Nos. 2, 14 and 18
are among the poorest because they have very shallow germs and are low in feeding value.
The white, starchy appearing material lying just below the germ has the very lowest
feeding value of any part of the kernel. Nos. 17, 15 and 11 show a very small amount of
this material, while Nos. 1, 2, 12 and 19 show a great deal and should be discarded for
seed purposes.

The upper row (Nos 21-37) show the depth of the germ when the kernels are split
into lengthwise through the middle of the germ. Nos. 21, 24, 27, 28, 29, 33 and 35 show
very deep germs and are from ears rich in protein and oil. No. 35 being from the ear
richest in protein of 2,000 tests, while Nos. 22, 23, 36 and 37 are from ears very poor in
feeding value it will also be noticed that the germs are very small.

*Note.—Chemical analysis shows that the per cent of oil and protein is
higher in the germ than in any other part of the kernel. Thus we can
see the importance of a deep kernel and a broad, deep, well filled germ.*

of the planter. If the corn is uniform the planter should give the desired
number of kernels at each drop. If the number of kernels dropped is irregular this corn should be resorted to remove irregular or discarded
kernels.

There is no one thing that would do more to increase the yield of
corn on every farm in Iowa than the careful selecting and sorting of the
seed both in the ear and after it is shelled, and then stay with it until
the planter will drop the desired number of kernels at least ninety times
out of 100 tests. It may be necessary to have the plates of the planter
drilled or get new ones or take more care in sorting out the large, small
and irregular kernels. The main thing is to stay with it until the work is
satisfactory.

The preparation of the seed corn and testing of the planter should be
done during the latter part of February and the forepart of March. If
this important work is put off until April or May it is very likely
neglected, as is too often the case. This is simply a matter of good business management and no one can afford to neglect it.

After the corn has been sorted, shelled and thoroughly tested in the
planter it should be put in sacks (about a bushel in each sack) and hung

up in a dry place in the loft or where there is a thorough circulation of air and where it will be free from mice.

4   3   2   1

The kernels on ear No. 1 are too thin and those on ear No. 4 are too narrow, while those on ears Nos. 2 and 3 are too broad and thick. Ears of this kind should be discarded for seed purposes, as no planter can be set to drop the kernels evenly. The planter tests with this corn showed a variation in the dropping all the way from 1 to 6 kernels per hill.

About the twentieth of April a thorough germination test should be made. There are many methods of doing this and any of them will be satisfactory. The important thing is not to fail to make the test. About 100 kernels should be taken from each sack by running the hand down into the corn so as to get a fair average sample.

May we all exercise the utmost care in selecting the seed for this year's crop, give it the best cultivation we can and hopefully look forward to an increased yield and a corresponding improvement in the quality of the corn harvested.

CHAIRMAN: We have with us Professor Macbride of the State University, President of the Iowa Park and Forestry Association.

PROFESSOR MACBRIDE: Mr. Chairman and Gentlemen: I am very glad to appear before you, if just for a moment. I became so much interested in what you were discussing that I almost forgot

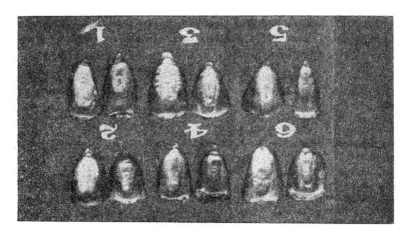

Kernels showing large and small germs, taken from different ears of corn. The left hand kernels in all pairs come from ears with low feeding value and should be discarded for seed purposes, while the right hand kernels with large germs come from ears with higher per cent of oil and protein.

what I came in here to say. I do not see that you could do anything better than to keep up this discussion. However, I came in here delegated to bring you greeting from the latest ally you have in the culture of this magnificent state. The latest organization which comes to your assistance to do, as I trust, the same sort of work that you are trying to do, is the Iowa Park and Forestry Association. There would not seem to be much need to say anything to the farmers of Iowa in regard to either parks or forestry, especially as these farmers are represented here this afternoon; and for this reason; the men who have made Iowa one magnificent park from one side of it to the other, and from river to river, are men who are naturally interested in all that I and my colleagues have sought to promote; and I believe, and I have found it true, that the men who are furthering the ordinary processes of agriculture (who are striving for improved culture of the field), in the state of Iowa are by no means backward in finding out the way to make their homes more beautiful and their lawns more beautiful, and how to find the best trees for planting about their grounds and premises. Indeed, I have found in every community that the man giving the most attention to the field and what he raises there is the man who is most interested in those things that make for

beauty and the permanent happiness of our people. We consider
that forestry and park improvement go hand in hand with scientific farming; that forestry is in its way the highest and best kind
and type of agriculture, and we believe that in this agitation we
are helping you; and we believe that you will help us a great deal,
and I am here to say that you are cordially invited to come out,
each and every one of you, and become each a member of the
Iowa Park and Forestry Association, and so help more and more
to make this one of the finest lands not only on this old planet,
but in all the fields of time.

Gentlemen, I thank you.

(Meeting here adjourned.)

Jersy Bull Silverine Coomassie, owned by J. E. Bobbins, Greenburg, Indiana, and
shown at the Iowa State Fair, 1902.

STATE AGRICULTURAL CONVENTION AT DES MOINES, WEDNESDAY, DECEMBER 10, 1902.

The convention convened in the rooms of the Department of Agriculture in the capitol, at 10 o'clock on this day, with President Frasier in the chair.

The first order of business was the appointment of a committee on credentials. The president appointed the following committee on credentials: John Ledgerwood of Decatur county, J. I. Nichols of Muscatine county and B. L. Manwell of Black Hawk county.

Vice-President Morrow was called to the chair and President Frasier delivered the following address:

PRESIDENT'S ADDRESS.

J. C. Frasier, Bloomfield, Iowa.

We have assembled here today to report what we have done since our last annual meeting, and to elect officers for the ensuing year. I am glad to be able to report that the financial condition of the Iowa department of agriculture is good. The expenditures on the State Fair Grounds for the year 1902 were large, in round numbers about $27,000 in addition to the $37,000 appropriated by the legislature for the building of the live stock pavilion. Forty-five thousand dollars was the total cost of this building, and while it is a large amount of money, I think it is worth many times its cost to the live stock interests of the state. And it is a building that every citizen of our state may justly be proud of. I think this convention should extend a vote of thanks to the Twenty-eighth General Assembly for its liberality in voting an appropriation of $37,000 for the erection of this building.

Two new cattle barns were built, one with stalls for 108 head of cattle, costing $3,281.76, and the other was built the first three days of the fair costing $631.17. A new dry air closet costing $3,775 was erected and brick sidewalks, crossings and curbings at a cost of $2,171.82 were also built. The secretary in his report will give you a full and complete statement of the cost of all improvements and repairs for the year.

The fair of 1902 was a success in every respect. The exhibits in all departments were good. The cattle show was the best ever seen at any state fair and for the first time in the history of the society the people could see the exhibit with comfort.

While it rained Monday, and looked gloomy enough Tuesday forenoon to give us all the blues, the gate receipts for those two days were good; but Wednesday was a record breaker and more money was taken in on that day than on any other day in the previous history of the society.

The attractions were furnished by Paine of New York and Chicago, both for afternoon and evening, and were a success, proving that night attractions will pay if you get the proper kind. No doubt the attendance at night would have been much larger had our transportation facilities been greater. However, the street car company did the best they could to handle the immense crowd, but it was a physical impossibility to get the people home before twelve o'clock on Tuesday and Wednesday nights.

Some improvements will no doubt be made during the year 1903 and perhaps it is not necessary for me to suggest what should be done as the board of directors know as well as I do what is needed. But if I may be allowed to make some suggestions, I would say continue the walks begun this year and build a brick building for the electric light plant. North of the street, running north of the live stock pavilion, where the electric light plant now stands the plant is surrounded by wooden buildings and in case of fire in that part of the grounds, this valuable plant would very likely be destroyed and no means left for lighting the grounds. I think the time has arrived when the Iowa State Fair should exclude all side shows from the grounds. The only excuse that ever could have been made for them was the need of the revenue received, but that is no longer an excuse.

In severing my connection with the department, I wish to thank you for the honors conferred upon me, and to the members of the board I owe a debt of gratitude for the many courtesies and favors shown me. I shall always look back with pleasure to the many hours that I have labored with you.

Wishing each one a happy and prosperous life, and to the department success, I again thank you.

Secretary Simpson read his report as follows:

SECRETARY'S REPORT.

J. C. Simpson, Des Moines, Iowa.

Following the last annual convention and meeting of the State Board of Agriculture, at which meeting I had the honor of being elected secretary, the first work to be given our attention was the collecting and editing of material for the second annual "Year Book." Desiring to have the copy in the hands of the state printer before the usual legislative rush, this was found to be no small task. The first copy was delivered to the printer January first. Very little typesetting had been done by the time the legislature convened and work on the "Year Book" was suspended, the printing to be done for the general assembly being given preference over it. This is usually the case during the winter when the legislature is in session. As this is an off year it is to be hoped that the printing can be done and the book placed in your hands before corn planting time. Although the copy was furnished promptly it was the first day of May when we received the first books for distribution. They should be out by the first of March, and this we hope to accomplish this year.

In preparing the "Year Book" of 1901, a radical change was made in the usual style, by dividing the copy into parts, placing each article as nearly as possible under its proper head, and by thus grouping the different subjects, hoping thereby to popularize it. From press and other comments received we believe our efforts along this line met with some favor. More than five hundred requests for the "Year Book" after the supply was exhausted, have been received.

The work of preparing the copy for the third annual "Year Book" is now under way, and it is our earnest desire to improve this over the one of last year. It is the intention to use in this book several cuts made from photographs of Iowa farm scenes, and animals shown at the last state fair. Members of the state board and this convention are requested to aid in this work by suggesting where pictures of model farm scenes, improvements and live stock may be obtained. While I do not intend offereing a premium for these pictures, I trust you will assist in making the "Year Book" as attractive as possible by making suggestions and assisting in collecting the views. A few good cuts will in no way detract from its usefulness and my experience has been that a book is read and studied much more if it is well illustrated.

FARMER'S INSTITUTES.

We expect to devote a number of pages in the forthcoming "Year Book," to a report of the Farmers' Institutes. At the last session of the legislature an amendment was passed to Section 3, Chapter 58, Acts of the Twenty-eighth General Assembly, giving to each farmers' institute in the state a vote at the annual State Agricultural Convention, provided such farmers' institute has been organized at least one year, and has reported to the Secretary of Agriculture not later than November first, through its president and secretary of executive committee, that an institute was held according to law, the date thereof, the names and postoffice addresses of its officers. They are also to furnish the state secretary of agriculture with a copy of the program of each institute hereafter held and where addresses are read before such institute one or more of these in written or printed form. No proxy given by any delegate elected by a farmers' institute shall be recognized by said convention. This we hope will bring the agricultural interests of the state more closely together, and to insure a larger gathering at the annual State Farmers' Institute and Agricultural Convention.

We have prepared a blank which we ask the secretary of each farmers' institute to fill out, giving the county in which an institute is held; topics discussed; place of holding last meeting; place and date of holding next meeting; names of officers, etc. This is the only way a complete record of every institute in Iowa can be secured. This information is to enable us to answer innumerable questions relative to the date, location and program which are almost daily called for. The co-operation of the officers of each institute will greatly facilitate this work, and will be appreciated by this office.

CROP SEASON.

The past season has been quite a contrast to that of 1901; however, we believe the object lessons taught our agricultural people by these extremes, will fully compensate them for any decreased yield of farm products. It is our intention to ask some of the leading farmers over the state to contribute a paper for the "Year Book" on "A dry vs. a wet season from the standpoint of the farmer." This will bring out some very interseting discussions that should be of much value, in the future, under similar conditions. The crop report for 1902, compiled by the Iowa Weather and Crop Service will be published in the "Year Book" in full.

THE SILO.

Considerable space has been given to the discussion of the silo by the agricultural press of the past few months, which would indicate that farmers are seeking information on this subject. Several farmers of the state who have used the silo, have been asked to contribute papers on the silo for the "Year Book." There are men in Iowa who have been using the silo for the past ten or fifteen years, who now say they hardly see how they could get along without it. In the "Year Book" we will publish an experiment conducted at the Illinois Station by Prof. Mumford, on silage for the beef steer, in which he states that there are nine distinct advantages in a system of silage feeding over that of shock corn in wintering calves intended for beef production, as against three disadvantages.

ALFALFA FOR IOWA.

Alfalfa has never been raised in Iowa except in small tracts, and it is a question whether the acreage can be materially increased. I notice by the last report on crops from Nebraska, the tonnage of alfalfa in that state this year is but little less than that of hay. If the acre age in Iowa can be increased there is no question but what those who have soil on which it can be grown will be greatly benefited. It is well known that the soil of this state, as a whole, is not adapted to the growing of alfalfa, but there may be hundreds of acres in Iowa that will produce as good a crop as that of Nebraska. It has been grown successfully for a number of years along the Missouri river bottoms in the western part of the state. Several people from that part of the state have been asked to contribute a paper for the "Year Book," and give the public the benefit of their experience. The question of "Successful growing of alfalfa in Iowa," is one that every farmer will have to solve for himself. It would be well worth his time to experiment on a few acres, for there are few crops that will bring the same returns acre for acre.

LIVE STOCK AND CORN JUDGING.

The short course of stock judging conducted by the college at Ames the past two years, has proven so successful, that it is not now a question of whether enough students can be enrolled from among the farmers of the state to make it pay, but what to do with all those who wish to attend. It would not be surprising if the enrollment for the course the first two weeks in January would be from 600 to 700. Farmers who have fed cattle all their lives have said, that they never really knew how to judge them until after they had attended one of these short courses.

There will be a school of corn judging, and all those who contemplate attending should select a dozen ears of their best corn and take with them when they go in order to have the corn passed on by competent judges. This will enable them to compare the corn grown at home with that of others, and will in many cases show where improvement can be made. Iowa grows 9,000,000 acres each year, and we are satisfied that those who attend this school for two weeks will know more about corn. A difference of five bushels per acre over the whole of Iowa would amount to $20,000,000 a year, and this can be accomplished by being better able to select the right kind of seed corn. Professor Holden who will have charge of this work is without doubt the most eminent corn specialist in the world.

The amount of money expended in attending these courses will prove one of the best investments of a life time. The actual expense including railroad fare, board and everything else will be less than $25.00.

IMPROVEMENTS FOR 1902.

After the last annual meeting several members of the board were discussing the improvements to be made on the fair grounds. Each had his idea of the improvements that were the most necessary, but were all of one opinion in stating that the time had arrived when the state should make appropriations for permanent improvements on the fair grounds. The management had long felt the need of a stock pavilion. This was brought before the board at their January meeting, and by a unanimous vote it was decided to ask the legislature for an appropriation of $37,000,000 to erect a suitable building. The bill met with a cold reception at the hands of some of the members at first, but after investigation they were convinced that the state was badly in need of such a building on the fair grounds. We are pleased to state that it passed the house by a unanimous vote. It met with some opposition in the senate, but when put upon its final passage there were but two votes against it.

It was the fifth day of May when the board met to open the bids and award the contracts for the erection of this building. When the bids were opened it was found that the cost would be from seven to eight thousand dollars more than the appropriation. Regardless of this, by a unanimous vote of the board it was decided to award contracts, and draw on the funds of the department to meet the deficit. The building was erected in less than four months, and was ready long before the opening day of the fair. Many favorable comments on the building were made by the exhibitors and visitors at the fair, as well as by the exhibitors at the horse show which was held in the building two weeks after the fair.

The judging of cattle and horses was carried on in this building, beginning at nine o'clock Tuesday morning, and ending with the last class on Friday afternoon. The contrast was most marked by the old-timer, who weary of pushing, struggling and standing around the ring, witnessing the contests of a few years ago, now settled himself comfortably under the roof of the grand new stock pavilion, free from the scorching sun and inclement weather. Not by word or thought did he censure the members of the legislature for their action in providing a building for the greatest industry in Iowa.

The program should be so arranged at the next fair, that the horses and cattle will not be shown in the arena at the same time. It is dangerous and accidents should be provided against before they occur. In this respect we were very fortunate this year, much more so than at the Illinois fair where a very serious accident might have occurred.

From eleven to one o'clock on Tuesday, August 26th, the building was given over to the old soldiers who had prepared an excellent program. Hon. A. B. Cummins and United States Senator J. P. Dolliver appeared on the program at this gathering and entertained those present by short addresses. The veterans should be given the standing invitation to continue this as a feature of the fair for Old Soldiers' Day.

The board had arranged to dedicate the building on Monday afternoon at one o'clock, but owing to the disagreeable weather the ceremonies were postponed until the same hour Wednesday. Governor Cummins dedicated the building on behalf of the state and spoke at length on the greatness of the state and its resources. He quoted some interesting figures showing that in the United States there is employed as fixed capital in manufactures a little more than $5,000,000,000, while in agriculture there is invested more than $20,000,000. This address as well as that of Hon. W. F. Harriman, who accepted the building on behalf of the State Board of Agriculture will be found printed in full in the annual "Year Book."

DRY AIR CLOSETS.

The two dry air closets built on the grounds had proven to be satisfactory in every respect, so the board deemed it advisable to erect a third this year. The building cost $3,775, a slight increase over the cost of the former. These dry air closets have solved the sewerage problem for the grounds and is a great improvement over the old system.

STREETS.

Much work was done on the streets this year in the way of grading and putting on cinders and gravel. Much difficulty was experienced in doing this work properly, on account of the heavy rains which at times washed away the gravel before it had time to settle. However, we were able to materially improve them, and with a little work of this character each year they can be put in excellent condition. There was an effort made at one time, advocating the paving of the streets with brick, but this after deliberation did not seem advisable. It would cost thousands of dollars. This money could be better expended in permanent buildings, which would be of much more benefit to the fair.

BARNS.   ..

During the fair of 1901 a large tent had to be erected to make room for all the cattle we had on exhibition, so at the board meeting last winter it was decided to put up a new barn. This action of the board was carried out by the executive committee and a barn 120 by 160 feet was erected. In this we put fifty-four large double stalls, which made room for 108 head of cattle. The barn complete cost in round numbers, $3,200. With this additional space it was hoped to stable all the cattle that would be on exhibition. In this we were agreeably disappointed, and at the last minute another barn had to be erected to make room for all that were coming. This barn was very hastily put up in one day, but since the fair it has been rebuilt and is first class in every respect. This gives us thirteen barns for use in the cattle department, but if the entries keep on increasing, it will not be long before the board will be forced to build new ones.

The department purchased the Iowa Producers' Building in the fall of 1901. This building was repaired and turned over to the superintendent of the machinery department. He now informs me that it is hard to rent space in the building on account of its location and recommends that it be moved to a location more accessible to the public.

About the time of the purchase of the above mentioned building, a deal was made whereby the department came into possession of the building formerly owned by the Burlington Railway Company. This was fitted up as an office for the secretary and treasurer. The old secretary's and treasurer's office was remodeled to be used for police headquarters. Comfortable bunks were put in, and while it does not have the appearance of a Pullman sleeper in the interior it answers the purpose quite as well.

The dwelling on the grounds occupied by the superintendent was in a very bad state of repairs and was rebuilt this season.

The poles supporting the wires of the electric light plant were many of them rotten and it was practically necessary to rebuild the line. Some of the wires and lamps had to be replaced. In addition to this we purchased a dozen arc lamps for use in lighting the stock pavilion.

About three-quarters of a mile of brick sidewalk was laid. I think the public fully appreciated this on the first day of the fair, when we had one of the hardest rains of the season. This walk we slushed with cement filling up the cracks which makes it as solid as a pavement.

The Iowa State Fair for 1902 was the greatest the state has ever seen. It was not only the best fair ever held in Iowa, but the greatest ever held in the West. The receipts were larger than ever before received at an Iowa fair. The total aggregate amounts to nearly $63,000. On Wednesday during the fair of 1896, the day's receipts amounted to a little over $19,000, which was the largest ever received in one day up to the present year. On Wednesday of the fair this year the receipts were over $21,000, As stated before the total receipts for the fair, in round numbers, were $63,000, and the total premiums and expenses were $43,000. This you will see leaves us a balance of $20,000 from the fair of 1902.

On Monday the prospects for a good attendance looked gloomy. The rain began early in the morning and continued all day long until late in the evening. One would have thought by studying the faces of the members of the board on this day, that they were all preparing to attend the funeral of very dear friends. In estimating the success or failure of the state fair, no matter what the number of entries or quality of exhibits may be, it is judged by the cash to be found in the treasurer's office. If one had examined the books in his office after the first day, it would not have taken long to have seen, that another day or two of the rain, would have made a dismal failure of the Iowa State Fair for 1902 from a financial standpoint, and this in the eyes of the public in general would have been sufficient.

On Tuesday morning, however, the skies cleared and the remainder of the week was ideal weather. The race track had been left in a frightful condition and it was late on Tuesday afternoon before we were able to start any races, and even on Wednesday the track was so soft that a great many horsemen refused to start their horses. We had received a very large list of entries, more than ever before, and the condition of the track interfered with what would have otherwise been the best race program ever seen on the Iowa State Fair grounds. .

The horse exhibit at the fair showed improvement over last year, but was not up to what it should have been, especially in the draft classes. The superintendent informs me that he conversed with many of the large horse breeders during the fair, and they assured him they would make an exhibit another year, since we have the stock pavilion in which to show their horses. The large increase in the number of entries at the Illinois state fair this year was largely due to the stock pavilion, so I was informed by their superintendent of horses. We hope as much for our horse department another year.

Never before in the history of the Iowa State Fair has so great a lot of cattle been gathered together as at the 1902 exhibition. It was the strongest in numbers and best in quality ever witnessed in the show ring. Over 800 head of cattle were on the grounds, and this certainly demonstrates Iowa's rank as the first cattle state of the union. The exhibitors were generally satisfied with the awards.

Iowa leads the world in its swine exhibit. This year the number of entries were over 900, and the number of hogs on the grounds being something over 1,700. I believe I am safe in saying that at least 70 per cent of the hogs shown at our fair, change hands before being taken from the grounds. One exhibitor this year informed me that he received over $800 for the thirty-two he brought to the fair.

The sheep exhibit was rather light but of good quality. The number of entries were as large as could be expected from a state that raises as few sheep as Iowa. However, I should state that the exhibit consisted of some of the best flocks in America, from the states of New York, Michigan, Illinois, Wisconsin, Nebraska, Minnesota and Iowa.

The machinery display excelled all past exhibitions of this kind, and if there was one feature of the fair that more than another indicated the great prosperity that the state is enjoying, it was this department. It is one of the great educational features of the fair. Implement dealers, farmers and live stock men spent many hours in this department and the exhibitors all seemed pleased with the interest shown in their exhibits. The space set aside for the department presented a far different appearance from that of a few years ago, when many of the large manufacturing. concerns signed an agreement not to exhibit at state fairs.

The exhibits in the agricultural, horticultural, dairy and art departments were up to the usual standards. While the showing of corn was not as good as it would have been had the season been less backward, it was much better than was looked for a few weeks before the fair. The county exhibits were especially good this year, and the display of fruits in the horticultural building has seldom been excelled.

The poultry exhibit of the fair this year was the largest ever shown and attracted more attention than in previous years.

CHANGES IN PREMIUM LIST FOR 1903.

I wish to call the attention of the members of the state board to a few changes in the premium list which I would recommend for another year. Several years ago a 10 per cent entry fee was enacted for all entries made. This worked a hardship on many exhibitors, some of them paying as much as fifty or sixty dollars in entry fees and receiving no premiums. This rule was changed later on and instead of charging the fee on each entry made, the ten per cent was deducted from all premiums awarded, thus eliminating the entrance fee from those not receiving premiums. Having conversed with many of the exhibitors this year, before and since holding our fair, at the Illinois State Fair and the International Live Stock Show, I find them almost a unit in condemning our rule which takes from them 10 per cent of their premiums. So far as I have been able to learn, from an examination of the premium lists of other state fairs, the Iowa fair is the only one that now exacts this ten per cent, and I now believe that for the best interests of our fair in the future this rule should be abolished.

Another matter that should be given careful consideration by our state board, is the advisability of issuing a catalogue of the cattle and horse exhibit. The only criticism that was made on our stock exhibit this year was the absence of a catalogue that would enable the people occupying seats in the pavilion to identify the animals shown. The press has been unanimous in expressing their opinion that a catalogue should be issued for our next fair. I am well aware that the efforts along this line in previous years were not successful, for the reason that it was very difficult to get the exhibitors to send in their pedigrees. I believe they now realize that the best results cannot be obtained without a catalogue. It is true we would be compelled to close the entries in these departments at least two weeks before the opening day of the fair, and this would probably shut out some exhibitors the first year, but the benefit the public would derive from the use of the catalogue would more than make up for the loss thus sustained. If a catalogue is to be issued a pair of scales are needed to weigh the stock and have their weight marked on the cards tacked on the stalls and used by the attendants in the show ring.

IMPROVEMENTS FOR 1902.

There are a number of improvements that should be made on the fair grounds; far more than the finances of the department will permit. The new board will have a surplus of $30,000 at their disposal. It would be unwise to reduce the surplus below $12,000, which amount should be set aside so as to be able to meet any emergency which may arise. A large sum of money is necessary each year in keeping the old frame buildings in repair. Most of these buildings have been on the grounds for more than sixteen years, and many are now in a very bad state of repairs. After this it can be readily seen that the board will not have a very large sum to be expended in the erection of permanent buildings. Cold water paint used judiciously on some of the buildings would add greatly to their appearance especially on the sheep and swine barns and the fence around the race track. Then put a few ornamental bridges across the creek in place of the old ones.

The sidewalk should be extended and more crossings put in, so that in case of rain such as was experienced this year, it would be possible for the people to visit the grounds without wading in mud to their shoe-tops. A few hundred feet of sidewalk laid each year would soon put the grounds in such a condition that it would be a pleasure to visit the grounds on a rainy day.

Trees would add greatly to the comfort of the exhibitors, and visitors on the main part of the ground, and a number should be planted each year.

The hog and sheep men have long wished for suitable buildings in which to judge their animals, and I believe this should be among the first of the improvements to have consideration from the board. The exhibit that the hog men have made the past few years certainly entitles them to a better place to show their hogs than we now have. The same can be said of the sheep exhibit. While not so large in numbers as the hogs, nevertheless the quality has been good, and we should encourage a larger exhibit by giving them a building in which to show their sheep and a place where the public can be comfortable while watching the judge tying the ribbons. A smaller building would answer the purpose in this department.

COUNTY AND DISTRICT FAIRS.

This has been a remarkable year for the county and district fairs of the state. I believe that I am safe in stating that at least half of the fairs had to postpone their opening day on account of rain, or were brought to a sudden close for the same reason. Strange to say, notwithstanding the wet weather, the receipts from the seventy-nine fairs reporting this year were larger than from the eighty-two reporting in 1901. The total amount of the premiums paid were about $5,000 less. We attribute this to the rainy weather which prevented people from bringing in their exhibits. Columbus Junction district fair of Louisa county still leads in the largest amount paid in premiums, paying this year about $2,000 aside from speed. By studying the financial statement of the county and district fairs published in the "Year Book," you will find invariably that the fair having a good speed program pays more premiums in the other departments.

LOUISIANA PURCHASE EXPOSITION.

Preparations should be commenced at once for an exhibit at the Louisiana Purchase Exposition to be held in St. Louis in 1904. Iowa is a part of the territory purchased just one hundred years ago from France and will be prominently identified in every way with this greatest of all expositions. The general assembly has wisely appropriated $125,000 that the state may be properly represented, and a commission of thirteen members consisting of men prominent in state affairs have been appointed by the governor. It is the intention of this commission to erect on the ground at St. Louis in the location set apart and said by those who have seen it to be most desirable of any assigned to states, a building to cost about $50,000. This is to be the home of the Iowa people, and as Goveruor Larrabee, president of the commission, says: the latch string will always be out not only for Iowa people, but for the friends of Iowa as well. The commission intends to make an exhibit in every line of the state's industries and asks the State Department of Agriculture to take preliminary steps toward aiding in this work. Agriculture has always been a prominent feature in Iowa exhibits at the various expositions held and the state department should excel herself in this coming meeting at St. Louis. Few Iowa people have anything of an idea of the magnitude of the exposition to be held in St. Louis in 1904. St. Louis's world's fair will be approximately twice as large as any former international exposition. The Centennial Exposition at Philadelphia covered 236 acres, the Paris Exposition of 1899-1900 336 acres, the Columbian Exposition at Chicago, 633 acres, the Pan-American at Buffalo 350 acres.

THE ST. LOUIS WORLD'S FAIR WILL COVER 1,200 ACRES.

The construction cost of the Paris Exposition was $9,000,000; that of the Columbian Exposition $18,322,000 and the total cost of the Pan-American Exposition was $10,000,000.

8

The estimated cost of the St. Louis World's Fair will be $30,000,000. This you know will mean $40,000,000 by the time the work is completed.

Before the exposition gates are open May 1, 1904, the city of St. Louis will have expended the enormous sum of $20,000,000. Of this amount $5,000,000 was appropriated for the fair through the municipal assembly, her citizens raised $5,000,000 additional by private subscription, and by popular vote at a special election October 22d, the charter amendments were carried, which will enable the city to expend $10,000,000 for street paving and other public improvements.

The work in progress at St. Louis at this time, eighteen months prior to the opening of the fair, shows it to be further along than did the world's fair at Chicago twelve months prior to the opening. The Iowa commissioners urge that immediate steps be taken by the state department of agriculture so that the exhibits in the way of agricultural products may be planned for at the time of the spring planting.

I herewith submit as a supplementary report a statement of the financial condition of the department at the close of the fiscal years, December 1. 1902:

Money coming into my hands as secretary and paid to G. D. Eellyson, treasurer, as shown by his receipts:

Speed entries	$2,762.50
Exhibitors' tickets	1,530.00
Insurance—loss and returned premiums	101.33
Booths in stock pavilion	520.00
Advertising in premium list	245.00
State appropriation for stock pavilion	37,000.00
State appropriation for insurance and repairs	1,000.00
Speed suspensions	111.50
Protest money forfeited	20.00
Railroad coupon tickets	3,804.50
Interest on deposit	1,040.33
Short-Horn Association, special premiums	625.00
	$48,760.16

SECRETARY'S ACCOUNT WITH G. D. ELLYSON, TREASURER.

Receipts.	Credit.	Debit.
To cash on hand December 1, 1901	$34.244.93	
From W. C. Brown, Supt. Horse Department	487.00	
From C. E. Cameron, Supt. Seed Department	1,328.30	
From S. B. Packard, Supt. Cattle Department	743.00	
From W. M. McFadden, Supt. Swine Department	436.50	
From Jno. Ledgerwood, Supt. Sheep & Poultry Dpts.	179.80	
From W. W. Morrow, Supt. Machinery Dept	948.75	
From R. T. St. John, Supt. Agricultural Dept	132.00	
From M. McDonald, Supt. Dairy Department	427.51	
From M. J. Wragg, Supt. Horticultural Dept	37.50	
From J. P. Manatrey, Supt. Art Department	1,131.10	

Receipts.	Credit.	Debit.
From T. C. Legoe, Supt. of Gates................	416.75	
From J. W. Wadsworth, Supt. of Privileges........	5,162.00	
From John Cownie, Supt. Electric Lights	125.00	
From J. C. Frasier	3.00	
From Donald Hill, Chief of Police	12.75	
From James H. Deemer, Supt. of Fair Grounds ..	1,375.40	
From J. C. Simpson, Secretary	48,760.16	
From Ticket Sales	42,415.25	

Disbursements.		
By expense warrants paid—1901-1902...........$	86,206.54	
By premium warrants paid—1901-1902............	21,787.91	
By cash on hand, December1, 1902..............	30,372.25	

	$138,366.70	$138,366.70
Cash on hand December 1, 1902 ....$30,372.75		
By outstanding warrants, Dec. 1, 1902.. 151.35		

Total credit for Dept. Agriculture.....$30,220.90

SECRETARY'S ACCOUNT GENERAL EXPENSES 1902.

1901 bills paid ....$		94.25
Finance committee		89.20
Board meetings...................................		1,115.10
Superintendent fair grounds—salary		600.00
Printing		1,520.91
Fair ground expense		1,138.13
Ex-Secretary's salary		157.29

Improvements and repairs.		
Repairs on Iowa building ....$	96.00	
Cattle barn No. 12	3,281.76	
Cattle barn No. 13	631.17	
Repairs and new roof on horticultural building.......	485.50	
Dwelling house	1,397.71	
Grading streets around stock pavilion, Iowa building, etc., and hauling gravel, cinders, roller, grader, etc.	1,958.47	
Electric lights..............	1,225.75	
Sidewalk	2,071.82	
Cement floors in stock pavilion not included in contract	185.10	
Secretary's and treasurer's office	344.22	
Police headquarters	156.00	
Cattle sheds	115.59	
Dry air closet ....;	3,775.00	
Swine pens	300.00	
Improvements and repairs during fair	·507.40	
Miscellaneous improvements and repairs	2,116.09	18,821.78
Express and telegrams		81.37
Silver cups, medals and engraving		185.41
Office supplies		84.83

Dues American Association Fairs and Expositions	25.00
Insurance	1,092.50
Postage	450.00
Special committee work	541.85
Stock pavilion ($7,635.34)	44.635.34
Advertising	1,662.53
Telephones	75.85
Executive committee	134.40
Paid out on collection from suspensions	228.80
Clerical work	407.75
American Trotting Association dues	75.00
Attractions	5,673.74
Admissions returned	58.00
Music	563.75
Decorations, etc	221.50
Auditing committee	52.20
Scavenger work	162.00
Police	1,102.25
Marshals	110.00
Horse department	252.35
Speed department	323.25
Cattle department	395.16
Swine department	199.85
Sheep and poultry departments	211.20
Machinery department	181.76
Agricultural department	339.45
Dairy department	361.14
Horticultural department	206.35
Gate department	629.50
Ticket department	177.76
Privilege department	201.70
Treasurer's department	534.80
Electric light department	274.80
President's department	75.30
Premiums 1902	4.50
Agricultural meeting 1902—Joint agent	11.00

$86,139.15

Report of Treasurer G. D. Ellyson:

DES MOINES, IOWA, December 8, 1902.

Report of receipts and disbursements of G. D. Ellyson, treasurer of the Iowa State Board of Agriculture, for the year 1902.

RECEIPTS.

Cash on hand December 1, 1901	$34,244.93
Gate receipts	30,942.75
Amphitheater receipts	3,789.75

Live Stock Pavilion Iowa State Fair Grounds, in course of construction, 1902.

Quarter-stretch receipts	3.25
Evening admission receipts	1,496.00
Evening amphitheater receipts	5,851.50
Railroad tickets receipts	3,804.50
Special tickets	332.00
Round up tickets	416.75
Superintendents privileges	5,162.00
Superintendents horticulture	37.50
Superintendents agriculture	132.00
Superintendents swine	436.50
Superintendents sheep and poultry	179.80
Superintendents horses	487.00
Superintendents machinery	9,948.75
Superintendents electric light	125.00
Superintendents speed	1,328.30
Superintendents dairy	427.51
Superintendents fine arts	1,131.10
Superintendents grounds	750.40
Superintendents cattle	743.00
Secretary	7,540.33
State appropriation	37,000.00
President	3.00
Chief of police	12.75
Interest	1,040.33
	$138,366.70

DISBURSEMENTS.

Expense warrants	$86,206.54
Premium warrants	21,787.91
Balance	30,372.25
	$138,366.70

Respectfully submitted,

G. D. ELLYSON, *Treasurer.*

DES MOINES, IOWA, December 8, 1902.

To Whom it May Concern:

This is to certify that G. D. Ellyson, treasurer of the Iowa State Board of Agriculture, had on deposit in this bank subject to check at the close of business January 5, 1902, $30,372.25.

D. F. WITTER,
Vice-President.

Mr. A. H. Grissell of Guthrie county moved that the president appoint a committee on address of the president and reports of secretary and treasurer, which motion prevailed.

The president appointed on such committee, A. H. Grissell of Guthrie county, S. B. Packard of Marshall county and James Nowak of Poweshiek county.

Mr. Grissell moved that the date for the Iowa State Fair of 1903 be August 21st to August 29th inclusive, which motion prevailed.

Mr. St. John moved that the convention be now adjourned until 2 o'clock p. m., which motion prevailed.

AFTERNOON SESSION.

Pursuant to adjournment the convention met at 2 o'clock p. m., with President Frasier in the chair.

Meeting called to order and convention listened to the reading of the report of the committee on credentials as follows:

REPORT OF COMMITTEE ON CREDENTIALS.

Adair Agricultural Society—Walter Scholes.
Black Hawk County, La Porte District—B. L. Manwell.
Bremer County—E. M. Reeves.
Buena Vista County Agricultural Society—C. E. Cameron.
Cass County Agricultural Society—S. W. W. Straight.
Clark County—W. W. Williams.
Crawford County—J. I. Gibson.
Dallas County Agricultural Society—H. H. Crenshaw.
Davis County Agricultural Society—T. D. Doke.
Decatur County—C. W. Hoffman.
Delaware County Agricultural Society—L. G. Clute.
Floyd County—John R. Waller.
Franklin County Agricultural Society—T. W. Purcell.
Fremont County—I. W. Omer,
Greene County—Mahlon Head.
Grundy County Agricultural Society—E. A. Crary.
Guthrie County Agricultural Society—A. H. Grissell.
Hardin County Agricultural Society—Robert Smith.
Ida County—W. J. Scott.
Jackson County Agricultural Society—C. W. Phillips.
Jasper County Agricultural Society—C. W. Campbell.
Jefferson County Agricultural Society—E. R. Smith.
Keokuk County—What Cheer district—T. C. Legoe.
Kossuth County Agricultural Society—J. W. Wadsworth.
Lyon County—James Walpole.
Madison County Agricultural Society—T. J. Hudson.
Marion County—Lake Prairie district—Chas. Porter.
Monona County—H. L. Pike.
Monroe County—G. P. Cramer.

Montgomery County Fair Association—G. M. Hull.
Muscatine County—Union district—J. I. Nichols.
Polk County—Chas. W. Britten.
Poweshiek County— Malcom district—Jas. Nowak.
Poweshiek County—Grinnell district—J. E. Van Evera.
Scott County—George Metzgar.
Sioux County—Sioux Valley district—Emmet Brown.
Union County—W. W. Morrow.
Wapello County—Ben S. Benson.
Winneshiek County Agricultural Society—Thos. Graham.
Wright County Agricultural Society—W. C. Brown.
Improved Stock Breeders' Association—W. M. McFadden.

FARMERS' INSTITUTES.

Ida County—J. C. Preston.
Scott County—M. H. Calderwood.
Audubon County—A. H. Edwards.
Calhoun County—Henry Parsons.
Jones County—W. C. Monroe.

John Ledgerwood,
B. L. Manwell,
J. I. Nichols,
Committee.

J. I. Gibson moved the adoption of the report as read. Seconded by Wadsworth and motion prevailed.

The report of the committee on the address of president and reports of secretary and treasurer was read as follows:

To the President and Members of the Agricultural Convention:

We, your committee, to whom has been referred the reports of the president and secretary of the Department of Agriculture, beg leave to submit the following:

We heartily indorse the administration of the outgoing president, J. C. Frasier, and congratulate the state that during his term of office the affairs of the department have been attended to with unprecedented success.

The thanks of the convention are due, and hereby are tendered to him, as a faithful officer, for his zealous and efficient work. That during the term of office held by the president, J. C. Frasier, important improvements have been made at a large expenditure of money, which was under his direct supervision, and we therefore commend him for the admirable manner in which the plans of the department were carried into execution and for the economical expenditure of the department's funds.

We fully indorse the idea of excluding all sideshows of an objectionable nature, but there may be shows that are entirely unobjectionable, that are not only entertaining, but instructive, and add to the attraction the fair. We, therefore, suggest that the society use due discrimination in the selection of these shows.

The secretary's report is a very comprehensive outline of the year's business and contains many valuable suggestions which are highly commended by your committee.

Your committee wish to commend the secretary for the admirable executive ability he has displayed in carrying on the business of the department the past year, and we also desire to commend him for the promptness with which he completed the entry books of the fair, and placed them in the hands of the judges of the different departments, thereby hastening the business of the fair.

We also commend G. D. Ellyson, the treasurer, for the careful and judicious handling of the funds of the society, and recommend that he be accorded the thanks of the directors of the Iowa State Fair.

A. H. GRISELL,

S. B. PACKARD,

JAMES NOWAK.

Mr. T. C. Legoe moved that the report of the committee be adopted, which motion prevailed.

Convention then proceeded to the election of officers.

Gov. S. B. Packard of Marshall county placed in nomination for the office of president for the ensuing year, W. M. Morrow of Union county, and moved that, if there were no other nominations, the rules be suspended and the secretary instructed to cast the unanimous vote of the convention for Mr. Morrow. This motion prevailed and the secretary so cast the vote, and President Frasier declared W. W. Morrow duly elected president of the Department of Agriculture for the ensuing year.

M. J. Wragg placed in nomination for the office of vice-president C. E. Cameron of Buena Vista county, which motion was seconded by W. J. Scott of Ida county.

Mr. Wragg moved that if there were no other nominations, the rules be suspended and the secretary instructed to cast the full vote of the convention for Mr. Cameron, which motion prevailed. The secretary cast the vote and the president declared C. E. Cameron duly elected vice-president of the Department of Agriculture for the ensuing year.

George Metzgar of Scott county placed in nomination for director from the Second district, C. W. Phillips of Jackson county, to succeed himself, and moved that the rules be suspended and secretary instructed to cast the unanimous vote of the convention for Mr. Phillips, which motion prevailed. The secretary cast the vote and the president declared C. W. Phillips duly elected director from the Second district for the ensuing two years.

John R. Waller of Floyd county nominated for director from the Fourth district, R. T. St. John of Mitchell county, to succeed himself. There being no other nominations the secretary was instructed to cast the unanimous vote of the convention for Mr. St. John. The secretary so cast the vote and the president declared Mr. St. John duly elected director from the Fourth district for the ensuing two years.

George P. Cramer of Monroe county, placed in nomination for member of the State Board of Agriculture from the Sixth congressional district, T. C. Legoe of Keokuk county to succeed himself. There being no other nominations, on motion of Mr. Cramer the rules were suspended and the secretary instructed to cast the vote of the convention for Mr. Legoe. The secretary so cast the vote and the president declared Mr. Legoe duly elected a member of the State Board of Agriculture from the Sixth district for the ensuing two years.

C. W. Hoffman placed in nomination for member of the State Board of Agriculture from the Eighth congressional district, John Ledgerwood of Decatur county, to succeed himself. There being no other candidates the rules were suspended and the secretary instructed to cast the full vote of the convention for Mr. Ledgerwood. The secretary so cast the vote and the president declared Mr. Ledgerwood duly elected a member of the State Board of Agriculture from the Eighth congressional district for the ensuing two years.

J. I. Gibson placed in nomination for a member from the Tenth congressional district, J. W. Wadsworth to succeed himself and moved that the rules be suspended and the secretary instructed to cast the full vote of the convention for Mr. Wadsworth. The secretary so cast the vote and the president declared Mr. Wadsworth duly elected a member of the State Board of Agriculture from the Tenth congressional district, for the ensuing two years.

Mr. C. E. Cameron placed in nomination Mr. H. L. Pike of Monona county for member of the State Board of Agriculture from the Eleventh congressional district to fill the vacancy caused by the election of himself as vice-president. There being no other nominations, on motion the rules were suspended and the secretary instructed to cast the full vote of the convention for Mr. Pike. The secretary so cast the vote and the president declared Mr. Pike duly elected a member of the State Board of Agriculture from the Eleventh congressional district for the ensuing year.

There being no further business, on motion of Mr. Ledgerwood the convention was adjourned.

J. C. SIMPSON, Secretary.

MEETING OF THE STATE BOARD OF AGRICULTURE.

Thursday Morning, December 11, 1902.

Board met on call of president at 9 o'clock with President Morrow in the chair.

Meeting called to order by the president and on roll call the following members were found to be present: Dairy Commissioner H. R. Wright, State Veterinarian P. O. Koto, President W. W. Morrow, Vice-President C. E. Cameron, Secretary J. C. Simpson, Treasurer G. D. Ellyson and the following named directors: J. P. Manatrey, C. W. Phillips, W. C. Brown, S. B. Packard, T. C. Legoe, M. J. Wragg, John Ledgerwood, J. W. Wadsworth and H. L. Pike. R. T. St. John came in a few minutes later.

C. T. Jones, clerk of the supreme court, appeared before the board and the following newly-elected members were sworn in: W. W. Morrow, C. E. Cameron, John Ledgerwood, J. W. Wadsworth and H. L. Pike.

R. T. St. John and C. W. Phillips appeared before the clerk and were sworn in later.

The board then went into executive session and proceeded to the election of a secretary.

J. W. Wadsworth moved that the secretary pro tem cast the unanimous vote of the board for J. C. Simpson for secretary and that the salary be $1,500 per year, which motion prevailed. The secretary pro tem cast the vote and the president declared J. C. Simpson duly elected secretary for the ensuing year. Mr. Simpson was called in, informed of his election and assumed the duties of the office.

M. J. Wragg moved that C. S. Relyea be chosen assistant secretary at a salary of $75.00 per month. Motion prevailed.

Mr. C. E. Cameron placen in nomination for treasurer, G. D. Ellyson to succeed himself and moved that the rules be suspended and the secretary instructed to cast the unanimous vote of the board for Mr. Ellyson. The secretary so cast the vote and the president declared Mr. Ellyson duly elected treasurer of the State Board of Agriculture for the ensuing year.

The minutes of the last session of the board were read and on motion of S. B. Packard were approved.

The board then proceeded to the election of a chief marshal.

M. J. Wragg presented the name of T. J. Hudson of Madison county. Mr. McDonald presented the name of W. W. Williams of Clark county and Mr. Manatrey presented the name of T. D. Doke of Davis county.

Mr. Manatrey moved that we proceed to ballot and that the first ballot be an informal one. This motion prevailed.

Result of informal ballot: Total number of votes cast fifteen, of which Hudson received six, Williams two and Doke seven.

The first formal ballot was then taken with the following result: Total number of votes cast sixteen, of which Mr. Doke received nine, Hudson six and Williams one.

Mr. Doke having received a majority of the votes cast was declared elected marshal for the fair of 1903.

Mr. Ledgerwood moved that we proceed to the election of two assistant marshals and that we vote for only one man at a time.

For the first ballot Mr. Hudson and Mr. Williams were placed in nomination.

The result of the ballot was as follows: Total number of votes cast sixteen, of which Mr. Hudson received fourteen and Mr. Williams received two.

Mr. Hudson having received a majority of the votes cast was declared elected to the position of assistant marshal for the fair of 1903.

For the second ballot the following named gentlemen were placed in nomination:

Mr. Ledgerwood presented the name of C. M. Akes of Decatur county, Mr. Wadsworth presented the name of W. W. Williams of Clark county, Mr. Manatrey presented the name of Harry Smith of Jefferson county.

The ballot resulted as follows: Total number of votes cast, seventeen, of which Mr. Akes received thirteen, Mr. Williams three and Mr. Smith one.

Mr. Akes having received a majority of the votes cast was declared elected assistant marshal for the fair of 1903.

For the office of chief of police, Mr. McDonald placed in nomination Donald Hill of Buena Vista county. On motion of Mr. Brown the rules were suspended and the secretary instructed to cast the full vote of the board for Mr. Hill. The secretary so cast the vote and the president declared Mr. Hill elected to the office of chief of police for the fair of 1903.

Mr. Cameron placed in nomination for superintendent of grounds, Mr. J. H. Deemer to succeed himself and on motion of Mr. Brown the rules were suspended and the secretary instructed to cast the full vote of the board for Mr. Deemer. The vote was so cast and Mr. Deemer was declared elected superintendent of the fair grounds for the ensuing year.

Mr. McDonald moved that the salary of the superintendent of grounds be fixed at fifty dollars per month for six months of the year and at seventy-five dollars per month for the remaining six months. Mr. St. John moved to amend by fixing the salary of superintendent at $800 per year, which amendment was seconded by Mr. Ledgerwood. A roll call was demanded on this which was taken with the following results: Ayes, thirteen and nays two, so the amendment was declared carried and original motion prevailed as amended.

Mr. Packard moved that the salary of chief marshal, assistant marshals, chief of police, gate keepers, ticket sellers, superintendents, assistant superintendents and all other assistants be the same as for the year 1902. Seconded by Cameron and motion prevailed.

Mr. Packard moved that the selection of superintendents for departments for the ensuing year be referred to the executive committee, who shall report their selections at the afternoon session for the approval of the board and that the chair appoint the standing committees. Motion prevailed.

The secretary read a letter from Mrs. E. E. Kyle of Mt. Vernon, Iowa, regarding the loss of lace pieces at the last state fair, in which she asked the board to reimburse her to the amount of fifty dollars for the above named pieces.

After a statement to the board by Manatrey who was superintendent of the department, that the loss was in no way the fault of the superintendent or his assistants, but was due to the carelessness of the party exhibiting the lace, the claim was disallowed.

A committee from the Commercial Exchange appeared before the board and asked that the old Iowa Producers' building be moved to a suitable location and that it be used for exhibits from Iowa manufactures.

Mr. F. R. Conaway, secretary of the Iowa Louisiana Purchase Commission, appeared before the board and made a short address setting forth the plans of the commission for an exhibit at St. Louis.

Mr. Cameron moved that General Rule Number Nine of the premium list be amended by striking out the words of the first and second lines thereof, "ten per cent deducted from all cash premiums paid."

Mr. Manatrey moved that the board adjourn until 1:30 p. m., which motion prevailed.

AFTERNOON SESSION.

Board met at 1:30 pursuant to adjournment.

President called meeting to order and on roll call the following members were found to be absent: Cummins, Koto, Ellyson and Wragg. Koto and Wragg came in later.

Secretary read the report of the executive committee on the assignment of superintendents and committees appointed by the president, as follows:

Auditing committee, J. W. Wadsworth, C. W. Phillips and W. C. Brown.

Superintendent of tickets, C. W. Phillips.

Superintendent of gates, T. C. Legoe.

Superintendent of privileges, J. W. Wadsworth.

Superintendent of electric light and power plant, John Cownie.

Suprintendent department A, horses, mules and ponies, W. C. Brown.

Superintendent department B, speed, C. E. Cameron.

Superintendent department C, cattle, S. B. Packard.

Superintendent department D, swine, W. M. McFadden.

Superintendent departments E and F, sheep and poultry, H. L. Pike.

Superintendent department G, implements and machinery, John Ledgerwood.

Superintendent departments I and J, agriculture, pantry and apiary, R. T. St. John.

Superintendent department K, dairy, M. McDonald.

Superintendent departments L and M, fruits, plants and flowers, M. J. Wragg.

Superintendent department N, exposition building and fine arts, J. P. Manatrey.

STANDING COMMITTEES.

Committee on resolutions, Packard, McDonald and St. John.

Committee on powers and duties of board, Cummins, Morrow and Cameron.

Committee on fungus diseases in grains, grasses and plants; the adulteration of foods, seeds and other products, Stanton, Wragg and Packard.

Committee on dairy industry and products including fraudulent imitations thereof, Wright, Ledgerwood and Manatrey.

Committee on contagious diseases among domestic animals, Koto, Legoe and Pike.

McDonald moved that the report as read be adopted. Seconded by Ledgerwood and motion prevailed.

Mr. Ledgerwood moved that we allow nothing to be sold in the stock pavilion except the catalogue containing a list of the stock entries, and that nothing be allowed sold, peddled or distributed in the amphitheater except the score card of the races. Motion prevailed.

Mr. Legoe moved that the president appoint a committee on the revision of the premium list, and that said committee report to the board tomorrow. Motion prevailed.

The president appointed the following committees:

On Rules—Legoe, Ledgerwood and Morrow.

Horses and Speed—Cameron, Brown and Simpson.

Cattle—Packard and Wadsworth.

Sheep and Poultry—Pike and Ledgerwood.

Agricultural Department—St. John and McDonald.
Dairy Department—McDonald and Wright.
Art Department—Manatrey and Legoe.

Mr. Cameron moved that our reserve fund be placed at $12,000. Seconded by Ledgerwood.

Mr. Wadsworth moved to amend by placing the reserve fund at $15,000 and that the same be placed on deposit with interest bearing certificates with the proviso that the same may be drawn at any time after the fair without releasing the interest.

The roll call on the amendment offered by Mr. Wadsworth resulted in the amendment being lost and the original motion by Mr. Cameron then prevailed.

Mr. Wadsworth moved that Tuesday, August 25th, be Old Soldiers' and Children's Day, which motion prevailed.

Mr. McDonald moved that the executive committee be instructed to secure a plan for a swine pavilion and that the same be submitted to the board at their next meeting for approval. Motion prevailed.

Mr. McDonald moved that the executive committee be instructed to dispose of the old boiler, dynamo and piping in the dairy building, and that the dairy building be sealed up to the square. Seconded by Wright and motion prevailed.

Mr. Mills and Mr. Redhead appeared before the board and had a hearing regarding the use of the stock pavilion for the holding of sales.

Phillips moved that the executive committee be authorized to enter into a contract with responsible parties, for one hundred or more trees to be set out on the fair grounds. Seconded by Wragg and motion prevailed.

Mr. Packard offered the following resolution and moved its adoption:

Resolved that the executive committee be and are hereby authorized to ask for bids for the printing of 20,000 premium lists and that they enter into a contract with the lowest responsible bidder for the number required.

Mr. Packard moved that the matter of renting the stock pavilion for the purpose of holding sales, etc., be referred to the executive committee with power to act, which motion prevailed.

Packard moved that we now adjourn until nine o'clock tomorrow morning. Motion prevailed.

FRIDAY MORNING, DECEMBER 12, 1902.

Board met at nine o'clock a. m., pursuant to adjournment with President Morrow in the chair.

On roll call the following members were found to be present: Wright, Cameron, Morrow, Simpson, Phillips, Brown, Packard, Legoe, Wragg, Ledgerwood, McDonald, Wadsworth and Pike. St. John and Manatrey came in later.

The secretary read the minutes of yesterday's board meeting which were approved.

The president presented the bond of G. D. Ellyson, treasurer, in the sum of $50,000, signed by G. W. Marquardt who had qualified in the sum of $100,000.

Mr. Packard moved that the bond of Mr. Ellyson be approved, which motion prevailed.

The committee on rules made a report recommending the following changes:

1st. GENERAL RULE NUMBER TEN: All entries close Saturday, August 22d, at ten o'clock p. m., except in the speed, horse and cattle departments; provided, that all entries sent by letter and mailed prior to ten o'clock p. m., Saturday, August 22d, shall be entered if received by the secretary before Monday, August 24, 1903, at nine o'clock a. m.

2nd. GENERAL RULE NUMBER ELEVEN: All entries in departments A and C, horses and cattle, shall close on Wednesday, August 5, 1903, at ten o'clock p. m., and all entries in these departments A and C must be mailed before ten o'clock p. m., Wednesday, August 5th, and received by the secretary on or before ten o'clock p. m., August 8, 1903.

3rd. GENERAL RULE NUMBER SIXTEEN: Hay, straw and grain. A depot for hay, straw and grain will be established on the grounds. Hay and straw delivered in the bale and sold at retailers' city prices by the State Board of Agriculture.

4th. GENERAL RULE NUMBER TWENTY-SIX: The chief of police shall have police supervision of the grounds, under control of the president and state board, etc.

9

General rule thirty-seven stricken out.

Paragraph eight, of general rule number forty-one, stricken ont.

The president presented the bond of Mr. Simpson, in the sum of $10,000, signed by Fletcher Howard and G. S. Gilbertson who has qualified in the sum of $20,000. On motion of Mr. Wadsworth, the bond was approved and placed in the hands of Mr. Morrow for safe keeping.

Paragraph number eight under general rule number forty-six stricken out.

On motion of Mr. Packard, judging in departments A and C is to begin at nine o'clock a. m., on Monday, August 24th.

Mr. Brown reported from the committee on A and C as follows:

Recommends that the last sentence in the rule in class sixteen Shetland Ponies, be stricken out, and on vote of the board it was so ordered.

That the words "or more" in the "Get of Stallion" or "Produce of Mare" in all classes be stricken out. On vote of the board it was so ordered.

That the premiums in the "Get of Stallion" and "Produce of Mare" in classes One, Two, Three, Four, Five, Six, Seven, Eight, Nine and Ten be changed to $20.00 in place of $10.00 and Silver Medal. On vote of the board the change was so ordered.

On motion of Mr. Wadsworth that class seventeen, Jacks and Jennets, be stricken from the premium list, the motion prevailed.

The committee recommended the adoption of the following saddle class in lieu of class fifteen:

Gelding four years old or over $20 $10
Gelding three years old and under......................... 20   10
Stallion four years old or over........................... 20   10
Stallion three years old and under four................... 20   10
Mare four years old or over............................... 20   10
Mare three years old and under four....................... 20   10
Champion Stallion, mare or gelding........................ 50

HIGH SCHOOL HORSES.

Stallion, mare or gelding any age......................... 50   25

Mr. Wadsworth moved that eight thousand dollars be appropriated for the speed department, which motion prevailed.

Mr. Packard moved the adoption of the recommendations as reported by Mr. Brown, which motion prevailed.

Report of S. B. Packard on the cattle department as follows:

That class number forty-three be stricken out.

That class number forty-one, old list, fat stock, read as follows:

GRADES AND CROSS BRED.

Class number —: Steer or spayed heifer, two years old and under three, $15, $10, $5.

Class number —: Steer or spayed heifer one year old and under two, $15, $10 and $5.

Class number —: Steer or spayed heifer under one year old, $15, $10 and $5.

HERDS.

Class number —: Group of three steers or spayed heifers, consisting of one steer or spayed heifer two years old and under three; one steer or spayed heifer one year old and under two; one steer or spayed heifer under one year old, owned by one exhibitor, $25, $15 and $10.

Class number —: Champion steer or spayed heifer, competition limited to first prize winners in classes number —; —; —, $20.

FAT STOCK—PURE BREDS.

Must show certificate of register.

Class number —: HEREFORDS. Steer or spayed heifer two years old and under three, $15, $10 and $5.

Class number —: Steer or spayed heifer one year old and under two, $15, $10 and $5.

Class number —: Steer or spayed heifer under one year old, $15, $10 and $5.

HERDS.

Class number —: Group of three head of steers or spayed heifers, consisting of one steer or spayed heifer two years old and under three, one steer or spayed heifer one year old and under two; one steer or spayed heifer under one year old, owned by one exhibitor, $25, $15 and $10.

Class number —: Champion steer or spayed heifer, competition limited to prize winners in classes —: —; —, $20.

Note.—Same classes for Short-Horns, Aberdeen Angus and Galloways.

GRAND CHAMPION.

Class number —: Best steer or spayed heifer, competition limited to animals winning championship honors in the above classes, $50.

Mr. Packard moved that the recommendations as offered by the cattle department be adopted, which motion prevailed.

Mr. Manatrey moved that department N be left to himself for revision, with the proviso that not more than one hundred dollars be added. Seconded by Cameron and motion prevailed.

Mr. Ledgerwood moved that class fifty-nine be stricken out. Seconded by Brown and motion prevailed.

Recommendations of R. T. St. John on the agricultural department:

That class number eighty-seven, premium be changed to twenty dollars.

That class number ninety, premium be changed to twenty-five, fifteen and ten dollars.

That class number ninety-one be reduced to pecks.

That class number ninety-three, premium number 926 be changed to read "One mammoth squash."

That class number ninety-four, premiums number 951, 952, and 953 should be $6, $4 and $2.

That class ninety-nine, premiums to be $40, $20 and $10.

Mr. Manatrey moved that the recommendations as presented by Mr. St. John be adopted. Seconded by McDonald.

Mr. Wadsworth moved to amend that they should be adopted with the exception of class ninety-nine, which shall be left as it is. Amendment was seconded by Mr. Ledgerwood and was declared to have carried after which the original motion by Mr. Manatrey prevailed.

Mr. McDonald moved that premium number 1163 of the premium list be made to read as follows: "$25, $20, $15, $10 and $5, respectively, to the five tubs scoring highest." Motion seconded by St. John and prevailed.

M. J. Wragg presented the recommendations for changes in departments L and M as follows:

In rule three, department L, after *district* add the following:—As follows:—Counties of the northern district—Allamakee, Winneshiek, Howard, Mitchell, Worth, Winnebago, Kossuth, Emmet, Dickinson, Linn, Osceola, Sioux, O'Brien, Clay, Palo Alto, Hancock, Cerro Gordo, Floyd, Chickasaw, Fayette, Clayton, Dubuque, Delaware, Buchanan, Breemer, Black Hawk, Butler, Grundy, Franklin, Hardin, Wright, Hamilton, Humboldt, Pocahontas, Calhoun, Buena Vista, Sac, Cherokee, Ida, Plymouth, Woodbury and Webster.

Counties of the Central district:—Jackson, Clinton, Jones, Cedar, Linn, Johnson, Benton, Iowa, Tama, Poweshiek, Marshall, Jasper, Story, Polk, Boone, Dallas, Greene, Guthrie, Carroll, Audubon, Crawford, Shelby,

Monona, Harrison, Pottawatamie Cass, Adair, Madison, Warren, Marion, Mahaska, Keokuk, Washington, Muscatine, and Scott.

Counties of the southern district:—Louisa, Des Moines, Henry, Lee, Jefferson, Van Buren, Wapello, Davis, Monroe, Appanoose, Lucas, Wayne, Clarke, Decatur, Union, Ringgold, Adams, Taylor, Montgomery, Page, Mills and Fremont.

In premium number 188 the words "or numbered" be stricken out.

In premium number 1190 strike out the words "not less than."

In class number 126, premium number 1202, substitute the following, "for bunches of grapes of varieties not named above, premium limited to twelve varieties, first $1, second fifty cents.

Premium number 1203 after the word "grapes" add "if deemed worthy." First $1.00, second fifty cents.

Premium number 1213 strike out the word "Comfort" and add the word "Hunt."

Premium number 1214 strike out the word "Deaton" and insert the word "Surprise."

Premium number 1215 strike out the word "Hammer" and insert the word "Terry."

Premium number 1218 substitute as follows, "Best plate not named on list, not exceeding seen varieties, each plate first one dollar, second fifty cents."

Premium number 1219 strike out the word "eight" and insert the word "six."

Premium number 1221 after the word "Japan" insert the words "and hybrids."

Department M. Add the following rule "Members of the same firm or family will not be allowed to take both the first and second premiums."

Class number 130 as follows:

Premium number 1224—$30, $15, $10.

Premium number 1225—$12, $6, $3.

Premium number 1226—$15, $8, $4.

Premium number 1227—$4, $2.

Premium number 1229—$4, $2.

Premium number 1230—$5, $3.

Premium number 1232—$5, $3.

Premium number 1236—$8, $4.

Premium number 1237—$4, $2.

Premium number 1239½ "Best specimen of any rare, novel or new plant, $6, $3.

Premium number 1240—$4, $2.

Premium number 1241—$4, $2.

Premium number 1243—$4, $2.

Premium number 1245—"Best new and original floral design" $30, $15, $8.

Premium number 1246—"Best display of cut flowers requiring green house culture—$20, $12, $6.

Premium number 1246½—"Best display of cut flowers from open ground—$15, $10, $5.

Premium number 1247—$8, $4.

Premium number 1248—$5, $3.

Premium number 1249—$5, $3.

Premium number 1249½—"Best display of cactus, dahlias, $5, $3."

Premium number 1250—Best display of gladiolus, not less than thirty named varieties, first $15, second $10."

Premium number 1250½—"Best display of gladiolus, without being named, first $6, second $3."

Premium number 1250 3-4—"Best display of flower spike of gladiola, first, $2, second $1.

Premium number 1251—$5, $3.

Premium number 1253—$6, $4.

Premium number 1254—$4, $3.

Premium number 1275 1-2—"Best specimen of any new, rare or novel plant, first $5, second $3, third $2.

In class 132 add the following "Most beautiful bouquet, first $3, second $2,

Wadsworth moved that the recommendations as read by Mr. Wragg be adopted, the premiums not to be raised to exceed fifty dollars, which motion prevailed.

Mr. Packard offered the following resolution and moved its adoption, which motion prevailed.

Resolved, that Albert Head be permitted to remove the cottage, known as the 10th Iowa Cottage, from the fair grounds at any time between now and July 4, 1903.

Mr. Legoe moved that we adjourn until 1:30 p. m.

AFTERNOON SESSION.

Board met pursuant to adjournment at 1:30 p. m., with President Morrow in the chair.

On roll call the following members were found to be absent: Wright, Cummins, Koto, Ellyson, Manatrey, St. John and Wragg. St. John and Wragg came in later.

McDonald moved that the executive committee and the superintendent of swine be authorized to revise the swine department as thought best.

Wadsworth offered the following resolution and moved its adoption:

Resolved, that the executive committee be instructed to get estimates on what repairs are needed on the buildings now on the fair grounds; also to obtain plans and estimates of cost of a swine judging pavilion, a green house and a building for the electric light and power plant and submit the same at the next meeting of the board.

Courtesy of Wallaces' Farmer.
Sunshine, first prize junior yearling grade Angus steer at the recent International live stock show; owned and raised by Silas Igo, Palmyra, Iowa.

Phillips moved that the executive committee be authorized to confer with parties desiring to erect machinery buildings on the fair grounds, and if satisfactory arrangements can be made regarding the location, style of building, lease of ground, etc., that the committee report the same to the next board meeting for action. Motion prevailed.

Cameron moved that each elective officer of the board appoint four policemen, except Wragg and Ellyson, who shall appoint four mounted police each.

Wadsworth moved that the chair appoint a committee on per diem and mileage. Chair appointed as such committee, Wadsworth, Ledgerwood and Pike.

McDonald moved that the executive committee represent the state board before the Louisiana Purchase Commission of Iowa, and motion prevailed.

Phillips moved that the elective officers of the state board constitute the board of management for the state fair of 1903. Motion prevailed.

Legoe moved that when this board adjourned that it be to meet on the third day of March, 1903.

Report of committee on per diem and mileage as follows:

	Days.	Amt.	Miles.	Amt.	Total.
W. W. Morrow	6	$24	82	$ 8.20	$ 32.20
C. E. Cameron	6	24	140	14.00	38.00
J. P. Manatrey	5	20	118	11.80	31.80
C. W. Phillips	4	16	...	......	16.00
W. C. Brown	6	24	102	10.20	34.20
R. T. St. John	6	24	195	19.50	43.50
S. B. Packard	6	24	58	5.80	29.80
T. C. Legoe	6	24	100	10.00	34.00
M. J. Wragg	5	20	16	1.60	21.60
John Ledgerwood	6	24	89	8.90	32.90
M. McDonald	6	24	65	6.50	30.50
J. W. Wadsworth	5	20	123	12.30	32.20
H. L. Pike	3	12	...	......	12.00
J. C. Frasier	3	12	113	11.30	23.30
					$412.10

On motion meeting adjourned.

J. C. SIMPSON,
Secretary.

MEETING OF THE STATE BOARD OF AGRICULTURE.
TUESDAY, JANUARY 28, 1902.

Board met pursuant to adjournment, with President Frasier in the chair. The roll being called the following members were found to be present: Ex-Officio members, Gov. A. B. Cummins; President of Agricultural College, W. M. Beardshear; President J. O. Frasier, Secretary J. C. Simpson and directors as follows: J. P. Manatrey, C. W. Phillips, W. C. Brown, R. T. St. John, S. B. Packard, T. C. Legoe, M. J. Wragg, John Ledgerwood, M. McDonald, J. W. Wadsworth and C. E. Cameron.

Minutes of board meeting in December read and approved.

Mr. Wragg moved that we take up the matter of electing an assistant secretary. Motion prevailed.

Mr. Brown moved that C. S. Relyea of Storm Lake, Iowa, be elected assistant secretary, at a salary of seventy-five dollars per month ($75). Motion prevailed.

Committee appointed at last meeting to investigate the matter of redeeming coupon tickets from old soldiers reported as follows:

Mr. President and Gentlemen of the State Board of Agriculture: We, your committee, to whom you referred the matter of redeeming railroad coupon tickets from old soldiers, beg leave to report that we have had the same under consideration, and deem it advisable and for the best interests of the department, that we will redeem railroad coupon tickets, good for one admission at our gates, from all old soldiers presenting same at the Treasurer's office on the fair grounds, on *Tuesday, August 26th*, (this being Old Soldiers' Day), *but will not redeem old soldiers' tickets given out by this office free.*

C. W. PHILLIPS,
M. J. WRAGG,
J. C. SIMPSON, Committee.

Mr. Wragg moved the adoption of the report as read, which motion prevailed.

Mr. Legoe made the following report from the committee appointed to investigate the matter of selling the coal underlying the state fair grounds:

Your committee appointed to look up and report on the advisability of asking the legislature to enable the State Board of Agriculture to sell the coal beneath the surface of the state fair grounds report as follows:

First—That we find the coal vein where mining has been done, near the fair grounds; is from three and one-half to four feet thick; that the roof is reasonably good for this district.

Second—That from the best information we can get, we find that the coal vein is from one hundred to two hundred feet below the surface of the ground, and that the condition of the roof is such in this district that it would not be advisable to take out any coal from under the buildings now on the ground, nor from beneath the surface of any ground where buildings are liable to be erected in the future, and further, that all any event no coal should be mined from under any of the low land in said fair grounds.

Third—We find that the usual price paid for coal fields where the coal is from three to four feet in thickness, to be from twenty-five to one hundred dollars per acre, and this price usually includes surface rights for railroad switches, and sufficient rights to locate shafts and top works on.

Fourth—We find that before any offer could be had for the coal underlying the state fair grounds it would have to be prospected by boring holes, to find out the quantity and the quality and the nature of the roof overlying said coal vein.

Fifth—That in all probability the number of acres of coal that could be mined and not interfere with the buildings on the fair grounds would not in any event exceed one hundred and fifty acres, and that it would not bring a sufficient price at this time to justify the sale of the same; that there is no question but what coal will sell for a much higher figure in the near future than it will now. Therefore your committee recommends that we take no steps to secure legislation to enable the board to sell the coal underlaying the state fair grounds.

                                    J. C. FRASIER,
                                    W. W. MORROW,
                                    J. C. SIMPSON,
                                    T. C. LEGOE,
                                               Committee.

Mr. Simpson moved the adoption of the report as read. Motion prevailed.

Mr. Wragg made an oral report in regard to switching facilities on the fair grounds and the progress he had made with the Chicago Great Western people.

Mr. Packard made the following report from the committee on rules:

DEPARTMENT OF AGRICULTURE.

Following is the bill that passed the Twenty-eighth General Assembly, establishing the department of agriculture:

A bill for an act to create a department of agriculture, and repeal sections sixteen hundred and fifty-three (1653), sixteen hundred and fifty-four (1654), sixteen hundred and fifty-five (1655), sixteen hundred and fifty-six (1656), sixteen hundred and fifty-seven (1657), sixteen hundred and seventy-four (1674), sixteen hundred and eighty-two (1682), sixteen hundred and eighty-three (1683), of the code, and chapter forty-two (42) of the acts of the -Twenty-seventh (27th) General Assembly, and amend sections sixteen hundred and seventy-nine (1679), and sixteen hundred and eighty-one (1681) of the code, and making an appropriation therefor.

Be it enacted by the general assembly of the state of Iowa:

SECTION 1. For the promotion of agriculture, horticulture, forestry, animal industry, manufactures and domestic arts, there is hereby established a department to be known as the "department of agriculture," which shall embrace the district and county agricultural societies organized or to be organized under existing statutes, and entitled to receive aid from the state, the state crop and weather service, and the offices of the dairy commissioner and state veterinarian.

SECTION 2. The department shall be managed by a board, to be styled "the state board of agriculture," of which the governor of the state, the president of the State College of Agriculture and Mechanic Arts, the state dairy commissioner, and the state veterinarian shall be members ex officio The other members of the board shall consist of a president, vice-president, secretary, treasurer and one director from each congressional district, to be chosen as hereinafter provided.

SECTION 3. There shall be held at the capitol on the second Wednesday of December, 1900, and annually thereafter, a state agricultural convention composed of the state board of agriculture, together with the president or secretary of each county or district society entitled to deceive aid from the state, or a regularly elected delegate therefrom accredited in writing, who shall be a resident of the county; and in counties where there are no agricultural societies the board of supervisors may appoint a delegate who shall be a resident of the county. The president or an accredited representative of the following named associations shall be entitled to membership in the said convention, to wit: the State Horticultural Society, the State Dairy Association, the Improved Stock Breeders' Association and the Swine Breders' Association.

SECTION 4. At the convention held on the second Wednesday in December, 1900, there shall be elected a president and vice-president for the term of one year; also one director of the board of agriculture from each congressional district; those from even numbered districts to serve two years and those from odd numbered districts to serve one year. At subsequent annual conventions, vacancies occurring from death or other causes shall be filled for the unexpired term; and the board may fill any vacancy in office until the next annual convention.

SECTION 5. In connection with the annual convention, either preceding or following the day on which the officers are elected, the board may hold a State Farmers' Institute, for the discussion of practical and scientific topics relating to the various branches of agriculture, the substance of which shall be published in the annual report of the board.

SECTION 6. The board shall have general supervision of the several branches, bureaus and offices embraced in the department of agriculture; and it shall be the duty of the board to look after and promote the interests of agricultural education and animal and other industries throughout the state; to investigate all subjects relating to the improvement of method, appliances and machinery, and the diversification of the crops and products; also to investigate the reports of the prevalence of contagious diseases among domestic animals, or destructive insects and fungus diseases in grains and grasses, and the plants, the adulteration of foods, seeds and other products, and to report the result of investigation, together with recommendations of remedial measures for prevention of damage resulting therefrom. It shall be the duty of the Iowa Agricultural Experiment Station to co-operate with the department of agriculture in carrying on these investigations.

SECTION 7. The president, vice-president and secretary shall constitute an executive committee, which shall transact such business as may be delegated to it by the board of agriculture. The president may call meetings of the board when the interests of the department require it.

SECTION 8. The board shall have full control of the state fair grounds and improvements thereon belonging to the state, with requisite powers to hold annual fairs and exhibits of the productive resources and industries of the state. They may prescribe all necessary rules and regulations thereon. The board may delegate the management of the state fair to the executive committee and two or more additional members of the board; and for the special work pertaining to the fair they may employ an assistant secretary and such clerical assistance as may be deemed necessary. All expenditures connected with the fair, including the per diem and expenses of the managers thereof, shall be recorded separately and paid from the state fair receipts.

SECTION 9. The department of agriculture is hereby authorized to take and hold property, real and personal, derived by gifts and bequests and the president, secretary and treasurer shall have charge and control of the same, subject to the action of the board, and shall give bonds as required in case of executors, to be approved by the board of agriculture and filed with the secretary of state.

SECTION 10. The board shall elect a secretary for the term of one year whose duties shall be such as usually pertain to the office of a secretary, under the direction of the board. He shall keep a complete record of the proceedings of the annual agricultural convention and all the meetings of the board; he shall draw all warrants on the treasurer and keep a correct account thereof; he shall compile and superintend the printing of the annual report of the state department of agriculture, which shall be entitled "Iowa Year Book of Agriculture," and shall include the annual report of the dairy commissioner, the State Dairy association, and the Iowa Experiment Station, the annual report of the state veterinarian, the Iowa weather and crop service, and the Iowa Improved Stock Breeders' association, or such part thereof as the executive committee may approve, and such other reports and statistics as the board may direct, which shall be published by the state; he shall perform such other duties as the board may direct.

SECTION 11. The Iowa Year Book of Agriculture shall be printed and bound in cloth and in such number as the executive council may direct, to be distributed as follows: One copy to each state officer and member of the general assembly; ten copies to the state library and ten copies to the libraries of the State University and the State College of Agriculture and Mechanic Arts, one copy to each library in the state open to the general public, one copy to the president and secretary of each county and district society, and one copy to the board of supervisors of each county in which there is no agricultural society, and the balance as may be directed by the board of agriculture. The executive council shall receive competitive bids for he printing and binding of the Year Book and let the contract to the lowest responsible bidder; such bidding, however, shall be confined to concerns in Iowa, and to firms and corporations paying the union scale of wages.

SECTION 12. The present officers and directors of the State Agricultural society, upon taking effect of this act, shall be, and they are hereby made and constituted officers and directors of the department of agriculture, who with the ex officio members named in section two (2) hereof. shall have full control and management of the department of agriculture until the members of the state board of agriculture are elected, as provided in section three (3) of this act.

SECTION 13. The office of the department of agriculture shall be in rooms eleven (11) and twelve (12), in the capitol building; the said office shall be entitled to such supplies, stationary, postage and express as may be required, which shall be furnished by the executive council in the same manner as other offices are supplied. The salary of the secretary shall not exceed fifteen hundred dollars ($1500) per annum; and when the board deem it necessary it may employ an assistant at an expense of not more than seventy-five dollars ($75) per month.

SECTION 14. The board shall elect a treasurer for the term of one year, whose duties it shall be to keep a correct account of the receipts and disbursements of all moneys belonging to the department of agriculture, and shall make payments only on warrnts signed by the president and secretary thereof, except in payment of premiums. He shall execute a bond for the faithful performance of his duty, to be approved by the board and filed with the secretary, and shall receive such compensation for his services as shall be fixed by the board, not exceeding one hundred ($100) per annum.

SECTION 15. The elective members of the state board of agriculture, for attending the meetings of the board and for the special work pertaining to the holding of the state fair, shall be allowed four dollars ($4) per day and five cents per mile in going and returning from the place where the businss is transacted, the claim for which in·all cases shall be verified and paid as provided in section eight (8).

SECTION 16. A finance committee consisting of three members shall be appointed by the executive council, whose duty it shall be to examine and report on all financial business of the department of agriculture prior to the annual convention thereof, and make their report to the governor. No member of such committee shall be a member of the board. A reasonable compensation, not exceeding four dollars (4), to each member for each day actually and necessarily engaged in te performance of their duties, and neccessary expenses incurred, shall be allowed such finance committee, to be audited by the executive council and paid out of any funds in the state treasury not otherwise appropriated. Such report shall be edited under the direction of the executive council and published in accordance with the provisions of one hundred ·and sixty three (163) of the code, and acts amendatory thereof.

SECTION 17. The premium list and rules of exhibition shall be determined and published by the board prior to the first day of April in each year.

SECTION 18. That section sixteen hundred and fifty-three (1653), sixteen hundred and fifty-flour (1654), sixteen hundred and fifty-five (1655), sixteen hundred and fifty-six (1656), sixteen hundred and fifty-seven (1657), sixteen hundred and seventy-four (1674), sixteen hundred and eighty-two (1682), and sixteen hundred and eighty-three (1683) of the code, and chapter forty-two (42) of the acts of the Twenty-seventh General Assembly, be and the same are hereby repealed.

SECTION 19. That section sixteen hundred and seventy-nine (1679) of the code, be and the same is hereby amended by striking out the eleventh line thereof the words "said society," and inserting in lieu thereof the words "department of agriculture;" that section sixteen hundred and eighty-one (1681), of the code, be and the same is hereby amended by striking out of the fourth line thereof the words "agricultural society," and inserting in lieu thereof the words "department of agriculture."

SECTION 20. That where the words "board of directors of the state agricultural society, occur in the code, or the acts amendatory thereto, the same shall be construed to mean and refer to the state board of agriculture; 'and the words "state society" and "state agricultural society,"⸲ shall be construed to mean and refer to the department of agriculture.

SECTION 21. There is hereby appropriated annually, from and after the first day of January, nineteen hundred and one (1901), for the support of the office of the department of agriculture, twenty-four hundred dollars ($2400), and for insurance and improvements of buildings on the state fair grounds the sum of one thousand dollars, or so much thereof as shall be necessary, and the auditor of state shall ·draw a warrant therefor upon the order of the department of agriculture, signed by the president and secretary thereof, in such sums and at such times as the board shall deem necessary. The state shall not be liable for the payment of premiums offered by the state board of agriculture, nor for any expenses or liabilities incurred by said board except as expressly provided in this act.

RULES.

DUTIES OF THE PRESIDENT. The president shall take the chair at the hour to which the board shall have adjourned, call the members to order, order the roll of members called by the secretary. Six members shall constitute a quorum for the transaction of business, but a less number may adjourn in the absence of a quorum.

2. He shall preserve order; may speak to points of order in preference to other members, rising from his seat for that purpose; and shall decide questions of order, subject to appeal to the board by any two members, and upon such an appeal no member shall speak more than once, unless by leave of the board.

3. He may state or put a question either sitting or rising.

4. In the absence of the vice-president he shall have the right to name any member to perform the duties of the chair; but such substitution shall not extend beyond the day.

5. All committees shall be appointed by the chair, unless otherwise directed by the board.

6. The president shall vote in all cases, and if after he has voted, the board shall stand equally divided, the question shall be decided in the negative.

7. All questions relative to the priority of business to be acted upon shall be decided by the president without debate.

8. Every member who shall be in the room of meeting shall vote unless excused by the board, whenever a question is put.

9. The yeas and nays shall be called upon any question upon the demand of two members.

10. After a motion or resolution offered is stated by the president or read by the secretary, it shall be considered the property of the board, but may be withdrawn at any time before decision or amendment, by leave of the board.

11. Every resolution or motion shall be reduced to writing, if the president or any member desires it, and may be read by the mover or secretary.

12. Any member may call for a division of the question, when divisible, but a motion to strike out or insert shall be indivisible.

13. When a question has once been decided, it shall be in order for any member of the majority to move a reconsideration thereof on the same day, or any day of that session of the board.

14. When two members arise at the same time, the president shall name the member who is first to speak.

15. No member shall speak longer that ten minutes at any time nor more than once on the same question, except by leave of the board.

16. Nine o'clock in the morning shall be the hour of the meeting of the board, unless otherwise ordered.

17. No rule shall be dispensed with or suspended without the consurrence of two thirds of the members present; nor shall a rule be rescinded without one days' notice being given on the motion therefor; but a new rule not in conflict with the existing rules, may be added by a majority vote.

18. On question of parliamentary law governing the board, where the rules are silent, or do not cover any point, Cushing's Manual of Parliamentary Law shall govern.

STANDING COMMITTEES.

1. Executive Committee.

2. Auditing Committee.

3. Committee of Resolutions.

4. A committee on the powers and duties of the board, of which the Governor of the state shall be chairman.

5. A committee on fungus diseases in grain, grasses and plants; adulteration of foods, seeds and other products; the president of the State College of Agriculture shall be chairman.

6. A committee on the Dairy Industry and Products, including fraudnient imitations thereof; the State Dairy Commissioner to be chairman.

7. A Committee on Contagious Diseases among domestic animals. the State Veterinarian to be chairman.

8. All committees when not otherwise stated, shall consist of three members.

ORDER OF BUSINESS.

1. Call of the Roll.

2. Reading of the minutes of the previous meeting. The reading of the minutes may be dispensed with by a vote of the board except once each day.

3. Communication or petitions.

4. Reports of Standing Committees.

5. Reports of special committees.

6. Unfinished business or business on the secretary's desk.

7. Introduction of resolutions.

8. Reports of the officers of the State Board of Agriculture.

9. Reports of the superintendents of the departments of the state fair.

10. New business.

11. Adjournment.

OTHER OFFICERS.

The duties of the vice-president, secretary and treasurer, shall be such as are prescribed by law and required by the board.

STATE FAIR.

1. There shall be an assistant secretary and such clerical assistance as the board shall direct.

2. A chief marshal and two assistant marshals.

3. A chief of police and such number of policemen as the board shall direct.

4. The superintendents of the departments shall be selected by the executive committee subject to the approval by the board.

5. The assistant superintendents shall be nominated by their respective superintendents, and be approved by the board.

6. The state fair shall continue to comprise the following departments: 1. Tickets. 2. Gates. 3. Concessions and Privileges. 4. Electric Light and Power. 5. Superintendent of Fair grounds. A. Horses, Ponies and Mules. B. Speed. C. Cattle. D. Swine. E. Sheep. F. Poultry and Pet Stock. G. Machinery, Implements, etc. I. Grains, Seeds and Vegetables. J. Pantry, Kitchen, etc. K. Dairy Products. L. and M. Fruits, Plants and Flowers. N. Mechanical, Textile Fabrics, Fine Arts, Boys' and Girls' Departments.

The general rules and regulations to govern the fair shall be promulgated in the premium list each year with necessary revision. When revising, the board shall require the report of the last superintendent of the department under consideration read first.

Mr. Bearshear moved the adoption of the report as read by Governor Packard, seconded by Simpson and motion prevailed.

Mr. St. John moved that the secretary be authorized to have the rules published in pamphlet form, five hundred in number, seconded by Mr. Wragg.

Mr. Legoe moved to amend St. John's motion, by printing the rules in the premium list. Seconded by Cameron. Roll call resulted in a negative vote, so amendment was declared lost.

The roll call on the original motion resulted as follows: Affirmative, Frasier, Simpson, Phillips, St. John, Packard, Wragg and Ledgerwood; negative votes as follows: Cummins, Manatrey, Brown, Legoe, McDonald, Wadsworth and Cameron. The vote being a tie the president declared the motion lost.

Mr. Packard moved that we proceed to the revision of the premium list.

Note by Secretary —The full proceedings of the State Board as regards to the revision of list was eliminated from the Year Book, but can be found in the records in the secretary's office.

10

Mr. Manatrey moved that the matter of the Des Moines Tent and Awning Company, who asked for additional space, be turned over to the superintendent of the privilege department.

Mr. Brown moved that Mr. A. L. Lynnes from Plainfield, Iowa, be allowed four dollars ($4.00) for third premium awarded at the last state fair and never paid. Seconded by Cameron and motion prevailed.

Mr. Manatrey moved that the secretary be authorized to collect the premium paid to Mr. J. P. Allison of this city, which was not due him and which he has never been unwilling to give up. Motion prevailed.

The secretary presented petition from the swine breeders asking that a dormitory be built for them on the fair grounds. Board took no action in the matter.

Motion to adjourn was declared in order, and board stood adjourned until 2 o'clock p. m.

J. C. SIMPSON,

AFTERNOON SESSION.

Board met pursuant to adjournment.

Roll call and all present except G. D. Ellyson, treasurer.

Mr. Plummer appeared before the board and asked for an indorsement as superintendent of the agricultural department at the St. Louis exposition.

Mr. Wragg moved that it is the sense of this board that we take no action at this time in the matter of recommending any one for the appointment as superintendent of the agricultural department at the St. Louis exposition. Motion prevailed.

Report from the committee appointed to draft rules and regulations governing the police at the state fair as follows: See rules in premium list 1902.

Mr. Packard made a report of recommendations for the cattle department for the fair of 1902, as follows:

Gentlemen:—I beg herewith to submit a detailed report of the receipts from the rent of stall in the cattle barns at the last state fair. As you are aware the exhibits of cattle exceeded the space available in the eleven cattle barns equal to the stall room in thee such barns. I have therefore to recommend in view of a still larger exhibit of cattle at the next state fair that four additional barns of similar capacity be erected for use. For convenience in identification of the stock housed in the open sheds I recommend that the stalls be numbered as they are in the cattle barns. The need of a pavement about the hydrants near the cattle barns with the necessary drains to carry off the water used in washing stock is most urgent. The cattle exhibitors complain vigorously against existing conditions so I recommend that the needed improvements be made. Acknowledging with thanks the uniform courtesy officially and personally accorded me by you and the other officers as well as by the members of the department of agriculture. S. B. PACKARD,

Superintendent of Cattle.

By unanimous consent Rule 10 was made to read as follows: "The base for computing age and ownership of all entries will be September 1, 1902."

Mr. Packard moved that we offer a sixth premium of $2.00 in the beef classes and Red Polled class. Seconded by St. John and motion prevailed.

Mr. Hippee appeared before the board and made a statement in regard to the Street Railway Company coming into the grounds.

Mr. Cameron moved to adjourn and motion prevailed.

J. C. SIMPSON,

Secretary.

WEDNESDAY MORNING, JANUARY 29, 1902.

Board met pursuant to adjournment, with Vice-President Morrow in the chair.

Roll call found all members present except President Frasier and Treasurer Ellyson. President Frasier came in while the minutes were being read.

Minutes of Tuesday's meeting were read and approved.

Mr. Ledgerwood presented recommendations from the former superintendent of the sheep department.

Mr. Wadsworth moved that a suitable show ring be fenced for judging sheep. Seconded by Ledgerwood and motion prevailed.

Mr. Wadsworth moved that Mrs. Ada Newquist be paid the money on premium No. 2143. Seconded by Manatrey and carried.

Mr. Packard moved that the money be refunded to Mr. J. A. Stamen, on exhibitor's ticket. Ticket purchased at the last fair and on account of his not getting his butter at the fair, he has returned the ticket and asks that the money be refunded. Motion lost.

Mr. St. John moved that the secretary be authorized to draw warrant to Mr. Van Houten, in acordance with resolution at last meeting. Motion prevailed.

Courtesy of Wallace's Farmer.

One of the prize Aberdeen Angus bulls shown at Iowa State Fair, 1902.

Mr. Newman, Grand Master of the Iowa I. O. O. F., appeared before the board and asked that the board grant the use of the fair grounds for the Canton encampment in September.

Mr. Morrow moved that the president, secretary, superintendent of privileges and superintendent of machinery be appointed a committee to divide the grounds between the machinery department and the privilege department. Seconded by Brown and motion prevailed.

Mr. Manatrey moved that the proceedings of the Iowa Park and Forestry Association be published in the year book, to be edited by the secretary. Seconded by Wragg and motion prevailed.

Mr. Cameron moved that the request of Mr. Newman for the use of the fair grounds for the canton be referred to the president and if it is found that we have the right to grant such privilege the same be granted. Seconded by Wragg and motion prevailed.

Mr. Wadsworth moved that we adjourn until 1:30.

AFTERNOON SESSION.

Board met pursuant to adjournment. Roll call and all members found present.

The board consumed considerable time in discussing the improvements to be made on the fair grounds the coming year, and at 3 o'clock Mr. McDonald moved an adjournment until 3:30. Motion prevailed.

Mr. Hollenbeck appeared before the board and made a statement in regard to bill for moving hay barn. Packard came in later.

Motion to adjourn until 9 o'clock tomorrow morning prevailed.

J. C. SIMPSON,
Secretary.

THURSDAY MORNING, JANUARY 30, 1902.

Board met pursuant to adjournment, with President Frasier in the chair.

Roll call and all members present except Gibson, Ellyson, Phillips, St. John and Packard.

Minutes read and approved.

Mr. McDonald moved that the bill of Mr. Hollenbeck be allowed for $130, amount O. K. by Deemer, which was the contract price for moving the hay barn. Motion prevailed.

St. John came in at this time. Packard came in later.

Mr. Wadsworth moved that the printing of the premium list for 1902 be awarded to the Iowa State Register, they being the lowest responsible bidders. Motion prevailed.

Mr. Wadsworth moved that the executive committee be authorized to make a contract with our treasurer for loaning our money. Seconded by Brown and motion prevailed.

Mr. Cameron moved that the secretary be instructed to ask the executive council for a new carpet for the rooms. Seconded by Brown and motion prevailed.

Mr. Packard moved that the matter of the street car contract be referred to the executive committee, and that they be empowered to draw a bill to secure necessary legislation to allow the street car company to extend their line into the fair ground. Seconded by McDonald and motion prevailed.

Governor Packard presented communication to be sent to the Hereford cattle breeders in regard to holding sale on fair grounds as follows:

Having considered the application made by Mr. C. A. Stannard in behalf of himself and other breeders of Hereford cattle for permission to hold a sale of cattle at the fair grounds during the next state fair, the State Board of Agriculture will allow the sale to be made as requested subject to the rules of the board. Inasmuch as the department will have stabling room only for the cattle on the grounds for exhibition, and being without sale pavilion the breeders interested will be required to supply tents for stabling and selling such cattle at their own expense. Suitable ground space will be given for the necessary tents without charge, and the fees provided under rule 15, stock sales, will not be exacted.

Managers of other breeds of cattle dsiring like selling privilege will be allowed to make sales during the next state fair, provided timely notice is given to the superintendent of cattle.

Mr. St. John moved that the communication presented by Mr. Packard be adopted. Motion prevailed.

Governor Packard offered a resolution in regard to improvements for the next year as follows:

Resolved, That the executive committee take up the matter of improvements needed at the State Fair Grounds and are hereby authorized to have constructed certain buildings and to have work performed as follows, to-wit:

1. A dry air closet the size of the one recently erected.

2. An addition to the Horticultural building upon the plan as presented by Superintendent Wragg.

3. Four cattle barns the size of the other cattle barns.

4. To pave with cement sidewalks to the extent of 5,000 lineal feet of suitable width.

5. To erect suitable buildings to be used as dining halls at a cost not exceeding $1,500.

6. To make all needful repairs to the buildings and improve the roads and grounds as may be needful for the use of the next state fair.

Mr. Wragg moved that the superintendent of the grounds prepare fifty signs calling attention to the fact that there was a fine for hitching to trees. Motion prevailed.

Mr. Manatrey moved that we adjourn until 1:30. Motion prevailed.

AFTERNOON SESSION.

Board met pursuant to adjournment, with President Frasier in the chair.

Roll call and the following members were found to be absent, Phillips, Wragg and Legoe.

Mr. Cameron moved that the executive committee be authorized to build a closet, not larger than the one last year, on the street running to the south gate. Seconded by Morrow and motion prevailed.

Mr. St. John moved that the plan presented by Mr. Wragg for an addition to the horticultural hall be built at a cost not to exceed $1,500. Seconded by Manatrey and motion prevailed.

Mr. Manatrey moved that two cattle barns be built, the same size as those on the grounds. Seconded by McDonald.

Dr. Gibson moved a substitute, that the executive committee be authorized to build four cattle barns if found necessary. Seconded by Phillips, and upon roll call there was six affirmative votes and eight negative, so substitute was declared lost.

Roll call on original motion resulted in an affirmative vote.

Mr. Ledgerwood moved a reconsideration of the resolution passed on building an addition to horticultural hall. Seconded by Morrow and motion prevailed.

Mr. Wadsworth moved that the executive committee be authorized to expend not to exceed $3,000 in building cement walks on the fair grounds. Seconded by Ledgerwood.

Mr. Manatrey moved to amend the foregoing resolution, by stating that the executive committee be authorized to build brick walks if they see fit.   Seconded by Morrow.   Roll call had, there was found to be four affirmative votes and eight negative, so amendment was declared lost, and the original motion carried on roll call.

Mr. Packard moved that the sixth proposition as read in the resolution be approved, and that the executive committee be authorized to purchase a roller if they think necessary. Seconded by Gibson and motion prevailed.

Mr. Gibson moved that we have night attractions. Seconded by Morrow and motion prevailed.

Mr. Gibson moved that the matter of night attractions be left with the executive committee.   Seconded by Brown.

Cameron moved to amend by allowing the Executive Committee to expend $2,500, if found necessary for night attractions. Seconded by Brown.   Dr. Gibson accepted the amendment and the motion prevailed.

Dr. Gibson moved that the executive committee be authorized to secure good day attractions. Seconded by St. John and motion prevailed.

Mr. Manatrey moved to adjourn which motion prevailed.

J. C. Simpson,
Secretary.

FRIDAY MORNING, JANUARY 31, 1902.

Board met pursuant to adjournment with President Frasier in the chair. Roll call and all members found to be present.

Minutes of yesterday's session read and approved

Mr. Manatrey moved that the executive committee be empowered to purchase such amount of advertising matter as they think necessary.   Motion prevailed.

Mr. Manatrey moved that we now take up the motion made by St. John on yesterday in regard to building an addition to horticultural hall, which motion was deferred from yesterday until Mr. Wragg could be present. Seconded by Brown.

Mr. Cameron moved to amend by inserting that the matter be left to the executive committee and the superintendent of the horticultural department. Seconded by McDonald and amendment prevailed.

Mr. McDonald moved the the executive committee be empowered to build additional cattle barns if found necessary, in addition to the two voted. Seconded by Gibson and motion prevailed.

Mr. Wadsworth moved that the chair appoint a committee on per diem and mileage. Motion prevailed.

Chair appointed Wadsworth, Ledgerwood and Cameron.

Mr. Packard moved that we adjourn until 2 o'clock p. m. Motion prevailed.

AFTERNOON SESSION.

Board met pursuant to adjournment with Vice-President Morrow in the chair.

Roll was called and all members were found present or came in soon afterward except Manatrey.

Mr. Wadsworth made the report from the committee on per diem and mileage as follows.

	Days.	Amt.	Miles.	Mileage.	Total.	
J. C. Frasier	7	$28.00	113	$11.30	$ 39.30	272
W. W. Morrow	6	24.00	82	8.20	32.20	273
J. P. Manatrey	6	24.00	118	11.80	35.80	274
C. W. Phillips	5	20.00	...	......	20.00	275
W. C. Brown	6	24.00	102	10.20	34.20	276
R. T. St. John	6	24.00	195	19.50	43.50	277
S. B. Packard	6	24.00	58	5.80	29.80	278
T. C. Legoe	7	28.00	100	10.00	38.00	279
M. J. Wragg	5	20.00	16	1.60	21.60	280
John Ledgerwood	6	24.00	89	8.90	32.90	281
M. McDonald	6	24.00	65	6.50	30.50	282
J. W. Wadsworth	6	24.00	123	12.30	36.30	283
C. E. Cameron	6	24.00	140	14.00	38.00	284

$432.10

Mr. St. John moved that the report as read be adopted. Motion prevailed.

Mr. Packard made the report of the committee on resolutions
as follows:

The committee on resolutions desires to bring to the notice of the
State Board of Agriculture the painful news of the death of the wife of
our valued colleague, the director of the Tenth congressional district,
Joseph W. Wadsworth of Algona, which occurred at the family home on
the fifth day of this month.

The members of this Board sympathize deeply with our colleague in
this great loss and terrible sorrow which has come to him, to his daughter and son; to a vast circle of sorrowing relatives and friends in the
death of Emeline A Wadsworth, the wife, the mother, whose Christian
life and example has so much endeared her and which will be ever
present in their memory.

Resolved, That the officers and other members of the Board tender
our most sincere condolence and heartfelt sympathy to Joseph, our
brother member, and to his children so severely stricken in sorrow and
offer our prayers that the Divine and All Merciful One may vouchsafe
consolation and comfort to sustain and reconcile them to their loss.

Resolved, That this tribute be recorded in our minutes and a copy
sent to the family at Algona.

On the twenty-fourth day of December, Frank N. Chase died at his
home at Cedar Falls, after a somewhat prolonged and painful illness.
Several of our membership have served with our brother in the later
years of his life. He was elected as a director in 1882, serving as such
until elected vice-president in 1894, and brought to the society his very
valuable judgment and painstaking efforts, which contributed greatly to
its success since its permanent establishment at Des Moines. In the
preparation of the Iowa exhibit at the exposition at Chicago in 1893 and
Omaha in 1898 his was the master hand and to him a most generous
meed of prise has been accorded. To those who best knew Frank and
by whom he was best loved, outside of those having kindred ties, his
sunny and genial temperament endeared him to his friends like a
brother. To enumerate the virtues of one who as husband and father
has been in his home circle all and everything that a wife could wish,
and that a son and daughter could desire, being upright in citizenship,
devoted to his church, and reverently worshipful to God; to the mourn-
ing family the members of the State Board of Agriculture tender their
sympathy.

Resolved, That a copy be sent to the widow of our departed friend
and be recorded in the minutes of the proceedings of the Board.

Your committee on resolutions beg leave to submit the following
resolution respecting the death of the Hon. Peter Melendy, who was an
honored member of this society of agriculture, being its vice-president from
the year 1863 to 1865 and its president from 1865 to 1869 and its treasurer for the year 1871. He was one of three who held the office of presi-

dent for four consecutive years, the others being the Hon. Thomas W. C. Claggett and the Hon. George G. Wright. Mr. Melendy had the welfare of this society always in view until death removed him from his labors here to life eternal on October 18, 1901, at Cedar Falls, Iowa.

Resolved, That in his death his family is bereft of a kind and loving husb'and and father, the state and city where he resided, a progressive citizen, and our society one who gave to the cause of agriculture six years of unremitting labor to advance the interests of this society, and we share and sympathize with the family in this their great bereavement and loss.

Resolved, That these resolutions become a part of our records and that the secretary be instructed to forward a copy of the same to the grief-stricken family of the deceased.

The president announced committees as follows as per rules and regulations adopted.

No. 2—Auditing committee, Cameron, Wadsworth and Brown.
No. 3—Resolutions, Packard, McDonald and St. John.
No. 4—Governor, Frasier and Morrow.
No. 5—Beardshear, Wragg and Manatrey.
No. 6—Norton, Ledgerwood and Packard.
No. 7—Gibson, Phillips and Legoe.

Mr. Cameron moved that the executive be empowered to act on all business that may come before them in the absence of the board.

Board adjourned to meet at call of president.

J. C. SIMPSON,
Secretary.

EXECUTIVE COMMITTEE MEETINGS.

MARCH 21, 1902.

Present, Frasier, Morrow and Simpson.

Committee went to the fair grounds and looked over the matter of proposed improvements.

Ordered Mr. Deemer to fix up the old secretary's office for police headquarters.

Ordered the C., B. & Q. building to be remodeled for the secretary's and treasurer's office; also to put brick pillars under the porch.

Ordered Mr. Deemer to extend the gravel walk running from the street car entrance to the street in front of the C., B. & Q. building.

Ordered Mr. Deemer to fix the poultry house in accordance with the wishes of the poultry exhibitors.

Ordered gravel put on the streets.

Secretary was authorized to issue warrants on pay roll of Mr. Deemer when O. K. by him.

APRIL 10, 1902.

Committee met with Frasier and Simpson present.

The committee were busy looking after the improvements at the fair grounds.

Proposition from Botsford & Maher in regard to advertising on the grand stand and fences, was before the committee, and they accepted the same, authorizing the secretary to draw up a contract in accordance with their proposition.

APRIL 21, 1902.

Present, Frasier, Morrow and Simpson.

Received plans and specifications from Reeves & Baillie, architects, Peoria, Illinois, for stock pavilion, and proceeded to advertise for bids, to be closed May 5, 1902.

Visited fair grounds and ordered Mr. Deemer to put new roof on the horticultural building; get new poles for our electric light plant; to build bridge across ditch southeast of the producers' building; grade a road along the north side of the building; paint the producers' building.

APRIL 22, 1902.

Present, Frasier, Morrow and Simpson.

Mr. Taft, representing the American Warming and Ventilating Company, was before the committee and submitted plans and specifications for a dry air closet to be erected on the grounds.

Mr. Morrow moved that Mr. Frasier be authorized to personally superintend the improvements to be made on the fair grounds this year. Motion prevailed.

Mr. Morrow moved that we accept the proposition of the American Warming and Ventilating Company, to erect a dry air closet on the fair grounds, and make repairs on the one erected in 1901, on the above said grounds, for sum of $3,775, in accordance with plans and specifications submitted herewith. Motion prevailed.

MEETING OF THE STATE BOARD OF AGRICULTURE.
MAY 5, 1902.

Meeting called to order by President Frasier, and on roll call all were found to be present, except Mr. Cameron who came in a few minutes later.

Mr. St. John moved that the opening of the bids be postponed for the present. Motion prevailed.

Mr. Packard offered the following resolution and moved the adoption of the same.

Whereas: The secretary of the State Board of Agriculture, by direction of the Board, has invited bids or proposals for a stock pavilion on the State Fair Grounds, in terms and conditions as follows:

PROPOSAL FOR STOCK PAVILION ON IOWA STATE FAIR GROUNDS.

Sealed proposals will be received at the office of the secretary of the State Board of Agriculture, Des Moines, Iowa, until 12 o'clock m., on the fifth day of May, 1902, and immediately thereafter opened, for all labor and materials required in the erection and completion of a stock pavilion, to be erected on the State Fair Grounds, Des Moines, Iowa, in accordance with the drawings and specifications prepared by Reeves & Baillie, architects, Peoria, Illinois.

Proposals received after the time stated will be returned unopened to the bidders. Copies of the plans and specifications will be on file at the office of the secretary of the State Board of Agriculture, and also at the architect's office on and after April 21, 1902.

The work to be commenced as soon as practicable after acceptance of bid. All iron work to be delivered on the ground not later than July 1, 1902, and erected not later than July 15, 1902. Bids on iron work will be received separately.

The building to be completed by August 15, 1902, under penalty of $50 per day forfeit.

Each bid to be accompanied by a certified check for 5 per cent of amount of bid. Satisfactory bond for 50 per cent of amount of bid will be required.

The State Board of Agriculture reserves the right to reject the lowest or any or all bids, and to waive any defects or informalities in any bid when it is deemed in the interest of the Board to do so.

Each bid must be enclosed in an envelope sealed and addressed to Mr. John C. Simpson, secretary of the State Board of Agriculture, Des

Moines, Iowa, and indorsed on the envelope "Proposal for Stock Pavilion." Pavilin."

By order of the State Board of Agriculture.

JOHN C. SIMPSON,
Secretary.

And Whereas: The hour named, 12 o'clock, meridian this 5th day of May, A. D. 1902, has expired, at which time sealed proposals were required to be in the hands of the secretary.

Therefore Be It Resolved: That John C. Simpson, secretary, in the presence of the Board now in session, proceed to open the sealed envelopes which have been received indorsed "Proposals for Stock Pavilion," in the order of their receipt at this department.

The secretary proceeded to open the bids in the following order. (Amount of each bid to be found on file in this office):

Charles Weitz & Sons, Des Moines, Iowa.
American Bridge Company, Kansas City, Mo.
Des Moines Bridge and Iron Company, Des Moines, Iowa.
Capital City Brick and Pipe Company, Des Moines, Iowa.
Joliet Bridge Company, Joliet, Illinois.
Modern Steel Structural Company, Waukesha, Wis.
John W. Evans & Sons, Bloomington, Illinois.

Mr. Legoe moved that we accept the bid of the Des Moines Bridge & Iron Company, Des Moines, Iowa, for all iron and steel work to be in the stock pavilion, it being the lowest bid according to plans and specifications, for $14,850.00, subject upon their execution of a satisfactory bond. Seconded by Brown and all voted in the affirmative.

Mr. Legoe moved that the contract be awarded to Charles Weitz & Sons, Des Moines, Iowa, for the construction of the stock pavilion complete, except the iron and steel work, and the setting of the same, for which a reduction in his bid is made of $14,850; also the using of Legrand stone in the place of the Gray Canon stone specified, for which a reduction in his bid is made of $200; also the omitting of the finishing coat of paint on the structural iron, for which a reduction is made in his bid of $600; and the using of square edged selected local paving brick, laid in black mortar, for all faced brick work instead of the common brick specified, for which an addition to his bid is made of $820, making the amount of the contract as accepted $26,518.98, provided a satisfactory bond is given and contract executed according to the plans and specifications of said building. Seconded by Brown and all members voted in the affirmative.

Governor Packard offered the following resolution and moved its adoption:

Resolved, That the executive committee are hereby authorized to sign the contracts awarded this day for the erection of the stock pavilion on the State Fair Grounds; to approve the bonds required of the contractors; and full power is hereby given said committee to supervise and approve the work when completed, to make contract with the architects for expenses for working their plans and supervision.

. Mr. Gregory, representing the Pain Manufacturing Company of Chicago, Illinois, appeared before the board and presented a proposition in regard to putting on attractions for our fair.

Mr. Manatrey moved that we reject the offer of the Pain Manufacturing Company. Seconded by McDonald, and upon motion of Cameron further consideration of the matter was deferred until the next morning, when the motion was called up and passed rejecting the offer of the above named company.

Mr. Wragg moved that the addition to the horticultural hall be deferred for one year. Seconded by McDonald and motion prevailed.

Mr. McDonald moved that the board adjourn until 9 o'clock to-morrow morning.

MAY 6, 1902.

Board met at fair grounds and proceeded to select a location for the stock pavilion, and decided on the location standing north and south, east of the street running to the Rock Island gate.

Minutes of the yesterday's meeting read and approved; also of the January board meeting.

Mr. St. John moved that the motion requiring the executive committee to put down all cement walks be rescinded. Seconded by Wragg.

Mr. Legoe moved to amend as follows: That that part of the motion requiring the executive committee to build cement walks be rescinded and that the executive committee be authorized to use either brick or cement for said walks as they deem best. Mr.

St. John accepted the amendment and the motion prevailed as amended.

Mr. St. John moved that the executive committee be authorized to expend not to exceed $1,200, in repairing and rebuilding the dwelling house on the fair grounds, occupied by the superintendent of the grounds. Seconded by Wragg and all voted in the affirmative. Absent, Frasier, Manatrey and Brown.

Mr. McDonald moved that the Executive Committee be authorized to procure material to build a cattle barn 60x120 feet, not to exceed twelve feet high, to be built by day labor. Seconded by Wragg and motion prevailed.

Mr. Wragg moved that Mr. Frasier be superintendent of construction of the improvements to be made on the fair grounds this year. Motion prevailed.

Mr. Ellyson moved that the secretary be instructed to confer with the secretary of the State Board of Health, and appoint a janitor, and that the preference be given to an old soldier. Seconded by McDonald and motion prevailed.

Mr. Morrow moved that the president appoint a committee on per diem and mileage. Motion prevailed and president appointed Wadsworth, Ledgerwood, and Legoe.

Mr. Cameron moved that Monday, August 25th, be Dedication Day for the new stock pavilion, and that the executive committee and two other members be a committee on ceremonies, and that a special invitation be issued to members of the lgislature, state officers, congressmen, United States senators to be in attendance on that day. Seconded by Ellyson and motion prevailed.

President appointed on above committee in addition to the executive committee, Mr. Cameron and Mr. Packard.

Mr. Morrow moved that the members of the State Board of Agriculture be appointed a committee on reception on the day the stock pavilion is dedicated.

11

Committee on per diem and mileage reported as follows:

NAME.	DAYS.	AMOUNT.	MILES.	MILEAGE.	TOTALS.
J. C. Frasier.	4	$ 16.00	113	$ 11.30	$ 27.30
W. W. Morrow	3	12.00	82	8.20	20.20
J. P. Manatrey.	2	8.00	115	11.80	19.80
C. W. Phillips	2	8.00	.	.	8.00
W. C. Brown.	4	16.00	102	10.20	26.20
R. T. St. John.	4	16.00	195	19.50	35.50
S. B. Packard	3	12.00	58	5.80	17.80
T. C. Legoe	4	16.00	100	10.00	26.00
M. J. Wragg	2	8.00	16	1.60	9.60
John Ledgerwood	3	12.00	89	8 90	20.90
M. McDonald.	3	12.00	65	6.50	18.50
J. W. Wadsworth	3	12 00	123	12.30	24.30
C. E. Cameron.	3	12.00	140	14.00	26.00

Mr. Cameron moved that we adjourn. Motion prevailed.

J. C. Simpson,
Secretary.

Courtesy of Wallace's Farmer.

A prize Hereford bull shown at the Iowa State Fair 1902.

MEETING OF BOARD OF DIRECTORS, IOWA STATE BOARD OF AGRICULTURE.

Friday afternoon, August 29, 1902, at 1 o'clock p. m. in the president's office on the fair grounds.

President Frasier was in the chair and upon roll call the following members were found to be present: President J. C. Frasier, Secretary J. C. Simpson, Treasurer G. D. Ellyson and Directors S. B. Packard, John Ledgerwood and C. W. Phillips.

Pay roll of W. M. McFadden, superintendent of the swine department, was presented, allowed and placed on file, on motion of Ellyson.

Pay roll of G. D. Ellyson, treasurer, was presented and on motion was allowed and placed on file.

Bill of W. H. Erwin, assistant superintendent of grounds, was presented, allowed and placed on file on motion of C. W. Phillips.

Pay roll of C. W. Phillips, superintendent of tickets, was presented and on motion of Ellyson was allowed and placed on file.

Pay roll of John Ledgerwood, superintendent of sheep and poultry departments, was presented and on motion of Ellyson was allowed and placed on file.

Pay roll of Hon. S. B. Packard was presented, and on motion of Ellyson was allowed and placed on file.

Pay roll of J. W. Wadsworth, superintendent of privileges, was presented and on motion of Mr. Packard was allowed and placed on file.

Mr. Ellyson moved that the itemized bill attached to Mr. Wadsworth's pay roll, be allowed, which motion prevailed.

Protest from Mr. H. Lefebure, Fairfax, Iowa, against award in Class No. 9, to McLaughlin Bros., was presented and found to be in regular form, accompanied by check for $20.00.

Phillips moved that the premium awarded to McLaughlin Bros. be withheld until Mr. Lefebure had time to prove charges made in said affidavit.

Mr. Ellyson moved that the pay roll of T. C. Legoe, superintendent of the gates department, amounting to $535 be allowed, which motion prevailed.

On motion the board adjourned to meet at 6:30 p. m.

EVENING SESSION.

! Board met pursuant to adjournment with President Frasier in the chair.

Upon roll call the following members were found to be present: Frasier, Morrow, Simpson, Manatrey, Phillips, Brown, St. John, Packard, Wragg, Ledgerwood, McDonald, Wadsworth, and Cameron.

Mr. McLaughlin and Mr. Lefebure appeared before the Board and made statements regarding the protests filed by Mr. Lefebure.

Mr. Phillips moved that Mr. Lefebure be given forty days in which to substantiate his evidence, which motion prevailed.

Mr. Wragg presented his pay roll, as superintendent of the horticultural department, and on motion of Phillips the same was allowed and placed on file.

Mr. Wragg moved that the pay roll of Mr. St. John, as superintendent of the agricultural department be allowed, which motion prevailed.

Mr. Manatrey moved that the bill of Mr. St. John for his assistant be allowed, which motion prevailed.

Mr. Wadsworth moved that the bill of McLaughlin & Company of Chicago for booth in the agricultural hall amounting to $10 be allowed which motion prevailed.

Phillips moved that the pay roll of Mr. W. C. Brown, as superintendent of the horse department, be allowed, which motion prevailed.

Mr. Morrow moved that the pay rolls of McDonald, superintendent of the dairy department, be allowed, which motion prevailed.

Mr. Ledgerwood moved that the meals for judges in the cattle department, be allowed, which motion prevailed.

Mr. Brown moved that the pay roll of Mr. Cameron be allowed. which motion prevailed.

Mr. St. John moved that the pay roll of Secretary Simpson for clerical work in the secretary's office, amounting to $183 be allowed, which motion prevailed.

Mr. McDonald moved that the pay roll of Mr. Cownie, superintendent of the electric light department, be allowed, which motion prevailed.

Mr. Manatrey moved that we adjourn to meet at 9 o'clock, a. m.

SATURDAY MORNING, AUGUST 30, 1902.

Board met pursuant to adjournment, with President Frasier in the chair.

Upon roll call the following members were found to be present: Frasier, Morrow, Simpson, Manatrey, Phillips, Brown, Packard, Legoe, Wragg, McDonald, Cameron, Ledgerwood and Wadsworth. Mr. McDonald moved that the bill of Phillips for meals for his assistants be allowed, which motion prevailed.

Mr. McDonald moved that the pay roll of Mr. Manatrey be allowed, which motion prevailed.

Mr. McDonald moved that the itemized bill presented by Mr. Wragg for advertising, amounting to $5, be allowed, which motion prevailed.

Mr. Wragg moved that the pay roll of Mr. Morrow, superintendent of the machinery department, be allowed, which motion prevailed.

Mr. McDonald moved that the police pay roll amounting to $1,082,25, be allowed, which motion prevailed.

Mr. Legoe moved that the bill of Mr. George C. Inlow, for $3.50 for tent for gate department, be allowed, which motion prevailed.

Mr. Cameron moved that Mr. Cownie be allowed $25 for expenses during the fair, which motion prevailed.

Mr. McDonald moved that the president appoint a committee on per diem and mileage, and the chair appointed Cameron, Wadsworth and Ledgerwood.

Mr. McDonald moved that the executive committee be authorized to buy a road scraper for use on the fair grounds, which motion prevailed.

Mr. McDonald moved that the bill presented by Mr. St. John for meals for his assistant, be allowed which motion prevailed.

Mr. Morrow moved that Mr. Simpson and Mr. Ellyson be allowed $24 each for office expenses during the fair, which motion prevailed.

Mr. St. John moved that Mr. Frasier be allowed 100 days' time for services in superintending the work of erecting the new stock pavilion, which motion prevailed.

Mr. St. John moved that a vote of thanks be tendered to Mr. Frasier for his work in superintending the live stock pavilion, which was unanimously passed by the board.

Mr. Cameron presented the report of the committee on per diem mileage, and moved its adoption, which motion prevailed.

NAME.	DAYS.	AMOUNT.	MILES.	MILEAGE.	TOTALS.
J. C. Frasier .	16	$ 64.00	113	$ 11.13	$ 75.30
W. W. Morrow	17	68.00	82	8.20	76.20
J. P. Manatrey.	19	76.00	118	11.80	87.80
C. W. Phillips	18	72.00	...	......	72.00
W. C. Brown.	19	76.00	102	10.20	86.20
R. T. St. John	19	76.00	195	19.50	95.50
S. B. Packard	17	68.00	5%	5.80	73.80
T. C. Legoe	17	68.00	100	10.00	78.00
M. J. Wragg	19	76.00	16	1.60	77.60
John Ledgerwood	18	72.00	89	8.90	80.90
M. McDonald.	18	72.00	65	6.50	78.50
J. W. Wadsworth.	26	104.00	12%	12.30	116.30
C. E. Cameron .	16	64.00	140	14.00	78.00

C. E. CAMERON,
JOHN LEDGERWOOD,
J. W. WADSWORTH,
Committee.

Mr. St. John moved that the executive committee be authorized to make a contract with the street car company to extend a temporary track into the fair grounds for the week of the horse show, which motion prevailed.

Mr. Cownie presented a clock to Mr. J. C. Frasier, president of the State Board of Agriculture, on behalf of the members of said board, in words as follows:

Mr. President: The Iowa State Fair of 1902 has closed, and painstaking, faithful and efficient work, supplemented by a bright sun and clear skies, kindly vouchsafed by an allwise Providence, have made it possible to place this year's fair at the head of all those that have preceded. The fair of 1902 will be ever memorable in the history of Iowa, as it marks an epoch that insures still greater prosperity to the wealth producers of the state.

By the erection of the live stock pavilion renewed energy will be given to the improved stock breeders of our own and neighboring states, and with the facilities and comfort now afforded for witnessing the judging of horses and cattle, we may hope that in the near future swine and sheep, agricultural machinery, grains, fruits and flowers, will be recognized in like manner by the erection of buildings planned with the same regard to durability, elegance, convenience and comfort as the new live stock pavilion that was dedicated last Wednesday.

To you, Mr. President, the people of Iowa owe a debt of gratitude for the interest you have taken in the erection of the pavilion, your constant, careful supervision of all material and labor has been rewarded by a building that is a credit to our state, combining as it does architectural beauty, ample size, strength and durability.

. With the excellent record you have made while connected with the State Board of Agriculture as director, vice-president and president, as superintendent of privileges, of tickets and of construction, your co-workers had hoped to have the benefit of your example and counsel for at least another year. But it having become known that you have determined to positively decline what was already assured, a unanimous re-election to the position of president for another, your associates desire to tender you, as a slight token of their appreciation of your services to the Iowa State Board of Agriculture, this beautiful clock, which I now have the pleasure of presenting to you.

Place it upon your mantel, and as you look upon it from day to day it will revive pleasant memories of the years you spent with your fellow members laboring to build up the agricultural and manufacturing interests of our great state, that is already in the front rank with everything that adds to the moral, intellectual and material advancement of our people.

On behalf of your fellow members of the Iowa State Board of Agriculture I desire to express to you and yours our best wishes for your future. May a long, prosperous and pleasant life await you, and rest assured that the personal friendships you have made among the members. of this Board will only end with life itself.

On motion Board adjourned.

J. C. SIMPSON,
Secretary.

PART III.

REPORT OF THE IOWA WEATHER AND CROP SERVICE.

John R. Sage, Director.

METEOROLOGICAL SUMMARY FOR THE YEAR 1902.

BAROMETER. The mean pressure for the year was 30.01 inches. The highest observed pressure was 30.96 inches on January 28th at Dubuque; lowest pressure 28.67 inches on February 28th at Davenport. Range for the state, 2.29 inches.

TEMPERATURE. The mean temperature for the state was 47.8 degrees which is 0.6 degrees above normal. The highest temperature reported was 98 degrees on July 30th at Charles City. The lowest temperature reported was 31 degrees below zero on January 27th at Atlantic, Range for the year, 129 degrees.

PRECIPITATION. The average amount of rain and melted snow for the year as shown by complete records of 99 stations was 44.31 inches, which 14.01 inches above the normal, and 19.69 inches above the average amount for 1901. The greatest amount recorded at any station for the year was 58.80 inches at Columbus Junction; least amount recorded, 20.14 inches at Sioux City. The greatest monthly rainfall was 18.04 inches at Grand Meadow, Clayton county, in May; least amount, a trace at Cresco, Howard county, in March. The greatest amount in any consecutive 24 hours was 9.96 inches at Allerton, August 25th and 26th. The average number of days on which .01 or more of rain fell was 100.

WIND AND WEATHER. The prevailing direction of wind was northwest. Highest velocity reported, 74 miles an hour in Sioux City, from the north on April 25th. Average daily wind movement 211 miles. There were 145 clear days, 109 partly cloudy, and 111 cloudy days.

JANUARY.—The monthly mean temperature for the state, as shown by records at 112 stations, was 22.4 degrees, which is 5.3 degrees above the January normal. By sections the means were as follows: Northern section, 20.4 degrees; central section, 21.9 degrees; southern section, 24.8 degrees. The highest monthly mean was 27.5 degrees at Keokuk; lowest monthly mean, 17.4 at Cresco. The highest temperature reported was 63 degrees at Pella, St. Charles and Thurman on the 7th and 8th; lowest temperature reported, 31 degrees below zero at Atlantic on the 27th. The average monthly maximum was 52.7 degrees; average monthly minimum, 20.9 degrees. The greatest daily range was 56 degrees at Guthrie Center, average of the greatest daily ranges, 34.4 degrees. The average precipitation for the state as shown by the records of 129 stations, was .88 of an inch, which is .34 of an inch below the normal for January. By sections the averages were as follows: Northern section, 0.84 of an inch; central section, 0.98 of an inch; southern section, 0.88 of an inch. The largest amount reported was 2.83 inches, at Ridgeway; least amount , 0.19 of an inch, at Mt. Pleasant. The greatest daily precipitation reported was 1.51 inches, at Ridgeway on the 20th. The average number of days on which .01 or more precipitation fell was 4. Prevailing direction of the wind, northwest; highest velocity, 38 miles per hour from northwest at Sioux City on the 2d. Average number of clear days, 17; partly cloudy, 8; cloudy, 6.

FEBRUARY.—The monthly mean temperature as shown by records of 110 stations, was 17.6 degrees; which is 4.1 degree below the February normal for this state. The monthly means by sections were as follows: Northern section, 16.6 degrees; central section, 16.8 degrees; southern section, 19.3 degrees. The highest monthly mean reported was 22.2 degrees at Thurman; lowest mean, 12.8 degrees at New Hampton. The highest temperature reported was 62 degrees at Humboldt on the 27th; lowest reported 21 degrees below zero at Galva on the 2d. The average monthly maximum was 52.2 degrees; average monthly minimum 14.2 degrees below zero. The greatest daily range was 46 degrees at Elkader; average of greatest daily ranges 32.5 degrees. The average precipitation for the state, as shown by the records of 128 stations, was 0.73 of an inch, or 0.33 below normal. The averages by sections were as follows: Northern section, 0.69 of an inch; central section, 0.74 of an inch; southern section, 0.75 of an inch. The largest amount reported was 2.39 inches at Belle Plaine; least amount 0.02 of an inch at Thurman. The greatest daily precipitation reported was 1.40 inches at Belle Plaine on the 27th. Average number of days on which .01 or more precipitation fell, 4. Prevailing direction of wind, northwest; highest velocity reported 46 miles per hour, from northwest at Sioux City, on the 28th. Average number of clear days 13; partly cloudy 8; cloudy 7.

MARCH.—The monthly mean temperature for March as shown by records of 101 stations, was 39.1 degrees, which is 5.9 degrees above normal. The monthly means by sections were as follows: Northern section, 36.9 degrees; Central section, 39.3 degrees; southern section, 41 degrees. The highest monthly mean was 44.5 degrees at Thurman; lowest, 34.9 degrees at Larchwood. The highest temperature reported was 79 degrees at Winterset on the 25th; lowest, 12 degrees below zero at Estherville on the 17th. The average monthly maximum was 69.4 degrees; average monthly minimum, 1.5 degrees below zero. The greatest daily range was 46 degrees at Sibley, Monticello and Thurman; average of greatest daily ranges, 34.6 degrees. The average precipitation for the state was 1.45 inches, as shown by the records of 121 stations. This amount is .30 inch below normal. The averages by sections were as follows: Northern section, 1.20 inches; central section, 1.73 inches; southern section, 1.42

inches. The largest amount reported was 4.33 inches at Cumberland; least amount, 0.13 of an inch at Algona. The greatest daily amount reported was 3.00 inches at Cumberland on the 10th. The average number of days on which .01 or more precipitation was recorded was 7. Prevailing direction of wind, southeast; highest velocity, 58 miles per hour at Sioux City on the 16th. Average number of clear days, 9; partly cloudy, 11; cloudy, 11.

APRIL.—The mean temperature for the state as shown by the records of 114 stations, was 48.2 degrees, which is about 1.3 degrees below the normal for April. The highest monthly mean was 53.1 degrees at Thurman. and the lowest, 44.2 degrees at Estherville. The means by sections were as follows: Northern section, 46.3 degrees; central section, 48.1 degrees; southern section, 50.3 degrees. The highest temperature reported was 96 degrees at Clarinda, on the 20th; lowest, 9 degrees at Larrabee on the 7th. The average monthly maximum was 87.5 degrees; average monthly minimum 18.9 degrees. The greatest daily range was 59 degrees, at Glenwood; average of greatest daily ranges, 39.5 degrees. The average precipitation for the state, as shown by the records of 130 stations, was 1.71 inches, or 1.50 inches below normal. The averages by sections were as follows: Northern section, 1.34 inches; central section, 1.60 inches; southern section, 2.19 inches. The largest amount reported was 4.15 inches at Bonaparte, Van Buren county; least amount reported, .40 of an inch at Glenwood. The greatest daily rainfall reported was 2.95 inches, at Sioux Center on the 25th. The average number of days on which .01 inch or more of rain fell was 5. The prevailing direction of the wind was northwest; highest velocity reported was 74 miles per hour, from the north at Sioux City on the 25th. The average number of clear days was 14; partly cloudy, 11; cloudy, 5.

MAY.—The mean temperature for the state as shown by records of 107 stations, was 63.8 degrees, which is about 4.1 degrees above the normal for May. The highest monthly mean was 67.8 degrees, at Keosauqua, and the lowest 59.0 degrees at New Hampton. The means by sections were as follows: Northern section, 61.8 degrees; central section, 64.0 degrees; southern section, 65.6 degrees. The highest temperature reported was 97 degrees at Sigourney on the 20th; lowest 25 degrees, at Cresco, on the 10th. The average monthly maximum was 88.7 degrees; average monthly minimum 38.4 degrees. The greatest daily range was 50 degrees, at Pacific Junction; average of greatest daily ranges, 37.7 degrees. The average precipitation for the state, as shown by the records of 127 stations, was 5.39 inches, or 1.42 inches above normal. The averages by sections were as follows: Northern section, 6.69 inches; central section 5.02 inches; southern section, 4.46 inches. The largest amount reported was 18.04 inches, at Grand Meadow, Clayton county; least amount reported was .87 inch at Washta. The greatest daily rainfall reported was 5.45 inches, at Grand Meadow on the 18th. The average number of days on which .01 inch or more of rain fell was 13. The prevailing direction of the wind was southeast; highest velocity reported, 50 miles per hour, from the south, at Sioux City, on the 20th. The average number of clear days was 10; partly cloudy, 12; cloudy, 9.

JUNE.—The month was unseasonably cool, especially in the last half, The daily mean temperature as shown by the records of 113 stations was 65.2 degrees, which is 4.8 degrees below the June normal. The means by sections were as follows: Northern section, 64 degrees; central section, 65.4 degrees; southern section, 66.3 degrees. The highest monthly mean was 69.2 degrees at De Soto; lowest, 60.2 degrees at Cresco. The highest temperature reported was 97 degrees at Keosauqua on the 10th; lowest, 32 degrees at Sibley on the 22d. The average monthly maximum was 89.9 degrees; average monthly minimum, 38.4 degrees. The greatest daily range was 42 degrees at Larrabee. Average of greatest daily ranges, 33 degrees. The average precipitation for the state as shown by the records of 120 stations was 7.16 inches which is 2.90 inches above normal. The averages by sections were as follows: Northern section, 5.54 inches; central section, 8.11 inches; southern section, 7.83 inches. The largest amount reported was 16.04 inches at Grundy Center; least amount reported, 1.46 inches at Sheldon. The greatest daily rainfall reported was 6.60 inches at Buckingham on the 5th. The average number of days on which .01 inch or more of rainfall was reported, 14. Prevailing direction of wind, southeast and northwest; highest velocity reported, 48 miles per hour from the west at Sioux City, on the 15th. The average number of clear days was 8; partly cloudy, 11; cloudy, 11.

JULY.—The monthly mean temperature for the state, as shown by records of 108 stations, was 73.1 degrees, which is 0.6 degrees below normal. By sections the mean temperatures were as follows: Northern section, 71.9 degrees; central section, 73.3 degrees; southern section, 74.2 degrees. The highest monthly mean was 76.5 degrees at Keokuk; lowest monthly mean was 70.2 degrees, at Alta, Fayette, New Hampton and Northwood. The highest temperature reported was 99 degrees, at St. Charles on the 17th; lowest temperature reported, 41 degrees, at Clinton on the 1st. The average monthly maximum was 92.9 degrees; average monthly minimum, 50.9 degrees. Greatest daily range, 43 degrees at Plover; average of greatest daily ranges 30.4 degrees. Average precipitation for the state, as shown by records of 125 stations, was 8.67 inches, which is 4.99 inches above normal. The averages by sections were as follows: Northern section, 8.35 inches; central section, 8.84 inches; southern section, 8.82 inches. The largest amount reported was 13.57 inches, at Odeboldt; least amount reported, 4.87 inches, at Keokuk. The greatest daily rainfall reported was 6.25 inches, at Ovid on the 17th and 18th. Average number of days on which .01 of an inch or more was reported 13. Prevailing direction of the wind, southwest; highest velocity reported, 47 miles per hour, from the south, at Sioux City, on the 5th. Average number of clear days, 14; partly cloudy, 10; cloudy, 7.

AUGUST.—The monthly mean temperature for the state, as shown by records of 109 stations, was 69.1 degrees, which is 2.00 degrees below normal. By sections the mean temperatures were as follows: Northern section, 67.4 degrees; central section, 69.2 degrees; southern section, 70.6 degrees. The highest monthly mean was 72.8 degrees at Council Bluffs; lowest monthly mean, 65.2 degrees, at Dows. The highest temperature re-

ported was 98 degrees at Perry, on the 19th; lowest temperature reported, 37 degrees, at Sibley, on the 11th. The average monthly maximum
was 91.2 degrees; average monthly minimum, 45.0 degrees. Greatest daily
range, 46 degrees at Toledo; averages of greatest daily ranges, 29.9 degrees. Average precipitation for the state, as shown by the records of
123 stations, was 6.58 inches, which is 3.51 inches above normal. The
averages by sections were as follows: Northern section, 5.45 inches;
central section, 6.76 inches; southern section, 7.52 inches. The largest
amount reported was 15.47 inches at Columbus Junction; least
amount reported, 1.57 inches, at Dubuque. The greatest daily rainfall
reported was 6.96 inches at Allerton on the 25th and 26th. Average number of days on which .01 of an inch or more was reported, 11. Prevailing direction of the wind, southeast; highest velocity reported, 44 miles
per hour, from the northwest, at Des Moines, on the 19th. Average
number of clear days, 11; partly cloudy, 11; cloudy, 9.

SEPTEMBER.—The monthly mean temperature for the state as shown
by records of 103 stations, was 59.1 degrees, which is 5.2 degrees below
normal. By sections the mean temperature was as follows: Northern
section, 57.9 degrees; central section, 59.3 degrees; southern section, 60.2
degrees. The highest monthly mean was 62.6 degrees at Burlington; lowest monthly mean, 55 degrees at New Hampton. The highest temperature
reported was 88 degrees, at Denison, Sibley, Sigourney and Council Bluffs
on the 2d and 7th; lowest temperature reported, 23 degrees at Galva on
the 11th. The average monthly maximum was 82.5 degrees; average
monthly minimum, 31.7 degrees. Greatest daily range, 50 degrees at
Galva; average of greatest daily ranges, 37.0 degrees. Average precipitation for the state, as shown by the records of 118 stations, was 4.35
inches, which is 1.36 inches above normal. The averages by sections
were as follows: Northern section, 3.63 inches; central section, 4.49
inches; southern section, 4.93 inches. The largest amount reported was
10.41 inches at Ottumwa; least amount reported, 1.65 at Clear Lake. The
greatest daily rainfall reported was 4.31 inches at Chariton on the 30th.
Average number of days on which .01 of an inch or more was reported,
9. Prevailing direction of wind, northwest; highest velocity reported,
41 miles per hour, from the northwest, at Sioux City on the 8th. Average
number of clear days, 15; partly cloudy, 6; cloudy, 9.

OCTOBER.—The monthly mean temperature for the state, as shown
by records of 112 stations, was 53.5 degrees, which is about 3.00 degrees
above normal. By sections the mean temperatures were as follows: Northern section, 51.4 degrees; central section, 53.5 degrees; southern section 55.7 degrees. The highest monthly mean was 58.4 degrees at Winterset; lowest monthly mean, 47.3 at Plover. The highest temperature
reported was 83 degrees at Ida Grove and Council Bluffs on the 10th and
22d; lowest temperature reported, 20 degrees at Plover on the 14th. The
average monthly maximum was 77.6 degrees; average monthly minimum,
27.28. Greatest daily range, 46 degrees at Sibley; average of greatest
daily ranges, 35.7 degrees. Average precipitation for the state, as shown
by records of 130 stations was 2.54 inches, which is .26 of an inch above
normal. The averages by sections were as follows: Northern section,

1.24 inches; central section, 2.60 inches; southern section, 3.78 inches. The largest amount reported was 6.66 inches at Newton; least amount reported, 0.28 of an inch at Sioux Center. The greatest daily rainfall reported was 3.71 inches at Newton on the 17th. Average number of days on which .01 of an inch or more was reported, 5. Prevailing direction of the wind, northwest; highest velocity reported, 42 miles an hour, from the southwest, at Des Moines on the 25th. Average number of clear days, 16; partly cloudy, 8; cloudy, 7.

NOVEMBER.—The monthly mean temperature for the state, as shown by records of 108 stations, was 41.2 degrees, which is 8.4 degrees above normal. By sections the mean temperatures were as follows: Northern section, 38.1 degrees; central section, 41.8 degrees; southern section, 43.7 degrees. The highest monthly mean was 48.2 degrees at Keokuk; lowest monthly mean, 35.4, at Sibley. The highest temperature reported was 79 degrees, at Carroll on the 1st; lowest temperature reported, 4 degrees, at Chester, on the 30th. The average monthly maximum was 69.5 degrees; average monthly minimum, 16.0 degrees. Greatest daily range, 46 degrees, at Denison; average of greatest daily ranges, 31.4 degrees. Average precipitation for the state, as shown by the records of 127 stations, was 2,13 inches, which is .71 of an inch above normal. The averages by sections were as follows: Northern section, 2.08 inches; central section, 1.04 inches; southern section, 2.37 inches. The largest amount reported was 4.19 inches, at Stockport; least amount reported, .16 of an inch at Sioux City. The greatest daily rainfall reported was 2.20 inches, at Charles City, on the 14th. Average number of days on which .01 of an inch or more was reported, 7. Prevailing direction of the wind, northwest; hignest velocity reported, 42 miles per hour, from the south, at Sioux City, on the 7th. Average number of clear days, 9; partly cloudy, 7; cloudy, 14.

DECEMBER.—The monthly mean temperature for the state, as shown by records of 109 stations, was 20.1 degrees, which is 3.5 degrees below normal. By sections the mean temperatures were as follows: Northern section, 17.4 degrees; central section, 20.4 degrees; southern section, 22.4 degrees. The highest monthly mean was 27.0 degrees, at Keokuk; lowest monthly mean, 14.6 degrees at Alta and Estherville. The highest temperature reported was 59 degrees, at Albia, on the 1st; lowest temperature reported 20 degrees at Estherville on the 26th. The average monthly maximum was 47.2 degrees; average monthly minimum, 10.9 degrees. Greatest daily range, 41 degrees at Charles City and Sheldon; average of greatest daily ranges, 30.8 degrees. Average precipitation for the state, as shown by records of 123 stations, was 2.23 inches, which is 0.85 degrees above normal. The averages by sections were as follows: Northern section, 2.32 inches; central section, 2.13 inches; southern section, 2.24 inches. The largest amount reported was 5.51 inches at Ridgeway; least amount reported, .67 of an inch at Ottumwa. The greatest daily rainfall reported was 2.15 inches at Le Mars, on the 20th. Average number of days on which .01 of an inch or more was reported, 8. Prevailing direction of the wind, northwest; highest velocity reported, 50 miles per hour, from the northwest, at Sioux City on the 24th. Average number of clear days, 9; partly cloudy, 6; cloudy, 16.

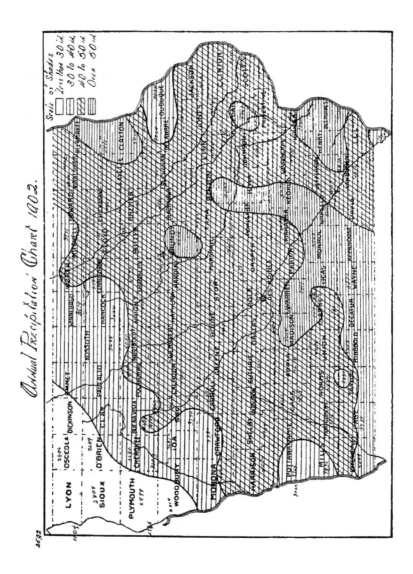

REVIEW OF THE CROP SEASON 1902.

January, 1902, was warmer than usual, the daily mean temperature being about five degrees above normal, and the average precipitation for the state was below normal. February temperature averaged about four degrees below normal and the precipitation was less than the normal amount, the larger part coming about the close of the month. The winter as a whole was about as moderate and favorable as the average in this section.

March was warmer than usual, the mean temperature ranging from four to seven degrees above the normal. Wintry weather of considerable severity prevailed from the first to the fourth and from the fifteenth to the nineteenth, but the balance of the month was mostly springlike and unusually favorable for early farm operations. The soil was in excellent condition for plowing, and seeding of spring wheat and oats was well advanced before the close of the month. The season opened from ten days to two weeks earlier than the average in this section. The cold wave and high wind, prevalent from the sixteenth to the eighteenth, caused some damage to winter wheat in the southern and central counties, and delayed spring seeding in all parts of the state. The average precipitation was below normal, but there was ample moisture to facilitate plowing and for germination of grain.

April was slightly cooler and drier than usual, the abnormal conditions prevailing for the most part through the first and second decades. The last decade was seasonably warm, and copious showers relieved apprehensions of a serious drouth. The worst features of the month were the frequent dust storms and strong gales, which caused considerable damage to windmills, trees and light structures, and wrought some injury to newly seeded grain crops in exposed localities, by uncovering the grain or blowing the loose soil into drifts. The conditions, however, were generally favorable for field work, and more than usual progress was made in seeding and preparing the ground for planting corn. In southern localities the planters were started about the twenty-eighth to thirtith of April. The germination of small grain was retarded by the cold and dry weather in the first half of the month, but there was considerable moisture below the dry surface to quicken the growth when the soil became warmer during the last decade. At the close of the month the grain crops were making a fair stand and the outlook was generally promising. The foliage and bloom on fruit trees appeared very near the normal period. There was a fair prospect for apples, plums and cherries, but peach buds were not in evidence, and the smaller fruits did not give promise of full average crops. Pastures and meadows were late in starting, but the growth was fairly good at close of April.

In marked contrast with the preceding month, May was warm and showery. The daily excess in temperature was about four degrees. The average rainfall for the state was 5.39 inches, which is 1.42 inches above normal. There was great inequality in the distribution of rainfall, ranging from .87 of an inch at Washta, Cherokee county, to 18.04 inches at Grand Meadow, Clayton county. The area of the marked deficiency was limited to a small portion of the northwest district. The northern section received the heaviest rainfall, and the eastern half of that section the bulk of that amount. But the soil was very dry, and in excellent condition to absorb and retain a goodly portion of the copious moisture; and despite the interruption of frequent rainy days the work of planting corn progressed rapidly between showers, so that before the close of the month the corn area was practically planted. The seed was generally good, and a fair stand of corn was secured, with not more than the usual amount of replanting. Cultivation was begun early, and in portions of the state where the rainfall was about normal, or less than normal, the crop was most thoroughly cleaned and made most satisfactory progress. Generally corn was rated in high condition on June 1st. The copious rains, though not so favorable for corn planting and cultivating, were highly favorable to grass in pastures and meadows, and caused a heavy growth of all small grain crops. Except in portions of the northwest district spring wheat, oats and barley showed a tendency to rankness, causing apprehension of damage by lodging and rust. The potato crop was generally very promising at close of the month, and garden truck was seldom in better condition at the corresponding date.

June was an abnormal month in respect to temperature, amount of rainfall and excess of cloudiness. The daily average temperature for the state was about five degrees below normal, and the daily average of the last decade was about eleven degrees colder than the first decade of the month—a reversal of usual conditions. At the central station the records show only 49 per cent of sunshine for the month, and about 75 per cent of mean relative humidity. On the mornings of the 21st and 22d frost was observed at numerous stations, with some damaging results in the northwest district. The average rainfall was 7.16 inches, which is 2.90 inches above normal. The heaviest amounts were recorded in the central district, and the lowest in several counties of the northwest district. One striking feature was the fact that showers fell in some portion of the state every day in the month. The average number of clear days for all stations of record was only eight, as against an average of twenty-two cloudy or partly cloudy days. As a result of these abnormal weather conditions farming operations were greatly retarded, and in the wettest portions field work was wholly impracticable except at short intervals between showers. On the river bottoms in the central counties many thousand acres of corn, small grain and meadows were flooded and the crops practically ruined. But despite all the drawbacks fully three-fourths of the corn acreage had been fairly well cultivated, and the average condition of early planted fields was promising at close of the month. The oats crop grew unusually rank on rich lands in all sections where the rainfall was at or above normal, and there was a tendency to rust. At close of the month oats and spring wheat were filling well, and were standing up remarkably well, though bulky in straw. Winter wheat, rye and clover harvest was begun, but the wet weather was unfavorable for securing hay and grain. Potatoes, pastures and garden vegetables made great advancement. The wet weather was very favorable for new seeding of grasses.

In respect to temperature, July was about normal, the average for the state being seventy-three degrees; but the month broke all records as to amount and distribution of rainfall, frequency of showers, severe wind squalls and extent of overflow of the principal rivers of the state. The average precipitation was 8.67 inches, or about 5 inches above normal, and the reports of all stations of record showed an excess. As in the preceding month of June, the records showed a measurable amount of rainfall every day during the month, at one or more stations. These adverse conditions greatly retarded the cultivation of late corn, and harvesting the matured crops of hay and small grain. The saturated grain fields were rendered too soft for operation of harvesting machinery. The heavy storms of rain and wind caused lodgment of oats, wheat, barley and grass to a much greater extent than was ever known in previous years, and this added greatly to the labor and difficulty in securing the heavy burdens of grain and hay. There was, therefore, a much larger percentage of loss of acreage and damage to quality of these crops than was ever known in this state in recent years. But despite these unusual drawbacks, by strenuous labor between showers, the farmers secured a considerable amount of hay in fair condition, and the small grain crops were put in shock or stack. Corn in upland fields that had been well tilled was in fair condition, being bulky and heavily eared. Potatoes exceeded all recent records. All kinds of garden truck made heavy growth. Apples suffered materially from windstorms.

The abnormal features prevalent in June and July continued throughout the larger part of August, the cool, cloudy and showery weather making altogether the wettest and most unfavorable season for cultivating crops and harvesting hay and grain that has been experienced in Iowa during the past thirty-three years. The daily mean temperature for August was two degrees below normal, and the average rainfall, 5.58 inches, —— 3.51 inches above the normal amount. Cool nights, cloudy days, frequent showers, excessive humidity of the air and saturated soil, retarded the ripening of corn and rendered it well nigh impossible to carry on the usual harvest operations. At the close of the month corn was about two weeks later than usual, with rank growth of stalks and very heavily eared. The late planted portion of the crop was green as in June, and its immature condition indicated the need of a full month of warm and dry weather to bring it to the stage to withstand killing frosts. The oats crop suffered greatest damage in shock and stack, and a very large percentage has been ruined. Spring wheat was injured, but the total loss was not so great. Barley was discolored and much of it rendered unmarketable. The hay crop was badly damaged, but there was partial compensation in the growth of very heavy aftermath. Potatoes suffered materially by rot and blight of tops.

The month of September was also cold, cloudy and wet. The daily average temperature being five degrees below normal and the rainfall,

12

4.35 inches, was 1.36 inches above the average for that month. The generally saturated condition of the soil retarded field work, and corn and other unripened crops made slow progress toward maturity. The period of low temperature from the eleventh to the thirteenth, with frost and ice in all districts, caused great injury to belated corn, especially on low ground and in the northern half of the state, where the crop was least advanced. All reports indicated very heavy damage from the untimely frosts and continued prevalence of unseasonable weather.

October was nearly normal in amount of rainfall, though portions of the central and southern sections received a considerable excess. The temperature was about three degrees above normal and there was a fair amount of sunshine. In large areas the soil was too wet for plowing, and many corn fields were not dry enough for harvesting the crop. November was warmer than usual, with excess of moisture, humidity and cloudiness. The conditions were measurably unfavorable and at the close of the month fully 25 per cent of the corn crop was still afield and much of it was lying on the ground and covered with snow. The wintry conditions prevalent throughout December afforded but little opportunity to secure the unharvested portion of the crop.

The season was generally very productive in respect to the bulk of all soil products, but the quality has been much impaired, and a large percentage of small grain and corn was practically destroyed. The final reports show a full average yield of corn in bushels per acre, but fully 55 per cent of it was below the merchantable grade, and its value in the markets was correspondingly low. Pasturage has been unusually heavy, though in quality it was below the normal standard. The potato crop, as a whole, was much better than in recent years, though there was some loss from rotting. Apples yielded more abundantly than was anticipated in midsummer.

CROP REPORT JUNE 1ST.

Reports of county and township correspondents show the following results as to the number of acres and average conditions on June 1st of staple farm crops at the outset of the crop season of 1902:

Corn.—The total number of acres planted appears to be 9,208,980—an increase of 521,500 acres, or about 6 per cent, as compared with the acreage of 1901. The average condition of corn in respect to stand and vigor of plant on June 1st was rated at 97 per cent, as against 90 per cent on the corresponding date last year. Due consideration should be given to the fact that since June 1st both the acreage and condition of corn have been materially lowered by the excessive rains in extensive areas of the state, causing damaging erosion of slopes and flooding of bottom lands.

Wheat.—The acreage of winter wheat is shown to be only 48,449 acres, which is very nearly the amount returned by township assessors last year. The number of acres of spring wheat is placed at 1,152,985 acres, which is 14,695 acres above the area seeded in 1901. The condition of winter wheat is rated 96 per cent, and spring wheat 99 per cent.

Oats.—Acreage, 3,770,620 acres—a decrease of 28,600 acres, compared with last year. The average condition of the crop is placed at 98 per cent, as against 89 per cent at same date last year.

Barley.—Number of acres, 594,670; decrease, 9,490, compared with last year. Condition, 100 per cent, as against 93 in 1901.

Rye.—Number of acres, 53,150—a slight decrease; condition, 99 per cent.

Flax.—Number of acres seeded, 94,760; decrease, as compared with last year, 9,380 acres. Condition of crops, 98 per cent, as against 89 per cent at corresponding date in 1901.

Potatoes.—Acres planted, 138,484—an increase of 2,184 acres. Condition, 103 per cent, as against 95 per cent June 1, 1901.

Meadows.—Number of acres, 2,515,000; decrease since last year, 176,-550 acres. Condition June 1st, 96 per cent, as against 90 per cent last year.

Pastures.—Number of acres, 7,820,140 acres, a decrease of 287,300 acres, compared with last year.

Condition of Live Stock.—Cattle, 96 per cent; sheep, 97; hogs, 96; spring pig crop, 92; horses, 97; foals, 98.

Secretary Greene, of the State Horticultural Society, issued for June 1st the following summary as to condition of fruit: Apples, 65 per cent; American plums, 51; cherries, 40; currants, 70; grapes, 70; red raspberries, 42; black raspberries, 57; blackberries, 47; strawberries, 63 per cent.

TABLE No. 1—IOWA CROPS 1902—NUMBER OF ACRES BY COUNTIES.

COUNTIES	Winter wheat—acres	Spring wheat—acres	Corn—acres	Oats—acres	Rye—acres	Barley—acres	Meadows—acres	Pastures—acres	Flax—acres	Potatoes—acres
Adair	173	12,466	103,070	30,109	30	625	31,920	95,040		1,740
Adams	700	5,580	71,680	17,875	60	650	25,590	73,740		826
Allamakee	1,190	5,220	39,800	38,850	1,390	5,860	34,290	94,260		1,390
Appanoose	320		56,60	6,930	820		37,720	108,390	550	560
Audubon		22,800	52,680	33,430	80	2,850	21,640	62,620		930
Benton	50	2,800	124,860	66,60	80	15,870	32,540	93,680		1,490
Black Hawk	15	860	95,900	55,300	970	8,650	26,9 0	79,950		1,710
Boone	60	7,390	117,60	46,130	430	800	19,690	74,720	30	1,140
Bremer	50	890	62,950	51,850	310	60	19,920	87,290		1,500
Buchanan	13	60	88,710	48,370	110	2,790	30,960	87,870		1,490
Buena Vista		10,570	115,890	56,110	150	7,120	16,920	75,290	1,490	2,000
Butler		2,90	110,340	72,610	1,010	3,920	18,780	70,170	270	1,480
Calhoun		12,320	118,880	57,500	210	4,690	11,860	87,690		1,255
Carroll	215	23,120	123,180	54,750	155	3,270	19,430	66,880	810	2,050
Cass	320	20,850	113,550	35,250	145	1,000	25,870	73,120	90	2,500
Cedar		970	117,760	40,110	580	10,470	36,260	27,610		1,280
Cerro Gordo		3,810	90,120	74,950	530	6,060	21,750	84,270		1,450
Cherokee		28,810	119,970	47,780		7,060	20,480	67,380	3,450	1,572
Chickasaw	210	2,070	54,820	59,110	130	190	21,790	77,280	320	1,120
Clarke	350	90	57,400	15,60	125	190	36,650	80,510	6,510	470
Clay	750	8,100	99,700	40,580	770	25,080	17,040	67,040		1,170
Clayton	160	6,060	88,500	64,320	1,950	6,430	37,280	135,110		2,160
Clinton		2,730	123,440	42,420	1,350	4,010	39,400	103,510	4,950	1,410
Crawford		43,170	122,940	38,830	90	3,340	30,110	106,190	310	1,770
Dallas	230	6,490	103,770	38,330	240	800	23,860	85,940		1,150
Davis	630		55,480	18,940	1,460		45,650	114,090		670
Decatur	930		63,310	17,820	300	40	37,320	103,040		640
Delaware	25	1,410	100,320	44,380	410	5,470	37,830	96,910		1,320
Des Moines	2,660	250	68,460	26,00	200	120	19,010	61,580	50	1,520
Dickinson		16,930	42,640	23,380	2,310	24,650	6,970	35,070	5,150	565
Dubuque		3,180	67,440	47,60	920	2,60	34,170	91,260		2,290
Emmet		15,760	54,570	25,650	150	17,560	9,200	37,230	2,576	2,450
Fayette	165	2,620	99,410	65,880	350	6,860	50,170	14,510	2,306	2,160
Floyd	19	1,950	87,470	65,610	550	8,110	21,050	62,200	4,110	1,760

Franklin	1,150	1,230	63,520	18,930	4,090	420	75,930	99,180	6,200	3,300
Fremont	1,000		52,460	21,730	810	640	14,400	121,510	4,870	120
Greene	1,120	192	65,860	18,730	2,880	100	48,880	106,310	8,993	73
Gay	1,900	140	66,620	21,880	13,310	80	52,300	103,920	8,630	107
Guthrie	1,066		72,810	23,640	1,495	105	33,240	84,540	11,840	30
Hamilton	1,170	230	73,460	17,020	1,170	90	54,280	103,170	8,980	
Hancock	920	4,180	51,430	16,520	5,800	410	26,720	84,500	12,480	
Hardin	1,200	250	79,870	19,410	2,030	85	54,430	98,470	13,890	40
Harrison	1,770		88,960	7,820	510	190	13,840	123,240	100	1,480
Henry	710		84,540	24,180	400	1,940	25,640	70,820	41,550	24
	1,100	7,192	55,300	38,910	5,190	60	58,510	52,650	1,800	
Humboldt	790	1,660	43,810	12,590	2,270	40	33,390	63,120	17,90	
Ida	1,020		52,890	21,110	4,010	30	30,130	88,940	23,380	250
Iowa	1,316		92,810	39,370	6,280	225	38,610	99,030	2,90	166
Jackson	1,390		132,590	40,010	3,240	1,730	39,920	81,010	3,120	50
Jasper	2,730		91,290	25,950	660	210	40,950	102,600	11,420	1,089
Jefferson	750		99,890	23,360	1,140	2,090	21,710	78,860	260	520
Johnson	1,580		103,570	38,950	3,330	1,680	38,940	116,320	1,050	
Jones	1,070		106,790	38,480	4,090	560	32,210	84,520	1,150	66
Keokuk	1,160	4,80	96,180	34,280	2,990	2,030	35,780	108,850	840	
Kossuth	1,410		90,560	17,400	17,460	470	82,820	129,800	28,690	9,970
Lee	1,660		92,360	34,500		2,610	23,390	59,020		50
Linn	7,940		110,950	45,270	1,850	320	47,850	106,540	1,550	2,020
Louisa	890	910	63,710	14,360	360	2,510	24,260	74,940	510	350
Lucas	510		84,580	38,380	220	800	13,300	59,720	210	
Lyon	1,330		38,630	5,690	47,320		27,320	77,280	61,670	230
Madison	1,265	90	104,910	37,130	1,350	280	23,500	90,100	6,250	520
Mahaska	1,420		93,310	26,230	839	50	32,959	103,180	2,460	425
Marion	1,190		102,497	1,010	930	720	29,832	105,350	4,810	
Marshall	1,640	7,510	77,630	28,300	2,166	70	45,740	115,540	15,400	450
Mills	1,166	210	67,590	16,670	240	320	11,885	104,400	12,870	
Mitchell	1,670		56,550	30,600	11,940	360	43,180	64,920	2,980	302
Monona	1,310		90,880	3,860	320	250	13,560	119,380	34,310	690
Monroe	540		99,870	30,880	230	950	10,130	46,610	110	390
Montgomery	1,000		64,730	20,300	6,390	160	12,380	95,90	15,90	
Muscatine	2,870	1,910	68,420	21,810	29,350	1,460	21,050	72,280	2,160	
O'Brien	810	2,360	64,280	15,170	39,770	90	41,160	107,630	26,090	
Osceola	1,070		27,920	10,270	1,310		28,540	56,540	25,310	6,929
Page	1,210		85,010	15,360	10,286	550	21,970	131,650	7,450	
Palo Alto	3,310	2,890	60,340	7,580	8,90	470	47,790	79,650	8,210	
Plymouth	1,300	650	82,810	13,510	7,760	240	42,80	137,220	98,410	150
Pocahontas	2,390	2,480	71,180	10,300		430	51,890	106,020	7,750	485
Polk	3,150		73,240	22,440	540	130	32,580	112,900	11,60	310
Pottawattamie	1,400		122,560	30,950	3,720	450	28,690	215,730	46,825	100
Poweshiek	760		111,910	37,500		115	44,270	114,060	2,970	445
Ringgold	1,270	1,910	107,530	51,290	8,400	286	22,670	126,090	54	
Sac	4,870		72,400	24,190	26,200	85	88,740	81,730	13,010	
Scott	1,610	200	62,220	23,060	2,610	720	41,580	119,950	8,200	50
Shelby	1,470		72,010	29,220	29,220	70	23,160	125,720	36,250	
Sioux		685	55,150	10,870	33,210		41,500		83,300	

TABLE No. 1—IOWA CROPS 1902—CONTINUED.

COUNTIES.	Winter wheat—acres.	Spring wheat—acres.	Corn—acres.	Oats—acres.	Rye—acres.	Barley—acres.	Meadows—acres.	Pastures—acres.	Flax—acres.	Potatoes—acres.
Story		4,430	110,010	49,100	510	970	21,210	69,230		1,060
Tama		10,300	118,140	45,120	110	26,340	30,670	95,420		1,590
Taylor	2,595	410	85,080	18,123	580	1,130	33,830	86,820		1,180
Union	70	610	66,140	18,130	130	290	36,770	78,030		1,125
Van Buren	2,940		50,190	18,250	1,580		34,930	108,350		490
Wapello	730	170	60,850	18,020	1,170	350	30,890	89,780		1,440
Warren	90	6,940	96,590	21,870	350	1,110	34,340	93,440		1,230
Washington	780	325	98,400	38,970	1,160	3,630	34,722	93,260		840
Wayne	50		73,690	16,630	520		59,100	105,840		525
Webster		12,490	111,290	66,110	190	2,090	12,240	81,820	520	1,330
Winnebago	150	20,750	48,870	33,920	60	4,070	11,410	42,240	3,223	780
Winneshiek		7,620	72,770	68,460	200	11,790	30,600	83,010	8,430	1,340
Woodbury		58,780	143,930	25,250	140	2,500	11,630	72,110	540	1,480
Worth		5,590	38,880	46,280	190	8,830	17,450	51,090	10,410	1,500
Wright		11,540	83,060	58,450	130	4,450	15,273	56,010	1,930	1,050
Totals for state	48,449	1,152,085	9,208,680	3,770,624	53,150	591,070	2,515,000	7,820,110	94,767	128,484

CROP REPORT JULY 1ST.

Following was the estimated condition of crops July 1, 1902:

Corn, 92 per cent, a decline of 5 points since June 1st; winter wheat, 96; spring wheat, 97; oats, 95; rye, 98; barley, 97; flax, 99; potatoes, 108; hay crop, 99; pastures, 107; apples, 65; plums, 50; grapes, 65.

At the corresponding date in 1901 the averages were as follows: Corn, 90 per cent; winter wheat, 98; spring wheat, 93; oats, 85; rye, 95; flax, 94; barley, 93; potatoes, 92; hay crop, 76; pastures, 80; apples, 51; plums, 70; grapes, 90.

The blanks issued for the July report called for a revised estimate of the acreage of corn, compared with the number of acres harvested last year; and reporters were requested to make due allowance for reduction of acreage as the result of excessive storms and floods since June 1st. The tabulated report showed a material reduction, the revised aggregate for the state being 8,693,900 acres, which amount is 504,780 acres less than the estimates of the previous month.

CROP REPORT AUGUST 1ST.

Reports of crop correspondents of the Iowa Weather and Crop Service showed the following average condition of the staple farm crops August 1st:

Corn, 93 per cent; spring wheat, 84; oats, 83; barley, 89; flax, 91; hay, 100; potatoes, 107; apples, 66; plums, 51.

In 1901 at the corresponding date the averages were as follows: Corn, 55 per cent; spring wheat, 84; oats, 75; barley, 83; flax, 74; hay, 70; potatoes, 34; apples, 35; plums, 40.

FINAL CROP REPORT DECEMBER 1, 1902.

Average Yield Per Acre, Totals for the State and Average Prices, December 1, 1902.

Following is a summary of crop reports received from the corresspondents of the Iowa weather and crop service, showing the average yield per acre and totals for the state of staple farm products for the past season, and the average prices at the farms or nearest stations December 1, 1902. As the larger portion of the season's output will be consumed on the farms, and marketed in the form of beef, pork, mutton, horses, dairy and poultry products, etc., the actual value of the crops is materially higher than is shown by the figures representing the local prices obtainable at this time.

The Corn Crop.—In bulk, expressed in bushels, the corn crop is reported to be a little above the ten-year average, the yield per acre being about thirty-four bushels, and the total for the state grown on an area of about 8,700,000 acres, is 296,950,230 bushels.

On account of the unfavorable character of the crop season, and the unusually variable condition of the corn crop a special report was called for in answer to inquiries as to the average yield of hard and soft corn, the percentage that is sound and merchantable, the local price of sound corn and the feeding value of the softer portion of the crop. The tabulated reports show the following results of this investigation: Dividing the state into three sections, or belts three counties wide crossing east to west, we find that in the northern section (thirty counties) the sound corn is estimated at 29 per cent; in the central section (thirty-eight counties) it is 48 per cent; and in the southern section (thirty-one counties) the average is 64 per cent. For the state as a whole the average condition appears to be 47 per cent sound and merchantable, and 53 per cent graded as soft, chaffy or unmerchantable. The total yield by sections is as follows: Northern section, in round numbers, 73,000,000 bushels; central section, 129,000,000 bushels; southern section, 94,000,000 bushels.

The average local price of the sound corn is reported to be 35 cents per bushel, and the average feeding value of the softer portion is estimated at 22 cents per bushel.

This serves as a basis for estimating the total value of the corn crop this year in round numbers at $83,000,000. Last year the yield was 227,-000,000 bushels and the value $113,000,000. In 1900 the total yield was 345,000,000 bushels, and the value, at the current prices, $93,000,000.

Wheat.—The acreage of winter wheat is small, and the total yield appears to be only 825,045 bushels, an average of eighteen bushels per acre. In spring wheat the yield is thirteen bushels per acre and a total of 12,680,800 bushels. The total yields of both winter and spring wheat is 13,-532,845 bushels. The quality of the wheat is generally poor, on acount of the very wet harvest, and the price of winter wheat is reported to be 55 cents, and spring wheat 52 cents. The total value of the crop appears to be $7,002,-640. Last year the yield was 18,295,000 bushels and the value was $10,-976,000.

Oats.—This crop suffered greater damage than any other cereal from effects of excessive rains, and it has been impracticable to secure reports as to the extent of total loss, and the quality of the grain that was secured in condition to repay the cost of threshing. The returns from correspondents indicate an average yield of thirty-four bushels per acre from the portion of the crop that was secured and threshed. Making a liberal deduction from the acreage planted in each county we have a total of 92,907,960 bushels, as against 114,000,000 bushels last year, and 138,000,-000 bushels in 1900. The average local value of this year's product appears to be 24 cents per bushel and the total $22,297,910. Last year's oats crop was valued at $40,209,000.

Barley.—Estimated yield per acre, twenty-five bushels, and total yield, 15,380,940, valued at 33 cents per bushel, or a total of $5,075,710. Last year's crop was 14,654,000 bushels, worth $6,447,000.

Rye.—Average per acre, seventeen bushels; yield, 882,830 bushels; worth 40 cents per bushel, and the total, $353,132. Last year's crop, 859,-630 bushels, valued at $411,762.

Flax.—Product, 725,350 bushels; yield per acre, eight bushels. Value about $1.00 per bushel. Last year's crop, 916,880, worth $1,182,000.

Potatoes.—Product, eighty-one bushels per acre; total yield, 12,051,-670 bushels. Price, 34 cents; total value, $4,097,567. Last year's product, 5,098,000 bushels, valued at $4,588,000. In 1900 the crop was 10,850,000 bushels, worth $4,340,000.

Hay (tame).—Product, 4,439,040 tons—an average of 1.8 per acre. Value, $6.80 per ton; total value, $30,171,592. Last year's output, 3,711,000 tons, valued at $30,721,000.

Hay (wild).—Average yield, 1.3 tons per acre; total yield, 1,202,860 tons, worth $5.50 per ton; total value, $6,615,730. Last year the product was 1,268,700 tons, worth $7,992,000.

The estimated value of sweet potatoes is about $320.000. Sorghum, $250,000; broom corn, $40,000. Timothy seed is estimated at $750,000; clover seed unknown and not ascertainable as to value.

Corn fodder in shock and fields probably worth half as much as last year, or about $10,000,000.

Pasturage; bulky, early and late, and worth at least $35,000,000.

Fruits and vegetables are estimated at $9,500,000, which is a conservative figure.

TABULATED CROP SUMMARY.

CROPS.	TOTAL PRODUCT, BUSHELS.	FARM VALUE DEC. 1, 1902.
Corn	296,910,230	$ 83,432,708
Wheat	13,512,845	7,012,640
Oats	92,907,900	22,297,930
Barley	15,181,940	5,075,710
Rye	882,830	353,132
Flax	755,150	755,350
Potatoes	12,051,670	4,097,567
Hay (tame)	*4,439,940	30,171,592
Hay (wild)	*1,202,860	6,615,730
Sweet Potatoes	....	320,C00
Sorghum	....	259,000
Broom Corn	....	40,000
Timothy Seed	....	750,000
Corn Fodder	....	10,000,000
Pasturage	....	. 36,000,000
Fruits and vegetables	....	9,500,000
Total soil products	....	$ 215,722,339

* Tons.

As to the corn crop, it is proper to add that a considerable percentage is still ungathered and subjected to the vicissitudes of the weather, which at this time is unfavorable for securing the full product. The figures as to all the crops are submitted as the best that can be secured at this time, under exceptional conditions.

The grand total for last year was $274,000,000, and in 1900 it was in round numbers $229,000,000.

FINAL CROP REPORT, 1902.

Average per acre and totals by counties.

COUNTIES	CORN Yield per acre	CORN Total yield, bushels	WINTER WHEAT Yield per acre	WINTER WHEAT Total yield, bushels	SPRING WHEAT Yield per acre	SPRING WHEAT Total yield, bushels	OATS Yield per acre	OATS Total yield, bushels	RYE Yield per acre	RYE Total yield, bu.	BARLEY Yield per acre	BARLEY Total yield, bushels	FLAX SEED Yield per acre	FLAX SEED Total yield, bu.	POTATOES Yield per acre	POTATOES Total yield, bushels	TAME HAY Yield per acre	TAME HAY Total yield, tons	WILD HAY Yield per acre	WILD HAY Total yield, tons
Adair	30	3,058,560	25	4,320	10	94,650	30	601,820			30	15,600			120	208,800	1.5	47,880	1.0	1,650
Adams	38	2,769,600	19	13,300	11	61,380	35	534,450	18	2,880	25	16,250			150	123,900	1.5	38,380	1.0	1,720
Allamakee	27	1,074,600	12	14,280	9	46,980	25	870,000	18	19,240	25	146,500			70	97,500	1.5	48,430	1.5	2,410
Appanoose	35	1,902,100	15	4,900			30	159,300	10	8,210					100	56,000	1.5	56,530	1.0	1,680
Audubon	33	2,752,860			13	283,530	30	669,360	20	1,200	30	85,500			90	93,000	1.5	32,460	1.2	7,250
Benton	35	4,075,050			12	33,600	30	1,205,300			25	306,510			90	134,100	1.5	48,810	1.5	1,680
Black Hawk	35	2,416,680	15	225	15	10,200	33	945,400	15	14,550	25	163,000			105	179,550	2.0	53,825	1.5	14,120
Boone	28	2,997,620	13	2,089	15	74,850	30	1,026,250	15	5,590	23	11,730			85	96,900	2.0	29,530	1.5	16,140
Bremer	25	1,523,750			13	8,450	30	95,520	18	5,280	20	30,400			83	124,500	2.0	39,840	1.5	16,530
Buchanan	28	2,451,300	16	190	15	25,650	33	1,067,840	20	2,200	30	11,490	8	10,320	80	119,200	1.5	61,920	1.5	15,270
Buena Vista	30	3,356,700			8	84,560	33	1,422,630	15	2,250	25	213,600	8	2,160	70	127,400	2.0	25,380	1.0	20,130
Butler	30	2,180,680			8	98,560	27	1,742,700	15	13,650	25	90,500			91	140,600	2.0	37,560	1.5	18,210
Calhoun	35	3,948,700			8	253,640	31	1,039,500	18	3,780	20	76,200			90	112,500	2.0	23,720	1.5	29,330
Carroll	33	3,965,940			12	231,720	31	1,185,440	20	2,860	23	65,400			92	188,600	1.8	34,950	2.0	21,700
Cass	35	3,504,610	18	3,870	12	13,580	27	843,300	18	2,790	26	21,160			85	196,200	2.0	38,850	1.0	10,390
Cedar	40	4,508,800	14	4,480	14	38,100	30	866,970	15	8,700	21	246,220			52	66,560	2.0	72,520	1.0	950
Cerro Gordo	33	2,874,900			10	259,290	31	1,436,540				109,830	7	24,150	70	101,500	1.8	43,500	1.5	19,320
Cherokee	35	4,198,950			9	28,980	32	1,146,900	18	6,360	30	138,000	7	2,170	110	172,600	1.8	36,860	1.5	18,210
Chickasaw	35	1,536,300			14	1,802	32	1,507,520	20	1,340	25	183,600	7	45,570	60	67,260	1.8	39,220	2.0	19,520
Clarke	35	1,932,350	22	4,625	20	81,000	28	391,320	18	2,750	23	4,370			115	54,450	1.5	54,910	1.5	620
Clay	26	2,525,900	18	6,300	10	54,600	22	1,042,550	18	13,860	30	692,400	5	9,750	60	70,200	1.5	25,560	2.0	31,200
Clayton	32	2,554,500	15	11,250	10	27,300	31	1,353,280	16	34,560	30	192,900			80	172,800	1.5	55,920	1.5	4,120
Clinton	33	3,868,530			10	474,870	35	772,090	14	21,600	20	80,260			75	107,750	1.5	59,100	1.0	6,560
Crawford	30	3,459,300	20			97,350	32	837,460	20	1,260	25	76,130			70	123,990	1.5	45,220	1.5	12,210
Dallas	39	3,303,850	20	4,600	15		31	871,720	16	4,800		101,250			70	80,500	2.0	47,720	1.0	10,210
Davis	40	2,125,200	18	12,600			36	509,120	16	23,300					110	73,700	1.4	61,870		
Decatur	36	2,668,850	20	16,740	17		35	533,050	20	4,640					130	83,200	2.0	52,240	1.5	1,00
Delaware	36	2,763,600	20	500			31	685,720	16	7,380	30	164,100			100	158,400	2.0	75,660	2.0	12,150
Des Moines	28	2,223,940	20	53,200		20,570	32	661,680	20	46,300					100	152,000	2.0	28,510	1.0	1,020
Dickinson	40	1,179,920			16	152,370	36	1,091,840		3,200	28	690,200	8	41,200	60	33,600	1.8	12,540	1.5	24,110
Dubuque	40	2,488,400	17	7,040	16	50,880	35	1,337,350	19	17,480	32	65,920			102	231,290	1.8	61,500	1.2	4,280
Emmet	30	1,540,230			11	145,860	33	747,450	12	1,680	32	455,040	8	20,560	120	73,200	2.0	18,420	1.5	42,250

Fayette	2,862,300	20		32	52,400	31	1,491,720	15	52,400	30	5,250	205,800	70	7	16,175	151,220	2.0	46,340	1.5	15,230
Floyd	3,076,920		3,300	35	21,840	35	1,837,150	20	10,200	25	202,750	90	10	41,100	158,400	1.8	37,890	1.5	12,250
Franklin	3,138,960	16		33	99,200	35	1,882,630	15	6,300	22	89,980	48	8	9,840	55,200	2.0	37,800	1.0	13,910
Fremont	4,415,980	17	64,600	38	81,770	27	504,000	22	14,080			150			136,500	2.0	43,460	2.0	10,285
Greene	3,166,010	12	1,200	31	61,080		921,240	20		25	72,000	70			28,400	2.0	37,420	1.5	15,122
Grundy	3,138,560	10		33	85,110	30	1,247,759	20	60	22	294,060	110			188,100	2.0	43,700	1.0	16,210
Guthrie	2,803,420	20	2,140	33	11,100	30	802,200		2,100	25	37,350	105		1,840	111,300	1.5	35,430	1.5	11,120
Hamilton	2,793,600			35	65,340	28	1,124,480	21		25	25,744	90	8		57,980	1.8	34,040	1.3	24,110
Hancock	2,425,750	9		30	102,100	32	1,263,040	20	8,610	25	145,000	63	5	20,910	57,900	1.7	29,730	1.5	23,230
Hardin	2,886,720	11	800	31	130,790	31	1,220,330	21	1,640	24	48,720	92	8	1,840	32,990	2.0	32,990	1.1	20,110
Harrison	3,591,680	18	33,600	32	578,250	25	442,886	16	3,040	25	14,250	140			247,860	2.0	15,640	2.0	23,210
Henry	2,432,800	15		26	2,880	23	641,000	14	27,165	28	8,000	106			75,260	2.0	48,365	1.0	293
Howard	1,539,150	14		31	28,350	30	1,203,600	18	1,080	23	145,380	55	12	86,280	59,950	2.0	58,350	1.0	14,110
Humboldt	1,959,960	12	450	33	205,080	32	772,480	18	720	25	52,210	50	7	11,620	39,500	1.8	22,660	1.2	22,800
Ida	2,853,600	15	2,250	36	254,520	33	795,960	20		35	140,350	68			91,680	1.8	31,620	1.0	5,080
Iowa	2,828,350	15	2,720	36	31,350	20	774,840	20	4,500	25	157,000	60			89,080	1.8	78,710	1.2	2,140
Jackson	3,051,600	17	850	37	46,800	27	843,360	18	31,140	25	97,080	60			83,400	1.8	72,010	1.0	2,910
Jasper	3,283,320	17	18,510	40	2,860	30	889,650	15	4,140	28	18,480	53			141,690	1.8	46,700	1.0	1,820
Jefferson	4,332,860	19	9,880	40	17,850	19	548,300	19	31,350	31	35,340	120			90,240	1.8	42,040	1.0	1,610
Johnson		19			13,800	30	928,200	18	31,920	27	92,930	115			181,700	1.8	70,110	1.0	1,560
Jones	4,235,700	19	12,540	40	258,210	33	927,930	18	10,080	32	130,88	102			115,360	2.0	76,960	1.2	3,220
Keokuk	3,235,880	12		40		24	978,60	20	40,600	25	64,480	70	7	29,260	98,700	1.5	61,700	1.0	560
Kossuth	2,615,400	9	159,520	28		42	1,246,820	21	9,870	24	350,980	130			215,860	1.8	26,100	1.0	49,620
Lee	2,927,120	15		31	23,250	31	643,840	18	44,370	42		111			217,280	1.5	62,00	1.5	240
Linn	2,442,530	15	34,340	35	7,640	33	439,320	17	5,730	24	44,400	92			90,101	1.7	81,480	1.5	7,510
Louisa	1,928,480	17	7,040	34	2,520	35	927,850	19	12,070	20	7, 20	91			40,920	2.0	24,410	2.0	2,260
Lucas	2,328,410	15		31	826,950	35	636,810	15				93	11	10,010	129,360	1.5	57,940	2.0	1,120
Lyon	2,556,200	13	4,600	34	68,250	26	705,000	16	4,200	25	1,283,520	90			113,500	1.6	66,830	2.0	14,230
Madison	3,140,940	14	9,360	36	34,410	33	620,500	20	800	22	28,750	95			134,900	1.8	41, 90	1.2	2,810
Mahaska	3,557,522	22	9,250	35	52,910	32	1,127,680	19	10,080	30	18,260	78			92,820	2.0	42,020	1.2	1,620
Marion	3,586,839			33	169,540	30	356,460	16	1,400	25	27,900	58	8	60,080	95,120	1.5	42,450	1.2	1,230
Marshall	3,928,400	16	7,200	32	154,410	35	1,221,760	18	6,080	22	653,750	110			127,600	2.0	33,340	1.2	3,700
Mills	1,959,040			35	35,760	32	474,600	17	5,760	25	273,250	60			160,210	1.5	39,780	1.3	7,120
Mitchell	3,752,920	14	5,470	34	452,340	35	354,550	14	4,25	33	135,630	60			160,800	1.8	7,720	1.5	3,022
Monona	1,836,400	18	15,180	40	1,760	35	311,400	18	17,110	25		125	8	60,080	55,450	1.5	61,760	1.2	29,110
Monroe	3,672,410	22	7,800	38	159,100	30	701,750	15	2,400	33		125			99,500	1.8	36,540	1.2	500
Montgomery	3,016,020	20		42	38,810	30	311,400	20	17,840	70	191,700	100			200,920	2.0	43,622	1.5	2,010
Muscatine	3,485,790	12		33	289,080	38	1,507,680	20	1,800	28	788,220	60	12	22,920	74,400	1.5	22,750	2.0	26,240
O'Brien	1,653,630	9	103,930	30	216,000	29	769,660	15		23	817,740	50	8	18,810	49,500	1.5	13,350	1.5	17,120
Osceola	1,892,160	11		32	81,950	25	537,500	16	8,800	22	30,139	120	8	17,120	128,400	1.8	27,640	1.2	5,120
Page	2,626,160	12		34	82,100	33	1,346,070	15	7,050	30	359,800	72	10	6,500	72,620	1.5	11,310	1.5	34,160
Palo Alto	5,155,680		17,980	39	1,144,920	35	1,396,850	15	4,800	30	291,600	45	4	9,920	238,322	1.5	27,020	1.2	45,370
Pocahontas	2,973,600	8	10,670	30	57,410	31	1,327,920	15	6,450	31	240,505				58,500	1.8	20,600	1.0	41,240
Polk	4,586,820	12		40	132,730	33	795,960	20	2,600	26		120			167,300	2.0	40,390	2.0	11,240
Pottawattamie	8,289,200	13		32	561,840	35	1,229,550	20	2,350	25	14,040	70			378,000	2.0	61,900	1.0	16,210
Poweshiek	4,189,880	14	560	32	35,640	31	1,058,100	20	3,640		93,000	73				1.8	56,250	1.2	1,060
Ringgold	3,461,160	14	4,340	38		30	623,720	13	1,700	25		82	8	1,600	79,800	1.8	81,200	1.2	1,120
Sac	4,204,550	14	1,400	35	156,100	35	1,106,360	18	12,960	25	203,750				116,840	2.0	42,380	1.2	21,250
Scott	2,721,680	20	8,900	34	123,000	30	604,800				630,250	100	8		487,000	1.5	34,590	1.5	7,120

FINAL CROP REPORT 1902—CONTINUED.

COUNTIES.	CORN Yield per acre	CORN Total yield, bushels	WINTER WHEAT Yield per acre	WINTER WHEAT Total yield, bushels	SPRING WHEAT Yield per acre	SPRING WHEAT Total yield, bushels	OATS Yield per acre	OATS Total yield, bushels	RYE Yield per acre	RYE Total yield, bu.	BARLEY Yield per acre	BARLEY Total yield, bushels	FLAX SEED Yield per acre	FLAX SEED Total yield, bu.	POTATOES Yield per acre	POTATOES Total yield, bushels	TAME HAY Yield per acre	TAME HAY Total yield, tons	WILD HAY Yield per acre	WILD HAY Total yield, tons
Shelby	30	3,274,500			12	386,520	27	580,500	15	1,050	23	60,030			72	115,920	1.8	52,530	1.2	12,230
Sioux	35	4,204,200			10	802,600	33	1,161,910	17		24	725,040	10	6,850	90	132,300	1.5	16,200	1.5	27,340
Story	32	3,360,330			17	75,310	32	1,251,200	12	8,670	25	24,250			85	90,100	2.3	48,780	1.2	6,400
Tama	31	3,352,340	15	38,850	12	123,600	25	1,027,840	13	1,320	24	531,360			93	147,870	1.6	49,070	1.7	9,300
Taylor	33	2,711,940	15	1,050	13	5,330	35	453,000	16	7,540	25	27,120			120	141,630	2.4	81,190	2.0	3,140
Union	38	2,272,040	18	51,120	12	7,320	35	524,550		640		7,250			110	123,200	1.8	55,380	1.2	1,560
Van Buren	43	2,158,170	20	14,600			40	730,000	20	31,600					150	73,500	1.5	52,390	1.0	1,920
Wapello	35	1,965,250	19	1,710	13	2,210	29	493,580	16	18,720	22	7,700			90	129,600	1.8	55,060	1.0	310
Warren	38	3,442,410	20	15,630	13	90,220	28	612,350	15	4,750	20	21,800			85	104,550	2.0	68,650	1.3	420
Washington	40	3,974,800	16	1,440	16	5,200	40	1,124,800	20	23,220	32	116,160			87	73,080	1.6	57,090	1.0	310
Wayne	40	2,843,600			15	1,050	35	388,550	18	9,360					150	78,750	1.8	94,560	1.2	520
Webster	38	3,839,020			14	146,860	33	1,521,630	14	2,660	22	45,980			80	105,600	1.5	18,360	1.0	40,120
Winnebago	30	1,400,100	16	2,400	12	224,520	40	916,490	20	5,820	27	81,400	9	27,090	90	70,200	1.8	17,110	1.2	33,120
Winneshiek	31	2,224,870			15	114,300	32	1,064,800	15	2,100	27	291,330	10	72,300	80	107,200	1.8	71,280	1.5	17,150
Woodbury	33	4,749,690			10	587,800	31	689,750	15	3,040	28	64,400	11	5,940	120	177,600	1.5	17,440	1.2	14,210
Worth	21	894,240			9	50,310	35	1,946,800	15	1,950	26	229,580	10	104,100	58	87,000	2.0	34,900	1.5	16,240
Wright	25	1,976,500			8	84,320	30	1,303,500			25	115,150	9	17,370	57	59,850	2.0	39,540	1.6	27,110
Total for state		296,950,230		852,045		12,680,800		92,937,960		882,830		15,380,910		755,350		12,051,670		4,439,940		1,202,860
Av. per acre	34		18		13		31		17		25		8		90		1.8		1.3	

PART IV.

IOWA STATE COLLEGE OF AGRICULTURE AND MECHANIC ARTS.

A TEN DAYS' COURSE IN AGRICULTURE FOR THE BUSY FARMER.

By W. H. Olin.

Professor Curtiss, as the director of the work in agriculture, and Professor Kennedy, as professor of animal husbandry in the Iowa State College at Ames, decided in 1901 to offer to farmers of the state who could spare the time in January to come to the college, a ten days' course in the study of farm stock, using all the college facilities for this work. Fully two hundred responded to this invitation the first year.

Last year Professor Curtiss added corn judging to the course. This met with such success that this year Professor Kennedy in charge of live stock judging and Professor Holden in charge of the corn judging classes arranged the work in four periods of two hours each, while the classes were divided into two sections. This gave each section four hours each day for corn and four hours for stock judging.

This short course school was held during the midwinter vacation— January 5th to 17th, just when farmers could best get away from home and the professors could give all their time to the work.

The good work done preceding years caused an increased enrollment of earnest, zealous farmers with their sons who came "to do business."

Nearly every county in Iowa was represented, while corn-growing and stock-raising farmers from Canada, Mexico, Virginia, Kansas, Wisconsin, Missouri, Ohio, South Dakota, Minnesota and Illinois came to share with them the practical instruction given at this school, taxing both the agronomy and agricultural husbandry departments to handle the large classes.

More than three hundred and fifty students were regularly enrolled taking full work in both departments, while those only present for part time made the attendance over four hundred.

WORK IN CORN JUDGING.

The corn school was held in the college dining hall, the largest room in any building on the campus. Here forty tables provided room for 160 students in a class, giving two samples of corn of ten ears each for every student.

Farmers owning from one hundred to one thousand acres of land came to this school that they might learn how to make their seed selections for the coming season. Men sixty years of age entered this corn work with all the energy of the sturdy farm youth working by their side.

All took the work with such unbounded enthusiasm that no one was left simply to "browse around."

Hundreds of samples of the very best corn obtainable in the whole corn belt, representing all the present standard varieties, were given the classes for study.

This work consisted in the study of a unit ear, then a group of ten ears, kernel characteristics, breed characteristics and finally sample scoring and variety differences.

A barren stalk.

This diligent work at the corn tables was changed when the students became somewhat weary, chairs were drawn from under the tables, and the class was seated while Professors Holden, Shamel and Stevenson gave helpful, instructive talks on important and essential things to know about breeding and improving corn.

Mr. James Reid sent the school two ears of his model type of Reid's Yellow Dent as now improved, together with an ear of the type from which this corn was developed, over fifty years ago.

Mr. Nims of Emerson, Iowa, originator of the Legal Tender corn, and Mr. Thad. Chester of Champaign, Ill., whose father procured his Leaming corn from the originator of this variety, gave the corn school the benefit of their experience with corn and Professor A. D. Shamel gave the school the history of the standard varieties here studied by the students.

Most helpful discussion on proper methods of preparing, planting and cultivating corn were given in the inspiring "experience meeting" held from time to time in the afternoon sessions under direction of Professors Holden and Shamel. The work in the class room, the talks and discussions all brought out these facts:

1. Vitality of all seed corn should be tested. This alone enables one to secure healthy, vigorous plants. Unless 97 per cent of seeds germinate, best not to use this corn.

2. Shape and size of kernel planted all important in getting a good stand. A good planter illustrated this by using uniform and irregular kernels and noting uniformity in number of kernels dropped in the first instance, and the irregularity in the number dropped in the second instance, when irregular kernels were used or those of different shapes and sizes.

Students at work in corn judging at the Short Course School at Ames.

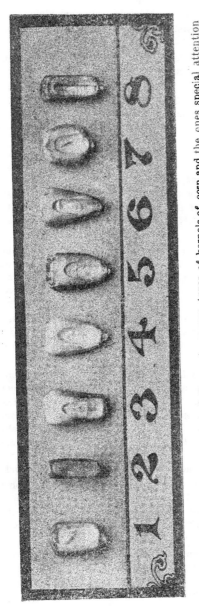

The above cut shows a few of the most common types of kernels of corn and the ones special attention was called to at this winters Corn School.

While number one (1) is too nearly rectangular, it is a kernel with a large germ and high feeding value a. Number two (2) gives a side view of this same kernel showing it to be full at the tip and of uniform thickness. Numbers six (6)

Numbers three (3), five (5) and represent the types in order named Numbers six (6) and even (7) represent objectionable types, both being too low in feeding values. Number six (6) gives open spaces at cob, while number seven (7) usually gives wide rows on the outside and both yield too low a proportion of corn to cob.

Number eight (8) is a type of kernel hard to handle in the average planter so as to obtain a uniform stand.

3. Character of ear, condition of corn and percentage of corn to cob, all important in working up good, marketable corn and good yields.

4. The acre the unit for all tests, be it quantity, quality, or special characteristics.

The value of this work in corn is clearly shown by the experience given by a farmer who attended the corn school last year. He says:

"I came here last winter, went home and picked out a bushel and a half of seed corn from seventeen bushels I had reserved for seed. This bushel and a half I shelled and prepared for planting by discarding all large and all small grains. My seed corn when finally ready to plant, was uniform in size of grains. I secured an unusually good stand, and a yield of over seventy-five bushels per acre, which was exceptionally good for this last year (1902). This superior yield I attribute wholly to the knowledge gained here this last winter."

Mr. R. S. Hooper, foreman of a large corn and stock farm in Missouri, could scarcely say enough of the value he felt the school of 1903 would prove to him, while Mr. E. G. Butler, from the far-famed and historic Shenandoah Valley of Virginia, told the writer of this sketch·

"I never dreamed there was so much to be learned about common corn. It is one of the staple crops in our valley and I am going home to put in practice the things I have learned here. They have been of great value to me, and will revolutionize our methods of raising corn in Virginia."

The corn school closed with an examination; those passing a satisfactory test were granted corn judging certificates by the agronomy department of the college. Two hundred and fifty students took this examination.

The *Iowa Homestead* offered $68 in prizes for the best corn exhibited by students enrolled in the school and $32 in prizes to the best corn judges shown by the examinations. This together with the enthusiasm developed in the school led to the organizing of a Corn Growers' Association. The objects of this association are: "Improvement and development of varieties of corn adapted to Iowa; to encourage better and more thorough methods of cultivation; to secure better seed and to aid in the organization of local clubs for the study and improvement of corn."

The state has been divided into three primary districts and each of these into a number of subordinate districts with an executive officer in each. Two hundred and seventy-five dollars has been subscribed for premiums at the corn school in 1904 and the members confidently hope to raise the full amount to $1,200 before the close of the year.

A Grand Champion Prize has been promised by the *Wallaces' Farmer*, Mr. A. E. Cook of Odeboldt promises a Trophy Prize, Mr. Whiting in charge of the Agricultural exhibit for Iowa at the World's Fair at St. Louis, Missouri, will give another Trophy Prize and still others are in sight.

Mr. Grant Chapman of Bagley was elected president, Mr. George S. Forest Miles, secretary-treasurer and Mr. Asa Plummer of Maxwell as vice-president of the new association.

THE STOCK JUDGING SCHOOL.

The stock judging pavilion proved too small for the number seeking this work. The college has excellent animals in all classes of farm stock for class study as well as practical work in feeding and breeding.

The work the college is doing in breeding for certain types and specific purposes in sheep, hogs and cattle proved as interesting as the judging of the animals themselves. Professor Kennedy was assisted in this work by Professor C. F. Curtiss, Dean of Agriculture and Professor E. C. Marshall, assistant in animal husbandry.

Dr. J. Perchbacher of Janesville, Wisconsin, gave a demonstrated lecture on horseshoeing. Dr. McNeal of the Iowa Station staff gave a lecture on anatomy, Mr. George Heyl, of Washington, Illinois, lectured on swine, while Mr. Dobson of Marine, Iowa, brought over some light roadsters and gave an illustration of high action in horses. One horse represented the quality that tops the New York market and is valued at $3,800. The three roadsters made an interesting contrast with the three Percheron draft horses sent out from the Frye Horse Farm.

Probably the most attractive features of the live stock work were the slaughter test and block demonstrations given at the close of the course. Mr. M. F. Mullins, foreman of the killing department of the Agar Packing Company of Des Moines gave the students an object lesson in slaughtering that revealed the science as well as the art of his profession. Mr. Mullins holds the championship of the world on speed in slaughtering animals.

For this work the following animals were provided:

1. The yearling grade Angus, Thistle, a prize winner in his class at International, 1902, winner of the Angus Special, and one of the three animals with which the college won grand champion herd prize over all other breeds.

2. A fat Angus heifer purchased in the Omaha market.

3. The best market topper that could be obtained in Omaha, January 12th.

4. An old cow representative of the canner type of beef.

With Thistle, the expert butcher showed how Christmas beeves are slaughtered and dressed for the block. He proved a veritable artist with the knife as with deft and rapid swinging strokes, he rolled back the black fur from the carcass. When the carcass was halved, using the butcher's knife as pencil, chisel and mallet, he decorated the carcass with holly sprays.

13

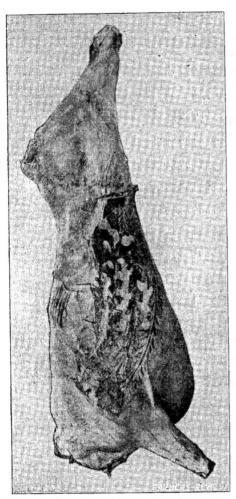

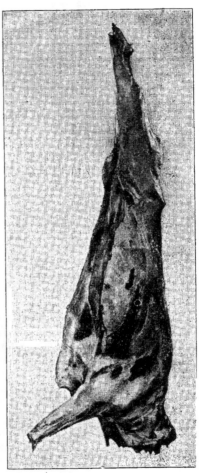

Half Carcass of Thistle (which meat dressed out 69 per cent of salable meat).

Half Carcass of Canner Cow (which dressed out 43 per cent of salable meat).

With the canner cow, Mr. Mullins gave the students some idea of what he could do when he had conveniences for his work. It was just 70 seconds from tne time he began skinning the head until it was completely dressed and severed from the body; from severing of the head until the carcass hung on the hooks, skinned, dressed and halved was six minutes and four seconds, and from the time the canner fell to the floor, was bled, dressed, halved, thoroughly washed and hung on hooks dressed for the block, 17 minutes. With few conveniences for rapid work, still this was undoubtedly the greatest exhibition of humane, skillful and rapid slaughter work ever given before a body of students.

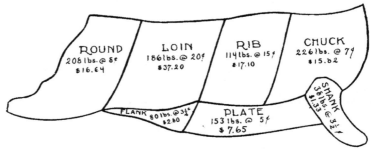

Diagram showing Thistle's carcass cuts with value of each.

After being in the cooler forty-eight hours, the meat was brought out placed on tables in middle of stock pavilion and Mr. John Gosling, undoubtedly the greatest beef expert in this country, gave a demonstrative lecture upon it.

Mr. Gosling showed the composition of the different types of beef, gave the students the points of beef, and with his expert cutter, Mr. C. F. Eckert, of Weber's market, Kansas City, Missouri, cut up the 3,000 lbs. of meat before him and showed the students the different kinds of beef in one and the same animal.

The "eye" of the beef was pointed out, the hanging tenderloin explained, the regular roll, Spencer roll, the shoulder cloy, sweet bread explained, that delicacy to so many meat eaters and so on through the butcher's cuts.

The seven distinctive block cuts are here given of Thistle, with weight of each and value as fixed by Mr. Reid of the Ames local market. The value of careful cutting by making the loin and rib cuts, the high priced cuts of all animals, was interestingly shown. As Mr. Eckert measured with eye and knife to so divide that he would make the greatest possible percentage of high priced cuts and at the same time give each one good quality, the lecturer remarked: "The proper cutting of the beef carcass often means many dollars, for from the same quarter comes the porter house worth 17 1-2 to 20 cents per pound and a low priced cut worth 3 1-2 to 6 cents per pound. The turn of the knife may mean many cents a pound less to the butcher or a poor quality to the consumer."

The weights, percentages and market value of the four animals used for this work are given below:

	MARKET VALUE.	LIVE WEIGHT.	DRESSED WEIGHT.			PER CENT. DRESSED.
			Fore quarter.	Hind quarter.	Total.	
Thistle.....................	....	1,480	274	237	1,022	69.
Angus heifer....... ...	$ 4.40	1,330	204	204	816	61.3
Fat steer..................	5 00	1,390	193	207	800	57.5
Canner cow.	2.70	980	109	108	424	43.2

THISTLE ON THE BLOCK.

CUT.	WEIGHT LBS.	MARKET VALUE PER LB.	VALUE OF CUT.
1. Loin........	186	20 c	$ 37.20 ⎱
2. Ribs...............	114	15 c	17.10 ⎰ *
3. Round..	208	8 c	16.64
4. Chuck	226	7 c	15.82
5. Plate	153	5 c	7.65
6. Flank	80	3½c	2.80
7. Shank....................	38	3½c	1.33
Total cuts.	1,005	......	$ 98.54
Hide........	90	5 c	4.50
Tallow	119	2 c	2.38
Total products.	1,214	....	$105.42

*High priced cuts, 29.35 per cent.

Live weight 1,480
Dressed weight................. 1,022
Net percentage of beef 69

Mr. Gosling showed the students with Thistle's carcass, that when they felt the back of a beef animal and found as they supposed flesh, they were feeling no muscular tissue whatever for flesh never gets over the backbone. It is spine fat that is felt. This spine fat on Thistle was from one inch to one and one-half inches thick. He also showed that much coarse muscle or gristle is due to the animal being range fed. Elk and deer meat is never marbled on account of the constant use of the muscles. Thistle was cited as an excellent illustration of well marbled meat.

The fact that the fat Omaha steer was rated in the market at 60 cents per hundred *more* and dressed out 3.8 per cent *less* than the fat heifer was commented on; also it was noted that the heifer dressed out more yellow in color. Heifers usually dress out a smaller per cent than the same weight of steer.

Mr. Gosling is a forceful teacher, a clear demonstrator and as expert a judge of good beef on the hoof as on the hook.

The editor of the *Farmer's Review*, Chicago, speaks for all, when he says: "We are going ahead of the world in this kind of work. Nowhere else have students such grand opportunities for study along both scientific and practical lines, and the Iowa educators deserve all the fine reputation and renown that is accruing to them." They have not only fed animals that are good enough to win, but animals that dress up well as it

Views of cuts of beef in the slaughter test and demonstration at the short course in judging live stock held at the Iowa Agricultural College.

is possible for animals to dress. This is shown by the recent victory at the International Live Stock Exposition; on foot, and by the block test at Ames, where Thistle dressed out no less than 69 per cent net to gross weight. To most of the young men who enjoyed the privilege of viewing these carcasses the sight must have been novel and interesting. From the time of this exhibit they will possess different ideas on the subject of beef production and the lessons learned cannot but benefit them in their future work on the farm. They have seen how the different cuts are selected how quality is appraised, that good beef is marbled with fat, what proportion the cheap cuts bear to the high priced ones, how the fore quarters weigh out compared with hind ones, how the tallow of a well fed, early matured beast looks, compared with that of a tough old canner, and we expect also have learned how good beef feels. The latter is a point sometimes forgotten in teaching the business of judging meat, but the skilled meat cutter can tell, by merely running his fingers lightly over a freshly cut rib roast, exactly what class it belongs in and how it will "eat on the table." The trained finger tells the grain of the meat and that silky quality that is only found in well fed, choice young meat.

Each evening during the ten days the students gathered in a mass meeting for lectures and general discussions.

While the work in this course can in no way be equal to the training given in the longer course, it does broaden the one who can come,

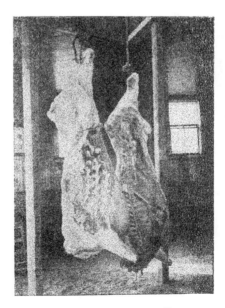

Carcass of Angus steer, Thistle, killed during
beef dressing demonstration at Ames.

gives him many new ideas, makes him a greater student of his farm work and thus, in the end, a better farmer, a stronger citizen, a nobler man.

One of the immediate results of the work in corn is a series of co-operative experiments planned at the short course school. Prof. Holden purposes to purchase choice seed corn and send to those who have signified their desire to co-operate with him in seeking to establish over the state standard varieties of pure bred corn best adapted to that particular locality. He is seeking to have these experiments carried on in each county in Iowa. It will undoubtedly be of incalculable value to this, one of the leading corn states in the union. Hearty co-operation with Professors Kennedy and Holden on the part of Iowa farmers in feeding steers and growing corn means added value to the intrinsic worth of our "Hawkeye State."

PART V.

IOWA IMPROVED STOCK BREEDERS' ASSOCIATION.

TWENTY-NINTH ANNUAL SESSION.

The twenty-ninth annual convention of the Iowa Improved Stock Breders' Association convened in the opera house at Newton, Iowa, January 21st, at 1:30 p. m. The meeting was called to order by Secretary E. H. White. A letter from President W. M. Mc-Fadden was read, stating his inability to be present.

Mr. Forest of Miles was appointed temporary chairman.

ADDRESS OF PRESIDENT.

W. M. McFadden.

The underlying principle of live stock breeding is supposed to be "like begets like." For some years we have been rapidly developing the idea that farming and stock raising is a profession, and that numerous scientific principles are the basis upon which successful farming is conducted, but the experiences of the past two years by Iowa farmers are calculated to shake both these theories.

It is doubtful if the history of agriculture in this state has ever seen two years so remarkably different in all respects. A year ago we thought we had laid by many rules and helpful hints for dry weather; all our experience, all our study had been along the line of what was best to do to combat the troubles and annoyances incident to a dry season. All of these carefully cherished rules must now be decidedly rusty—if not entirely washed away.

I think the records show the greatest amount of rainfall during the past season that has ever been recorded in Iowa. These two seasons have brought into play all the different rules, hints and suggestions that any kind of a previous season has ever before suggested. What we learned in 1901 we found little or no use for in 1902. The crops that were successful, the methods of handling stock that were just right in one year would totally fail the next.

In no other business or profession, it seems to me, is there so constantly coming up questions to be met and settled that are entirely new.

It is the necessity for the exchange of experiences, and barter of ideas that makes such meetings as this interesting and instructive. Time was when the Iowa Improved Stock Breeders' Association was the leading one of its kind in the United States. That it is not so today certainly is not because the need for it is gone.

I believe that some line of action should be decided upon here that will properly present this matter to our next legislature. This organization should be one in keeping with the agricultural interest of the greatest state in the union.

The organizations in our sister states, such as Minnesota, Illinois and Nebraska, are recognized and encouraged by the legislatures of those states in a substantial manner. A bill on this subject was before our last legislature and there is but little doubt but what it would be favorably acted upon by the next legislature if it is properly presented. I hope this meeting will not adjourn without some decisive action on this matter.

Certainly there is not a farmer or stock grower in the state of Iowa who does not take great pride in the position attained by our agricultural college. That it is in the forefront of agricultural colleges was clearly demonstrated at the recent International Show at Chicago. The record made there clearly demonstrates what a commanding position we hold in stock breeding and farming.

This great live stock center of Newton should be exactly the right place to inaugurate a movement which shall result in giving us an organization of improved stock breeders that will as thoroughly and properly represent Iowa's position as an agricultural state, as does our agricultural college. The need for an organization of this kind never was greater than at present. New problems are coming up to be solved all the time, and the recent sharp advance in lands in Iowa calls for better and more careful farming than ever before. The methods heretofore in vogue, in many places, will not do for the future and if we are to maintain the position we now occupy, advancement and education along agricultural lines must be the watchword.

There is one feature of live stock breeding and improvement that many farmers and breeders overlook. A farmer may get the idea that the ordinary kind of stock he has been raising has not been profitable, and for this reason he will buy a good thoroughbred male. The first cross is, if at all judiciously made, almost always surprisingly satisfactory. The test, however, comes as to whether he can see the necessity for keeping on in the same direction. It is rare indeed that such improvement can be noted by any succeeding cross. The owner is quite likely to conclude that he has not been so fortunate in securing a good male as in the first instance, and owing to this fact he loses his enthusiasm, and his stock begins to go back.

Very few farmers, comparatively, realize the necessity for the constant use of improved blood. They do not realize that the introduction of improved blood is necessary to guard against the natural deterioration that comes from bad crosses, poor feed and unfavorable seasons.

The popular idea is, that if a sweepstakes male and female at our state fair could be crossed together, the result could be nothing but satisfactory. As a matter of fact, the animais may not be at all suited, either in form or in blood lines, to cross together, and it is very often the fact, that the coupling of these very best animals is attended with extremely unsatisfactory results. Old breeders realize to its fullest extent the danger and liability as to what is known as a bad cross; then, a very great proportion of our really good animals are ruined by a lack of care. We hear a great deal about the danger and damage from over feeding.

There are a great many who even go so far as to say that the animals shown at our state fairs should be only in breeding condition.

I undertake to say that ten animals are ruined by lack of feed to where there is one that is injured by over-feeding. The facts are, that the injury from over-feeding comes more often from the way it is taken off than in the way it is put on. It is these bad crosses, the unfavorable seasons and the lack of care that is constantly working to reduce the standard of excellence of all breeds of stock. They are kept up only by the intelligent care and mating of the really successful breeders.

It is the efforts of the few that are necessary to maintain the improved standard of any breed of stock. There are so many influences that tend to deterioration in all breeds of stock that make necessary the improved stock breeder. These things are true in the same degree with grains and grasses. This feature of agriculture is just coming into its own, and the study of it is developing the fact, that we must have pedigreed seedsmen as well as pedigreed stockmen. Some have had the idea that such a high state of perfection would be reached with certain breeds of live stock, that further improvement would be impossible, and that the general standard of excellence would be so high that the improved breeder would lose his business. Nothing could be further from the real facts in the case than this. It often requires more skill and good care to maintain a herd to a high standard of excellence than to put it there in the first place. In fact, the real test of the successful breeder comes when he has put himself at the very top. So few are able to stay there once they reach it.

What is true of a herd is true in a broader sense of a breed, and the necessity for this battling against deterioration will always remain. This demonstrates the great need of an organization such as this that shall be a permanent power for good in Iowa, and I hope that some action will be taken at this, the twenty-ninth annual meeting, to place the association in a position to properly represent our peerless Iowa, the leading agricultural state of the union.

The following committees were appointed:

Resolutions—F. F. Failor, E. H'. White and T. M. Flynn.

Location—G. W. Burge, E. H. White and Stustman.

Officers—D. L. Howard, II. R. Parsons and C. W. Norton.

A conference committee was appointed to meet a similar com-mittee from the Short-Horn Association, to define a breeding animal. The following named gentlemen were appointed on such conference committee: Flynn Donahey, Forrest and Parsons.

THE FARMERS' INSTITUTE.

F. F. Failor, Newton, Iowa.

The County Farmers' Institute is the preliminary school to all agri-cultural advancement and improvements, and provides the opportunity for study and the attainments of knowledge in all the various branches pertaining thereto; with the advancing prices in land and higher priced labor, it becomes necessary to raise less stock and better ones, to be-come skilled in the art of breeding and feeding, and to understand the relative value of different kinds of feed, both as to cost and feeding value.

No branch of business in the world today is receiving so much atten-tion from outside sources as is given to agriculture. First, the Secre-tary of Agriculture which adds prestige and dignity to the industry, second, the agricultural colleges and experiment stations where the fu-ture farmer can gain a thorough knowledge of all the little details, where experiments are carried on and a careful record of the results given as a guide for future operations.

In the improved methods of farming we have the same source of knowledge as in the improvement of live stock, viz., through the experi-ment stations at our agricultural colleges.

Our government is sending men all over the world in the search of grains, grasses and live stock suitable to the varied climates and soils of this great country, such as the reindeer from the far north, macaroni wheat for the great wheat belts of the northwest, and many varieties of grasses from the arid district of the West, in fact, when you come to con-sider what this government is doing for the farmer, it is astonishing. Government inspection for meats, tariff legislation for the protection of infant industries, especially sugar, duties on live stock that we can pro-duce, and free entry of improved stock for the betterment and building up of our herds.

It might be no more than fair to look at the other side a moment. What the farmer is doing or has done for the government. When he tide of emigration took its westward course, this westward country was but a howling wilderness, and but for the hardy pioneer who braved the hardships and privations of frontier life, we would not have a school-house on every hill, and a meeting house close by.

As the country became more settled, capital was interested in build-ing the great railroads that gird the country from east to west, and the wilderness was made to blossom as the rose, and the vast plains where the bison roamed free from the sight of man is now thickly settled with happy homes and prosperous farmers.

The farmers' wives and daughters should be interested in these county institutes. They should take part in the program and discuss the best methods of housekeeping, and instruct their unfortunate sisters in the art of inducing their husbands to have all next summer's wood nicely cut and stored away to fortify against the days when time is precious and important farm work is pressing.

They should also tell their sisters how to induce their husbands to see the necessity of doing the milking and help get the water ready on wash day, and many other duties the husband owes his patient helpmeet, for the Lord knows she has enough to do without adding any of those things to her never ending daily duties.

The American farmer is the predominating element of this country, and I feel free to say that if all her forces could be marshaled under one common head, they could control the commerce of the world. How long would it be until the more densely populated portions of the old world would be in distress for want of bread, if this country would withhold the shipment of grain alone, to say nothing of the semi-luxuries such as our meats and packing house products, and the real luxuries as wines, fruits and many other articles. I mention these things that the young farmer may realize the grand position he occupies in this grandest of all nations on earth.

The most unfortunate fact is that we don't half live up to our privileges in this country. Too many of our young farmers are content to take up the work just where their fathers left off, and continue it in the same old way. This is an age of progression, and while old methods may have done very well at the time, under the new order of things, they are out of date.

The remedy is at hand, however. Every agricultural paper is full of good suggestions bearing upon good farming and improved methods of feeding and stock raising. Read those papers, young man, study the experiment station bulletins, think and then act. Attend the Farmers' Institute, learn to make two blades of grass grow where but one grew before.

"Do noble things, not dream them all day long and thus make life, death, and that vast beyond, one grand sweet song."

EVENING SESSION.

ONE OF THE ESSENTIALS.

J. W. Johnson, Albia, Iowa.

The first I knew of the circumstances which led up to my present situation was that I was on the program for a paper and the above subject assigned me. I felt toward the committee as Pat Murphy did the Cruickshank bull. He had just come over—that is Pat, the bull had been imported the year before—and was making across the pasture. Whether it was his red hair or verdant hue that angered his majesty, the bull made after him. Pat made wild strides for salvation and was ready for the final leap over the fence when the polished horns of the thoroughbred caught him amidships and tossed him over. He lit in the brush and dust bit the ground, scraped his shins and got up saying something not recorded and as he smoothed down the ruffled places he looked back over the fence at the bull, who was bowing and pawing and making great ado. "You old divil," said Pat, "you need make no apologies to me, ye did it a purpose."

But on second thought we have taken it more kindly and forgiven them. There is need of great care at times like this for, "we have known I stand in the presence of men who have done much for the material too much that was not so," and we are always asserting it for the truth. prosperity of the great commonwealth of Iowa, indeed who rank with the most eminent in the great fine stock industry of the whole country. Whether it be in the cabinet or congress or the public service, or national politics or the fat stock snow, or wherever it be, Iowa's thoroughbreds are all right and will continue to be, for our whole people are alive and thinking, wide-awake and working along all lines.

There are many essentials on the farm. The first to suggest itself is the farmer's wife. Mr. Farmer is quite apt to believe that he is "it." but the gentle, patient, bright woman that stands by him in life's picture is just as essential as he. My mother was a farmer's wife and my wife a farmer's daughter, so that it is not theory, but sweet experience I am talking. The lady of the white house is all right in her place, "the new woman" has added many charms to modern life, but the farmer's wife is more essential to your prosperity and business than any element or factor mentionable. A farm without a home would be a drear and a desert place. There mould be mould, dust and decay, it would be sunshine without vitality, leisure without pleasure, life without refinement, without the farmers' wives. Forget her not. In the struggle and toil of the day, in the rush for wealth, smile upon and love and cherish the noble woman who is wife and mother in your farm home. Says Tennyson: "Happy he with such a mother; faith in womankind beats with his blood, and trust in all things high comes easy to him." It was woman who was last at the cross and first at the tomb, and so it is with the true woman in every trail.

The agricultural experiment stations of the country, fifty or more are essential to the farmers' and stock breeders' business. Perhaps no class of men dote more on "practical experience" than farmers, and true it is that when you work out a thing for yourself and get the right answer, it's complete and satisfying. Josh Billings says there is one thing peculiar about a self-made man—he's always proud of the job. But jokes aside, the most practical, the most progressive, most successful farmers, stock-men, creamerymen, keep a sharp eye on the experimental work of the agricultural colleges. They solve new problems quick and by better methods than can be done anywhere else, for they have the facilities and exist for that end. What George Washington recommended a century ago, Cyrus C. Carpenter of Iowa, when in congress, framed into law, which in 1887 was passed, appropriating money as a perpetual aid to agricultural experiment work in connection with the land grant colleges.

The value of this work the country over can be estimated approximately by taking our own splendid institution at Ames as an example. While such eminent men as the lamented McKinley, President Roosevelt, James Wilson and others endorse and foster agricultural experimentation, and so long as we see the splendid results of the work, study it, follow it, swear by it. They discovered certain facts that lead to economy of labor, or saving in feeds, or increased production of grains or grasses, or better methods in cheese and butter making or develop better varieties of fruits and vegetables, or produce a Shamrock for the fat stock show, or beat the world on fine stock judging. Why not keep up with the experiment station? The Ames boys are filling good positions everywhere at fine salaries, or, if doing work for themselves on some broad western farm, are succeeding like eminent "captains of industry" which they are. Put your sons into these short courses in dairying or stock judging, or, better still, give them a full course that covers these vital subjects of botany, chemistry, zoology, geology and 'a that. It will broaden them, polish them, quicken them, give them confidence in self, and enable them to cope with the powerful competition of today, whether brains or brawn, whether statecraft or commerce or field sports. Who have preferment in places of trust and emolument? It is the educated as against the uneducated, 100 to 1. (*The Inter Ocean* some time ago published an editorial in which it is claimed that college trained people had advantage over the unschooled 700 to 1.) When Daniel Webster's father told him he was to have his wish gratified, he would send him to college, he fell upon his father's neck and wept for joy. There are Iowa boys who carry with them this burning desire which if you gratify you will add jewels both to your crown and theirs. Lincoln once met a ragged urchin on the street and said to himself, "You can't tell what possibilities are buttoned up in that old coat," and at that moment he drew a picture of himself and did not know it—did not seem to know.

"The One Essential" for this hour's discussion is dairying as a neces-sary adjunct of stock raising and general farming. Shakespeare says "learning is but an adjunct to ourself," but since learning is life, since knowledge put to use is power, since it is the truth that makes us free, the comparison is conclusive. We would never know "which side of our bread is buttered" if it were not for the dairy cow. She has been the mortgage lifter, the wealth producer, the constant friend of the Iowa farmer for many years. Nobody will deny the truth of my statement, but there are so many, especially among stockmen, who will not milk. In fact stock breeders have retarded dairying and their own business of breeding and selling fine stock because they have directly and especially indirectly discouraged dairying.

You have persistently refused to milk the cows of your herd because you say you want fine, fat calves for the show ring and auction block and they cannot be produced without they run with the dam. To save time let this be admitted as to show cattle and the highest blood for private sale, yet it is a serious question if such handling of cows as this is not breeding out or turning dormant the milking power of the animal, to say nothing of the fact that fine, fat calves are raised by hand from the warm separator milk supplemented by oat meal, oats, corn, bran and good pasture at various stages of growth. But stockmen indirectly have crippled the dairy (and their own business as well) because their example is contagious. Other men who are not breeding thoroughbred cattle copy the example and contend that it does not pay to rob the calf of the fresh full milk of the dam, and so thousands of Iowa cows that cost from $18 to $25 each to keep them are carried through the year to raise $15 calves. Farmers see this finally and get discouraged with the business

Courtesy Wallaces' Farmer.
One of the prize Short-Horns at the Iowa State
Fair 1902.

and decide to give up cattle. That hurts the fine stock industry and you are yourselves in part to blame. You pay little or no attention to that phase of the trade. You do not breed for milk because you have blinded your eyes to the necessity of a double purpose, or all purpose cow. The average farmer must have that kind or none.

The man who keeps sheep gets both of clip of wool and a lamb per ewe, and a fine carcass from the weathers. The man who raises colts uses his mares on the farm and gets two products, while hogs reproduce themselves more often and thus return values, and the genaral farmer and the man who raises grade cattle cannot afford to use the cows for but the one purpose, and your business is hurt when they do it.

If farmers will handle the cows as they should be they will not only get just as good a calf, and 100 to 250 pounds of butter in a year, but will get a third more of product, surplus of warm milk from the separator for pigs and chickens. Vast sums of money are wasted every year in Iowa because of this mismanagement. In Albia and vicinity butter has sold for almost two years at from 16 to 35 cents a pound, and if 2,000 cows were put onto the farms of Monroe county and handled skillfully they would not adequately supply the demand for good butter.

We would not draw here a dark picture. We picked up for Sunday reading on January 18, 1903, a copy of the Iowa Agricultural Report of 1864 and looked it carefully over to find out about the Iowa dairy at that time, but the thing was not mentioned. Then we thought a moment and recalled that it was severalyears later than that before John Stewart of Manchester started the first gathered cream creamery, and not until 1876 did he achieve the distinguished victory over all the world with his Iowa butter at the Centennial. Before that it had been known in the eastern market as "prairie grease." Then came the era of invention and expansion, the building of creameries and cheese factories, until the combined number in the state reached nearly one thousand. We built them whether there were cows in the neighborhood or not or ever would be. We bought all the cans and tanks and churns and curious appliances suggested by all the Chicago and New York houses, and thus were thousands of dollars unwisely invested in the business. Meanwhile the counterfeiter was getting in his work and butterine and other patent stuff were being sold as genuine butter, and here again the fine stockmen halted and said if they use our tallow to make oleomargarine it will make tallow prices better, guess they can use fraudulent butter if they don't know it, and so the dairy met with another backset. Pardon a personal allusion, but it was your speaker who from the platform of the National Dairy Association in Cincinnati in 1883 first called the hog butter business by its right name and made the old thing come out into broad daylight and show its bristles. The scene was dramatic. There were 350 men present from twenty-seven different states. The paper was read at 2 o'clock and the discussion closed at 5:30, after men from Denver, St. Louis, New Orleans, Richmond, New York, Boston, Philadelphia and Chicago, to say nothing of brave Colonel Littler of Iowa, who defended the Iowa creamerymen against the charge they for years before were using oleo oil in their creamery churns to swell the butter output of Iowa, had taken part. Mr. Coleman of St. Louis, afterwards Mr. Cleveland's secretary of agriculture, and Professor Taylor, who was afterwards Mr. Coleman's expert chemist in Washington took part in that discussion. You know the history of butterine since that time. State and national legislation has been called in. The thing had been branded and colored and labeled and taxed and is now under better control (Dairy Commissioner Wright says there is almost none at all sold in Iowa), but these are some of the ups and downs of dairying in the past.

Let me name two incidents which go to show that dairying is improving. In 1885 I represented Iowa, along with C. A. Houston of Linn county (the state forgot to pay us for that service, though fully authorized and appointed by ⎣he governor), at the world's fair at New Orleans, and when the dairy butter was examined (258 packages, that required two and one-half days' work), I assisted the committee and kept close watch of their work. There were not twenty-five packages in the entire lot that could be called fine, and not seventy-five that ever had been, though the age of the goods was somewhat against the quality of the product.

Last week I assisted in judging thirty-eight exhibits of butter at the Mahaska County Farmers' Institute and 75 per cent was fine and 90 per cent was as good as the best at New Orleans. From these facts, and they are the facts, the art of butter making is surely improving.

A strenuous effort should be made at all these meetings to educate the people in these matters. There is untold loss in Iowa because of mismanagement in dairying. De do not complain of Iowa, for she leads all others as a dairy state. In 1902 Iowa produced 80,000,000 pounds of creamery butter, and 60,000,000 pounds more on the farms and in private dairies. Of this about two-thirds was shipped out of the state, making a return of nearly $20,000,000. Nothing was taken from the soil. Millions of dollars worth of milk and cream were consumed at home. The total milk, cheese and butter product of the state for 1902 will reach above $40,000,000. Can it be thought that this is not important?

There are many things that can be done to improve the business. Do not increase the number of poor cows, but breed and select and train until we have better cows. Instead of 135 pounds of butter per cow it should be 250 to 300 pounds. There are and always have been too many creameries. Every factory that makes money must make a large amount of butter. If farmers will keep hand separators and take the cream from the milk and large quantities of water and make the business easy. Then the milk and large quantities of water and make the business easy. Then sell the cream to the creamery or the ice cream man in the city or make butter for the city market as the circumstances seem to warrant. This will improve the quality of the product, for the separator takes out impurities that nothing else will, the cream can be better shielded from bad company (onions, potatoes, the pups, boots and old clothes in the milk room and a hundred things that rob butter and cream of its fine flavor.) We do not advocate any special cow except a good dairy cow. If she be a good beef animal all the better. The farmer needs both. The question of profit in the dairy will be settled if the double purpose cow is well handled—feed, shelter, cleanliness, separator, in fact, utilizing all the product. Thus done, dairying is the one essential.

THURSDAY FORENOON.

BLACK THINGS ON THE FARM.

J. S. Trigg, Rockford, Iowa.

The question of color in our domestic animals cuts no small figure with many men in the selection of varieties to keep. There is probably more than one breeder of Short-horn cattle present who is wedded to red as a standard color for his stock, when the facts are that a large proportion of the prize winners at our stock shows, of this breed, are any other color than red, some of the top-nothers being roan, while pure white is associated with some of the best Short-horn pedigrees in the country. The color fad may easily be carried to extremes, and in many cases is. Uniformity of color in a herd is desirable, in that such a herd is thus more attractive in appearance, and the way to easily obtain it is partly the object of this paper.

Speaking of the colors of domestic animals we note that among the most valuable are the black ones. This color not only harmonizes with the green of the fields, but in this northern latitude bespeaks a degree of hardiness suited to our variable climatic conditions. There is the black Percheron horse—he of the shiny, silky coat, powerful as a locomotive, gentle as a kitten, true as steel, sound as a dollar; no curby, splint-legged, balky brute, without pedigree. a product of chance, where man's intervention thwarted nature in her effort to secure the survival of the best. Hitch three of these horses to a sixteen-inch sulky plow, and, as we saw last fall, put a pretty girl in a sunbonnet up on the seat to drive them, and just see her turn over four or five acres in a day, while her town sister was fretting over the cut of her new sacque or discussing some ethical problem at some woman's club. There is a girl worth having, as well as a team—a black-eyed, black-haired beauty—gritty, independent, resourceful, helpful and rich in good health, good looks and executive ability. Hitch two of these horses up and the residents of the town will all say: "There goes Jones and is $500 team."

Then there are the "Doddies," the Ethiopian kings of the beef tribe, broad-backed, smooth lords of the blue grass, royal bullocks, whose juicy, marbled flesh will glut the carnivorous appetite of some old wide-paunched gourmand in English ducal halls, who with their near relatives, the Galloways, represent the best and most modern machines for converting blue grass, clover and corn into money, and besides have a way of taking all the prizes at the state fairs.

Then there is his excellency, the Poland-China hog—the western farmer's mortgage lifter and barn builder, and the begetter of more healthy bank accounts than any other animal. Black as Erebus, he roots out and sleeps away his brief existence, revelling in unlimited clover, milk and corn, until the very luxurious riot of living, as the man, simply hastens his end. He not only pays the mortgage and builds big red

14

barns, but he puts a surrey in the carriage shed, a piano in the home, sends the boys and girls to college, and helps pay the preacher and convert the heathen. Your Chester Whites and Jersey Reds are to him as commoners to the aristocrat—poor relations.

In a smaller way in the poultry yard no breeds of fowl will be found more profitable or handsomer in general appearance than the Black Spanish and Langshans—prolific egg producers.

But better than all these is the rich black soil of these Mississippi valley farms. What a soil this is!—the bed of the prehistoric ocean, which has hoarded for ages the accumulated detritus of mighty glacial forces, which in ages past robbed the mountains of their primal fertility and stored it up for us; just as now and then some old pirate's pot of illgotten gold, long buried, is turned up by the plowman of today. No state in the union possesses so large and uniform an area of this black and treasured wealth of the past as Iowa; farm after farm, section after section, county after county, from Minnesota to Missouri, from river to river, every acre fertile, every farm a garden spot. Just as in a side of leather, or in a boiled ham, the best cut is toward the center, so the very best of this good, black soil of the Mississippi valley is found in Iowa—a soil alike indifferent to excess or scarcity of rainfall, a soil which like an old friend can always be depended upon, reliable as a Scotch Presbyterian elder, as easily pleased as a child, generous as heaven, responsive as its own fair girls, forgetful of wrong or neglect as a sister of charity, prolific as the hoary ocean, dabbled in by infancy to make mud pies, acquired as a precious heritage and lived from by the matured man and welcomed by him as a last resting place when the day of life is done.

Black things on Iowa farms are good things; they are the state's best gifts. With them she is gracious, liberal, responsive. You son of toil, wearing out a miserable existence among the stumps, rocks and gravel hills of the east, battling with nature in her most unkindly moods, come here, where the rows of corn are half a mile long, two ears on a stalk, where cows have twin calves and hens lay double-yolked eggs, where the cyclone goes north of us, the blizzard west of us, the drouth south of us, and the untimely frost east of us. Iowa's black soil begets her black horses, black cattle, black pigs and poultry, and the color, somber though it be, has become the insignia of her unequalled agricultural prosperity.

THE OUTLOOK FOR THE BREEDER OF PURE BRED CATTLE.

Albert Harrah, Newton, Iowa.

As long as there is an Iowa farmer who persists in breeding scrub cattle, just so long is there an outlook for the breeder of pure bred cattle. For the war on scrubs is a war of conquest to be waged until the last scrub is exterminated from the Iowa soil. This is a strenuous fight, but I rejoice in the advancement made during the past five years. In traveling through the country, I can see the work of grading up is going on and you will find but few herds, even among the small land owners of Iowa, where there is not a marked improvement in the quality of their cattle. The breeding of pure bred cattle has assumed an intensely practical basis. There can be no hap-hazard work for the successful cattle breeder of the future. His success depends upon intelligent action, adaptability for the business, a constant application to fortify against all weak points, economy in management, intelligent and economical feeding, a scientific knowledge of mating, and from first to last a conservative financial policy. Too many of our young breeders take their cue from breeders well advertised and strong financially, and are led into the error of buying cattle beyond their means, and from the start are handicapped by debt. I consider that the breeder of pure bred cattle is under moral obligations to give honest advice and most hearty support to every customer that buys his cattle. For every man that engages in the business and makes a failure has a widespread depressing influence on the trade.

Note the difference. A man or a dozen men may make a complete failure in handling the promiscuous scrubs of the country and their failure is accepted by the public as a matter of common occurrence, and no criticism is made, and the business moves along just the same. But let a breeder of pure bred cattle make an assignment and the fact creates an illusive argument used without limit against the business. It is true, a breeder has many unjust and unreasonable things to contend with in his trade. But after all they only prod a breeder up to more careful methods in his business and his complete success in business depends largely upon broad-minded and liberal treatment of customers.

While the present improvement in the quality of the cattle bred and handled by the average farmer of Iowa is encouraging, it has not kept pace with the wonderful transformation on the range. The ranchmen who wrestled with his conscience several years ago to nerve himself up to buying even grade bulls is now buying thoroughbreds and will not use a grade, and the dividing of ranges and creating a larger number of cattlemen will necessitate the breeders establishing shipping points in the ranch country where the average cattle man can buy one or more bulls at a time, as these men will not, neither can they afford the expense of single shipment.

Money consideration after all is the basis of all cattle breeding, and while there is a profound inspiration in the breeding of pure bred cattle developing the highest type of agricultural life, yet we naturally drift back to the "profit and loss" page of the ledger, and the average breeder has to reckon from this point no matter what his ambition may crave.

With the satisfactory results of our experimental stations at our command there are many questions simplified, as but few breeders can afford independent experimental tests of various feeds and proccesses.

I am infidel to the fad of importing. You may ask what would we have done without the imported blood. I acknowledge its past virtue in the line of improvement, but in my judgment we do not need the imported blood today to improve our cattle any more than we need the imported blood to improve our people.

The exhibition at our international show of beef production commands the admiration of the old world, and from now and henceforward we wield the sceptre and wear the crown before the civilized world along this line. I maintain, therefore, the outlook for the breeder of pure bred cattle in Iowa is encouraging if practical, economical methods are adopted. We are an important factor in the commercial transactions of the country, subject to the reverses and depressions of finance and hence governed by the fluctuations of trade, the same as all industries.

We have an important and desirable mission in the cultivation of new territory where we will have a market for our surplus stock. Our work must be aggressive like every other good work. To this end our best thought and judgment should be displayed.

I do not desire to boast of our superiority over our sister states adjoining us. The reliable statistics of our agricultural department show our standing. We have the motto of success inscribed upon our banner. I enjoy the proud honor of having lived in the grand state fifty years, a half century of development.

Spiritual discernment could hardly have portrayed the magnificent growth of this period. It is simply grand to me to be one of the fortunate number who have lived this past fifty years, and I bless the memory of my father for possessing the spirit of conquest, and desire for bettering the condition of his family that caused him to sever his boyhood connections in eastern Ohio and push out into this "Beautiful Land."

I predict a magnificent future for our industry. A careful, conservative, intelligent course is demanded and to the breeder of pure bred cattle in Iowa will be allotted a full share of the credit due every breeder in this grand union.

THE ODEBOLT EXPERIMENT.

R. J. Kinzer, Ames, Iowa.

Mr. President and Members of the Iowa Improved Stock Breeders' Association: There has been so much said and written about the Odebolt experiment during the last year that it seems like threshing old straw over again in discussing it at this meeting. The agricultural papers all over this country have reviewed it in their columns and pointed out its great value to the cattle feeders of the country and I shall only endeavor to give you a brief review of some of the minor details.

About a year before this experiment started, Professor Curtiss began looking around over this state for a place to do some experimental feeding under ordinary farm conditions. Many of the experiments at the Iowa station as well as at other stations, have been conducted on so small a scale that they have been of little value to the practical feeder. And the Iowa station was very fortunate in securing the facilities offered by the Brookmont farms where there was ample room for the feeding of carload lots of cattle under conditions no better, if as good, as the Iowa feeder gives his cattle. The Brookmont farms are located six miles north of Odebolt in Sac county. Here Mr. Cook has 7,351 acres of land all in a body. He has it divided into farms of one-half section each with buildings and feed lots on each farm. Three of these feed yards lying nearest the ranch headquarters were selected as the places for this experiment. On farm No. 14, one-fourth mile west of the headquarters, three loads were fed. On No. 3, one-fourth mile south, three loads were fed and on No. 16, one-half mile east, five loads were fed. Yards of as near the same size and with as near the same accommodations as possible were selected. The object of the experiment was to determine the value, if any, of feeding by-products and condimental foods for the production of beef, and it was planned to feed eleven lots of cattle. Lot 1, on corn alone, Lot 2 on corn and oil meal, Lot 3 on corn and cotton-seed meal, Lot 4 on corn and gluten meal, Lot 5 on corn and gluten feed, Lot 6 on corn and germ oil meal, Lot 7 on corn and dried blood, Lot 8 on corn and Iowa Stock Food, Lot 9 on corn and International Stock Food, Lot 10 on corn and Standard Stock Food, Lot 11 on corn and grass. The by-products and condimental foods were furnished by the following companies: Old process oil meal was used, furnished by the Midland Linseed Oil Co. of Minneapolis, Minn. The cottonseed meal by the American Cotton Oil Co., of Chicago. The gluten feed, gluten meal and germ oil meal were furnished by the Glucose Sugar Refining Co. of Chicago. The dried blood by Swift & Co. The Iowa Stock Food by the Iowa Stock Food Company of Jefferson, Iowa, and the International Stock Food by the International Stock Food Co. of Minneapolis, and the Standard Stock Food by the F. E. Sanborn Co. of Omaha. These products were all delivered free of charge at Odebolt. Mr. Cook furnished the cattle, yards, corn and roughage and they were fed under the direction of the experiment station or rather under the direction of the companies furnishing the food, that is as to the amount of grain and by-products or condimental foods their respective lots were to have. But they were all to have the same kind of corn and roughage. With this in view, 220 head of steers were selected from some 500 head which Mr. Cook had running in his stalkfields and on a light ration of snapped corn at the time. The steers were very common grades, Angus, Hereford and Short-horns, two years old. They were purchased by Mr. Cook from the Bartlett-Richards Cattle Co. in western Nebraska. The 220 head were divided as evenly as conditions would permit into eleven lots of twenty head each, each lot consisting of one Hereford, four Angus and fifteen Short-horns, or steers showing some evidence of such blood. This division was made two weeks before the experiment began and the cattle were placed in their respective yards. This was done that they might become accustomed to their yards and all be under practically the same conditions when the feeding started. On the tenth, eleventh, and twelfth of March, each lot was driven over the scales and an average of these three weighings was taken as the starting weight. The feeding started on the eleventh. All the grain feed that each lot had was carefully weighed, mixed and placed in labeled sacks at the elevator and hauled to the feed lots. It was the intention to start the cattle on corn and cob meal but owing to delay in getting the macinery necessary for crushing, the snapped corn feeding was continued until the thirtieth of March. On the twenty-first of March, a little shelled corn was added which was gradually increased until the twenty-seventh, when the feeding of corn and cob meal was begun. The first day's feed on March 11th was three hundred pounds of snapped corn to each lot in addition to five pounds of each of the various by-products and one pound of the various stock foods to their respective lots. On March 28th, the grain ration was two hundred pounds of shelled corn, one hundred pounds of snapped corn, 40 pounds of corn and cob meal to each lot, with 17 pounds of oil meal, cotton-seed meal, gluten meal, germ oil meal and dried blood were given to their respective lots. Twenty-four pounds of gluten feed was fed to lot 5 and the stock food lots were each receiving two pounds. The amount of shelled and snapped corn was gradually decreased and the corn and cob meal increased and on April 9th, each lot was receiving 450 pounds of corn and cob meal, lot 2, 38 pounds of oil meal; lot 3, 29 pounds of cottonseed; lot 4, 38 pounds of gluten meal; lot 5, 66 pounds of gluten feed; lot 6, 38 pounds of germ oil meal; lot 7, 20 pounds of dried blood; lot 8, 2½ pounds of Iowa Stock Food; lot 9, 2 pounds of International Stock Food, and lot 10, 2½ pounds of Standard Stock Food. The corn and cob meal did not give satisfactory results as it proved too binding a ration with nothing but wheat straw for roughage and on April 16th, coarsely ground meal was added to the ration. This was gradually increased until May 8th, when the corn and cob meal was all taken out and corn meal alone was fed from this in connection with the various by-products and condiments.

Each lot was now allowed all the grain it would readily clean up and they were eating from 460 to 480 pounds of corn meal, lot 2 having an additional 60 pounds of oil meal; lot 4, 60 pounds of gluten meal; lot 5, 70 pounds of gluten feed; lot 6, 60 pounds of germ oil meal; lot 7, 20 pounds of dried blood; lot 8, 2 pounds of Iowa Stock Food; lot 9, 2 pounds of International and lot 10, 3 pounds of Standard Stock Foods. The feeding continued in about this manner until the experiment closed, June 13th, when the various lots were eating from 480 to 520 pounds of corn meal, with lot 2 eating an addition of 80 pounds of oil meal; lot 4, 76 pounds of gluten meal; lot 5, 76 pounds of gluten feed; lot 6, 80 pounds of germ oil meal; lot 7, 20 pounds of dried blood; lot 8, 2 pounds of Iowa food; lot 9.2½ pounds of International and lot 10, 3½ pounds of Standard stock foods. The racks in each yard were kept well filled with wheat straw, some of which was not of extra good quality. The straw was never weighed but so far as I was able to see, there was practically no difference in the amount each lot consumed.

Lot 1 was fed on corn alone. As a rule they were always ready for their feed and had fairly good appetites to the end although they did not shed off quite as early or look as sleek as some of the other lots. They weighed at the beginning an average of 1,042 pounds and made a gain of 2.71 pounds per day, shrunk 55 pounds in shipping, sold for $7.45 and dressed 58.8 per cent. The cost of 100 pounds gain was $10.71. Net profit $14.49.

Lot 2 with a ration of corn and oil meal were the heaviest lot of all at the start, averaging 1,082 pounds. They gained 2.51 pounds per day at a cost of $11.02 per hundred pounds, they shrunk 54 pounds in shipping, sold for $7.50 and dressed 60.6 per cent. This lot fed nicely all along and were the first cattle to shed. They stood the feeding of corn and cob meal better than most of the others, and dressed out better than any of the others excepting lot 5, which just equalled them, $14.85.

Lot 3, on corn and cottonseed meal. After being on feed 42 days, these steers showed signs of sickness and three of them died. This made it necessary to drop this lot from the experiment. The cottonseed meal men claim this was not due to the cottonseed meal but the cattle were fed exactly the same kind of corn meal and wheat straw from the same stack as the other lots, none of which showed any signs of sickness. The average analysis of 35 samples of cottonseed meal as reported by Professor Henry in his work on "Feeds and Feeding" shows 8.2 per cent water, 7.2 per cent ash, 42.3 per cent protein, 5.6 per cent crude fiber, 23.6 per cent of nitrogen free extract and 13.1 per cent of ether extract, and the analysis of the meal which we were feeding, made by Dr. Weems, shows 9 per cent water, 7.4 per cent ash, 41.3 per cent protein, 7.8 per cent crude fiber, 18.9 per cent nitrogen free extract and 15.6 of ether extract. The cattle were feeding nicely and only eating 2½ pounds of cottonseed meal per head daily when the first symptoms of sickness appeared. They were making a gain of 2.38 pounds per day at a cost of $9.84 per hundred. During July and August while still at the Brookmont farms, I fed a bunch of yearling steers as high as seven pounds of cottonseed meal per day without bad results but they were only on this feed about forty days and they lacked a few pounds of making as good gains as a like lot on corn meal alone. My experience with cottonseed meal has therefore been quite unsatisfactory but I am not prepard to say that the cottonseed meal was or was not the cause of this trouble as it has been fed by others in larger quantities and for longer periods without bad results, and in many cases giving very satisfactory returns.

Lot 4, on corn and gluten meal, were a very even lot of cattle and took kindly to their feed from the start, averaging 1,075 pounds and making a gain of 2.92 pounds per day at a cost of $9.34, shrunk 62½ pounds in shipping, sold for $7.65 or five cents above any other lot, dressed 59.6 per cent. Net profit for steer $17.99.

Lot 5, on corn and gluten feed, were a little slow in taking hold of their feed at the start. They did not seem to like the gluten feed until they became accustomed to it, but during the latter part of the test they fed very satisfactorily. They weighed 1,025 pounds at the start, made an average gain of 2.88 pounds daily at a cost of $9.65 per hundred, shrunk 50 pounds in shipping, this being the lightest shrink on any lot.

They sold for $7.60 and dressed 60.6 per cent, equalling the oil meal lot in this respect. Net profit per steer $17.60.

Lot 6, on corn and germ oil meal, never took hold of their feed with the relish that the other lots did and were very slow feeders all through the test. They weighed 1,075 pounds average at the start, made an average gain of 2.32 pounds per day at a cost of $11.64 per hundred, shrunk 71 pounds in shipping, sold for $7.40 and dressed 60.3 per cent. Net $12.16

Lot 7, on corn and dried blood. The best feeding steer in the whole 220 head was in this lot and also some of the poorest feeders. At first they turned away from the dried blood when it was scattered over the snapped corn but later when mixed with corn meal they seemed to like it and ate it with a relish and were never off their feed. They weighed 1,062 pounds at the start, made a gain of 2.42 pounds daily at a cost of $11.08, shrunk 63 pounds in shipping, sold for $7.60 and dressed 59.5 per cent. $15.36.

Lot 8, on corn and Iowa Stock Food, weighed 1,015 pounds at the start, made a gain of 2.30 pounds per day at a cost of $10.51, shrunk 60 pounds in shipping and sold for $7.40. They were the lightest lot of cattle in the test but fed fairly well all through, dressing out 59.6 per cent. Net profit $13.89.

Lot 9, on corn and International Stock Food, fed very slow on the start but did better toward the close. They averaged 1,016 pounds, made an average gain of 1.97 pounds at at cost of $13.41, shrunk 72 pounds in shipping, sold for $7.20 and dressed 59.6 per cent. Net profit per steer, $6.33.

Lot 10, on corn and Standard Stock Food, weighed 1,030 pounds, made an average gain of 2.17 pounds per day at a cost of $11.95, shrunk 67 pounds in shipping, sold for $7.00, the lowest price of any lot and dressed 58.7 per cent. According to the instructions given by the company furnishing the Standard Stock Food, these cattle were fed but once daily, receiving the whole of their grain ration in the morning. Net profit, $5.52.

Lot 11, on corn and grass, average 1,053 pounds at the start, made a gain of 2.49 pounds per day at a cost of $10.20 per hundred, and as would be expected of grass cattle they shrunk 84 pounds in shipping, which was the heaviest shrink of any lot. They sold for $7.55 which was within ten cents of the top, dressing out 59.3 per cent. This lot was fed exactly the same as lot 1 until April 17th, when they were turned on a 24-acre pasture. The grass was very short at this time and they were still allowed access to straw. Net profit per steer, $14.97.

There was very little difference in the gains made by the hogs following the different lots. Twenty hogs were placed in each lot at the beginning and no extra feed was given them. At the end of eight weeks, when the cattle were being fed corn meal, half of the hogs were taken from each lot Those following the grass cattle made the best gains. This was perhaps largely due to the amount of feed they got from the grass. Careful check was kept on each lot while they were being shipped, also in the Union Stock Yards and until they were hanging in the coolers. They were purchased by Nelson Morris & Co. and they reported that lot 4 exhibited the best carcasses though there was very little difference in this respect.

Experiments to be of the greatest value must be several times repeated and as this work will be duplicated this year, we will wait for the results of the next test before coming to any definite conclusions as to what is the most economical grain ration for the production of beef.

AFTERNOON SESSION.

The committee reported as follows:

The committee on location wished to leave the matter of location to the president and secretary and it was so left.

Officers: W. F. Harriman, Hampton, president; E. H. White, Estherville, secretary; vice-presidents, First district, B. R. Vale, Bonaparte; Second, G. S. Forest, Miles; Third, W. H. Warburton, Independence; Fourth, A. W. Avery, Mason City; Fifth, G. H. Burge, Mt. Vernon; Sixth, A. Stuart, Newton; Seventh, C. F. Curtiss, Ames; Eighth, S. A. Converse, Cresco; Ninth, Harvey Johnson, Logan; Tenth, D. L. Howard, Jefferson; Eleventh, Peter Mouw, Orange City.

The committee on resolutions presented the following:

Resolved, That it is the sense of this institute that our laws should be so amended as to secure to the farmer and stock raiser better protection from the depredations of dogs, and we ask our representatives to use their best endeavors to secure the passage of a law which will impose a sufficient tax on dogs to reduce their numbers and to raise a fund sufficient to pay all damages caused to domestic animals by the depredations of dogs.

Resolved, That we approve the action of the commissioners of the Iowa-St. Louis Louisiana purchase exposition in their efforts to make a creditable showing for the state of Iowa, and hereby pledge them our support and will use all means at our command to assist in the carrying out of the same.

Resolved, That we favor a much larger appropriation by the legislature than has been made, in order that we make a showing in keeping with our position as compared with other states.

Resolved, That this association tender its thanks to the professors of the Iowa Agricultural College for their able and instructive addresses on this occasion. That we tender our thanks for and express our highest appreciation of the general work of the college and the efforts there put forth in the cause of live stock improvements.

Resolved, by the Iowa Improved Stock Breeders' Association, That we extend to the citizens of Newton our hearty thanks for their kind reception and express our high appreciation of the royal entertainment afforded the members of this association.

The conference committee's report defined a breeding animal as follows, and their report was adopted:

At one of the early sessions the question of what constitutes a breeding animal and the disputes that arise between buyer and seller was discussed quite fully. A committee was appointed consisting of Messrs. Frank Flynn of Des Moines, E. S. Donahey of Newton, Geo. S. Forest of Miles and H. D. Parsons of Newton, to draft and prepare a statement defining a breeding animal. This committee reported as follows:

"A bull 12 months old or over during the years of ordinary usefulness shall be considered a breeder when, not being allowed to run at large with the breeding herd, he will get with calf at least 70 per cent of all the regular breeding females he may serve during the breeding season. In cases of disagreement between buyer and seller a trial of six months shall be given a bull and during the period of such trial both parties must agree that the bull is receiving proper care, both as to fed, ration, water and exercise. Shall be kept isolated from the breeding herd except at such times as a cow is in heat. Such cow shall be left only until she has been properly served, then removed from the bull.

"A cow shall be considered a breeder; first, if she has at foot a calf that was carried full period of gestation (about 280 days) and (in the hands of the seller) not served by a bull since the date of birth of such calf. Second, a cow that has remained quiet for four full periods from the date of last service; provided that she has carried her last previous calf to full period of gestation (about 280 days) and that she has never been a habitual aborter, and that the last previous calf was not more than seven months old at time of last service.

"A heifer that has never produced a calf shall be considered a breeder, if after coming in heat regularly has not been served more than four times and has remained quiet for four full periods from date of last service."

This is a matter of considerable importance and we advise our readers, both breeders and farmers, to preserve this resolution, which was adopted by the association. It will serve as a guide in determining disputed questions in the future.

IS IT PROFITABLE TO KEEP SHEEP ON OUR IOWA FARMS?

A. J. Blakely, Grinnell, Iowa.

This is a very practical question. Keeping live stock, especially fine stock, may be done by some people to a limited extent, not chiefly for the money there is in it, but for the love of the beautiful animals, just as one keeps a flower garden. But the practical, money-loving American farmer who has many uses for his dollars will not long consent, and should not, to raise crops or keep any class of stock, which in his opinion does not yield a good profit.

Hon. J. B. Grinnell, who was the owner of several farms and a man of extensive observation, used to say he never knew a man who kept sheep and stuck to the business who did not make a success. That is more than he or anybody else could truthfully say of continuously raising and keeping cattle, hogs or horses. But the question is not whether everybody and at all times who keeps sheep here in Iowa succeeds in making good profits, but rather whether with good judgment and attention to business, keeping sheep is and probably will be profitable with our climate, rich soil and advanced prices of land.

Some people have claimed when land was only half or two-thirds as high as now that land was too high to keep sheep here. But men have continued to keep sheep in Iowa, and on the best and highest priced farms and to make money at the business. It may be still more profitable to keep sheep in the Dakotas and in Colorado and Montana, for it is well known that large fortunes have been made and are being made in some of those regions in keeping sheep on a large scale, where there are large wheat stubble fields and extensive ranges of free grass, better fortunes in fact than are made by the cattlemen in the same localities.

But if Iowa lands are too high for sheep raising, they are also too high for cattle and hogs, though cattle and hogs have ruled higher the past year than for thirty years. But fat sheep and lambs have also brought good prices, and are now fully as high as a year ago. Chicago quotations for January 9, 1903, show choice native wethers $4.75 to $5.00, choice native yearlings $5.00 to $5.25. Choice light native ewes $3.90 to $4.00. Heavy ewes $4.25 to $4.40. Choice lambs $5.80 to $6.00.

I think if we take a series of ten years together it will commonly be found that there is not much difference between the market price of fat sheep and fat cattle, if we compare all classes, wethers, fat ewes, yearlings and lambs, with steers, fat cows, heifers and calves. The fat cattle are now about $1.00 per hundred less than a year ago, still choice fat steers are now considerably higher than fat wethers and yearlings, but fat cows are about the same as fat ewes.

It has been proved at our experiment stations that as a general rule it requires about the same amount and quality of feed to grow and fatten a given number of pounds of sheep or mutton, as of cattle or beef. According to this rule ten sheep at two or two and one-half years old weighing 130 pounds each have eaten the same amount of feed as a steer or heifer of the same age and weight, 1,300 pounds.

Suppose now we compare ten choice two-year-old wethers, weight 1,300 pounds, with a choice two-year-old 1,300-pound steer. The steer would sell in Chicago for about $6.30 or about $82.00. The wethers for about $4.80 or about $62,00, or $20.00 less than the steer. But this difference of $20.00 is more than compensated by the twenty fleeces which the ten wethers have produced in the two years, which should weigh ten pounds each, or 200 pounds, and would now bring at home fully 20 cents per pound, or $40, making $20 in favor of the wethers. The quotations on wool January 1, 1903, are just about the same as in May, 1900, when I sold for 21 1-2 cents at my home my 400 fleeces of Delaine unwashed wool weighing ten to fourteen pounds each.

If we compare fat ewes with fat cows the wool is the profit of the sheep over the cows, while lambs bring nearly as much by the hundred as steers.

It is wonderful that the prices of fat sheep have been so well maintained, when the receipts of sheep the past year have been so heavy— more than 20 per cent more than in 1901.

Steers and hogs were so very high last summer that many of the sheepmen thought they were not making money fast enough and sold off their flocks and rushed around and brought stock steers at much higher prices than they were worth two or three months later. It is quite probable that if they had kept their sheep they would be better off next summer. The outlook for sheep and wool has not been so bright for many years. All reliable statistics show that the amount of wool on hand in the United States and in the world is much less than for many years. The annual consumption of wool by woolen mills has greatly increased the past three years. More than twice as much wool was used last year by the United States mills as six years previous, while we produce no more wool in this country than in 1893. The terrible seven years' drouth in Australia, formerly the largest wool producing country in the world, has greatly lessened the sheep and wool production there. The Argentine Republic, which produces more wool than the United States, has during the past few years changed the character and quality of her wool. Formerly keeping sheep wholly or mainly for wool only, their sheep were the smallest size merinos, but the very low price of wool a few years ago, and the European demand for mutton shipped in cold storage, induced the flock owners there to cross their ewes with the large coarse wool rams from England. They have now made two or three coarse wool crosses. They could not get the large, good-bodied Delaine rams, now raised to some extent in this country. The production of fine wool in the world being thus greatly diminished it must be and already is in great demand with higher prices. In fact all grades of wool are higher, the result of which will be that flock owners will hold on to their sheep this year and this will advance the price of mutton.

While the general rule holds that it takes about the same amount of feed to produce a thousand pounds of beef as a thousand pounds of mutton, it often happens that sheep can be kept on cheaper feed. Sheep eat a larger variety of plants or weeds than cattle and readily convert even noxious weeds into wool and mutton. The common ragweed, which some years grows thick and high in cattle pastures, is greatly relished by sheep. They eat it like clover. A few years ago I bought a forty acres which was thoroughly infested with cockleburs. Two years later none were to be found. The sheep exterminated them.

Turnip seed can be sown with oats or barley. The turnips make but little growth until after harvest, but in August and September sometimes make a large growth, which can be fed off by the sheep, and often proves to the sheep owner as valuable as the grain crop. The turnips cost only the seed.

Lord Bauff, prize Short-Horn Bull, owned by Geo. Ward, Hawarden, Iowa, and shown at the Iowa State Fair, 1902.

Rape also can be sown with the small grain, or in the cornfield the last time the corn is plowed and commonly yields an immense amount of best pasturage in the fall.

For a month during the hottest period of our drouth in the summer of 1901, with the thermometer many days in succession 100 degrees and over, my 500 Delaines were turned out of my shortened blue grass pastures and into my cornfields commencing at the time when the corn first silked out, where they thrived on the grass and weeds (which had got some start in the wet June) and on the lower leaves of the corn, doing the corn crop no injury, but rather helping it. When in the last of August the ears bent down to their reach I returned them to their pastures, which would have been very bare of feed had they been cropped by the sheep during the time they spent in the cornfields. If they had remained longer and pulled down some of the ears, there would have been little waste, for they shell off and eat what they pull down.

Sheep can be well fattened in less time than cattle. The 100-day fed steer is not finished; but sheep in very moderate condition can be well fattened in 100 days.

Another element of profit with sheep is the increased fertility which they give to the soil. No other stock equals them in this respect. Increased fertility means better crops.

While good sheep with good management are profitable on our best lands in Iowa, sheep with light fleeces or with poor mutton qualities will not pay anywhere, any more than the breeding, keeping and fattening of inferior scrub cattle, or keeping a dairy of twenty cows that produce no more butter and cheese than ten good cows well fed and well managed. Yet there are many such inferior flocks of sheep, many such poor herds of cattle and such dairies in Iowa. Nothing short of the use of better sires and better care and management will ever save such stockmen from poverty. If they don't reform they must sell out or be sold out and go out of Iowa hunting for cheaper lands, where they think it will pay to keep stock. They will find cheaper lands and poorer lands, but they will never succeed until they mend their ways.

I think the average weight of Iowa fleeces does not exceed six and one-half pounds. A single cross of native and medium and coarse wool ewes with a good Delaine ram will add two or three pounds to the weight of fleece, and greatly improve its quality and also improve the shape, constitution and fattening qualities. Great improvement in the carcass can also be made by the use of pure bred rams of the English breeds.

When these improvements are made, certainly no one will approximate the truth who asserts that sheep cannot be profitably kept on our best Iowa farms.

THE OUTLOOK FOR THE BREEDING OF PURE BRED SWINE.

O. W. Browning, Newton, Iowa.

Preliminary remarks are like a hog's head and ears—quite essential but we do not want any more of them than are necessary.

I feel honored in having my name on this program, but I realize that there are others here from a distance who are to speak this afternoon and I hope to present my subject in the shortest time possible and do it justice.

The immediate outlook for pure bred swine is like the Indian's sign of rain—clouds all round and pouring down in the middle. A strong demand for desirable stock at remunerative prices. But what of the future? The demand for breeding stock comes largely from the pork producer. Iowa is well adapted to producing pork. She is surrounded with the greatest pork producing territory in the world and with which we have excellent railway connections.

Hogs require for their best development plenty to eat and drink, some exercise and a comfortable place to sleep. Exercise is best secured in the pasture, where the hogs combines business with pleasure. Conditions in respect to pasture are getting better every day. Farms are being fenced hog tight throughout, so that every field can be used, if desired, as a hog pasture.

Corn is well called king of the field, but the king must have his queen and to modest blooming glorious clover may well be accorded this proud distinction; and when they are harmoniously united in the bonds of the balanced ration what marvelous results are produced!

There was a time when the $10 pig was largely in evidence. The past few years have seen the passing of the $10 pig and the $1,000 hog. Both served a good purpose in advertising improved stock. Twenty dollars for a pig and $100 for a hog are safe prices which represent value received on both sides of the deal.

There are those who speak lightly of pedigree, but the well informed buyer insists on having this much-abused article with the stock he buys. There is only one animal in my mind who can be said to carry the pedigree on his back and that is the thoroughbred razor back.

Comparing cost of beef and pork production we find the advantage of the hog quite in favor.

In experiments at Ames covering three years of time, with six breeds of swine and twenty-two different lots of hogs, it required on an average 4.23 pounds of dry matter to make one pound of gain. The highest amount required being 5.06 pounds and the lowest 3.19 pounds. With young cattle the amount of feed required to make one pound of increase ranged from 7.27 pounds to 20.54 pounds, the average being 9.70 pounds.

There is one item that must not be overlooked. It is the most important from a financial standpoint in the whole business. That item is printer's ink. Transportation and printer's ink are the greatest moving agents in this progressive age. In this respect Iowa is perhaps favored beyond any other state. In the way of farm papers Iowa stands in the foremost rank. Now a newspaper is a baited hook. The subject-matter is the bait, while the advertising matter is the hook. The value of a paper as an advertiser depends largely on the character of the bait. If it is wholesome and attractive we may expect the hook to do effective work. From this point of view Iowa papers are of the best. There is one feature I never like to see in a farm paper and that is the whisky advertisement.

Imagine, if you please, *Wallaces' Farmer* with Uncle Henry's Sunday school lesson on one page and on the opposite page a flaming advertisement of four full quarts of Rocky Mountain Rye for $3.20 put up expressly for family use (that would tickle the devil himself). That is not the Iowa idea, and Iowa's influence is so strong that it is not safe for even an Omaha farm paper to carry a whisky advertisement.

Now, to sum it all up, with the best facilities for producing good stock, a good market near at hand and the best of advertising mediums, surely the outlook for the breeding of pure bred swine in Iowa is bright.

BY-PRODUCTS.

J. J. Ferguson, Chicago, Ill.

In the ordinary work of the farm there is a wide difference today between the methods in vogue and those used even ten years ago. The application of mechanical skill and invention has led to the perfection of many labor-saving devices, which greatly reduce the cost of production of our staple farm products. These changes have come quickly, but naturally. Until within recent years the stockman was feeding practically the same foods that were fed by the breeders and feeders of the old country one hundred years ago. In the matter of foods, both human and animal, our people are extremely conservative and wisely so. They must first be shown that the new are superior to the old by actual experiment before they will make a change in this line. We have become quite accustomed to various health foods offered to a hungry public for human use. Perhaps the health food crank is the first to pave the way for innovations with human and animal food stuffs.

Two factors have been at work leading to the introduction and general use of new foods for our farm animals. The first of these was high priced land. The high priced land of the Middle West means high priced feed. The high priced foods of the farm in many cases have not met with a correspondingly high price for the finished meat stuffs into which they were converted in the form of beef, mutton or pork. This first factor creates a demand and the second factor in the near future will prove largely instrumental in supplying this demand.

In all our manufacturing concerns today the watchword is economy. Such a thing as waste is practically unknown in the modern factory. Nowhere is this more true than in the case of the modern packing house, which admits at one door the steer, the hog, or the fat wether and sends out from its loading platform every thing in the shape of finished meat products for which a demand has ever been created. In many cases the product has been made first and the demand has followed. For years we have been accustomed to the use of dried brewer's grains from various by-products resulting from the manufacture of different human cereal foods. Germany and France have been leaders in this kind of work, but it is only within the last five years that any large amount of attention has been directed towards the various by-products of the packing house as being suitable for use as animal foods. It is true that the various brands of ground bone have been used for poultry food for some time, but until recently nothing has been done in the way of converting blood and meat by-products into palatable foods.

Swift & Company were among the first to see the great future which lay in store for this line of production. At the present time they have a line of no less than eight standard products which are listed as animal food. These include two brands of tankage, two of blood meal, one of meat meal, two of bone and a combination feed made of meat and bone.

Prof. C. S. Plumb, late of the Indiana Experiment Station, now of the Ohio State University, was one of the first men to realize that much of the material going out from the packing house in the form of by-product might be economically utilized as animal food. His first work was done in feeding tankage to hogs, the results showed that a proper combination of this food with corn effected a saving of nearly 2 cents per pound in the cost of making a pound of pork. These results were a surprise not only to Professor Plumb, but to Swift & Company, who furnished the material for the experiment. Visitors to the first International exposition were much interested in Professor Plumb's "Tankage Hogs." Iowa Experiment Station was the next station to follow up this line of work. A carefully conducted experiment was outlined for the purpose of comparing tankage and other packing house by-products with corn as food for hogs. The results of these experiments have already been published in bulletin No. 65 of the Iowa station. On page 222 the following summary is made· "That a ration consisting of five parts corn and one part Swift's Tankage yield over 34 per cent greater net profits than a ration of corn alone."

These experiments were a revelation to the farmers and feeders of the country. The greatest problem before the feeder today is the question as to where he can find the cheapest source of protein. The corn plant is and must continue to be the foundation for successful feeding. Corn in the Middle West supplies fat and carbohydrates in large amounts at low cost, yet we find while corn contains a fair amount of protein, it is nowhere in proper proportion in relation to the constituents named. The farmer who is feeding only corn to his steers or hogs, literally, must have "corn to burn." For years it has been a difficult matter to know where protein could be obtained at such cost that the farmer could afford to sell some of his corn and buy a protein feed with which to properly balance the remainder. The results of experiments quoted have surprised the oldest practical feeders of many states and would seem to indicate that the solution lies ready at hand in the large output of by-products prepared in the packing house. Many men object to the use of animal foods in the shape of blood meal or tankage. We do not find this objection well founded in actual practice. Hogs will greedily eat all kinds of refuse coming fresh from the slaughter house. Many people have objected to the use of slaughter house fed animals,. owing to the danger of disease infection. Packing house foods are free from this objection. In their manufacture they are subject to such a high temperature that any germs which might cause trouble are destroyed. In the first place, every animal which goes into the packing house has passed a careful inspection by officers of the United States bureau of animal industry, so that the danger of infection is reduced to a minimum.

These foods are cheap, clean and highly concentrated. It is not necessary to handle a large bulk in order to get the food constituents required. We do not believe in tablet rations, but recommend a wise and carefully planned system of feeding, by which an animal will get plenty of bulky food and at the same time plenty of nutritive material. The

15

following table will give a better idea of the relation existing between some of these feeds and the ordinary feeds of the farm. These analyses are authentic:

FEED.	PER CENT PROTEIN	LBS. PRO-TEIN IN ONE TON.
Corn..	.08	168
Wheat Bran	.12	240
Oil-Meal (O'P)...	.29	580
Cottonseed Meal	.37	740
Swift's Digester Tankage.................................	.60	1,200
Swift's Blood Meal	.87	1,740
Swift's Soluble Blood Flour...............................	.87	1,740

One of the by-product foods mentioned above is likely to become of great interest and importance to practical dairymen. We refer to soluble blood flour. This preparation has been tried and proven to be an excellent food to develop rapid growth in young calves feeding on skimmed milk. Different stations have found that blood meal absolutely cures and prevents scours, which causes so much trouble with skim milk fed calves.

Digester Tankage is a food for hogs only. It is made from pure meat scraps thoroughly dried and carefully ground. Hogs eat it greedily and, as noted before, make large and satisfactory gains.

Meat Meal is a product of higher grade meat scraps dried and ground, and is meeting with a large demand from poultrymen who wish cheap winter eggs. Every practical poultryman knows that no food is a better egg stimulant than meat scraps fresh from the butcher shop. Such scraps cannot be stored except in refrigerators during hot weather, so are not available to many poultrymen. Many of our best breeders of pure bred swine are thoroughly alive to the fact that if they are going to develop bone in their breeding stock, they must make a radical change in the methods of breeding, feeding and treatment. It has been a practice in Great Britain and Germany for many years to feed swine especially early in life, liberal rations of ground bone. Ground bone contains a large amount of digestible protein from 20 to 25 per cent, and is rich in phos-phates, containing from .50 to 55 per cent. It will be readily seen that this material affords the swine breeder valuable help in overcoming the serious defect in this breed stock. In conclusion we would say that we believe that a great future is in store for the use of animal foods. We believe that it is a matter of only a few years until every available material from our great packing house will be converted into palatable and nutritive foods for the growth and maintenance of farm live stock.

LEGUMES IN IOWA.

James Atkinson, Des Moines, Iowa.

A study of the principal crops grown in the state of Iowa will reveal the fact that most of them are non-nitrogenous in their nature, that is, they are lacking in those elements and compounds that are required for flesh production. We can grow abundant fattening foods, and if such were the case that we had only mature animals to feed there would be little need for anxiety on the part of feeders to introduce other foods, for the reason that no crops gives so many pounds of nutrients per acre as the corn crop if this crop is properly cared for. But the majority of our peo. ple whether engaged in fitting animals for the block or the raising of pure breds, are obliged to rear their own animals and because of this there arises the necessity of growing crops that furnish a large propor. tion of protein or flesh forming substances. In supplying these it may be said that one class or family of plants stands alone because of one characteristic which it possesses this being the large proportion of nitro-gen in the form of protein which legumes contain. While we value the legumes because of their high feeding value it is of great importance incidentally that these plants are not soil robbers in the sense that this term could be applied to such crops as corn, oats, barley, wheat, timothy and rye. However, because legumes enjoy the power of extracting nitro-gen from the air and storing it up in the soil it must not be presumed that these crops will increase the fertility supply unless they are fed on the farm and the manure returned to the soil. In other words, a legume crop will take more nitrogen out of the soil than it will extract from the air and store in the roots. But if the whole crop is fed the soil is benefited to the extent which nitrogen is taken from the air and stored in the roots.

At the present time our most important legume is red clover. It is an important crop because of its great feeding value, containing, as it does, a higher proportion of protein than is found in any of our cereals, while at the same time it is well adapted to the condtions of the entire state. In spite of its adaptability, however, there are those who experi-ence great difficulty in obtaining a stand, while, on the other hand, there are those who seldom fail when they attempt to give it a place in the rotation. Because of this it might be well to consider a few of the most important points that are to be observed in getting a stand.

In the first place we will say that it is seldom practicable to seed in the fall, there being too much danger that the young clover plants will be killed during the winter or early in the spring. Wherever winter wheat is grown this furnishes one of the best nurse crops with which to establish clover. However, as there is but a small area of winter wheat in the state, we might almost pass this subject over, although it may be said that when seeded in this way clover should be sown just as early as possible in the spring and afterwards thoroughly .harrowed in. Three good harrowings will not only cover the clover seed so as to induce a uniform stand, but it will also do the wheat good by the breaking up of the crust and the formation of a surface mulch.

As a nurse crop we place barley next to winter wheat, the variety known as Success being specially adapted to the purpose of establishing clover. This is due to the fact that it grows light in the straw and matures very early. The soil in this case should be thoroughly prepared on the surface, and it will always be found to be advantageous if the soil is plowed in the fall where it is the intention to sow clover in the spring. As a rule too little attention is given to covering the seed properly. One of the best methods which has been called to my attention is that of sow-ing the clover seed after the surface soil has been thoroughly prepared and afterwards sowing the grain by the use of the disc press drill. In this way the clover seed is covered by the soil that is turned back by the disc, and more than this, the young plants make their appearance between the rows of grain. Where a drill is not available if the soil is properly prepared it will seldom do any harm to disc in the seed.

Early, oats may be used as a nurse crop and while this crop tends to dry out the soil to a greater extent than wheat or barley; yet it often happens that it may be cut even earlier than the other crops. If oats are to be fed to farm animals it does no harm to cut them before they are thoroughly ripened, the early taking off of the crop being of great advantage to the young clover.

After getting a stand the only precaution that should be taken the first year is not to allow the clover to make too much top and also not to pasture it too bare. A certain amount of top affords a much needed protection to the root, while too much top is liable to smother the crop. No mistake is more common than that of pasturing first crop clover too closely.

In the past the farmers of Iowa have had but little success with alfalfa, and even at the present time there are few who take much stock in this crop. However, it must be conceded that considerable has been added to our knowledge as to how this crop should be handled during the last year or two. We have generally been under the impression that it was adapted to light soils in the semi-arid region, but such is not the case. We have in mind a number of fields of alfalfa that are producing their three or four cuttings a year on soil that is comparatively stiff in texture. In fact it has been found that soils with a clay subsoil are especially adapted to the production of alfalfa, the matter of chief im-portance being good drainage. In the past our soils have not been inocu-lated with the organism that enables this crop to extract nitrogen from the atmosphere, and because of this the plant in the majority of cases have not grown strong, generally resulting in a diseased condition. It now seems to be practicable to introduce a little soil from fields where alfalfa has been successfully grown, this being sufficient to entirely change the character of the plant. In many instances all that is neces-sary to do is to scatter a few hundred pounds of this soil on the upland, the organisms being spread from this to the lower land by the surface water.

Alfalfa should be sown in the spring as early as possible, on fall plowing that has been well worked on the surface in the spring, and it should be sown without a nurse crop. The seed should be sown at the rate of twenty pounds per acre, and so much the better if a drill is used in the seeding, in which case half this amount of seed should be sown in one direction and half in the opposite direction. In all probability the crop will require cutting back two or three times during the first season in order to destroy the weed growth. This, however, does not seem to injure the alfalfa, but, on the other hand, seems to strengthen it by bringing about greater root development. It seldom happens that a crop can be secured the first year. When once established it is usually possible to obtain from two to four cuttings annually even in times of drouth, this being due to the fact that the roots penetrate the lower soil and subsoil where there is always a supply of moisture. It must be kept in mind that alfalfa is primarily a hay crop and should seldom, if ever, be used as a pasture. It is true that there is little danger in pasturing hogs and horses, but ruminants are so liable to bloat that the losses generally make the pasture too costly. The hay is exceedingly rich in flesh forming material, and is in itself almost a balanced ration. We have in mind a few farmers living in the state of Kansas who have been successful in fattening steers on alfalfa hay alone.

A list of clovers would not be complete unless it included the mammoth and alsike. These, however, are crops of less importance than those mentioned. The alsike is primarily adapted to lands that are not thoroughly drained. It furnishes a good quality of pasture and hay, but on upland where the drainage is good the yield per acre is not large enough to justify seeding it in any considerable area. However, it has considerable value when sown in mixed pastures. Mammoth clover matures much later than the common red and grows considerably coarser, although it makes a large yield per acre. Under Iowa conditions the red clover will be found to give better satisfaction than the mammoth.

There are two other legumes that are coming into prominence somewhat slowly in the state of Iowa, although there is no question in my mind but what they will finally take a prominent place in our rotations. I refer to the soy bean and cow pea. These crops are drouth resisting in character and produce grain that is exceedingly rich in flesh forming material, the beans containing about the same percentage of protein as our rich concentrated meals. When varieties are developed that are adapted to the conditions of the state it will be found that protein can be grown in this form more cheaply than it can be purchased in the form of our rich meals, and if this can be done there is no reason why farmers of Iowa should not undertake the growing of these crops to be fed in conjunction with corn, which is our best fat-producing food. At the Iowa Experiment Station a yield of thirty bushels per acre of soy beans has been obtained, this being equivalent in feed value, so far as protein is concerned, to 110 bushels of corn.

A number of methods may be employed in putting in these crops. In Kansas they are usually planted about as far apart in the row as corn, the seed being dropped so that the plants are two or three inches apart in the row. However, my experience has been that on our soil it is practicable to put the rows just half this distance apart. This may be done by adjusting the corn planter to drill, and driving the planter every second time across the fields so that the tongue is over one of the planted rows. When crops are put in in this manner they generally require a little attention by way of cultivation, this being given with a one-horse cultivator. These crops may be cut with the mower and threshed with an ordinary threshing machine after removing the concave and a number of the cylinder teeth. It is true that the labor involved in handling these crops is somewhat different to that which we are accustomed, but when it becomes apparent that it is to our advantage to take up these new lines of production there can be little doubt but what the necessary change will be made.

THE FARMER AND THE STATE FAIR.

H. C. Wallace, Des Moines, Iowa.

The great annual festival known as the state fair should enable the observant visitor to determine with considerable accuracy both the character of the people and of the principal industries of the state in which it is held. Originally it was probably a sort of "harvest home" festival, or rather the outgrowth of such festivals of the earlier time, where folks from different parts of the state could get together, renew old acquaintances and make new ones, enjoy a few days away from home cares and the daily grind, meet other people and absorb from them new ideas, and in general to enjoy themselves. To make such a festival attractive, entertainments of various sorts were provided. To add a personal interest premiums were offered for excellence in the arts and industries. Wherever the buying public congregates in numbers the man who has goods to sell takes advantage of the opportunity to make a display of his wares, and this feature soon lent interest to the state fair. As the population of a state increases, the state fair evolves, if it evolves at all, from a sort of basket dinner, harvest home, horse-trot and big pumpkin show, where everybody knows everybody else and calls him by his first name, to one of the greatest educational institutions of the state and a place where in a few days' time the stranger can get a better idea of the real character of the people of the state, and of its material resources than in many weeks spent in traveling through it.

It cannot be said that the visitor at our Iowa state fair, even if he puts in all of the time conscientiously, can get as broad an idea of the resources of the state as they warrant. He has, for example, very little opportunity of learning of our mineral resources, our pearl button industry, our shipbuilding, and many of the great manufacturing industries. But the man who attends this fair and goes away without being thoroughly impressed with Iowa's greatness as an agricultural and live stock state, and with the superior intelligence and orderliness of her people, has used his eyes and ears to little purpose.

As the Iowa state fair each year is considered, whether he wills it or not, a sort of weather vane which indicates which way the wind is blowing for the farmer, the latter is vitally interested in the fair. He wishes to attend it, to take a part or all of his family, to send his boys. He has a right to ask and to expect that it be clean, wholesome, instructive, so that when they return home they will have a feeling that the time and money was well spent. He has a right to expect that the fair will solicit his attendance and that of his family with clean hands; that it will not expose them to unwholesome temptations; that its influence will be instructive and calculated to teach things they ought to know; that due provision will be made for their comfort; and that the young people especially will not be lead into acquiring information and habits which they should not acquire.

While the farmer has a right to expect all this, he sometimes forgets the old maxim that "a stream cannot rise higher than its source," and that the Iowa state fair has its source on the farm. If it falls short of what it would be, the farmer himself and he alone is to blame for it. It is to be remembered that this annual fair is an institution of the state. While it is recognized as belonging largely to the agriculture of the state and its control is therefore delegated to a representative body supposed to be elected largely by the farmers, nevertheless the state itself as a state stands back of it. An admission is charged, and the fair is expected to largely pay its own way; but as its mission is to foster and encourage industries and to afford object lessons which cannot be seen anywhere else, the obligation of the state to stand behind it financially is never ignored by the legislature when properly appealed to. If, therefore, the Iowa state fair fails to be what it should be, if it falls short of what the farmer has a right to expect of it, the farmer himself is mainly to blame.

Whatever may be its shortcomings, at the present time, it may fairly be said that the Iowa state fair compares favorably with those of other western states. The fairs of Illinois and Minnesota may be said to excel it in some respects, mainly in the provisions which have been made for housing the people and enabling them to see the exhibits to advantage, and the superior advantages they have—one because of its being an older state, and the other because of its location between two great rival cities —to draw a larger attendance. But considered from every standpoint of what a fair should be, the Iowa state fair measures up well. And it should. As an agricultural fair it should excel them all. It is located in the center of the best all around agricultural state in the union. The grounds are of great natural beauty, and well adapted to the purpose. The railroad facilities for reaching the city at which the fair is held are excellent; and it comes at a season of the year when the weather is favorable and when the farmer can leave home for a few days with very little disarrangement of the farm work.

During the past two or three years the fair has been vastly improved There is room for still greater improvement. Until last year the farmer who wished to even see, let alone get an intelligent idea of the cattle and horse exhibits was compelled to stand around in the sun and struggle for a place at the show ring, elbowing his neighbor, crowding the cattle and giving the judges barely sufficient room to work. Last year the new live stock pavilion was built, with seating capacity for a large number of people and a roomy ring for a show ring. One fair has demonstrated not only how much this pavilion was needed, but how badly at least two more are needed, one for horses and another for the hogs and sheep. I am informed that the plans for one of these are already under way and that no doubt the other will come soon.

With these pavilions but one more improvement will be needed to enable visitors to derive the full educational benefit from the live stock exhibit; a complete catalogue of this exhibit, giving name, breeding, age, weight and owner of each animal, and placards both at the stall and show ring to enable the spectator to identify the animal. I understand the management contemplates the issuance of such a catalogue at the coming fair.

An equally urgent need is for a similar building for the agricultural products, suitably arranged, well lighted and conveniently located where people cannot get past it, instead of being compelled to hunt it up. A comparison of the exhibits of grain, grasses, fruits, etc., at the Iowa and Illinois state fairs is not favorable to Iowa; and while the fact that the Iowa fair is held a month earlier accounts in a measure for this, most of it is due to the inadequate facilities for suitably displaying the exhibit. Agriculture at the Iowa state fair should obtrude itself.

More large, covered buildings are needed to protect the visitors from the inclement weather, and a thorough system of paved streets, walks, etc. Such thorough provision should be made for the comfort of the visitor that he will attend the fair rain or shine, and not be governed by the condition of the sky at 3 o'clock in the morning of the day he expects to start. I speak of these things not by way of unkind criticism, but to bring them to the attention of the farmer as part of the job that belongs to him in the work of making the Iowa state fair what it ought to be.

The fair is governed by the state board of agriculture elected by delegates from the county fair societies and from the county farmers' institutes. This board is made up of members elected from the congressional districts, a part being elected at each annual meeting. It is therefore a board that should be close to the farmer; and if it is not, it is the farmer's fault.

Many of the troubles of the fair in the past have been due to the failure of the farmer, and of the breeder, to recognize his responsibility to it. The right to criticize, after the fair is over, has been exercised a good deal more freely than the right to take part in its government before the fair is held. The right to kick because something has not been done is exercised oftener than the right to help do it. For example, for two or three years both farmers and breeders complained bitterly of the inadequate facilities for showing cattle and horses, and yet I believe I can count on the fingers of one hand if not on my thumbs the number of farmers and breeders, aside from members of the legislature and of the board, who personally lent a helping hand to get the new pavilion from the legislature.

To make such a fair as the state of Iowa ought to have, all agricultural influences in the state must pull together. The farmer and the

breeder must see to it that strong men are sent from the county fair associations and from the institutes, as delegates to the annual convention of
the state board of agriculture. And when these men elect the board,
everyone must stand ready to help, loyally and effectively, to secure improvements and everything else that is needed. The present board and
secretary have done excellent work for the fair. Let the farmers and
breeders hold up their hands and they will do still better in the future

Courtesy Wallaces' Farmer.
An Iowa State Fair Winner, 1902.

PART VI.

FARM CROPS AND LIVE STOCK.

A. THE SILO.

THE SILO AND THE BENEFITS TO BE DERIVED FROM THE USE OF SILAGE.

Alson Secor, Forest City. Iowa.

The silo is the most economical building a farmer on high priced land can build. It has long been regarded as a luxury for the well-to-do dairyman, but in reality it is the poor man's necessity. If the "well off" dairyman cannot afford to be without the silo, how much less can the man of small means. The silo is no fad or new fangled thing. It is true that very few farmers have one, many never saw one, and no small number ever heard of such a thing. The original method of construction made them so costly that few could afford a silo. That is not so now since the introduction of the stave silo. Most anyone can afford a silo just as well as he can a corn crib and granary. By its use he can soon save enough to pay for it. Wherever a good silo goes up it stays up. No one has reported having had a good silo and discontinued its use because it was unprofitable. In most cases the number of silos on the farm keeps increasing. This speaks volumes.

What benefits are to be derived from their use?

I. The silo saves the whole crop of whatever goes into it. There is a small percentage of loss but it is not so great as from the use of any other method of preserving crops. It is well known that in saving corn fodder there is a considerable loss because the dry leaves break off and blow away; the fodder spoils more or less in the shock; the cattle do not eat all the stalk; and if shreded there is liability of further loss in the stack unless the day of shredding was just right.

Take the clover, pea or bean crops generally made into hay. There is a loss of the best part (the leaves) in curing, with great possibility of loss in the stack from bad weather, spontaneous combustion, mould, mice and worms. Loss in feeding for stock do not like to eat the coarse stems. Put these crops in the silo and everything is saved regardless of weather and everything is eaten by every kind of animal.

2. The silo contains more feed in a given space than any other receptacle. It is evident that five acres of corn put into a silo wet will occupy less space than the same area stacked dry.

3. It utilizes waste products. This year, because of excessive rainfall, the cornfields became very weedy. Cut the corn with a binder and the weeds go into the shock, but they are not eaten. Pasture the cornfield and the weeds are not eaten. Cut corn and weeds with binder and run the whole thing into the silo and every weed is consumed. The fields of soft corn this year have been a burden to many farmers. It has kept them very much puzzled to know what to do with the crop. It spoils in the shock; will not keep in the crib. They must feed it a load at a time which means some winter corn picking. The man with a silo can save it and rest easy.

4. Silage produces better results than the same product fed dry. The agricultural chemist says there is no difference in the feeding value of silage and fodder. The highest authority (the animal that eats it) says there is a difference in favor of silage. The silage fed animals show by their sleek coats a better thrift. Silage makes cows give more milk, and makes the steer fatten cheaper than on dry feed.

5. The silo makes the farmer more independent of weather conditions than any other method of saving a crop. Weather is the whole thing in harvesting clover for hay, corn for fodder, or in shredding it. Weather cuts quite a figure with these feeds after the harvest is over. Silage can be made in the rain. Weather does not affect it after it is in the silo. It is easier and more agreeable to go into the silo and get feed when the weather is bad than go out and chop shocks out of the snow, or open a stack in the rain.

6. It is the cheapest kind of harvest, and the cheapest kind of feed. The cost of feed is the cost of production plus the cost of harvest, plus the value of the loss and waste. The cost is about the same whether you make clover into hay or silage. The work of curing and harvesting will about offset the work of running through the cutter. However, the loss in the silo is not equal to the loss in the stack. Up to harvesting, the cost is the same whether the corn is to be siloed or otherwise saved. There is a saving of time in cutting for the silo, for the binder can work when the dew is on or before, during or after a rain, and nothing spoils, while the corn must be dry if cutting for the shock, and consequently the binder cannot put in full time. The silo takes the corn off the field and you are ready for manuring and plowing. No shocking, no husking, no stacking, no swearing over corn stalks in the manure.

7. The silo adds to the acreage of the farm without buying more land, and adds to the stock capacity of the same. Anything that will present a man with a few acres of high-priced land is worthy of some consideration. The silo reduces pasture acreage and gives that to the tillable portion of the farm. It can supplement pasture feed all summer long, and more cows can be kept on less land. The same is true in reducing the meadow acreage. An acre of corn makes more feed than an acre of pasture or meadow.

Joseph E. Gould told the Ontario dairymen that "It does not pay to keep cows walking up and down the field looking for pasture, and tramping it down at the same time. I can supply feed at less cost in other ways. Silage is the basis of my feeding. I have only twelve acres of pasture on the whole place (110 acres). I consider it much cheaper to grow corn for feeding than to have cows wandering about the pasture field. I have thirty-one cows and fed silage 351 days last year." Any dairyman with silos can tell the same story.

Does the dairyman get a silo because he is rich, or does the silo make him rich?

I have made no effort to go into detailed description of the silo, or give the capacity, cost of construction or filling. The cost will vary with local conditions and any one interested will get books on the subject. There are many methods of construction and destruction, use and abuse, all of which the authorities will tell you. All I care to say is, if you build, build right. Don't be reckless or penurious.

The silo has been a blessing to many a man; it will be the same to you, whether you are dairyman or stockman, whether you raise cattle, sheep, hogs or poultry.

SILO EXPERIENCE.

F. D. Pierce in Wallaces' Farmer.

In 1887 I commenced farming in Iowa. My first purchase was 240 acres of land within a short distance of town. In 1890 I bought another 250-acre farm adjoining the first. From the first I realized that one of the chief problems for the Iowa farm to solve was how to get the most out of the corn crop. It was evident to me that to leave the large amount of animal food contained in the stalks of the corn in the field to bleach and wither was a great waste and one no up-to-date farmer would permit. Consequently I began to try the different methods then in vogue of utilizing this part of the corn plant, and of all those methods none of them were satisfactory until I came to the silo.

The great drouth of 1894 was what finally brought me to the point of building my first silo. I had a large stock, among them some forty cows from which I was making butter to supply a trade in town, and how to get them through the winter without considerably augmenting the amount of feed then growing upon the farm I did not know unless a silo would help me out. Consequently I ordered a No. 16 Smalley ensilage cutter after having disposed of an old one I had been using for cutting dry fodder, and set the carpenters to work to build by first silo. This was a box 16 feet square in one side of my basement barn extending from the ground to the roof, a height of 30 feet. I had barely commenced work when I was called to the Pacific coast by the illness of a daughter and did not return until the box was finished ready for filling. The workmen did a pretty good job but failed to use timber and nails enough to make the walls capable of resisting the great pressure brought against them when the silo was filled, so I have had some trouble from the walls bulging. The cost of correcting this mistake, however, was not great, and in every respect the silo was a success. The inside construction was originally of two thicknesses of shiplap with resin paper between. Year before last this was supplemented with another thickness of shiplap with paper behind it. In each corner a 12-inch plank beveled to fit runs from top to bottom and cuts off that much of the angle. The doors are arranged one above another with a distance of some three feet between opening into a chute which permits the silage when thrown from any of the doors to fall in the alley way in front of my cattle. The result of that year's filling was so satisfactory that during the summer of 1895 I built two others on the same plan in my barn on the other place with the exception that as the barn had no basement these silos were but twenty feet deep. Experience soon showed that the depth was not sufficient to give the best results. While we were able to make pretty good silage even in these shallow silos the silage was so much better and loss so much less from spoiling in the deeper one at the other place that a year ago I excavated to a depth of 7 feet in the bottom of these silos and built a wall of stone and cement below the sills. This had the desired effect, as the silage from last year's filling was vastly better than ever before. These three wooden silos, constructed at a comparatively small cost, are giving very good satisfaction, and others like them I have no doubt will give like satisfaction where, for any reason, a farmer does not care to use the money to build better ones. I believe, however, that the round silo is the best, and last season built one of this description 30 feet in depth and 17 feet inside diameter. This silo is located outside of a shed fitted with mangers for feeding young cattle and opens into the alley in front of these mangers. The shed is part basement, having a 5-foot wall on the side next to the silo. The lower 10 feet of this silo is built of stone and cement, 9 feet of it below the surface of the ground with the bottom of the silo about 5 feet below the floor of the feeding alley. Above the 10 feet of stone work is a frame of 20-foot 2x4 studding 12 inches from center to center, lined inside and out with thin lumber made by resawing No. 1 fencing. Outside of this is a layer of paper and a covering of common house siding. Inside this woodwork is a lining of brick and cement about 5 inches thick, the inner surface flush with the inside of the stone work below and whitewashed inside with cement. The capacity of these four silos is about 450 tons and it requires about forty-five acres of average corn to fill them.

Up to last year I had run my cutter with an old ten-horse sweep power of which I owned a fifth interest, using five horses. But on account of the greater amount of work to do I last year discarded this power and bought a ten-horse power gasoline engine, and this year I have laid aside my old cutter to be disposed of and have secured a new No. 20 machine.

As to the advantage of siloing corn over any other method of saving the crop I think there is no question. Experiments have shown that a much larger percentage of the crop can be saved than by **any** other method and its value is still further enhanced by the succulent condition in which it is placed before the animal consumes it. With dairy cows, of which we keep between fifty and sixty, we know of nothing that will take its place. With it the flow of milk is larger, the cows' coats are better, they shed earlier and come out in better condition in the spring than with any other food we have ever used. Nor are results any more favorable with cows than with young stock. We begin to feed it to our calves as soon as they will eat, and that is as soon, if not a little sooner, than they will eat any other kind of roughage, and we continue to feed it to them until they are sold or our supply runs out. Last winter we carried through something like fifty head very largely on ensilage and we never had young cattle do as well without feeding much more grain than this bunch received. Aside from these advantages there is the fact that when a field of corn is once in the silo there is nothing else to be done with it but to shovel it out to the cattle, a much easier and pleasanter task than placing the crop before them in any other form. Then, to, the field is cleared early in the season and can be plowed and sown to any other grain or any other thing done with it that one desires.

As to the cost of siloing as compared with other methods of harvesting the crop the difference is not so great as one would think. With seven men and eleven horses we can put up from six to eight acres per day, which is about as fast as it can be harvested in any other way. With a smaller machine than ours less help would be required and a correspondingly smaller amount of work can be done. We keep a man in the silo to spread and tramp the corn (which, by the way, we find very essential), and one man to feed the machine, a man in the field with the corn harvester and as many teams and wagons, with one man to a team, as is necessary to keep the machine going. We use low truck wagons with the bed of a hayrack, and the man handling the team can pile on as much as the team will haul without anyone to load. We think we save money by binding the corn instead of handling it loose. The man with the team, by keeping a knife in his hand while unloading, can cut the band as he throws the bundle to the feeder, so that no band cutter is required. It took us some time to learn all these things, but now that we have them learned the process is much more simple and much cheaper than when we first began.

From my eight years' experience with silos I have no hesitancy in recommending them to others. I do not believe a farmer can make a better investment than to build one or more silos, according to the size of his farm ,and procure either alone or with one or two of his neighbors the necessary machinery to fill them. If one has neighbors with whom he can work harmoniously the partnership plan has many advantages and will be found satisfactory, I think, in most cases. As to the kind of a silo to build, it depends, I should say, somewhat upon circumstances. If the means are not available, or cannot be reasonably secured, to build one that will last for a long term of years practically without repairs, then build a cheaper one. The less expensive silo will give good results for some time and will do much towards putting the farmer in shape to build a better one when this is gone. Where one has means I believe the better silo is the thing, such a one, for instance, as the round one I built last season. In this there is no wood work to come in contact with the moist silage except the doors and inner edges of the door frames. Consequently if the outside is kept painted it will last almost indefinitely. It seems to me that the time has come in all our buildings when we ought to build not only for the present but for the future—for those who will come after us. I do not believe one can leave a better inheritance to his children than a well built silo. This is my word on the silo, and if any reader of the *Farmer* gathers anything from it that is of value to him my purpose will have been accomplished.

SILAGE AS A FEED FOR THE DAIRY COW.

S. Remington in Kansas Farmer.

Silage may be fed with advantage to all classes of farm animals, such as milk cows, horses, steers, mules, sheep, hogs and even poultry.

The feeding of silage can be traced back for centuries. The semi-barbaric people in different parts of the world have known and practiced this method of feeding. They buried their feed in underground pits to save it for the future and to save it from their enemies.

Silage should not be fed as an exclusive coarse feed to the farm animals but should be mixed and fed with some other roughage, such as hay, straw, etc., and should not be fed more than twenty-five or thirty pounds per head daily where the keeping quality of milk is an important consideration. In feeding the dairy cow, always feed after milking as the peculiar silage odor will be apt to affect the flavor of the milk.

Silage exerts a very beneficial influence on the secretion of milk. Where winter dairying is practiced cows will usually drop considerably in the flow of milk toward spring if fed on dry feed and cause a loss of milk during the whole lactation period. Where silage is fed there will be no decrease in the flow of milk before turning out to pasture in the spring, and the cows will be able to keep up the flow of milk until late in the summer or fall when they are dried up before calving.

Silage has the same effect as green fodder or pasture. A failure in feeding silage to cows comes from its being improperly prepared or fed in a poor manner to cows that are confined to the one feed.

There is good evidence at hand showing that where good silage is fed in moderate quantities it will produce an excellent quality of milk and butter. According to the butter experts, silage not only in no way injures the quality of the butter but better flavored butter is produced by judicious feeding of silage than can be made from dry feed.

The combination in which corn silage will be used in feeding milk cows will depend a great deal on the local conditions. It should be fed with a fair proportion of nitrogenous feeds, such as wheat bran, ground oats, corn cob meal and clover hay. Silage furnishes a uniform quality to be had during any time of the whole year, hence it is succulent food, it is nature's food, and aids the digestion and the general health of the animal.

CLOVER SILAGE EXPERIENCE.

Alson Secor in Wallaces' Farmer.

Perhaps the inquirer for silo experience that is not full of boast may be enlightened a little by my experience with clover. The mistakes of the first year are very impressive and may be a good lesson for others. I bought a factory stave silo—Philadelphia patent—12x24 with the intention of putting clover in for summer feed but the silo did not arrive in time so I made hay of the first crop. Had but little corn and the dry weather made that too valuable to put in silo so I run second crop of clover in.

It was past middle of September when I went to work. Got a corn shredder with blow stacker run by steam engine, but the shredder was not made for green stuff and the stacker clogged unless the machine was fed slowly. Got nicely started when the fall rains set in and almost every ton was soaked. The second day the rain stopped the machine and I quit using it. The silo was then two-thirds full. It rained so that nothing could be done until the eighth day after the machine left, when three of us picked up what was already cut in the field. The silo is in the corner of hay barn, two feet in the ground. We pitched the green clover uncut into the hay mow then over into the silo, one person inside to pack it. We filled within about five feet of top. Some of the last was almost as dry as hay. Some are frostbitten.

Other things prevented further work although I had enough clover left to fill it. The silo was left just as it was when we quit hauling. It should have been wet, weighted and sown with oats, but it wasn't. When it quit settling it was about 16 feet full. You see there wasn't enough weight there. It should have been refilled until it couldn't settle any more. Being the first and only one around here to use a silo, it was the wonder of the people. Very few knew what a silo was. Had plenty of visitors during the filling. Nearly everybody ventured to say it would burn up. They thought I was a fit subject for the asylum when I continned to run in green clover wet with rain. It did get hot, of course, and cooked the clover. It could be smelled for a long distance until cold weather came. Visitors continued to come to see it, but I did not open it until the first part of January. About three feet of spoiled silage was on top. It had dried out too much and being loose the air penetrated quite deep. Had I begun feeding earlier it would have been better. But I had reasons for waiting. I wanted to test the silage and was letting my cows go dry so as to see its effect.

They had had no grain since last winter, and nothing but clover hay this winter. In fact, I had begun feeding hay in July, so they were on dry feed six months before I opened the silo. They were going dry very fast. They were as constipated as horses. They had no relish for hay any longer. When I put silo before them they went at it greedily. Fed moderately at first of course, but the second week they were getting all they could eat twice a day, morning and night, with hay at noon. I tried everything with it and all animals went at it without having to learn to like it. The silage was sweet and nice. It made me hungry for a mess of greens to smell it. The brood sows get two feeds of silage and one of corn and the fat hogs get two of silage and three of corn. They will leave corn any time for silage. As a hog feed it has saved quite a corn bill this winter—and I believe it is better for them to have both.

In a few days the cows looked better and their bowels were more laxative. They increased on flow of milk as the three following examples will show: First cow, a heifer milked six months: During the five weeks before feeding clover silage this heifer gave a weekly flow of milk of 66.3, 77.8, 72.3, 71.7 and 67.2 pounds respectively. For the first five weeks on clover silage her milk record was 74, 76.5, 77.1, 79.1 and 84.3 pounds for each respective week. Second, an old cow milked five months, weekly record before feeding silage, 85, 87.4, 81.7, 83.2 and 79.5 pounds. Record after feeding silage, 86.3, 84.7, 84.3, 89.3 and 95.6 pounds for each succeeding week. Third, an old cow fresh four weeks before feeding silage. Record for these four weeks in their order 138.6 (bred tis week), 117.7, 95.91 (bred again), and 97.9 pounds. For the five weeks following the weekly milk record is 112.3, 118.9 (bred), 115.2, 114 and 120.4 pounds respectively.

These samples from the herd are sufficient to show the practical side of silage feeding. The cows will go on grass in good condition. They are not only holding out in the flow but gaining a little as the weather gets warmer. The same cow did better last winter, but I fed bran, gluten feed, oats, and corn and cob meal and fed heavily. There is no doubt but that they would have done much better this winter had they received grain with the silage, but at present prices I could not get myself to believe it would pay. Next winter I will feed grain of my own raising and grinding and silage run through my own cutter. so I think it will be cheaper.

There is this to learn from my experience: Clover keeps better cut up fine. If not cut it should be well packed and air excluded from the top. Clover is not a hard keeper if the silo is a good one and clover is cut fine. By the way, before getting my silo I figured in every way and found that I could buy a factory made almost as cheaply as I could make one—one that might be a failure as a money saver. It took two days for two of us to set it up—and it cannot collapse. It is there to stay until rotted out.

16

"Make hay while the sun shines," but make silage in any weather. There was no spoiled silage when I got to that which was run through the shredder when it was soaked with rain.

I see no reason why second cutting of clover cannot be mixed with corn silage. I surely put my clover in late enough. Next year I will use corn as my clover will be run out, but when I get more clover I will not hesitate to put it in the silo if I need it. It is not every summer we have such perfect clover haying weather as last and the silo may come handy. Sometimes when I overfeed and feed too late the milk is tainted with a sweetish taste and odor. It is due partly to the lack of ventilation in the old barn. The cows breathe silage odor all day and night. But much of the odor is taken out by the separator. By being careful there is none whatever. If I were a cattle feeder instead of a dairyman I would not hesitate to use the silo. I had three cows that were of no use to me. The first I sold to a butcher without having had any grain. The second and third had corn for two weeks to put a finish on them and it was amazing how they did fill out. It was no trouble to sell those to the butcher though they were out of a dairy herd. Silage, corn, and quick finish.

SILAGE OR CORN FODDER.

Farmer and Breeder.

We are frequently asked, "Why put up a silo when good corn fodder contains as much nutriment as silage?" says A. W. Trow in St. Paul *Farmer.* While corn fodder is a cheap and valuable food, it would be as reasonable to ask, why not feed the cows the peat that is dug from the words have not always fallen on barren soil, though the interest taken in cent of nutriment and there are scores of unwholesome things that are rich in food elements which are worthless for feeding purposes for the reason that they are unpalatable and indigestible. While nutrient is an indispensable qualification of a food it is valueless when it is in a form that is unpalatable and it is not only worthless but a detriment if the animal's digestive machinery is unable to assimilate the nutriment. Food must first be good enough to eat, and then digested before the nutriment can be turned into milk or meat. Herein lies the great advantage of silage over the dry fodder. Silage is so palatable that stock eat every portion of the corn plant, while fodder in dry form is not unusually over half eaten, especially if the stalks are coarse. The silage being so impregnated with water and the cooking process which it goes through in the silo renders it very digestible. While stock thrives on green grass alone, this same grass in dry and woody form is not so palatable or digestible, and consequently much grain must be added to keep the stock in as good condition as they will keep on grass alone. The drying process deprives the grass as well as the fodder of its succulence. It takes from the plant much of its laxative and corrective qualities which are so essential in producing milk and healthy animal development. Silage is to dry fodder as grass is to hay. It is through silage that we get the equivalent of grass in winter. The succulence of silage or roots are as essential to economical bovine assimilation as fruit and vegetables are to the health-fulness of mankind.

THE SILO AN ECONOMICAL FACTOR IN BEEF PRODUCTION.

The Breeders' Gazette.

For a long time The *Gazette* has steadily urged upon its beef-pro-ducing readers the wisdom of considering the silo as a factor in their business. Communications appearing from time to time show that our wire grass sloughs, as the chemist finds that peat contains a large per the matter is far less than it should be. The common practice of fattening steers in the West must rapidly change from the present time forward because of the changed conditions which confront our stockmen. The day of cheap corn seems forever past. The enormous use of corn for other purposes than feeding farm animals and the expanding foreign demand for this grain have extended markets hitherto of small capacity. The time has gone by when the stockman can give his steers what roughage they need in the shape of cornstalks or hay and then supply each animal with a half-bushel of ear corn to crunch at its leisure. Twenty-eight pounds of shelled corn now represents too much cash to constitute the daily allowance of the fattening steer if a smaller amount of this grain or some other combination less costly will produce the same result.

The silo offers the greatest adjunct to the more economical feeding of steers now available to stockmen generally. It does this through the stor-age of the whole plant—ears, stalks and leaves—in a direct, economical and most palatable form. With the silo and the corn harvester at his command the corn-growing steer feeder will harvest his corn crop just before frost comes in the fall, running the harvested bundles of corn forage ears and all through the feed cutter and on into the silo. The mass of finely-cut material carefully compacted undergoes fermentation which decreases its feeding value somewhat, but leaves the material— ears, cobs, stalks and leaves—all in a most succulent toothsome form for the cattle. Fed as silage not a pound of the corn plant need be wasted, the coarser stalks all being consumed as well as the ears. Under this system the fields are cleared of their stalks and there is no husking of the corn as heretofore. The additional labor of shelling the corn and grind-ing it, as practiced on many farms, is no longer necessary for that part of the corn crop placed in the silo. In winter time a bushel of the silage twice a day furnishes the steer all of the roughage he requires during the earlier stages of fattening together with the needed portion of grain, un-less there be fed a little bran or some such material additional. As the fattening period progresses the steer needs less roughage and more grain. To furnish this corn purchased for the purpose or raised on the farm, matured and husked, is used. The grain portion of the corn silage being less hard than corn from the crib is much relished by the steer and more easily masticated than is dry corn. It also differs in taste from dry corn and thus furnishes variety, an important factor in economical feeding. The succulent cornstalks fed in silage form tend to keep the body of the fattening steer in a most healthful receptive condition for the nutrients furnished by this and the other feeding materials supplied. Corn silage is to the steer in winter what fresh grass is to him in summer time or what roots would be. Many a stockman wishes he had roots for his fattening cattle, but he does not grow them, holding that their cost is too great for the returns secured. And he is right, as he can furnish a succulent feed in corn silage at a cost less than half that of roots measured by the nutrients furnished the cattle in the two feeds.

The indifference of the beef producer to silage as a helpful factor in his business has doubtless been fostered by several causes, one of which was the fact that in the past this feed has been most used by practical dairymen. The meat-maker seems to have thought that a feeding stuff which was so good for dairy cows must of necessity be of little use in his feeding operations, which he regarded as quite different from those of the dairyman. Again, the claims for the silo have been exaggerated by some of its foolish friends who were not content to state facts and reasonable possibilities concerning silage, but who drew the long bow whenever occasion offered both in the press and on the lecture platform. Fortunately silage has outlived its fool friends as a feed for the dairy cow and now is about to win its way in the feeding of steers.

Silage will prove useful in a high degree for the summer feeding of steers. The blue-grass pastures which supply ample grazing for streets in May and June fail to afford sufficient succulent feed later on in the season. If not over-stocked there may be an abundance of half-dry grass. but there is not the proper supply of real green feed. Then, too, our summer drouths seem more frequent than in the past and often through the month of August the steers on pasture make little or no gains because of the scant supply of feed then available. The stockman who has a large supply of silage on hand will find it possible in summer time to use this material to great advantage just as many provident dairymen are doing. Many dairymen now hold that the silo is a more useful adjunct in their farming operations in summer time than it is in winter. With a good feed of silage and some grain additional once a day in August the steer should make use of what pasture is available and show steady satisfactory daily gains. Those making "baby beef" or pushing their steers to the utmost fully realize that not a day can be lost under their system of management. It will hardly do to make use of dry feed in midsummer without either satisfaction or profit. To such feeders the silo offers a boon as yet but little realized or appreciated.

We have dealt with the silo as though its main use was for that period when the steers are being finished for the market. It is more useful, if possible, with cows suckling their calves and with young growing stock whose bodies need this kind of feed to put them in the best condition for utilizing whatever other food may be furnished them. Silage is especially valuable for young and growing cattle. The *Gazette* strongly urges its beef-producing readers to consider the wisdom of adding the silo to their equipment for economically conducting their business.

THE ILLINOIS EXPERIMENT STATION ON SILAGE.

Wallaces' Farmer.

We have intimated that the beef breeder would sooner or later, and the sooner the better, have to consider the question as to whether or not it will pay him to feed part of his corn in the shape of a silage. As aiding him in this investigation, we publish the conclusions from an experiment conducted at the Illinois Station by Professor Mumford. These conclusions are not to be read over but to be studied:

"There are nine distinct advantages in a system of silage feeding over that of shock corn in wintering calves intended for beef producing. To offset this there are three disadvantages. The advantages are that silage is taken off the ground when the soil is dry and cannot be damaged, that the manure is saved, that the quality of the feed is not affected by bad weather, that calves are in better thrift and flesh in the spring, that more rapid gains can be secured, that steers can be fed without hogs in case of cholera, without considerable loss; that more pounds of beef can be produced per acre with silage, that a larger proportion of the meat produced is beef; that corn may be harvested earlier in the season.

"The disadvantages are that a greater acreage of crops other than corn is needed to supplement silage than shock corn, that warmer quarters must be provided silage fed steers and that silage feeding involves more capital and labor."

SUMMARY OF THE TEST.

"1.   The results secured in this experiment were from a yield of ten tons of corn silage per acre and 32 bushels of shelled corn and 1.68 tons of corn stover per acre.

"2.   Of the 50.60 tons of corn put into the silo, but 43.09 tons were available for feeding, there being a loss of 7.51 tons. Two tons, or about four per cent were spoiled silage taken from the top of the silo and 5.51 tons or 10.88 per cent were shrinkage in gross weight.

"3.   The gross weight of the silage available for feeding was about three times as great as that of shock corn.

"4.   In the feeding of 5.33 acres of silage to calves 8.69 acres of crops other than corn were used. In the feeding of 5.33 acres of shock corn to calves 5.68 acres of crop other than corn were used. This difference may or may not be found unavoidable.

"5.   It requires a third longer time to feed an acre of corn silage than an acre of shock corn.

"6. The average number of pounds of meat made per acre from a system of silage feeding where oats and hay were used as supplementary feeds was 385.35, where shock corn with oats and hay were fed 337.91 pounds—a difference of 47.45 pounds per acre in favor of a system of silage feeding.

"7. So far as the cost of harvesting and feeding crops for the production of beef is concerned, in the net profits of the enterprise, it should be borne in mind that it will probably require nearly twice as great an expenditure of labor and capital in a system of silage feeding as in a system of shock corn feeding.

"8. The silage-fed steers were much better in thrift and flesh at the end of the experiment than were the shock corn-fed steers.

"9. In case of the silage-fed steers 97.69 per cent of the meat produced was beef and 2.31 per cent pork. In case of the shock corn-fed steers 84.22 per cent of the meat produced was beef and 15.78 per cent was pork. This clearly shows that pork production is an important factor in a system of feeding shock corn for beef production, while it may be entirely eliminated from a system of silage feeding for beef production practically without loss.

"It should be noted that the silage-fed lot consumed less feed than the shock corn lot and less feed per pound of gain whether beef alone is considered or beef and pork combined. The amount of dry matter required to produce a pound of gain of meat where the corn was fed in the form of silage was 6.52 pounds; where fed in the form of shock corn it was 8.57 pounds.

"11. With an average daily ration to each steer in lot 1 of twenty-six pounds silage, two pounds oats and 4.55 pounds of mixed hay, an average daily gain of 1.68 pounds was secured for a period of eighty-eight days. With an average daily ration to each steer in lot 2 of 13.22 pounds of shock corn, two pounds oats and four pounds mixed hay an average daily gain of 1.42 pounds was secured for a period of eighty-eight days.

"12. Under conditions comparable with those prevailing in this experiment one steer would be able to make an average daily gain of 1.68 pounds for a period of six months on .82 of an acre of silage, oats and hay, of which .31 of an acre would be devoted to corn for silage, .23 of an acre to oats and .28 of an acre to hay. One steer receiving shock corn, oats and hay would be able to make an average daily gain of 1.42 pounds for a period of six months on .92 of an acre, of which .45 of an acre would be devoted to growing the corn, .23 of an acre to oats and .24 of an acre to hay, making a difference of .26 of a pound of meat per day per steer and one-tenth of an acre of land for the season both being in favor of the steers receiving their own corn in the form of silage for the period indicated."

SILOS AND SILAGE.

H. B. Cowles, Topeka, Kan., Before Oak   Grange   Institute.   Kansas Farmer.

A silo is a more or less air-tight structure used for storing feed in a green and succulent condition. Ensilage, or silage as it is usually called, is the stored crop.

The history of the silo dates back to antiquity, the semi-barbaric people of the old world having been known to bury their fodder in underground pits to preserve it for future use and to hide it from their enemies. But the first silo in the United States was built by F. Morris of Maryland as recently as 1876. The number of silos now in the United States is estimated by F. W. Woll at over 300,000, located mainly in the dairy sections of the country.

THE ROUND SILO.

Silos are built of all sorts of shapes, ranging from a hole in the ground to expensive stone and cement structures. I have had experience only with the round wooden stave or tub silo, and will confine myself to that type. I think it at once the cheapest and the easiest to construct. It is at the same time the most durable of them all except, perhaps, the stone and cement silo; and this for the reason that it dries out immediately the silage is removed, and does not hold moisture like those with thicker walls.

In planning a silo be sure to not make it too large, as a little has to be fed off the top each day after the silo is opened to keep it from moulding. Sixteen feet in diameter is about right for thirty head in warm weather. To accommodate the required number of tons, build the silo tall, thirty feet or more above ground and six feet or more below, if you are not troubled with water.

I think the best lumber to use is 2 by 6 cypress, beveled and also tongued and grooved. Cypress is great lumber to warp, and the matching helps keep it in shape. You will save a good deal of money by ordering your lumber some months before you want to use it, so that it can be gotten out of the mill down south. The dealers here do not carry silo lumber in stock.

HOW TO BUILD A ROUND SILO.

If you plan to put it down in the ground a few feet, have the dirt excavated and a smooth, circular wall laid up; if cemented, so much the better for smoothness, but I do not yet see that the acid in silage rots the rock and mortar, as some claim. Have the sill gotten out of the planing mill. It will come in sections about four feet long sawed out of 2 by 10 plank. "Float" it in mortar, and then lay a second sill over it, breaking joints, and spike the two together thoroughly. Have this ready when the lumber arrives, so that it may be set right up before the staves get warped.

As cypress comes in short lengths, you will have to make the silo two stories high, so to speak. In my last silo I used fourteen and sixteen-foot staves for each story, alternating first a long one and then a short one. Plumb your first stave carefully, and brace it thoroughly. Then set the others one by one, toe-nailing the bottom and nailing a ⅜-inch batten around the top as you go to hold the staves in position. After completing the circles, put in two or three hoops, and repeat the operation, placing a fourteen-foot stave on top of a sixteen-foot, and a sixteen-foot stave on top of a fourteen-foot, so making a two-foot splice in the middle.

For hoops I used three to six strands of No. 9 galvanized wire well twisted into a rope with an eye-bolt twisted on each end. For tightening, pass the eye-bolts through a twelve-foot 4 by 4 oak scantling, and screw up the nuts. I used eight wire hoops on the first story, and four on the second. Over the matched ends of the staves at the splices I used two flat iron hoops about four inches wide and perhaps 3-16 inch thick.

On my first silo I used some round iron and some flat iron hoops. Both were trublesome to put up and to keep up, besides costing about ten times as much as the wire hoops. Some people advocate using woven wire fencing for hoops, fastening oak scantlings at each end and drawing the scantlings together by means of bolts with a bur on each end. It is said that the coil in fence made of hard steel wire, like the "Page," is sufficient to take up the slack when the staves shrink, and keep them under tension, whether wet or dry.

THE EMPTY SILO.

A tub of this size, when empty and thoroughly dry, is a very shackly concern, difficult to keep either in shape or in place. After letting mine blow down a few times, I have put around the top and the middle wooden hoops, made of twelve-inch cypress, one-half inch thick, four-ply, breaking joints, and well bolted and spiked. To further prevent the changing of shape under stress of wind, I have put a triangle inside at the top made of 2 by 10 plank and well braced and bolted to the wooden hoop. With these precautions it looks as if with three or four long and strong wire ropes for guys, it may be practicable to keep the silo on its foundation and in an approximately cylindrical shape.

DOORS AND ROOF.

When the hoops are on and drawn tight, cut out the doors on the side from which you want to feed, two feet square is large enough. Cut on a bevel all round, cleat the pieces of staves together, and simply set the door in place from the inside to be held by the silage. I have one door above the splice and two below. It is not necessary to put a door near the top, as the silage will settle six feet or more after it is filled

As to the roof, I am somewhat like the Arkansas man who could not mend his roof when it was storming and did not need to when it was not. A roof is a matter of comfort, and not of necessity in keeping the silage.

Such a silo as I have described, thirty feet above ground and six below, with a diameter of sixteen feet inside, will hold about 155 tons of silage. and will ccst for labor and material about $200.

FILLING THE SILO.

The silo being ready, it may be filled with any green crop. Corn is the most important silage crop for this section of the country. It may be put in the silo whole, or shredded, or cut in short pieces, the cut fodder being the easiest to handle in filling and feeding. The cost of putting corn in the silo is in the neighborhood of 50 cents per ton.

The force needed for a quick job, besides the engineer and the man with the cutter, is about this:

One band cutter.

One man in the silo.

Four men and teams, with low wagons.

Two men in the field to help load.

A corn binder in the field, with the necessary men and horse power.

This force should be able to put the corn in the silo as fast as binder will cut it. Binding is a great advantage in loading, and a still greater advantage in unloading. With loose fodder, one cannot throw off fast enough to keep the cutter running smoothly. Even feeding is highly important if a blower is used for elevating, because the high speed developed when the cutter becomes empty shakes both engine and cutter badly. With bound fodder much larger loads can be hauled, and the driver can always have a bundle ready for the feed table, one man being able to throw off a ton in five minutes.

ADVANTAGES OF SILOING CORN.

The advantages derived from siloing the corn crop are many, the principal one being the greatly increased amount of feed to be obtained from an acre. The corn should be cut at a stage in its growth when it is at its best, preferably about a week before it would do to shock. According to analysis, corn fodder loses in digestibility very rapidly as the corn approaches maturity. So the corn is secured at its most digestive stage, and preserved in this shape with a loss of not more than .2 per cent. In fact it does not look as if there is any loss in feeding value; for stock certainly eats silage up cleaner and with a better relish after it has stood in the silo a month than when it is fed directly from the field, either whole or chopped. I think this is largely due to the fact that the corn is steamed and partially cooked in the silo. Then, too, the cattle like it warm, especially in cold weather. My cattle prefer corn silage to the finest clover of alfalfa hay or any other roughage I ever tried.

In handling the corn crop in the usual way of shocking in the field, the loss begins before it is cut and continues until it is fed out, amounting under the most favorable circumstances, according to calculations of the Colorado experiment station, to from 31 to 55 per cent of the original nutrient matter. In siloing corn this loss is stopped before it begins, and in addition the corn is rendered more digestible in the process.

There are other minor advantages, such as getting the ground cleared early, greater convenience in feeding, and so forth.

SILAGE FOR STEER FEEDING.

Wallaces' Farmer.

We have from time to time called the attention of our readers to the question as to whether it will pay to feed steers on silage. Heretofore silage has been considered first-class feed for dairy cows and it was supposed that the silo was the peculiar heritage of the dairymen. It may be somewhat surprising to them that quite a number of silos have been put up in Iowa and adjoining states this year to be used for steer feeding purposes. The more thoroughly we discuss the question of utilizing the entire farm where dairying is a specialty, or the growing of stock cattle, or the farm where dairying is a specialty, or the growing of stock cattle, or the feeding of steers for the market. At the meeting of the Live Stock Breeders' Association at Bloomington, Ill., Professor Henry had something to say on this subject that is worthy of the attention of our readers, as follows:

"Great Britain has given to the world its finest breeds of beef cattle indeed, practically all of them have come from that favored island. In developing these cattle to their present high degree of perfection roots have played a most important part. The English winters are short and so the cattle are much of the time on pasture. Instead of subsisting on dry feed while housed or in the yards, their cattle have always had roots to take the place of fresh grass when deprived of that most important feed article

"But the American farmer cannot grow roots. He has been told again and again that he should do so—he has tried it at times, but always given up in despair. Too much time must be spent on an acre of root crops to permit of growing them economically or successfully. Our machinery has been developed wonderfully for the production of crops of corn, reducing the labor of production to the minimum. There is no machinery, however, which will materially aid our farmers in cutting down the cost of producing root crops. While we have had cheap corn to help us in our cattle feeding operations, the English farmer has had root crops to aid him, and thus one has offset the other in some fair measure. In the Mississippi valley we have a continental climate, which forces us to take our cattle from the pastures, so that they must remain in feed lot or stable from five to seven months in the year. We all believe this to be a hardship. We would prefer to have our cattle upon succulent feed, but we have heretofore seen no way that we could satisfactorily provide for it. Handicapped as we have been in the past, we now have an open door through which we may pass into conditions fully as favorable as those offered the British stock man. Let us seriously consider the introduction of the silo as a factor in economical beef production.

"Experience and experiment have both shown that the dairy cow will give a larger yield of milk upon a given amount of dry matter in the form of succulent silage than in the form of dry forage. The difference is not large, but it is still enough to leave no doubt in the matter. Experiments several times repeated have shown that corn silage is as effective with the dairy cow as the mangel wurzel or the turnip. Indeed, if there is any superiority between roots and silage made from Indian corn it is in favor of the silage. The steer feeder has in some way deluded himself in the past with the thought that while silage might be satisfactory for the dairy cow, the steer for some reason needed something different. Now a little reflection should show us that if silage is such a good thing for the dairy cow giving milk and for her calf after it has become a few months old, and for growing heifers, then it ought to be a pretty good thing for cows of the beef breeds suckling their young, for young stock of the beef breeds and finally for fattening steers.

"To show that roots are not superior to corn silage for steer feeding let me here introduce the results of an experiment at the Ontario Agricultural College, conducted by Professor Day. A bunch of twelve steers was divided into two groups of six each. One was fed corn silage, hay and meal; the other roots, hay and meal. The roots consisted of turnips and mangels. The meal and hay allowances were alike for both lots. The same amount of silage was fed as roots. Between the dates of November 30 and April 26 the six steers fed silage gained 1,464 pounds, while the six steers fed roots gained 1,407. Day concludes his report with the following points:

" 'The steers receiving silage made slightly larger gains than those receiving roots. It required less dry matter to produce a pound of increase in weight in the case of the silage-fed steers than in the case of the root fed steers. In this experiment, therefore, corn silage scored a decided advantage over roots.'

"Let us now consider the matter in a somewhat general way. First we come to the breeders of pure bred-stock. Such must have their breeding cows in good flesh and yielding an abundance of milk for the nourishment of their young. A beef cow should be a good milker, the same as a dairy cow. Now, if silage is such an excellent food for the dairy cow, it must be likewise valuable for the cow of the beef breeds when suckling her calf and so long as the production of milk is necessary. A calf should have succulent feed in winter if it is to advance the most rapidly. With such animals the flesh should be soft and yielding, and not dense and hard, the skin pliable and the coat soft and silky. Succulent feed tends to this condition. Corn silage is a succulent feed, and it is as much relished by cattle as are roots. Corn silage will do all for the beef bred cow and for young animals that roots will accomplish.

"Then for the fattening steer. Under ordinary conditions steers now come into the feed lot without having previously received grain, and from the pasture lands. The change to the dry feed lot, with its bunk and feed rack is sudden and always more or less damaging. Heretofore we have thought that there was little or no remedy for this condition. The feeder has been forced to follow the dangerous and expensive practice whether he would or not. With corn silage he has a perfect substitute for roots. Leaving the pasture and coming to the feed lot, the steer finds before him

a mass of chopped ear corn, leaves, husks and stalks, all moist and appetizing. After a little experience he shows his appreciation of this prov-
ender by burying his nose deeply into the mass, filling his mouth quickly
and showing contentedly. Later he is found lying down ruminating in
contentment. This new feed, moist as pasture grass, has a satisfactory
taste. His grain is taken with more satisfaction because he has had a
partial fill of moist, appetizing food. He gets considerable grain in the
silage in the shape of broken ear corn. These fragments are easily masticated and the grain must be quite easily digested since it is thoroughly
softened. We all know that the heavy use of corn burns up the steer. This
dry, intensely rich, heating food, while greatly relished, is at the same
time of a more or less destroying character. Georgeson at the Kansas
experiment station showed us that when steers were fed on dry shelled
corn that some of the grains passed through the animals without absorbing as much water as it could naturally take up. How can such corn be
properly digested? It is true that the steer fed on corn makes large daily
gains, but at what a heavy cost! When from twenty-five to thirty pounds
of corn are fed per day it required something like ten pounds of the
grain to make a pound of gain. And does it pay?"

The question will arise as to how silage should be fed. Professor
Henry suggests that it be as rich in ears as possible and that the steers
be allowed to have all they want of it at the first with two or three pounds
of bran or oil meal sprinkled over it, and with all the dry forage that they
like. He would then gradually add broken or crushed corn and gradually
increase this to eight or ten pounds per day and when the fattening period
is about two-thirds over to ten or twelve pounds, gradually reducing the
silage in order to harden the beef and meet the demands of the butcher

Now, do not all commence to build silos. The silo is not the thing
for the inexperienced feeder, but we do not think there are any of our
experienced feeders who feed from one to five carloads that cannot afford
to put up a cheap stave silo and make the experiment. We have personally
no doubt as to the profit of an investment of this kind, but we do not
care to urge our readers who have no experience in beef feeding to undertake new enterprises until they see for themselves tat it will pay.

SILAGE FOR STEERS.

Wallaces' Farmer.

A number of our steer feeders are investigating the problem of feed
ing steers in part on silage, and for their information we quote from the
experience of Mr. Humphrey Jones of Washington Court House, Ohio. He
commenced with 178 steers on the day he finished filling his silos, October 7th, last year. The steers were taken off dry pastures, where they
were losing flesh. and weighed 1,159 pounds. A week was taken in getting them used to the silage. when they consumed forty-five pounds per

head per day in the first thirty days and gained fifty-five pounds each with no other feed than dead grass, of which they ate but little.

The second month they were fed a third of a full feed of shock corn in connection with what silage they would eat, less in amount than the previous month, and this month made a gain of seventy-five pounds per head.

They were then put in dry lots and fed ten pounds of clover hay in addition to the corn fodder. He commenced selling about the first of February and sold in three different lots, but the result of the entire feeding period, ranging from 120 to 150 days, was a gain of 2.25 pounds per day and consumed, estimating the silage to contain 10 per cent of its weight in ear corn, less than one-half of the corn which he had been accustomed to feed heretofore. He adds that it costs no more to put the corn in the silo than in the shock and that it costs only about one-fourth as much to feed it as it does shock corn. Part of this ensilage was a mixture of corn and soy beans from which better results were secured as might be expected, than from the pure corn ensilage.

He has also carried through the winter about 300 head of 900-pound steers on ensilage alone with better results than he had ever secured with stock cattle wintered on hay and fodder. He regards the ideal feed for fattening 1,000-pound steers to be all the clover hay and corn ensilage they will eat, and about fifteen pounds of corn per day with a little oil meal added during the last month. Stock steers, yearling, and two-year-olds get along nicely without any grain at all and can be wintered, in his judgment, in this way better than under the old method.

While we have never had any experience in feeding steers on silage. we sort o' feel it in our bones that this is to be the coming method and hope to be able before long to add our own experience to that of others

---

B. ALFALFA.

ALFALFA IN IOWA.

O. H. Barnhill, Shenandoah, Iowa.

In the arid and semi-arid regions of the west alfalfa is one of the most profitable crops that can be grown. Here in Iowa, where conditions are so different, it is a question whether it pays to grow alfalfa, and, if so, in what cases. It makes good hay, and plenty of it, but so does red clover.

Alfalfa is not a success as a rotation crop to restore fertility. Unlike red clover, it is a perennial and does not attain its full size until the third year. Red clover will occupy the ground one year sooner, thus saving a year's time. The other objection to alfalfa as a rotation crop is the great difficulty of ploughing it up. With a sharp plough and four good horses it is a big day's work to plough one acre of alfalfa sod.

Admitting the superiority of red clover as a rotation crop to **restore** fertility, there remain only two uses for alfalfa—permanent meadow **and** pasture. I have never seen alfalfa thoroughly tested for pasture, **but** see no reason why it would not be a success. Doubtless it will not stand very close pasturing, but that will injure any grass or forage **plant.** Alfalfa is the main reliance for pasture in the drouthy west and doubt. less it would prove valuable for that purpose here in Iowa. It begins **to** grow fully as early in the spring as blue grass and keeps green late **in** the fall. Unlike blue grass, it does not stop growing in midsummer, **when** most needed. In two weeks' time it will make a good growth in **dry.** weather. Its long roots extend several feet down into the sub-soil, **mak.** ing it largely independent of drouths.

As a permanent meadow alfalfa is doubtless superior to either clover or timothy. F. C. Woodford of Page county has a large alfalfa meadow on the fertile bottom of the Nishnabotona. Mr. Woodford figures on three cuttings of two tons each, making six tons each year, valued at $6 a ton. or $36 for one year's crop. These figures may be realized in exceptional cases. but I believe one ton a cutting and $4 a ton, or $12 an acre, would be a fair estimate for an average field, one year with another.

The quality of alfalfa hay is of the highest. Our stock prefer it to any other. Horses will often leave bright timothy for musty, half rotten alfalfa One objection to alfalfa is this: If there is a long dry spell after it has been cut it will make a very poor growth and go to seed. At such times it will often make not more than a half ton an acre. There is no use in waiting for it to grow larger, for when it blooms it quits growing. The proper time to cut is just as it begins to bloom. If the cutting is delayed much longer the stalks become hard and woody. It is so used to having its head cut off that it thrives best when cut very often, say three to five times a year. Another objection to alfalfa for hay is that it cures very slowly and not if perfectly dry when put away it will become musty. However, a light rain or two while curing does not seem to damage it very greatly. It takes longer to cure than clover, but is less injured by rain.

As far as a permanent alfalfa meadow is concerned, what need is there for a permanent meadow, unless one desires to raise hay for **the** market A little timothy or prairie hay is nice to feed work horses, **but** for the great bulk of our hay we may safely rely on red clover. We **must** raise clover in order to keep up the fertility of our land, and so we have a large quantity of clover hay on our hands, whether we prefer it to other hay or not. If there is not sufficient clover hay for roughness, it **will pay** better to save the corn fodder and feed it from the shock or shredded than to raise alfalfa for hay. As a supplemental forage crop, sorghum for fodder is probably better than alfalfa. It grows a heavy crop in a few months, instead of two years, and can easily be ploughed up the same fall.

EXPERINCE WITH ALFALFA.

—

W. S. Kelley, Mondamin, Iowa.

My experience in growing alfalfa dates back to 1894, when I sowed thirty pounds of seed on one and a quarter acres of fall plowing, after cultivating and harrowing the ground. Sowed broadcast and covered with a harrow. It was cut three times the first year, yielding about four tons during the season.

The second year it was cut three times, yielding seven, six and four loads respectively.

Since that time we have gradually increased our acreage up to thirty-five or forty acres. I have sown it in a variety of ways and have never had a failure. Broadcast on fall plowing and disced in and harrowed in and drilled in. Sown with and without a nurse crop (I prefer this way).

When sown with a nurse crop (barley) I always mow it for hay when in the milk stage about June 20th. A nice crop of hay can then be secured early in September.

On light or thin soil the drill is best. On rich soil broadcast give best results. Have sown on spring plowing and also disced it in on stock ground. I can stand in the fence corner and throw the seed and get a stand, so can anyone. I never heard of a failure to seure a stand. The failures all come in the after treatment. Were I asked to point out the way to successful alfalfa culture, I would nail up but two sign boards. On one I would put the words MOW IT. On the other I would put the words MOW IT. Now that is all there is to it. Run the sickle on the ground and mow it every three or four weeks the first year if the weeds or fox-tail grass (its greatest enemy) equal it in height. If these do not bother mow it every six weeks, beginning about June 15th. There is no danger of any weeds or grasses interfering with it the second or subsequent years. It will take care of itself.

It has given me on the first year an average yield of three to four tons per acre. The first crop is weedy but the second and third are of first-class quality. I mow my old alfalfa four times and the average yield during all these years has been over seven tons per acre. It does best on a level surface with a porous sub-soil. Do not sow on thin hilly land; it will disappoint you; the growth on such land will not justify the frequent cutting it must have to keep it at its best.

Twenty-two to twenty-five pounds of seed per acre is required to secure a good stand. I sow early in the spring about oats sowing time. How long it will grow without reseeding I do not know. The oldest piece under my observation has now passed its eighth year and looks as vigorous as at four years old. It will not grow a seed crop in this state every year. I secured a crop of five bushels per acre in 1901 which was sold for six dollars per bushel. I let the third crop go to seed. The second crop is removed about July 4th.

From experience and observation I am firmly convinced alfalfa will grow on all the alluvial soils of the state, and on 'all that portion of the state where we have the "drift" soil and on all other rich land where there is no hard pan underneath or atleast within 8 or 10 feet of the surface.

My farm is located on the Missouri river bottom and the soil is a light clay locally known as "gumbo," a very porous sub-soil with quicksand and water ten feet below. The soil is rich beyond measure, and has the decaying vegetation of ages mixed through it.

ALFALFA IN ILLINOIS.

Joseph Wing in Breeders' Gazette.

The most valuable bulletin ever issued on alfalfa growing has just come from Prof. Cyril George Hopkins, of the agricultural station and college of Illinois. It is not possible in these columns to give more than an incomplete summary of this bulletin and we urge our readers, whether they intend or wish to grow alfalfa or not, to get the bulletin, for a study of it is fascinating and reveals many truths underlying the growth of crops, and especially legumes, most interesting and valuable. Alfalfa has not often been a success in Illinois. Failure has been written over most fields where it has been sown. Why is this? It is not the climate that is to blame, nor is it the soil, nor can it always be due to bad treatment of the plant. What then is the secret of this mysterious failure of the best of all foliage crops?

Let me here stop to pay tribute to the memory of B. F. Johnson, Champaign, who in the late eighties experimented with alfalfa and secured on his city lot a fine stand and a magnificent yield. He urged the general sowing of this crop and became almost bitter because farmers heeded him not. There were two reasons, doubtless, why his words fell on unheeding ears. First, he was ahead of his time, far ahead of it. Agriculture in Illinois meant then corn, blue grass and cattle. No one knew except in a vague way of alfalfa; the use of protein in stock foods was not understood; agricultural writers were not much appreciated and whoever knew a prophet to have honor in his own land? The next reason doubtless was that other men sowing alfalfa, incited by his experiments, did not reach the same results. The crop for them was difficult to get started, slender of growth, choked by weeds and grass, unfit for hay when left until "aying time," and disappearing after a few years of neglect Why, only a few weeks ago Professor Shamel spoke lightly of Mr. Johnson's alfalfa experiments because there are today to be found but a few plants in his once well-heralded plot! There are other things of value that will not endure the company of weeds and the contemptuous neglect of those who should cherish them. I have no doubt that Mr. Johnson himself was at a loss to explain why his own alfalfa grew so luxuriantly in his city lot and his friends' crops grew so poorly on rich prairie fields

Here is the probable reason: City lots are manured easily; they receive dust, litter, everything, and among other things doubtless Mr. Johnson's alfalfa plat secured the bacteria which the alfalfa roots need to enable them to feed on the free nitrogen of the air. The right bacteria is to the alfalfa plant what the bait can is to the small boy; it helps to catch fish. The fish is the atmospheric nitrogen. Alfalfa plants are greedy devourers of nitrogen. The protein of which alfalfa is composed is largely made up of nitrogen compounds; without bacteria it is powerless to feed on the free nitrogen and must fall back on the fixed nitrates or ammonias of the soil. That is why alfalfa revels in barn-yard manures; they feed it, and often, too they carry to it the bacteria that it needs.

But alfalfa must have mineral elements, too—potash and phosphoric acid and lime, and it seems from this bulletin that all these are rather deficient in Illinois prairie soils, the phosphorus seeming to be the most deficient. Lime, no doubt, is mainly useful in sweetening the soil and making it a fit place for the abode of the bacteria; anyway we know they will not thrive in a sour soil nor in a drowned-out soil, and that brings up another idea: Is it not true that failure with alfalfa often comes from the saturated condition of the soil in winter, when few Illinois tile-drained farms are really dry enough for things to breathe in them? There are regions in the gravel belt where drainage is perfect, almost too perfect maybe for drouth conditions, and there to establish alfalfa successfully it is only needed to know how to feed it and to introduce the right bacteria into the field.

Now take up the bulletin and study the tables of results a little. Table 5 shows that without any treatment the first cutting made at the rate of 1,313 pounds to the acre. With bacteria added to the soil the yield was 2,563 pounds—almost double, you see, and that is not all. Had the plots continued without bacteria their condition would have become rapidly worse rather than better. But let us lime a plot; the result is encouraging, 1,438 pounds of hay without bacteria and 2,875 with it. Lime then pays well on that soil. Now try lime and phosphoric acid; the result is 1,938 pounds; when bacteria are added to this we get 3,625 pounds—very nearly three times the result of the untreated plot!

Take up another matter—the amount of nitrogen that the alfalfa plant can secure from the air. When no bacteria are present the amount is nil. When they are present the amounts fixed in one cutting vary from forty to fifty-four pounds per acre. That means you are gainer through the season of at least 100 to 200 pounds to the acre of nitrogen. What does that mean, reduced to dollars and cents, to the man who needs more fertility, larger crops on his farm? It means from $20 to $40 the acre of fertilizing value given him by the alfalfa meadow! Do not stare incredulously; it is true, gospel truth, scientific truth, practical truth, proved by more than one practical experiment. I have often said that alfalfa was the greatest soil enriched known, but that unfortunately, it would not enrich poor soils because it would not thrive on them. It has enriched Woodland Farm beyond our expectations and put our bank account out of red ink.

17

But how are you going to get your alfalfa fields inoculated? The easiest way seems to be to secure a few bushels of soil from an alfalfa field already charged with the right bacteria and sow it over the land at the rate of a bushel or two to the acre. The bacteria rapidly spread if soil conditions are right, and that means dryness, air penetration, lime enough to correct acidity, phosphoric acid enough to supply the mineral needs of the plants. And what are these bacteria? I do not know. They are too small for my eyesight. Professor Hopkins says of them: "A single alfalfa plant may contain hundreds of tubercles upon its roots; a single tubercle may contain a thousand million individual bateria."

I feel now that I have been most remiss in not pushing this idea of soil inoculation more than I have, for it is doubtless the secret of many failures. As to what alfalfa is doing now in Illinois Professor Hopkins gives numerous instances. Among them is the experience of W. R. Goodwin, Jr. (associate editor of The Gazette). His alfalfa is near Naperville on the Du Page river. Two acres on bottom land were seeded in April, 1900. A good stand resulted and a satisfactory growth the first season. During 1901 four large crops were cut, a total of twenty-one tons of field cured hay by actual weight, making the total yield for the season of ten and one-half tons per acre of excellent forage. Other instances are given and alfalfa culture in Illinois is doubtless now on a firm footing on the bottom round of the ladder. What shall hinder it from assuming great proportions as the value of alfalfa hay to be fed with corn becomes better and better known?

ALFALFA IN IOWA.

T. C. Cole, Thurman, Iowa.

Alfalfa growing in Iowa is no longer an experiment. It is now well known that it succeeds in the alluvial valleys of the state and likewise can be successfully grown on rolling uplands that have usually been considered too dry to be safe for general farm crops.

It is strange, yet true, that alfalfa has been grown for more than a century, and yet it is a plant that is not fully understood, although its great value has been partly realized by many interested farmers.

It is a well known fact today that the man that possesses an alfalfa field has a veritable gold mine. He has deposited some seed in the fertile Iowa soil, and it but remains for him to handle it intelligently to obtain from it much wealth.

It is a surprise to note what a variety of soils alfalfa can be grown on with varying degrees of success—sandy, sandy loam, black rich, yellow clay, gumbo, but never on sloughs or swamps. There is much to be learned about this wonderful plant as to the most successful methods of planting, curing and stacking, and also feeding.

We have yet to meet that man that knows all about it. We are at least sure of one thing, that it is one of the greatest forage crops in Iowa for all time to come, and that its good points cannot be too highly praised. My own experience in raising alfalfa has been somewhat limited, though I have had abundant opportunities to observe what others are doing with it.

I sowed my first piece four years ago about the first of May, had a fairly good stand, but a better stand of weeds. These I mowed and left on the ground, which proved to be a mistake, as the weeds were so heavy they killed the alfalfa where it was densely covered. In the fall it stood in patches, but the partial stand was so luxuriant, and looked so inviting to hungry stock that I pastured it, which proved to be another misake. In the spring following, it was so scattering and thin that I plowed it up and planted with cane seed, which, as I afterward learned, was still another mistake; I should have disced and resowed. My second effort which has proven a success, was made two years ago on creek bottom land, on soil which has naturally a mellow surface, and a sub-soil as porous as a sieve. It was a five-acre plat that was thickly studded with elderberry bushes. The ground had been previously corned from year to year for more than forty years. I plowed the ground the first of May, harrowed and sowed the seed broadcast, twenty pounds to the acre; then harrowed it twice and rolled the ground. The seed came up very evenly, and likewise the weeds, which were cut three times during the summer. Did not get any crop the first year.

I sowed the seed alone, as I do not consider a nurse crop necessary and the weeds were all removed at each cutting. Alfalfa must have air and sunlight. I learned from my former experience that a very small bunch of weeds or hay will kill every spear under it. I let to go into winter quarters with a good growth for protection from freezing. Did not pasture any the first year. This, the second year, I have cut that hay the fourth time and have pastured it after the last cutting with cattle, horses and hogs, and that after the frost came. Have not had any trouble with bloat. While I did not weigh it all as it was harvested, yet enough was weighed to satisfy me that it yielded at the very least calculation two tons to the acre the first three cuttings, and one ton at the last, making seven tons for the year. I mentioned above that this five-acre piece was thickly set with elders. These elders have all disappeared. Four cuttings per year is too many in one year. I have never seen this mentioned in print, but my opinion is that alfalfa will kill out elders, and if this be true, it is the only known crop that will kill them out, and that, too, without pasturing. My opinion further, too, is that alfalfa will grow wherever elders will grow.

One of my intimate acquaintances has been raising alfalfa during the past three years on land situated on the bank of the Missouri river. There is on this farm three different kinds of soil. One sandy, one gumbo and a streak of white sand. He cut it three times the first year. The first crop was thrown to the stock because of the weeds, but the second and third crop was put into the barn. Had eight acres and it yielded a ton to the acre at each cutting. He sowed that piece the middle of April, sowed twenty-five pounds to the acre. The ground was in oats the year before and summer plowed. In the spring harrowed once, sowed the seed broadcast by hand, then harrowed twice and then rolled. The second year cut it five times and got two tons to the acre at each cutting. That was the dry year of 1901. This year cut it four times and it yielded two tons to the acre at each cutting.

The first cutting was the hardest to cure; the leaves would get dry before the stems. I have another friend living on the Missouri river bottom, whom I frequently visit, and from whom I caught the "hay fever" that has been raising alfalfa for a longer period, some seven or eight years.

This he harvests, bales and hauls a distance of ten miles and sells enough each year from each acre to more than pay for the land on which it grows, and it is all gumbo at that. Before I was much acquainted with the plant I asked him one time what he fed it to. What would eat it. Oh, he says, everything on the place will eat it, and we make tea out of the leaves and drink it ourselves. It tastes much like store tea and is very much cheaper. It is needless to say this man is getting rich raising alfalfa, and that in Iowa.

Someone in high authority has said that the utility and great value of alfalfa is beyond question No one at this stage of the business disputes its value. The fact that it grows everywhere in the state, on hill, valley, slope and table is now conceded. The only difference is in the producing capacity of the various locations. The rich valleys just exactly situated are the greatest producing lands for the crop, but the hill and high table are producing good crops successfully. It is coming, brother farmers, and if you want to be in the procession, you can's climb into the band wagon too quickly.

AN ALFALFA SEED BED.

The Homestead.

The drouth of 1901 aroused much interest in drouth-resisting plants. Since much of the clover was killed out during the dry spell, the interest naturally centers around other legumes that are more hardy, more especially the alfalfa. Without even giving this crop a trial on a small area many persons are about to undertake its production on a large scale. To those who have determined to grow alfalfa there is no reason why they should be cautioned at this stage of the proceedings. However, we would like to point out a few conditions that must be complied with right in the beginning if a reasonable degree of success is to follow.

A better seed for alfalfa may be prepared on fall than on spring plowing, and we would strongly advise the use of such a soil. It should be prepared the very first thing in the spring after the surface is dry enough to work without puddling. The importance of this is not always appreciated, and it is not uncommon to find alfalfa being seeded after the spring cereals. Our reason for emphasizing this matter is that the immediate surface dries out much more rapidly as the season advances, and as the seed is too small to bear a deep covering there may not be sufficient moisture to induce germination. It must be remember that weed seeds are getting in their work just as soon as the soil thaws out, and unless the seed is sown, early weeds will be given just that much start.

Another matter of great importance is that of preparing a most perfect seed bed. We know no better use that can be made of the roller than on this very occasion. This will smash any small lumps that may be on the surface, and prepare the seed bed in the best possible manner for te reception of the seed. Under such conditions it will be an easy matter to insure a uniform covering of the seed. There is still another matter that is frequently overlooked in sowing small seeds of this kind, and that is given too little covering. Where the drill is available we would strongly advise its use. It will do much more good than harm if all the seed is covered to a depth of one inch. The common harrow may insure such a covering to part of the seed, but much will receive consid-ten pounds of seed per acre in one direction with the drill and the same erably less while some will be left entirely bare. A good plan is to sow quantity in the other direction. An alfalfa crop put in as above described will generally keep pace with weed growth, and where such is the case one is generally pretty sure of a stand.

SUCCESS WITH ALFALFA IN ILLINOIS.

Orange Judd Farmer.

Farmers who have tried to grow alfalfa in Illinois have met with somewhat indifferent success. Theoretically the soil ought to produce large crops. The Illinois experiment station several years ago began a series of experiments to determine what was lacking. Alfalfa was grown in pots and treated in various ways. A little later field experiments in twenty-five different sections of the state were inaugurated. The results of these tests published in bulletin 76, indicate that alfalfa can be success-fully grown if the soil is infected with the bacteria which are found in tubercules on the roots of the alfalfa. If these are not present the soil must be exceedingly rich and receive a liberal application of barnyard manure of nitrogenous fertilizers. Even the rich black soil of Illinois does not furnish sufficient available nitrogen to produce profitable crops of alfalfa.

In some sections of the state alfalfa has been grown successfully for some years. The soils from these fields are thoroughly infected with the alfalfa bacteria and can be used for inoculating new areas. In the experiments conducted by the station this infected soil was applied at the rate of from 320 to 1,920 pounds per acre, the heavier applications being the most effective. Prof. C. G. Hopkins states in the bulletin that where lime is applied at the rate of 400 pounds per acre in connection with 100 pounds of infected soil, the inoculation will be very satisfactory in a year or two. The infected soil can be secured from Kansas or Nebraska if it does not seem desirable to get it from Illinois. The application of two or three hundred pounds of phorphorus fertilizer, such as steamed bone meal, raw bone meal, rock phosphate, in autumn, would be advantageous and profitable.

For successfully growing alfalfa in Illinois, the soil should be well drained and prepared as well as for corn. The seed should be sowed in April, but May is also a fairly satisfactory month. Fair results have been secured from sceding in June or even in August, but later seedings are more liable to be injured by drouth or freezing. Sow broadcast at the rate of twenty pounds of seed per acre, and cover about half an inch deep with a light harrow. The more common practice, however, is to sow alfalfa with a slight seeding of beardless barley or oats, cutting these nurse crops early. The soil infected with bacteria is put on at the same time, at the rate of one hundred pounds per acre. If the lime is to be applied, four hundred pounds per acre should be sown broadcast. The seed and soil containing bacteria and lime should be applied at the same time and worked in with the harrow.

The first scason cut alfalfa whenever it seems to stop growing vigorously. This must be done regardless of the size of the plant. If weeds come up quickly, run over the field with the mower and let the clippings lay on the ground. In no case should they be allowed to produce seed. The second season cut the alfalfa when about one-tenth the heads are in bloom. This should be practiced even though the crop is a light one. Subsequent cuttings are much more satisfactory than if the alfalfa is allowed to reach full bloom. The last cutting should not be very close to the ground, because of the danger of winter killing.

The experiment station advises farmers to try a few acres of alfalfa and to apply infected soil to at least a small plot. The infection enables the alfalfa to feed upon the supply of free nitrogen in the air, greatly enriching the land on which it grows, as well as producing heavy crops of forage. On the limestone soils of the state it will not be necessary to add lime.

ALFALFA IN SIOUX COUNTY, IOWA.

C. W. Carter, Grinnell, Iowa.

My experience in sowing and growing alfalfa is very limited, but eminently satisfactory so far as it extends.

Along the Rock river in Sioux county the top soil is a dark loam with enough sand to make the soil quick and warm in the spring. This soil varies in depth from four to ten feet, and under this is a gravel or pure sand for perhaps ten feet more; permanent moisture is found in large quantities in this sand and gravel.

About the twentieth of April, 1901, I sowed in this bottom land two tracts of about two or three acres each. I instructed my man to sow twenty pounds of seed per acre, without a nurse crop. One tract was sown on fall plowing, well disced and harrowed just previous to sowing. I did not get a good stand on this tract and the pigeon grass was so thick that the dry season following caused the young alfalfa to die out so that I plowed it up. The other tract was on land less sandy and of better soil; on cornstalk land well disced. The seed was sown thereon and harrowed in. I secured a very good stand, but felt that it would have been better had I sown twenty-five pounds of seed per acre. This tract was mowed twice that season, securing quite a fair amount of hay that was about half pigeon grass, but as the weather was unfavorable and the hay not good, no account was kept of it. In the spring of 1902 I contracted with the renter on the farm to cut this tract three times and pay me $2 per ton for the hay, by measure, counting seven feet each way, or 343 cubic feet for a ton, to be measured as soon as sacked. While this measurement so soon after sacking would not weigh out a ton when fully cured, we supposed we made the price low enough to balance the shrinkage. The tenant cut, sacked and measured the hay himself, and reported as follows: First cutting, June 20th, 2,432 cubic feet; second cutting August 5th, 2,240 cubic feet; third cutting, September 15th, 2,352 cubic feet; total, 7,024 cubic feet, or twenty and one-half tons. The ground measured two and two-thirds acres. If one-fourth is deducted from this amount for shrinkage, you still have almost six tons per acre.

The hay is well liked by all kinds of animals in preference to any other kind of roughness. I think that in the northwestern part of the state, where the rainfall is lighter than farther east, and where the soil is so loose and so well drained that at least twenty-five pounds of seed per acre should be sown, and that better results are obtained by sowing on cornstalk land. The clay sub-soil on the western slope is, in my judgment, well adapted to alfalfa, and that it will be profitable on a very large portion of the land.

ALFALFA GROWING IN IOWA.

D. B. Nims, Emerson, Iowa.

I came from Jones county, Iowa, in 1874 to Mills county. When I had been here a year or more I noticed on the farm of one of my neighbors (to me) a new forage or hay plant. Upon inquiry I learned that the plant was alfalfa. The man who introduced it into this part of Iowa was a German farmer by the name of William Huelle. He formerly lived in Saxony, Germany. From there he moved, in 1867, to Illinois. Here alfalfa was tried, but the soil conditions not being suitable, it was not a success. From Illinois he moved, in 1873, to near Emerson, in Mills county. Here he sowed on his own farm the alfalfa seed he had brought with him from Germany. This is the Swiss alfalfa.

There is another variety (the French) which grows coarser in stem, and leaf, and is not relished so much by stock, and that sometimes winter-kills. Farmers from all around watched suspiciously the habits of this plant. Some thought it would be a success, but others doubted. The old German went right along and sowed one field after another. It proved to be a success. Soon other farmers tried it, cautiously at first, and then with confidence. When there came a dry season and clover and timothy failed, the alfalfa fields were as green as June. It has now long since passed the experimental stage and forms a part in the rotation of the best farms.

The fact that three or four good crops of the very finest of hay can be cut each year from the same field commends it to every thinking man. It is no unusual thing to cut two to three tons per acre at least three times a year.

Since southwest Iowa farms have reached $100 per acre (and even more) we cannot afford to keep forty acres in timothy and clover to obtain what can be raised on twenty acres if sown to alfalfa. I have grown quite a plot for the past ten years, and must confess that it beats all other forage plants two to one. There are various methods of preparing the soil and sowing the seed. Perhaps the most common (and a safe way) is to wait in spring until all danger of frost is past, then plow the ground as for corn, harrowing immediately after plowing until the soil is very fine and mellow. Then sow ten pounds of seed broadcast or drilled, lightly. If sown broadcast, harrow after sowing, the same as for wheat. Sow no nurse crop with it, but cut and haul off the weeds say about three times during the summer.

You may get quite a sprinkle of hay at the third cutting. The following season you should get at least two good cuttings. There is another way to sow it, which I like better, and that is to clear a field of small grain as soon after harvest as possible and plow and thoroughly pulverize and then drill in with pressed drill five to eight pounds of seed per acre. If the season is favorable you will get a fine stand, and it will get such a vigorous start before freezing weather that it will not winter kill. By this method you can grow a small grain crop (barley preferred, as it gives a chance to get your alfalfa sowed earlier), and you do not have any weed crops to mow the first year and you should get two pretty good hay crops the first full season.

The twentieth century farmer must be an intensive farmer, more than an extensive, and I know of no way in which you can nearer "make two blades of grass grow where one gred before" than by growing alfalfa. Alfalfa has come to stay. It is the ideal feed fed to fattening cattle. It is great feed for all growing stock. Even hogs in winter eat nicely cured alfalfa with avidity, and for milch cows I know of nothing better in the forage line to increase the flow of milk.

Before I leave this subject I wish to state the only fault I have to alfalfa and that is, it is not safe to use it as pasture for cattle, as it is more liable to cause clover bloat than red clover, but horses can pasture it with no danger. When it comes to curing it for hay it should be cut as soon as the blossoms show plentiful, and as soon as thoroughly wilted and before it is dry should be cocked up in small cocks and left (if the weather will permit) about three days before stacking or putting in the mow, but if rainy weather should catch it before curing, it will stand twice the abuse that any other tame hay will and yet make pretty good hay. The aim is to so cure and handle as to save all the leaves. Great is alfalfa in southwest Iowa!

SOWING BARLEY WITH ALFALFA.

The Homestead.

A subscriber from northern Iowa inquires if it is advisable to sow barley and alfalfa together. As a rule alfalfa does much better when sown alone with a nurse crop, although we well realize that farmers will give up the use of their land for one year somewhat reluctantly. We have known instances, however, where one bushel of barley per acre and twenty pounds of alfalfa have given splendid results, although this cannot be depended upon, taking it one year with another. The best plan is to prepare the soil as early in the spring as possible and sow the alfalfa at the rate of twenty pounds to the acre. If a drill is available so much the better, in which case ten pounds of seed should be sown in one direction and the same quantity in the opposite direction. The idea of using the drill is to insure a perfect covering and the germination of all the seed. Alfalfa sown in this manner may require cutting back two or three times during the season, as weeds are very apt to grow strongly unless a nurse crop is used. However, this cutting back does no harm, but rather seems to establish a strong root growth.

C. CORN.

CORN CULTIVATION AND BREEDING.

Kansas Farmer.

W. H. Stevenson, before the Illinois Corn Growers' Association.

There are many men today, in every state, who have toiled long and diligently to increase the average yield of corn per acre, but there has ever been few—very few—among the number who have endeavored to accomplish this important work by systematically breeding corn. We can readily understand why this is so. It has been comparatively easy to investigate improved methods in planting and cultivating, but what time and patience and study have been required to breed aright? And yet, by reason of its inherent capacity for variation, corn improvement opens to every intelligent farmer a large and exceedingly fertile field for practicable and profitable investigation and work.

Corn sustains such a vital relation to the agricultural interests of our country and the world, owing to its value as a food, both for animals and men, that its breeding along practical and scientific lines, is a matter of the greatest importance. Therefore a knowledge and application of the principles of breeding are as important and fundamental to success in producing desirable types of corn as in bringing our various breeds of live stock to a more perfect development.

BREEDING PLANTS MUCH LIKE BREEDING ANIMALS.

Within recent years it has been found that the work of improvement in plant life and animal life can be conducted along similar lines by similar methods.

To the great breeders of the past are the stockmen of the present indebted for the choice animals in their flocks and herds. What would be the type and quality of our live stock today had not Bakewell, Collings, Bates, Booth, Cruickshank, Webb and other breeders during the past century and a half studied animal life and form, and through careful selection, mating and breeding, pursued with persistency during many years, laid such an admirable foundation for our modern live stock industry?

Successive generations of sheep and cattle, upon a thousand hills, in both hemispheres, have borne the impress of these master breeders' handiwork, in feature, form, quality and other characteristics.

THE REWARDS.

And now we believe that in the fulness of time the day has arrived when the reward is as certain and as great for those who will give their energy and time to the improvement of our farm corps as that which crowned the efforts of the pioneer in live stock improvement. The breeding and improvement of corn is of such great importance and can be carried on so successfully and profitably by the intelligent and enthusiastic farmer that we deem this work worthy of the most careful and thoughtful study.

Successful corn breeding is inseparably linked with three all-important factors in crop production. These are fertile soil, proper methods of cultivation, and improved seed. Unless they are the very foundation on which the corn breeders' efforts are based, failure and disappointment must follow.

MISTAKES OF THE FARMERS.

The farmers of the great corn belt a generation ago apparently believed that the virgin fertility of the soil was inexhaustible. With little thought, regarding the penalty which te immutable laws of nature inevitably exact from every soil robber, these pioneer farmers raised corn after corn, wheat after wheat, or corn after wheat, producing large and profitable crops of each. The wonderful productiveness of the soil encouraged and fostered a system of grain growing and soil robbing, which in time, threatened to completely exhaust the fertility of the land. When the pioneer farmer discovered that he had worn out his fields and that they would no longer produce profitable crops, he made haste to move to a new section. But, in these later days, there is little available new corn land for the younger generation. In many sections the children of the early settlers are today striving to solve the problem of restoring the fertility to the soils.

WE HAVE LEARNED.

Many have learned that a one-crop system of farming assuredly brings poverty and want to any community. Many, too, have advanced a step and now realize how much more steady the profit is in meat and milk than it is in corn and wheat; how much better corn pays in cattle, hogs and sheep than when sold to the grain buyer. When all grain growers master this one underlying principle in successful agriculture a new and brighter era will come most speedily and with a promise of reward rich almost beyond comparison. The problem, then, before every corn grower is to keep up the fertility of his soil in order that he may continue to produce profitable crops. We offer a few special methods by which the mechanical as well as the chemical condition of the soil may be improved at the same time that profitable crops are produced.

IMPROVE THE SOIL.

The leguminous crops, e. g., soy beans, cow peas, clover and alfalfa furnish one of the best means of building up soil fertility. They are grown under widely different conditions and are especially beneficial to the soil and valuable as feeds.

Increased yields of from five to fifteen bushels per acre a re frequently reported where corn follows one of the legumes in a rotation. The great value of leguminous crops is based on the fact that they furnish the cheapest food for stock and the cheapest manure for the soil. This is true because they obtain from the air nitrogen, a substance necessary for plants and animals alike, which costs in the form of fertilizers and feed stuffs fifteen to twenty cents per pound.

The soy-bean and cow-pea have been found to be as valuable as ordinary red clover hay and the crop is harvested in much the same way. in rich, black prairie loam the soy bean is more successmul than the cow-pea. The latter, on rich land, produces an excessive growth of vine with very little seed.

However, these leguminous crops cannot be rotated with corn indefinitely when the entire growth is annually removed from the land. They add much to the available nitrogen in the soil, but they do not add potash and phosphorus. Continuous cropping of any kind will sooner or later exhaust the land. Therefore it is important that every corn grower heed the warning of waning fertility and speedily learn that there is no such thing practicable as maintaining fertility without live stock. Barnyard manure, when carefully cared for and applied to the fields is the best of fertilizers for the corn grower. The use of commercial fertilizers. the growing of legumes and the turning under of green crops are helpful but they only delay the inevitable loss of fertility in the fields in which they are used.

CULTURE.

The second important factor in the production of a corn crop is the culture. This includes the preparation of the seed bed, the planting and the cultivation. Conditions of soil and climate vary to such an extent that no fixed rules can be given regarding the depth and time of plowing, discing and harrowing. The preparation of the seed bed, however, should be such as to provide fullest measure, moisture, heat and air which are absolutely essential for the germination and healthy development of seed corn. A large number of experiments have been made to secure valuable data regarding such important points as the distance apart of the hills, the number of stalks in a hill, and hilling versus drilling. All of these items contribute, in part, to the success or failure of the corn crop, but, here again, so many conditions enter into the problem that we can do little more than call attention, very briefly to three or four facts which may prove valuable as guide posts to the corn grower who would profit by the accumulated evidence of many investigators.

Year after year the trend has been to increase the number of hills per acre and decrease the number of stalks in a hill. There are good reasons for this change from the planters, three feet ten inches wide, or even wider, to those three feet six inchs wide, and less. Two and three stalks in a hill give a maximum yield and the ears are usually larger and more fully developed. In addition, a three foot six inch planter drops 3,556 hills per acre, or 316 hills more than a three-foot eight inch planter. If each hill produces two well developed ears this represents an increased yield of six or seven bushels per acre. Drilling is very often practiced on rich, new land quite free from noxious weeds. Under these conditions an increased number of stalks per acre give very satisfactory yields. However, when grass and weeds threaten to seriously interfere with proper cultivation of the drilled corn it always prove best to a dopt the hill system. A series of experiments at the Illinois station, repeated with different soils, varieties of corn in seasons. show that the average yield for the two systems is practically the same. In view of the great advantage in favor of the hilled corn during the period of cultivation we must grant that it is the most practical system for nearly all conditions.

DO MORE THAN KILL THE WEEDS.

We cultivate the corn to kill the weeds, to improve the physical and chemical conditions of the soil, and to conserve moisture. Careful plowing, dragging and harrowing improve the physical condition of the soil by making it finer and looser, thereby affording a larger feeding area for the roots of the plants. Chemical improvement is brought about by admitting a larger quantity of air into the soil. This process increases the fertility by hastening the formation of available plant food. An adequate supply of moisture is an essential condition for the growth of corn. The amount of water used by the corn crop during the growing season is enormous. An idea of the total moisture needed is gained from the fact that 310 pounds of water are required for every pound of dry matter. During the hot summer months, the period of the least rainfall, the growing crop requires the major part of this vast quantity

French Coach Stallion owned by Carroll French Coach Horse Co., Carroll, Iowa, and shown at Iowa State Fair, 1902.

of water, and it is during this time that the great reserve supply of moisture in the soil finds its way to the surface by capillary attraction and evaporates rapidly. Now the point is, will the corn grower permit the loss of water which sustains such a vital relation to his crop? He need not permit it, for this evaporation can be retarded by stirring the surface of the soil and keeping it light and porous, the loose soil serving as a mulch. The pores in this soil are far too large for capillary action and the moisture fails to reach the surface. The corn grower, then, must cultivate more frequently, and less deeply, too, as we shall find, in order that while killing the weeds, he may preserve the moisture for the corn roots and spare the corn roots to gather the moisture.

Many successful corn growers have found it very profitable to continue cultivation after the corn is too nigh for the regular two-horse cultivators. They go between the rows with a one-horse cultivator, or drag, while the ears are setting, and thus maintain a dust mulch. This work is of value only in the dry season.

Root-pruning or cutting off the roots of the corn plants effects serious injury to the crop and demands the thoughtful attention of the majority of corn growers. The loss from this source is so great and yet so frequently entirely overlooked that we desire to offer a few figures which will clearly show the importance of a system of cultivation which does not cut and injure the roots of the corn plants.

The results of three years' work in testing the effects of root-pruning were as follows:

```
Not pruned ..........  .............................62 bushels per acre
Pruned two inches deep ..........................60 bushels per acre
Pruned four inches deep .........................45 bushels per acre
Pruned six inches deep ..........................30 bushels per acre
```

The experiments explain the reduction of the yield which almost invariably follows deep cultivation.

SEED CORN BREEDERS.

The third factor in the growing of a corn crop is the seed corn. It is in this connection that the possibilities in corn breeding are most pointedly emphasized. With few exceptions, only in the past decade have earnest euorts been put forth in the way of systematically breeding corn. More than half a century ago a few men, realizing the far-reaching importance of well-bred seed corn, began to improve their strains of corn by careful selection and cultivation. Their labors, prosecuted amid innumerable difficulties and discouragements, finally gave to the corn growers of the United States improved varieties of corn. They are today the very foundation on which rests much of the advancement which has been made in establishing our most valuable pure-bred varieties of corn. One of these pioneer breeders, J. S. Leaming, of Wilmington, Ohio, as early as 1825 began to select and breed the variety which now bears his name. This corn was brought to Illinois, the shape and size improved by selection and breeding for desirable characteristics, and today this variety is the most widely grown of all yellow varieties. The valuable results accruing from these long years of breeding are proved by the records made by the Leaming corn in a series of comparative variety tests of yields per acre which began in 1888 at the Illinois experiment station. During this long period this variety has maintained its lead as the best yielder. Another pioneer breeder, Mr. James Riley, of Thorntown, Indiana, more than a quarter of a century ago selected the best white corn in his state for a foundation line and by persistently weeding out the barren stalks and other undersirable types in his corn fields he s.cceeded in producing the valuable strain of corn known as the Boone County White. This variety is widely grown and has been a potent factor in improving the corn in many sections. The truth is, there is ample proof that careful breeding and selection give more profitable types of corn. We have referred to the splendid achievements in improving the various breeds of live stock. The profit to American farmers from their well-bred herds and flocks has reached millions of dollars. Practical corn growers who have put improved breeds of corn to the test are unanimous in their statements that we may obtain results, equally valuable and profitable, from highly bred varieties of corn. This is not theory or speculation. Abundant evidence of the most reliable character is available to prove that well-bred seed corn increases the yield per acre, improves the quality, and advances and fixes desirable types in the varieties. The average yield of corn per acre in the great corn states is about thirty bushels. This fact shows that our farmers are not at the present time producing a maximum yield. If every hill of corn at the average distance of planting, three feet six inches by three feet six inches, produced a single pound of corn the yield would be about fifty bushels per acre. Here we have an increase of twenty bushels over the average and yet if each hill contained two or three stalks, the most profitable number, and each stalk bears a well developed ear the yield would reach nearly a hundred bushels. Can we not find a reason for the low average in the fact that every stalk does not produce an ear and that many of the fruitful ones give ears dwarfed and greatly lacking in development and soundness?

BARREN STALKS.

One of the factors which directly contributes to this reduction of yield is the abnormal number of barren stalks in our corn fields. It is a matter of surprise to one who has not noted the fact that careful counts establish the average number of barren stalks at 30 per cent. Many speakers on dairy subjects have long advised the weeding out from milking herds the unprofitable cows, because they not only fail to return a profit themselves but often absorb that afforded by their superior stable companions. Is there not as strong an argument in favor of eliminating this excessive number of barren stalks from our fields? They are little better than weeds; serve no good purpose; doubtless take quite as much fertility from the soil as the fertile stalks, and the labor and expense of growing them fully equals that of the desirable ones. It is extremely difficult to find in any crib even a very limited number of ears of corn uniform in shape, size and other characteristics. Nearly all of them are deficient in length or circumference, have poorly filled butt and hips and shallow or rounded kernels. Only in the cribs of of those who have improved their corn by selection and breeding is it possible to secure samples approaching that degree of uniformity and trueness to type which is so valuable and an indication of good breeding and prepotency. The value of this uniformity is not a fictitious one. A farmer can cultivate and care for a field of corn which has been planted with improved seed without expending a dollar more than his neighbor who persists in planting corn without any prepotency other than that which tends to reproduce its own undesirable characteristics.

If, then, with pure-bred seed the yield can be increased five bushels, or even one bushel, per acre, which one of these men, think you, will most certainly be rewarded for his diligence in business? Ah, yes, perhaps you say, how easy it is to figure these increased yields and profits! But are the facts fully in accord with these very interesting figures? Let us see. Will we accept unimpeached the testimony of scores of our business-like, practicable corn-growers? There can be no more trustworthy authority. Within recent years a large number of farmers have profited by planting pure-bred seed corn. Their report of results are interesting and to the point.

One of these men, a renter, decided to plant his own unimproved seed corn, for he believed that he could not afford to purchase pure-bred seed altough he had unbounded confidence in the prepotency and value seed corn, for he believed tnat he could not afford to purchase pure-bred seed to plant half of the land, and thus the improved and the unimproved were grown side by side in the same field, and the cultivation and soil conditions were practically identical. The results, as given to me are not surprising but fully in keeping with those which we may reasonably expect when these conditions exist.

The number of barren stalks was 50 per cent less in the well-bred corn and the yield at least six bushels per acre more. But the profit in this case will not end with the cash larger income from this one crop. Enough well-bred, prepotent seed was secured to plant the entire acreage this year and thus the profits from that first small outlay for seed corn will be materially augmented by the increased yields from succeeding crops.

Another farmer planted eighty acres with Boone County White. The yield from this field was nearly twenty bushels per acre more than that from any other field on the farm. The seed from these eighty acres cost $25 and the farmer figures that the net profit from the investment amounted to the handsome sum of $600. No comment is necessary.

Pure-bred seed corn will increase the yield per acre. The important point for our consideration is the fact that corn breeding is not for the few. This work, which must prove of unbounded value to corn producers, is not hedged about by impassable barriers. Far from it. On the contrary the system of breeding is so simple and practicable, and, withal, so scientific and profitable that it cannot fail to appeal strongly to every thoughtful corn-grower who is intent on maintaining a leading position in corn production.

The system of breeding is as follows: Buy pure seed, in the ear, of the variety selected for improvement, from a reliable breeder. This plan insures seed of the best type and gratest prepotency and enables the grower to start at the point which it has taken the breeders many years to reach. Examine the bushel or more of corn very carefully and select

Bird's-eye view of Iowa State Fair grounds and buildings looking east.

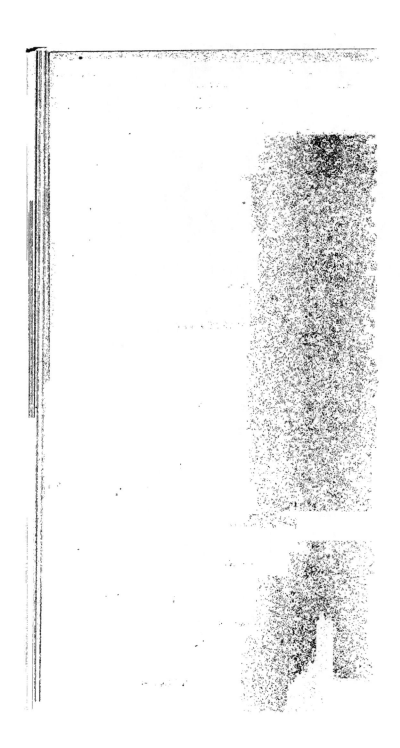

thirty or forty ears for the breeding plat which show the greatest number of desirable type characteristics. Shell off the tips and butts of these ears and plant three kernels in a hill by hand, carefully covering with a hoe. When the hills are three feet six inches apart each way a field twenty-eight rows wide and one hundred and twenty-seven hills is an exact acre. This is a field of convenient size and shape. Plant each row with corn from a single ear. The corn which is left can be planted around the seed plant to protect it from foreign pollen. The most difficult problem is to keep the variety pure and free from all mixture. The difficulty arises from the fact that pollen from other fields will drift for a long distance. The breeding plat, therefore, should be in an isolated spot, if possible, or surrounded for a distance of forty rods with corn of the same variety. This is an important point for the reason that cross fertilize with inferior and barren stalks, even of the same variety, is detrimental to the development of desirable variety characteristics and the weeding out of unavoidable types. The best corn land on the farm should be selected for the breeding field. The preparation of the seed bed should receive most careful attention and should be of such a character as to insure favorable conditions for germination and plant growth. The cultivation should be such as will conserve moisture and remove all weeds without injury to the roots. As soon as the tassels appear and the ears begin to set, it is necessary to go through the field several times, every other day and remove all weak, inferior and barren stalks and suckers. It is impossible to give too much care to this work, for every inferior and barren stalk produces pollen which will fertilize the seed of the plat. Cross fertilization of this kind must be prevented; otherwise, little progress can be made toward establishing a prepotency for the production of fruitful, vigorous stalks which develop uniform ears of desirable type and quality. At the Illinois station, in five years, as a result of this weeding out process, the per cent of barren stalks has been reduced from 60 per cent to 12 per cent. In the fall each row should be husked separately. Examine the ears from each row and select for next year's breeding field from those rows producing the largest proportion of ears true to type. The ears which have produced this large proportion of desirable ears must be prepotent. It is the business of the corn-breeder to improve his corn by selecting and planting these ears which have inherited this prepotency.

When this plan is pursued and the same type of ear selected year after year, a marked improvement in type and quality gradually adds to the value of the variety for seed purposes. If the breeding has been for the purpose of changing the composition of the kernel, the results may mean much to feeders, stockmen, and glucose factories. This is true, for if the per cent of protein can be increased by breeding, the corn becomes more valuable as a feed for live stock because it is more nearly a balanced ration. On the other hand, an increase in the oil content is of great importance to the glucose factories and by decreasing the per cent content of these elements a larger per cent of starch is obtained.

18

After the best ears have thus been selected for next year's breeding
plat, the farmer will have a large quantity of well-bred seed for planting his entire acreage. In this way he can economically provide himself
with choice seed corn every year which he has gradually suited to his
that it is very difficult and expensive to obtain seed corn of this quality
that it is very difficult and expensive to obtain seed corn of this quality
when they seek to secure it from others.

The vitality of all seed corn should be tested. Only vigorous seed
with strong germinating power can be depended upon for a full stand.
The following is a simple and practicable method of testing for vitality:
Fill an ordinary china plate with sand and saturate it with water
Select three kernels from each ear, one from near the tip, one from
near the middle, and one from near the butt. Place the kernels in
the sand point down, and turn a smaller plate over the first to prevent
too rapid evaporation of moisture. Set the plate in a warm room. Keep
a record of the time and number of kernels sprouted. If the seed is of
high vitality at least 95 per cent should germinate within five days.
If this result is not obtained better seed should be secured.

In concluding this subject I would not in any sense underestimate
the importance of the work of many farmers, which has for its object
an incrased yield of corn per acre. You will agree with
me, however, that the practicable system of corn-breeding which we have
outlined gives greater promise of yielding a suitable reward in profit
than any other. That a larger number of farmers may enjoy a share of
this reward is my reason at this time for making this plea in behalf of
the better practices in breeding and improving our varieties of corn.

SELECTION AND PRESERVATION OF SEED CORN.

*H. J. Webber, Chief Plant Breeding Laboratory U. S. Department Agri-
culture, in Orange Judd Farmer.*

The question with corn growers is how to increase the yield at least
expense. This can probably be accomplished in two ways, either by improving the methods of culture or by improving the varieties cultivated.
As long as we continue to cultivate corn on an extensive scale, it is not
probable that the methods of cultivation can be very greatly improved.
However, the other factor of improvement is surely within the reach
and practical application of every corn grower. The fact that improvements of the greatest importance can be secured simply by the process
of selection is evident from the fact that the great majority of our best
varieties of corn, such as Leaming, Boone County White, etc., are the
results of careful selection of seed, carried on systematically through a
series of years.

The keynote of proper seed selection is to select seed from the best
individuals among the many. The proper selection of seed corn can be
made only in the field. Experience has shown that in different individ-

ual plants differ in vigor, productiveness, etc., and that to secure increased yield, seed must be selected from those plants which produce the heaviest. In selecting seed, the best available field of the variety desired should be gone over before the husking, and the ears of those individuals which are the most productive and best meet the grower's ideal variety should be husked for seed.

Before starting to select the seed, the grower should clearly determine with character of plant he desires, whether the stalk should be tall, or short and stocky, whether the 'ears should be long and slender or short or large in diameter, whether one ear or two ears per stalk is desired. In general an ear of medium length, 10 to 12 inches, and of large diameter, with comparatively small cob and long, deep kernels, is desired. It is also important that the ears selected be well filled both at top and butt.

Having the ideal well in mind, the grower should go over the best field very carefully and gather sufficient seed for the next year's planting, taking ears only of the kind desired and from the most productive and vigorous plants. Some growers who in a very hasty way follow the above methor of seed selection, have a seed corn box attached to the wagon while husking, and when a good plant is found, the ears are thrown into the seed box and retained for seed. This method is not to be commended, as in the haste of husking, sufficient attention cannot be given to the comparison of characters which is necessary to make a satisfactory selection.

To obtain the best results, the field from which the selection for seed is to be made should be gone over carefully just before the silks begin to appear, and all small, imperfect and non-productive stalks cut out, in order to insure that all ears formed will be fertilized from pollen from productive stalks. If this practice is found too burdensome, it can of course be omitted, but is certainly of importance if the best results are desired.

A second factor in the production of seed corn which should probably not to be disregarded is that of obtaining seed which in all cases has been cross-pollinated. Results obtained by various experiment stations and the department of agriculture show that cross-fertilization is very necessary in corn in order to retain the vigor. If stalks are inbred with their own pollen for about three generations, they become almost sterile, and in a single generation very marked differences in production can be observed. It is a very easy matter to insure that seed corn has been cross-pollinated by going through the field just before the silks begin to appear and cutting the tassels off the stalks on every other row. The seed corn can then be selected from the detasseled rows, on which it is certain that every ear has from necessity been cross-pollinated. Detasseling, while simple of application, requires considerable time, and, as in the case of cutting out small and barren stalks, can be omitted from the method of selection adopted if found to be too burdensome.

As to the preservation of seed corn, methods differ. An ordinary and inexpensive way is to leave a few husks on each ear and then tie two ears together by the husks and hang them over poles or ropes in the top of the granary or barn, or anywhere in a dry, well-ventilated place. If the corn is perfectly dry when husk, every grower knows that it can be preserved in a granary in bulk without serious injury. Kiln-drying of seed corn is claimed by some growers to be of decided value in securing first class seed, and while this method of treating seed corn is doubtless desirable where the necessary facilities are at hand, yet it is certainly not necessary that corn should be kiln-dried in order to give an excellent percentage of germination and good vigorous plants.

WHEN CORN SHOULD BE PLOWED DEEP.

Homestead.

Much of the experimental data that accumulated during recent years on the subject of corn cultivation has tended to conclusively prove that shallow plowing is followed by better results than is deep plowing. While this is true in a general way yet it must not be understood that under no conditions is it a good policy to plow corn deeply. There are many instances this year where deep plowing will give much more satisfactory results than will shallow. The exceedingly heavy rains that have fallen in some districts have not only kept the soil in a saturated condition until weeds made a strong growth, but have compacted the soil in such a way as to leave it in a baked condition. Where the heavy rains fell before corn planting it frequently necessitated the complete preparation of the soil over again, and in some cases this has been performed as many as three times. Our attention has been called to instances where it was necessary to plow the soil twice in order to prepare a proper seed bed.

Where compaction of the soil has taken place after corn has been planted and rainfalls have been so frequent as to prevent plowing at the proper intervals it may be absolutely essential to plow or cultivate much more deeply than would be suggested by the correct theory of corn cultivation. This may be necessary even after corn has attained considerable growth, and under such conditions we would not hesitate to lay corn by after plowing it to a depth of four or five inches. Such a stirring as this may tend to destroy a few surface roots, but on the other hand this injurious effect would be much more than compensated for by the destruction of weeds and the free aeration of the soil that it would bring about. There will be many instances this year where the shallow shovel plows will be discarded, owing to their utter disability to destroy the strong weeds and loosen the soil.

While as a general thing the four shovel plows are generally being displaced by the six or eight shovel implements, nevertheless there are instances when the former will do much more effective service than the latter, and we believe that the conditions prevail this year under which the four shovel plows are having their innings.

FERTILIZING CROPS FOR CORN LAND.

A. D. Shamel in Wallaces' Farmer.

The question of fundamental importance to the corn growers is how to maintain fertility of the soil in order to produce profitable crops of corn. The most successful farmers of Illinois who have had long experience with all methods of fertilizing are convinced that commercial fertilizers are not practical for producing corn crops. If the crop is produced by commercial fertilizers the crop cannot be sold for enough to pay for the fertilizers.

Some other method for maintaining the fertility of the soil must be found. It has been found that leguminous crops as clover, alfalfa, soja beans and cow peas, are valuable crops for putting the soil in condition for corn. They add to the supply of nitrogen in the soil, and by their root development improve the mechanical condition of the soil. It is also likely that they bring up the fertility of the sub-soil to the surface soil where the corn plants may use it. However, it is being found that in spite of rotations of corn and clover, when the crops are taken off the field, year after year, the soil grows gradually poorer and poorer until it will no longer produce profitable crops. There is no escape from the fact that the crop must be fed to stock, and the manure carefully conserved and spread on the fields.

Such a plan is found to restore and keep up the fertility of the soil. So true is this that in many sections where the soil has been exhausted by wheat farming, wheat is being abandoned, and corn and clover crops grown instead. On many of the poor fields it is found to be impractical to secure a profitable stand of clover. So that the corn growers are turning to some other, not so precarious crop, which will add to the fertility of the soil, furnish a valuable protein feed to be fed with corn and improve the condition of the soil. Wherever clover and alfalfa can be grown no better crops have been found. But for other conditions, two valuable and successful crops have been introduced from China and Japan. These crops were first introduced in the south where they gave results beyond the anticipation of everyone. They have been carried north to the northern line of Michigan, and certain varieties have been found to succeed under all conditions.

These crops are the soja bean and cow peas. The soja bean is adppted to the prairie soils, and the cow-pea to the clay and upland fields. On rich soils the cow pea runs to vine and does not seed. On such soils the soja-beans reach their fullest development. Thousands of acres of these crops are now grown in Illinois, and their cultivation extending rapidly over the entire state.

The two crops are cultivated and harvested in a smilar manner. They yield when raised for seed, from 12 to 25 bushels per acre which is worth about $2 per bushel. They yield from 2 to 5 tons of hay per acre which is recognized by experienced stockmen to be as valuable as clover hay. It is rich in protein and is fed with corn. It has been the invariable experience of several hundred farmers whom I have interviewed, that a crop grown on land increases the yield of the succeeding corn crop from 10 to 18 bushels per acre. The influence of the crop on the soil can be seen to the row in the field of growing corn the next season.

It has been found that the seed can be drilled in between the rows of corn, about three rows between two corn rows, just after the last cultivation and produce a large amount of feed and beneficial effect on the soil.

When planted for a crop the seed should be drilled in on land prepared as for corn, after corn planting time. As they were originally tropical or semi-tropical crops they should be planted later than corn. The rows can be drilled in with a wheat drill about sixteen to eighteen inches apart, or with corn planters; if with corn planter the rows should be doubled. If grown for seed, drill the width of corn planter rows. The ground shall be harrowed after planting, two or three times, and after the plants get a good start they shall need little or no cultivation.

The soja bean crop can be cut with a mowing machine, as the first berries are turning brown, allowed to wilt a day, then put in barn. The hay will come out as fresh and bright as when put in the barn. Keep the barn closed, and handle as clover hay. The crop makes a very valuable hog feed in August and September. It can be cut off or the hogs turned in the field. Experienced hog men who have used this crop recognize a most profitable feed especially for young stuff. Cow-peas are harvested with more difficulty. The vines are hard to handle. They are more easily fed by "hogging off" in the field. Old "self-reapers" are successfully used to cut this crop.

The variety is very important. For soja beans the medium or dwarf are the two varieties that will mature in central and northern Illinois, and Iowa. For cow peas, the Early Black Eye, Black and Red Ripper varieties are giving the best results.

Before planting the seed should be tested in sand or earth. They contain so much oil that they are likely to heat and be destroyed. If the seed is saved from the field it ought to be fire dried. A good plan is to sow a small field. Allow the plants to mature and save your own seed. Otherwise the seed should be secured from some reliable grower.

HARROWING CORN.

Homestead.

In the corn belt of the United States there are two methods in vogue for raising this important crop. One is by plowing, accompanied by surface planting, while the other may be confined in the limits of the word listing. Both methods have their advocates, but, regardless of the advantages and disadvantages of each, the harrow fills the important place as an implement of cultivation in either method. We refer to the ordinary steel frame harrow commonly called a drag.

Within the last few years the tests made with a surface cultivator as an implement for conserving moisture have brought out much favorable comment. We refer especially to the mere stirring of the surface which not only should be done lightly but often. No implement on the farm is of greater value in the corn field than the harrow. While it is not altogether advisable to lay too much stress on the individual season when drouth prevails, yet at the same time it is never a mistake to take such precautions as will conserve the moisture of the soil to the greatest possible extent.

What we have to say about harrowing corn, then, will apply to its effect in holding the moisture as well as to the destruction it will work in the weed pests. As to the time when corn ground may be profitably harrowed we wish to say that we refer to its free use before as well as after the corn is planted. Harrowing the ground before the planting is of much benefit to the future crop. Many farmers lose sight of this, believing that when a field is fairly level that more work expended upon it is labor wasted. This is certainly a mistake, for if the farmer has time a harrowing after every beating rain before the crop is in the ground does much to bring about conditions that will favor the rapid growth of the corn after it is planted. It loosens the surface crust, which is generally in a puddled condition after heavy rains, and leaves behind a mulch-blanket which prevents the evaporation of soil moisture. It is generally advisable to use the harrow as soon after a rain as possible, but of course the soil must not be puddled. If the surface is left until it is dry the harrow will have little effect by way of mashing clods or leaving the right kind of surface mulch. In the prairie states it is often said that one extreme follows another, and sometimes very quickly, too, and, however much moisture the soil contains one week, perhaps ten days or two weeks after much of this may have been evaporated, if provision has not been made for its conservation.

If the corn fields have been thoroughly harrowed before planting this implement need not again be used until the plants are large enough to withstand the wear and tear of the harrow. However, the ground should in no instance be harrowed when wet. We also doubt the wisdom of its use when there is any considerable amount of trash on the surface, as many of the young plants are liable to be injured by dragging rubbish over them. This year on account of the large area of corn being cut up last fall such obstacles will not be so generally in the way and because of this and the fact that the importance of conserving the moisture has been emphasized by a recent experience we look forward to a greater use of the harrow in the corn field this year than ever before. While we are aiming to conserve moisture by the use of the harrow we will also accomplish much in the destruction of noxious weeds.

WHEN TO CUT CORN.   .

The Farmer, St. Paul.

The best time to cut corn is a disputed question. Perhaps it always will be, for in this singular world "the thing that hath been is that which shall be." When the scientists begin to see eye to eye on the question, then other scientists will begin to look at the question through a different lens, and will therefore see it differently. But the time is coming when the concensus of opinion in this matter will be sufficiently unanimous to be taken as a safe guide by the masses.

The best time to cut corn, probably, when the stalk and ear are wanted, is when the ear is just passing out of the glazed stage to the stage of completed ripeness. The nutriment is then all in the stalk and ear together. When corn is cut at that stage, the ear is not likely to shrivel, and the stalk has a palatability far ahead of that which is possessed by the stalk which is allowed to cure on the ground before it is cut. If corn could all be cut at that stage it would be well, but where a large acreage is to be cut, so that cutting it is going to cover several days, may be well to begin when the crop is not yet quite ready, as before it is all cut some of it will be a little too ripe. Especially would such a course be wise if the corn is to be fed in the stalk and ear without any preparation for the feed lot.

Of course if corn is reared only for the grain, it would be better to have the crop fully matured before it is harvested. In fact it would not need any other harvesting than removing the ears. The stalks would be left standing. The ears can then be removed at the convenience of the grower, as is commonly done now. But this involves the wasting of much of the stalk, if not indeed all of it. This is a grievous waste. Are we not right in saying this? If we are not we would like to be corrected. We would like to advise for the best in this matter.

We often wonder that so little regard is paid to palatability in corn fodder, and indeed to other fodders. It is here that mistakes are made through following the analysis of the chemist blindly. The chemist can tell us about the food contents, but he cannot tell us whether the animals will relish these food factors. If the animals will not eat them, they can be of no earthly use to them. In the cutting of all fodders there is a time when they reach the stage beyond which palatability waves. This point should not be passed in the cutting of the crop when it can be prevented. What a grand thing it would be if all the corn in this Northwest could be cut and shocked at that stage that would fit it for making food that farm animals would at with much relish.

Let it not be concluded then that corn is corn anyway, no matter when it is cut. And when it is cut just at the right stage and put up in small shocks? Are they not right? After it has stood two or three weeks and then four or five shocks are put into one, it will stand up nicely against storms and will keep nicely until it is fed. This means work, but is it not work that will pay, and pay well?

D. CLOVER.

MAMMOTH OR COMMON RED.

Wallaces' Farmer.

We thought that we had said over and over again all that we know about clover years ago, but we find that if we reply to the questions asked by our readers that we will have to tell the same story over and over again as long as we edit the paper, not because the old subscribers do not get the facts clearly before them, but because of the constant accessions of new subscribers to whom we must begin preaching the clover gospel from the beginning. An Illionis correspondent writes:

"Is the mammoth variety suitable for hay and will it not produce the second year? If you sow in the spring without a nurse crop, do you usually get a crop of hay or seed the first year?"

Mammoth clover is a large variety which in the latitude of Iowa, Missouri, and Illinois will not produce a crop of hay and a crop of seed the first year on account of the shortness of the season. Sown at the same time in the spring, it is from two to three weeks later than the common red and it will not bloom the first year as the common red clover does; hence, the way to determine whether you have sown mammoth or the common red is to notice whether it blooms in late August or September. The mammoth simply keeps on growing. The common red will bloom and often produce as much as half a crop of seed if the season be favorable.

When mammoth and timothy are sown together, they will be ready for cutting at the same time; that is, the mammoth will be in bloom and about one-third of the heads turned brown when the timothy is in its best condition for mowing. This is one great point in favor of growing mammoth clover. With the common red, you must either cut your timothy before it makes the best hay, or you must wait until the heads of the clover are all brown and the stalks become woody and you are compelled either to sacrifice the best of the timothy or the best of the clover.

The disadvantage is that on rich land the mammoth grows too rank and lies down and hence does not make a good quality of hay. Besides, the growth is so rank under those conditions that timothy has little or no show the first year. The mammoth should be sown with timothy, therefore, on thin land or on rolling clay lands where it will not grow too rank and will not smother out the timothy. By smothering it out, we do not mean destroying it altogether but simply covering it up so that it makes too little growth the next year after sowing. The next year it will usually be found that you have about a third of a stand of clover and a magnificent growth of timothy, so that the second year's mowing will give a very superior quality of hay, mostly timothy; that is, if you sow these together in the spring of 1903 with a nurse crop and mow it in 1904, you will have on rich land a vast yield of mammoth and a small show of timothy, but in 1905 you will have a magnificent development of timothy and probably about one-half or one-third as much mammoth clover.

Mammoth clover is more nearly a biennial than the common red. If you sow mammoth clover and timothy in 1903 and pasture off your mammoth clover in 1904 up to or about the 10th of June in the latitude of southern Iowa and northern Missouri, extending clear through Illinois and Indiana and one hundred miles west of the river into Nebraska you can usually take a fine crop of seed ranging from two to five bushels per acre. After that you will find very little mammoth clover. All that will remain the next year will be the seeds which for some reason did not come up in 1903 but came up in 1904, and by the time the timothy will have taken such a hold on the land that these will not grow too large or coarse to make good hay.

The common red clover if sown in the spring of 1903 with a nurse crop, will come in bloom that fall, provided the stand is good and the season favorable, and will always under these circumstances give fine fall pasture. In a season like 1902, it will give from one to two tons of a hay crop and frequently about a half a seed crop, if allowed to stand for seed. This, however, we do not advise, as the maturing of the seed will thin the stand. It should, therefore, either be pastured or cut for hay. The next year it will produce a crop of hay in June and, if the season be favorable, a crop of seed in the fall. The bulk of the crop will be clover the first year, but if allowed to stand a year later will be two-thirds timothy and one-third clover, that third year clover being for the most part from seed which did not grow the first year.

However, we are inclined to believe that in our common red clover seed there are two or three varieties which can be distinguished by the color of the blossoms, some being a deep red, or scarlet, others being paler, about the color of the mammoth, with an occasional pure white one. Our seed breeders will in the course of time separate these varieties and give us at least three distinct varieties of red clover. We are inclined to believe that one of these at least is a short perennial. If the common red clover is kept from going to seed it becomes a short perennial and will continue three or four years, whereas the mammoth clover is more nearly a biennial.

It should be stated, however, that with both varieties of clover, a seed crop depends on insect fertilization; hence there are some seasons in which there will be an almost total failure. We have never been able to get a good crop of seed of mammoth clover in any year when there was an abundance of white clover and alsike in bloom in the neighborhood in the first half of July, the reason, we believe, being that the Italian bees and their grades do not visit the mammoth clover and hence do not fertilize it. We have known seasons of this kind when in our mammoth clover we would not find a honey bee in a rod square when it was in full bloom, the only fertilizing agency being the bumblebees. If the winter has been such as to insure a large crop of bumblebees, then you can get a crop no matter

what the alsike and white clover may be doing, but if it is a short bumble-
bee year you need not expect any clover seed unless it is visited by these
larger varieties of the common honey bee.

Again, we have never been able to secure a bumper crop of seed from
mammoth clover when sown on rich bottom land, nor for that matter,
of the common red, for the reason that a very great luxuriance of stalk
prevents the proper seed development. ,Even on uplands we have often
found that the thinner spots where there was a short growth of the common red clover produced not only the most seed but the best seed.

Where a man grows either variety for fertility he should plow under
the second year; that is, if he sows his seed in the spring of 1903 and gets
a good stand and cuts it for hay or for seed in 1904, then he should plow it
up in the fall of 1904 or early in the spring of 1905 and harvest his crop
of nitrogen. As stated in the paper a week or so ago, it will pay him to
plow the spring sowing under late in the fall or early the next spring. It
will pay him better if h'e can let it stand a year longer and get a full crop
of nitrogen, for it must be borne in mind that one of the great reasons
why we grow clover is to store the soil with nitrogen sufficient for two
good corn crops. He will get a good crop of nitrogen with a good stand of
clover during the one summer but a better crop if he will let it stand two;
then, however, it should be plowed up if fertility is the main thing he is
after.

We expect to make an experiment next year of which our readers
shall have the full report whether it be a success or failure. We regard
our failures on our own farms as quite as valuable to our readers as our
successes, however they may be on us. We sowed this spring on
some drained bottom land with winter wheat and have secured a most
elegant stand. We will plow this under in the spring and put in corn,
which we expect to follow with winter wheat provided we can get the corn
cut in time, then seed this down to clover again, thus making a two crop
rotation. We would not do this on thin uplands and we do not ask our
readers to follow our example until they find out the result. We regard
our own farms as in a certain sense experiment stations carried on in
farmer-like fashion in order that we may test our theories under ordinary
farm conditions.

SPRING GRAIN AND A CATCH OF CLOVER.

Homestead.

At this season of the year there is always more or less activity among
farmers to ascertain which is the best way to get a catch of clover when
sown with small grain. The older some farmers get the less faith they
have in some of their own methods and the older a country grows the
more attention is being paid to a clover crop. Of late years there have
been many failures to get a good stand of clover and there is always inter-

est in this topic. It would seem that the more this question is agitated the more interesting it becomes. In the preparation of the seed bed for clover one should not lose sight of the demands for such a crop and be governed too largely by the desire to get a crop of grain on the same ground where there is to be a start made for a crop of clover. On most farms small grain is put in on ground that had been to corn last year and it will be necessary to clear it from stalks and trash, if it is not to be plowed, which is not always advisable. If possible to do so it is better to break the stalks when the ground is frozen and when sufficiently dry they should be raked (not raked at) and burned so as to be out of the way of working the ground and also out of the way of the first crop of hay that is to come off the field. Both clover and small grain needs a solid seed bed and this is not always obtained by spring plowing. When the soil is in a good condition for drilling and discing it should be disced and harrowed down smooth, then the clover seed and oats are to be put in with a drill. This will appear to be a great deal of trouble but it will pay to take some trouble in obtaining a good stand of grass. The oats and grass seed can be put in at the same operation if the right kind of drill is employed. Some drills will work all right in this kind of ground even if there are a few stalks left on the field, others will not do so well.

Many mistakes are made in the quantity of seed used and the quality as well. It should be remembered that the main crop expected is the clover crop and the oats should be put in so as to be a protection to the young grass and not as a main crop. Let the seed oats be selected and thoroughly cleaned so all the grain will grow, then set the drill to put on four or five pecks of oats to the acre. If the clover seed has been selected with the same view to good quality it should be sown at the rate of one bushel to five acres, otherwise the seeder attachment should be set to sow one peck per acre. We know we are treading on dangerous ground and that a great many farmers will feel that we are advocating a wasteful practice, but experience along just exactly this line has convinced us that this is the best way to do on soil such as is found in the greater part of the central West.

In growing all kinds of crops it is very naturally to be expected that we are growing crops for profit and not to see how easily and economically crops can be put in. There will be as much gain in having one stalk of oats yield one hundred grains of oats as there will be in having four yield that number and save three stalks cumbering the ground and impeding the growth of the clover.

When two or three bushels of seed oats are sown on an acre a large number of the oat plants are of but little consequence and a great deal of the young clover is killed out on or about the time the oats are harvested. which condition is liable to occur in any case when the weather conditions are such as to endanger the young plants. When clover has been put in as above the ground will not dry out as it will when plowed and the young plants will have more growth, which are two conditions in its favor. The only reason for stirring ground to obtain a seed bed for any kind of grass crop would be for the purpose of getting the surface of the ground level and to get rid of the stalks, trash and stubble. If these conditions can be obtained in any other way besides plowing the ground, we would take advantage of them.

THE VALUE OF ONE-CROP CLOVER.

Wallaces' Farmer.

By one-crop clover we mean clover sown this year, 1902, and plowed under either this fall or early next spring for the purpose of producing additional crops in 1903. We are often asked what is the value of this clover used in this way, purely as a fertilizer. Our uniform reply for the past five years has been that it is not of as great value as if allowed to grow another year, used for hay and pasture and the roots and aftermath turned under, but that it will pay for the cost of the seed and labor and pay well. We have tried it on a large field on our own farm, but not having a check plot (a part of the field on which no clover had been sown but in other respects equal), we are not able to state the exact profit. All we know is that we raised a bumper crop of corn and we ascribe much of it to the value of the clover turned under.

We don't know of any experiments in a large way conducted by any station in this country for the purpose of determining the value of one-crop clover as a fertilizer. The experimental farm at Ottawa, Canada, has gone into this matter somewhat extensively under the direction of Dr. Saunders and Professor Frank Shutt, and from a recent bulletin we are able to present some facts that are quite worth the attention of our readers in the states. These experiments were not made in fields but in plots of from one-twentieth to one-fortieth of an acre each and while in this plot culture, there is room for mistakes and it is not so satisfactory as field culture, yet where they are conducted with care and a sufficient number of them are so conducted the results are fairly reliable.

In the spring of 1897 this station sowed plots of one-twentieth of an acre each to spring grains, wheat, barley and oats. The soil was a sandy loam of fair quality which had been manured the year before. Four of these plots had clover sown with the spring grain and four, one adjoining each of the other four, were without clover. All the plots were plowed in October. In the spring the land was harrowed and sown to the same variety of oats with the following results: The plot on which wheat had been sown with clover in 1897 yielded at the rate or 1,610 pounds of straw and 19 bushels 4 pounds of oats more per acre than that sown without clover. On the plot on which barley had been sown with clover in the spring of 1897 the increase over the field without clover was at the rate of 730 pounds of straw and 7 bushels 2 pounds of oats per acre. On the plot on which a different variety of barley had been sown with clover in 1897 there was an increased yield of

1,090 pounds of straw and 7 bushels 2 pounds per acre. On the plot on which Banner oats had been sown with clover in 1897 there was an additional yield of 2,850 pounds of straw and 10 bushels 30 pounds of oats.

The reason for the small increase in two of the plots was because the land was of much inferior quality as compared with the others. The result of these tests show that the average yield of grain on the four plots with clover exceed by 11 bushels one pound per acre the yield of those on which no clover was used. Bear in mind that this is what we call one-crop clover, sown in 1897 and turned under in the fall.

The next year these plots were again sown to Mansury barley. Without going into details it is enough to say that the average increase the second year over plots of the same character that had not been sown to clover in 1897 was 8 bushels 31 pounds. On this the station comments as follows:

"These results are indeed remarkable. They show in the case of the plots under consideration that the plowing under of a single crop of clover sown with the grain in 1897 produced a wonderful increase both in straw and grain. The crop of straw when compared with the adjoining plots on which clover had not been sown was increased 78 per cent in 1898 and 35 per cent in 1899. The grain was increased 28 per cent in 1898 and 29 per cent in 1899."

In 1899 the station plowed a field of four acres four inches deep. The soil was a sandy loam of medium quality. On two acres of this land barley had been sown in the spring of 1898 and with it ten pounds of clover seed. One acre had been in brome grass. Half an acre had been sown to a mixture of pasture grasses with clover and half an acre to a mixture of pasture grasses without clover. It was sown to Bavarian oats with the following result:

The acre of oats after brome grass yielded 33 bushels, 8 pounds. The half acre after pasture grasses without clover yielded 36 bushels, 16 pounds; the half acre after pasture grasses with clover 46 bushels, 4 pounds; the half acre after pasture barley with clover yielded 43 bushels, 28 pounds, or a difference of 10 bushels, 4 pounds per acre in favor of the crops grown after plowing under clover.

A similar line of experiments were conducted in the year 1900 with the following results: The crop grown was New Zealand oats. The increase in the yield after wheat with clover was 1 bushel 52 pounds; after barley with clover 2 bushels 12 pounds; after oats with clover 2 bushels 12 pounds per acre. On this the station comments:

"This yield was the smallest at any time obtained where clover had been plowed under and was probably due in part to the fact that the grain with the clover was sown a week later than usual and the subsequent growth of the clover was light and unsatisfactory."

A similar line of experiments in plots continued in the year 1901. There were six plots in number, two sown with wheat, two with barley and two with oats; and one of the plots in each case sown with clover and one without. After the grain crop was taken off the clover was allowed to grow, plowed under in the middle of October and the land harrowed twice and seeded with Banner oats in the spring of 1901. There was an increase in the plot following wheat of 2 bushels 12 pounds over the plot that had no clover; of 4 bushels 24 pounds in the plot sown to barley and the same amount in the plot sown to oats. In other words, the plot sown with clover gave an average of 43 bushels 31 pounds per acre while those without clover gave an average yield of 40 bushels, or 3 bushels and 31 pounds in favor of the clover plots. There was also an increase of 827 pounds of straw per acre in favor of the clover plots.

Similar experiments were conducted with the corn in 1898, 1900 and 1901, the corn being used for fodder, with a difference in favor of the plot sown with clover of about 40 per cent of the yield in 1900. Taking the average of eighteen experiments made with corn in these years there was an average gain in the weight of the green crop from the use of clover of three tons 1,694 pounds per acre.

In 1899 similar experiments were made with potatoes, after one-crop clover sown on land which had previously been in barley, peas and carrots, with the result of a difference in favor of the crop where clover was used of about 28 per cent. Similar experiments were conducted in 1900 with the result that the three plots sown to clover gave an average of 317 bushels 7 pounds per acre, while those without clover yielded an average of 283 bushels 47 pounds, or a difference in favor of the plot sown with clover of 33 bushels 20 pounds per acre. This experiment was again repeated in 1901, in which case the clover plots yielded at the rate of 423 bushels 40 pounds per acre, while those without clover yielded 391 bushels 20 pounds, or a difference of 32 bushels 20 pounds.

Various experiments were conducted for the purpose of determining whether the sowing of clover with spring grain lessened the yield of the grain. After three years of experiments the conclusion is reached that the growing of clover with grain as a nurse crop had no perceptible influence on the yield of grain.

The results of these experiments are cumulative in their character. While the results vary, there is in every case an increased yield of grain and potatoes that more than compensate for the cost of seed and labor.

The only risk the farmer runs in sowing clover solely for fertility is in not securing a stand and of losing the stand after he has secured it. There is practically no risk in securing a stand of clover in the natural clover country in any ordinary season, if he will only secure good seed and, as we pointed out in a recent article, cover it deep enough to secure sufficient moisture, but not so deep as to exclude the air. There are seasons when the wisest man on earth can't hold a stand of clover, but by using ordinary judgment he can hope to in four years out of five.

If farmers will quit talking about nurse crops and talk about strangling crops, or as we head a farmer at an institute the other day call them, "curse" crops, and will quit sowing late oats or wheat and will sow early oats or wheat or give the clover the full use of the land, and in the case of threatened damage to the clover from very dry weather, mow and pasture them before they have time to rob the clover of moisture, they can get a stand every year without fail except such years as 1894 and 1901.

Someone, however, rises to remark that clover will kill out some years. So it will, but even if it does kill out the residue will far more than pay for the cost of seed and the sowing, even if the seed cost ten dollars a bushel. The Canada station has experimented along this line and found that when clover was entirely kiled there was an addition to the nitrogen content of the soil in the residue, that is, in the shriveled, brown foliage and roots in the upper nine inches of soil of from 58 to 81 pounds per acre, or the equivalent in the nitrogen value of five tons of barnyard manure per acre. In other words, by sowing clover with your grain, even if it does kill out, you get the equivalent of barnyard manure at the rate of about twenty cents a ton, or about what it would cost to put it on wagon and spread it on the field.

Therefore, answering in advance a number of questions we are sure will come up, we would say that if you have no place to put corn next year except on your clover sown last spring, don't hesitate. Under our conditions we believe it pays better to let it stand the second year and get a crop of hay and seed and then turn it under. Where this is practical we advise it.

Our own experience has shown that a three-ton crop of clover is the equivalent of about forty bushels of corn per acre in two years, or say ten dollars per acre; four bushels of wheat the first year, four bushels of flax. We believe that every acre of clover of a good stand sown last spring and turned under late this fall or next spring will be good for from fifteen to twenty bushels of corn next year and possibly more. We don't know of any cheaper way of getting corn than by sowing plenty of clover and plowing it under either the first year or the second.

We believe that in the above we have presented the important facts in the case for the consideration of our readers and that they can be relied upon.

WHEN TO CUT CLOVER.

Homestead.

If all other operations on the farm could be set aside during the hay making season it would be an easy matter to prescribe in detail the course to follow in the cutting and curing of clover. It frequently happens, however, that attention must be given to other matters, especially to the cultivation of the corn crop, so that haymaking is carried on when it will most conveniently dovetail into what are seemingly more important operations. However, in a general way one should endeavor to cut his hay crop when it will furnish the largest amount of good food. No crop is more easily spoiled than clover, and no crop will furnish such excellent hay for all kinds of farm animals as will clover if it is cut at the right time and afterwards properly cured. Those who have observed the nature of a clover plant will have noticed that the head on top of the main stem comes out first, while the two lateral heads come into bloom from ten days to two weeks later. It is a very common thing to hear the advice given to cut clover when it is in full bloom, but in our estimation the "full bloom" period is somewhat an indefinite term. Some seasons clover may appear to be in full bloom for a period of about a month, and yet during this time the quality of the hay may have materially deteriorated. When the first heads have attained their full size and bloom clover is in a very succulent condition, and if cut in this stage will be somewhat difficult to cure, owing to its large water content. If climatic conditions were favorable at such time and other operations on the farm so adjusted as to allow a few days' haying when the clover is in this condition it would be advisable to begin cutting. But unless the weather were well settled and the corn ground in ideal condition it would be much better to delay cutting until the first heads were just beginning to turn brown. At this stage the second pair of heads will be coming in bloom. While in this condition clover could still be made into nutritious, palatable hay. There might be the slightest deterioration in the quality, owing to a somewhat increased percentage of crude fiber, although the lessening of the water content would so materially assist in the curing process that the lessening of the value of the hay would be an unimportant factor.

To leave clover much longer and allow the first heads to turn completely brown is to cause a decrease in the per cent of digestible protein and also an increase in the amount of crude fiber present. On the other hand, hay made from overripe clover is not nearly so palatable, and as a result is not so freely eaten by animals.

HOW TO SECURE A STAND OF CLOVER.

Wallaces' Farmer.

We have written so much about clover growing for the last fifteen years that we had assumed that the farmers who had been reading after us know everything that we knew about it, and possibly more too. When, however, we attend an institute, we did last week, the same old questions come up. The farmers want to hear that clover story once more. We will try and make it so plain and simple that a child can understand it.

First, secure seed that is not spoiled; in other words, seed with germinating power; or to put it plainer still, clover that will grow. Any clover seed will grow if you give it a chance. Any clover seed will grow if it has not been frozen or otherwise spoiled. To know just what per cent will grow, get a soup plate from your wife, fill it with sand; then pour water on it till it runs off, then count out 100 clover seeds and put them on the sand. Borrow a pie pan from her, turn it upside down over it and

19

set it under the stove. In a week count how many sprouts you have or how many grains have grown. That will give you the per cent that will grow the first year. You are likely to find in the course of two or three weeks more seed sprouted. These are the seeds that will not grow the first year, but will grow the second, the "hard shells," so to speak. Now you know what your seed will do if you give it a chance. This seed cannot help but grow next spring if you give it three things; heat, air and moisture, all three. If you give it heat and moisture by putting four inches of ordinary soil on top of it, it will not grow, because there is no air. If you give it air and heat by leaving it in the sack, it will not grow because it has no moisture. If you give it moisture and air by putting your soup plate and pie pan in the refrigerator where the temperature is below 32 it will not grow. You must give all three, not one or two, but all three.

Now the only question about getting a stand of clover is furnishing these conditions. If you do not put it over two inches deep in lighter soils, or over one inch deep in clay soils, it will get all the air it needs. April or May will give it all the heat it needs. Now what you want is to give it the moisture; in other words, to so arrange the seed bed that it will have moisture, heat and air. If you will thoroughly prepare the seed bed and cover the seed from half an inch to two inches according to the moisture content, in the month of April or farther south the last of March, you will have the required conditions, and that clover seed will grow. It can't help it, and you can't keep it from growing unless you deprive it of one of these three conditions.

We will now point out how many farmers fail to give these conditions. We saw any number of farmers last April sowing clover seed on top of the ground. We sowed some ourselves. We examined it and found that only an occasional seed was growing. It was lying on top of the ground and was not growing, of course. It was sown on wheat and we harrowed it thoroughly. That clover started to grow because we had furnished the conditions. That sown by our neighbors started to grow too, but not until the moisture was furnished by the May rains. Our harrowing of the ground furnished the moisture and gave it a start; that was all. But if no heavy rains had come in June or since, the clover sown on top of the ground would have been there yet. It would have stayed there until next year and then if undisturbed would have grown. Why? Because moisture was not furnished.

Clover seed will grow in very wet springs and on very wet land without covering. Under these conditions sufficient moisture is furnished. If it is not furnished, it will not grow and you can't make it. Some farmers fail to provide the conditions by sowing it on lumpy, cloddy land. Moisture is not furnished because the lumps allow it to dry out before the clover gets soaked up and ready to start. It may possibly sprout, but through lack of moisture it will die. There is no trouble in getting good clover seed to grow, if you give it these conditions, and only those grains that are furnished these conditions will ever grow.

This, however, is not the difficult matter in practical clover farming. Clover needs moisture, heat and air to start growing, but to continue this growth it must have light and heat above as well as moisture below, and just here is where most farmers fail. They sow clover with a "nurse crop," so-called. That nurse crop, generally oats or spring wheat, is a rank grower and so shades the ground that the plant cannot have sufficient light. The leaves of the plant can't do their work in darkness. The growth is made through the leaf by taking up the carbon dioxide, or as it is generally called, the carbonic acid of the air, dissolving it by means of its green coloring matter, exhaling the oxygen and using the carbon to build up the plant, for this is absolutely necessary. Unless it gets light and plenty of it, the plant can't grow, and just in proportion as the nurse crop,

Group of Short-Horns, winners of the Grand Beef Herd prize at Iowa State Fair, 1902. Owned by G. M. Casey, Clinton, Missouri.

so-called, shuts off the light, just in that proportion does it weaken the clover plant, the weakness being shown by the lack of color in the leaf. Therefore if you use a nurse crop, use one that grows as slender in the stalk as possible, with as narrow a leaf as possible, and that matures as early as possible. It is for this reason that we advise sowing the earliest kind of every kind of spring grain whether wheat, oats or barley, when used as a nurse crop for grass seeds. The reason why so muay farmers succeed in getting a stand of clover when putting it on rye or winter wheat or oats and using these as grasses, is because the constant cropping of the grass by the cattle keeps down the "strangling crop" (for that after all is the true name of the nurse crop so-called), and permits the young plants to have the light they so much need. Weeds act in the same way, and the only reason why we sometimes recommend sowing some kind of grain with clover when the land is very foul instead of giving it the full use of the land, is because it is more satisfactory to mow oats for hay than weeds to prevent their strangling the clover.

Another reason why we object to sowing any kind of clover with rank growing spring grain is because when grown as a grain crop these are removed about the 15th to the 20th of July in the latitude of central Iowa, and the full blaze of the hot sun is allowed to fall on the delicate, sickly clover plants that have been struggling for an existence. This is just like taking a boy out of the sick room and making him do a full day's work in the harvest field. This explains why so many stands of clover apparently good up to that time perish. It does not, however, explain it fully. These crops have been making very heavy drafts on the soil moisture. It requires 500 pounds of water to make a pound of dry oats; wheat and barley about 400. Our readers can readily see why when the supply of moisture is short, the clover is robbed, consequently has little root development, and no wonder it dies when the nurse crop is removed, unless the ground is full of moisture. This explains why heavy rains during harvest save a prime stand of clover which would otherwise perish.

If our readers who are planning to have a stand of clover next year will read this over two or three times till they fully understand it and then put it in practice, we will not have half the complaints we have had in years past of failures in the stand of clover from various causes. Bear in mind that clover that has germinating power will germinate if given the conditions of germination; that the main thing required in the spring is moisture, and that it must be put down in the soil deep enough to get the moisture, but not so deep as to exclude the air. Bear in mind further, that the seeds absorb the moisture from the particles of soil around them. Hence they must be in close contact with that soil, which can only take place when a good seed bed has been prepared. That is, when the soil is finely pulverized, so that the clover seed can get right up next to the particles of soil and get the moisture that it needs. A thoroughly prepared seed bed is one of the first requisites, therefore, in securing a stand of clover. Where you can get your seed bed so thoroughly prepared that every grain will grow, you don't need more than five pounds of clover seed to the acre. We usaully recommend eight pounds, because we are talking to men, many of whom don't prepare their seed bed; some because the circumstances are such that they can't do it, others because they don't try to do it. In these cases you must sow pretty nearly twice as much seed as you expect to grow.

BREEDING CLOVER.

Twentieth Century Farmer.

The aggregate value that has come from improvement of live stock and plants is so great that there can hardly be any adequate conception of it. A large part of the wealth of the agricultural world can be traced to this source. Never have efforts been as great or activity so marked as at the present time. If the man who causes two blades of grass to grow in place of one adds to his own and his country's wealth, then Prof. De Vries of the Amsterdam university, Holland, has earned the right to be called the benefactor of the agricultural world by breeding a clover that uniformly has five leaves on each clover stem instead of three, the usual number. He has accomplished this by a process of selection and isolation carried on for a period of ten years.

It is a common belief that the finding of a four-leaf clover is an auspicious event and will bring good fortune to the possessor. Five-leaf clovers and even six leaves are sometimes found. Prof. De Vries found some of these and carefully transplanted them to a greenhouse. After careful breeding for a number of years he got seed enough to begin field culture. So from this beginning the farmers of Holland now raise crops of the five-leaf clover. The leaves of clover are the part that have no waste and are richer in food elements than the clover stems. In the new five-leaf there are no more stems than there were in three-leaf, so in that part there is two-fifths gain.

Prof. De Vries has put in ten years of his life on what would seem a small thing, but the results show that his labors have been of great value to the world. This is only one of the numerous experiments in plant breeding that are in progress at all our experiment stations. We shall expect that the result of these studies of plant life will result in the future, as they have in the past, in increased crop production by breeding plants that will give a larger yield and those that will better flourish in our climate.

E. RAPE.

THE PLACE FOR DWARF ESSEX RAPE ON THE FARM.

Wallaces' Farmer.

What is Dwarf Essex Rape?

It is a plant of the cabbage brossica family; not a common cabbage, however, but a turnip that does not have any turnip on the root, but puts its substance wholly in the stock and leaves. It is a biennial like the cabbage and turnip, which grows one year and lives over winter in climates suitable, and produces a crop of seed the next year. In the United States east of the Rocky Mountains and north of latitude 40 degrees, and perhaps even further south, the severe freezing of the winter kills it; hence, the seed is all brought from England or Holland or from the states on the Pacific coast, where the mild winter enables it to survive. There is therefore, no danger of it becoming a weed and polluting the land like wild mustard. You may be dead sure of the northern winter killing any Dwarf Essex Rape that may be left over if indeed your stock will allow any of it to survive after the first of December.

Of what use is Dwarf Essex Rape, anyhow? says the new subscriber. Its use is for pasture. It may be sown as early as oats and from time to t'me until August, whenever the soil has sufficient moisture to sprout the seed. We advise sowing it under the following circumstances: First, we advise plowing up and sowing to either rape or to a mixture of oats and rape, or wheat and rape, or all three, any lots around the barn or other buildings that are rich and liable to grow up to weeds or on which there is an insufficient grass stand, for use as a hog pasture. We are dead sure that treated in this way these lots would become revenue producing instead of growing up with unsightly weeds and will give as large a revenue where hogs are on hand as if they were cultivated in corn with the greatest care, and with a great deal less labor. In fact, the very cheapest thing, as well as the most profitable, to grow on these lots is Dwarf Essex Rape alone or combined with the grains above mentioned. There is not the slightest doubt about this being a paying proposition. Our new subscribers, as well as old, can take this on faith and act accordingly. Corn is scarce this year and high in price, and you may just as well get the value of a crop of corn in advance, beginning to harvest it as soon as the rape is six or eight inches high as pay out money for feed for your hogs until a new corn crop comes.

A good many farmers for the past two years have picked up an extra five dollars per acre on oats fields by sowing, either with the oats or after the oats have fairly started, from three to five pounds of rape seed per acre. We do not, however, advise this so positively and would prefer sowing after the oats, sowing the oats in drills, and covering with a light harrow say after the oats are two or three inches high.

The objection to sowing with the oats is that if the oats should be a thin stand, the rape will make such a rapid growth as to prove a serious inconvenience at harvest; or if the oats should grow rank and should lie down, the rape will come right along through and harvesting might be a serious trouble, if indeed it is at all practicable. The end to be secured is to have the rape growing not more than stubble high until the oats are harvested. If that end is attained, and the farmer must make up his own mind as to how best to attain it, he is sure of an aftermath, whether he has grass seed with his oats or not, that will be worth from three to five dollars per acre to him provided he can pasture it down with sheep. Quite a number of farmers who do not have a sheep on the place have adopted this method on twenty and forty-acre fields and after they remove their crops of oats they go into the markets, buy a carload of sheep, pasture it down, then ship them as fat sheep to market, and have in several cases that have come to our knowledge realized five dollars per acre for this pick-up crop at a total cost of not over twenty-five to forty cents per acre for seed.

The third method of using rape is by sowing it at the rate of from three to five pounds per acre in the corn fields just prior to the last working. If there is sufficient moisture to secure germination this will pay every time. There will not, however, be a rank growth of rape until the frost kills the corn blades, as rape does not grow rapidly unless it can have the full sunlight. In any case, however, if a stand is secured, the rape will be worth more than the cost of the seed sown in keeping down weeds, and will always bring its full value by means of its rapid growth after the frost has stopped the growth of the corn.

This should not be done, however, where it is intended to sow the land to winter wheat, as the full benefit will not be secured in time for wheat sowing, and besides the rape will interfere somewhat with the drill in sowing the wheat. Where it is intended to husk the corn and pasture the stalks, a practice which we hope we will live long enough to see entirely out of date, there should be no hesitation in sowing it, as the only risk will be in not securing a stand. It will be of great advantage to cattle ,and tend to prevent impaction of the stomach or what is sometimes known as blind staggers. It will also be a very great advantage where sheep are fattened in the corn field, as with rape, corn blades, weeds and corn, sheep will make a growth that will surprise and delight the owner.

If our new subscribers will experiment with Dwarf Essex Rape in one or all of these ways, we are sure they will be paid many times over for the cost of their subscription to Wallaces' Farmer and will wonder why they have never subscribed for the paper before.

SOWING RAPE IN GRAIN FIELDS.

Homestead.

Investigation reveals the fact that valuable plant food constituents are lost when soil is allowed to remain bare after a cereal crop is removed. In view of this, there is a growing tendency in favor of keeping some crop growing on the soil throughout the summer and autumn. It has been determined, for example, that by sowing rape along with cereals in the spring there is produced a most excellent fall pasture for sheep and hogs, so that fertility which otherwise might be wasted is utilized in the production of mutton and pork. The manner of seeding is very similar to that by which clovers and grasses are established. The soil should be well prepared on the surface in order to insure a uniform covering of the seed. It is the practice of some to mix rape seed at the rate of two or three pounds per acre with oats or barley and sow all together at the same time.

Another plan is to sow broadcast by hand or with a grass seeder just in front of the grain drill. This will insure a good covering of the seed and will in all likelihood give the rape a strong start. The only objection to either of these methods is that in case the season should be wet there is a little danger that the rape will outgrow the cereal and thus interfere with harvest operations. However, this rank growth occurs so seldom that it is hardly necessary to take any precaution to prevent its occurrence. On rich soil splendid results are obtained when the rape is sown ten days or two weeks after the cereal crop, and covered by the use of a light harrow or a weeder. We say a "light" harrow because experience has demonstrated that unless the soil is very firm the harrow will tear out rather too much of the grain crop, although we have frequently seen this method recommended without any qualification.

If a stand of rape is secured it is never advisable to pasture too early after the removal of the crop. The returns will be much larger at the plants are allowed to get up six or eight inches before stock is turned on. This affords opportunity for the establishment of a vigorous root system so that close cropping will not be such a serious setback to the crop. When handled properly we have known cases where rape seeded in the above manner yielded as high as eighteen tons per acre by the end of October. In most instances the amount of pasture produced will run over ten tons per acre if the seed bed has been properly prepared in the spring. Although this may seem to be somewhat exhaustive of fertility yet lands that have been handled in this way generally prove to be very productive the following year. The rape roots lock up food materials that would otherwise be lost, and in turn by their decay liberate plant food for the following crop. Even should the rape not be used by stock but simply plowed under the soil would be much benefited by its growth.

RAPE IN FEED YARDS AGAIN.

—

Homestead.

A subscriber from Mediapolis, Iowa, sends the following inquiry:

"I have two feed lots each containing two acres. One was seeded to rye last fall, while the other is simply growing up with weeds. I expect to raise fifty or sixty pigs this summer and have no feed for them, and would therefore like to sow one lot with rape, but know nothing about the crop. Please inform me how to sow it to get the best results."

The above question is specified and we take pleasure in giving a specific answer. Besides we are always pleased to champion the cause of this most wonderful plant, rape. The yard that has not been seeded to rye should be disced up just as early in the spring as the soil will work nicely without puddling. After getting the surface in good condition sow about four or five pounds of rape seed per acre broadcast and cover well by the use of the harrow. If these instructions are carried out there will be a strong growth of rape in four or five weeks, at which time hogs may be turned on. We know persons who make a practice of allowing their hogs to have access to the rape right from the start, while others prefer to let it grow seven or eight weeks. Of course it never is a good practice to cut any crop back too severely until it has a strong root development. In the case cited we would prefer to use the rye section until the rape had made a growth of nine inches or one foot. In this connection we would like to proffer a little advice concerning the yard in which the rye is growing. It will be an excellent plan to sow two or three pounds of rape seed per acre among the rye just as early as possible in the spring, and afterwards harrow in the seed. It will do the rye no harm to give two or three strokes with the harrow, while this will insure the germination of the rape. As the rye becomes woody quite early in the spring the rape will come on and will keep up the supply of fresh pasture. Wherever yards are likely to be left to grow up to weeds we would strongly advise using the means we have described of making them productive.

F.　SOJA OR SOY BEANS AND COW PEAS.

SHOULD THE SOY BEAN CROP BE GENERALLY INTRODUCED?

Homestead.

' Possibly not more than one reader out of every thousand is growing the soy bean, so that at first blush such a subject as the above may seem irrelevant to their conditions. There is one thing about this plant, however, that immediately commends it to the attention of thoughtful farmers, namely its ability to add fertility to the soil. By this we do not mean that a crop of soy beans may be grown and removed from a soil, at the same time enriching its supply of plant food, but we do mean that if the product is fed upon the farm and proper care is taken of the manure the effect will be to increase rather than to decrease the productive power of the soil, owing to the fact that nitrogen, one of the most expensive elements of plant food, is taken from the atmosphere and stored in the land by the bean roots. As agriculture progresses greater emphasis will be placed upon the production of such crops, and we are fast approaching the point where we will believe in "balanced rotations" just as much as we do in "balanced rations." It would sometimes appear that the difficulties connected with getting a stand of clover are insurmountable, and where conditions are adverse to the establishment of biennial legumes it is possible that annuals may be made to take their place. The bean belongs to the latter class and we believe that it will find a place in the rotation of not only the south, but of the middle and north-central west. In fact it has been demonstrated that this crop will do quite well wherever the cereals grow.

But the soy bean has other qualities to commend it for general culture beside its ability to increase soil fertility. It is specially worthy of consideration because of the large amount of valuable food that may be grown on an acre, and especially are its products valuable to stockmen of the corn belt. As is well known, corn is a one-sided food, and and is not adapted to the needs of growing animals, that is, when fed alone. Even for fattening purposes nearly all really successful feeders supplement their corn with the rich commercial meals, especially toward the finishing period. To bring up this side of the ration involves considerable outlay so that the production at home of those foods which are rich in flesh forming materials would cheapen meat production. Now the soy bean is almost as rich in flesh forming elements as the commercial meals, while at the same time it is palatable to all classes of farm animals, so that the importance of such a crop to the dairyman or to the feeder is at once apparent. It is true that the value of a bean crop depends upon its ability to yield as well as upon the quality of its product, and this is the very point where its introduction has met with the most opposition. It must be remembered that it takes time to acclimate any crop, and as the soy bean is not indigenous to America, we must exercise a little patience about its introduction. Southern seed will not mature in the north the first year any more than would corn, but the crop is gradually creeping northward. To a very large extent we have yet to produce varieties that are adapted to our great variety of climatic conditions. Nearly all the experiment stations have succeeded in establishing varieties that are suited to the special set of conditions found in their vicinity. This is forming the nucleus seed supply for the northern and western states. It is no uncommon thing to get a yield of fifteen hundred pounds per acre, and even as high as four thousand pounds have been obtained. It is true that the bean crop requires special attention but when it is possible to obtain a yield like the above of such rich products, the expenditure of a little extra labor is justifiable. We would not advise anyone to undertake to grow this crop on a large scale the first year, but so far as we are able to look into the future, having in mind what our needs will be, we heartily endorse its introduction. Should our subscribers become interested in the matter and require specific instructions on the subject of preparing soil, seeding or handling of this crop, we shall be pleased to give it our earnest attention.

SOJA OR SOY BEANS.

Wallaces' Farmer.

We are having a number of letters from correspondents in Iowa and Illinois as to the best methods of growing soja, or as they are commonly known, soy beans. As this crop was first introduced into the west by Professor Georgeson, of the Kansas station, whose three years residence in Japan as professor of agriculture enabled him to ascertain the merits of the crop, we naturally turn to the Kansas station for the most reliable information for western growers, and we do not know that we can do better than to quote from their bulletin of March, 1900, as follows:

"The soy bean should not be planted until the ground becomes warm and the danger of severe frost is over. While the plants may not die if the seed is put in earlier, they do not thrive. No extra growth is gained by too early planting, and the weeds are more likely to grow and make more cultivation necessary. We usually begin putting in soy beans as soon as we have finished planting corn. The beans should be planted in rows thirty to forty-two inches apart, with the single beans dropped one to two inches apart in the rows. One-half bushel of seed per acre is required. The ground should be in good tilth, and the weeds thoroughly killed just before the beans are planted.

"We prefer surface planting. Shallow listing is some times successful, but we have lost several crops from listing by heavy rains falling before the beans came up, filling the furrows so full that the young plants were killed. Several Kansas farmers have reported good stands by listing, then filling the furrow nearly full with the cultivator and planting the beans in the shallow furrow that is left.

"The beans may be planted with a grain drill or with a corn drill, having the plate drilled to drop right. At the college we plant with an eleven-hole grain drill, stopping all holes but the two outside ones and the middle hole. This puts the beans in rows thirty inches apart. We prefer this distance, where the teams are trained to work in narrow rows.

"We cultivate the same as corn, using the two-horse cultivator with small shovels and taking great care not to ridge the ground. Level culture is necessary to harvesting a full crop. The ground should be kept clean, free from weeds and grass, and we prefer the shallow tillage which secures a good earth mulch.

"The crop should be harvested when the pods turn brown and before the beans are fully ripe. If left until the beans become thoroughly ripe, the pods will open and the beans will be scattered on the ground.

"The only satisfactory way we have found for harvesting the crop is to cut the plants off just below the surface of the ground and rake them into windrows with a horse rake. Where not over ten acres are grown this cutting can be done by removing the shovels from a two-horse cultivator and bolting to the inner shank of each beam a horizontal knife about eighteen inches long, the knife set out from the cultivator and sloping back from point of attachment to point so as not to clog. Any blacksmith can make these knives. With such an arrangement two rows are cut at a time, the knives being set to cut the plants just below the surface."

As to yield, the same report says:

"The Early Yellow soy bean, planted in the spring, with yield from ten to twenty bushels per acre, depending upon the soil and season. The college farm is upland. In 1898, thirty-five acres of soy beans were grown, with an average yield of thirteen bushels per acre. In 1899 seventy acres gave an average yield of fifteen and one-half bushel per acre. With sufficient moisture to germinate them, a crop of soy beans can be grown after wheat and oats have been harvested. In 1896, the yield on the college farm on ground after wheat was eight bushels per acre; in 1898, six and one-fourth bushels. With linseed meal at twenty-five dollars per ton, these crops after wheat would be worth $6 and $4.68 per acre. In addition to these returns we received the benefit of increased yields from succeeding crops.

"Farmers with better ground than ours report a yield of twenty bushels per acre, using our seed."

From the same bulletin we gather a summary of experiments as to the value of soy beans for feed for live stock. Experiment No. 1, pigs weighing 188 pounds, fed one-fifth soy bean meal and four-fifth Kaffir corn meal, showed a saving of 13 per cent in the amount of feed required to make 100 pounds of gain:

Experiment No. 2, pigs weighing 122 pounds, fed the same ration, showed a saving of 27 per cent by adding beans to the Kaffir corn.

Experiment No. 3 showed a gain of 31 per cent by adding soy beans to Kaffir corn in the proportion of one-third soy bean meal to two-thirds Kaffir corn meal and showed a gain of 24 per cent by adding the bean meal to corn meal.

Experiment No. 4, hogs weighing 126 pounds, fed nine weeks on a ration of four-fifths Kaffir corn meal and one-fifth soy bean meal, showed a saving of 37 per cent; that is, 37 per cent less grain was required for 100 pounds of gain. This experiment was repeated on hogs weighing 140 pounds, fed fifty days, and showed a saving in feed of 33 per cent by adding soy beans to Kaffir corn.

From all that we can learn, there is a gain not only in weight, but in thrift, muscle, and vitality by feeding soy beans to hogs intended for breeding purposes. Some farmers plant their soy beans at the last planting of corn by drilling or dropping them by hand between the rows from four to six inches apart, and cover them when they plow the corn the last time, then hogging the patch down.

COW PEAS AND SOY BEANS IN CORN.

A. D. Shamel in Breeders' Gazette.

A large number of inquiries in regard to sowing cow peas and soy beans in corn have been received this spring. Our experience has been that these crops, by adding directly to the supply of nitrogen through the root tubercles, are of great value to the fertility of the soil and through their extensive root development break up and loosen the subsoil. It is further true that the roots in penetrating the sub-soil tend to bring unavailable plant food to the surface soil where it can be used. Experiments and experience have shown that these crops are extremely valuable for feeding purposes, being rich in protein and minerals, and thus promote development of bone and muscle in young animals.

To get a stand of these crops in corn the best plan.is to drill in the seed just after the last cultivation. An ordinary three-row wheat drill will do the work very satisfactorily or a corn drill or a small one-horse drill of any sort may be used. The seed should be drilled in deep enough to reach the moist earth. Three rows are the best number to drill between two rows of corn. Drill the seeds about one inch apart in the row. At this rate one bushel of seed will sow an acre. Seed may also be broadcasted just before the last cultivation. The cultivator will cover the seed with moist earth and they will usually sprout quickly. The difficulty with this method of seeding comes from the fact that many of the seeds will not be covered evenly and many such seeds will not grow. It is customary when sown broadcast to sow about one and one-half bushels of seed per acre.

The varieties of cow peas best adapted for this method of planting are the Extra Early Black Eye, Clay, Red Ripper and the Whippoorwill. With a favorable season these will make a growth of vines two or three feet in length, but will not mature seed. Sheep or hogs turned into such a field will clean up the vines to the last vestige, leaving the manure scattered in the best possible shape for improving the fertility of the soil. If it is not convenient to turn stock into such fields the vines can be plowed under in the late fall or early spring. If plowed under in the spring the field should be disced before plowing in order to work the stalks into the ground and cut them up in such a way that they can be successfully turned under. A heavy freeze will wilt the plants so that the pasturing should be done as early in the fall as possible.

The best variety of soy beans for this purpose is the Medium Early Yellow. Great disappointment has been occasioned by farmers securing seed of the mammoth or very late varieties which will not mature in the latitude of central Illinois and are of little use for this purpose. The green soy bean matured at this station last season and produced a crop of seed of about eighteen bushels per acre. The soy bean is particularly desirable for sowing in corn, making an upright growth and flourishing particularly well in the corn rows. Last season on the station farm the beans were found to grow from two to five feet in height. They developed tubercules as large as small marbles and put the soil in splendid shape for the future corn crop. Owing to the fact that these plants will wilt down in freezing they do not interfere in husking the corn.

The great value of cow peas and soy beans to the soil comes from the fact that they come on in the corn field after the corn crop has ceased to draw on the plant food in the soil. During the latter part of the summer the organisms in the soil liberate plant food and continue this work until cold weather. If some crop does not take up this fertility it is likely to be lost through leaching or evaporation. By securing a stand of cow peas and soy beans in the field they not only do not interfere with the growth of the corn crop, but actually conserve the plant food for the use of future crops which otherwise might be lost.

HOW TO RAISE SOY BEANS IN THE NORTH.

Wallaces' Farmer.

There is a common impression that soy beans can be grown successfully only in the latitude of Kansas, Missouri, southern Iowa, and central Illinois. Waiting at a depot in northern Illinois a few days ago a farmer came in with a sack of as fine soy beans as we ever saw, grown right up by the Wisconsin line. Soy beans have matured in the last year or two in northern Iowa, and there is no reason why they may not be tried in those latitudes and we have no doubt that as the soy bean moves further north it will, like corn and other grains, adapt itself to the climate, becoming earlier with the shorter seasons, probably yielding smaller but paying crops to the man who would sow them wisely.

"Tell us about these beans," we hear some farmer say. The soy bean is a native of Japan, where nearly two hundred varieties are grown, according to the environment of the particular locality. There are very small varieties for table use, larger varieties for the growth of the soy bean as a grain, and still larger for ensilage and for hay. At the Kansas experiment station they have been grown, to our personal knowledge, for ten or twelve years, much as corn, only in drills, and in rows thirty-two inches apart, and narrower if the farmer has a tool with which he can keep them cultivated.

If cut for grain, they must be cut below the surface of the ground with a bean harvester, or with a corn plow with blades attached to it which answers the same purpose, cured and thrashed. The yield may run from ten bushels to twenty-five per acre, much the same as wheat. For forage, they may be sown broadcast, or in drills, cut with a mower, and cured like clover hay.

The soy bean is a nitrogenous plant, as rich in nitrogen as oil meal, and exceedingly rich in fat. In time some manufacturers will buy these beans, extract the fat, and sell it for olive oil straight from Italy, and sell soy bean cake to farmers in lieu of oil cake or cotton-seed meal. Mixed with corn, the soy bean would make excellent silage and would avoid the necessity of buying bran or oil meal. Professor Georgeson, who first introduced these beans, told us ten or twelve years ago that he regarded an acre of soy beans equivalent in feeding value to five tons of bran, and we do not believe his estimate is far out of the way.

Some farmers have adopted the method of having a boy drop soy beans between the corn rows at the last plowing and using these as feed for thoroughbred pigs. We have not the slightest doubt, where the moisture is sufficient to secure germination, that they will make pigs grow, shine and dazzle the eyes of the buyers without making them gobs of fat. In other words, they neutralize the effect of the corn diet.

We do not advise everybody to sow soy beans this year, but we do advise them to think about it, and if they can secure seed, of the earlier varieties in the northern section of our territory, and the medium and late varieties in the middle and extreme south, to experiment with them in a small way and thus find out their value for themselves. The province of the agricultural paper is not to work out details, but to give hints and suggestions and discuss general principles

HOW TO SOW SOY BEANS.

Homestead.

During the last few weeks we have had something to say on the value of the soy bean crop. We find now that some of our readers have purchased seed and wish information on the manner in which it should be sown or planted. In some instances the ordinary grain drills gives satisfactory results, although we have seen a number of drills that would not sow beans without splitting them. However, it will take but a short time to investigate the matter before taking the drill to the field. In case the beans are not split by the "feed" of the drill it is a good plan to stop the spouts so that the rows will be planted from twenty-four to forty inches apart. The practice in southern districts is to put the rows about the same distance apart as corn, although in northern areas exceedingly satisfactory results are obtained when the rows are placed twenty-four to thirty-two inches apart. When sown in this way the crop should be freely cultivated, which will in turn destroy all weeds and conserve moisture.

Where the ordinary grain drill breaks the seed and no other form of implement is at hand with which to put in this crop the corn planter may be pressed into service. It should be adjusted to drill instead of check. Some prefer to leave the rows the full width of the planter apart, although on rich soils we believe the yield will be increased by putting the rows half of the width of the corn planter apart. This may be done by driving the planter with center over the last row every second time across the field. Of course where there is nothing but the ordinary corn machinery it would not be advisable to put the rows so close together, but where the one-horse cultivator is at hand we believe, as we have said before, that the yield will be much increased when the rows are placed half the width of an ordinary corn planter apart.

In no case should soy beans be planted before the soil becomes warm. As the seed is somewhat large it is a good plan to plant fairly deep. If the soil is dry at the time it will do no harm to put it down to a depth of three inches. However, where there is considerable moisture in the surface two inches or two and a half of covering will bring the plants up a little quicker.

THE TIME TO SOW SOY BEANS AND COW PEAS.

Wallaces' Farmer.

An Iowa correspondent writes:

"I have been reading all the articles in relation to soy beans and cow peas in your most valuable paper and I find that you advise culti-vating, but I do not remember reading with what kind of a tool the cow peas were cultivated which were planted in rows from 18 to 22 inches apart. I want to sow a field of ten acres next spring to soy beans and oats to cut flor hay and I would like to know the month in which to sow. I also want to put in some cow peas. Please advise me when they should be sown, how much to the acre, and if they are to be cultivated, with what kind of implements. This is asking for a good deal of advice at one time, but I want to prepare early and make my first trial a success."

There seems to be a good deal of confusion in the minds of farmers who have had no experience with cow peas and soy beans as to the time of sowing them. Bear in mind that both these plants are hot weather plans and, therefore, should not be sown with oats or any other spring grain which requires early sowing. Neither of them should be planted until after corn planting when the ground is warm and the weather hot. We would sow cow peas broadcast, and if the ground is thoroughly prepared weeds will not interfere until the cow peas take full possession.

The Kansas method of cultivating soy beans is to drill them in rows wide enough apart to admit of cultivation with the regular tools on the farm. Thirty-two inches is about as close as you can put them; then cultivate as you would drilled corn. They should be about four inches apart in the row. If any one can devise a method of cultivation at narrower distances it would be better. The soy beans can be mown with a mower if cut for hay, but not if grown for seed, as the stalk becomes almost like wood. The Kansas way of harvesting is either with a bean cutter which cuts them off below the ground, or with a cutting knife attached in lieu of the shovels on an ordinary corn plow, which cuts them below the surface of the soil.

COW PEAS AS A SUBSTITUTE FOR CLOVER.

Wallaces' Farmer.

In our last issue we printed a communication from a correspondent of Calhoun county, Illinois, describing the growth of cow peas in that section, their great feeding value for sheep, goats, and he might have added hogs, and suggesting that they might be used to great advantage as a substitute for clover in sections where for any reason clover does not thrive.

This is in accordance with the views we have held for some time on this cow pea question. There are sections in Missouri and south central and southern Illinois where clover does not do as well as in latitudes farther north, and for two reasons: the winters are open and there is freezing and thawing during most of the winter months and the soil is a heavy clay, which turns into hardpan in the next county, for hardpan, like milk sickness and fever and ague, is usually found in the county adjoining. This stiff, tenacious clay lifts the clover out of the ground, and while it does well during the spring and summer, it does not carry through the winter and hence is not available except for plowing under as a first crop.

This is not a fatal objection to growing clover, for the fertility alone developed in the first crop is ample payment for the seed, but it is an objection none the less, but will be less of an objection when farmers come to realize the value of even a first crop of clover as a source of fertility. Alfalfa cannot be grown under these conditions and hence the cow pea is the best substitute for clover of which we have any knowledge.

Careful readers of *Wallacees' Farmer* must have noticed that in the last two or three years this cow pea is coming north. We planted a small quantity as an experiment this year and while planted late and badly cared for, nevertheless they yielded a fine crop of peas, showing that it can be used with profit in central Iowa. Farmers in northern Iowa, almost up to the Minnesota line, have furnished us from time to time with samples of well matured cow peas, and it may, therefore, be safely stated that the cow pea will flourish in northern Illinois and we have but little doubt in southern Wisconsin. The cow pea adapts itself to climatic conditions even more readily than corn and in time varieties will be developed that will grow wherever corn will grow.

The cow pea is a hot weather plant and therefore must not be planted until after corn, and as it will not stand frost it must be used either as a grain or a forage crop before the first frost. The cow pea belongs to the same order of plants as the clover; that is, it is a legume, and as such obtains its nitrogen from the atmosphere and fertilizes land exactly in the same way and with the same ingredients as clover; hence, it can be used as a substitute for clover wherever for any reason clover does not do well.

As a grain crop it is superior to clover and fully its equal as a forage crop the first year. It is strictly an annual and all the benefit comes in the year it is planted or sown and within ninety days of sowing. It can, therefore, be used not merely as a fertilizer, but as pasture for dairy cows and as a substitute for early corn for hogs. It can also be used in the orchard and this is one of the places where we would suggest a trial. The cow pea will fertilize the orchard so far as nitrogen is concerned and can be sown at the last cultivation, say in June. It can either be harvested for forage, or for seed, or the hogs can be turned in to gather the crop and leave the haulm to lie as a winter covering.

20

In southern Illinois and Missouri it can be drilled in at the rate suggested by our correspondent, a bushel per acre, following a crop of fall wheat or rye where the land has not been seeded to grass, and after harvesting the crop in any of the ways above suggested, the land can be plowed for the corn the next year, and while it may not add as much fertility as a crop of second year clover, it will not be far from adding as much fertility as a crop of yearling clover, which, as above stated, will be worth at least the cost of the seed.

As farmers in northern Illinois, Indiana, and Iowa come to understand the value of cow peas, there will be a great demand for seed. Heretofore farmers who have experimented with seed have been obliged to get it from the southern states. Our corresponedent's suggestion that seed from Missouri and southern Illinois will be far better for northern farmers than seed grown farther south is entirely correct.

As to the varieties, perhaps there is none better than the whip-poor-will. There are about fifty varieties of the cow pea, which is really not a pea but a bean, and as the plant moves north there will be a still wider variation and a general adaptation to northern conditions. We shall hear a great deal more of cow peas in farm institutes in the future than we have in the past and its cultivation opens a very fine opportunity for experimentation.

G. CATTLE.

THE CATTLE INDUSTRY OF THE UNITED STATES.

Paper of Hon. James Wilson, Secretary of Agriculture, read before the Central Short-Horn Breeders' Association, Kansas City, February 4, 1902.

The condition of the cattle industry in the United States at this time is a subject for congratulation. There is a demand for all classes of cattle at prices far above those which have ruled in recent years. Beef cattle, dairy cattle and pure-bred cattle all may be marketed on terms favorable to the breeder and feeder.

When we consider the depression and encouragement which existed in this industry but a few years ago, we can only marvel at the change which has been brought about in so short a time. And this change has occurred, not as a result of disasters to the industry, not as the result of losses or sacrifices of animals, but in spite of the fact that we have maintained a stock of cattle unexampled in the history of the country for numbers and values.

The preliminary census figures which have been made public are surprising. They show a much larger number of cattle than many writers anticipated. They demonstrate that during the years of the last decade, when it was supposed the stock of cattle was being depleted, it was really increasing. And now it would appear that we actually have more cattle, and also more in proportion to population, than we ever had before.

The same number of breeding cattle gives us a much greater annual product of beef now than it did fifty years ago. The stock of cattle has been improved; it is more precocious; bullocks are marketed at an earlier age; and the carcasses average heavier and better. With dairy stock there has been a similar improvement. The animals are more precocious, the average yield is better, and the annual product has greatly improved.

All of this, of course, is of advantage to the producer. It means that his breeding cattle are worth more money, that his sales bring him greater returns, and that his products are correspondingly larger.

These are the facts as we see them at this time. How can we explain the high price of cattle at a time when the numbers and products are greater than ever before? It cannot be accounted for by any variation in the crops of the country as a whole, or of any part of it; neither can it be explained by any variation in the amount of exports of cattle or cattle products. It is due principally to changed conditions in the United States; to the great and universal prosperity which prevails; to the increase in manufacture, and to the existence of a vast army of working men who are able to purchase and pay for the best beef, butter and cheese. We are manufacturing the iron and steel, the machinery, the textiles, and other finished products for the world, and are feeding directly and without any restrictions the laborers who are necessary to keep these enormous manufacturing enterprises in operation.

The statistics indicate that it is pre-eminently the development of the home market which has benefited the cattle market.

For many years our breeders have been working incessantly, with American energy and American intelligence, to establish in the United States the highest types of the best breeds of cattle. They have spent their money with a lavish hand for breeding stock; they have had the advantage of the most fertile soil in the world, and of a temperate climate favorable to animal life of all kinds. The cattle which they have produced have during late years held their own in the show rings with the best imported. It has seemed to me that we have reached a point where we might reasonably claim that we have as good cattle as exist in the country, and that we might assert our independence of foreign breeding stock.

Firmly believing that the development and high character of our pure-bred cattle warranted such assertions, I have taken steps to bring our animals to the country south of us, who are just reaching that stage of progress in animal husbandry where large numbers of such cattle are needed to grade up the native stock. I have had in mind particularly Mexico and Argentina as countries which must soon, of necessity, bring their cattle to the modern standard. But the people of these countries know good cattle when they see them and they want the best. It is useless to try and sell our culls in those markets. The first shipment of inferior stock will damage our prospects or perhaps ruin all chances of building up a trade. What is required is, first, confidence in our own stock, and, secondly, the determination that when the opportunity for shipment comes only the best cattle shall be permitted to go to represent us in these foreign markets.

There is still a sentiment among cattlemen in this country that we must have fresh blood from Europe to maintain the standards of our herds. This sentiment has been handed down by tradition from the early days when we began building up our herds; when many of the cattle imported were not as good as they should have been, and when our breeders were not as spillful as they are today. It has been kept prominent by the importers and dealers in imported stock, and by people who profited by such transactions otherwise than by the improvement of their cattle. I believe that I am right in concluding that this sentiment has no other foundation than tradition and personal interest at the present day, and I am going ahead upon that theory and trying to put our cattle into the markets of the world. But suppose, for the sake of argument, we accept the other view; would we not be asked at once by our prospective customers why they should not go to the same source that we are obliged to draw from? If our herds are not as good as the British herds, if they have not the quality of permanency, what argument can we use to induce people who want the very best to come to this country for our cattle? Should an American breeder find that a reasonably good animal had been produced abroad, having strains of blood corresponding with his line of breeding, I should expect him to try to gain possession of that animal, just as I should expect an intelligent Englishman or Scotch breeder to come to this country for an animal under the same circumstances, if he were not prevented by the rigid sanitary restrictions enforced by his country, and as they sometimes did before such restrictions were imposed. But the idea that foreign cattle as a class are better in the show ring or have greater prepotency than our cattle, is a fallacy which the American breeder should set about dispelling now and for all time.

We have within the United States the most varied soils and the widest range possible of climatic conditions, within the limits favorable to the high development of the domesticated animals. No doubt there are some sections which are especially adapted to the highest types of certain breeds. Our breeders should study this question, and they should try and unite the conditions of the soil, the condition of climate, the methods of feeding and treatment which are best suited to each particular breed. In that manner we shall produce animals of all breeds equal to any in the world—animals which are the product of their environment, and which, consequently, become more and more capable of transmitting their characteristics to their offspring. It is not surprising that the highest types of animals bred in distinct countries, under the peculiar conditions which exist there, should in certain instances after being brought to this country, show some falling off in succeeding generations, as a result of the violent change in their environment. But this deterioration is not permanent, if they are properly managed; and when the herd recovers from the shock of being transplanted to a totally different climate, it is the more valuable on that account, for it is then acclimated, as we say, or, in other words, it has become adapted to the different conditions of life.

Now, as you know, the climate of the original home of the British breeds has marked peculiarities. The atmosphere of the island is laden with moisture, the summers are cool, the grasses grow rapidly and they contain a large proportion of water. It is quite different in most parts of the United States; but our conditions approach the conditions found in Mexico and South America. British breeds acclimated here may be taken from here to those countries with far less shock, with far less danger of deterioration and disease, than if taken directly from Great Britain. This is a point which should be understood by our own breeders, and which we should endeavor to impress upon the stockmen of other countries on the American continent.

Among the first questions, however, which we are asked by the governments of countries to which we propose to export animals are: Are they free from contagious diseases? and, can you guarantee that they will not be exposed to the contagion of any such diseases on their way to the ships which are to carry them? This today is the most important question to all governments that are willing to consider the advisability of admitting foreign animals to their territory. Most of you know how, on account of pleuropneumonia in this country, we lost the freedom of the British market for our live cattle over twenty years ago. Since that time our cattle have been killed on the docks where landed within a specified number of days. You can readily see that when our animals are once landed without the privilege of shipping to any other market, without the ability to hold them beyond the ten-day limit, our shippers are at the mercy of the English buyers. How many millions of dollars those restrictions have cost the American farmer never will be known; and all that we can say is that we have lost and are still losing an enormous amount of money because we permitted that disease to remain a few years too long upon American soil. We might just as well have stamped the disease out in 1870 as in 1890, and if we had done so, there would have been no occasion for these restrictions, which now have been permanently imposed. The reason we did not act sooner was that we listened to the counsels of a lot of noisy and insistent individuals who thought they knew all about the subject, but who really were densely ignorant of everything pertaining to it. They claimed there was no pleuropneumonia in the country; or admitting that there was such a disease, they were certain there was no danger in it, or, if they were forced to admit the existence of such a disease, they scouted the idea that the British would ever restrict the cattle trade on account of it.

We have had about the same experience in regard to sheep scab. It was scattered all over the country; the stock yards and markets were infected with it; all sheep in transit were exposed to it; and, notwith-standing the inspection, it would break out among our export sheep under the most inconvenient and embarrassing conditions. As a result of this, the British government applied the same restrictions to sheep as to cattle.

The same disease has been the means of shutting our sheep out of the markets of France and other European countries. Now we are getting sheep scab under our control, and with a few more years of intelligent work shall be free from it.

Much surprise has been expressed in some quarters with reference to a suggestion recently made by me that it might be well for us to consider whether the time had not arrived for following the example of Great Britain and entirely shutting out foreign live stock from our territory. We still have representatives of that same class of men who could see no harm

English Coach Stallion, owned by Truman Brothers, Bushnell, Illinois, and shown at the Iowa State Fair, 1902.

to come to us from nursing pleuropneumonia among our cattle twenty years ago, and who are equally positive today that no harm can come to us from any other disease. But it seems to me that with a stock of the finest animals in the world, with the largest number of animals that any country has ever accumulated, with a fabulous amount of wealth invested in these animals—an amount unexampled in the history of the world— it seems to me, I repeat, that we should take stringent measures to insure these animals and this wealth from the one danger to which they be exposed.

It is said that my suggestion to exclude live stock includes all kinds of animals—cattle, sheep, hogs and horses. Very well, if all kinds of animals are liable to bring destructive and disastrous plagues to our shores, why not exclude one kind as well as another? It is absurd to lock one door to a stable and leave another and equally convenient door open for thieves to enter.

If we follow the example of Great Britian, as suggested, we would not exclude horses; and yet there are many dangers connected with the horse trade. Glanders has been an ever present menace and source of loss for many years. Horses may also, it is believed, carry the contagion of foot-and-mouth disease. It may not be known to you, and yet it is a fact, that the Bureau of Animal Industry has been struggling for several years with an imported venereal disease of horses which has got upon the ranges of the Northwest, and which has so far defied all efforts for its complete eradication. As a climax comes the news of surra among the horses in the Philippines. Surra is a disease long known in India, of which we have heard little in the past, but with which we may become only too well acquainted in the future. Surra is caused by a small animal parasite which lives in the blood, and when once it gets into the blood of a horse it stays there for months and perhaps for years. It would, therefore, be not at all impossible for a horse harboring this parasite to be brought from the Philippines, or from India, or from any of the other Oriental countries where the disease exists, either directly to the United States, or indirectly by way of any of the European contries. Possibly the disease was carried to China with the horses of the troops from India; there it may have been communicated to the horses of the American army, and by these transported to the Philippines. What we know is that most of the horses in certain parts of the Philippines are affected this year and the disease is exceedingly fatal.

The parasite of surra is supposed to be carried from horse to horse by certain species of flies. Just what kind of flies these are or whether they exist in the United States is not definitely known. They certainly exist in the Philippines, and if they are not already here they may be introduced at any time. Surra is to horses what rinderpest is to cattle— a disease that spreads rapidly and is fatal in nearly every case.

Then why should we not adopt measures to protect our horses as well as cattle? Why should we continue to live in a fool's paradise, imagining ourselves safe, when we see these diseases existing in other countries, jumping from one country to another, and, with faster and more frequent communication between all parts of the world, ever getting nearer to us in point of time, and on that account more dangerous? We have seen foot-and-mouth disease jump from the continent of Europe again and again within the past two years, notwithstanding the prohibition of cattle, sheep and hogs; we have seen rinderpest jump to the African continent and spread over it like a sheet of flames, devouring the cattle and damaging the sheep; we have seen surra jump to the Philippines. Shall these diseases of other countries be no lesson to us?

There are other diseases new and strange to us existing in various lands which may or may not be capable of introduction into the United States. There is, for example, the horse sickness of South Africa, a most fatal and unmanageable disease; there is the Angora goat disease; there are various sheep and swine diseases, notably the erysipelas of Europe.

And finally there is tuberculosis, which is neither new nor strange to us. Tuberculosis is perhaps the worst of all animal diseases, because, like pleuropneumonia, it is a very insidious disease, entering a herd and progressing in it until most of the animals are diseased before its presence is suspected. Like pleuropneumonia again, when once it has entered a herd, it remains there during the existence of the herd unless stringent measures are adopted for its eradication. But its possibilities of danger are far beyond those of pleuropneumonia, because it attacks all species of domesticated animals—horses, cattle, sheep, pigs and dogs. Its greatest ravages are, as you know, with cattle and hogs. In some countries 40 to 50 per cent of the cattle and 3 to 4 per cent of the hogs are affected with it. In this country we have had far less than most other parts of the world, but the disease is increasing in most parts of the United States. This is shown by the federal meat inspection statistics, which since 1895 have covered over 30,000,000 head of cattle and 120,000,000 hogs. In 1895 the condemnation of cattle carcasses for tuberculosis equalled 407 per million; in 1901 they amounted to 1,285 per million, or three times as many. In 1895 the condemnation of hog carcasses for this disease equalled 29½ per million; in 1901 there were 352 per million or nearly twelve times as many. The inspectors are acting under the same instructions now that they did in 1895; and, making all allowances for the improvement of the inspection and its extension into smaller houses, where classes of animals are killed that are more likely to be affected, there is no escaping the conclusion that the disease has become much more frequent in slaughtered animals. What is the explanation of this fact?

In various countries the conclusion has been reached, after careful investigation, that tuberculosis was being spread by pure-bred animals purchased to improve the common animals of the country. Has that been the case with us? I know that this seems at first sight an ungrateful suggestion to bring before an association devoted to the production of pure-bred stock, but I believe that you have the strength, intelligence, and honesty to meet it squarely, and to take such measures as are necessary to guard against the dissemination of this disease by the cattle which you breed. When the department of agriculture began making tests of the pure-bred cattle coming into the United States from Canada, it found that 24 per cent of them were affected with tuberculosis; and in some of the tests made in Great Britain of cattle that importers desired to purchase, it was found that 50 per cent had the disease. How is it possible to maintain the health of our cattle if we continue to import that kind of breeding stock?

I present these facts plainly because you are the men who should, above all others, be interested in the welfare of the cattle industry, and

Display of fruit in Horticultural Department, Iowa State Fair, 1902.

because I desire you to know my reasons for establishing and continuing the tuberculin test of imported cattle. If anyone can give us a better and more certain test to determine which animals are affected, I assure you I should lose no time in adopting it.

And now a concluding word in relation to the South American market. When we turned our eyes toward Argentina as a promising market for our fine stock, we found the government of that country on the point of issuing an order excluding animals from all countries in which foot-and-mouth disease existed, or where sufficient precaution had not been adopted to prevent its entrance. That order was actually issued last May to remain in force for six months. The second order expires early next month. We did not suppose that this order would affect our cattle, as the American minister was authorized to certify that foot-and-mouth disease does not exist in the United States, and he was also instructed to explain the thorough system of quarantine which we apply to imported stock. The Argentine government held, however, that they had excluded British stock because they believed it might bring this disease, and, as we admitted British stock, they were of the opinion that consistency required them to exclude our stock, notwithstanding the quarantines and other precautions which we have adopted. The semi-official representative of Argentina visited the International Live Stock Exhibition at Chicago last December on the invitation of the officers and returned with a very favorable impression of our country and of our live stock. I have also sent a special agent to South America to ascertain the condition of their markets, and to give us full information as to the methods by which animals may be shipped and sold there to the best advantage. He has also been instructed to confer with the officials of the various countries and to explain to them that this government is ready to inspect animals that are to be exported, to make the required test, and to certify to their healthfulness. Considering the condition of international trade—that we have been buying an average of seven and one-half million dollars' worth of agricultural products while she has been buying less than $150,000 worth from us—it would appear that we may reasonably expect some plan to be devised by which our animals may enter that market.

If that is accomplished we must, on our part, see that they get the value of their money; that is, the stock which goes there must be first class and in a healthy condition. If we permit animals of inferior quality or those affected with tuberculosis to be shipped there, the returns will not pay expenses and we shall never establish a trade.

I thank the officers and members of the association for their kind invitation to attend this meeting, and for the future invitation to send a paper in case I should not be present in person. If it were not for the important business which demands my presence in Washington at this time, I should certainly have been with you. I am interested in your work. I admire the noble Shorthorn, and I hope you will maintain the breed in the position which it has occupied so long—unsurpassed among the beef breeds, unsurpassed as a general purpose animals.

THE RELATION OF THE BREEDER OF PURE-BRED STOCK TO THE FARMER AND FEEDER.

H. W. Mumford, Professor of Animal Husbandry, Illinois Agricultural College.

Read before the Kansas Improved Stock Breeders' Association:

For a long time we have believed that the relationship between the breeder of pure-bred animals to the feeder and market cattle has not been clearly understood. Breeders and feeders as well, have at times seemed to utterly disregard the possibility of mutual helpfulness and even of mutual dependency. The real place of pure-bred animals has frequently been lost sight of, which has led to practices that have not worked out for the best interests of breeders of pure-bred animals or the men whose rightful sphere of usefulness is producing animals for the block.

An active demand for good beef, coupled with a scarcity of prime steers, is bound to bring about relatively high prices for prime bullocks on hoof and hook. High prices for market beef-cattle invariably stimulate prices for pure-bred beef-cattle and as surely great activity in the breeding of the same. Usually the stimulation of this branch of the live stock trade, aided by the ever enthusiastic efforts and aggressive methods of stock-breeders, is, at times, beyond a point warranted by the actual conditions existing in the open market trade.

Prices of pure-bred cattle at the beginning of such an epoch are at times slow in reaching values fully warranted by the trade, due no doubt to the fact that producers of prime market-cattle and prospective breeders are conservative. Doubtless the lessons learned during recent years of depression in the trade are still fresh in their minds, but as time goes on, pure-bred beef-cattle sell at prices which no more indicate their actual worth to the feeder and farmer than do the prices of champion steers at fat-stock shows represent the actual condition of trade in prime steers. To be sure, we do not all look at these conditions out of the same eyes, nor do we all interpret them in the same way; but I take it that we are all interested in looking at and solving these questions in such a way that ultimately the breeder and feeder shall reap the greatest and most lasting profits.

There can be but little doubt that relatively high prices for pure-bred beef-cattle influences many—I was about to say young and inexperienced men—but I may as well not qualify it and say what is undoubtedly true, that relatively high-prices for pure-bred beef-cattle influence many men to embark in the breeding of pure-bred cattle that have no fitness either by nature, training, or experience for the work and consequently have no business meddling with it. Failure invariably attends those who thus embark in the pure-bred cattle trade. Many of these men fail not altogether because they lack experience, but because they are unable to own herds of a size that would warrant them being called breeders.

Some men seem to have formed the idea that the breeding of fine cattle is an easy thing. It is unfortunate that many breeders make no effort to dispel such folly with a prospective buyer on the ground. The sooner men generally know and appreciate that it is no child's play to breed fine cattle the better, and breeders generally will make no mistake in aiding to establish such principles.

We have but to look back over the generations of the past and single out here and there a man who has really been a breeder and improver of cattle. Without exception they have been men of rare judgment and intellectual attainments. Men who have not gone into the business as a diversion, men strong enough to bear up under discouragement, resourceful and quick to catch at suggestions of promise. I do not hesitate to say that these are the men to whom we owe our gratitude for whatever of merit exists in our pure-bred cattle today. These are the men who have during times of depression, saved our herds from utter annihilation; and, fellow breeders, it is to such men as these that we must look for whatever promise of permanency there is in this industry. Fortunate, indeed, is the man having but few cows, who is able to produce animals of outstanding merit. The rule is, and ever has been, that the breeding of fine cattle is a thing not to be trifled with, but gone into heart and soul, on a scale large enough to bring results. The dabbler invariably fails.

A failure in breeding pure-bred stock is very apt to be followed by a lack of confidence in pure-bred animals as a necessary factor in live stock husbandry, a conclusion as unfortunate as it is false. But you say the man who falls short of success in breeding pure-bred stock would fail as a breeder or feeder of market-cattle. This does not necessarily follow. The chances are that when a man fails in the breeding of pure-bred animals, we lose from the live-stock ranks an active man who may have been a success as a breeder and feeder of market-cattle, and as such increase the legitimate and rational demand for pure-bred bulls. Undoubtedly, we do not all agree as to the legitimate place of pure-bred animals in the live-stock trade of this country. We believe that there is no room for doubt as to the absolute necessity of the introduction of the blood of pure-bred beef-sires into the herds of farm and ranch where the object is the production of prime-beef.

When we say the pure-bred beef-sire, we at the same time infer the necessity of good blood being attended by individual merit. Granted that pure bred sire is a necessity, we believe it is equally true that the pure-bred cow is not essential, advisable, or possible as a factor in the production of the prime steer for the open market. The use of a pure-bred bull on a herd of high-grade cows need not add $2 each to the cost of calves intended as the foundation for prime steers, while if pure-bred cows were to be used, it would increase the cost of each calf $25, at a conservative estimate, or beyond a point which would be profitable to the producer. Looking at the proposition from this standpoint, the case is a clear one that the rational relation of the breeder of pure-bred stock to the feeder is one of furnishing him with pure-bred bulls rather than

cows. Whichever way we look at this question if we do so thoroughly
and with a desire to get at the truth, we must come to the inevitable
conclusion that the breeding and sale of pure-bred bulls is really the
backbone of the pure-bred cattle-breeding industry.

Pure-bred cattle are sold not as producers of market-cattle, but as the
foundation of breeding herds of pure-bred cattle, that shall in turn produce pure-bred bulls and cows. Breeders of pure-bred cattle everywhere
seem to have lost sight of the fact that every time a registered female is
sold, competition is invited; but some one may say, why not invite and
even encourage competition? I can only answer this by saying that in my
judgment it is not necessary to invite, much less encourage, competition
in this line. A business that is naturally as attractive as the breeding
of pure-bred beef-cattle, that promises fair interest on the money invested, does not need any "drumming up." Besides, the kind of competition that is secured by inexperienced men embarking in the business
under the influence of a stimulus of high prices is not the kind of competition that will tend to furnish a normal and staple market for pure-bred
beef cattle. Our judgment would be to eliminate as far as possible this
element of competition by discouraging rather than encouraging the indiscriminate founding of herds by men who you have great reason for
believing will fail in the undertaking.

True, they furnish a present market for a few females, but where
failure is inevitable, they are bound to do the business, and the breed you
represent, immeasurable harm. Undoubtedly, I will be considered as
preaching a queer doctrine and one that will not work, by suggesting that
breeders discourage the sale of cattle for which they have demand.

We have but to look back over the history of this industry in the past
to satisfy ourselves that a failure of a majority of breeders to recognize this
principle of forcing a large number of females on the market when there
is a demand for them by experienced breeders, is not wholly but partly
responsible for periodical slumps in the pure-bred cattle trade. We confidently believe that if a united effort were directed along this line by
breeders of pure-bred cattle the country over, we should have continuous, staple and profitable market for all of our good cattle, a condition
which would make steady improvement possible. As it is, we nicely
prepared for breeding some good cattle when suddenly we find we cannot
afford to do so, owing to a slump in prices. Again, the breeder of pure-
bred cattle may well ask, what are we to do with the females we breed if
we are not to sell them? We concede that this is the most difficult question you could propound; however, it is not unanswerable. Many of the
breeders have no doubt observed the opinion expressed by Col. Woods
in his letter to the *Breeders Gazette*, and later by many breeders as to
the advisability of having one-third of our bull calves castrated. We are
not prepared to say that this is the right thing to do, as we do not believe this proposition strikes at the root of the whole matter.

That we have a large number of pure-bred beef-bulls going onto the
market that ought not to, we admit, and still, looking at it from the

standpoint of the breeder and feeder of market-cattle, practically every pure-bred bull now produced could be used to advantage. Not so, of course, from the standpoint of the breeder of pure-bred stock. While this is true for the present, the time is surely coming when there will be no market at all for inferior pure-bred bulls even to the producer of market cattle. The sale of a pure-bred bull to a breeder of steers, even if that bull is not one of high individual excellence, is pretty sure to work such improvement in a common herd of cows that the purchaser of the first pure-bred bull is certain to want another and a better one later on.

Unless we have a smaller per cent of inferior bulls produced in our pure-bred herds in the years to come, we will not have these better bulls to meet the demand of the breeders of market cattle. Certain it is that there ought not to be as large a proportion of inferior bulls produced in our pure-bred herds as there is.

Let us consider briefly why this is so. First of all, we will agree that no matter how well selected a herd may be, both as to cows and to bulls, and at the same time granting that the herd has been carefully managed as to housing, feed, and the like, there is bound to be, now and again, an inferior bull produced. Second, as long as we have, and we shall always have, men who dabble in the business without experience and judgment sufficient to properly care for their herds, we shall have too many inferior bulls. Third, I might say the most potent factor of all, inferior cows breed inferior bulls. This last cause or source, from which spring inferior bulls, is worthy of our most thoughtful consideration. I say, with Col. Woods and all the rest, let us castrate all unworthy bulls, but let us send the dam of all inferior bulls to the slaughter house before the bull gets large enough to "take by the horns." Granting that one-half of the calves dropped in a herd are bulls, and the other half heifers, there would be approximately the same number of males and females that ought not to find their way to the breeding-herd. In fact, there ought to be a closer and more discriminating selection of heifers than bulls, as a large per cent of the bulls are expected to produce a worthy representative of the race.

For sake of argument, however, let us consider that if 33½ per cent of all the bulls offered for sale in the country should be castrated then we hold that their dams should not be allowed to produce; while the dams of an equal per cent of heifers should not be permitted to go to the bull. This would take care of 66 2-3 per cent of the females bred. We believe there would be little trouble in disposing of the other 33 1-3 per cent of the females annually produced in any breeding-herd.

Nor need the heifers turned to the butcher need be without their value to the breeder. Is it not true that we as breeders should make a more careful study of the carcasses of some of the cattle we are producing and calling pure-bred? We think so. Recently we heard one of the best, if not the best, informed men on fat cattle, on both hoof and hook, say that "Our improved breeds of beef-cattle were getting to contain so large a per cent of fat that they were not as profitable from the butcher's standpoint as a plainer-bred steer, and so far as quality is concerned a plainer bred steer's carcass would have sufficient quality if the steer has been properly fed and ripened." Here certainly is food for thought for real breeders; and by real breeders I mean, not dealers and speculators who buy cattle in one sale to sell in another, perhaps before the cow would have time to produce a calf, but men who buy cattle in numbers sufficient to found a herd with the determination of improving certain characteristics of the breed.

Recognizing their proper functions in the live stock trade, the breeder and feeder must be brought into closer relationship and work more for each other's interests. Both are absolutely necessary, neither one could successfully prosecute their branch of this vast and growing industry without the other. Intelligent co-operation is always to be prefered to coertion.

Finally, farmers and feeders should not, and probably do not, look upon breeders as waiting and watching for their scalps; and on the other hand the breeders should not, and doubtless do not look upon farmers and feeders as their possible victims.

THE MOST PROFITABLE TYPE OF BEEF STEER.

W. L. Schubert, Rockport, Missouri.

(Missouri Bulletin, State Board of Agriculture.)

An animal to be most profitable for a beef steer must be an early maturing one, one that fattens quickly, and lays on lots of flesh. In order to lay on flesh the animal must have a form which has plenty of room for flesh. This form must, therefore, be broad, square and blocky. Also to lay on much flesh the steer must be a good feeder, one that will eat lots of food and utilize that food for making flesh. To get an animal that is a good feeder we want one that has what is known as good quality, that is a loose, pliable skin covered with fine glossy hair. Why? Because it has been found that animals having a loose, pliable skin covered with fine glossy hair do feed better than those with a tight skin covered with bristly hair. Fine, smooth bones are wanted in a profitable beef steer so as to get a large per cent of flesh from him when he is dressed, and not a pack of large rugged bones. A profitable beef steer must be one that will lay his flesh on the parts which bring the most when sold at the butcher shop. And this a steer cannot do unless he is so formed that the parts, on which the best flesh is, developed so as to hold plenty of it.

I will now endeavor to describe the qualities a profitable beef steer should have and tell why they should be such.

The head should be short and small because it does not contain any valuable flesh and because a short head invariably goes with a short, thick set body.

The forehead should be full, broad and high so as to show intelligence.

The mouth should be large and the muscles of the jaws well developed so as to indicate a good food grinding apparatus.

The eyes should be full, bright and clear because this indicates great vitality and vigor, two of the most important qualities.

The neck should be short, thick and set firmly on the shoulders because this indicates a short, thick set body and a tendency to lay on flesh.

The shoulders should be compact and well covered with flesh so as to give smoothness of form and flesh on fore quarters.

Strong, stright and wide-apart forelegs are wanted to give a good foundation for the fore quarters. Legs should be short because they are not worth much and anyhow short legs are stronger than long ones. The chest should be wide, deep and thick through the heart so as to give plenty of room for the most important organs of the body, namely, the heart and lungs. The brisket should be deep and moderately projecting and breast wide because they go with a well formed chest.

The girth of the animal should be large because this indicates a good chest. The crops or that portion just behind the withers, should be full because this is one of the valuable meat portions.

The back must be short, straight and broad. Short because a short backed animal is an early maturing one. Broad so as to give room for lots of flesh. ᠊raight so as to give good support.

Ribs should be well sprung and arched in order to give plenty of room for the digestive organs. It is a well founded fact that a large, deep chest and a capacious stomach are good indications that an animal has the capacity to utilize large quantities of food and make rapid progress in fattening. The ribs should be well covered with flesh because this is a good indication that the animal fattens well.

Wide hips are wanted because wide hips go with a broad loin and the loin is the most costly portion of the beef. Loin should be full and thick for the same reason.

The rump should be long, level and wide so as to give plenty of room for rump steak. The thighs ought to be full and well fleshed in order to yield plenty of good round steak.

The flanks should be full, low and thick, because if they are the thighs will generally be full and well fleshed.

The hind legs should be short and straight so as to give good foundation for hind quarters. The tail should have a smooth base, fine bone, and a fine hair switch. Smooth base so there will be no fear of having lumpy patches of fat gathered there. This is very objectionable because it spoils the looks of the steer and looks go a long way in affecting the sale of an animal. Fine bone in the tail indicates that the animal is fine boned.

Then, after all this, we want an animal that has some life in it. One that will always be there ready to eat. And one that is not wild. Because a wild one is bothersome, and besides he is wasting flesh while running and jumping everywhere.

Now we might ask in what breed will we find such a steer? Well, there is no distinct breed of animals best for beef purposes, but any of the Short Horns, Herefords and Aberdeen Angus breeds will do, because they first originated in England where they were bred strictly for beef purposes. These are the beef breeds of today, and a steer of any of these breeds and having the qualities already described will be the most profitable beef steer.

POUNDS OF CORN, POUNDS OF GAIN.

W. A. Henry in Breeders' Gazette.

A Livonia, Ind., correspondent writes:

"On the average how many pounds of gain may be expected from each 100 pounds of corn fed to fattening steers? How many pounds of pork will hogs make from 100 pounds of corn? How many pounds of pork will hogs make from droppings of steers from each 100 pounds of corn the steers get?"

Fattening steers will require from 400 to 1,500 pounds of corn for 100 pounds of gain. For short periods and when on pasture, 400 pounds of corn may put on 100 pounds of gain. For long periods they will probably take at least 600 pounds. In winter when on dry feed steers will require from 600 to 800 pounds of corn for 100 pounds of gain when feeding period is comparatively short—say three months. Where steers are fully fed for as long as six months or 180 days, they will require from 1,000 to 1,500 pounds of grain for 100 pounds of gain. Our correspondent may feel dissatisfied with the indefinite statements here made, but it is impossible to give exact figures in cases like this where so much depends upon the quality of the steers as to breeding, their condition as to fatness when the feeding experiments begin, the ability of the feeder to successfully nurture his animals, etc. On the average it may be said that it requires 1,000 pounds of grain for 100 pounds of gain when steers of fair quality are being thoroughly fitted for the market. Fattening hogs require about 500 pounds of corn for 100 pounds of gain. The limits are from 400 to 600, depending upon the condition of the hogs at the beginning of the fattening period, the length of the period, etc.

In answer to the third question, the writer submits the following taken from his book "Feeds and Feeding." It is the report of an experiment which he conducted a number of years ago to learn the value of the droppings of steers for hogs following the steers. In this trial a bunch of twelve steers was divided into two lots of six steers each. The first lot was fed shelled corn, and the second cornmeal. Each steer received thirteen pounds of corn or cornmeal daily, and half as much more wheat bran additional, making about twenty pounds of grain per head daily. Three hogs weighing 175 pounds each were placed after each lot of steers to work over the droppings. The hogs were further fed from the trough enough corn to supply their apparent wants. As a check in experiment three similar hogs were placed in a pen and fed all of the corn they would consume. The following table from "Feeds and Feeding" summarizes the trial:

SUBSISTENCE.	FEED FOR 100 POUNDS GAIN.	PER CENT CORN SAVED BY PIGS EATING DROP-INGS OF STEERS.
Pigs in pen	564 lbs.	....
Pigs following steers getting corn meal.	479 lbs.	15
Pigs following steers getting whole corn......................	272 lbs.	52

It will be seen that the hogs kept in the pen and fed corn required 564 pounds of corn for 100 pounds of gain; the three hogs following the steers getting cornmeal required 479 pounds of corn fed in the trough to enable them to put on 100 pounds of gain. Here was a saving of 15 per cent, because of the droppings of the steers. Where the hogs followed the steers getting whole corn there was required only 272 pounds of grain fed in the trough to give 100 pounds of gain. Thus there was a saving of 52 per cent by allowing three hogs to follow six steers fed shelled corn and bran. Had we fed these hogs a little middlings, ground oats or something to add variety to the ration, we would doubtless somewhat have reduced the pounds of feed required.

Helpful as the above is, it does not answer our correspondent's inquiry directly. For this purpose we must refer to the only available experiment, that made by Georgeson at the Kansas Station several years ago and likewise reported in "Feeds and Feeding." In this experiment Georgeson divided a bunch of ten thrifty steers into two lots of five each, giving the first shelled corn which had been soaked until it had begun to soften, while the second received dry shelled corn. Both lots were confined in open yards, with sheds for shelter, and received the same roughage. All statements of the corn fed are based on the weight of dry corn. The trial began Nov. 7, lasting five months, with the results shown in the table:

FEED.	AVERAGE WEIGHT OF STEERS.	TOTAL CORN EATEN.	WHOLE GAIN.
Dry corn	1,033 lbs.	16,244 lbs.	1,468 lbs.
Soaked corn.....	1,033 lbs.	15,787 lbs.	1,652 lbs.

The table shows that the steers fed soaked corn did not consume quite as much grain as the other lot, yet made a better gain. In this trial there was a saving of 15 per cent by soaking shelled corn.

Fortunately Georgeson placed eight thrifty shoats, averaging eighty-eight pounds per head, with each lot of steers, to pick up the corn voided in the droppings. At first they subsisted entirely on such corn,

21

but later, when they had grown larger, they were supplied with additional grain from a trough, with the following results:

SUBSISTENCE.	EXTRA CORN FED.	TOTAL GAIN OF LOT.	CORN FED EXTRA PER 100 POUNDS GAIN.
Shoats following steers fed—			
Dry corn.........	1,272 lbs.	747 lbs.	170 lbs.
Soaked corn	1,272 lbs.	685 lbs.	200 lbs.

The above shows that shoats secured much of their feed from the droppings, and that the droppings from steers getting dry corn gave the best returns.

By combining the data of feed and gain with both hogs and steers we ascertain the gain required for the combined gain as follows:

	TOTAL GRAIN FED TO STEERS AND SHOATS.	TOTAL GAIN OF STEERS AND SHOATS.	CORN FOR 100 POUNDS GAIN.
Steers fed dry corn with shoats following	17,516 lbs.	2,215 lbs.	791 lbs.
Steers fed soaked corn with shoats following	17,059 lbs.	2,267 lbs.	752 lbs.

Combining the feed for steers and shoats and likewise the gains of both, we find that 791 pounds of corn were required for 100 pounds of gain of steers and shoates where the steers were fed dry corn, and 752 pounds of grain for 100 pounds of gain with steers and shoats where the steers were fed soaked corn. This shows a net saving, by soaking corn for steers, of about 5 per cent.

From the above data we deduce another table entirely to our purpose in making this reply. Let us assume that 500 pounds of corn would have put on 100 pounds of gain with the hogs used in this experiment had they been fed entirely on corn supplied them in the pen. This is the only assumption we will have to make, and it is an entirely reasonable one in this case. On the basis that 500 pounds of corn would put on 100 pounds of gain, the 1,272 pounds of extra corn for the hogs directly would have made 254 pounds of gain. Subtracting this sum from the total gains made by the hogs in each case, we have the gains which should be credited to the corn the hogs secured from the droppings of the steers. Dividing the total corn fed the steers in each case by the gains of the hogs due to the corn in the droppings, we get the following summary table:

	WHEN DRY CORN WAS FED TO STEERS.	WHEN SOAKED CORN WAS FED TO STEERS.
Corn fed to steers for each 100 lbs. of net gain made by hogs following them	3,800 lbs.	4,150 lbs.
Net gain made by hogs for each 100 lbs. of corn fed to the steers............	3 lbs.	2.4 lbs.

The above table shows that in this experiment for each 3,300 pounds of dry corn which the steers consumed the hogs made 100 pounds of gain, or 100 pounds of corn fed to the steers produced three pounds of gain in hogs following them. Where soaked corn was fed it required **4,150** pounds of corn fed to the steers to produce 100 pounds of gain in hogs working over the droppings, or 100 pounds of grain fed to the steers produced 2.4 pounds of gain with hogs working over the droppings of steers so fed.

The writer has answered at considerable length, hoping that the figures given will be appreciated by stockmen generally, for they bear on a question of great importance throughout the corn belt.

THE YOUNG CATTLE BREEDER.

Wallaces' Farmer.

Among our readers throughout the west there are doubtless many hundred young men who are debating the advisability of starting in the pure-bred cattle business. One of these has submitted to us the following:

"Will it pay a young farmer who has a quarter section Iowa farm with fair improvements and practically out of debt to go into the business of breeding pure-bred cattle? If your answer is yes, should he buy just good average cattle of good breeding but not fancy or should he buy some of the higher priced kinds of the more fashionable breeding but no better individually? I have a liking for good stock, but want some advice before going into the business of breeding pure-breds."

I would advise a young farmer in circumstances such as described by all means to engage in the business of breeding fine cattle, but in a conservative manner. He must not think he has to have all the highest priced cattle to be found. Buy good individuals, well bred ones. By this I do not mean that he must have pure Scotch or pure Bates among Shorthorns, but the good old-fashioned kind, such as Rose of Sharons, Young Marys, etc., well topped out—cattle that have come up through breeders whose name opposite the name of an animal in the catalogue is a guarantee of itself that the animal must have been a good one. Then as circumstances will permit and conditions seem to require, add one or two fancy bred ones, so that in time he will have young things to suit all classes of buyers. In selecting a bull to head his herd, the utmost care should be taken. It would be well for him, being a novice in the business, to go to some breeder in whom he has utmost confidence and get him to assist in the selection. I have no hesitancy in advising a young man, one who has a natural love for fine stock, to engage in the business. Years ago when I first started breeding Shorthorns in a very modest way I fed steers and milked cows for the milk and butter they would produce, and also for a period of years during the great depression. In all kinds of cattle, my Shorthorns paid me far better than either my milk cows or steers. F. A. EDWARDS.

Webster county, Iowa.

I believe it will pay a young farmer who owns a quarter section of land to breed pure-bred cattle. Care should be taken to select only animals of good type and good breeding, disregarding fashionably bred individuals of undesirable quality. Many young farmers cannot become expert breeders and it will pay to ascertain by experience of what is the young man in question. After becoming familiar with pedigrees and if the business is to his liking, let him purchase a few choice cows, always using a well bred bull of quality and individuality. It will pay any farmer to breed his grade cows to a choice bull. It will pay to breed pure-bred cows to the best bull obtainable. A man could not afford to buy a choice bull for two or three cows, but if he had a few choice cows, only two or three, and a herd of what would be termed good breeding cows he could then afford to buy the best bull he could find, selecting the bull first and then buy him as reasonable as possible. In this way he could soon build up a herd to his liking, and at comparative little expense.

E. H. WHITE.

Emmet county, Iowa.

In reply to nis query in regard to whether it will pay a young farmer nearly out of debt to go into the raising of pure-bred cattle, my answer would be most emphatically yes. I do not know anything he could go into that would pay him better. To be sure, he must be a good practical man, keep all records straight, and not be afraid of work. I would advise for the start to buy some of the plainer bred females of good individuality, but the bull I think should be both well bred and a strong representative of his breed. If the young man attends to his business and buys at least five females on the start, at the end of ten years he will find himself surrounded with a grand lot of females (bulls sold as fast as old enough to keep down expenses of herd) that he can sell and buy enough more of this high-priced land to complete his section, and be all out of debt and some more besides. I might add here that land is worth $80 an acre here or better.

WARREN E. REYNOLDS.

Whiteside county Illinois.

In regard to your reader wishing advice as to whether it will pay a young farmer who has a quarter section of Iowa land, and practically out of debt to go into the business of breeding pure-bred cattle I would unhesitatingly say yes. There are many reasons and I shall not attempt to give them all. This is a question that should interest every farmer in Iowa, whether he be a large or small farmer, whether wealthy or in moderate circumstances. If he be one of the farmers in moderate circumstances, he needs the improved cattle all the more. The wealthy farmer can get along better with inferior stock than can the farmer of moderate circumstances. Pure-bred cattle are the poor man's friend. Never before was the Iowa farmer in a position where he is literally forced to give his careful consideration to the value of improved live stock. Iowa land that not many years ago sold at $25 to $50 per acre now commands from $50 to $100 and upwards. With land at present prices we must have the best improved stock obtainable. We must raise better crops, we must learn to feed these different crops to the best advantage to our stock to obtain the best results possible. We cannot afford to keep an inferior class of mongrels and scrubs on our farms to feed these crops to. One only needs to look at the difference in prices paid for cattle on the Chicago and other markets to see that the improved cattle are bringing prices that pay a much better profit to their owners than does the plain or common class of cattle. Besides there is a pleasure in feeding good animals. I would advise every young man owning 160 acres of land to start raising pure-bred cattle. He should not jump head-long into the business and buy a lot of high-priced fancy cattle to start with. What I mean by fancy cattle are those of fashionable pedigree that the old established breeders hold very high in their estimation. They can afford to keep them as their reputation as breeders are established. The young farmer should not pay attention to fads and fancy pedigrees but let individual merit and quality be ever in his mind when selecting his foundation cattle, and let pedigree and family be a secondary consideration. By the selection of a few good females and a good male to head his herd it will not be long until his farm will be stocked to its capacity with a fine herd of cattle. As he continues in the business his herd will become better and better, as it is quite natural to retain good females and let the poor ones go. Also he can from time to time add other females as he desires from the sale of his male stock. In this way a farmer of moderate means can soon possess a good herd that will be a source of pleasure and profit.

The great secret of success in the breeding of fine cattle is in starting with the right ideal and sticking to it. Examine well the merits of the different pure-bred beef breeds and when your selection has been made persevere to the end in the work of their better development and your efforts will be crowned with success.   H. J. HESS.

Black Hawk county, Iowa.

———

Replying to your query, I would say that I am firmly of the opinion that a young farmer who has a quarter section of land and is practically out of debt cannot do better than to go into the business of breeding pure-bred cattle. I would not advise buying the high-priced kinds to start with. Get good useful cattle of good breeding. Use nothing but the best obtainable bulls. With proper management there can be no question as to the result. There is always an unlimited demand for a good article and the young man who starts out with pure-bred stock is bound to succeed.   N. P. CLARKE.

Stearns county, Minn.

INFLUENCE OF SHELTER ON STEERS.

H. J. Waters, Missouri Experiment Station, in Breeders' Gazette.

It has been accepted without argument that animals when exposed to cold require more food per unit of gain, since a larger proportion of the food is used in maintaining the heat of the animal body than would be required if the cattle were comfortably sheltered, and there is necessarily less left for the production of animal tissue. It is a trite saying that boards furnish a cheaper shelter than corn and hay and that coal is cheaper fuel for stock than feed.

Despite the fact that these propositions have been generally accepted as true and have in the main gone unquestioned the beef feeder of the Middle West has not provided the warm, commodious barns for his steers on full feed that would logically follow if he proposed to carry his operations on with the greatest economy and according to the most approved methods. It is unquestionably true that these feeders are among our most intelligent and progressive farmers and business men and are in most cases possessed of ample means to provide whatever shelter would promise a certain and sufficient return for the money invested. The fact, therefore, that they were not universally providing barns for their winter feeding operations and the further fact that the limited experimental results on record were conflicting and uncertain induced the Missouri station to take this work up some years ago with a view of carrying it far enough to reach some definite conclusion. A brief summary of the results of several years' work will perhaps prove of interest.

In all but one of the experiments three lots of cattle were used, one of which was sheltered in a barn, one had access to an open shed and one was fed in the open lot without shelter of any kind. All were natives that had been handled enough to become gentle and were dehorned. The steers sheltered in the barn were confined in a reasonably tight but well-ventilated frame building with plank floor and were allowed to run loose. They were kept well bedded. During pleasant weather they had the run of a small lot from about 8 o'clock in the morning until 4 in the afternoon and were turned into the lot for water every day, but in stormy weather they were returned to the barn as soon as they had finished drinking in the forenoon and afternoon.

The open shed used in all these experiments was of the ordinary form, closed on the north, east and west, but open to the south, with a dirt floor, which was kept as dry as possible with bedding. These sheds opened into lots of about the same size and exposure as those into which the cattle sheltered in the barn were allowed to run. They were fed and watered in the shed, but allowed free access to the lots at all times and in all kinds of weather. The open lot had a southern exposure, as did all the other lots, was enclosed by a barbed wire fence, was about the size of the lots adjoining the sheds and barn and contained no grass. Cornstalks were thrown in one corner to give the steers a dry spot on which to lie.

The first trial lasted from November 1, 1897, to February 13, 1898, 105 days, five two-year-old steers being in each lot. Results:

	BARN.	OPEN SHED.
Corn eaten, bushels	172	187
Hay eaten, pounds	4,575	5,204
Gain per lot, pounds	772	903
Daily gain per steer, pounds.	1.47	1.72
Gain per bushel of corn, pounds	4.50	4.83
Digestible dry matter per pound gain	12.9	11.8

In this case the steers in the open shed consumed nearly 9 per cent more corn and nearly 14 per cent more hay, but gained 17 per cent more. In other words, a bushel of corn produced on steers in the barn 4.5 pounds of gain and 4.83 pounds on those in the open shed. In the second trial, lasting from November 2, 1898, to February 18, 1899, 109 days, four steers in each lot, a bunch of steers which was required to stay in the open lot was added to the experiment, with the following results:

	BARN.	OPEN SHED.	OPEN LOT.
Corn eaten, bushels	100	219	208
Hay eaten, pounds	5,521	4,360	5,475
Gain per lot, pounds	1,010	1,250	1,250
Daily gain per steer, pounds	1.83	2.30	2.29
Gain per bushel corn, pounds	5.32	5.73	6.15
Digestible dry matter per pound gain	10.92	9.02	9.24

In this case the steers in the open shed ate 15.3 per cent more corn than did those in the barn, but gained 24.2 per cent more and ate considerably less hay. Those in the open lot ate 6.5 per cent more corn than did the barn steers and about the same amount of hay and gained 23.7 per cent more. A bushel of corn produced:

In barn ....5.32 pounds of beef
In open shed..5.73 pounds of beef.
In open lot..6.15 pounds of beef.

THE SKIM-MILK CALF.

Wallaces' Farmer.

It is an old story that we have told over and over again, but the large increase in our subscription list compels us to tell it again. It is possible to grow a skim-milk calf which at six months old will be of equal value to one that runs with the cow. On $60 land it is not profitable to keep a cow for the chance of a calf unless it is a pure bred and has a breeding value over and above its meat value; therefore, you must get out of the calf raising business or else learn to grow calves by hand.

Thousands of farmers say this cannot be done. With all due respect to them, we say it has been done for generations and is being done by thousands of farmers, and is being done now more successfully than ever before, because thousands of farmers have learned how to do it. If our readers would take our advice and understand why we give the advice, they can do it, and do it at least as successfully as their grandmothers did long before they were born.

The first thing to get in your mind is that nature, or the power behind nature, loves young things, whether calves, or pigs, or colts, or babes, and that it provides for them in the mother's milk a balanced ration. Where man for any reason disturbs the ration, as he does in taking the cream off milk, he must restore the balance in some other way. Another thing to learn is that nature, or rather the power behind nature, feeds all young things warm milk, about 100 degrees Fahrenheit, and a third thing is that it feeds the milk sweet and often. And still another thing to learn is that in the first milk nature provides an aperient or physic and a tonic or stimulant, and gives the youngster this at the very first pull and starts it off in its career free from the mecomium or effete matter contained in the bowels at birth.

Keeping these facts clearly in mind, how shall we go about it to grow the skim-milk calf? First, see that it has not merely milk at the start, but its very own mother's milk. Give it the physic and the stimulant which nature has provided, and none other. Either let the calf suck for two or three days or milk its own dam and give it that milk, and give it to it at blood heat. Keep this up for ten days. The milk by that time is fit for use and you may begin adding a little skim-milk at 100 degrees temperature, and in the course of ten days more get it down to a skim-milk diet. As you decrease the full milk, add a little ground flax seed. Or, if you cannot get the ground flax seed, then give it a mixture of ground oats and corn, adding a little at a time.

The best way to acquaint it with this is to take a little in your hand and after it has drunk its milk put your hand in its mouth and let the stupid youngster get the idea that there is something good besides milk. After thirty days you can give it corn meal alone as a balance, and after it is sixty days old it does not need anything but sweet milk (you can gradually accustom it to taking it cold in the summer time) and good clover hay or grass.

Put your calves in stanchions, which you can easily make with palings and bolts. Sixteen inches is sufficient space for a calf, and the readiest way to make a stanchion is to take the middle board off a three-board fence and put it above, add another board below, and between these put in your stanchions, using bolts. In front of the stanchions place the trough with divisions every sixteen inches, and in this feed each calf its milk, and after the milk the grain, and let them stand there until after their mouths are dry, then give them good clover hay in the winter or grass in the summer. This, with a dark place to which they can retreat in fly time, and close observation, will enable any man who wants to to grow a first class skim-milk calf. A skim-milk calf grown without a balanced ration is a delusion and a snare. With a balanced ration it can stand up in the feed lot alongside a steer that had the full use of the cow and defy any man to tell t'other from which. We know this, because we have seen it done, had it done on our own farms, and therefore know that it can be done. All that is lacking is the "know how," and that "know how" can be easily obtained.

To do all this, you must have your creamery sterilize the milk. It must be brought back to you sweet, and if it is not then you have a settlement to make with that creamery. They may have a settlement with you at the same time and insist that you bring your milk sweet to the creamery. If so, take your medicine like a little man, correct your faults, and then insist that they correct theirs. Tell them that you cannot allow your calves to suffer either on account of their carelessness or on account of the carelessness of the driver.

We cannot go on raising common calves on the cow now that land is from $60 upwards as we did when land was only $25 of $30. Neither can we go on growing pessimistic, disconsolate, pot-bellied, spindle-shanked calves and call them skim-milkers. The farmers of the west must wake up if they are to get good revenues from high-priced land.

RIGHT MILKING.

Homestead.

A matter of farm economy often overlooked is that of right milking. Anybody on the farm who can squeeze a stream of milk out of a cow's teat is set at the task. And those who do not know how, provided they are a part of the farm's working force, are made to learn. Milking is a chore not requiring much strength, and on the ordinary farm considered as not requiring great skill. If the cows have any milk the ordinary milker can get it. What more is asked?

When butter is sold for 12 cents per pound there is no incentive to painstaking milking. But where milk or butter has become one of the farm's staple products care in milking is worth while. The large number of cows on some farms, to be sure, requires all the help available. But the youngsters and inexperienced men should be well taught before they become regular helpers.

The first principle of teaching should be cleanliness. A milker with clothes so grimy that particles of dirt and dust fall into the milk, and whose hands could be benefited by soap suds, needs a lesson; ditto the person who sticks his fingers into the milk pail or milks on his hands so as to wet the cows' teats. In addition to cleanliness on the part of the milker, care in thoroughly brushing off the cows' udder should be insisted upon and particular care that neither through kicking, switching or otherwise, none of the stable's filth gets into the milk. The best way to guard against such accidents is to have the stable clean.

After cleanliness comes efficiency. It includes good ways of holding the teat, rapidity and thoroughness of milking. The teat, if not too short,

should be grasped with the whole hand, the index finger and thumb pressing, as the hand closes, a little more firmly than the lower fingers, thus
forcing the milk downward instead of upward. Milking with the thumb
and one or two fingers, slipping them down the teat, is to be condemned,
since it is neither quicker nor easier than the whole hand way and calls
for the filthy practice of wetting the teats. Thoroughness means getting
the last and richest drop. It is necessary to milk dry, all dairymen know,
if the cow is to be kept up with her milk. Rapidity of milking, unless it
be violent, stimulates the milk flow.

Finally comes the treatment of the cow; it is of great importance.
with the nervous cow, perhaps of first importance. Singing of a boister-
ous kind, whistling, chattering, loud talking, to say nothing of rough handling, certainly does not make the cow more comfortable and therefore
cannot be conducive to a full steady flow of milk. And do not treat the
cow to an indifferent milker every day and to irregular hours of milking.
Because of mere changing about of milking we have frequently noticed
in herds of fifteen or twenty cows a decrease of 10 per cent in a day's
milk. Let each cow become acquainted with her milker and let the
milker stick by her.

All of these things—cleanliness, efficiency and careful treatment of
the cow—are matters of economy; for if all the cow has it to be gotten
from her, and the product is to be marketed in first class style, they must
receive attention. They must be taught the new milkers.

MILK AS A BY-PRODUCT.

Homestead.

An experiment conducted at the Iowa Experiment Station a few
years ago indicated that the cost of raising a steer from the time of birth
until two years old, or at least until he is ready for market, is about $50.
This includes all the food eaten during the entire time, even the pasture,
reckoned at the prevailing market prices of foods. Sometimes we are
inclined to think that an animal at the age of two years old that is worth
$50 for beef is a fairly good one, and when marketed at this age, for
this money, it is clear that there is no great profit in the business. In
the experiment cited the animals sold for $12.20 over and above the en-
tire cost of feeding them through the whole period. This does not mean
that the only profits on feeding in this case was $12.20 per head, because
all foods fed during the entire period must be credited at their full
value. The farmer, therefore, has not only marketed his food at a profit.
but he has, in turn, a large amount of manure which may be returned to
the soil.

The point that we have specially in mind, in this instance, is that
large profits were made from the milk which the dams of these steers
produced during the feeding period. The record of two cows in the herd

is given. in which it is shown that in one instance a pure-bred Short-Horn cow produced 7.464 pounds of milk in a year, containing 3.59 per cent of butter fat, yielding 312½ pounds of butter. The cost of her feed was $20.50, while the profits over and above the food fed was $28. Another individual, the dam of one of the steers in the experiment, produced **5,791** pounds, which made 257.8 pounds of butter, her feed costing $17 during the period, the produce selling at a net profit of $24. The two individuals whose records have been given are taken as average representatives of the herd. Another cow in the same herd has the following record: Nine thousand one hundred and thirty-six pounds of milk, testing 3.79 per cent, yielding 404 pounds of butter. The cost of her feed was $25, while the net profit in this case was $43.

These figures demonstrate, beyond a doubt, that it is possible to combine beef making and milk qualities in one animal, and when this is found there is no more profitable animal to be found on the average farm of the middle west. Without the steer, which sold for something over $62, there is a good profit on the product of the cow alone. There are persons who at the present time are making money on a straight beef animal, where no attempt is made to manufacture dairy products from the milk. However, among the Short-Horns and other breeds it not uncommonly happens that most excellent milkers are found, in which case it will not only pay to feed for beef, but will also be profitable to feed for milk. We believe that the ideal poor man's cow is one that will produce a good animal for the block and at the same time more than earn her living with her dairy products. The specialist of course should have his special purpose cow.

TREATMENT OF MILK FEVER.

Homestead.

Despite the best precautionary measures owners of dairy cows may expect to have some cases of parturient paresis (milk fever) to treat, but these will be mostly in newly purchased cows or in the first flush of grass, when many will have considered it unnecessary to feed as advised for winter calving. A very few heavy milking cows will be likely to "go down" with the disease. Incidentally it may be stated here that the preventive treatment already given in this department applies to the spring calving cow upon rich grass as well as the winter-fed, stabled cow—both should have the doses of iodide of potash prior to calving, and the spring cow should have dry food and bran mashes, but no green grass for two or three weeks prior to calving if she is considered likely to suffer an attack of milk fever. When, just after calving—in from twenty-four hours to four days—the cow is observed to be restless, off feed, stepping up and down with hind feet, running her tongue out, drying up suddenly in milk flow, staggering in gait and costive in movements of the bowels, it may be taken for granted that she is coming down with an attack of milk fever. It is rare indeed that the veterinarian is called at this stage of the trouble. Were he present in time he might possibly abort the attack by the immediate administration of stimulants and alternate doses of tincture of aconite and fluid extract of belladonna (poisons that we could not advise farmers to administer), but as a rule the cow is down and probably unconscious before he arrives, or the attack is noticed by the owner. Unless an experienced veterinary surgeon can be called in at once the owner should proceed to treat the case in the following manner: The first point to be attended to is to place the cow upon her breast bone (sternum), for if allowed to lie for any length of time upon her side she will bloat and die from suffocation or will regurgitate food, which often gets into the windpipe and lungs. When this occurs such an accident usually leads to fatal pneumonia even if recovery from milk fever apparently follows treatment. The cow should be propped up in the position mentioned by means of sacks filled with straw or hay, and a similar sack should be placed under his chin to keep it fairly level. Medical treatment consists in injecting into the udder a solution of two to two and one-half drams of iodide of potash in one quart of freshly boiled and filtered water. Boil and filter the water first, then stir in the iodide of potash, and when milk-warm infuse it into the udder as follows: Have on hand for the purpose five feet of small rubber hose in one end of which has been fitted a glass funnel, and in the other end a large milking tube. Wash the udder thoroughly with warm water, soap and carbolic acid (3 per cent solution) and place it upon a rubber sheet. The udder should have been first milked out, and when this has been done it will be found an easy matter to insert the milking tube into each teat in succession to infuse an equal amount of the iodide of potash solution into each teat by pouring it into the funnel from a bottle and allowing it to gravitate into the teat gradually. The udder should afterwards be massaged thoroughly, and this should be repeated every hour until the solution is no longer noticed to "gurgle" in the udder. In addition to this simple treatment the cow should be given copious injections of soapy warm water, per rectum, every two hours. No medicine should be given by the mouth. In such cases the patient has lost the power of swallowing, and when a drench consisting of two or three quarts of warm water, containing Epsom salts or other medicines, is poured into the mouth a large portion of it goes into the trachea, although the cow may seem to swallow. The urine should be withdrawn by means of a catherer every six hours if the cow is unable to stand. If she is not up in the twelve hours after the first infusion of iodide solution repeat the dose—two drams for medium cow, two and one-half drams for large cow, in one quart of warm water. Hypodermic injections of strychnine may be given by a veterinarian in addition to the above treatment.

WINTER FEEDING FOR THE WEANLING CALF.

Wallaces' Farmer.

An Illinois correspondent writes as follows:

"Within the next few weeks hundreds and thousands of young calves will be taken from the cows and put on feed for the first winter. Please advise farmers through the columns of your paper how and what to feed, and how to care for these calves during the first winter."

Our correspondent of course refers to calves that have run with their dams morning and evening, calves that have had little, if any, grain feed during the summer, and have been dependent upon their mothers' milk and what grass they cared to eat. When these calves are weaned at the close of the grazing they usually weigh from three to four, and some even five hundred pounds, and are in good flesh fit for veal; but in a month or six weeks after the sudden change from milk and grass to grain and grass, they present a sorry spectacle. Calves that have been kept in the yard and suckled morning and evening usually fare much better, be· cause if their owner has had any sort of gumption he has been giving them more or less grain which they have learned to eat; and in that case the change is not nearly so sudden.

Our first experience in handling calves of this kind, was a sorry one The calves were high grade, averaging nearly five hundred pounds at weaning time. They were put the last week in September in a good pasture with plenty of bluegrass dried on the ground. In our greenness we ordered them fed a full feed of corn, and thought we would have baby beef in a year. A heavy rain came on, soaking the ground thoroughly. Warm weather followed, and the result was a very rank growth of soft blue grass. In ten days thereafter, out of thirty calves six died of blackleg. The calves were then removed to an oat field in which there was a good deal of voluntary growth; turned back again in a week to blue grass pasture, and four more died of blackleg. Those calves did not make any baby beef, although they made splendid two-year-old feeding steers.

This experience will suggest the first point in the management and that is, not to make a sudden change at weaning time from milk to grain. If you have calves running with the cows and entirely acquainted with grain, shut them up and let them suck morning and evening and through the day let them have free access to oats and corn. Until the change is made, it would pay to grind the grain, say bleached oats, shriveled wheat and old corn and at the same time let them have access to some good hay. Let the weaning be done gradually. Two milk rations a day at first, then one, then one every other day, every third day, and then quit altogether.

Now that the calves are weaned the question arises: When does the owner intend to market them? In six months or a year as fatlings, or in two years as feeders? If he intends to sell them as baby beef at a year or sixteen months old, the feed required would be one thing. If he intends to sell them at thirty months old for feeders, another ration will be required. If he intends them for baby beef, we would feed about all they will eat up clean from start to finish. The ration should be corn and oats, or damaged or shriveled wheat, about half and half, with good clover, alfalfa hay or corn fodder. If we had alfalfa hay, we would not feed any small grain except as a variety. If clover hay, we would feed a little oats or wheat or ground rye. If we had corn fodder without clover, then we would certainly make half the grain ration oats screenings or bleached wheat.

We speak of these grains now, because over a large section of our territory there is a very large amount of wheat that will not sell for over 40 cents, and a great deal of oats that will not sell for more than 10 or 15 cents. A good calf will give more for this than the grain dealer at the station. If properly cared for otherwise, this ration will bring the calves through in good high flesh the next spring. We would continue the grain on grass and would never stop feeding grain until they were ready for market, whether that was in June, August or October. When calves fed in this way reach a weight of 1,100 to 1,200 pounds, ordinarily they should go. The time of marketing, however, will depend on prices.

If we intended these calves for feeders merely, we would feed the same ration, but only about half as much of it. We would aim to keep them gaining at the rate of not less than a pound a day during the first winter. A pound and a half might be made without getting them too fat. We would continue this grain feed until grass became solid, or in other words, nutritious. We would then discontinue it until the succeeding winter and would then put them on a half ration, keeping up a steady gain, and let them have another season of grass.

Which of these two methods of feeding is the most profitable depends on circumstances too various to describe. Suffice it to say that the man with a large amount of pasture and the farmer on a large farm will probably make more money by growing these calves as feeders, while the man on a small farm with plenty of grain of his own growing, if he is a scientific feeder, can make more money by the shorter method. The care required other than above mentioned would be good, comfortable out of door shelters, protecting them from wind and rain, good bedding and an abundant opportunity for exercise in the sunlight. All calves. whether intended for lighter feeding or stock feeding should be vaccinated for blackleg, especially in Missouri, southwestern Iowa, southeastern Nebraska and Kansas.

We would feed calves that are intended for beef precisely the same as steers. If they are intended for dairy purposes, however, we would feed quite differently. We would separate them from the steers, and while we would give the steers plenty of corn, we would give the calves intended for dairy purposes as little as possible. In neither case would we grind it except for the first ten days or two weeks, while we were making the change. A calf's time is not of much value, and it may as well grind its own corn. If in health, it will not pass any corn undigested until nearly a year old, and hogs following it would starve to death on that kind of waste. We would feed the heifer calves intended for dairy purposes, oats and damaged wheat only, except in the severest cold weather when we might give them a little corn. We would not aim to make these calves fat, simply good growing order, and would expect them to come out in the spring from fifty to one hundred pounds lighter in weight than steers of the same age and quality. We would, however, keep up the grain feed as in the case of the steers, until the grass became properly nutritious.

The same correspondent asks how we should feed a young bull calf during the first winter. If he intends him for sale, we would feed it as we would the steers intended for beef, but if we intended to keep him for our own use, we would put him in with the heifers, possibly giving him an additional feed of corn in order to make a more rapid growth. He will have to associate with females all his life and he may as well get used to them, no great hardship in his case. The ration, however, of a bull calf or any other kind of stock intended for breeding purposes, should not be a fattening one, but a ration the object of which is to develop bone and muscle, and the highest possible degree of vigor.

BUTTERMAKING AS A PROFESSION.

Professor G. L. McKay, Iowa Agricultural College.
Monthly Bulletin, Missouri State Board of Agriculture.

This is an age of combinations and concentration of capital. It is also an age of specialists. The general purpose man must necessarily fall to the rear. Every man should be educated along some line of business. While I am a strong believer of adaptability, I cannot think that the man who has made a success as a specialist would have made a failure at any other business if he had applied the same energy and thought to it.

Success in any business never comes by chance or luck. Chauncey Depew, being asked by a young man what was the secret of success replied: "My boy, there is no secret to it. It is just dig, dig, dig." Edison, being asked to give the definition of genius, answered: "Two per cent is genius and ninety-eight per cent is hard work." On another occasion when this great inventor was asked if he did not believe that genius was simply inspiration, he replied: "No, genius is perspiration." The editor of a western newspaper sent to all the successful men in his city this question: "Why is it that not more of our young men succeed?" And one answer came in this laconic phrase: "Because too many of them are looking for white-shirt jobs." Possibly this was a homely way of saying it, but it is true in many cases, especially with many of our college graduates. Some imagine that because they have a college education they must necessarily get an easy, high-salaried position. It is well to have a technical education, but it is also well to have a manual train-

ing. Lord Bacon says: Learning should be made subservient to action."
We need a knowledge more of how to do things than how to explain
things. The world today is looking for men who can turn out the finished
product.

The time, we hope, is past when it is considered a disgrace for a man
to work with his hands. No man would be so irreverent as to say that the
man, Christ, was lacking in brain power or in manliness, yet we find him
a carpenter, toiling with His hands.

Study the lives of all successful men and the story will be found in
each case exactly the same. The methods vary as they must, but the
actual basis of every successful life is the persistent hard, hard work of
years and many a personal sacrifice. This is not always apparent simply
because we are all too apt to look at a man when he has achieved his
success. But there was a struggling period.

Thoroughness in everything is the keynote of success. As Mr. Bok,
the distinguished editor of the Ladies' Home Journal, says: "A thorough
workman never says, 'There, that will do' but 'there, that is it.' " And
this is what every young man in business should learn: that absolutely
nothing is good enough if it can be made better, and better is never good
enough if it can be made best. We frequently hear men complain that
there is no use in doing extra work, that their employer does not appreciate it. They work merely like an automatic machine with no interest or
heart in their work. As a rule the fault is more often with the employed
than the employer. There are exceptions to this as to any rule, but as a
general thing a man gets paid about what he is worth. The man who
most loudly complains of being underpaid is frequently the man who is
overpaid.

I find it much more difficult to get men to fill the high positions than
it is to get men for ordinary positions. A. T. Stewart used to say that he
had always plenty of vacancies in his store which he could not fill,
although he wanted to, for $10,000 employes. The same condition exists
today in many other branches. Let an important position open in any
branch of business and it is very difficult to find a competent man to
fill it.

A universal precept and rule of success which, spoken long before
universities were thought of, applies to academic studies as it does to
every action and decision of human life: "Whatsoever thy hand findeth
to do, do it with thy might." No work is worth doing badly; and he who
puts his best into every task that comes to him will surely outstrip the
man who waits for a great opportunity before he condescends to exert
himself. We are not all adapted by nature to be physicians or lawyers,
so it is well for the young man to find the line of work for which he is
best adapted, and then use all his energy to make it a success.

The creamery business of today opens up a large field for intelligent young men who are not afraid to work; men who are willing to work
with their hands as well as with their heads. In fact the man who successfully operates a creamery must be an all around good fellow. The

dairy business is practically in its infancy. We know very little about milk or its production. I think it was Ex-Governor Hoard who said that the laboratory of a cow was one of the darkest places in the universe. The success of the creamery depends more on the buttermaker than on anyone else. Many things that to the careless maker seem of little importance, to the intelligent maker are of the greatest importance. The condition is quite evident to anyone who visits a large number of creameries. In some creameries we find every evidence of prosperity. The maker meets the patrons with a "Good morning" and a pleasant smile, and weighs and samples the milk as it should be done. The creamery is in first class order and there is a pleasant atmosphere everywhere. It is a pleasure to visit such a plant. Contrast this with a creamery where we find everything in a dilapidated condition, with an untidy maker at the head of it, patrons dissatisfied and the complaint is made on every side that the creamery business does not pay and the patrons think that the creamery men are among the greatest rascals in existence. This is what is preventing the creamery business from progressing as it should. Jealousy among farmers has destroyed more creameries than all other things combined. More faith in mankind is needed. I believe there are very few dishonest men in the creamery business. If one-tenth of the dishonesty that is printed in the sensational papers was true, the business of the world would be seriously affected.

When we consider that only 5 per cent of the world's business is done on a cash basis, we find that business men must have faith in mankind. How frequently we hear farmers in a community find fault with the creamery in their section and do everything they can to injure the operator's business, when in reality the very presence of a creamery in their neighborhood is enhancing the value of their land from $3 to $5 an acre in many cases.

With your permission I will review the butter business from the time the milk is received up to the finished product. The weighing of milk, which seems of little consequence to some makers, is a very important place in the creamery, and a place where the head maker should always be found in the morning. Here is the opportunity of coming in contact with the patron and doing missionary work that will educate him to furnish a better product. It also gives the maker a knowledge of the condition of the milk that he is to handle that day. The importance of taking a correct sample of milk is quite an item in keeping patrons good natured and satisfied. More dissatisfaction exists over the testing than any other business in connection with the creamery. If milk is allowed to stand only a few moments in the weighing can, and a sample is taken without carefully stirring in the cream, the result will be an inaccurate test, which may defraud the patron of the creamery. The leaving open of milk jars, as frequently happens, after samples are taken, will not give accurate results, as evaporation of moisture is taking place all the time. I have known samples of this kind to cause a variation of 2 per cent. And take up the question of testing milk. The testing machine must run perfectly smooth and at a certain speed to insure correct results. Sulphuric acid.

22

should also be of a certain specific gravity. These things require skill.
The heating of milk for separation is not receiving the attention it should.
It was my privilege at the great national convention to try and point out
the defects in the butter exhibited. I found possibly from 30 to 40 per
cent of the flavor was injured more or less by the use of live steam for
heating milk. It was an easy matter in most cases to select the butter
where live steam had been used before reading the method of making,
many using the exhaust steam from the engine to heat the feed water for
boiler. Here we found the cylinder oil transmitted to the milk from the
boiler, this giving a decided oily flavor to the butter. The use of boiler
compounds showed injurious effects also. Why live steam should be used
for heating milk at the present time is a mystery to me. Many of the live
steam heaters not only injure the flavor by transmitting impurities from
the boiler, but the heating is not sufficient to give the best or desired
results. The heating of milk helps the fluidity of the fat globules. The
quick, flashy heating of milk has very little effect on the fat globules.
Therefore the separation of milk is not as perfect. Milk should be heated
for some time before the separation to get the best results. There is still
room on the market for a good heater. The centrifrugal separation of milk
is a wonderful process. Think of a separator bowl making from six thousand to ten thousand revolutions per minute. Here we see sweet milk put
into the machine and skim-milk and cream immediately separated. Most
any machine will skim clean to a certain limit if the machine is run perfectly smooth and at the proper speed. A little vibration of the machine
causes a remixing of the cream, and no separator will skim thoroughly
clean that vibrates. This is where some makers in large creameries lose
possibly more than their wages. The next thing is cream ripening, which
is possibly the most important step in the whole process, as this is a factor that largely controls the flavor, and flavor is the quality that distinguishes butter from lard, tallow or any other fat. Flavor does not come
by chance. Take the national six-month contest just ended, and we find
that John Sollie of New Sweden, Minn., got an average score of 98.12.
This was not brought about by chance nor entirely by the good milk furnished by the patrons. This maker informed me that he carried as many
as seven or eight starters during this contest. Here we find him selecting the kind of bacteria that produces the best flavor.

A starter of any kind is only adding enormous quantity of a species of
bacteria that we expect to predominate in the final product. This takes
skill and hard work on the part of a maker. Starters of any kind are
quite difficult to carry forward, as every detail must be attended to punctually. The maker must also have smell and taste well cultivated so that
he will be able to detect the slightest change or off-flavor. He must also
have some knowledge of the principles of bacteriology. A few years ago
it was largely chance-work for a maker to win two high scores in succession. Now we find makers who use pure cultures and have a knowledge
of the scientific principles of cream ripening, scoring high in most every
contest. It is asked, does all this care and trouble pay? I would say,
"Yes." As the value of the butter may be enhanced as much as 2 cents

per pound. The churning and working of butter is another important factor which does not receive the attention it should from the creamerymen of the country. We have a law limiting the per cent of water in butter to 16 per cent, yet we find the chemical analysis of butter in the six-month contest is something less than 12 per cent. The maker who is able to incorporate between 15 and 16 per cent of water in his butter will increase his yield nearly four pounds to the hundred. Take an ordinary make of 500 pounds per day and we will have a difference of twenty pounds. Twenty pounds at 20 cents per pound will give us $4.00, quite an item on a man's wages. Here is where skill comes in.

The dry butter or that containing a low per cent of water does not sell any higher than the medium and in some cases not as high. I tested butter in the London market and found the French rolls and Danish selected which sold highest in the English market to contain about 5 per cent more water than the New Zealand butter, which brought 3 or 4 cents per pound less. In this case the New Zealander was losing four or five pounds of butter per hundred and also losing in price. I asked Professor Siegleke why the Danes incorporated so much water in their butter and he answered that butter was supposed to be plastic and intended to be spread on bread. While I do not like to see slushy butter, I think that from 14 to 15 per cent of water can be incorporated with good results. It is almost impossible to form any conclusion of the amount of water butter contains by the looks of it. Frequently butter than seems slushy will contain very little water under chemical analysis. Professor Stork has been working on this subject for a number of years and he has been unable to fully explain why some samples of butter have a very dry appearance and at the same time contain a very high per cent of water, some samples testing as high as 18 or 19 per cent. We do not know when a lot of cream is churned at a time that the overrun will be much greater than when a small quantity is churned. This is possibly due to the fact that when a small quantity of cream is used the fat globules are thrown together more compactly and do not hold the same amount of water, as when a large amount is churned. There are several other conditions that influence the yield, which the skilled maker understands. A large creamery cannot place an accurate estimate on a good, intelligent maker. We have one large creamery in Iowa that is getting as much as one and three-quarter cents per pound above western extras for their butter. They could pay $3,000 per year and still have a big profit left.

Employers frequently do not realize the value of a good buttermaker. In any ordinary large creamery a maker could lose as much as $100 per month without the employer knowing it, and in some cases the maker being able to detect the cause. A few years ago while traveling on the train I got interested in a gentleman's tale of woe about the trouble they had in their community in closing up their creamery. I got so interested that I finally purchased this old plant and I will say right here it would take a very strong tale of woe to make me purchase another one. However, I fitted up this old plant with modern machinery and placed a young man from the college in charge. I had implicit faith in his ability. It was a very difficult field in which to put any maker, as a' co-operative creamery had made a failure and a private individual had made a failure. Nevertheless this young man went among the people with a pleasant smile but with a strong determination to build up the business, and he succeeded beyond expectations, thus showing what the right man will do in the right place.

Afterwards this young man left to take charge of one of the largest plants in Iowa at $1,200 per year. We did not think we could afford to pay such high wages, so put on a cheaper man. The result has been disastrous to our income as well as to the patrons of that creamery. Not many months ago this same young man was offered $1,800 per year as buttermaker, thus showing that the services of good men are usually appreciated and rewarded accordingly. If you have a good maker, do not wait for him to ask for a raise, as a $5.00 per month raise given unsolicited will be more appreciated than a $10.00 raise demanded. The creamery business today needs the best talent that can be secured. College graduates should not hesitate to take up this line of work, as there is certainly a bright future for highly skilled workmen who are adapted for this business.

CATTLE IN RUSSIA.

Peter Jensen in Breeders' Gazette.

Russian cattle are very much inferior to our beef breeds. The grain fattening of beef is almost unknown. In summer the very nutritious wild grasses of the steppes fatten beef rapidly and in winter the hay made from these grasses alone makes tolerably good fat cattle.

Meat is not eaten nearly as much or as often as in our own country or in England; in fact the peasant rarely eats it, except on Sundays or holidays, and then in limited quantities only. "Salo," a kind of dry salted pork, is used for the flavoring of his daily soup or "Borshtsh." On the large estate mutton is used mostly. The steaks you get even at first-class hotels are not nearly as savory as those from our corn-fed beef.

It seems surprising that Russia with her vast resources for grazing and feeding should not supply all of western Europe with meats. One adverse circumstance is the very slow and unsatisfactory railway transportation. Although the Russian railways are owned and managed by the government the officials treat the farmer and stockmen of the lower classes very harshly and unless the usual "donation" is forthcoming, will often delay cattle in transit. I observed this while in Russia a year ago. Several of the small cattle cars, each only containing eight head, were standing on a side track. The cattle were evidently very hungry; they were very gaunt and were bellowing most pitifully. I saw the owner standing near the cars looking very crest-fallen and finally asked him in Russian what the matter was.

He took off his greasy cap and addressing me as "Your Worshipful Honor" related his tale of woe. He had come into the division; station two days ago and had not been able to get out. He had already offered a large "bonus" for an engine but the officials demanded a much larger sum. I asked him what he would do. His reply was characteristic of the long-suffering Russian; he said "Boch znaiet. God only knows. I have not the money to give him and must trust to God." In our country a little "cussing" or a message to the general manager of the road would probably have brought quicker relief.

There are several distinct breeds of cattle in Russia. The universally grey "Ukraine" cattle are found all through south Russia and up to Charkow. They are very nimble and enduring, with handsome horns and of a beautiful silver gray color. They are used for hauling and plowing and all farm w᷈ k and are the main stay-by of the small farmer and are employed by the hundred of yokes on the large estates. They hardly ever reach the block until they are worn out and old and of course make poor eating. The Kalmuck cattle are red and not as tractable as the former; they are somewhat heavier in build and make fine beef while young. The German Russian colonists have imported a number of Swiss bulls to improve the milk breeds and have been very successful in this respect although these cattle are like our Jerseys and not beef breeds.

I believe Russia is on the eve of being opened to western enterprise and industries, and when this day comes our packers will undoubtedly enter this new field and with their usual energy show the Russian how to slaughter cattle, hogs and sheep and how to make the most of their great opportunities that are now lying dormant. For years to come, however, Russia will not be a serious competitor to our meat industries in the markets of the world.

"JUST A LITTLE CORN."

Homestead.

Many years ago when the fat stock show was held on the Lake Front, Chicago, when some of the fattest cattle were exhibited of that day, one of the exhibitors, Mr. Gillette, of Illinois, was asked what he fed his cattle to put them in such good flesh. His answer was "Just a little corn," and no one could find out any more from this king of the show ring. Later, when Mr. Moniger, of Iowa, showed some very fine cattle in the same old building he was asked about the same question. His answer was, "Well, I just feed them a little corn and some grass." At the later international show if hundreds of exhibitors were to be questioned as to the ration used they would answer, "Just a little corn."

Corn fed in a systematic way is one of the best feeds on earth to put a finish on cattle. It is equally as good for sheep and no one regards it as dangerous when fed to hogs to put on that finish that will make them valuable in a market where really good pork is in demand. In the corn belt may be found the best cattle for market purposes. Cattle that are not finished with corn are bought by feeders and taken to the corn belt to be finished and when they return again to the market they are scarcely recognized as being the same cattle.

Now the question is being agitated as to whether the states and territories west of the corn belt can make beef, button and pork without the aid of corn. To demonstrate this there is a movement on foot to give a show of live stock fitted for the market in a locality where there is no corn. There are those who believe it can be done and that good beef can be produced that will equal that produced in the corn producing states and at a lower cost. This show is to be held in Denver, Colorado, and the time set for the first exhibition being in February, 1903, and all the states and territories of the west will be asked to contribute cattle, sheep and hogs, raised and fed in the west in whatever way the competitors may decide, and each competitor will be required to tell how he did it.

The cost of such a show would come not far from $10,000 and a committee on organization has been appointed consisting of the leading stockmen of Colorado. We are informed that about $2,000 has already been raised. It is not the intention to limit the exhibition to fat stock but feeders as well. Western stockmen are very enthusiastic over the proposition. That the fat stock should look as well as these people would like to have it we are afraid they will have to feed "Just a little corn."

H. THE HORSE.

MARKET CLASSES OF HORSES.

George M. Rommel, Expert in Animal Husbandry, Bureau Animal Industry, U. S. Department of Agriculture.

BUREAU OF ANIMAL INDUSTRY—BULLETIN No. 37.

The growth of the horse market during the past few years, its present healthy tone, and the apparent promise of a continuance of these conditions for at least a considerable time to come, warrant the bestowal of time and attention, not only upon the general demands of the market, but also upon rather detailed examinations of the various kinds of horses that are wanted.

In this article the market classes are generally referred to in the colloquial terms of the market. This, it is thought, will, to a considerable extent, tend to prevent confusion and misunderstanding. Aside from casual references, no attempt is made specifically to discuss breeding or fitting for market.

For convenience, all points of an anatomical nature are grouped under the head of "Conformation" Although according to the generally accepted usage by the best authorities on score-card practice and live stock judging, this is a somewhat broad use of the term, it is not technically incorrect, and the advantages gained by the elimination of details that might prove wearisome will, it is believed, warrant such treatment.

The classifications here considered are made as comprehensive as possible, embracing the views of dealers in all of the principal markets of the country. All the classes mentioned will not be found present in all markets, nor will all markets have exactly the same qualifications, but these differences are so slight as to be practically unimportant.

Especially in regard to size and weight, it must be borne in mind that the figures given are not arbitrary. Not only will they vary in different parts of the country with different markets, but dealers in the same market will differ in their ideas as to the exact sizes and weights of the various classes. With this, as with all points, the attempt has been made to strike an average—to obtain a consensus of opinion, as it were. It is always to be remembered that "doctors differ," both as to the symptoms of a patient when ill and as to his normal appearance and proper conduct when well.

Prices are seldom mentioned here, for the reason that they are subject to continual fluctuations and any that might be quoted would be serviceable only for the time of writing. Such information is accurate only when gained from regular market publications, and is easily obtained.

For specific information regarding contemporaneous market conditions there is no better or more easily approached source of information than the commission firms and dealers on the market, whose courteous assistance, it should be mentioned, has made this bulletin a possibility; and no better school for practical instruction can be imagined than an auction ring in one of our great horse markets on a sale day during the height of the season.

PRIMARY CONSIDERATIONS OF THE MARKET.

A general observation of the horse markets in the United States reveals very different conditions from those existing in the early part of the last decade. Before going into details and ascertaining the kind of horse that the several demands on the market require, three facts present themselves for consideration.

First—The market is seen to be on a much firmer basis than it was in the years from 1893 to 1897. Not only are prices much higher, but, generally speaking, the competition among buyers is keen, and a serviceably sound, well-set-up horse of the right type, in good condition, can almost always be disposed of at a profit to the producer.

Second—One is impressed with the pronounced scarcity of animals of the better grades, especially among light horses. Dealers cannot satisfy the demands that come to them for high class roadsters, coach horses and saddlers. Even among "business horses" a higher price must often be paid than buyers desire, and it is said that this has even led some large establishments to send agents into the country to take advantage of the natural differences between farm and market prices. To a casual observer this is, perhaps, the most striking feature that presents itself. A change from a condition of over-production and panic prices to one of scarcity and strong prices has come about within the course of less than five years.

Third—Going more into the details of the market, we find a pretty well-defined system of classification. Buyers are on the market to get horses of a certain type, and thus have created "classes." It is true that there are still thousands of horses every year that are shipped in simply to be gotten rid of—to sell for whatever they will bring; yet they are, as a rule, sold at a loss, and the only horses that sell at satisfactory prices are those that conform to the requirements that buyers demand.

The reasons for these conditions are rather definitely understood, but a brief review of them here may not be out of place.

CAUSES OF THE DEPRESSION OF THE LAST DECADE.

Going back of the firmness of the present market, the causes of the low prices and over-production that preceded it present themselves.

PASSING OF THE STREET-CAR HORSE.

The recent depression of the horse business began about 1890. Up to that time immense numbers of animals were in demand for street-car use. A fairly good animal was used, but there was no certain fixity of type. This trade absorbed very many horses that had always constituted the overwhelming majority on the market—the small chunks and the general-purpose animals; and with the introduction of the cable car and almost immediately after, the sweeping substitution of electric cars for horse cars in nearly all the large cities, these immense numbers of horses were thrown on the market without a demand for them, and the public was suddenly confronted with a condition of extreme over-production. This, however, would only indirectly affect the higher grades. Extra individual horses maintained a fairly good scale of prices, and never at any time were they such drug on the market as the commoner sorts.

The severest test to the market horse was yet to come. Strongly organized conditions might have tided over the effects of over-supply that the falling off of the demand for the street-car horse brought about, but the punishment was to be made all the more complete by the financial panic of 1893.

THE FINANCIAL PANIC OF 1893.

The great panic that began in this year, but whose influence was felt most severely in the horse-producing sections two years later, was really the most effective cause for the breakdown in the horse market. The cheaper grades fell still lower and the higher classes began a descent in prices that forced men out of the business and had a most disastrous effect in creating a general distrust of the horse, not only on the part of men who were already engaged in his production, but also with prospective producers. All classes of stock were affected, but it was the horse breeders who had the worst "scare," and it was freely predicted that horse raising would never again exist as a factor in live stock husbandry.

THE BICYCLE AND THE ELECTRIC CARRIAGE.

On the heels of the panic came the bicycle and in a few years the electric carriage followed. The bicycle influenced particularly the demand for cheap drivers—the inferior grades—and naturally intensified the downfall of prices. However, though for a time the growing use of the bicycle brought about a decline in the use of horses, its effect was hardly so severe as appeared; certainly it was not permanent. The use of the bicycle became most widespread among persons who could afford neither to purchase nor maintain a horse and among those who constitute a large part of the patronage of livery stables. If it has severely affected the horse in any capacity, it is by the inroads that liverymen claim it has made on their business. The most effective force for furthering the downfall in prices was simply fright, which brought about an unnecessary unloading of horses on a market already over-supplied. The results after the lapse of a few years, and the adjustment of the bicycle to its proper place as an important economic factor, with the return of the business to normal conditions, give ample reasons for such opinions.

Experience with automobiles has shown that in their present state of development their effect on the horse market is not serious. For business purposes they have not yet been found to be entirely satisfactory, whereas the bicycle has become an invaluable adjunct of business. At present the "auto" is the least dangerous of all the deterring influences that operate against the horse market.

CAUSES FOR PRESENT SCARCITY.

DECLINE OF HORSE BREEDING.

The lack of confidence in the horse-breeding business which resulted from the depressing influences of the panic period undoubtedly brought about a decline in the breeding of the best grades. This cannot be shown very accurately, for the twelfth census has reported the largest number of horses in the history of the country. By a careful study of the market conditions, however, it is evident that a more exacting market has found an inferior grade of horses from which to draw its supply. Misfits and culls are common enough, but they are not in demand. The scarcity that exists today is most apparent among the better grades of horses, and we are forced to the conclusion that these horses have rapidly decreased in numbers, while unsalable, inferior sorts have increased. The period of low prices caused men to stop breeding good horses, but failed to stop the progress of the scrubs.

THE EXPORT TRADE.

Almost coincident with the beginning of the panic of 1893, a new force began to operate to offset the disastrous conditions of the horse market, so that while this date marks the beginning of the severe downfall in prices, it also marks the beginning of their revival.

The world's fair year (1893) brought to the United States among its visitors those whose search for good horses for export, directed toward the great markets of the west, was to be the rejuvenating force that would once more place the horse in his rightful position as a revenue producer for the farm._ The effect of the demand they created was an almost instant rise in prices of the better grades. Inferior sorts were only sympathetically affected, for it is not profitable to ship anything but "toppy" animals. The growth of exports was tremendous. From about 3,000 in 1893, they have increased fifteen times over in seven years, and to all appearances the demand is by no means yet satisfied.

The exporters entered the market with a call for horses of definite qualifications that have been rigidly adhered to. Hodgepodge methods would not and cannot pay in supplying this market.

The following statement of exports for the fiscal years 1890 to 1901, inclusive, shows an enormous growth:*

Exports of horses for the fiscal years 1900 to 1901.

1890	3,501
1891	3,110
1892	3,226
1893	2,967
1894	5,246
1895	13,984
1896	25,126
1897	39,532
1898	51,150
1899	45,778
1901†	64,722
1901	82,250

The demand for so many animals for export very greatly increases competition, and, as it represents a much broader field for the market to cover than formerly, it is a second cause for the apparent scarcity of good marketable stock. This trade is the means by which surplus stock may be marketed and good prices maintained. If no more horses are produced than are needed for our own uses, it will generally happen that the export trade cannot exist; for home buyers can nearly always pay better prices than exporters, and it is easily seen that, when the supply is short, a strong market may exist independent of foreign demand. Information received within the last two months indicates that such conditions are largely present at this time. There is still a large demand from abroad, but prices have risen to such an extent that this trade has been very much diminished.

---

* From reports of Bureau of Statistics, Treasury Department.

† The shipments to Africa during the last two years are largely responsible for the great increase for the years 1900 and 1901. This is shown as follows:

For fiscal year ended June 30, 1899	127
For fiscal year ended June 30, 1900	10,220
For fiscal year ended June 30, 1901	37,465

These exports, developed under abnormal conditions, must not be looked upon as permanent.

GROWTH OF THE LOCAL DEMAND.

With the growth of the export trade, the great increase in the demands of the local market has required horses in large numbers. The increase of population, with a growing love of a good horse, and the wonderful growth of business, call for many more horses than were needed for such purposes in the early "90's." The exacting nature which characterizes the foreign demand is also coming to be a notable feature of the home demand.

This third cause—the local demand—combined with the export trade, makes a broader market. Undoubtedly, there are as many horses in the country now as ten years ago, though of an inferior quality, but relatively there is a great scarcity.

GENERAL CONSIDERATIONS OF THE MARKET—WHAT CONSTITUTES A MARKET CLASS

By a market class we mean the demand that exists for a horse of certain characteristics definitely specified. We find the requirement that certain work shall be done in certain ways. This requires a horse of certain size, conformation, style and action, and becomes more exacting as time goes on and the demand for such a horse increases. For this reason it is readily seen that classes on the market at one time may be cut off by reason of a change in the kind of work to be done or a cut off by reason of a change in the kind' of work to be done or a change in the method of doing it; such, for instance, as the substitution of electricity for horses as a motive power for street railways. On the other hand, we have an illustration of the creation of new classes in the opening up of the English demand for the omnibus horse. The increasing demand for hunters for both the local and export trade and the brisk trade in polo ponies are also instances in such conditions. The kind of work and the manner in which it is to be done, therefore, develop the buyer's demands and thus create the market class.

WHEN WILL A HORSE SELL WELL?

The question naturally arises, When will a horse sell well? This is answered in describing the requirements of the various classes, which is done elsewhere in this bulletin. An animal will be in good demand when he meets the qualifications of a market class; the more clearly he does so the greater demand there will be for him and the higher will be his selling price; and a horse that goes into a class because his breeder was successful in breeding him for that class is much more likely to sell profitably than one that drops into a class as the result of an accident in breeding, handling, or fitting for the market. A breeder must determine for himself whether he can produce such a horse and dispose of him at a profit. That he will find a good demand for animals of the right type is quite certain. The individuality of the horse himself, then, will indicate his class.

GENERAL ESSENTIALS OF A MARKET HORSE.

Before taking up the details of the various classes it may be well to consider the essentials that all classes must have—the requirements of a drafter as well as a coacher, or of a busser, as well as a cob, roadster or saddler.

AGE.

Mature and well-broken horses are always the best sellers. A year or two spent in waiting for a horse to develop and educating him means an expenditure of time and money on the part of the purchaser which is, as a rule, undesirable, unless the horse is bought specifically for the purpose of fitting him for the finished market. The ideal age is five years, buyers usually purchasing animals ranging from five to eight. The classes vary somewhat in this respect. A horse intended for draft purposes may be marketed somewhat sooner than a harness horse or saddler.

BREEDING AND SEX.

The breed to which a horse belongs has very little influence on his selling price. All that is required is that he be a good individual of his class. A good horse always sells. Geldings are preferred somewhat generally to mares.

COLOR.

Color does not figure so strongly as many would lead us to believe. Almost any color with excellence to back it will sell well, except white, flea-bitten gray, "mealy" bay or any other color that might be termed "washed out." Among drafters, no special color seems to have a preference; with harness horses and saddlers, bays, browns and chestnuts have first preference, but grays and blacks sell readily if "good." Well-matched teams, both in harness and draft classes, usually bring higher prices than if sold singly.

CONDITION.

Condition is very often overlooked. It is absolutely essential that a horse be in good condition (well fed) to bring what he is really worth. This is particularly true of animals of the draft type. Whether it increases the animal's real value as a worker is not necessary to consider. The market demands high condition and pays those men well who cater to it. The great lack of condition is shown by the the fact that many horses are sent in for sale only to be reshipped to the country for further feeding. Condition is almost as essential as fat on a steer, and its absence cuts from 25 to 50 per cent from the selling price of a horse. The requirements of the market in this line are well worthy of notice.

DISPOSITION AND INTELLIGENCE.

Every class calls for an animal of intelligence and good disposition, willing to pull at a good rate or set a fast pace on the driveway, and capable and cool-headed in an emergency. The use of horses on crowded streets, often among large numbers of pedestrians, makes the latter particularly essential. The need of these qualifications is more important in some classes than in others.

THE MARKET HORSE IN DETAIL.

SOUNDNESS.

The most important requirement of a market horse is "serviceable" soundness; that is, he must have no chronic disease that will unfit him for work of a general nature. He must be sound in wind and in limb, able to do a reasonable amount of work without undue fatigue or premature breakdowns. The majortiy of the horses sold from a great market go to the city trade and are compelled to do their work on hard, unyielding pavements, pulling heavy loads, or developing speed that is an even greater strain on the feet and legs. The average period of usefulness on city streets of a horse that was sound at the start is not more than five years, and it is manifestly evident that this time will be materially decreased if he begins this work in an unsound condition. Broken wind, sidebones, unsound hocks, and all the various other ills that a horse is heir to should be strenuously guarded against, as they greatly diminish his value.

CONFORMATION.

The next requirement, then, is a conformation that will enable an ani-mal to do hard work with a minimum of wear, and give him the longest possible period of soundness. Special emphasis should be placed on the foot, which should be of medium size, with hard and dense horn, plenty of height to the heels and plenty of room between them, a large elastic frog, and a nicely hollowed sole—in short, a sound, durable foot. The pastern slopes well, corresponding to the slope of the shoulder. These conditions—with flat, fully developed muscles, strong, well-developed joints, strongly supported knees and hocks, clear, clean-cut tendons stand-ing well out from the leg, and dense bone of a quantity sufficient to sus-tain the weight of the horse—will give a limb well calculated to with-stand the wear and tear of a city pavement.

Joining the fore and hind quarters we must look for a deep, fairly wide, and compact middle piece, with ample room for chest organs, and no pinching at the waist. Too much width should be avoided, as the action of the forelegs is almost sure to be bad with such a conformation. A short back is generally sought, especially one which shows the least pos-sible amount of space between the last ribs and the hips, giving a "close coupled" horse. This is almost as essential as a sound foot. A long loose-ribbed, open-jointed, wasp-wasted animal is especially to be avoided. Such a conformation indicates a lack of strength and forecasts an early breakdown. The shoulders should be deep and smooth, and hind quarters deeply muscled, wide and well rounded. A sloping rump is always un-sightly and detracts both from the use and the value of the horse, for it stands to reason that such a conformation cannot furnish the same amount of muscle that a nicely rounded one can. The tail should be set high and smartly carried. Prominent shoulder points, hips and buttocks are objec-tionable.

The neck should be clearly outlined, of moderate length, and well muscled, with a good crest. The head should be clean-cut and of moderate length, with a rather small ear, much breadth and fullness of fore-head, a large, clear, full, intelligent eye, and a wide-open nostril, showing good lung power and consequent stamina. The mouth should be of good size, with sound teeth, and firm lips of medium thickness.

Over all these must be an abundance of muscle laid on smoothly and nicely rounded. Quality is highly essential, and the mistake of growing size without it will be found expensive. A close connection between qual-ity and stamina is very clearly recognized by horsemen.

HORSES FOR DRAFT.

Any horse the purpose of which is to draw large loads, whether at the walk or trot may be spoken of as a "horse for draft." Common usage has fixed the term "draft" on horses of specified weight and size, but there are other classes on the market whose conformation is what has come to be known as the "draft form," but which differ from the drafter in the matter of size and weight and the manner of performing their work. The drafter proper works always at a walk, while other classes of horses of draft type do their work mainly at the trot. As we go along, the close relationship between the different classes of this group should be noticed, for it is one of the most interesting and instructive features of the market.

THE DRAFT HORSE.

Size and weight.—The weight that will characterize a horse as a drafter will be that above which he cannot work at the trot without waste of effort and horseflesh and below which he can work more econom-ically by hauling smaller loads at increased speed. This weight is pretty generally conceded to be 1,600 pounds in fair flesh. The height of a drafter will vary from 15.3 hands for the smaller sorts to 17.2 hands for horses of great weights.

The importance of weight in a drafter must not be overlooked. His purpose is solely that of heavy work, pulling great loads at the walk, and to fulfill this requirement most perfectly the first essential is weight with, of course, proportional size. Without weight the immense loads that are to be hauled over our city streets could not be moved, and careful obser-vation of the average prices has shown that, other things being equal, draft horseflesh is worth about $25 for every additional hundred pounds it can show over 1,600 pounds.[*] It is also essential that as much as possible of this weight be bone and muscle. Though many buyers unquestionably demand fat, and the truth is that a horse cannot sell for a creditable price unless fat, the effective value of a horse as a worker should not be lost sight of.

Conformation.—His conformation should enable the animal to make his weight as effective as possible, and, at the same time, assure a rea-sonably long period of usefulness. For this purpose, he must have a rather short, heavy neck and a shoulder sloping enough to take the collar well, but not so straight as to cause a "post leg" and bring about prema-ture unsoundness. The back should be short, well muscled, and strongly

[*]Craig. Judging Live Stock, p. 34.

Interior view of new Live Stock Pavilion, Iowa State Fair Grounds, during progress of stock judging.

coupled to the hind quarters, which should be nicely rounded, smooth and plentifully supplied with muscle. Particular attention should be paid to the hock. The legs must be moderately short and have a supply of bone sufficient to support the weight and work of the animal, and, of course, must be sound. A short leg, with low-set knees and hocks, is one that will stand wear and tear and usually goes with a strong, closely coupled body. Head and neck should be proportionate to the size of the horse. The whole appearance should be massive.

Action.—The action of the drafter is confined almost exclusively to the walk. For this reason the walk is of vital importance. Rapidity of step and length of stride enable him to cover considerable ground in the least possible time. Straightness, smoothness, regularity and lack of friction enable him to do this with the least possible wear and injury to himself. The trot should possess all the merits of the walk.

Demand.—Horses of this description are in strong demand for use in city streets of America and Europe. The great packing houses, brewing companies, wholesale houses, and heavy dray and transfer companies buy this class of horse, differing slightly in weight, according to the purpose to which it is to be put or the desires of the purchaser.

The rougher, plainer drafters are used for the coarser work of the cities, where the style of a team is of no particular importance to its owner. The lumber trade takes such a horse, often buying animals that are blemished or even unsound.

The horse used for the American city trade is also in strong demand for the export trade to England and the continent.

THE LONDON VANNER.

The horse known in England as a van horse is very largely purchased on the American markets. He is simply a good, "toppy" American drafter, such as has already been described weighing from 1,600 to 1,800 pounds, and standing from 16 to 16.2 hands, with a strong, compact body on short, strong legs, with sound, healthy feet. He is used to draw heavy drays, vans, etc.

THE SCOTCH, OR GLASGOW, VANNER.

This horse is about the same as the English as to weight, though he may be lighter, and is more upstanding—that is, on longer legs. His work is the same as that of other classes of horses intended for moderately heavy city work.

The horse that the Englishmen term a "cart horse" is extremely rare on the American market, and, when found, not always of the best quality. He should stand 16.2 to 17.2 hands, and weigh 2,000 pounds and upward.

THE EXPRESS HORSE.

After the drafter, the remaining classes of the draft type are distinguished by the fact that their work is done almost exclusively at the trot. The first of these is the expresser. This is one of the best and highest classes on the market so far as individual excellence is concerned, and horses that fill the requirements are always in demand at strong prices. An expresser is the best finished of all of the minor draft classes.

Size and weight.—The size and weight vary somewhat, as a matter of course, but, as a general rule, an expresser stands from 15.2 to 16 hands, and weighs from 1,250 to 1,500 pounds, or even more, the weight varying with the kind of work, wagon, etc., to which the horse is to be put. In some cases a team hitched to an express wagon will be seen showing all the characteristics of the true drafter, but, as a rule, these horses are for heavy dray work, and are not looked upon as representative expressers.

Conformation.—The most pronounced type of expresser is a rather upstanding horse with strong, closely coupled body, considerable width of chest and hips, sound, clean limbs, and particularly sound, healthy feet. Special stress is placed on the health, quality and conformation of the foot. Excepting the class following (the bussers) no class of draft type has to undergo the same amount of strain on the feet as the expresser. Hauling a loaded wagon at the trot soon tells on any but the best organs of locomotion.

When an expresser is said to be upstanding the inference should not be that he is what could be denominated "leggy." This extreme is to be absolutely avoided, and as between the two, a horse with short legs is much preferable. Buyers demand a sensible medium. The most striking features in the conformation of an expresser are (1) his high finish, with considerable weight—"a draft horse with coach finish," and (2) his rather upstanding appearance as compared with other draft classes.

Action.—His work makes the trot of an expresser his most important gait. It should, above all things, be straight, frictionless, as smooth as possible, and quick and regular. The walk must be similarly developed.

Demand.—The express companies constitute the ruling factors in the trade for this class of horses, but other lines of business that require an extra good light-delivery horse find in the expresser such an animal as they desire. The lighter teams of the packing companies are heavy expressers, weighing from 1,450 to 1,550 pounds.

Fire companies buy horses very much after this type, getting a somewhat "toppy" animal that shows much intelligence and courage. Police horses come from somewhat similar sources.

ENGLISH TYPES.

Much is heard of English "light vanners" and "parcel carters." These are simply the English forms of what we call expressers, changed somewhat to conform to English requirements—that is, with legs as short as possible. The two names are used for practically the same horse.

THE OMNIBUS HORSE.

Size and Weight.—A typical busser stands from 15.1 to 15.3 hands, and weighs from 1,200 to 1,400 pounds.

Conformation.—In form he is a compact, rugged little horse with all the characteristics of the true draft type, set on short, strong legs, with ample bone, more or less feather, and sound feet. He should carry a fairly high head and show some style.

Action.—The work of this class is performed almost wholly at the trot, and, accordingly, we will look for a horse that is a "straight line mover"—that is, straight and true in movement. He should have plenty of activity with a moderately attractive action, but especially with a trot that is quick, straight, elastic and smooth—a true, frictionless gait.

Demand.—These horses are used in large numbers on the streets of foreign (especially English) cities to draw the omnibuses that are a common means of transportation. Some are employed in the trade of American cities demanding a light, stocky, active horse for miscellaneous purposes. He fills to some extent, the call for a general-purpose horse, but he should not be confused with the horse quoted as "general purpose" in market reports. The prices that bussers are bringing show not only the strength of the demand but the camparatively small supply.

THE TRAM HORSE.

Trammers are very little different from the bussers except that they are rather plainer, an inch or two smaller in size, and correspondingly lighter, but they should have as much weight as possible for their height. They are used on the tramways of European cities.

ARTILLERY HORSES.

Contracts for horses for the army artillery service often give an outlet for small horses of the draft type weighing from 1,100 to 1,250 pounds. They are not of any particular line of breeding, being often of the blood of the light breeds, but they must fill very exact requirements to be acceptable. Two classes are generally recognized, one for light and the other for heavy artillery. Quite large numbers are purchased for use in the British army, a horse answering the description of a light parcel carter being taken for this purpose.

The specifications herewith given for the United States artillery horse will be seen to be those of an expresser without the weight:

(Article 1142, United States Army Regulations, 1901.)

"The artillery horse is required for quick draft purposes, and should move the carriage ordinarily by weight thrown into the collar rather than by muscular exertion.

"The animal must be sound, without blemish or defect, well bred, of a kind disposition, and free from vicious habits, a square trotter; well broken to harness, and gentle under the saddle, with easy mouth and gait, and with free, prompt action at the walk, trot and gallop; otherwise to conform to the follow description:

"A gelding of uniform and hardy color, in good condition, from 15¼ to 16 hands high; weight of the lead horse not less than 1,050 pounds and that of the wheel horse not more than 1,200 pounds; from 5 to 8 years old, head and ears small, forehead broad, eyes large and prominent, vision perfect in every respect; chest full, broad and deep; fore legs straight and standing well under; shoulders sufficiently broad to support

23

the collar, but not too heavy; barrel large and increasing from girth toward flank; withers elevated; back short and straight, with broad, deep loins, short coupled with solid hind quarters; hocks well bent and under the horse; pasterns slanting, and feet sound and in good order. Long-legged, loose-jointed, long-bodied, and narrow-chested horses, as well as those which are restive, vicious, or too free in harness, or which do not, upon rigid inspection, meet the above requirements in every respect, will be rejected."

HORSES FOR HARNESS AND SADDLE.

In taking up the class which, excluding cavalry horses, might be termed "pleasure horses," in contrast with the previous group, the classes which are used almost exclusively for business purposes, we come to the horse that brings by far the highest market prices when of a high degree of excellence, but whose breeding has been attended with more disastrous failures than any other; the horse that is the ennoblement of equine virtue when it approaches perfection and that in the embodiment of uselessness and insignificance when poor. More "tinkering" has been done with trotting, coach and thoroughbred blood than with any other, and it is safe to state that the unintelligent, indiscriminate, and improper use of sires of these light breeds has had more to do with the development of an unsightly mass of scrub horse stock than any other cause.

Stand by the auction ring of any great horse market and observe closely the horses that fail to bring prices sufficient to cover cost of production. In the great majority of cases trotting blood predominates if any breeding at all is noticeable. Ask a dealer what is the breeding, if any, of most of the large numbers of the unclassed horses on the market, his answer will be: "Trotting and coach blood." This is not because draft blood is more valuable or that the blood of the light breeds is not wanted, for the great cry of the market at present is that good drivers and saddlers are extremely scarce. It is because performance and style are much more difficult to acquire in breeding than size and weight. It is because men with a fascination for the race track attempt to produce trotters without the slightest regard for nature's laws, and no disappointment or failure seems sufficient to bring them to realize their folly. Breeding to a trotter without system and study, but only in the hope of getting a speedy foal as a possibility or an accident, is "playing with fire." The breeding of light horses requires not only a considerable amount of capital, but demands a knowledge of horses of the very highest order. It necessitates concentration of effort and years of waiting and planning. It is not every man that brings such qualities to bear when he takes a 1,600-pound draft mare to a 1,200-pound harness or saddle stallion, and it is largely because of this, and not on account of the breeds themselves, that so many poor horses are forced on the market.

A high-class roadster, coacher or saddler is by far the most difficult horse to produce that the market calls for. In addition to careful plans of breeding and high individual excellence in the resulting progeny, a course of handling, mannering and training must be pursued before the horse will figure as a really marketable animal.

These facts must be thoroughly understood if a man would breed light horses for market.

Three pretty well-defined classes, each with several sub-classes of more or less distinct demarcation, make up this type. Speaking of the group as a whole, we find that all the virtues of which a horse is possessed must be found in this animal. The higher grades must be perfectly sound in wind and limb, free from blemishes of any kind, and extremely stylish in appearance. Disposition and education are very important; the uses for which he is intended and the conditions surrounding him require that he be kind, gentle, cool-headed in emergencies, and well mannered, yet full of spirit and energy.

DRIVERS.

ROADSTERS.

Size and Weight.—The typical roadster stands from 15.1 to 15.3 hands high and weighs from 950 to 1,150 pounds.

Conformation.—We note now a very radical difference from the heavy horse. The roadster is more upstanding, not so wide, and entirely lacks the massiveness of the drafter, but is deep of chest and middle. In extremes of roadster form, especially when in racing condition, there is a prominent appearance of angularity that, though not unpleasing, is a sharp contrast both to the form of the drafter and as will be shown later, to that of the coacher.

It is highly essential that feet and legs be not only sound, but of that correct conformation that will prevent unsoundness to the greatest possible extent. The pasterns should be sloping and strong, and the shoulder deep and sloping and extending well into the back. The withers are high and sharp, the back strongly muscled, short, and closely coupled, and the hind quarters long and heavily muscled. The bones from elbow point to knee (forearm) and from stifle to hock (leg) should be nearly twice as long as the cannon bones in their respective limbs, thus giving long leverage and muscles that are long, and therefore quick to respond and placing the fulcrums of these levers close to the ground, giving strength steadiness, and poise. The neck should be of medium length* to long, joined to the shoulder, and clearly defined, with a clean-cut throatlatch. The head should be fine and clean-cut, with an erect, neat, medium-sized ear, a full, clear eye and full, good-sized nostrils. Stamina is an essential of this class, and, as an indication, a high degree of quality will be looked for.

Action.—There are two opinions prevalent in the market regarding the trotting action of a roadster. One places more emphasis on its approach to the extremes of coach action, while the other regards moderately

---

* It is questioned by good judges and expert buyers whether it is possible to get a neck too long in a horse of any class.

high action as essential, but does not carry it to the point where speed is sacrificed. This latter idea carried out will develop the long, reachy action that tends to increase speed; it will develop the class of horse that will closely approach the true trotter and it will at the same time be less wearing on the horse. The former will branch off in an entirely different direction, with the coach horse as its ultimate end, if much speed is also present, will entail a severe strain on the horse. In other words, as between action and speed in a roadster at the trot, some will place more importance on action, while others will seek to develop speed, and will buy accordingly. As a roadster, strictly speaking, is a horse whose purpose is to draw a light rig on the road at a fairly high rate of speed for a considerable length of time, the latter idea is technically more nearly correct. All-around and not extreme action is desired. It must be prompt, straight, and frictionless, whether at the trot, the pace, or the walk.

Demand.—Roadsters are in demand for city use or country use, and for any purpose where a horse is wanted for fast driving to a light road wagon or run-about.

THE STANDARD-BRED HORSE.

Size and weight.—The standard-bred trotter or pacer is the horse of the foregoing class more highly specialized and always eligible to registry in the trotting register.

Conformation.—This shows the extreme of speed production, and is the result of years of breeding for the sole purpose of increased speed. It is the roadster type carried to the farthest known limit. A better description of the type was never made than the one comparing the conformation to that of the greyhound.

Action.—The sole purpose of action in the Standard-bred horse is for the development of the greatest speed with the least possible expenditure of energy. The most important essentials are straightness, smoothness, and reach.

Demand.—Eligible trotters and pacers are in demand for racing purposes, both amateur and professional, and for the breeding stud.

COACHERS.

The connection between the coach horse and the roadster is extremely close, the difference between the two groups being chiefly those of conformation and action.

COACH HORSES.

Size and weight.—A typical coach horse stands 15.2 to 16 hands and weighs from 1,100 to 1,250 pounds.

Conformation.—A coacher is considerably heavier, smoother and more compact than a roadster. The conditions of his work, of course, require soundness as an absolute essential. His legs are clean-cut and well muscled, with sloping pasterns and shoulders; the back short, closely coupled to the hind quarters, and smoothly muscled. The hind quarters are well packed with muscle; smooth, and rounded, not straight and angular as in the roadster. A smooth, well-filled, evenly-rounded quarter is regarded with much favor. The tail should be set well up and carried high. In the shoulders the same point of smoothness and lack of angularity are required. The withers should be high and thin, the neck smoothly joined to the shoulders, long and clean, with a full crest, the head fine and of medium size, with fine ears, a full, clear eye, and large open nostrils.

Quality is as important in the coacher as in the roadster, and for similar reasons.

Action.—Conformation and action are absolutely essential to a coach horse and to each other; that is, a horse cannot lay claim to merit as a coacher unless he has both of these qualifications. Proper conformation should first be present, for then the animal may be trained to act fairly well, but if a fine actor is rough and "weedy" in make-up no amount of feeding and care can give him form and style.

In discussing the coach action the necessity for the legs to be moved straight and true is perhaps the first thing to be considered, for the extreme flexing of the legs, especially at the knees, makes it all the more difficult for the horse to move them in a straight line, and thus increase the danger of injury to himself by interfering, to say nothing of the unsightliness of faulty action. The fore legs are flexed as high as possible and the feet extended with a sort of rotary motion that is very different from the long reach of the roadster.

The most difficult action to acquire is at the hocks. That of the knees may be developed by training and shoeing, but high, elastic hock action is well-nigh a hopeless proposition unless bred in the horse. It may be easily inferred that it is far less common than first rate knee action. The hocks should be flexed without any deviation from a straight line, the feet carried in much the same manner as in front and placed directly in front of their former positions, with as little jar as possible At all time a coacher must "keep his legs under him." He does not extend himself as a roadster; there is not the long reach in front nor the swing behind.

A moderate degree of speed always gives added value to a coach horse, but much speed is not only not absolutely necessary, but is, according to the nature of things, usually out of the question. Much of the energy of the horse's effort is expended in lifting his feet as high as possible, and the combination of this effort with that of speed-making reach is asking too much of a horse, as it entails so great an amount of wear on the animal organism that it would soon give way.

While a coacher must be thoroughly sound, he is not required to have the great speed powers or endurance of the roadster. Short distances only are expected of him at a rate of from 6 to 10 miles an hour.

Demand.—The demand for a stylish animal for city driving takes all the available horses that come to the market. Some are exported, but the foreign demand has comparatively little effect on this class. The demand from the American cities is strong, the only complaint being that the right kind of horses are extremely difficult to find.

COBS.

Size and weight.—A typical cob stands about 15.1 hands and weighs from 1,000 to 1,050 pounds.

Conformation.—If anything, the cob is more compact and smoother than a coacher, and on somewhat shorter legs. He shows the highest possible amount of style and should be a horse of much beauty. "He is a nice, flashy, trappy-going little coach horse."

Action.—In action a cob has the highest development of any of the coachers, and has, especially, that sharp, snappy quality that horsemen call "trappy."

Demand.—Cobs supply the same class of trade as the full-sized coachers, and are used for the lighter grades of work to which a coacher may be put.

SADDLERS.

THE SADDLE HORSE.

Size and weight.—A saddler will vary considerably in the characteristics of size and weight, depending on the character of the work for which he is intended and the amount of weight he is to carry. As a general rule, a range of from 15.1 to 15.3 in height and from 1,000 to 1,150 pounds in weight will describe this pretty accurately.

A horse of 15.1 hands in height and 1,000 pounds weight makes what is called a "ladies' saddler"; or if a walk, trot and tenter horse, a "ladies' hack"; but for heavier riders the larger animals naturally are required, some men needing a horse standing over 16 hands and weighing 1,200 pounds or even more.

Conformation.—A typical saddler does not differ in form in any marked degree from other light horses. Many good saddlers come direct from harness stock. The principal requirements that are to a certain extent peculiar to this class are: (1) Sloping pasterns and shoulders; a straight pastern and shoulder is an added objectionable feature in a saddle horse, for it is almost certain to make a hard rider. (2) Moderately high and narrow withers, for the same reason; the height of the withers above the hind quarters should not be exaggerated—not more than an inch. The extension of the shoulder into the back and the shortness and compactness of coupling are extremely important.

The saddler shows, perhaps, more style than any other class of horses. He should have a high degree of quality, showing in each detail a ribbon-like smoothness from end to end. Shoulder should be smooth and even, the hind quarters will rounded and smooth. Rotundity of body is a marked feature. He is usually somewhat upstanding, and should have a high-set, smartly carried head and tail. An ideal saddler will naturally have a head that shows an unusual disposition and high intelligence, for the intimate relation between a horse and his rider demands thinking ability on both sides.

Action.—Two styles of a saddle action are demanded—the walk, trot, and canter action, and the gaits of the American Saddle Horse Breeders'

Association—the walk, trot, canter, rack, and running walk, fox trot, or slow pace. Any one of the last three of the second style is acceptable to breeders of this type, but the first four must always be present. The dictates of fashion have a good deal to do with a market demand for gaits. Just at present a horse with walk, trot, and canter only is somewhat preferred, but the American saddle horse will always be in demand as a very useful animal, and will be valuable in the production of saddlers, for training can bring out the desired action, and for intelligence and extreme style no breed will surpass him. Saddle action must, first of all, be sure. A horse inclined to stumble is dangerous. Following this we look for snap, moderate height, and particularly straightness and evenness in all gaits.

Demand.—Saddlers are in demand for both city and country trade, and are by no means equal to the demand.

HUNTERS.

Size and Weight.—The class of horses known as hunters is divided into "light" and "heavy" hunters; the former carrying ladies and light-weight men, and the latter able to take men of a weight up to 200 pounds. Naturally there will be many variations between these two classes, the requirements of each rider indicating the weight of his mount. A range of from 15.2 hands, with a weight of 1,100 pounds, to 16.2 hands, weighing 1,200 or 1,250 pounds, would be a fair approximation.

Conformation.—A typical hunter shows a conformation of a rather rangy order, but not loosely built, standing pretty well from the ground with legs of much bone, depending on the weight he is to carry. The shoulder should be deep; the body deep and full chested; "short above and long below," the barrel with a good development, but not paunchy—well built in every particular to be a ground gainer. Too much muscularity can hardly be present; the hind quarters should be especially long and deeply muscled. Thick necks are avoided; rather a thin, long neck with a good-sized intelligent head is preferred.

The hunter must show plenty of quality; stamina is absolutely necessary for work such as he is to perform. His head must show that high degree of intelligence and fearlessness that insure the confidence of his rider.

Action.—The most desirable feature in the motive power of a hunter is his jumping ability. Not only must there be the capacity to clear any reasonable obstacle that presents itself,* but this must be done gracefully and willingly. Of course, a straight, smooth, easy movement is always necessary. Speed adds much to the value of a hunter, especially if his rider has ambitions to gratify.

Demand.—This class of horses is in ready demand by persons of means who enjoy the sport of following the hounds. The same condition presents itself that is found in other classes of light horses, namely, that the price of a suitable animal will always be a long one. Riding to

---

* The usual height of the fences hunted over ranges from three to four feet.

hounds is gaining in popularity in this country and is an influential force in the development of the horse market.

THE THOROUGHBRED.

The breeding of thoroughbreds is rapidly assuming large proportions Many of the sales that have been held during the past year have averaged $1,000, even for yearlings, and fabulous sums have been paid for mature breeding animals, the large prices brought by the aged mares showing the strong demand that exists. The thoroughbred bears to some extent the same relation to the hunter that the standard-bred horse does to the roadster; that is, he is largely the producer of the hunter, the principal difference being that the hunter usually lacks the speed of a racer, and is not recorded in the stud-book.

POLO PONIES.

The three essentials of a polo pony are (1) weight carrying ability, with small size, (2) agility, and (3) speed. .

Size and weight.—The maximum height is 14.2 hands. The weight for such a height will be about 850 pounds.

Conformation.—Good bone and compact conformation are requisite. with as much muscle as possible. "Get quarters on him like a cart horse, if you can," said a polo authority. Short cannon bones, especially in the hind legs, give the horse a control of himself that enables him to turn with speed and agility. Perfect soundness and extreme quality are indispensable, for the strain of the game and the demands made on the pony's endurance are usually severe.

Intelligence and training.—Courage and intelligence are prime requisites with a polo pony. Quickness of sight and a keen enjoyment of the game make an animal still more valuable. Along this line it must be remembered that all ponies will not learn the game. Horses are differently constituted in this respect, and such things must be expected.

Action.—The principal requirement in action is agility. The pony must always have himself well under control, with the ability to come to a dead stop almost instantly from a run, and quickness that enables him to "turn on a dollar," as a Westerner puts it. Speed is also necessary, but agility first of all.

Demand.—Like the preceding class, the growth of a fascinating sport is rapidly opening up a market for another class of horses, and, like the hunters, polo ponies bring long prices when suitable for such work, and are sound. Most players have four or five horses constantly on hand, and some have twenty or thirty in their stables.

It is an interesting fact that no better polo ponies are found in the United States than Western "cow ponies" that are sound and well set up, with a few months' education in the rudiments of the game as a finishing school.

CAVALRY HORSES.

Troopers.—At uncertain intervals the market calls for horses to fill contracts with army authorities. The demand is not exceedingly large at any time and at no time is it steady. As a general rule, these horses are selected from the various classes of light horses. Foreign governments have executed orders to some extent for army stock, most horses that are regularly bought for this purpose going to England; and within the past two years immense numbers of animals have been purchased by British agents for use in South Africa, swelling the exports last year by over 30,000. Under no circumstances, however, can the army demand be looked upon as of such character as to affect the market steadily.

The best horses bought for army purposes in this country are for the United States army, those bought for home use by the British army next, and the stock for South Africa fall to the bottom of the scale. The United States army demands a practically sound and unblemished horse. The specifications for the cavalry horse follow:

(Article 1142, United States Army Regulations, 1901.)

"The cavalry horse must be sound and well bred; gentle under the saddle; free from vicious habits; with free and prompt action at the walk, trot and gallop; without blemish or defect; of a kind disposition; with easy mouth and gait; and otherwise to conform to the following description:

"A gelding of uniform and hardy color; in good condition; from 15¼ to 16 hands high; weight not less than 950 nor more than 1,150 pounds; from four to eight years old; head and ears small; forehead broad; eyes large and prominent; vision perfect in every respect; shoulders long and sloping well back; chest full, broad, and deep; fore legs staight and standing well under; barrel large and increasing from girth toward flank; withers elevated; back short and straight; loins and haunches broad and muscular; hocks well bent and under the horse; pasterns slanting, and feet small and sound.

"Each horse will be subjected to a rigid inspection, and any animal that does not meet the above requirements in every respect must be rejected.

"A horse under five years old should not be accepted unless a specially fine, well-developed animal."

MINOR CLASSES.

Strictly speaking, the horses mentioned below are not in market demand. They sell, however, if the price is low enough, and follow the natural result of such a condition of being dangerously near a losing investment to the seller.

GENERAL-PURPOSE HORSES.

A very large proportion of the horses on the market are what are known in stock yards reports and market quotations as "general purpose" animals. They are horses without any particular type, embracing misfits of all kinds of breeding, though not scrubs, as a rule, and usually being of fair to good quality without those characteristics that fit a horse for a market class. In many cases they may be serviceably sound—perhaps so in the majority of instances.

Such animls are used, as the name designates, for anything and everything, but the demand is not well defined, and the supply far too large to make this kind of horse a feature of the market other than by its numbers. The average prices for them are next to the lowest quoted.

SOUTHERN HORSES.

At most of the Western markets, particularly those on the Missouri river and at St Louis, there exists a good demand, strongest in the spring of the year, for a rather inferior grade of horses for the Southern trade. They range in quality from very inferior to very "nice" animals. They comprise mainly an assortment of practically unclassed horses, but as much of the roadster type as any. Many are sold as drivers, some as saddlers, the best grades usually going to Virginia. Prices range from $5 to $200.

PLUGS AND SCRUBS.

These wrecks of horseflesh seem out of place in a discussion of market classes of horses. Plugs are usually those animals that have come back from final sale after being worn out by long years of work. Scrubs are described by the name.

THE MARKET FOR RANGE HORSES.

This phase of the horse market is somewhat difficult to treat. When animals are sold on the market as "range horses," it is generally understood that they are unbroken branded horses brought in and sold in carload lots, usually going to the country to be broken, and finally resold as finished horses. On the other hand, if range men are equipped to break their young stock thoroughly and do not brand them, such horses sell as natives and strictly on their merits.

While the prejudice against a branded horse is not so strong as formerly, a brand still has a very cooling effect on the enthusiasm of a prospective buyer. The memory of the evil disposition of the old horses of this country and the frequently exaggerated stories of its presence today are constantly called to the attention of the public. However, it is safe to state that the character and disposition of the range horse and his individuality are being greatly improved by the enlightened policy of the more progressive ranchmen. His temper is being bettered by closer communication with man and better methods of handling, and the standard of breeding is being raised by the use of large numbers of pure-bred sires that have been brought in from the Eastern States and Europe. At the same time the wonderful quality and endurance of the native stock have been retained, and, however we may look upon the range horse personally we must admit that the foundation is there for a very excellent horse stock. The systematic experimenting that has been done by shipping rangers East as youngsters has been very successful, though grades of only average quality were used.

In speaking favorably of the range horse, the grades which are usually the offspring of pure-bred sires are meant. These represent what the range is able to do in producing horses, and show its possibilities in the best light, which is no more than fair. With the average old-time ranger —the cayuse, mustang, or Indian pony—only exceptional individuals are worthy of attention. In the main, there is no meaner kind of equine to be found than what is known in different localities under one or another of these names.

It cannot be said that even a large part of the range horses sold on the Western markets show much evidence of breeding. The work of improvement is yet in its primary stages.

The rangers divide into three fairly well-defined classes—ponies, saddlers and drivers, and chunks.

PONIES.

These are the descendants of the ancient stock that is known by the various names of cayuse, Indian pony, mustang, etc. They stand up 14.2 hands, weighing up to 750 or 900 pounds. Some of them are horses of quality, endurance, and intelligence, and make good riding animals.

These horses are very useful for herding cattle, often showing an intelligence and agility that is wonderful and frequently disconcerting to the rider. They also furnish some of the best material for polo work that can be found, especially when mares of good type are crossed with small thoroughbred sires. However, the cow pony that will make a good polo pony is not easily found. It is the exception, not the rule, that satisfies the buyer and brings the long prices. In such instances, the pony would not go on the market under the same condition as the ordinary ranger. He is the exception, but an exception that serves a valuable purpose for illustrating the possibilities of the best types of range stock.

SADDLERS AND DRIVERS.

These horses are the first as a range class that may show breeding.

The grades of coach, standard-bred and thoroughbred sires will come under this head. They could be described as horses standing from 14.2 to 15.2 hands and weighing from 900 to 1,100 pounds, with an occasional good one of larger size.

CHUNKS.

These usually embrace the draft grades, standing 15 hands and up, and weighing from 1,100 to 1,400 pounds. Extra individuals often weigh over 1,500 pounds.

DEMAND.

The larger number of range horses normally find their final place of consumption on farms and in small towns. The British government has bought thousands of them, and the United States army is often supplied with cavalry horses from these sources. Quite often branded horses will be found in the export stables.

SUNSTROKE IN HORSES.

Homestead.

When horses are working hard in the field or on the road in very hot weather they are apt to suffer an attack of sunstroke or heat prostration. In such cases the first symptoms which should warn the driver that trouble impends are as follows: The horse that has been sweating profusely gradually commences to dry off and becomes dry and hot. He has been working with vim and vigor, but now acts sluggishly and pants or breathes fast and with flapping nostrils. His ears drop, his nostrils are widely distended and his eyes appear red. Unless he is stopped at once at this stage he will go down and in excessively bad cases die in a few minutes. In other cases the above symptoms are associated with those of the colic and this form of colic is characterized by scouring and bloating. Having learned to detect the symptoms of impending sunstroke from the above description the next thing is to know what to do in such emergencies. Unhitch at the very first sign of trouble and if possible get the animal into a shady place under a tree where there is a breeze. Remove the harness and at once sprinkle him from head to foot with cold water from a sprinkling can. Keep this up steadily, but do not drench him with water from a hose. Place a compress of cold, wet cloths or sponge on his poll and keep this wet with water or vinegar and water. If ammonia is at hand let him inhale a little of it at once and depend upon stimulants for the balance of the remedial treatment. As a stimulant give at one dose an ounce of aromatic spirits of ammonia and four ounces of good whisky in a quart of water and repeat in half doses once an hour until it is seen that he has ceased to "blow" and flap his nostrils. If a thermometer can he had it will show when introduced into the rectum that the temperature has risen to 106 or even higher, whereas it should be 100 degrees in the normal state. By taking the temperature in this way once an hour it will be readily seen how the case is progressing, and if it commences to fail gradually all will go well, but if it increases bad results are in store for the patient and a veterinarian should be called in if possible. Seeing that the fever is so high some men are led to give tincture of aconite in these cases and this we consider to be the most dangerous procedure possible. In its place—and aconite should never be used by an amateur—an ounce dose of saltpeter may be given at the outset and repeated in two hours with great benefit in lowering the temperature and eliminating matters that might lead to future trouble after the urgent danger has passed. If our readers will make it a practice to keep stimulants on hand for such emergencies and use them at once and in large doses well diluted with water they will lose few horses provided that cold water can be had to spray with and apply to the head. The practice of applying a pack of crushed ice to the poll should be followed only when plenty of cold water cannot be had. It is more apt to produce brain trouble than is water and many a horse dies where it is used that would recover by sprinkling and applications of cold water to the head. In very bad cases we even inject cold water copiously into the rectum and find that this tends to reduce the great fever finally. Where colic is a complication the animal should be tapped on the right side and hyposulphate of soda in four ounce doses given along with the aromatic spirits of ammonia, but there is danger in giving laudanum or other narcotics in such cases. The pain will subside when the bloating and fever cease. Injections per rectum are useful in combination with the other treatment recommended where colic is present as a complication. It is the experience of all who have handled such cases that some animals apparently recovering from the severe symptoms turn out "dummies" afterwards. This is to be avoided by keeping up the cold packs for some days, placing the animal in a cool place where there is a breeze and administering iodide of potash in dram doses every four hours or saltpeter in half ounce doses in the drinking water or as a drench three times daily. Such cases as a rule follow the use of medicines like belladonna, or stimulants after the time for their proper use has passed. Bleeding is doubtless indicated at the outset of such cases where softening of the brain is threatened, but as a rule it is better not to bleed the average case where the other methods of treatment can be followed as advised. It should be remembered in this connection that the attack of sunstroke usually happens to the horse that is suffering from indigestion or to the middle horse in a three-horse team. From this it will be seen that it is of the greatest importance to watch the bowels of working horses in hot weather and avoid feeding corn or other foods that tend to produce indigestion at such times. Shade the horse's head and allow small drinks of cold water often, and change the middle horse frequently.

HOW TO GROW DRAFT HORSES IN THE MISSISSIPPI VALLEY.

Wallaces' Farmer.

Farmers in the Mississippi valley have never yet had the business of growing draft horses of the highest quality down to bottom, bedrock business principles. We have gone at it by fits and starts. Away back in the 80's we went into the business of growing draft horses with a good deal of enthusiasm, paid a large sum for imported horses, some of it wisely, much of it unwisely; bought oftentimes without judgment, without discrimination, paid good money sometimes for good horses and often paid good money for horses which ought to have been geldings hauling drays on the streets of London, Liverpool and Glasgow. Nevertheless, as a whole, the business paid.

It did not pay the farmer very well who started a horse ranch and kept a mare a year for the chance of a colt. No thoughtful man expected that, but it did pay the farmer who had work for his mares, who mated them with a first-class imported horse, and reared and educated the colt properly. It paid him and paid him well. Along toward 1891 or 1892, the business began to drag; it seemed as if there were indications of it being overdone. Then came the panic of 1893, the drouth of 1894, the doldrums of 1895, the presidential campaign of 1896, and the bottom fell out of the business. The bicycle came in, and the average farmer thought the business of growing horses was done forever.

We told them they were mistaken, told them in 1896 and in 1897 to buy all the good colts they could buy, to go to every sale and when a good draft colt was up, buy it, no matter what the other fellow would give, to buy it. The men who took our advice made money faster than they ever did on the same amount of live stock in their lives before, and since then most of us have been breeding horses in a haphazard way. They have been making us money, but some way we have been afraid something would happen; that the automobile, for example, would come in and take the place of the draft horse. Possibly it may to some extent, but not to the extent that would affect the price of your horse five dollars.

What, then, do we advise now? Just what we advised in the 90's. We advise the man on the eighty-acre or quarter section farm, who is following a regular line of farming to buy the best high grade mares he can buy, only be sure they are sound, with no defect in vision, no moon-eyed or ophthalmic mares, no unsoundness in wind, no limber-eared, disconsolate mares, but good, all around mares with plenty of size, perfectly sound, and with plenty of spirit. You may just as well do your farm work with this class of mares as with poor ones. They will not cost any more to keep, they will do just as much work, and they have a breeding value far beyond the ordinary scrub mare and not to be compared with one that is unsound, no matter how big they are, will do nearly as much work as geldings, and two out of three will produce fine colts if properly mated.

To the farmer who is out of debt, who really likes a good horse, we suggest that he buy pedigreed registered mares. At the present price they are about as cheap as any kind of stock on the market. If half a dozen farmers in any neighborhood would buy two mares apiece, registered, rattling good ones, and then form a horse company among themselves and buy the best stallion that they can find, they would have about as safe a money-making proposition as anything that we know of. For the registered horse can be grown by the farmer cheaper and better than by the foreigner or by the man who devotes a large farm exclusively to breeding horses. He has work for his mares. They will earn their way the whole year. All that the colt will cost him will be the service fee, the interest on the money invested in the mare, a couple of weeks' idleness at foaling time, and the feed of the colt until it is three years old. They will never see a time when a good brood mare or stallion three years old will sell for as little as the sum of these different elements of cost combined.

The breeder on the large farm must go to all this expense and besides the use of the mare for a year. He must lose a whole year's use; the farmer loses only ten days or two weeks' use of his mare. The work that she will give him will far more than pay for the year's keep. He can give more attention to two or three colts each year than the man who has a large stud farm and must depend on hired help. Nearly all our imported horses are grown in this way. The small farmer has the mares and he sells the colts at weaning time to the breeders who can grow them as he would steers

Have our readers ever stopped to think that it costs less to grow a colt to two or three years old than it does to furnish a fat steer of the same age? The service fee is greater in the case of the colt. The cost of keeping the weanlings the first winter is about the same. It costs less to keep a weanling colt the year around than it does the steer of the same age. The same may be said of the two-year-old, as you do not need to put 100 bushels of corn into the colt to fatten him to have him ready for the market; one-half the amount will be sufficient. You can winter-pasture the yearling and two-year-old colts, but you cannot winter-pasture the steers. They are probably a little harder on fences, a little harder on grass. but after a good deal of experience we would rather pasture the colt two years than the steer. He will make a better living by far under the same conditions. Why not, therefore, raise something you can sell for two hundred dollars instead of one hundred at the very top?

Think this over, friends, and do not be afraid that enough farmers will take our advice to knock the bottom out of the market. Even if our markets here were well supplied, we have the world for a market if we can only grow horses good enough. It does not cost more than half as much to raise a horse of a given quality in the Mississippi valley as it does in England, Ireland, Scotland or France. Let us get this business down to a practical, scientific basis.

Do not get scared at that word "scientific," for there never was anything done practically yet that was not done on a scientific basis, whether the man who did it knew it or not, for doing a thing scientifically is doing it right; that is all. Science is simply knowledge reduced to a system.

KEEPING FARM HORSES IN GOOD FLESH.

Homestead.

We believe that the average farm horse is underfed, not but what there are many instances where these are kept in the very pink of condition, but on the average, as we say, we believe they are underfed. We do not mean by this that animals get an insufficient supply of food to appease their hunger, but we do mean that the supply of nutrients in many cases is not sufficient to take the place of the wear and tear caused by hard work. This is especially true where corn alone is fed. While we know of many instances where good farmers feed corn alone during the entire year, yet in the majority of these cases farm animals are generally in a somewhat thin condition. Corn is a fat producing food, but when animals are working they need a large supply of lean meat producing food.

Some time ago a city physician informed us of the fact that he was un-able to keep his horses in good flesh, and asked our advice as to the method of feeding them. Upon inquiry we learned that corn alone was being fed. At our suggestion he changed the food to the following ration: A mix-ture composed of seventy-five pounds of oats, fifty pounds of corn and twenty-five pounds of bran, to be fed to the amount of fifteen or eighteen pounds a day per animal. To his surprise, although not to ours, the horses immediately began to gain flesh. Now this was due to the fact that the bran and oats in the new ration supplied a larger amount of flesh-forming material, so that horses doing a large amount of driving daily were kept in a much more muscular condition when on this food, while at the same time their appearance was much improved.

Work on the farm is generally much more erratic than that in the city, and under average conditions it is more difficult to keep work horses in the same bloom. However, if less corn were fed and the ration we have named above substituted we believe the horses would give more satis-factory service and at the same time appear in much better flesh. It is true that where one raises his own feed that a bushel of corn can be grown much more cheaply than a bushel of oats, and yet at the same time we believe that it will pay to compound a ration for the work horse in which oats is given a prominent part.

As to the quantity to be fed per day there is some little difference of opinion. We find that the United States cavalry horse weighing 1,000 or 1,100 pounds is fed twelve pounds of oats per day, while the German cavalry horse receives ten pounds per day. In Great Britain these horses when on severe duty receive from twelve to fourteen pounds of oats per day. Prof. Henry reports a case of draft horses at work receiving twenty-two pounds of grain per day consisting of thirteen pounds of oats, six pounds of beans and three pounds of corn. It will be seen that there is considerable variation in the amount of grain fed to horses under various conditions. However, it is our experience that the average farm horse weighing from 1,400 to 1,800 pounds will require from fifteen to eighteen pounds per day of a mixture composed of three parts oats, two parts corn and one part bran. Horses fed in this manner and given good, clean hay will do a heavy day's work and remain in good flesh.

I. SWINE.

HOW TO GET THE HOG ON THE MARKET TO THE BEST ADVANTAGE.

H. F. Hoffman, Washta, Iowa, before the Cherokee County Farmer's Institute.

This is a question that has been much discussed and belongs to that class of old ones that are ever new. As it is many sided, we only aim to give our opinion. It is presumed in this case, like most others, the first thing necessary is to get the hog to start with. This is much more complex problem and requires a far greater amount of judgment, care and skill than to fatten and market him. But as this may be considered foreign to the subject and could not possibly be presented and discussed in the space alloted for this paper, we will have to leave such matters as the selecting of sire and dam, etc., out of the question, but will simply say use the best at command. If we raise them, retain only the best as breeders; if we buy them, buy as good as we can afford; if we have only the price of one good one, better invest in the one than squander the amount on half a dozen inferior ones.

The process of producing the pig to start with, like fattening and marketing, is also many sided, only much more so. If anyone is at all skeptical about this last statement, they have only to read a part of the agricultural and swine journals, where they will find a vast number of articles on the subject where in many cases the methods advised are very conflicting and oftentimes misleading. So we do not wonder that the beginner after racking his brain over them becomes disgusted and asks himself where he is at. We do not want to be understood as saying there is not good advice in many of them, as we believe no stock raiser can afford to be without at least one good agricultural and live stock journal, for they are certainly great helps and indispensable; but no amount of study of theorizing will do the whole of it. We must get in the harness ourselves and use both brain and muscle to attain any degree of success.

We have tried to take the pig at birth and put him on the market to the best advantage but confess we cannot do it, and don't believe anyone else can. We cannot start with him later than 112 days farther back, when we would have the prospective dam in fair flesh and the pink of condition. We would aim to have her increase in flesh as maturity approaches and to do this would feed her liberally on a not too fattening food, with plenty of chance for exercise, with comfortable and well ventilated quarters and not too many together.

Having booked each service, we know when the critical time will arrive (there is no room for guess work here). Provide warm, dry quarters and make it a point to be with her, as there is nothing like getting started right. If she has been fed and handled as before indicated, her system

24

free from fever and constipation, she will not only do her work easily and quickly, but present you a litter of strong, vigorous pigs that will have the courage of their convictions and be ready from the start to put up a good lively scrap for their meals. If you think this too much trouble and choose to let her take her chances and some morning run onto a litter of dead pigs, have your swearing machine wound up and be ready to cuss luck, Providence or anyone except yourself. We do not mean to say there is no such thing as bad luck in the swine business, but much so attributed belongs to loose management.

If everything has come our way, we are now ready to grow, fatten and market the hog. We would give the pigs nothing to eat for the first two weeks at least except the food nature provides through the dam, and be careful they do not get too much of that as this is the most critical time in the life of the hog, being the age for such ailments as thumps, scours, canker mouth, bad teeth, etc. It is an easy matter at this time to blast the prospects of the finest litter. But as they soon grow older and with a fair sized litter the danger of overfeeding through the dam has passed by the time the pigs are three weeks old and a new danger arises Now be particularly careful not to underfeed the dam, as a pig once stunted never makes as good or profitable animal as if growth had not been checked.

By this time the youngsters will need a sort of lunch counter or place in the pen or yard where larger hogs cannot enter and there begin feeding them a little shelled corn and when they catch on, which will not take long we would add other feeds of a lighter mixture, as too much corn causes them to lay on fat at the expense of frame and vigor, of which the hog with no higher aim than the pork barrel needs a certain amount.

We would say first, last and always, don't let them stop growing for a day, and as the object sought is profit, we would use such feeds as would make the greatest gain at the least expense. It does not take an observing person long to determine what this feed is. It has been said corn is king, but we claim the title should rest with grass, as we are thoroughly convinced no amount of swine raising can be successfully carried on without grass, and the greater the variety the better. While we would not try to raise pigs on grass alone, we would not think of trying to raise them without it unless it might be on a dairy farm with plenty of skim milk in sight.

Give the dam the range of a good pasture with abundant shade and dry, comfortable sleeping quarters, a never empty cup of pure water, a box of salt within easy reach at all times, and, as we said before, feed that which will do the work the cheapest. For this last no ironclad rule can be laid down for what might be the proper thing at one time on account of price may be out of the question at another. So it becomes a question each one has to decide for himself. We would say that when good wheat or oat shorts are as cheap or nearly so as corn, would make it at least half of the grain ration and feed enough to make a good growth. See that they take exercise enough to avoid getting too fat until about six weeks before they are to be marketed, when we would increase the corn and diminish the lighter feeds except the grass, and would feed entirely for fat; and no feed has yet been found for this purpose that takes the place of corn.

At what age to market is another point each person must determine by conditions that prevail in each particular. We believe with the ordinary or small farmer who does not feed cattle, the better way is to have the pigs farrowed rather early in the spring and market them when seven or eight months old, and sell whenever they are fit to go no matter what the price may be.

We would observe the following rules: Give them a good pasture with good, clean grain and plenty of it, ground or whole, cooked or raw, as the conditions warrant; set the dog on all venders of stock foods and quack doctors with their wonderful cholera cures, and, in the words of Shakespeare, "throw physic to the dogs," use brains instead of drugs. In short, feed your hogs nothing you would not be willing to eat yourself; by this we mean feed clean grain and water and avoid the old-time swill barrel that is never quite empty, and by all means shun the ordinary house slop pail as you would a pestilence as it is too often the dumping place of nameless filths and is worth more on the compost heap than anywhere else. Finally, let us know our business, tend to our business, love our business, and success will follow.

CARE OF BROOD SOWS.

Forest Henry, in N. W. Agriculturist.

First of all, the brood sow needs plenty of exercise in the pure air and sunlight. This costs the farmer nothing and is of the utmost importance in keeping the sow healthy and vigorous.

If the sows are given warm sleeping quarters they are apt to make the most of it if they have nothing to induce them to take exercise. If they are allowed to do this they are apt to give us no end of trouble at farrowing time. The pigs come weak and sickly, and if the farmer succeeds in pulling them through they are only an excuse for a healthy pig.

To avoid this give the brood sows the barnyard to run in. They will work for hours rooting over the manure when otherwise they would be lying idle in the nests. This not only does the sows good, but has a very beneficial effect on the manure as well. They also get a considerable amount of feed that would otherwise be lost.

After the breeding season is over, the brood sow should have very little corn only in cold weather. Her feed should be very large of that kind that will promote bone, muscle and nerve growth. This can best be supplied on the farm by using bright clover hay, oats and wheat bran. The oats should be thinly scattered over the smooth ground, or what is still better, a tight feeding floor. The amount of corn fed should vary with the weather; more when the weather is very cold. Nature demands that the sow be fed liberally, but not on food that will fatten her.

It is a dangerous practice to let horses and colts run with the brood sows. The cattle will do no harm if they are dehorned. She should be provided with good warm sleeping quarters where she is not crowded. While she needs her daily exercise she also needs her rest at night.

Still another matter should be looked after, and that is that she should not be compelled to crowd through narrow gates, jump over bars or crawl through broken fences if you are depending on her to raise you a good litter of pigs next spring.

GROWING PEAS FOR FATTENING SWINE.

The Farmer, St. Paul.

In areas where peas will grow well, and where the growers have not yet introduced the machinery for harvesting them to the best advantage, why should not peas be grown on which to fatten swine in the fields where swine are to glean? Of course where fodder is wanted, the straw of the peas well saved would be worth more than the labor of harvesting the crop with the aid of a pea harvester, but even in the absence of such a machine, why should there not be much profit in growing peas for the object named? A good crop should run from 20 to 30 bushels per acre. Peas are not only one of the best fattening foods known, but they make a grand quality of pork. Two bushels of seed of the small varieties are wanted to sow an acre. There would be no other cost in growing this food after the seed was sown unless it should be in the harrowing the ground before the seed had come up. The pigs would do the harvesting. They could be turned in on a small part of the crop as soon as the pods were full. Then, when the crop was quite ripe, they could have access to all of it. By sowing at two or three intervals, the pigs would have ample supplies for two or three months. In less than that time they would be in fine shape for market. Other pigs to be fattened later could be allowed to glean after the pigs first turned in had gathered the larger share of the crop. The pigs thus gleaning would not need any other supplement than water. This they ought to have access to at all times, lest they should take injury from eating so many peas at the first that when they drank, the water would swell the peas and burst the stomach through distension. But this danger is only imminent at first. Have any tried the plan? It ought to work admirably in northern Minnesota and North Dakota. The crop will yield best when sown early, but it may also be sown later than other small grain crops and still do well. The pea crop would leave the ground richer in nitrogen than it found it. And the burial of the straw would add humus to the soil. Farmers, why would this not be a good scheme? Have any of you tried it? Then let us hear from you, please. If none have tried it, we will drive down a stake, and write on it, this scheme has been copyrighted by *The Farmer* for the benefit of its readers. If a farmer can get twenty bushels of peas from one acre, and if he can enrich his land in so doing at the same time, and if he can turn those peas into pork at no greater cost than that involved in plowing and harrowing the land and sowing the seed including the cost of seed, he is certainly engaged in a good business.

AGE FOR MATING SWINE.

A. J. Lovejoy, in Breeders' Gazette.

Subscribers in Norfolk, Va., and Greensboro, N. C., ask at what age a boar should begin to be used in service to obtain best results, and at what age should a sow be bred for best individual good of the sow and for the best and largest pigs.

If you want to get the largest size possible in your boar and sow individually do not use them till well on to maturity, or at least until they are a year old. This gives you a chance to get a large growth on either before being put to breeding and will in the case of the sow make her about sixteen months of age before she farrows. If well fed and properly cared for she would be a sow of 450 to 550 pounds and should farrow a litter of very strong pigs and of good size. The boar might, to be sure that he was a prompt server, be used to a sow or two as early as six or eight months, as sometimes when a boar is well fed and pushed to get a large growth and has never had a sow till a year old he will refuse to serve at first, and you might think him a failure. Patience is generally needed in commencing to use a young boar. After once used he is generaly all right and if so the older, up to a year, before giving him much service the better. You will, however, find that either the sow or boar will produce a better litter the second time than the first, and if the sow proves a good breeder and suckler I would recommend the raising of two litters a year from her till she is too old to produce well. In our own business we are great believers in old breeding animals, and sometimes keep them till ten to twelve years old.

As to the best feed for fattening pigs at the age of two months, and whether they should have a run on pasture or not, I would certainly say give them pasture by all means and all the good rich slop composed of shorts and milk, and shelled corn soaked, that they can eat. They will fatten and grow at the same time. If the pigs were of a weight of 100 to 150 pounds and you wanted then to get them fat for market as quickly as possible I would feed nothing but the corn and grass. Comfortable quarters secure from hot sun or cold storm should of course be had.

SKIM MILK AS A FOOD FOR HOGS.

Homestead.

The Tennessee Experiment Station has just completed a hog feeding test which demonstrates the importance of making good use of the by-products of the farm. One lot was fed water and corn meal alone for a period of sixty days. During the first half of the feeding period each hog received four pounds of meal per day, and hix pounds in the second half, from which he made sixty-two pounds gain or practically one pound per day. The pound in this case was made at a cost of 3.9 cents.

Each hog in lot two received twelve pounds of skim milk and four pounds of corn per day during the first thirty days, and twenty-seven pounds of skim-milk, together with five pounds of corn, in the second half. From this the gain was 138 pounds per head during the sixty days, or a daily gain of 2.3 pounds per head, made at a cost of 4.2 cents per pound. It must be remembered, however, that the cost per pound in the latter case was reckoned on the basis of skim milk being worth twenty-two cents per hundred pounds.

The item of greatest importance is that while 4.6 pounds of corn alone were required to make a pound of pork, it only required 2.1 pounds of corn, together with 11.2 pounds of milk, to make one pound of gain. Considering corn to be worth forty-eight cents per bushel skim milk had a value of 28.3 cents per hundred pounds. Not only were the gains made much more rapidly when skim milk was fed, but the slaughter contest revealed the fact that these had the most useful carcass, dressing 78.5 per cent compared with 73.6 per cent, as was the case in those fed corn alone.

GREEN CORN FOR HOGS.

Twentieth Century Farmer.

A more timely subject than regarding the feeding of green corn to hogs could scarcely be found at this time. Green corn as a food for hogs cannot be excelled if it is properly fed, but a greater amount of care and judgment must be used in feeding it than in feeding almost any other food, as easily accessible as corn will be this year. At this time it is even more necessary that this warning note be sounded than it has been for a number of years, for the reason that last year very few portions of the corn belt were favored with enough corn to feed at all; thus after the loss of a year's practice and experience in feeding a great many will have forgotten their well-learned lessons.

Undoubtedly the last year has been associated with the greatest scarcity of feed for stock that has been known in many years, but hogs, although thin, are in a very healthy condition. It would really be better if every year there was some method of inducing stockraisers to keep their breeding stock in thinner flesh. But now that green corn is here, many who have been anxiously awaiting its coming will unthinkingly throw it to their hogs in great quantities, even at first while it is soft and washy and while their hogs are not used to it. No better method of filling hogs with worms and thus laying the foundation for disease can be adopted. Than that there has been very little cholera among hogs in the last year, what better evidence do we want that too much corn is one of the primary causes of disease?

In the beginning of feeding green corn we would exhort that you exercise the greatest care and thus avoid disaster. While the corn is yet soft feed but very little, starting on no more than one stalk with one ear to a single mature hog. and feed younger hogs in the same proportion. As the corn matures the allowance may be increased to about three ears to each head at the end of a month. It is better to feed too little than too much. During the time that you are feeding green corn be sure to keep plenty of ashes and salt where the hogs can get at it whenever it is wanted; they will eat a great deal of it, which will serve to keep them free of worms to quite an extent. Also keep all watering places thoroughly disinfected. If there are any to which you have not been giving any slop it would be well to give them a "short" feed of slop about twice a week, and in it put some sort of a worm preventive. There are many recipes for using for worms that are very efficient, one of which we shall aim to publish soon, but if nothing else is easily accessible use turpentine, but do not feed anything with turpentine in it to pregnant sows.

It is our sincere wish that each one who raises hogs and expects to feed green corn will use enough discretion in doing so to avoid disease. The hog crop is short and the one who saves his hogs and cares for them well will fill his pockets with gold, but the one who throws green corn to his hogs promiscuously, regardless of quantity, will come to certain disappointment and loss.

There is no better feed than green corn if fed with care. The greatest danger is found in feeding it alone—that is, to hogs that are receiving no slop or grain allowance.

WHAT IS IT WORTH TO ALLOW HOGS TO FOLLOW CATTLE?

Wallaces' Farmer.

A Nebraska subscriber writes us that he has a neighbor who has pigs averaging from 100 to 125 pounds, for which he has to buy corn at 30 cents per bushel, and as he himself is feeding cattle and has not enough hogs to follow, he has allowed the neighbor to put his into the yard and wishes to know how much he should charge him.

It requires about 550 pounds of corn to make 100 pounds of pork. Therefore, the feed that the hogs get after cattle is worth as much to the owner of the hogs as the price of the corn he would feed them at 30 cents per bushel. The owner of the cattle has hog feed to spare and which is going to waste; therefore he can afford to allow these hogs to run after his cattle for a good deal less than the cost of feeding them corn. It ought not to be difficult for two neighbors to settle for themselves what is equitable as between man and man under such circumstances. The man who owns the cattle can afford to put pork on these hogs for less than 3 cents per pound and is just that much ahead, while the man who has the hogs can afford to pay 3 cents, as under ordinary circumstances it would cost him that in corn and bother in feeding besides. We suggest, therefore, that there would be no particular wrong done if he charged the owner of the hogs anywhere from 75 cents to 90 cents per month, depending on the gain the hogs were making. They should gain thirty pounds a month each on that feed and both parties are making money by the transaction.

BEST FEEDS FOR PIGS.

Twentieth Century Farmer.

D. W. May of the Kentucky experiment station issued an interesting bulletin entitled "A Comparison of Feeds for Pigs," of which the following is a summary:

Of the various feeds for pigs available to the farmers of this country, corn ranks first. It is a crop grown to some extent in all sections, is much relished by pigs, is easily handled and lays on fat rapidly. With these qualifications it is no wonder that it has largely superseded all other feeds and is used to a great extent as the single article of diet in the fattening ration. Not only has it become in most instances the sole feed given to pigs, but it has materially influenced the character of the animal in the corn-growing regions.

There is no doubt but that corn fed alone is in a great many instances unprofitable. Investigations have shown not only that pigs make a better gain per pound of feed, but that the animals are more thrifty and less liable to disease when fed a combined ration.

In the work herein reported certain feeds were employed which are available to the farmers of this state and which may be used to supplement the corn ration for pigs. Twenty grade Berkshire pigs raised on the station farm were divided into five lots of four each. The animals were from the litters of three sows of very similar breeding and were by the same sire. They were a very uniform lot of pigs and were divided into lots of nearly equal weights. They had been wintered on corn, and at the beginning of the experiment were in good flesh. The feeding was carried on in small pigeries, with a covered room for sleeping and eating and a small run 8x15 feet. The animals were supplied at all times with water, ashes, coal and salt. A little copperas was occasionaly added to the drinking water. The feeding was done twice daily, the animals being given all they would clean up well.

The feeds employed were corn, corn and soy bean silage, soy beans and dried distillery grains. In finishing the hogs there were used hominy meal, skim-milk, tankage and cottonseed meal. The first period covered ten weeks and the finishing period three weeks.

The results of these experiments, like those of several previously made, indicate that in feeding pigs corn should be combined with other feeds to get the best returns.

Experiments indicate that silage cannot profitably be substituted for a part of the grain ration with pigs. In this experiment it was fed in addition with some profit, giving quicker gains and keeping the animals in better condition.

Soy beans made an excellent pig feed mixed with corn in the proportion of 1 to 2. Being rich in protein it is recommended as an especially efficient addition to the ration when corn composes the larger part.

Dried distillery grains proved to be a poor pig feed except in small proportions. When fed as one-third or one-half of the ration with corn it was unprofitable. Where it composed one-fifth of the ration very good returns were obtained.

Cottonseed meal may be profitably used to finish hogs for market. In such cases it may be safely fed in quantities of one-half pound per pig daily and then omitted during periods of alternate weeks.

J. SHEEP AND GOATS.

SOME SHEEP TERMS.

Homestead.

The sheep industry in England and Scotland has become a leading one and there comes from these countries a great many terms as applied to sheep that are not fully understood by the average sheep owner, and since we have had a good deal to do with shepherds from Great Britain we here give a few of the terms that are most common among sheepmen of that country.

A new born sheep is called a lamb as in this country; if a male it is tup-lamb in Scotland. When castrated it is a hog-lamb, or a hogget, as it is sometimes called. A lamb goes by the name of a lamb in England until it is eight months old. After weaning and before it is shorn it is called in Scotland a tup-lamb or a tup-hog, and in England they are called ewe and wether tegs, according to the sex. In Scotland a ewe-hog after the first clipping is called a gimmer, a tup-hog, a shearling-tup; and weather-hog in dinmont. An animal called a gimmer in Scotland is called a theave in England until it bears its first lamb, after which it is called a four-teeth ewe; the year after it is called a six-teeth ewe, and after that it is called a full-mouthed ewe. The dinmont in Scotland answers in England to the word shear-hog until deprived of a fleece, when it is called two shear wether. A barren ewe is called a barren gimmer or an eild gimmer. When three times shorn a ewe is called a twinter-ewe; after the fourth shearing she is called a three-winter ewe. When a ewe ceases to give milk she is a yeld ewe; when removed from the breeding flock she is a draft-ewe; when put aside as unfit for breeding she is a gimmer or a draft gimmer. All drafts for fattening are called sheddings. tails or drafts.

In America we do not have so many names for the different kinds of sheep. A young sheep here is called a lamb until it is a year old. When its first fleece has been removed it is a shearling; when the second fleece is taken it is a two-shear and so on. The female is called a ewe and not a yeo, as some sheepmen are inclined to speak the name. A castrated sheep is a wether and the male is always a ram and not a buck. A buck is the male of deer and goats. A broken-mouth sheep is one that has begun to shed her teeth; a full-mouth sheep is one having eight adult front teeth. A pet lamb is a cosset lamb, and an old, broken-mouthed ewe is called a crone.

A great many of our readers would like to know the terms often used in the grading of wools in our wools markets, and we have grouped a lot of terms that are very plain to the wool dealer, but the sheepman is not fully acquainted with them. They are as follows:

Unwashed—Fleeces as shorn from unwashed sheep.

Washed—Fleeces from sheep washed in fresh water before shearing.

Scoured—Wool scoured in a warm alkaline solution and rinsed in clear water until entirely free from all foreign matter.

Fleece Wool—Wool shorn from the live sheep.

Pulled Wool—Wool pulled from sheep pelts.

Brushed (pulled)—Wool pulled from sheep pelts after being treated by a brushing machine.

Dead Wool—Wool pulled from the carcasses of dead sheep.

Cotted—Wool that, through disease, has loosened from the skin and become pelted so as to be in more or less clothlike patches on the shorn side.

Kemps—Coarse hairs scattered through the fibers of the wool—such wool is described as "kempy."

Yolk—The natural oil found in all healthy fleeces; more abundant in fine sheep than coarse; and in rams than ewes and wethers.

Condition—Refers to cleanliness. Fleeces losing the least in scouring are in best condition.

Character—Refers to length, strength of staple, luster, etc.

Combing and Delaine—Must be of full length, strong and of even strength throughout the fiber.

Clothing—Comprises the bulk of domestic wool. It should have good felting properties. but the fiber needs less strength in process of manufacture than is required for combing purposes.

Grades—Designate the size of the fiber. Fleeces are generally classed and described in trade as follows: Very fine or XX; fine or X: fine medium (below fine, but finer than medium); medium or three-eighths blood; low medium or one-fourth blood; coarse, braid.

If the staple is long gand strong enough for combing and worsted work they are still further designated by the addition of the words "delaine" and "combing," the finer grades being known as "delaine," those of lower grades as "combing"; as fine delaine, three-eighths combing, etc.

The grades of pulled wool corresponding to the fleece grades are as follows: Extra; fine A; A super; B super; C super; No. 1, low or coarse.

Unmerchantable—Not in condition to be classified or quoted in standard grades. In washed fleeces it generally refers to wools only partially washed.

Sorts—Should not be confounded with grades. The sorter spreads each fleece on a bench, breaking it in two, three or more sorts, the fleece may yield. The finer sorts in all fleeces are across the shoulders, the coarsest on the breech with, in fleeces not yet well crossed, a coarse strip on the top of the neck running up toward the ears, called the rick. The skirts are always inferior to the body of the fleece. The skillful sorter seeks the grades that will yield the sorts his mill requires.

Stuffed—Fleeces ignorantly or fraudulently put up, with tags, dung, dirt or other foreign substance inside them.

Cross-Breds—Fine wool sheep of Merino or Saxony blood yield fleeces of very fine grade. The native and mutton breeds are of larger frame and yield a much coarser fleece. Crossing the two breeds, if persistently followed, yields in time a uniform fleece in grade midway between the two extremes, generally three-eighths and one-fourth blood. These wools are often termed "cross-bred" wools, even long after the breed has become so persistent as to be known as a distinct variety, with a family name of its own.

WHY NOT KEEP A FLOCK OF SHEEP?

Wallaces' Farmer.

The average farmer in Iowa and adjoining states can keep fifty ewes on his place and grow from forty to fifty lambs and scarcely miss the feed that they require. The ewes could bring him from $1 to $1.25 per year in the shape of wool. The lambs, if they come in February and are well fed, should sell in June at from $3 to $5 per head, depending on the cost of getting them to the great markets. If they can be shipped at carload rates, they should bring him $4. In otherwords, the income from a ewe should be from $4 to $5, provided they are healthy. The feed consumed by five ewes weighing 200 pounds when kept in large flocks each will be about the same amount as that by a steer weighing 1,200 pounds. In small lots, however, a sheep will utilize a great deal of feed that a steer will not. In other words, they can be used as scavengers, not only for the benefit of the sheep but for the benefit of the land itself.

Why, therefore, are not sheep more generally kept on the average farm in the grain and grass states? One reason is that these farms are not as a rule fenced with sheep tight fences and hence sheep cannot be used, for example, for cleaning stubble fields, nor can lambs be pastured in corn fields to the fullest extent. The time, however, is past when a farmer can afford to do without fences around every field, sheep tight and horse high. When farms are worth from $50 to $100 per acre justice to them requires that they should be properly fenced and while a fence that will hold cattle and horses may be a legal fence, it is not the proper fence for a farm of that value. It is to be hoped that this objection will disappear in time.

Another reason is that cattle will not do well after sheep. This is a valid objection. They don't do well when a large number of sheep are kept on the same pasture. However, in a properly managed farm that number of sheep need not be kept much on the cattle pasture. They can be used as gleaners during the summer time and in the winter it does not matter.

Another objection is that sheep and hogs don't go well together. That also is a valid objection. The lamb is a foolish thing and is quite likely to allow the old brood sow to pull it through the fence and make an end of its usefulness. This objection can very easily be obviated by having separate enclosures for sheep and hogs.

The main objection, which is not a valid one, is that few farmers know how to handle sheep. This is one, however, that can very easily be overcome and a clear profit of from $100 to $150 a year on a flock of fifty ewes should be sufficient inducement for any man who is farming for dear life to learn how to handle them.

The sheep, of course, should not be of the special mutton breeds. There is a place for these, and a large place, but it is not on a small farm in connection with other stock. The medium breeds, such as Rambouillets and Delaines, may be kept to advantage on these grain farms, whether the tariff is high or low. This is especially true in regard to the Down breeds. While the tariff has been of some benefit to breeders of fine wool sheep, we believe it has done more harm to the breeders of mutton sheep by increasing the amount of mutton grown on the range, than it has ever done good.

DIPPING SHEEP.

Homestead.

As the time approaches when the sheep will be deprived of their warm coats of wool we hope that every sheep owner will make preparations to dip the flock. Some time ago we heard Richard Gibson, the Canadian authority cn sheep breeding, say: "A rich man may discard the use of dip; a poor man cannot afford to do so." This a fair statement of the matter. There cannot be the slightest doubt that it pays to dip sheep, not only for the purpose of ridding them of ticks, but also with the idea of stimulating growth of wool and production of mutton. A sheep that has been dipped grows more and better wool and puts on mutton faster than the sheep that is not dipped. Ticks cause irritation and keep the sheep from thriving so well and such irritation affects the wool crop and the increase in meat. At the same time it may be safely asserted that the modern, tar-product sheep dips stimulate an increased growth of wool and make the wool better in strength of staple. There has been a great deal of discussion for and against some of the sheep dips and notably regarding the lime and sulphur dip, which, while effective, has been proved to injure the wool; but we have not heard a word said against the tar-product dips for tick killing, general cleanliness and effectiveness and they certainly do not injure the wool, but as Mr. Gibson says, improve it and increase the annual crop. Where sheep are supposed or known to be afflicted with scab and have to be dipped on that account sulphur should be added to the solution of warm tar-product dip at the rate of sixteen pounds to the 100 gallons of solution and this will kill the scab mite and not hurt the wool, but the dipping should be repeated in ten days. Formerly it was a somewhat difficult and rather dangerous task to dip sheep. The commercial dips contained arsenic in some cases and wonderfully concocted home dips contained arsenic, lye, carbolic acid, corrosive sublimate, nicotine and a host of other things some of which might lead to death either by absorption through the skin or by getting onto the pasture grasses to be consumed by newly dipped sheep. All this has been done away with and we do not believe there is now a dangerous dip upon the market. Carbolic acid and tobacco are still used in some of the dips, but in such proportions and manner as to render them safe and effective, and it would be foolish, indeed, for any man to go to the trouble of making a home brew of alleged dip that might prove dangerous, hurtful or too expensive. The tar-product dips are cheap and come almost ready for use. All that is necessary in their preparation is the addition of water for ordinary purposes and the sheep may even drink the solution without danger, and do not suffer harm from getting it into their eyes. Further there are now handy dipping tanks, platforms and strainers on the market so that the work of dipping can be easily, properly and comfortably done. The best authorities claim that sheep should be dipped three times a year, and the first time is just after shearing when the coat is short and the dip

will get close to the skin, killing ticks, stimulating growth of wool and
at the same time to keep flies off and have a tendency to prevent mag-
gots about the tail and the depositing of gadfly larvae in the nostrils. The
lambs should be dipped shortly after the older sheep have gone through
the tank, for the ticks migrate to the lambs at this time and cause much
misery. It is also a good plan to make it a practice to dip every new
sheep brought onto the farm before allowing it to mix with the home flock.
If this were done by every sheep owner there would be fewer outbreaks
of scab. The railroad cars and shipping chutes are liable to be tainted
with scab mites, so that one is never sure that he is not bringing in the
disease with newly purchased sheep, and it is not enough to know that
they have been dipped before starting on their journey. When a man of
the reputation and experience of Richard Gibson says, "Dip three times a
year," he has good reasons for so advising and we hope that our readers
will follow his advice. The expense is light, but the gains are oftentimes
beyond measure.

ANGORA GOATS.

Homestead.

Modern skill, necessity and ingenuity have made it possible to utilize
every portion of the hog except its grunt and squeal, and it is asserted
you can sell every part of the goat except its scent. The latter statement
is made by Mr. John Collins, who manages an extensive goat farm in
Arizona. The number of goats on his farm he could not for the life of
him tell, he says. There might be 10,000, 20,000 or 30,000—he had no idea
how many. He is considered an authority upon the uses and abuses of the
goat. On his farm there is nothing but sage brush and cactus for the
goats to live on, yet no man, he claims, ever saw a dead goat, unless he
(the goat) came to a violent end. They will live and thrive where nearly
every other living thing would starve to death.

He started with 150 common goats, deriving the profit from the sale
of the hides. After a time these were crossed with Angora goats and
after two years the cross disappears and a perfect Angora goat remains.
The long hair of this goat is made into plush for furniture, sleeping cars
and similar uses. The hair next to the skin can be made into valuable
shawls. The meat of the kids is delightful when fresh, and is canned and
sent to Cuba, the Philippines, China and other foreign countries as canned
lamb. One tablespoonful of it equals three of the purest cream. One
great virtue of the milk is that it is a deadly foe to tubercula, and con-
sumptives by drinking it are often cured of the disease. In fine, no other
dumb animal has more valuable qualities than the goat. No stables are
required in which to house him. He takes care of himself; looks out for
his own shelter if he needs any, and is altogether an independent, profitable, happy-go-lucky kind of an animal.

WINTERING ANGORAS.

The American Angora and Stockman.

In former years when Angora goats were confined largely to southern and western states, in America, the question of wintering the animals was one which needed little consideration. Now the situation has changed. Nearly every state in the union holds some Angoras, and in those with rigid winter climates, the question of proper protection and feed is one of vital importance. Every farmer knows that other live stock require feed and sheds during the winter season, and he is just beginning to realize that Angora goats are live stock, and that if he wishes to get the most out of them, he must accord them the same consideration which he does the other domestic animals.

FOOD.

By preference the Angora goat is a browser and his instinct prevents him from doing well upon anything but the cleanest of a variety of food. Naturally he takes a bite of grass here and a few leaves there, then runs to the next bush. He travels rapidly and if allowed to run on the open range he will wander ten or twelve miles in a day. Knowing his natural instinct, one must see at a glance that where climatic conditions compel the breeder to shut the Angora in a small shed where he must feed upon corn stalks, etc., and depend upon butting his neighbor for exercise, that wintering an Angora goat requires some attention.

The goat should be allowed a good supply of clean roughness which should differ in variety if possible. One cow will eat about as much as twelve goats. The feed racks should be cleaned occasionally. It is important to feed nothing which contains burrs or other foreign materials which will get into the mohair and render it unsalable. Whenever the weather will permit, and Angora goats stand dry cold well, the goats should be allowed to forage for themselves.

Many farmers have learned that if they cut brush in the fall before the leaves drop and stack this brush or even leave it where it falls, that the goats clean off every leaf during the winter and require very little other food. The goats should not be starved, however, and if there is not enough nutriment in the roughness one is feeding, they should be given a little grain.

Goats, as well as sheep, bloat readily, and scour badly if they get too much grain before they are thoroughly used to it. Care is required to see that goats commence with small quantities of any new food and that they get to full feed gradually. Green alfalfa will bloat goats in less than an hour, if it is moist and the goats are not used to it. Dry grains such as barley and wheat have the same effect. Sometimes even after days of feeding, large quantities of grain will cause goats to scour. It should be remembered the goats with stomach worms and poorly nourished goats also scour, so that the causes of scouring should be determined before a remedy is attempted. The writer remembers a large flock of goats which he visited, which were dying of scours. The owner insisted that there was some disease among the goats, but upon careful examination it was decided that the goats were dying of starvation. A sufficient food supply soon remedied the trouble. A goat does not poison readily, as he eats only a small amount of each plant. Goats will die of poisoning, however, and precaution should be taken to see the poisonous plants are eliminated from the range.

CORN.

Where wethers or other goats are to be fattened for market, they should be treated about like sheep. This branch of the business is new and only a few corn fed animals have come into the market. Goat feeding for the market is practically in an experimental stage. Most of those who are feeding say that the goat eats as much or more corn than sheep. It does not take him long to get used to full feed. The Angora venison market is yet an uncertain factor. Good fat Angoras bring almost the same as sheep of the same quality. It does not seem to make any difference to the buyers whether the Angora is shorn or unshorn. There are a number of bunches of wethers being fed this season and we expect to give more details later.

SHEDS.

The goat must have exercise if he is to be kept in the best of condition. In some states the domestic animals are housed for from two to four months of the year. If it is necessary to confine the Angora he should have room enough to move about in. While in New Mexico a shed one hundred feet long by thirty feet wide, open on one or all sides will shelter 1,000 goats, yet in Wisconsin a shed of the same dimensions should be closed on all sides and should not be expected to house more than one-third as many goats. The goats should be kept comfortably warm and thoroughly dry. Sheds which are used for sheep will do for goats. The sheds should be kept dry. On cold nights, if the sheds are cold, the kids will crowd into corners to get warm and soon some of the kids will be crowded under others. If the pile gets too dense the lower kids smother and die.

SUMMARY.

1. Accord goats the same care which you do other live stock.
2. Give them plenty of clean food and exercise.
3. Keep them out of cold rains and provide dry sheds for them.

HOW MANY ANGORA GOATS TO THE ACRE.

Wallaces' Farmer.

We are frequently asked the question: How many Angora goats should be kept to the acre where the object is to clean up the brush? The Maine Experiment Station has been doing some good work along this line. It began in 1901' but gave the goats too much range and they did little clearing up. In May, 1902, they put one buck, six ewes and five kids in an acre of young wood land of a mixed growth, most of the trees three to six inches in diameter, with a thick growth of underbrush. In one year they have cleaned out the small underbrush completely and the ground under the trees looks as if it had been burned over, especially where there are alders or evergreens. They have eaten the leaves and sprigs of young bushes in preference to grass; have stripped the bark from every maple, killing those six inches in diameter. They have proven very effective in cleaning up brush or evergreen wood land. One acre of good brush will furnish twelve goats all they want for one summer. We would regard this as heavy grazing, but experience proves that if you want goats to clean up brush, you must put on plenty of them, from six to twelve per acre according to the quantity of brush available.

K. THE STATE FAIR.

DEDICATION OF THE STOCK PAVILION.

It was impossible to have the dedicatory ceremonies of the New Live Stock Pavilion, Monday, August 25th, on account of the inclement weather. Arrangements were made to carry out the program Wednesday at the same hour, and with addresses by Gov. A. B. Cummins, Senator W. F. Harriman and Senator J. P. Dolliver, the Stock Pavilion was dedicated in the presence of a vast multitude of admiring and applauding spectators.

Among the distinguished guests at the dedication were numerous members of the Twenty-ninth general assembly, which made the appropriation for the stock pavilion, and several of the Twenty-eighth. These occupied seats reserved for them on the speakers' platform, which was erected at the north end of the arena. Among the members of the last general assembly present were Representatives Secor of Winnebago, Moore of Davis, Coburn of Cherokee, Head of Jefferson, Calderwood of Scott, Hasselquist of Lucas, Teachout of Polk, Freeman of Pottawattamie, Greeley of Story, Blakemore of Taylor and Mattes of Sac; Senator Harper of Ottumwa and ex-Representative P. L. Prentis of Ringgold county and John Shambaugh of Madison county. Hon N. E. Coffin of Fort Dodge was among those that occupied seats on the speakers' platform.

25

PRESIDENT FRASIER EXPRESSES APPRECIATION.

President J. C. Frasier of Bloomfield, of the State Department of Agriculture, presided. Not les than 4,000 people looked on from the seats in the space outside of the arena, while 1,500 more thronged in the arena. After music by the Mitchellville orchestra, President Frasier called the assemblage to order and said:

Ladies and Gentlemen: We have met this afternoon to dedicate and set apart for the use of the people of Iowa, the largest and finest live stock pavilion in our state.

This magnificent building in which we are gathered was made possible by the liberality and wisdom of the last general assembly in making an appropriation for its erection.

On behalf of the state board of the department of agriculture I desire to express our appreciation and thanks to the members of the legislature and the governor for thus recognizing in a substantial manner the value and importance of the great live stock industry of Iowa.

Many are the purposes for which this beautiful and commodious building can be utilized and we may be pardoned for taking a just pride in a permanent improvement of this character that belongs to all the people of the state.

GOV. CUMMINS SPEAKS.

Governor Cummins was presented by Mr. Frasier as the first speaker. He was heartily applauded as he arose and at intervals throughout his address. At the outset the governor declared the imperative demands of the most successful fair ever held in Iowa had already dedicated the new building to the purposes for which it was designed. It seemed appropriate, however, publicly to recognize the great advance made in Iowa in the cause of animal industry and animal husbandry. "I congratulate the people of the state of Iowa," said the governor, "because the consummation of this project marks a new era in the upbuilding of the great interests for which this great building is to be used. I desire to compliment the members of the board of agriculture because it is due to their energy and wise prescience that this building has been made possible. The members of this board, I refer to the real members and not to myself, who am but an ex-officio member, are entitled to the profound gratitude and confidence of every lover of the cause of agriculture. I compliment the members of the Twenty-ninth General Assembly

New Live Stock Pavilion on the Iowa State Fair Grounds, viewed from the south-west.   Erected 1902.

because they were broad-minded and sagacious enough to see that a building of this kind was needed."

Governor Cummins said he wanted to invite the attention of those present to the grand song of triumph for Iowa that was to be found in the last census report. He proceeded to portray in the light of these figures some of the many points of supeiiority of the Hawkeye state. Comparing the importance of agriculture and manufacturing, he showed the fixed capital invested in manufactures was about five billions of dollars and in agriculture over twenty billions in the nation, while in Iowa there was a still greater discrepancy. In 1850, according to the reports at that time, there was farmed in Iowa a total of 824,622 acres of land. Now of the 35,-300,000 acres in Iowa, there is under cultivation a total of 34,574,-337 acres. The value of this land is now more than $1,700,000,000. The number of farms is 228,662 and the number operated by their owners is 147,305.

Iowa farm products have been increasing enormously in value in recent years. According to the reports of the crop bureau the actual cash value of Iowa farm products in 1899 was reported to be $365,411,528, which was twenty millions in excess of the value of the products in any other state of the Union.

The total gross income from farms is greater in Iowa than in other states. The figures for the best of the states, which figures include additions to farm property are: Iowa, $336,745,785; Illinois, $316,408,202; Texas, $253,896,328; Ohio, $201,144 284. There were no other approaching these in the total value of farm income.

In another way may this supremacy of Iowa be shown. The following figures show the value of all domestic animals in the states that led all others for the year 1900:

Iowa	$271,844,034
Texas	236,227,934
Illinois	186,856,020
Kansas	186,317,248
Nebraska	142,769,629
Missouri	154,295,363
Ohio	120,466,134
Indiana	105,048,423

In the number of neat cattle there is a similar gratifying showing. The figures for leading states are: Texas 9,428,196, Iowa,

.5,367,630, Kansas, 4,491,076, Nebraska, 3,176,243, Illinois 3,104-010. In dairy cows we find that Iowa is second only to New York in their number. In the number of two-year-old steers Iowa leads. In the value of neat cattle in 1900 Iowa stands well, being a close [second to Texas, but the value per head in Iowa was $26.55 against the value of $17.31 in Texas.

In closing his address Governor Cummins referred to the high moral and intellectual standing of the people of the state as more than keeping pace with its achievements in material things. He concluded by dedicating the new pavilion to the best interests of *the agriculture in the richest and best state in the union.

ADDRESS OF SENATOR W. F. HARRIMAN.

By invitation, I am granted the honor of representing the State Board of Agriculture, and of saying a few words in its behalf, informally accept-ing this beautiful and useful structure. I am confident that I bespeak the sentiment of every member of the board, in their individual, as well as in their official capacity, when I say that in accepting this valuable building from the state, they are afforded much gratification. And now, by the authority granted me, for and in behalf of the State Board of Agriculture, I proclaim that said board formally and duly accepts this commodious pavilion which has just been so eloquently dedicated to the great interests of Iowa.

I should not fairly represent the board, if I omitted to say, that in receiving the same into its charge and under its official control, it is with an earnest desire that the anticipations of those who so zealously favored its construction shall be fully realized; and that the great industries which the people of Iowa, by the construction of this substantial building, intended to promote shall not only be maintained in their present unex-celled high standing, but that they shall be advanced to a higher standard than is now within the knowledge of the people of any state or nation.

On my own behalf I desire to say that the completion of this valu-able pavilion upon the state fair grounds is the consummation of a long cherished desire of every member of the present board and of their imme-diate predecessors. It will materially aid in advancing not only the ani-mal industry, but other industries of this commonwealth.

It will not only be of great utility during the holding of the annual fairs, but under the careful supervision of the Board of Agriculture it should be utilized in connection with the barns and other conveniences now upon the grounds in the establishment of a permanent place for the holding of public sales of stock.

Iowa farmers and stock growers are the possessors of more fine herds than any other state or nation. They are liberal purchasers, as well as liberal sellers, of the best stock in the world.

This is certainly most favorably situated, being surrounded by the homes of more sellers and more buyers than any other location that can be selected with equal accommodations. The transportation facilities are all that can be desired, both to the city and to the grounds. It is on the line of several great through lines of railways convenient for the stockmen of the western states and territories, who are also liberal purchasers of Iowa's pure bred stock of all kinds.

The animal industry of Iowa is, indeed, of great importance, and is worthy of all the attention and all the consideration that the Department of Agriculture can bestow upon it, consistently with its duty to other important interests of the state.

The value of domestic animals in Iowa exceeds that of any other state in the union, and constitutes more than 1-11 of the total value of domestic animals in all the states and territories. The total value for all the states and territories being $2,981,722,945, and that of Iowa, $278,830,-096. Texas with nearly five times the land surface ranks second in value of this industry, but is excelled by Iowa by more than $35,000,000.

In years past we used to refer to the great commonwealth of Illinois as the leader of all the western states in everything that pertained to agriculture; and although it has an area of a thousand square miles more than Iowa, many cities, and the Union stock yards, within her borders, yet it had about $85,000,000 less value in domestic animals on her farms and ranches than Iowa had; and about two and a quarter millions head of neat cattle less than Iowa had the census year.

Iowa has more neat cattle than any other state, except Texas, which, as before stated, has about five times the area that Iowa has; and until recently it has made live stock raising its chief industry. But now, I understand, its chief industry is raising oil stock.

I must not dwell upon comparisons, although to me it is an exceedingly interesting subject. But I cannot resist the desire to propound the question, Is there any reason why Iowa should not have the best stock pavilion in America? and without waiting for an answer, for I anticipate that the reply of stockmen would be that there should be none, and will say that there is no reason why this grand state of Iowa, the leader in agriculture, leader in animal industries of all the world, should not only have the best pavilion on earth, but the best of everything that is essential to the welfare of her people.

Iowa produces the best of everything that it attempts to produce. In our opinion it has the fairest girls and the best boys, for the reason that it is an agricultural state; and it is close to the farm that this kind of boys and girls are generally found; and as our cities are all small, our people are necessarily close to the farm, consequently most of our girls and boys are fair and noble.

In my younger days, when I heard the statement, "Iowa is the best state in the union," I believed it to be but an impulse of the speaker's loyalty to his state; but I have long since learned that it is not the expression of an idle sentiment, but a conceded fact based upon such an abundance of proof that no one seeks to controvert the statement.

There are thirty-five and a half millions (35,504,000) of acres of land in Iowa. And according to the last census more than thirty-four and a half millions (34,574,337) acres, or 97.4 per cent, are included as farm lands. And nearly thirty millions (29,897,552) acres, or 86.5 per cent, are improved.

No other state in the union has so large a number of acres in farms, nor has any other state so many acres of improved land as Iowa has. It also has a larger per cent of improved lands in proportion to the total number of acres.

The value of live stock sold the census year exceeded that of any other state, and the total value of farm products exceeded that of any other state by many millions. I need not continue the citations of proof of the excellence and grandeur of Iowa. The character of her people, who are energetic and progressive, have had much responsibility in the attainment of the high standing and importance it now enjoys. Her past progress has been so rapid and wonderful that it has surprised our own people—her future development may astonish the world.

It is natural and proper that we extol the virtues and importance of our own homes and our beloved state. It is a principle and a characteristle which we have inherited all along the line of centuries from our ancient forefathers. While we love Iowa best of all, we are not unmindful of the attainments and importance of our neighbor states.

Illinois has the advantage of us in population, cities, manufacturing, etc., and furnishes us a market for a large portion of our surplus products. But time will materially change these conditions. Minnesota is drawing quite a number of our people within her borders, who having had experience in Iowa, know a good country when they see it.

Missouri has attained to a position of such importance that her citizens have the dignity to look one squarely in the face and assert that they are going to hold, in St. Louis, in 1904, the most magnificent exposition that the world has ever witnessed; and judging from the preparation that they are making and the energy that they are devoting to the matter they will dc it.

Our neighbor on the west, Nebraska, although twenty years our junior in statehood, is making wonderful advancement and producing results of which they may justly feel proud; and it is demonstrating what an intelligent people possessing the spirit of industry and enterprise may accomplish under favorable conditions. It is the abiding place of that eloquent gentleman who prefers silver to gold. It is also the home of other eloquent gentlemen, who prefer gold to silver. They have made a part of the state blossom like the proverbial rose, but it will be many summers before other parts of the state blossom much.

There are other interests beside agriculture and animal industry that are also of vital importance to our people. The opening sentence of the act creating this department is as follows: For the promotion of agriculture, horticulture, forestry, animal industry, manufactures and the domestic arts there is hereby established a department of agriculture.

This act passed both houses of the legislature, with only four votes in the negative, thus demonstrating that our people are deeply interested in all these matters.

The present Board of Agriculture is entitled to much credit for what they have already accomplished in the advancement of the first named industries; but we are all desirous that manufactures shall also advance more rapidly.

The last census shows that the total value of farm products in Iowa increased, the last decade, 129.6 per cent, while the total value of manufactured products increased only 31.6 per cent. Three per cent a year may be a healthy growth, but it certainly is not a rapid advancement. Time will not permit me to discuss this matter in detail, hence I will only say that there is no legitimate reason why manufactures shall not increase from 50 to 100 per cent during the next decade; and if there exist a reason that is not legitimate, it must be removed by statutory enactment by the state legislature, or by congress, or by both if necessary.

Our people are generous consumers of manufactured products, and we have the best of transportation facilities for reaching other markets, and we have an abundance of cheap coal and other material. Every person engaged in a pursuit is, directly or indirectly, interested in every other legitimate pursuit in the state. He has a special interest in his home city or town, and should, by every means in his power, encourage the upbuilding of a home market for his own products.

In several localities in this state corn is selling above Chicago market, and being manufactured into beef and pork at a profit. And this has been true for years, regardless of the quantity of the crop produced.

The same principle applies also to other products, and will always apply when the demand at home equals or exceeds the supply. I trust that the Board of Agriculture will, as soon as circumstances will permit, adopt some system for the dissemination of information pertaining to our resources and conditions favoring manufactures; and so far as it may deem expedient, co-operate with boards of trade, commercial clubs and municipalities in promoting a more rapid development of manufacturies in the state.

Some one has said that "Iowa leads in everything that is good." Whether this be true or not, I shall not attempt to determine, but it certainly leads in many good things. But if politicians are to be classed under the head of good things, I am sure that Iowa is left, for the good old state of Ohio produces more politicians to the acre than any other state in the union.

I trust I may be pardoned for referring to a matter that revives anew sorrow to the heart. The State Board of Agriculture has lost a highly esteemed and valuable ex-officio member by the recent death of Dr. Beardshear, who was president of the State College of Agriculture and Mechanic Arts. Dr. Beardshear was a great, generous-hearted, able man. Advanced agriculture has lost a zealous, faithful advocate. The college has lost a devoted, ceaseless worker. The state has lost a great educator. It will not be an easy task to fill the positions left vacant by his sad and untimely departure.

In conclusion I wish to add that in my opinion the money appropriated by the state for the construction of this much needed building could not have been better expended; and it will, in due time, return to the state treasury increased more than ten fold.

Those of us who have been in a position to observe some of the beneficial results of the annual meetings and the annual exhibitions, held under the present state organization and its predecessor, know of parties who are today exhibitors of some of the finest herds in the country, who assert that they received their first inspiration to produce such herds by attending the annual fair upon this ground; and who are now taking first premiums at the fairs and exhibitions held in every state in this circuit.

We also have in mind a young man who first attended our fairs as an interested spectator, who has since brought honor and credit to the state as an exhibitor of agricultural products at national and state expositions. These cases are only illustrations of the many instances that may be mentioned.

The State Board of Agriculture is deserving the gratitude of the state for its energy and perseverance in securing the completion of this building in a thorough and substantial manner, in so short a time and at a very reasonable cost.

It is to be hoped that the construction of this pavilion is but the beginning, and that the people of Iowa will insist upon other permanent improvements being made upon the state grounds; other improvements must be and I trust that in the near future the state will pay the premiums on exhibits, and every person will be permitted to enter the grounds during the annual exposition without admission fees, and be free to leave the grounds and return as may suit their convenience.

The great Iowa State Fair has not only national renown, but it is recognized by people of the leading nations of Europe. It has outgrown the significance of the name "Fair," by which it has been known in the past, and should henceforth be known as "Iowa's Annual Exposition."

I have in the past been criticized by some of my friends of being over-zealous in behalf of this organization. I wish to say that so long as it is as carefully and economically conducted as it has been for the past ten years, to my knowledge, and continues to accomplish the great results that it has accomplished I will endeavor to endure the criticism, and, if possible, increase my zeal with my increasing years.

I am constrained to believe that the people of this commonwealth possess today many, many millions of dollars as a result of the long continned efforts and labor of the State Agricultural Society, and its successor the Department of Agriculture. Much has been accomplished in the past; much more may be accomplished in the future.

SENATOR DOLLIVER CALLED OUT.

After Senator Harriman had concluded his address which was received with frequent outbursts of applause, Senator Dolliver, who had accompanied Governor and Mrs. Cummins to the pavilion, and who was seated with Mrs. Cummins at some little distance from the speakers' platform, was called for. He was not at first inclined to respond, but Governor Cummins left the platform and escorted him to the speakers' platform, where he was greeted with a hearty demonstration. He spoke briefly. He commended the last general assembly for providing for the construction of the pavilion. He said, amid laughter, the last general assembly in fact had done two excellent things, it had ordered this building and returned him to the Senate. He said he had been captivated by the extraordinary showing of statistics concerning Iowa's products given by the governor and Senator Harriman. He said he was pleased, too, at the reference by the governor to the moral and intellectual progress of the people of Iowa. "Our farms are good," said the senator, "but our folks are infinitely better. Side by side with the swift foot of material progress, the intellectual and moral side of this commonwealth has been developed." The speaker closed with the expression of two sentiments, one voiced in the old Hebrew quotation, beginning, "Thou hast crowned the years with thy goodness," and the other in the words, "God bless our commonwealth, not only on the farms and in the stores, but in our homes where the great forces are made for civilization and the progress of the world."

AS TO STATE FAIRS.

Homestead.

In some of the agricultural papers comments and criticisms regarding state fairs are making their appearance. Much latitude of opinion must necessarily be permitted as to what are the best features to be presented on such occasions. It is not an easy matter to decide, because of the diversity of minds to be pleased. There are those who will hold that everything which can amuse, instruct or in any way attract should be permitted. Others will contend that amusement features should be given little or no attention, but that instead every effort should tend towards instruction. Still others will contend that amusement and instruction should be so blended that those who were largely bent upon being instructed should also be amused, and those who thought only of amusement should be, consciously or unconsciously, instructed.   There are those who would sweep away the "Midway" features altogether.

The idea of a state fair, or any fair, national or international, is primarily instruction. To educate the people by the interchange of ideas, the displays of natural products, manufactures or the result of human

Display of vegetables from Lucas county at the Iowa State Fair, 1902.

thought as expressed in various accomplishments is the work which a fair is supposed to do. In carrying out such an idea, however, it is not necessary that everything should be done upon the lines of severity. Gravity does not accomplish more than smiles, and it is questionable if it accomplishes even as much. People can be instructed better through the medium of laughter than through the medium of tears. And even a little nonsense now and then is relished by the best of men. Let the practical be prominent, but do not discard the ideal merely because it perhaps can never be made practical. Let the fair be all things to all men. Let it be so diversified in its features that all will find some attraction—some in the way of amusement, some through instruction and some through everything that may be offered.

It should be borne in mind also that while the fair is a source of education it must be made to pay its way. It is easy enough to say that though some features may be attractive to a certain class and may add to the income of the management they should not be tolerated, nevertheless, because they fail to meet the approbation of another class. As long as they are not immoral and have only amusement for their merit why not admit them? Every one who attends a state fair does not care to listen to a scientific lecture. The mind just then may perhaps not be in unison with scientific thought. More hearty, healthy enjoyment could be obtained from watching the antics of trained monkeys or the pranks of dancing bears than could be obtained from a learned discourse upon the origin and destructiveness of a newly discovered insect. The insect lecture no doubt would be profitable to those who cared to listen, but to the generality of visitors one might as well lecture upon the best way of catching weasels asleep or how to ensnare birds by putting salt on their tails. The general visitor wants his instruction ready made. He does not want to reason it out. He sees the working of a machine or a live stock exhibit or a display of other products from the farm and he is not required to think. The instruction for him is there ready made and to his hand. So that whatever will instruct by way of exhibits and whatever will attract attention by way of amusement should be added to the program wherever possible. The days spent there are days of recreation. The visitor does not want to be burdened with the somber side of life. There has perhaps been enough of that already. What may be silly to one may be highly meritorious to another. The young are as much to be cared for, if not more so, than the old, and the fair should prove the common ground of instruction, amusement and profit.

Homestead.

The farmer who can attend a state fair and not enjoy himself certainly has a bad liver. I spent several days at a state fair recently and met scores of friends and readers of this paper. The exchange of ideas was mutual and beneficial. There was a mixture of enjoyment and red lemonade, flags and souvenirs galore. Machinery was there by the acre and nowhere on earth have I seen a better or larger display of all kinds of live stock. There is a steady improvement all along the line. It is at the fair where improvement can be observed. The man who is not improving his stock is going backward. Let there be a distinctive advance in merit, even though it be slow.

DOES IT PAY TO SHOW?

The Breeders' Gazette.

To show or not to show? that is the question. A subscriber in Iowa asks this journal if it will pay a young breeder of cattle to go into the show business. He states that the "nub" of the whole matter is as to whether the advertising secured in the show yard is worth what it costs, directly and indirectly. Below are submitted replies to this question from a number of the most prominent authorities in the United States:

W. P. Harned: It certainly does pay to show at least under two conditions: First, that the cattle possess real merit. Second, that the owner possesses a cool head and a generous spirit. The cattle will go through the critical test just before the ribbons are tied, and his head and spirit will pass through the trying ordeal just after they are tied. At this trying moment if he has a near friend who will feel his pulse it will help him to decide whether he may continue in the show business or not.

Right here let our young breeder take a lesson from the well bred animals which stand by halter under the trying scrutiny of the judge. They have walked in, and quietly walked out, without a murmur, whether they wear the badge of victory or not, and well bred cattle perform this duty with grace, usually well bred men try to do likewise. It is a great credit to a breeder, as a breeder, and a great credit to his herd to show some of his best animals and win. It is a strong proof of his judgment in successfully imitating blood lines which he may possess, yet he may be a great breeder and successful breeder and in many hotly contested fields win nothing.

A failure to win ribbons should not discourage a beginner in his new undertaking. If it is to be a life work every defeat should be a lesson.

"If at first you don't succeed, try, try again."

Few men win at first, but they learn lessons and win later. A successful show is to present before the public animals of real merit. It may be a very successful show and not a trophy won.

The inquirer wishes most to know if showing pays directly or indirectly. To this I would say it is not likely to pay directly. If he breeds successfully it is likely to pay indirectly. It is the true method to show the real quality of the herd. It is fame to win. It is high honor to show, and take defeat like a man without a murmur. Instances can be cited where great breeders and successful exhibitors in later years have taken the road home after their first show, broken hearted and bowed down in spirit. I think this is told of the late lamented Col. T. S. Moberly of Kentucky, who owned young Abbottsburn and whose herd was crowned with glory when he met his sad fate.

The late "Uncle Tommy" Westrope was a tower of strength in his later years, yet the writer saw him at a fair many years back where the showing was hot, and his credentials would have been weak, judged by his ribbons. The young breeder must learn that an ignorant public is apt to ridicule his first effort, rather than offer encouragement to persevere. It is a pity this is true. If he breeds improved stock he is a benefactor and it is the baser form of mankind that will offer a jeer instead of a word of encouragement.

John Letham: My idea is this: Next to a live advertisement the *Gazette* I want a winning steer and I will qualify that to a right good show animal, but the man who succeeds usually knows how to show his stock and also how to run his advertisement at the same time,,or he is willing to trust those who do know, viz., his herdsman, groom or shepherd and to some one in connection with the paper who knows his business. The two go hand in hand all the time.

Of course I know men who show a great deal and hardly even win a dollar and say it pays, but I never could see how it pays to show your stock to a disadvantage. These men are good talkers, business men when it comes to lobbying and cultivating; they meet the people, get them to visit them and furnish some particularly nice brand of cigars and by the way the good wife cooks her chicken they manage to make sales and call it a success. Why? Because they met these men when they had their stock at the fair. I cannot see how a man makes much unless he gets expenses while he is out—there is so much expense before leaving home and with bad results after getting home, so that unless you can pay out when gone I call it a flat failure showing and I never showed in my life when I did not, only in my first year with the Sussex, when we had no classification for them.

E. B. Mitchell: The question whether it pays to go into the show business must depend largely on the person. I think that all exhibitors who bring out good specimens of the breed, well fitted, will agree with me that it pays to show their goods. There is no question that a few men whom I could mention have made the show business pay directly: that is, their winnings have more than paid them for all labor and expense aside from the advertising received therefrom. Merchants in every line of business realize the importance of showing a good line of goods, and I can see no reason why the breeding of registered cattle should be any exception.

Experience has taught me that it is impossible to make a creditable show even though you may not be good enough to win without receiving more or less recognition from would-be customers. And if by chance one can develop and bring out just one animal that is a winner he will undoubtedly receive more than enough advertising to pay for all. It is remarkable how impressions last, as almost every exhibitor can tell you of sales made on the strength of your show possibly two years previous.

Again I believe that if the exhibitor will leave home with the determination to use his judgment unprejudiced and learn to see other cattle as he
sees his own (and he is unfit for an exhibitor until he can) the schooling
he will receive will more than pay him in qualifying him for the work
of breeding cattle. One of necessity must meet many strangers, thereby
extending his acquaintance, and usually wider acquaintance means more
business. The only way by which we can measure the standard of our
cattle is by comparison and I am quite sure there are exhibitors who
have not appreciated the merits of their animals until brought to the
show. I am quite sure the reverse is true. Some exhibitors have appreciated their animals more than anyone else, but such will generally come
back better the next year.

. L. McWhorter: Having followed the practice of exhibiting my cattle
at home rather than in the show ring during recent years I may not be
fully qualified to solve the problem of "to show or not to show." The
general public is disposed to judge of the merit or standing of a herd
by its winnings in the show ring and its relation to such winners. One
may breed and own as good or better cattle than the show ring afford,
but it is a problem how to demonstrate the fact to the buying public
except through the agency of the show ring. Meritorious animals that
have attained the most prominent positions in the shows of the country
are those most talked of and best known in live stock circles. The animals that win attain a prominence not otherwise attainable. Campaign·
ing a successful show herd is about the shortest route to prominence as
a breeder and gives advertising of unquestionable value to the owner of
the herd. It is, however, frequently dearly bought. When I look back
over the show yard history of Angus cattle in America I cannot but experience pangs oɪ regret when I think of the many prominent winners lost
to the breed by excessive and long continued fitting for show purposes.
A large percentage of the cows become shy breeders, chronic abortus or
wholly barren.

The loss among the bulls is hardly less noticeable. This may be a
fault of the present show yard methods and requirements, but we have
to take the show yard as we find it. "It is a condition and not a theory,"
as President Grover Cleveland said, and as such it must be faced by the
candidate for show yard honors. To win one must fit and fit heavily. To
fit heavily some top cattle will be ruined and lost to the breed. Show
yard contests remind me of war. War implies heavy preparation, hard
campaigns, strong rivalry and glorious victories. War affords quick
opportunities for honor, for glory and for victory and yet war is what
John Sherman called it. Its cost is not in money nor in effort, but in the
best life-blood of our country, and the same holds true in the show ring
contests of the country. They are both probably necessary evils and frequently worth the cost. The breeder with a reasonably large breeding
herd closely related to the individuals constituting a successful show
herd can, I believe, profit by showing them. At the present time fair

associations, breeding associations, stock yard companies and occasionally private individuals are very liberal in recognition of the interests of the show men. Thousands of dollars are annually showered upon them in addition to the advertising gained. These two sources of revenue, together with glory gained—the value of which is problematical—give a preponderance or argument in favor of showing one's cattle and yet the fact that my practice does not conform to the above conclusion will doubtless lead to the thought that I consider the subject a debatable one —and I cannot deny the allegation.

In a few years after embarking in the pure-bred cattle business I had out a successful show herd at district fairs, but discontinued showing and relied on the merit of my cattle and the advertising columns of the *Gazette* to sell my surplus. I have never shown cattle at a state fair, never sold cattle in a public sale, and never failed to move my surplus at prices that afforded reasonable profit. I have confined my advertising to one high class paper only. If your enquirer will buy and breed really top cattle, will give his customers fair and conscientious treatment, will place his cattle before the public in a proper manner through high class papers he can sell cattle without showing. Really good cattle generally find good buyers.

—

J. G. Robbins & Sons: We think any breeder who has the usual facilities for putting out a show herd should do so. One of the greatest secrets of success in any business venture is properly advertising that business, and no more effective way of advertising the cattle business can be found than through the medium of the show herd. We would not say that this way alone would be advisable, but used in connection with advertising in the live stock journals it makes sure work of it. No matter how small the herd, a few things should be fitted and exhibited at some of the many live stock shows of the country. If you are not able to go to state fairs at first go to the county fair. Get acquainted with the breeders and their ways and compare your cattle with those of others in the show yard. There is no educator equal to experience at the fairs And in beginning do not get discouraged if you do not win all you think you should, but see where the animal that beats you is better than yours. Then go home and begin getting ready for the next year. We are of the opinion that the advantages secured from the show herd in connection with a breeding herd are not fully appreciated by cattle breeders. Show your cattle and give the newspaper boys something to talk about and they will use it. Do not get discouraged, but remember "success comes to those who hustle wisely."

—

D. Bradfute & Son: Many conditions enter into this question. If the question was simply: Has it paid us? we can answer that fifteen consecutive years on the state fair circuit have proved the show business a very profitable one for us. In our opinion there are three good methods of advertising. Continuous and persistent advertising in several prominent stock journals (especially the *Gazette*) always pays. The little "one-horse farm papers" and local newspapers do not pay. It is well enough to stand in with these people, but as a business proposition it does not pay. Second, the continuous exhibition of choice specimens from the herd, especially of your own breeding, at state and county fairs and fat stock shows pays. The cattle must be selected with judgment, well fed, well groomed and well shown. In addition to all that it is important that the exhibitor always be a gentleman. The other fellow is just as anxious to win as you are. If you cannot take defeat gracefully stay out of the show ring. You should be a good judge yourself and know when you are beaten. Boast of your winnings all you like, but keep still about your defeats. The more fuss you make the more you advertise your defeats, which is very poor kind of advertising. If the sting of defeat is very sharp avoid talking much until the next day, especially to the judge and your victorious opponent. The average judge is as honest if not more so than the average exhibitor. Most beginners do not give sufficient attention to properly exhibiting their animals. Very few animals make a good show if left to themselves. If we had only one eye it would never be taken off the animal while under the judge's inspection. If you have two, keep one on the animal and the other on the judge. If we could only have a third eye to watch the other fellow's animal we would like it. If we had a dozen not one would have time to see the horse race or the balloon go up or the crowd. Keep your eyes open and your mouth shut. Both are very important. Remember you are as a traveling man exposing his samples to the public. Therein lies the value of exhibiting at the fairs. You can get a few hundred folks to come to your farm during a year, but at a big fair you expose your samples to thousands each day. If your samples are not very good the public will assume that what you have in store at home is certainly no better. Do not tell that you have better at home than you have at the fair. Some one may look at you as though he might doubt it. Be courteous to all people at all times. You cannot always judge a buyer by his looks. Now if you can be all these and do all these things everybody will be glad to recognize the merit of your animals and the stock papers will be glad to give you a lot of free advertising that will greatly aid you in your business the year around and make the show business a very profitable one.

Fifteen years' experience in exhibiting the Meadow Brook herd of Aberdeen-Angus cattle at the large fairs from New York to St. Louis has taught us that the foregoing are some of the essentials of success in exhibiting a show herd of cattle. How well we have learned our lesson is not for us to say here. The show business is one that has to be learned our lesson is not for us to say here. The show business is one that has to be learned by experience. Not many succeed in winning many prizes at the big shows the first year or so, but "success comes to those who hustle wisely," and come back each year a little better than the year before. It costs on an average from $100 to $200 for each large fair attended with ten head of cattle, besides the expense of fitting before starting. As our state fairs give only from $400 to $600 each breed and there are likely to be from four to ten herds in competition one can easily figure about how well he must do to come out even financially. Competition grows sharper each year and nothing of an ordinary character can now win at a state fair. It is best to begin with smaller fairs.

The third method of advertising referred to is the purchase of some noted animal at a record-breaking price and thus step suddenly into prominence. This method requires large means or a great amount of nerve it always seemed to us that the amount of free advertising given in such cases is out of proportion to the real merits of the case. The first two methods seem to us by far the best and most worthy of the true lover of good stock and the first method must be practiced in connection with the second to bring about best results. The man who is breeding and feeding winners at the big shows is certainly entitled to all the credit he receives at the hands of both the press and the public. It is in our opinion a business worthy of the best efforts of an honest man.

N. H. Gentry: In answer to the new beginner I would advise that he fit his animals up well and enter them at the shows. That is the quickest way for him to find out whether he has the right kind of animals or not. By comparing with others he will see at once, if he is any judge, just where he is and if he has the wrong ideals in his mind he will get them knocked out, and if he is disposed to learn and profit from others he will soon get set right in judgment. The show yard is a great educator, as it is only by comparison that we judge animals, good or bad. At home we are apt to be of the opinion that we have as good as any one and by entering the show ring and comparing our products with those of others we may find ourselves far behind. Again, nothing stimulates the development of our herds as much as the show yard. We think more of our animals, too, when we see them developed right. The old fogy idea that we must have animals in thin form to judge them to best advantage has long been proved erroneous. Not until an animal has been properly developed can anyone tell for a certainty how good it is or can be made. Development proves what is in them.

"Anything that is worth doing is worth doing well" will apply to showing as well as anything else. Nothing will advertise a breeder and give him an acquaintance quicker than showing, but the benefits he will derive from showing will depend on his efforts—that is, the quality of stock he shows and the development of it. Some breeders spend a life time almost in advertising to the world that they have a poor class of live stock by never showing anything in proper condition and also by showing a class of stock of low grade naturally. Such efforts are certainly worse than thrown away. Such breeders are simply advertising to the world by hard work and the spending of money, too, that they have nothing anyone should buy.

Charles E. Leonard & Son: The question has been asked by one who has recently commenced breeding cattle if it pays to go into the show

26

business. The amount of prize money offered annually by the various herd book associations and the many district, state and national shows is so great that the successful exhibitors find after the show campaign is over a good balance to their credit. Their reputation as breeders of a high class of stock has been greatly increased, their acquaintance extended and the value of the successful prize winners enhanced beyond their fondest hopes and thousands of dollars added to the value of the entire herd. In many instances beginners and young breeders who scarcely had a local reputation have bought, bred, fitted and so successfully exhibited such a high class of cattle that their reputation is now worldwide, brought about by their winnings in the great show yard contests. Such object lessons have these national and international shows proved that the intelligent and ambitious young breeders can learn and accomplish more as breeders, in a few years, than formerly was possible in a life time.

The best cattle from all sections of the country come into competition. Expert judges award the prizes. The live stock press, with the best talent at command, is present to commend or disapprove awards. All these advantages are more forcibly impressed on the exhibitors than on the non-exhibitors. In addition to these considerations for entering the show arena you have the consciousness of having done your duty in trying to advance the interest of the breed you think best. Certainly the successful exhibitor has the balance on the right side of the ledger.

It has not been an entirely losing game with the unsuccessful exhibitor. Probably too high an estimate was placed on the animals at home, which all are liable to do, but if they are honest seekers of light by the time they get through the grand circuit it will dawn upon them where they are or rather the estimate others placed upon their cattle will be understood and they will return home wiser for having been "shown." Though defeated do not become discouraged. Put more energy, means and ability into the business and success will crown determined efforts.

W. A. McHenry: To the question: Will it pay a young breeder to prepare his breeding stock for the show ring? I will say that in my opinion the money he would get out of it after paying the expense of fitting his herd, car fare and attendants from one fair to another will hardly pay the average exhibitor. But there is another element that enters into this matter which is equally as important as the money he receives—that is of showing his cattle to the general public. If he succeeds in winning with his cattle it advances his herd to the position of advertising what he has accomplished and thus leading the way to higher prices for his cattle. If a breeder is to talk he must have something to talk about and without a show yard record and show yard ancestry he has but little to back his cattle. I would therefore say, carry the young cattle along as best you can and if you find you have an outstanding winner take it to the fairs; this individual may gain for you a reputation as a breeder that will be valuable in the future.

John J. Steward: In reply to the question as to whether it pays to go into the show business I must say, from our own experience, yes, with these provisions: One must be ready for the show before going out. We must have some cattle of our own breeding, as that is where winning counts, increasing their value and the value of those at home.

The new men sometimes think if they pay high prices for cattle they can go right out into the show yard and make a success of it, and they often get badly disappointed, but when a breeder has produced something good enough to show, fits it carefully, and wins a ribbon on it, it almost doubles the value of the animal, besides giving the exhibitor about as good advertising as I know of, and since all the big breed associations have been giving so liberally at shows and fairs, by being careful and using good judgment, the exhibitor should be able to clear all expenses and soon make a little profit besides. Like all other successful business men, the cattle man must advertise his goods; the intending buyer (at least in Missouri) has to be shown. It does not count so much, no matter how good the individual merit or breeding of your animals if you keep them at home and talk or write about them; to get big values when selling, it seems generally one must get out in the ring and show them. The writer has known of several breeders who after exhibiting very successfully for many seasons, for some reason have decided to quit showing, and notwithstanding all they had done in the past, their successes were soon forgotten or overlooked or outshadowed by the new men who came into the field; and buyers have passed the old herds by and flocked to the comparatively new men in the business, so I think if one goes into the stock business to make it pay the best way to do is to exhibit your work.

———

Charles Gudgell: I regret very much that I have no positive convictions myself on the question as to whether it is profitable to a breeder to exhibit at the breeding stock shows. One can, of course, fancy conditions of success under which it would be profitable to do so, but taking the results as they usually come I am almost convinced at times that it does not pay in the end. To show without success would not be profitable in any event. Successful showing is now to a great extent a matter of fitting, which in the end is ruinous to the animals in shortening their period of usefulness if not entirely destroying the same.

———

Dr. Wm. W. Crane: Yes, it pays to show, a number of conditions being presumed. A man must have quite a good sized home herd above the show herd; they should be of the same general blood lines and same type. He should be right certain that he knows a show animal at home; he must know when an animal is in show condition; of his own knowledge he must know how to fit for the show yard, or in lieu of that knowledge he must have the ability and means to procure a fitter who does know the things mentioned. With these points taken for granted and many more that need not be recited I believe the advertising obtained and the acquaintances made at the ring side and during fair week will result in a reputation and as a consequence in sales, so that it pays to go into the show business. It is not necessary to win the first prizes to make it pay. If a breeder can put forward worthy cattle in prime condition he will make friends and admirers for his exhibit, though he may not win out on top. The awarding judges, acting in all honesty, may prefer a rival herd of a different type—perhaps a larger type—perhaps not deeper fleshed but rounded out till individuality is lost in fat. Understand show cattle must always be in high show condition, but if you do not believe in the stuffing process and resulting gross obesity you may safely show your independence by bringing your cattle into the show yard in that attractive state known as highly finished, showing their quality to their best advantage, plump, sappy, elastic, wearing blooming coats. With such a herd you may still fail of the blue ribbons, but in the lobby, which by the way is the appellate court in cattle contests, you will catch the eyes of some discriminative men who are seeking exactly the thing you are showing—prospective buyers, too—which the judges are not. Thus you will win renown followed by sales and find that it pays to go into the show business. When the conditions enumerated are absent a man had better stay at home with his cattle.

———

Edwin Reynolds & Son: Directly the benefit is not so great as might be expected, although an exhibitor can make expenses and considerable more to compensate for feed and labor, but indirectly benefit comes in from the advertisement received in the show yard, and this is worth many times the cost and trouble.

———

C. G. Comstock & Son: We think this question is like a good many others in that it cannot be answered for every one in the same way. We believe that the first essential factor is the breeder himself. If the conditions are such that he can give the time to it, if he is competent and sufficiently interested, we would say decidedly that it pays to show. In that case show by all means, but he should be a good judge of cattle and should understand the proper handling of them. If he has not all of this knowledge he should be capable of acquiring it by practice and observation. There are exhibitors who never will be able to do this. Our answer to the beginner would be what we believe he would receive from a professioual or a business man if he should write and ask him for his advice as to becoming a lawyer, doctor or a merchant, as the case might be. He would doubtless reply, "It depends upon yourself." We think it pays the right man if there are no personal reasons to prevent his giving the proper time to it.

Some of the breeders' associations are putting up sufficient money as premiums at the state fairs and association shows to pay him pretty well even if he is only fairly successful. The advertising he gets is something that cannot be calculated in dollars and cents, but it is valuable and of course increases in value with his success. Besides these direct results he benefits himself indirectly by helping the breed he reprsents and there is a compensation in the knowledge that he is improving the quality of his cattle and is the owner of some good ones even though they may no* all be first prize winners. It encourages him and makes him feel that he is on the right track.

Although it is not the point in question we would add that a man with good common business sense only may make a financial success iu handling pure-bred stock without being sufficiently versed in the business to become a successful exhibitor. There are many men who are doing this, some of them treating it as a side issue only. They have started with good foundation stock though and make it a practice to buy good sires as they need them.

Wm. T. Potts: My experience in the show business extending over a period of nearly twenty years convinced me that very few men make much if any money directly out of the show business, but any one with a good herd can make money indirectly by getting his cattle out where people can see them. But as the shambles are the end of all cattle I found that to castrate a few good calves each year and fit them for the fat stock shows was the best of all, though in fitting for the fat stock show a man must not think a calf too good for that purpose and castrate an inferior one. None of them are too good if you expect to win.

Jas. A. Funkhouser: Taking it for granted that the young man means to go into the business of breeding as a permanent one I think it pays to show. In conjunction with newspaper advertising it shows that we have what we represent. Again it brings us in contact with other breeders and gives us a much larger personal acquaintance with men in our own calling. But the most valuable of all the experience we get and the lessons we learn is the opportunity we have to compare our cattle with other men's cattle and our ideas with other men's ideas and thus learn the good from the bad.

W. C. Edwards & Co.: Speaking generally it is our opinion that it will not pay an inexperienced breeder to go into the show business. It is better for him to have quite a good deal of experience before he tries it and then he should only begin moderately, showing one or two animals at first. All who attend great shows going about intelligently acquire a great deal of knowledge, but perhaps the greatest experience is acquired by those who engage in showing.

There are many sides to this question. It is quite true that showing is a good method of advertising, but then there is showing and showing. It is our opinion that those who persistently show, fitting the best of their aged cattle for show purposes, considering the high fix in which they are now brought out, do so to the deterioration of their general herds and as a consequence many of the very best and most successful breeders never show. The excessively high feeding which is generally practiced in preparing animals for show purposes we regard as hurtful, but if the showing is confined to calves and yearlings or say young animals, we do not regard it as being so hurtful so long as proper methods are applied in feeding. If a large amount of succulent food is provided and not too much grain of a heating character we do not think it so hurtful. As a consequence of this belief after breeding for some years we showed aged herds for some two or three years and after having been victorious, carrying off first prizes at our various great shows, we retired and have since shown only calves and yearlings when we did show and to this practice we are confining ourselves. Further, we do not take much pride in showing anything except possibly a bull which is not our own produce. Very wealthy men who engage in breeding possibly for pastime as well as the hope that they may do good to the breeds they admire can engage in doing many things which the ordinary farmer-beginner cannot afford to do. For the ordinary beginner we would strongly recommend not going too rashly into showing and in no case to continue to show animals older than say two years, unless the practice of fitting animals for show purposes is largely changed from what is now generally being done. An excessively fat condition we do not believe in as being desirable in animals for breeding purposes.

S. F. Lockridge: To my mind it is largely a question of conditions. If the object is to bring cattle into public notice as soon as possible, in other words to advertise them, I know of no better or quicker way than by exhibiting them at the fairs and shows of the country. There is probably no more effective means of appealing to the judgment of men than by an object lesson. The animal speaks for itself and if it possesses the breed characteristics the breed is then prominently brought into public view in a way to leave the most pleasing and lasting impressions. Many a young man has had his ambition to become a breeder awakened by seeing the fine specimens of the bovine race on exhibition at his county or state fair and then and there resolved to replace the grade and scrub on his farm with a pure-bred herd. And naturally he seeks the owner of the herd whose cattle won his fancy and from him, in all probability, obtains his first purchases. So too many an older man who has spent his maturer years in the city amassing wealth sauntering through the show grounds sees the same exhibition that awakened interest in the younger man and the sight stirs within him memories of a time when he was a boy on the farm driving home the cows in the gloaming, while all around him the air was vocal with bird and insect life and redolent of summer sweets. So strong is the awakened old love that he never rests until he has renovated the old homestead and placed a pure-bred herd amid the scences of his younger years. In either case the owners of pure-bred herds are benefited, the breed is benefited, the country is benefited and the fact is emphasized that it pays to show.

On the other hand if the only object in exhibiting were the immediate pecuniary benefits to be derived from such display it is questionable taking into account the long course of preparation, the cost and risk of transportation, the high price of feed usually exacted at such times and the strong competition likely to be met with, whether the money value received would equal the outlay. Of course there are notable exceptions to this rule. But the money consideration should not in my estimation control if the best results are to be obtained either in the breeding or exhibiting of cattle. There is something inspiring to the soul of the true breeder in the thought that he is not only helping to keep his choice breed up to the standard it possessed when he began his operations, but that, regardless of pecuniary returns he is aiding largely to increase the merits of cattle as food-producing animals. Success along this line will bring its own reward.

So I would say to the beginner, procure, by breeding or otherwise, the best specimens of the breed of your choice, properly fit them for the show yard and exhibit them, not with the expectation of taking all the prizes offered, but for the good of the cause you have espoused as well as the advertisement of your own herd.

———

I. M. Forbes & Son: As to whether it pays to exhibit cattle or not we will say that while we have never done much showing we do believe that what showing we have done has been quite beneficial to us, and we believe that it is one of the best advertising mediums any breeder can have to show his breeding bull and his get if they are good enough to win a fair share of the prizes (and of course the more the prizes the more attraction to the herd). We have always doubted the propriety of showing an aged her as we have felt that it must be injurious to aged cattle to put them into extra high condition. Our showing has been confined to young things of our own breeding mostly, and we feel that it has been our best advertising.

———

Wallace Estill: If the young man has fully made up his mind that he is going to make the breeding of live stock a life business and will stay with it I answer yes. If not I think I would advise him to let it alone. In the first place there are many conditions required to make a successful herd of show cattle as well as to be competent to show them. Many a good animal has been turned down in the show yard because the show man was not competent and ought not to have been at that end of the halter.

The first year or two out the young show man will learn more about cattle and especially show cattle than he would ever know just to sit at home and breed them. Therefore I think it a fine education for the young breeder to show his cattle. Show cattle must have character, style, conformation and type, and the quicker he recognizes this fact and gets it into the herd the sooner he will be brought into prominence—and the advertising is great. My experience as a show man was the hotter the competition the more I learned and these lessons to a breeder from a breeder's standpoint are priceless. Now as to the advertising it gives and whether it will pay. I answer yes. A herd of successful show cattle will clear enough money to pay all expenses and to run a good "ad" in several of the best live stock papers, besides the advertising and the acquaintances you make that are useful to you.

F. A. Nave: From my personal experience I will say most emphatically it does pay to show cattle. Showing cattle will pay directly with a good herd and good herdsman to fit them and carefully managed. I think it is well for the beginner to start at the county and district fairs. The acquaintance with farmers and cattlemen at these shows is very valuable After some experience at the smaller shows one is better prepared to enter the field of the professional showman. Never be satisfied with just a place in the money, but always aspire and strive to the possession of a herd, or at least some individuals, to stand at the top. I do not favor overfitting cattle, but they must be in prime condition; and it is best that cattle make their reputation under three years of age. Then they are not ruined for breeders. The advertising gained in the show yard is the most effectual advertising, there is, and is gained without expense; and as i have before said the acquaintance of breeders, feeders and farmers gained in the show business is the most valuable of all and something money will not buy.

O. H. Swigart: If the end sought is immediate financial returns my answer is no. I have not had extensive experience in the show yard, but my observation is that the returns are remote rather than immediate. They are in advertising your own stock and incidentally the breed in which you are interested. If you are not endowed somewhat with the missionary spirit you would better not show stock, as the breeders and your competitors are more interested in making a fine display of the breed than they are in your financial welfare. "He who would save his life must lose it" is especially true in showing stock. That is if you are not willing to sacrifice immediate personal glory for the glory of the show, or if your disposition is to win for the sake of the money rather than for the glory of winning because you have the best, you will be disappointed and your fellow breeders will be disappointed in you as their representative. A "grouchy" man is not needed in the show yard. This dual character, representing both yourself and your fellow breeders, must be constantly borne in mind. From a selfish standpoint you have the only cattle and want to win on all. From a representative standpoint you must broaden out to want to see the best win whether you own it or not. From a selfish standpoint you will shut out your competitor on any technicality from the show yard. From a representative point of view you want to see the best show possible and unless the show is made better by excluding some one hesitate long before you do it, unless there is a positive offense in permitting him to show. Exclusion would help you to win money, but unless you have an ideal higher than winning money, unless you have regard for your competitor, unless you have regard for the breed you represent you will win neither money nor fame. The good opinion of your fellow breeder is a cash asset and that is won or lost in the show yard much more easily and more quickly than out of it, because the strife engendered there uncovers your better or worse nature and shows many latent qualities unknown in ordinary intercourse with your fellows.

To sum up: Showing stock does not pay directly and immediately hardly one time in ten, but it brings your name and herd before the public and if successful it puts you in position to advertise more effectively. A discreet advertiser must tell the truth. If you can truly say that in warm competition in the show yard your stock was successful under competent judges your advertisement appeals to the buying public, and they come and see what you have, and if what you have for sale is good enough you make sales. In this way you get a better class of buyers and make better sales. Besides all this you learn a great deal about breeding stock—the strong points and the weak ones of a breeding animal. You learn what to strive for and what to avoid. Your eye is trained. So is your hand. And with hand and eye you are given ability to form a more correct judgment. These indirect benefits are great. Many a man has had all the conceit taken out of him by the show yard test. At home on pasture or in his barn he thought his stock invincible. In the show yard by the side of really high class stock he recognizes faults he never dreamed of. And progress comes by this route.

Brookside Farm Co.: It pays to show and advertise cattle by all means. Whatever breed you fancy fit the cattle in the very best possible condition and you will be rewarded for time and expense. Every second inquiry for stock is: "I saw by *The Gazette* you were an exhibitor at such and such a state fair or at the international." Many other letters state: "I saw your cattle at the state fair last fall." Now if you do not show and get before the public you cannot expect *The Gazette* or whatever stock journal you advertise in to sell all your surplus stock. Come out; if you do not earn your expenses you will learn something for next year. Never count up your show experience nor your advertising in good stock papers. They will pay later on.

Thomas Clark: In answer to your inquirer I would not advise him to run the risk of fitting his older cattle, unless he is an expert feeder, as it is useless for any one to attempt to show nowadays with cattle poorly fitted and by so doing he would be very liable to spoil his older cattle for breeding purposes. But if he desires to show I would advise him to show younger animals. This would be less dangerous in injuring them as breeders. The reason I give this advice is that I do not think any one just starting a herd can afford to run the risk of spoiling his older females. As to the bull—there is little fear of hurting his breeding qualities; in fact, I would prefer to use a bull in high condition rather than in thin condition. As to the advertisement, if he shows and wins quite a few premiums, it is a good investment, but if unsuccessful it would be better to use a little more printer's ink than to attempt to show.

———

C. F. Rice: In reply to the inquiry of your subscriber in regard to whether it pays to show cattle I will say from an advertising standpoint I think it does, for you can realize from a fair campaign better results than from the same amount of money spent in any other way, but first you want a herd that either can win honors or stand along up the list and I would say show as near a herd of your own breeding as possible. A new beginner cannot do that. Take the show business from the financial standpoint and it is a failure, for if you can win the expenses of your herd you can think yourself fortunate, and there are more herds showing that are losing money than are winning their expenses.

———

Z. T. Kinsell: I will say as a breeder of registered cattle that it pays to go into the show business. I think it is a good advertisement and as such pays. At the fairs you will meet parties looking for cattle that would not come to your farm to see them. You can show them the kind and quality of cattle you have at home by what you have at the fair. You also get acquainted with some of the best breeders of your breed and they help advertise them for you. Some of the best sales I have ever made have been at the shows. I also get inquiries from parties who have seen my cattle at the fairs. Another great benefit in showing is in the comparison of your cattle with others; in this way you can see where your stuff is lacking and where they need improvement to meet the demands of the public.

To be a successful breeder you must breed the type that suits the buyer. It also pays to keep a few animals in show condition to show the visitors at your farm what your cattle will make when developed. At the shows you come in contact with the best breeders and feeders of the country, and I have always caught on to new ways of feeding and caring for my cattle that more than pay for the extra expense of showing. I may go to the state fair and not get a prize and still make money out of my showing as an advertisement. As a small breeder I have had no trouble in selling all I can produce. I find with the agricultural colleges, fairs and shows in educating the public as to what constitutes a good animal we must breed the best to get the prices that pay.

———

J. H. Miller: Whether it pays to show cattle depends greatly on the kind of cattle and the kind of man who is the exhibitor. Every breeder worthy the name strains every nerve and his bank account to raise the standard of his herd from year to year to get as near his ideal of perfection in animal form as he can. The nearer he gets to it, if it is the right one and in popular demand, will be the measure of his success as a breeder. The show yard to learn and unlearn along this line is the best place I know of. To the wide-awake beginner in the show business the experience gained will be worth a great deal of money. It will also give him a truer estimate of his own cattle. A prominent breeder has been quoted in answer to the question: "How is it, my friend, you have good cattle and make good sales, but are not a sensational winner in the show ring?" "Well, I will tell you. As I see my cattle at home I think the world cannot beat them, but when I come into the show ring I find I have forgotten to consider what the other fellow has been doing." And how true this is! So many breeders who see only their own cattle imagine they have the best on earth, but when they are measured beside the really good ones they are found to be quite common and are scarcely noticed. The common thing for this class of exhibitors to do is to accuse the successful one of trickery and to express a doubt as to the integrity and ability of the judge. The wise man will at once say to himself: "I must raise the standard of my cattle. I must breed and show as good cattle as any other man in my line or stay at home." He has now learned the kind and type of cattle and the condition necessary to win, and he goes to work, not in a half-hearted way, but in earnest, and it is this class of men that make a success.

Passing from the owner to his cattle more directly we find that traveling salesmen carry samples of goods they have for sale for the buyer's inspection. The great fairs of our country offer the fine stock breeder the best opportunity to show his samples to the public. In my experience among inquiries from prospective buyers they often add: "I saw your herd at a certain fair." It may have been several years before, but if they were favorably impressed with the cattle it seems to stick in their minds.

To the question: "Does it pay to show cattle?" my answer briefly is: If you have cattle good enough to win it does both directly in prize money and indirectly in advertising. There are many exhibitors who have made lots of money and the prize money alone has made showing very profitable, but the advantages gained indirectly in the way of advertising can scarcely be estimated. And even if the exhibitor does not get near enough to the front for the greatest cash awards or sufficient to pay all his expenses, still he may find his money and efforts well spent if he has a good class of cattle and there are many such that are outside the money at the greater fairs. The friendly rivalry of the show yard is a great incentive for a breeder to put forth his best efforts. It widens his acquaintance among his fellow breeders and is a good medium to bring his cattle into public notice.

————

Marion Parr: As to whether it will pay to go into the show business depends on several things. If your correspondent has on hand a good supply of stock for sale; if he has a herd that can go out and be ranked among the best of his breed; if he is a pleasant and agreeable man to meet who knows how to tell the good qualities of his herd and breed without disgusting those who hear him; if his breed needs advertising and last and most important if he does not have to neglect more important business it will probably pay him to go out with a show herd.

If on the other hand he is compelled to neglect other business; if he has only a fairly good herd he will hardly make his expenses. I have known quite a few exhibitors to have to send home for money to pay their expenses; on the other hand, I have known others who made a little money showing cattle. Still I have come to the conclusion that for my part the cheapest advertising I can do is in the best class of stock papers. Of course it is necessary for some one to show cattle to keep the respective breeds before the public. It is a good way to get acquainted with the best class of stockmen. It is also a good way to find out what kind of a herd of cattle you have. It is a good educator for those who engage in it. To your correspondent I would say the time is here when it will require a great deal of feed and attention to go out with a herd and win at any of our leading shows. Competition is very strong in the show yard now.

H. Brown: As the beef breeds of cattle have to be fitted to compete today do not show. As we showed them ten years ago, yes! In order to be successful in securing prizes today one has to feed from calves and crowd to the utmost limit regardless of the detriment to the animal by overdoing; and in the most of cases ruin both male and female as breeders. The custom has grown worse every year, until I have abandoned it. I was a constant exhibitor at all the leading state and national fairs for many years and met with success, but always stopped feeding when my cattle reached what I thought was the "danger line." But I always presented them in good bloom and today cattle in that condition would be classed as "not up in flesh," hence no particular advertisement to the exhibitor. Under no circumstances would I think of putting an aged herd of cattle in that flesh. A young herd can be fitted for a year or so if stopped at that time without serious results. And until a change in the rules of showing is inaugurated no man can afford to show, and but very few will do it. Good cattle are too scarce and worth too much money to be ruined in that way.

George Bothwell: In regard to the question whether it pays the breeder to show his cattle or not I will say it has paid me and paid me well. At the first show I did not win many prizes, but as it afforded me the opportunity of comparing my cattle with others it proved a great educator for me, and as time went on I bred and showed better cattle each year. I can look back now and see that if I had never gone into the show yard I would not have accomplished much as a breeder. As an advertising medium I believe it is the best and cheapest. I do not believe that a man should be discouraged if at his first show he does not win, but should try again. While the prizes may not pay his expenses of fitting the cattle for show I believe he will be amply repaid by getting his cattle before the public and becoming better acquainted with the breed and breeders. If he is successful in winning prizes he will be paid both ways.

Aaron Barber: Does it pay to go into the show business? is a question often asked by those engaged in stock breeding. In answer I can but relate my own experience. A person engaged in breeding fine stock as a business in order to make successful sales must first find his customers and then have the class of goods they desire to purchase. Exhibiting stock at the fairs brings the breeder face to face with those engaged in precisely the same calling. You form their acquaintance and see and know to a certainty the class of stock they are breeding. The breeder who is breeding and bringing out the best specimens of the various breeds show to a class of men who are constantly alert to find and purchase animals of rare merit. You have the opportunity of showing them that you are breeding and that you have this class of stock. In what other way of advertising can you so thoroughly attract this class of customers? There is another class of customers who are in want of plainer stock, not from choice but perhaps men of limited means; therefore the breeder who is breeding the plainer and cheaper animals finds his customers. The breeder has to depend on his sales for profits and to make sales he depends on his customers. To get customers he must advertise; advertising through stock journals keeps the breeder constantly before the people and exhibiting at the fairs demonstrates the truth of his advertisement. I would say to the breeder, exhibit your stock; bring them out in the best possible condition. While the money value of the premiums won may not be extremely profitable the acquaintance and advertising the breeder gets are of great value.

———

Stanley R. Pierce: I think your correspondent could not do a better thing for his business and for his breed of cattle than to show a few pure-bred steers of his own breeding and breed at our leading fat stock shows. The end of all pure-bred beef cattle is the block and in our breeding business we are trying to produce and sell pure-bred bulls that will sire good steers for Chicago and other markets. I think a good way for a beginner to sell these bulls is to first show some steers from his herd and if they can win in our best shows he will have no difficulty in selling bulls of the same breeding and individual merit at good prices to sire cattle for the leading markets. Besides your correspondent will have no trouble in selling his steers if well fitted for nearly as much as or perhaps more than they would bring if sold as bulls.

I am greatly in favor of fat stock shows. They are of great benefit to breeders of beef cattle. The small breeders can afford to castrate a few bulls and show steers, but they cannot all afford to fit and show a valuable herd of breeding cattle, and that is why the small breeders are unable to sell their bulls.

THE TESTIMONY OF SWINE BREEDERS IS PRESENTED.

A beginner in the business of breeding registered swine propounds the question as to whether it will pay to make exhibits at the fall fairs. The views of breeders thoroughly qualified by experience to speak authoritatively on the subject have been ascertained and are presented in a symposium which follows:

Wm. D. McTavish: If the beginner in the breeding of registered swine intends to make this his life work I would say it does pay to show, but if he is going into it only for a short time or while it pays well I should say no. The state fair is a great educator for the young breeder and although he may not win a prize, yet he will learn where he is weak and if he is made of the right kind of stuff right here is where it will pay. He will go home and set about improving his herd and not be content until he can win his share of the ribbons. Thus it often happens that a breeder's defeat in the show ring does him good in the long run. He finds out where he is, where some of his ideas are wrong and others all right. The first thing he must learn is to come out of the show yard as smiling as he goes in, whether defeated or victorious. It is a ve.y difficult thing to do, and only a showman can do it at times, but you must do it if you expect to attain any degree of success.

The sales made should more than pay all expenses. Right here in this matter of making sales is another important feature of the business. Never denounce another man's stock in order to sell your own; better by far lose patrons for the time being, for it will react against you an hundred fold. If the other fellow's stock is not up in quality with yours the public will notice it without your telling it. By observing these suggestions the new beginner will make many friends among his fellow exhibitors and visiting stockmen that will pay him well in after years. You must show the public what you have to offer if you want its full confidence and expect to realize good prices for your stock. If some one else shows stock of your breeding it will answer the same purpose, but this is out of the question with the beginner.

Thomas Bennett: In regard to showing hogs I would say to every young man going into the business, keep away from the fairs. I have known several good clean young men ruined forever, morally, physically and financially by attending the fairs with stock. It is a hard place for men settled in their habits, much more so for young men. I followed it for some years and know all about it. Shun it as you would a pesthouse. Besides, if a breeder of swine takes the circuit of the fairs nine times out of ten he will come home with a diseased herd, and the chances are that he will inoculate other herds with the stock he sells to his customers. I have quit the show business for years because I could not take the risk when handling as many hogs as I do. I know men who make a business of showing hogs at the fairs (they are not breeders) who ransack the country and buy the best they can find for show purposes, and when they get through showing sell the herd to the slaughterers—of course they sell some pigs but buy the most of them.

Some prize Herefords owned by J. A. Funkhauser, Plattsburg, Missouri, and shown at Iowa State Fair, 1902.

My own experience is that it pays better to advertise judiciously in some good clean agricultural papers, and I know of no better medium than *The Gazette*, which I find clean and straight in every particular. I have thought for some time that it would be the very best thing for swine breeders if all the state fairs would cease offering premiums for hogs, because every year they do more harm than good. The fairs are the means of spreading disease in all directions. Nearly every herd that was represented at one of the last very great shows went home in bad shape. It was kept very quiet, but nevertheless it is a fact.

I have passed the seventy-second milestone and would advise all young, middle- aged and old men to go to the state fairs; it is a good school if you keep your eyes open. You meet your friends, neighbors and loved ones whom probably you have not seen for some time. Keep sweet, be cheerful, and the fair may be a blessing to you.

———

Geo. S. Prine: It will pay to show pure-bred hogs, as there are many features connected with the business that can be accomplished in this way that would take years to reach otherwise. The wide acquaintance gained in so short a time with the practical experience in the selecting, fitting and the management of the show herd will be of great value to the beginner, and with a good herd carefully fitted and properly managed it will pay a liberal dividend on the capital invested, besides giving to the new man an advertisement that will be another profitable feature not to be overlooked.

To the young man I would say: "Go out and invest your money with skill in the accumulating of a herd, and lay your plans to exhibit at the best fairs and gain will result that will be of value to you and your business."

———

F. F. Failor: All would depend on the skill of the beginner as to his ability to breed and feed and bring out a show herd good enough to win in competition with breeders who have followed the business through years of experience, having met and overcome many disappointments. Not one man in a thousand could commence as a novice and win a ribbon at the first attempt, as the breeding and feeding of swine for show is as much of a trade as any scientific calling. My advice to a beginner would be to make an effort to get such animals of the breed he has as are in what he thinks prime show condition, and if possible take them to his own county fair, comparing them there with others of the same breed. If he meets with sufficient encouragement to justify him in taking them to the state fair by all means do so. This will be the best object lesson he can get at a reasonable cost, giving the novice a still better opportunity for comparison and doubtless point out to him his former mistakes.

The question is asked: "Does it pay to show?" Yes, it pays and it pays well if you have the winners or some of them. You will soon learn that there are others who know how to breed and feed hogs as well as yourself at a state fair. In giving my personal experience I will say that I fed and showed at our county fair for ten years before I had the courage to attend a state fair, and when I did so I never failed to get my share of the ribbons, and it paid me as an advertisement and gave me an excellent opportunity to dispose of my surplus stock at good prices.

A. J. Lovejoy: This is often a difficult question for the beginner in pure-bred swine breeding to determine. The fact that one has just embarked in the business of breeding pure-bred swine would seem to the writer evidence that he must in some way let the people know it, and from the standpoint of one who has in the last quarter of a century passed through the labyrinth and finally emerged into the open path I would certainly advise the beginner to commence at the fairs. The success he will meet with will depend entirely on what kind of stock he starts out with and how much pluck and good nature there is in him. Many men nowadays with some capital and good judgment pick up a few animals of show merit and at once start out and are in a short time close up to the old breeders who have spent a lifetime in getting well to the front. while others like the writer had to start with nothing but the good nature and pluck.

Well do I remember the first show I ever made. I had selected from the meager herd we than had enough to fill part of the classes at the fair, and had watched them from day to day and thought that there was not probably in the country anything to compare with them. The premium list had been studied till it was known by heart. Thoughts of how the animals would look when all washed up and driven into the ring had passed through my mind a thousand times; even the amount of money that would be won had been figured to a nicety. The day and hour came when the animals were called into the ring, with palpitating heart the last brushing was given and the pen was opened and out to the ring we went. Somehow the judge did not seem to see my pigs, or if he did his examination was not very critical, as he did not stop, but passed them, and in due course of time the ribbons were placed and none seemed to come my way. Of course I was disappointed, but if I was young and very green I had sense enough not to abuse the judge or condemn the association, but began to look around to see where my pigs lacked and to learn, if possible, why there were no ribbons coming to me. I could see several things that showed me that there was much to learn. and while I was out of pocket the expense of fitting and other incidentals I had been well paid, for I was a wiser if not a sadder man.

I had learned the lesson that all must learn—that "there are others" —and went home to come again the next year, which I did, and when at this the second trial in the show yard a ribbon or two came my way, even if the color was not just what was best, it was encouragement that was a tonic and a stimulant that worked well. To repeat the many trials and discouragements would tire the reader. The only object in mentioning these things is to caution the beginner that he must not launch out with the expectation of winning all the blue ribbons the first year. It took us many years before we were quite sure of getting our share if not all of them. It was the best way to advertise our stock and the best way to educate ourselves that was then and is possible, and there was always a chance to sell a few pigs and begin the long course of building up a trade.

My advice to the beginner, therefore, would be to fit the best animals he has or can buy and make the smaller fairs first for a few years, such as the county fairs, for the competition here is not so strong as at the great state and national shows. where one comes into competition with all the best in the country, and with those who know all the little arts of showing to the best advantage Above all things never abuse the judge or the association; it will not hurt them but reflect on yourself. A judge is or should be above reproach and should never favor any man to the detriment of another. It may look bad sometimes to the man who does not get just what he expected, but way down in his own heart he knows the other fellow had the right to get the blue.

In selecting animals for the show try to select only the best If you have but one, two or three that are of outstanding quality take them and fit them to the best of your ability, and leave those that are not quite as good at home. It is better to show a few and win than a whole bunch that are not strong enough to win. Always try to have them all of the same type, as the judge will keep as near one type in his selections as possible, for in no other way can he make his work an object lesson. The fact that all are striving to come as near the standard of excellence as possible would necessitate the discarding of those furthest from the standard. The writer has acted as judge at many of the largest shows of the country, has tried to keep as near the standard type as possible, and even has had in some instances to order certain animals back to the pens as not creditable to the breed. In conclusion let me say to the beginner: "By all means show your stock at the fairs; you will in this way build up an acquaintance that will in future years be of great value to you. Always show your stock in good fair show condition, but not overdone. Take your defeats good naturedly, be a gentleman, and as the years come and go you will find yourself growing stronger in the business, and among the fraternity. Be honest in your dealings, make every promise good and in time your only trouble will be to grow hogs enough to fill your orders."

Winn & Mastin: As to whether or not it pays to go into the show business at the fall fairs we have always considered that it paid well to show; that is, where the exhibitor has a creditable show and wins a fair share of the prizes To make a show at any fair with a poor or ordinary herd undoubtedly does such exhibitors more harm than good, but where a satisfactory herd is exhibited there surely must be great benefit and advertising obtained. To the beginner it is especially beneficial, for he can compare his exhibit with those of the older and more experienced showmen and thus learn wherein his hogs lack, and be better prepared the next year to make a successful campaign.

27

There are many beginners and inexperienced breeders who really believe they have good hogs until they have an opportunity to compare them with other hogs, when they find that they have entirely the wrong type, and there is no place that the prevailing and popular type of the hog can be learned so well as at a good show with a good judge. Showing also gives opportunity for breeders from the different parts of the country to meet and become better acquainted and undoubtedly furnishes advertising to the successful that cannot be obtained in any other way at any price.

The show yard is the test and those who are successful at a good show will surely have a good demand for their surplus stock and do well in the business of breeding registered hogs. The expense of fitting and showing is a large item, but in our judgment it is more than offset by the benefits derived.

———

Geo. Wylie: My answer based both on experience and observation is, yes, it pays to show. If the beginner looks at the mere money won at almost any of our fairs he may not be able to figure out an immediate profit. The new beginner needs first good stock, next to let the public know he has it. The public prints are good, but at the fair he gets advertising which may be expensive, but as a rule is worth more than it costs. He gets an acquaintance with men in the business, which is valuable. His stock is put in comparison with that of others and this should be valuable.

There may come a time when the breeder becomes so well known that he can sell all the good stock he can raise at good prices. Then it may not pay him to attend the fairs, but this is not the new beginner's case. I have observed in my experience with exhibitors that some of them would have better reputations if they had never attended any fairs, but these I am happy to state are a very small minority. Let the new beginner make up his mind in advance to take defeat gracefully if it comes. Do not "kick" on the judges; as a rule they are nowadays selected for their ability and know their business. Take your medicine and come up smiling next time and eventually you will be a winner.

———

Geo. W. Trone: It pays to exhibit swine at the fairs provided you have a first class lot. Success will depend largely as to how good a judge the beginner is of stock to start with. The next important thing is as to how good a feeder he is—not as to how much he can feed, but in knowing what kinds of feed to allow and how much of each kind to develop an animal to be of the first class. I do not mean to say that he can take any kind of a mongrel and develop it into a first class individual, but he must have the best blood that can be obtained.

Going to the fall fairs he will get acquainted with a great many men who want good stock and if he has a first class herd that will get the ribbons he will find that the people who want good stock will all get acquainted with him and then his returns will come in for years if he will advertise in good papers. Our herd has cleared us over $100 a week in premium money over all expenses for every week that we attended the fall fairs in the last ten years.

D. R. Perry: The profit to be had from showing pure-bred swine at our fall fairs depends very largely on the person engaged in the business

Polk county vegetable display at Iowa State Fair, 1902.

and his ability to breed and fit hogs for exhibition. If the breeder is a man of determination and intends to stay in the business I would say by all means enter the state fair contests of his own and neighboring states. While it has been truly said that showing does not pay in a direct way my experience has convinced me that it pays handsomely as an advertisement. In fact there is nothing that a breeder can do that will push him forward as much as to raise a sweepstakes state fair winner.

On the other hand if a breeder is a careless sort of fellow and is having his hogs looked after by a disinterested feeder I would not advise such a breeder to undertake to show at even a county fair, much less a state fair. The pure-bred swine business is very much like any other The person who gives it his very best attention 365 days in the year and advertises only what he really has, and then when his orders arrive delivers hogs that are exactly as he represents them to be will make a pronounced success and can well afford to fit some of his best specimens for exhibition.

Davis Bros.: What pay there is in showing swine at the fall fairs comes in the way of making sales. If an exhibitor is quite successful in winning premiums he will generally pay his expenses, but to show for premiums and not have stock for sale we would consider a poor invest ment.

H M. Sisson: Whether it will pay a beginner in the breeding of registered swine to go into the show business at the fall fairs will depend on the intelligence, energy and honesty of the beginner. He should be well informed as to pedigrees, should be intelligent, energetic and honest, and able to tell what a first class hog or pig is. The pedigree, size, form and color are essential if he expects success as an exhibitor. If the beginner has the above qualifications I see no reason why he should not be reasonably successful as an exhibitor and this will prove very beneficial to him as an advertisement if he is to be a permanent breeder.

L. N. Bonham: The show business depends so largely on the man that one cannot affirm that it will pay the inquirer to enter the contest. There are many who can succeed well as breeders and feeders of pure-bred swine who have little or none of the showman's talent. This is illustrated in two of the most noted of the pioneer breeders of Poland-China swine, viz., John Harkrader and D. M. Magee. The latter once told me that when he started on his Oxford Farm he would have paid any reasonable sum if he could have mated and fed hogs as successfully as John Harkrader. But Magee believed he could show hogs as well as any man, and Harkrader recognized this ability, and to encourage the dissemination of good blood he often lent Magee some of his best stock to be shown during the fair season and returned after the exhibitions, they dividing the premiums won. One liked to show, the other disliked it.

It is safe to say that unless one has talent as a showman and a liking for the business he will do as well financially to devote his energies to careful breeding and feeding. If he succeeds in producing high class stock he will find purchasers ready to pay a good price for it. With the modern sales ring and splendid facilities for advertising both by the press and the labors of auctioneers there is less need of fitting stock for the show yard than at an earlier day. To succeed in this way the breeder must also understand the art and value of advertising, which possibly is as rare a gift as that of excelling as a showman. Bringing one's name and stock to the attention of the public through the show yard implies a heavy outlay of time, feed and labor. It also means outlay in purchase of show animals to supplement those of one's own breeding.

Fitting and showing a herd lessens its value for legitimate breeding purposes and vastly increases risk of loss by disease contracted on the circuits and brought to the home stock. The absence of the owner of the herd from his family and farm and animals must be considered, and this is hard to estimate in dollars and cents. One must take all these things into consideration along with his chance of making a showing at the fairs that will be a credit. He must make a creditable showing or stay at home. The day is past when one can hope to win without a herd of high excellence and well fitted. One or two good ones may win and be admired, but the uniform excellence of the individuals shown is what tells of the skill and judgment of the breeder.

The showman who trusts to purchasing his show stock may follow the business a while for the fun of it, but he will find that a costly game which in the end will bring him little reputation as a breeder, but a wide reputation as a plunger. There is need of men who know how to breed and handle a herd from year to year so that their stock bears the stamp of their ideal and of their skill as breeders. When one has proved his skill and can bring forward animals of his own breeding of such excellence as to win a fair share of prizes then we want him to step into the show yard and set an example worthy of imitation by all legitimate breeders. The speculating showman who never wins on animals of his own breeding has been about as useful as Barnum or Robinson in stimulating breeders to higher effort and in elevating the standard of pure-bred animals. They may be a help to the show business, but they are a discouragement to the beginner and the legitimate breeder.

The inquirer will see that we do not think the path of the showman is strewn with roses or leads inevitably to success. It is beset with hard work and risks and dangers. Each must decide for himself. There is no danger that there will not be plenty of contestants for all liberal prizes fair managers may offer. The trend of things is for better equipment of fair grounds and for better accommodations for stockmen and for more liberal prizes.' There is all around great need of better appreciation of improved sanitary condition of pens and stables so that the valuable animals brought forward may be safe from contagion and even discomfort. Less outlay on showy buildings and greater study and expenditure to secure immunity from disease and loss to herds and exhibitors may be considered necessary to make the way to glory for the young beginner less dangerous. ·

John F. Stover: The answer to this question greatly depends on circumstances. If the beginner has selected good individuals of the right type for his breeding herd and understands mating them for the best results; then after he has produced pigs of the right type and understands feeding to develop for the show ring, and can produce animals of his own breeding good enough to win at the best state fairs, and also has a surplus of choice pigs to sell, then it certainly would pay him to show his stock, not just for the premiums alone, because they have been cut down too low. Winning the ribbons will find buyers for his surplus pigs at good prices. On the other hand if he had to buy his show herd and could not show good animals of his own breeding I would not consider it profitable to show.

A. S. Gilmour & Co.: We will say without any hesitation that it does not pay to show swine at fairs. The money expended in showing judiciously expended in advertising will, we think, pay a great deal better. Awarding premiums at fairs has become a much-abused system.

I. N. Barker & Son: We say without hesitation, it does pay. This answer is based both on our observation and experience. If the beginner has really good stock it costs a good deal of money. If he wishes to realize well on it he must sell for more than market prices. In order to do this he must let people know he has stock of a superior quality. The best way to do this is to place it on exhibition, where people can see it The fall fairs furnish a splendid place. The next best thing to do is to advertise.

STRONGLY COMMENDS SHOWING

Ed W. Monnier, Jo Daviess County, Ill., in Breeders' Gazette.

In answer to the question "Does it pay to show?" I say to any young man who contemplates following the breeding of pure-bred stock, it most certainly pays to exhibit at the leading county and state fairs. It brings your stock into competition with that of other breeders and furnishes an opportunity for direct comparison that you cannot otherwise obtain. If you get beaten at first, try again. It will be cheap education after all.

Do not waste time on the fairs where the judging is done by a committee of three selected from the crowd on the third day of the fair and whose pay is their dinner and the honor. It is seldom that three competent men can be found in that way and a competent man will object to serving on such a committee. No man is capable of judging stock unless he is interested in what he is doing and loves the work and some awkward work is even done in this way, but it is an improvement on any plan previously tried. Our fairs should be educational, and any award made should be backed up by reasons for it if necessary. The man who tries to please all and divide the premiums as evenly as possible among the exhibitors is not doing good work. Merit should win even though the bulk of the prizes go to one firm. The other fellows will learn in that way. On one accasion I called the attention of a judge to an award he had made and told him a certain prize should have gone elsewhere. His answer was: "That is not the way to make fairs." That kind of work in my mind is the way to ruin fairs.

If the young man is going to follow breeding let him go out and show. He will learn a great deal. Sometimes there will seem to be little compensation, but he will meet many breeders and find many customers he cannot otherwise touch. There are men who will buy only at the fairs and usually they are willing to pay good prices and any animal that has made a winning is usually in demand. He need not be in the ring every year, but let him see that he gets out when convenient and let him go prepared.

There is another sort of man you will meet at the fairs. That is the breeder who never shows but attends the fairs and then calls the attention of his friends he meets to how much better stock he has at home. Or if he ever owns an animal that has been a winner or bred one that in hands of others has been developed into a show animal he never ceases to boast of it at every opportunity. I remember on one occasion a friend said to me at a fair where I was showing: "I have better stock at home in the pasture than you are showing." I replied very shortly, saying: "I do not believe it." He was much older than I was and he seemed much surprised at my short answer and asked why I did not believe it. I told him that if he had better stock than mine he would show it. "Well," said he, "next year I will show you." And he did, but the color of the ribbons he won was red not blue. Now this man was honest, no doubt, but his stock looked to him much better at home in the pasture than when compared with others in the show ring. Afterwards when this man showed he brought out fewer and better animals and he finally boasted of beating me with an animal purchased of me.

The first show I ever made at a state fair I never won a ribbon, but it was the cheapest advertisement I ever made for it brought me in touch with a class of customers I could not otherwise reach and some of them have remained customers ever since.

If you do not win yourself you will get an idea of what it takes to win and will get nearer the front in that way.

L. MISCELLANEOUS PAPERS.

ABOUT CHOOSING AN OCCUPATION.

Hon. L. H. Kerrick in Breeders' Gazette.

It is a good thing for a young man to get it into his head that he is in the world to do business of some kind. If he should become possessed of such an idea rather early—even by the time he is eighteen or twenty years old—it is not going to hurt him. It would not hinder him from sleeping and eating well nor head off any genuine sport or recreation; and it might save him from a deal of foolish and dangerous indulgence and save him also from much waste of time or vigor by preoccupying him with manly aims and desires.

Every young man who may reasonably expect to do something and be somebody must sooner or later choose an occupation that he will follow for all there is in it. The world has little use for a man who is of no use to it. A business of some kind is the instrument through which a man expresses himself and with which he impresses himself upon the world. With a scythe in his hand a man cuts a good swath in the grass. It is with some kind of business in hand and of which he is master that a man cuts a respectable swath and leaves some mark where he passes through this earthly vale.

I would have the young man make choice of his occupation sooner, rather than later. We hear and read much now-a-days about waiting, going slowly. "Do not be in a hurry" they say, "to close down to any particular calling: it will dwarf your powers and narrow your views. Get larger ideas and broader views first." This kind of advice may be necessary in order to make room and demand for long-drawn-out university courses. "Large ideas" and "broad views" by themselves "cut no ice"; they have no edge nor point. A purpose single and early-shaped to master some great or useful art sharpens one's powers to hew out a way to fortune and to honor. I would not discourage schooling nor undervalue it. A young man with a strong purpose in mind to master some particular profession will have appetite enough for schooling; he knows that he will need it in his business and he will find time. enough to get enough of it.

If by waiting one could find out what by nature he is best adapted to do, then wait; but we have not noticed that men who wait until they are twenty-five or thirty to make a right choice of an occupation hit it oftener than they who start earlier. Indeed, we think we have observed that the earlier birds furnish the larger number of successes. Nobody knows any rule by which it may be certainly predetermined what business a young man is best suited to follow. If anybody has discovered a rule he carefully guards his secret. In rare cases boys and girls show a pronounced aptness for doing some particular kind of work. In such cases the inclination or aptness should be given full opportunity for development. Here is something approaching a rule in choosing an occupation: Other things being equal a young man will often do well to follow his father's business. But there are too many exceptions to call it a rule. However, if the father's trade or occupation has brought competence and honor to the family I would advise his son to look carefully to that business before choosing another. Part of his father's business the boy does not have to learn. He absorbs knowledge of it without effort: and then he will have _or his guide and instructor the man of all men in the world most interested in his success. I am sure young women, in ninety-nine cases out of a hundred, would better follow their mother's occupation.

Fortunately we are each of us wonderfully adapted to do almost any kind of useful work. We say a man has missed his calling because he has failed in business, but we do not know that he would have succeeded in another. If one succeeds in a particular calling he probably would have succeeded equally well in another. Whatever work is next to us. or, in other words, the work which we are "up against" and which most needs doing, we will generally find ourselves well suited to do. The world could not get on well and keep its work done up if that were not true. One stands the best chance of gaining success, honor and profit by taking up bravely whatever work or business is nearest to him and which most needs to be done. I well remember when the war of the rebellion came on we had no professional soldiers—none to speak of —but hundreds of thousands of soldiers were needed to save the nation. In just a little while farmers and lawyers and mechanics and every other kind became soldiers and no better were ever seen. I do not remember so well about it, because it happened several thousand years ago, but it is written that Nehemiah obtained permission of King Artxerxes to go and superintend the rebuilding or Jerusalem, whose walls were in ruins and her gates consumed with fire, and the remnant of the Jews that had escaped, that were left from captivity, were in a sorry plight. Nehemiah was no mechanic nor architect; he had been born rich and great, was cup bearer to the king, but he was resolved that the city and the walls of the city of his fathers should be rebuilt. So he went over to Jerusalem and gathered the remnants of his people together. They were mostly husbandmen who had escaped from captivity because they were not so easily rounded up as those in the city. Probably there were not among them a dozen bricklayers nor any soldiers; but they rebuilt those walls in an incredibly short time and defended themselves the while against fierce and cunning enemies. Nehemiah in his report of it says: "The people had a mind to work." Work that needs to be done is the kind a man can do "with a mind," if he is right minded, and what he does with a mind he does well. What was very peculiar and yet quite natural and sensible about the work of rebuilding those walls was that every fellow pitched into the breach right opposite his own house. not wasting time hunting for a place that might suit him better to work in. Tobiah, a scornful Amorite, saw the walls rising rapidly and he said they were no good; "even that which they build if a fox go up it he will fall down"; but they did not fall down, and so far as I know are standiug there yet.

But what has all this to do with choosing an occupation? This much: Any of us can do almost anything well that ought to be done, and we can do one thing as well as another. So when you are casting about for something that shall employ you profitably and honorably do not cast too long but jump in where you are needed most. If you wait until you are fifty you will not get a better pointer on a question as to what you are fitted for.

Then we might safely advise young men in this wise: If there is a great scarcity of lawyers in your part and likely to be for some years to come, if what lawyers you have are working full time, cannot do the business but have to turn large numbers of clients away, then study law if you want to. If there is a dearth of school teachers in your county or state, if school boards by all their efforts are still unable to find enough school teachers, then learn to teach school. If people are sick in you neighborhood and you have no doctors and none in reach and that condition seems to have some permanency, then by all means study medicine. Why not look at all kinds of business from this point of view? Where there is an opening for your services go in; where there is already a jam, a crush, keep out. That which should furnish the highest incentive to do your best work will be present where you are needed, but absent, wanting, nil, in any profession already over-supplied with laborers.

Anyone who will look about him just a little can see that almost every kind of business except farming is furnished with help far beyond the number for which there is any steady demand; the fact is notorious. Should any untoward thing happen to general business conditions, immediately thousands of people will be out of, or short of living employment in many trades or professions, but not in the business of farming. The farmer is sure of steady, living employment—sometimes more, sometimes less profitable, but always of living employment. Even if no one should want his products he can eat them and live. I am willing to go on record as saying that at this time all conditions point to farming as the most promising, the most inviting, the most profitable business for young men. For the young man already on the farm, who owns his farm or whose father owns one, the inducements to stay there far exceed those to leave it and engage in other business. If money be the measure, young men farmers are making more money than young men in other pursuits. If social standing be the measure, that is assured to the intelligent American farmer from this time forth. Farming is coming to its own, and socially the intelligent farmer is now regarded by good society the equal of any. I do not know of any business by which a young man may more easily and surely gain a home and a competence than by farming. It is practicable for the hired man even, who will save as much as he can of his wages, to lay up a thousand dollars in four or five years. The kind of hired man who saves a thousand dollars from his wages can easily get credit for as much more, if he needs it, and then he is ready to rent a farm and do business for himself. I have had intimate relations with several men who began not many years ago as hired men on the farm, who now live in their own good farm homes and are rearing their families in comfort and plenty and honor. Such cases are not exceptional. The isolation of farm life is passing. The telephone, rural mail delivery, better roads and the interurban car are doing the business.

We get so used to fooling ourselves. Just think of the isolation of the family of a man of moderate salary in a great city. In a cheap, cheerless flat, nine miles from the up-town house where the head of the family is employed; from early morning till late evening wife separated from husband, children from father, isolated by impassable social barriers from all except those of their own class, and fortunate if even a few congenial souls know of their existence. Compared with that environment the average farm neighborhood is a social elysium. It can be safely affirmed that there is no better, cleaner and more attractive business today than that of farming No business is making better progress than farming. Numerous recent discoveries of great importance in agricultural science and rapid advancement in general knowledge of agricultural processes mark this time and put agriculture in the front rank of progress.

If any young man suspects that he has brains enough to farm all right, with a surplus he could not employ in the business, let him try to learn what is known about agriculture and to keep up with the knowledge that is being daily added. It would be a pity for farming and a pity for the young man to turn down the business because he thought he had more brains than could be fully employed in it. A capable, intelligent farmer may enjoy more legitimate leisure than men in most any other kind of business. Among many more inducements to young men to choose farming for a business let me mention only this one. Every farm is an independent business concern, a business unit, and every farmer is independent, his own master and his own manager. Nobody is over him. He plans his own work and works out his own plans. Other kinds of business are concentrating more and more and nothing can stop it until it gets to the ^nd of the process, whatever that end may be. One head does the thinking and planning and gives orders and a thousand obey, begin or quit, rise or fall. as the head decides; but the farmer is the man that is his own master, politically, socially, economically free.

CROP ROTATION.

W. H. Stevenson in Breeders' Gazette.

Grain and live stock write the secret of the successful farmer's agricultural supremacy. Many interesting accounts have been published in your journal regarding the splendid achievements of the landed princes among our famers who have successfully based their extensive operations on this well established principle in farm management. Often, however, it is not possible for the owner of a small farm to work into his own system of management many of the features which are potent factors in bringing success to the extensive grain grower and stock feeder. It is therefore interesting to study the plans which are successfully worked out on a 100-acre farm of William H. Rowe and son Charles, in central Illinois. After long years of diligent study and experimental work, covering many branches of grain and live stock farming, they have adopted on their farm a system of rotation of crops and live-stock management which is at once so practical and profitable that it cannot fail to prove interesting to every farmer who would stand for the best in agricultural endeavor.

Their system is not the result of chance nor of an unbridled desire to test every new fad and passing scheme. Far from it. Methods full of promise are tried but rejected if found wanting An abiding interest in their work, a thoughtful study of the multitude of problems which ever confront the farmer and unceasing attention to every detail are the forces which have enabled them to establish their business upon a rational and paying basis On any farm,

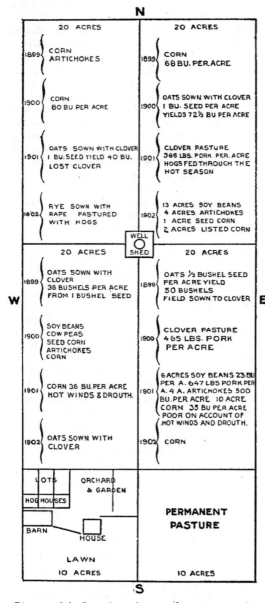

Diagram of the Rowe farm showing plan of crop rotation.

large or small, the farm home and its surroundings are of vastly greater importance than any system of crop rotation or improved breeds of live stock. Of what profit is it if the farmer maintain the fertility of his fields and builds up priceless herds and flocks, and yet fails to secure that most important factor in the building up of true and noble characters—the farm home—for who can measure the dwarfing, narrowing influences which constantly emanate from the cheerless, depressing homes found only too often on our teeming prairies and fair hillsides? Or who can estimate the inspiration and noble motives which flow from the pure, wholesome and beautiful farm homes in our land? Hasten the day when every farmer will plan his home and surroundings as wisely and thoughtfully as did this Illinois farmer. No luxury or extravagance in outlay here, but comfort, convenience and beauty. Only a comfortable farm house set in the midst of billowy blue grass, evergreens and noble forest trees, and yet what a haven of rest. Bank stocks and bonds may accumulate in ever increasing numbers and acres may be added to acres, but no investment of the farmer can equal in intrinsic value the farm home such as this one. The motto of this farm can be written in these words: "Richer fields and larger crops, the system of a wisely planned system of rotation and the feeding of the growth of the farm back to the land through live-stock."

When one by one the grain growers of our land master this one underlying principle in successful agriculture a new and brighter era will speed-i.y come. As shown in the diagram, ten acres of this farm are in permanent blue grass pasture and ten acres are devoted to the spacious lawn, orchard, garden and feed lots. Contrary to the generally accepted theory that a farmer cannot afford to "waste time" on a lawn,, garden or orchard, on this farm these interests receive intelligent care and add much to the comfort of the family and the annual income. The remaining eighty acres are fenced into four fields of twenty acres each. This is a hog farm and for convenience in handling the stock in the fields a shed and a well are located in the center of the tract. This shed is unique in design. In the winter it is closed except on the south. In the summer the north side, which is on hinges, is raised and thus a free circulation of air is at all times afforded. Fat hogs weighing over 300 pounds have safely been carried through the hottest weather with no other protection from the sun.

Oats seeded with clover, clover pasture, soy beans and artichokes and corn are the crops in the rotation which has made this one of the cleanest, most fertile and most profitable farms in the state. One bushel of seed oats per acre is sown broadcast on the land which was in corn the previous year. Clover seed is sown immediately after the oats and is well harrowed in. On this land, quite free from troublesome weeds, this light seeding of oats gives a satisfactory yield and affords the young clover light and moisture in greater abundance. This method of seeding has never failed to give a stand of clover except last year, when such extreme conditions of heat and drouth prevailed. The following year the clover is pastured with hogs the entire season. Few more interesting experiments have ever been conducted than those which have been carried on at this farm to determine how many pounds of pork an acre of clover pasture will produce. In 1900 over 100 fattening hogs were weighed into the twenty-acre clover field and an account kept of all the corn fed. At the close of the season the hogs were sold and the value of the corn fed was deducted from the receipts. The difference represented the cash value of the clover pasture and in this experiment was equivalent to 465 pounds of pork per acre. In 1901 an experiment conducted along the same lines gave a return of 366 pounds of pork per acre. These figures are interesting, for they show that it is possible to secure a large cash income from land even in years when it is growing a crop intended primarily as a source of available plant food. The third year the clover sod is plowed in the spring and the field planted to soy beans and artichokes. In 1901 six acres of well-matured soy beans were pastured with hogs. One hundred and thirty-two spring pigs were turned in the field about September 1. They ate the beans greedily and gleaned the field in a few weeks. They were exceedingly thrifty and made a gain equivalent to 647 pounds of pork per acre. This year thirteen acres of soy beans were raised and pastured. When the records of this experiment are made up doubtless they will show returns quite as remarkable and satisfactory as those of the previous season.

Mr. Rowe prepares the ground for soy beans just as he does for corn and about May 20 plants one-half bushel of Early Yellow beans with a beet drill in rows twenty inches apart. The crop is usually cultivated about three times with a one-horse cultivator and little or no hand work is required. The Early Yellow variety yields from twenty-five to thirty bushels per acre and is ready to pasture the latter part of August. Four or five acres of artichokes are raised each year and furnish a splendid food for the hogs through the fall and winter months. The hogs do their own harvesting and are benefited by the exercise required to root out the tubers The fourth year corn is raised following the soy beans. It is not surprising to find in these fields, which have grown several successive leguminous crops and been pastured summer and winter with hundreds of hogs, corn of the highest type and quality yielding seventy to ninety-five bushels per acre. A pure-bred variety of corn is raised and the demand for seed always exceeds the supply.

This is a hog farm. Twenty Duroc-Jersey brood sows are kept. The average number of pigs raised per sow for three years past has been eight. The pigs are farrowed in April and May and are turned off at fifteen or sixteen months of age weighing from 350 to 400 pounds. Permanent hog houses do not find favor on this farm. The modern individual farrowing pens are used. They are located in ample blue grass lots and afford comfortable and clean quarters for the sows and pigs. The sows raise one litter each year. After the pigs wean themselves the sows are fed to become thrifty and strong but not fat and heavy. An extensive pasture range and muscle-building foods are the factors which lead to success in carrying brood sows safely from year to year. This system makes it possible for the owner to keep a record of his own brood sows and turn off such as do not prove good mothers. It is advisable also to select for breeding gilts daughters of sows known to prove large even litters. Young sows carefully selected from such litters are this season suckling from nine to twelve pigs and show many of the excellent qualities possessed by their mothers.

As soon as the pigs are old enough to follow the sows they are turned into the clover field and from that day until they go to market the pigs are kept in the pastures and fields and are fed such rations as promote the greatest thrift and growth. The clover pasture is used until it begins to fail in the fall. The pigs are then turned into the soy bean field and when this in turn is exhausted the artichokes are available. This series of forage crops together with the blue grass afford excellent feed and pasturage the entire year. Pure air, pure water, plenty of exercise and a balanced ration are thus provided. They will bring success to many swine-raisers as they have to these Illinois breeders. There are no poorly-ventilated hog houses, muddy feed lots and wet disease-breeding straw stacks which serve as barriers to comfort and thrift. Doubtless this wise system of handling the herd has contributed largely to its freedom from disease. Cholera has broken out on the farm only three times in the past fifteen years. In every instance the loss has been very light. on the last occasion amounting to less than 1 per cent, although neighbors lost over 50 per cent. Whenever there is any indication of sickness in the herd corn is withheld and the hogs are fed on a scant laxative ration.

These thoughtful, hard-working Illinois farmers find opportunity 'o profitably employ their brains and hands on the small farm. They have succeeded in helping to solve some of the knotty problems which are ever before the farmer. Perchance this account of their system of maintaining the fertility of the land through live stock farming will help some earnest farmer to see more clearly the path which leads to success and give him renewed strength to push on with hope and courage.

WHY SHOULD FARMERS RAISE THOROUGHBRED POULTRY INSTEAD OF SCRUBS.

J. H Casey, M. D., Kansas City, Mo.
From Monthly Bulletin of Missouri State Board of Agriculture.

In considering the above subject, our reason must be actuated by various motives which will form the basis of our arguments. In the beginning of the twentieth century, when we look about us and notice the rapid strides being made in every branch of trade, in art, in science of all kinds, in the different professions, in all mechanical pursuits, in agriculture, horticulture, floriculture. in the marts of trade, and in fact in every calling that man is engaged in from which to gain a livelihood and to provide him with the necessities and luxuries of life, there is one goal which is the prime object of all efforts, and that is to accumulate wealth; all have this in view, directly and indirectly.

Money is the object sought; men of every clime bow before the "Golden Calf" and do homage voluntarily, to the best and easiest method of making money. The agriculturist or farmer shares alike in this ambitiou and naturally selects, or should select, the surest methods. He has one object in view when he selects his seed, or buys his farming implements; he visits the fairs, intent on gathering knowledge; he studies the market reports daily; in all his purchases of whatever he desires his one great object is to make and save money. Follow him as he starts out to purchase stock, cattle, horses, hogs or sheep. See him studying their points of excellence and their line of pedigree, then ask him why he does so? I will predict his reply, "Because their is money in the best." This, then, is one of the motives why the farmer should raise and keep thoroughbred poultry

If thoroughbred horses, cattle, hogs and sheep are better and will bring more money because they are better than inferior stock, or scrubs, the same rule is applicable to thoroughbred poultry. The quality which makes one head of stock better than another must be on account of its greater money making qualities, and why should this be so? Or in what manner can this be shown? The test is the market value in cash.

Thoroughbred stock, by universal testimony, is considered of the greatest value. Even to the untutored the word thoroughbred carries assurance of increased value. It has the ring of more money value, while the actual amount in money of thoroughbred poultry does not convey the idea of large sums, yet in the abstract, and by comparison, it is as great as in other stock. To the poultry fancier it means the best, and no farmer should ever be content without owning as good, or even better, than his neighbors.

In his argument he asserts that "One chicken is as good as another," but will he concede that the same rule holds good with other stock? How is one cow yielding four quarts of milk as good as one whose yield amounts to ten quarts? How is a cow whose milk contains but 2 per cent of butter fat as good as one in which the average butter fat exceeds 6 per cent? How is the "Razor back hog" or Arkansas as good as the "Chester white, Berkshire," or Poland China?—What is it that makes the difference? Is it not that the money producing qualities of the best is the result of the introduction of pure blood from animals that are known and recognized as thoroughbreds? And why does the fact of their being thoroughbreds insure the good qualities desired? Adulteration of any kind lowers the market value of all commodities. Dishonest persons resort to adulteration to compete with their neighbors, but the result is always the same as the good can be detected from the bad. Adulteration is the incorporating of an inferior and cheaper article with a good one in order to bring down the price of the best. This practice is widespread, and has for its results the overstocking of the market with an inferior quality of goods and a cheapening of values and prices, but it also has the effect of improving the values of pure articles and of making them more desirable on account of their intrinsic purity. The world at large acknowledges that the best of anything is worth having, because its money value is not as liable to fluctuation. For this reason thoroughbred stock is looked upon with favor, and must possess its good qualities.

But there are other reasons from those adduced to induce the farmer to raise thoroughbred poultry. We will assume that he pays some attention to his poultry and that to maintain them he must be at some expense. The cost of keeing pure bloods is no more than would be necessary with scrubs. Can this be proven in the abstract? I think it can. An inferior grade of cloth will not last as long as the best fabrics, because the materials of which it is composed are not as good as those in the latter, and in the scrub animals of mixed breeds the vitality or physical stamina is weakened and degenerated by inbreeding and crossing. This mixing of breeds is of such nature that unhealthy stock must be the result, and as a consequence the vitality is impaired.

This being the case,, extra kinds and amount of foods are required to sustain life to that degree which is necessary to insure the animal or the fowl's productive powers. Thoroughbreds, possessing as they do, healthy systems (without degenerated changes) k ept so by reason of careful breeding, require less food to retain their vital forces, they seek their living unaided, and are more easily kept up to the standard. In them there is no adulteration or inferior blood, hence their enduring qualities, necessitating a lesser outlay to maintain their health and procreative power. But there is an aesthetic side of the argument. The farmer who owns a fine herd of pure Herefords, a pen of fat, sleek Berkshires, a flock of heavily robed Merinos, takes a great amount of pride in showing them to his neighbors, comparing their fine points and extolling their physical qualities. He points with satisfaction to their money producing achievements, and plainly shows that the possession of such blooded stock is a source of greatest pleasure. Anyone is proud of the reputation of owning the best stock in the neighborhood.

While often the possesion of wealth is the means of furnishing pleasure, yet it is not the only one, and he who owns fine blooded stock, must and does enjoy such ownership better than the one who ignores the perfection of labor. In conclusion, I refer to one other reason which, I believe, carefully tabulated reports will prove, and that is the superior utility of thoroughbred poultry. This much mooted question has strong adherents pro and con, but I feel that conscientious breeders who have studied the matter carefully, will agree with me in the truth of the statement. By utility, I mean the quality of commercial productiveness. The fact of any animal or fowl being a thoroughbred carries with it the idea of being of perfect physical qualities, and as such capable of reproducing its kind with the same qualities, which are stamina, vitality and almost perfect productive powers. Such fowls show their superiority by increased egg supply, by greater reproductive power, resulting in more fertile germs and a larger proportion of healthy hatched progeny that are more easily raised on account of their hereditary stamina. These results are desirable because by them the credit side of the ledger is increased as well as

28

the profit side. To sum up, greater egg yield, greater number of chickens hatched and raised, thereby less expense in raising them, are arguments in favor of pure-bred chickens being of superior utility.

In this age of progress it behooves every farmer to progress and not to stand still. The successful farmer of today is he who has kept pace with the upward march of improvement in all its details. Brain work comes to the front,with its glorious results, and the old haphazard method of keeping poultry without profit is a thing of the past. In its place are found systematic business plans, resulting in success through the replacing on our farms of thoroughbreds.

BEES.

F. W. Hall in Wallaces' Farmer.

If there is anything near and dear to the human heart, it is something good to eat; and if there is anything better than honey—real good pure bee's honey—we have not yet discovered it. I shall not have much to say about honey, but will confine my talk mostly to bees. There are many varieties. both wild and domestic, but I shall deal only with the domestic honey bee. The leading facts in the breeding of bees ought to be as familiar to an apiarist as similar facts are to the breeder of domestic animals. To make a success of either, one must put his soul into the work and give attention to the many, many little details. This is especially true with bees, for successful bee-keeping is made up of little details. A few crude and half-digested notions, which were quite satisfactory to the old-fashioned bee-keeper will not satisfy the bee-keeper of today if he hopes to reap financial success. Our present conditions make a systematic management necessary.

Almost any locality where vegetation grows has "nectar" enough going to waste, within bee range, to supply a neighborhood with that delicious, wholesome, healthful article of diet—honey. Many little ailments might be averted in the family if honey was eaten with the regular meal, instead of so much other sweets. Honey is more easily digested than sugars and "all glucose" mixtures, and besides possesses a goodly amount of medicinal properties. Not only should a few bees be kept on every farm for the honey and wax, but for the part they play in the pollenization of plants, and especially fruit. Horticulture and "apiariculture" go hand in hand, their relations are mutual.

The honey bee can flourish only when associated in large numbers, as in a colony. Alone, a single bees is about as helpless as a new born babe. The hive has movable farmes in which the bees build their comb, suspended from the top bar of the frame. These combs are formed of hexagonal cells of various sizes, built out from a mid-rib, or septum, in which they raise their young and deposit their stores.

In a colony of bees is found a bee somewhat larger and considerably longer than the rest. In olden times this was called the "king bee" but this has since been discovered to be a "queen" instead. The queen is the only perfectly developed female in th colony and hence lays all the fcrtilized eggs. She can lay at will an egg that will produce a male or female bee. A prolific queen will lay at the height of the breeding season more than double her own weight in eggs every twenty-four hours. Good authorities claim to have had queens that would lay an average of six eggs per minute. This would be over eight thousand eggs per day. A queen that cannot be induced to lay over three thousand eggs per day usually gets her head pulled off and is superseded by one that will.

There are good and bad bees just as there are good and bad cattle The wide-awake apiarist will weed out those that are not profitable and will replace them with something that is profitable.

The queen is fed by the worker bees who keep her supplied with egg-producing food in the right amounts and she lays because she has to. She is not so much of a queen after all since she is not a ruler in any sense of the word, gives no commands, directs no movements, orders no work. She is not allowed to be idle but is fed by the rest as a sort of machine to produce eggs for the propagation of the race. The queen does not eat plain honey from the comb cells as do the other bees, but is fed, or rather stuffed, with a granular secretion very similar to the milk of mammals. This granular secretion is produced by the young bees and is fed to the queen and the young larva. The glands that produce it are useless when the bee is old enough to work in the field. The queen produces no wax but has a sting which she uses only on a rival queen, either in the hive or outside. The queens fight on sight and to a finish It is intensely interesting to watch them fighting a duel.

In the hive will be found several thousand smaller bees, known as workers, which are really incomplete or dwarfed females. Their office is to do the work of the hive and to bring in the food from the fields for the needs of the colony. It used to be said that bees did not make honey but gathered it. If man can be said to make sugar, then bees can be said to make honey. The nectar when first gathered is from eighty to ninety per cent water but when converted into ripe honey most of the water is absent. The chemist calls honey an inverted sugar or grape sugar. It used also to be supposed that bees manufactured wax from pollen and honey chewed together. Wax is a secretion on pretty much the same principle as fat is a secretion of the ox. The first condition necessary to wax secretion is a well filled stomach. Honey gathering and comb building go on simultaneously and when one stops the other ceases. When nectar no longer abounds in the field, it is wisely ordained that they should not consume in comb building the store they might need for wintering. The wax secreting organs, present only in the workers, are on the under side of the abdomen, four on each side called wax pockets, in which the wax is formed in tiny scales. It is interesting to watch the bees at comb building. They take the tiny scales of wax from the pockets and join them on the edges of the combs they are building.

Three sizes or kinds of comb cells are built—worker cells, drone cells and queen cells. There are fifty worker cells to the square inch and thirty-five drone cells in the same space. The queen cells are hung on the edges of the comb with the mouth or opening downward. They resemble a large peanut in shape. Any egg that will produce a worker bee will produce a queen if the bees feed the larva the proper amount and kind of food and change the shape and size of the cell to accommodate her extra size

The drones are the male bees and have no sting, produce no honey, secrete no wax, and do no other work in or out of the hive, but spend the whole time in gluttony and idleness. Healthy colonies usually destroy the drones when food becomes scarce. How wonderful the instinct that impels the workers to persecute and destroy those members of the colony which are no longer of service.

The time necessary for the transformation from egg to winged insect is sixteen days for the queen, twenty-one for the workers, and twenty-four for the drones. The queen lives about three years but may live five. The workers live thirty-five to forty days in the summer and from fall to spring. The drones live no longer than the season and are likely to be killed at any time.

WHY ARE LANDS ADVANCING IN THE WEST AND DECLINING IN THE EAST.

Wallaces' Farmer.

The fact that farm lands generally as far west as central Ohio are remaining stationary, or declining in value and sell in a great many cases at about one-half the price of twenty years ago, is a very great surprise to most western farmers and we are often asked why it is. It is important for the farmer to know the reasons for the decline in lands over large areas and their advance in other large areas in order that he may know how to shape himself to the ever changing conditions. We do not presume to be able to give all these reasons or to solve what is confessedly a surprisingly difficult problem, but we think we can throw some light on the situation.

Undoubtedly the first cause of the great decline in prices east of central Ohio is the opening up of the large comparatively level virgin areas in the states of Indiana, Illinois, Iowa, Nebraska, Kansas, parts of Minnesota, North and South Dakota, and Missouri. The extension of the great net work of railroads through these level, fertile, timberless lands has enabled their owners to produce all kinds of grain and live stock and lay them down in the centers of consumption in the east cheaper than the farmers in the eastern sections can afford to produce them. The reduction of railway freights has thus been to the advantage to the eastern consumer and the western producer and a great disadvantage to the eastern producer of farm products. We think there will be no difference of opinion on this point. It is not, however, the really vital point in the problem.

The most potent factor in the decline of farm lands in the manufacturing regions of the east is the surprising and unexpected; namely, the location of the farmer near the factory or the mine. When eastern farmers were voting high tariffs to foster the manufacturing industries in the hope of thus having a market at their doors, they did not foresee the result which now seems inevitable; namely, that they can drive farm population to the factory and fix a price for labor with which it is impossible for the farmer to compete. This, we believe, has done more to reduce the price of farm lands than western competition.

It seems to us a very plain proposition when stated clearly. The laborer lives in the village or city; he is paid by the day of so many hours. Whether he works eight or ten hours, the work is done, and he has the stir, the life and society of the city for relaxation. Hence, the farmer naturally prefers the factory, the railroad, the mine, to the farm, and the farm boy, unless he has an inherited instinct for country life, is apt to follow. He is more likely to enter into the higher branches and become a clerk, a bookkeeper, a salesman, or traveling man, but in any case he is taken from the farm. If he is an inventive genius, as New England people are to a great extent, he invents something that he can push for himself and thus be free from the long hours and isolation of the farm. He would not mind farming in the west where he can use machinery and, so to speak, bore with a big auger, but he does not like farming in the heavy soils and small fields among stumps and stones.

These causes have driven the more enterprising and ambitious boys from the farm and the farmer vainly tries to hire labor of a lower class to conduct his farm operations. It soon becomes unpopular in the neighborhood to be a farmer, farmers lose pride in it and thus the social element drives men away from the farm and of course depreciates the value of farm lands.

The third cause is the decline of available fertility of eastern lands, the result of the going out of the live stock business, except for dairying. This means inevitably a lack of humus in the soil because of the want of the continuous application of manure, and when the humus is gone out the available fertility is gone out, no matter how much of the real but unavailable fertility may remain. We have the authority of Mr. Whitney, Chief of the Division of Soils, United States Department of Agriculture, for the statement that these abandoned lands in New England show on chemical analysis as large an amount of real fertility as they ever have, and we believe it. The soil is simply out of physical condition because of the lack of manure, and this because it does not pay to feed cattle, and if they would feed there is no market except in the largest cities, and to be sent there profitably they must be sent by the car load. People in the farming regions of the eastern states eat Chicago beef. There are no butchers, but simply cutters; no cattle buyers because so few beef cattle are grown that it is difficult to procure a car load. As much as ten years ago we asked an old farmer in Pennsylvania why he did not sell certain dry cows. He replied: "Who would buy them?" We said: "The buyers, of course." "But," he said, 'there has not been a cattle buyer in this neighborhood for three months."

One can, therefore, readily see that where the eastern farmer has to compete with the farmer on level virgin lands with large fields in the west, with cheap long distance freights, and where he is not the influential man in the community; in other words, where the social and religious life is in the cities, and where cattle feeding is not profitable, land can not retain its price. It must continually fall until the reflex move sets in from the west, which can only be when western lands become too high, which they are likely to do in the near future.

We are speaking now only of general conditions. While the general run of farm lands have been falling in price until in a great many cases, and perhaps generally, they are not more than half as high as twenty years ago, there has been a very rapid advance in the price of such of these lands as were adapted to special styles of farming. Lands that will grow first-class tobacco, and especially under improved conditions, have advanced in value. The sandy lands of the Atlantic coast that are available for trucking have advanced in many cases five times as much as general farm lands have declined. The eastern farmer is obliged to become a specialist and do something in which his western neighbor can not beat him in the race. Land, however, will always be low the world over whenever it ceases to be fashionable to farm, or rather wherever the social drift is away from the farm instead of to it.

Two or three years ago the Maryland Experiment Station sent out one of its professors to investigate this question. He happened in our office at the same time with Mr. David Rankin, of Tarkio, Missouri. We told him here was a man who could throw more light on the subject than any man whom we knew, and asked Mr. Rankin to explain his operations. When he had finished, our eastern friend said: "What shall we eastern people do?" Mr. Rankin turned on his heel, and said: "Raise berries."

To illustrate further the social element in the thrift of farmers, we might refer to Mr. Whitney's testimony before the Industrial Commission, in which he goes on to state that in Lancaster county, Pennsylvania, lands that will grow wheat, corn, and tobacco are selling at from $125 to $250 per acre, while directly south there are two counties in Maryland that have exactly the same soil which sells at from $1 to $3 per acre in the forest and for $10 per acre cleared. These three counties were all surveyed by the government last year and the result of the survey was that the soils were as nearly as possible exactly alike.

Why this difference? Altogether a social one. A Lancaster county farmer farms his own land and lives off the farm, buying only his tea, coffee, sugar, salt, pepper, and clothing. The families are large and the boys and girls are all brought up to work on the farm. He sells nothing except tobacco and live stock. In that community enough men feed stock to enable a man to buy it by the car load and ship it to the cities. In Maryland, on the other hand, the farmer does not work the land. He would lose social standing if he did. He employs all the labor, has a superintendent, and lives in town; possibly has a tenant and gets a share of the crops. His corn is mainly fed to his work stock. His wheat is traded 'for flour. He buys his meat, his groceries and often his vegetables. The only thing he has to sell is tobacco, and the lack of live stock gives him half a crop of tobacco, whereas, his thrifty neighbor gets a full crop, sells almost everything, and buys almost nothing. This explains why lands are high even in some places in the east and sell for little or nothing in other places.

Possibly other influences are at work, but we present the above as the best explanation we can give of the seeming paradox that where lands are nearest manufacturing centers they are the lowest in price. The practical question with our readers will be: How much higher must lands advance in the west before the drift will be eastward instead of westward as it was a few years ago and northeastward as it is now?

RUT FARMING.

The Homestead.

It is human nature to get into ruts. We all do it. Ruts are simply confirmed habits, and the older the habit the harder it is to break it. We are all disposed to find fault with our neighbors for getting into ruts, the only difference being that we are in a different rut, though possibly a higher rut, ourselves. There are various kinds of ruts. A very large per cent of the farmers of the west are traveling along the soil-robber's rut. They have been following grain farming, planting corn after corn, or sowing small grain after small grain, year in and year out, and think they have made a great advancement when they alternate corn with oats or wheat. They will go on this way as thousands of other farmers have done until the soil refuses to grow paying crops, with debts accumulating and crop failures frequent, and only then will they be likely to get out of this rut.

The grower of common stocks looks at them complacently and points out the error of their ways, telling them they must get out of this rut and go to grass, save labor and maintain the fertility of the land by growing the common stock of the country, although unconscious that he is traveling in a little different rut, but still in a rut. He is of the firm conviction that the breed is in the feed, and that his stock is as good as anybody else's if he but feeds them as well, which he says he cannot afford to do. He wants stock that can endure neglect, that does not need to be pampered and babied, and maintains that all improved stock about himself, whether thoroughbred or high grade stock, is a delusion and a snare. He is bound to keep on in this line until debts accumulate, and he finds that he must either get out of this rut or get off the farm. A grade stock grower has much to say about the rut into which the grower of common stock, or, as he sneeringly calls it, "scrub stock," is traveling. He compassionates the poor fellow's want of foresight or sagacity, and urges him unceasingly to grade up, to grow stock worthy of the name, all unconscious that he, who, may be traveling in a rut, the only difference being that it is a different kind of a rut or that he is a little higher up on the hillside.   He has done wisely in growing only high grade stock, but he has been in the habit of feeding it and maturing it at a certain time, which habit when adopted, may have been the right one and productive of the best results.   Times have changed.   The market demands stock that can be matured earlier or later.   Prices of stock may have changed.   Prices of grain and the prices of lands may have changed, all of which require change in the management, which he would be able to do did he not employ the same sagacity and intelligence which formed the habit in the first place.   Not having adapted himself to the changed conditions, he can truthfully be said to be in a rut.

Nor is the breeder of improved stock always free from the charge of being in a rut.   He may have adopted lines of breeding which, for a time, worked admirably.   He may have crowded it to a point beyond which it will not work, and some change is required, possibly the introduction of new blood; possibly a change in the methods of feeding and management; possibly the introduction of a new breed.   It may be he has been the victim of one or the other crazes which affect even breeders of improved stock, and time has shown the folly of becoming a victim of these crazes. Whether a man is in a rut or not, depends upon whether he is using the best intelligence and the best information available for the conduct of his business.   The above remarks apply with equal force to almost every kind of business.   The world is full of "has beens" that were successful at a certain stage of the development of the business, but who carry into the present lines of action that which will not wear under new and improved conditions.

The only way to keep out of a rut is to be fully up with the times, not adopting all the theories and passing whims that may arise from year to year, but weighing carefully every new suggestion that is offered, first, in the light of its truth; second, in the light of its practicability, or, in the language of the apostle, "Proving all things, and holding fast to that which is good."   This is the only way to keep out of a rut.

FORMALIN—FORMALDEHYDE.

Wallaces' Farmer.

These are two more hard words of which farmers will have to learn the meaning.   We cannot help it.   Farmers will have to get the meaning of a whole lot of words fully fixed in their minds if they are to keep up with the times.

What is formaldehyde?   It is not necessary to for us to go into the chemistry of it further than to say that it is a colorless, volatile liquid about half-way between wood alcohol, or the alcohol distilled from wood, and formic acid.   Formic acid is the kind of acid that occurs naturally in ants and occurs also in nettles and is that which makes you jump when you touch them.   Formalin is a forty per cent solution of formaldehyde, so that when you ask for formalin you simply ask for formaldehyde forty per cent strong.

Why must the farmer know something about formalin? Because it will pay him. How? You ask. Well, one way is in getting rid of oat smut. We talked about that only a week or two ago, and we intend to repeat now what we suggested then and add a little more to it, for we are determined that so far as the *Wallaces' Farmer* folk are concerned, they must not grow smutty oats, at least if we can help.

We do not know how much they all lose every year by sowing smutty oats for seed; seldom less than five per cent, often twenty-five per cent. We will try to put this in a way that the farmer cannot help but see that it will pay him to get acquainted with formalin and use it. Professor Goff puts it in a better way than we have been able to do yet, when he says:

Suppose a farmer raises twenty-five acres of oats and receives a yield, without treating the seed, of forty bushels per acre, or 1,000 bushels. Now, if five per cent of the heads in this crop were destroyed by smut, his crop would have been 1,052 bushels of oats net gain, less the cost of thrashing if he had treated the seed. We will put the satisfaction of having good, clean oats with no smut in against the few cents that it would cost to thrash them and see how the account stands, if oats are worth 25 cents per bushel. It would cost him, say 60 cents for a pound of formalin, and perhaps four hours' work at 15 cents per hour; total, $1.20. He would have had 52 bushels more oats at 25 cents, or $13 less the cost of treating, or $11.80 net profit as a result of reading *Wallaces' Farmer* and taking its advice.

How to do it. Call around at your druggist's the next time you go to town and ask him if he has any formalin. If he does not have it, tell him that you and your neighbors are going to have clean oats next year and he had better buy a lot. Buy a pound of it and put it into a barrel of clean water, holding about forty-five gallons, and stir it up. Then get out your seed oats, spread them about three or four inches thick on the barn floor, take your sprinkling can and sprinkle, then stir them up until you get all the grains wet, then put on another layer and sprinkle that, then shovel them up into a pile and spread gunny sacks over them until the next day, spread them around once or twice until they are dry, then sack up until you are ready to sow. Now that is all there is to it. Had you not better pick up this $11.80 net profit for every twenty-five acres of oats you are going to sow next year?

But this is not all. You are going to plant some potatoes next year and you will have need for more formalin and you will need a stronger solution this time. If you have only a small amount of potatoes to plant, fill the barrel only one-third full of water and put in a full pound of formalin. Before you cut your potatoes, and before they are sprouted, put in as many as it will hold and have all the potatoes covered with the solution. Let them stay there for three or four hours, then take out, cut and plant. You can use this solution five or six times.

Now, be careful. Do not use the potato solution for grain smut. That is. do not put your oats in the strong solution. It is too strong for that. Do not fool with the oats solution in dealing with potatoes; it is not strong enough to do the business.

VALUE OF GALLOWAY ROBES.

Homestead.

In a recent report published by the Kansas State Board of Agriculture the above subject is discussed at some length by Mr. F. McHardy. According to Mr. McHardy the skins of the Galloways make better robes than those from the buffalo providing they are dressed to the proper thickness so that they are pliable. In the early days, this dressing process was not well understood, but great improvements have been made, and are now being made, along that line. Galloway hides are not only being used for robes, but are also manufactured into overcoats, sacques and capes, and these are dressed by a furrier who takes all the coarse hair out, making them equal to skins of the otter.

All fur-bearing animals have this coarse hair. When they go into water this laps over the fur and prevents water from penetrating to the hide. This is the same theory which explains why a Galloway will stand out all day in the rain and yet remain dry. An instance is given where a Galloway heifer stood out during a cold, wet, wintry night along with some Short-Horns. In the morning the Short-Horns were in a pitiful condition, while this heifer seemed as unconcerned about the condition of the weather as if it were June. A close examination of the Galloway heifer in this case revealed the fact that the skin was absolutely dry.

Still another instance is given of a three months old calf that remained out during one cold night on the north side of a building. The next morning this calf was found with three or four inches of snow over the back, but when disturbed proved to be as lively as a rabbit. The temperature during the night had reached twenty degrees below zero, while the wind blew at the rate of forty miles an hour. These instances are given to show the true character of the Galloway hide for robe making purposes. A hide that will protect an animal under these circumstances will surely give satisfactory service when used in the form of a robe.

AGRICULTURE THE MASTER SCIENCE.

A Hayseed in Breeders' Gazette.

"A fine display; there must be something in farming?"

"Maybe, but it is only fit for 'Hayseeds!' "

Such were the remarks that greeted my ears as I took a seat in a lunch room at one of our fall fairs. As I am somewhat of a "Hayseed" myself these comments from two city visitors put my thoughts in action. Here was food for thought. I had come to take food for the body, and I had been supplied with food for the mind. Everything in nature calls for food—the growing plant, the animal, the human, all need food, and without it all material life will shrink and perish. Is it not even so with the mind, unless supplied with its peculiar food? Was I not therefore fortunate? I had been supplied with two kinds of food, so having satisfied the needs of the body I put on my thinking cap and went forth to view again some results of the labors of "Hayseeds."

As I passed down the lines of fine cattle, through the pens of sheep and swine, and among the stands where were displayed the various products of the field, I asked, "Why should the term 'Hayseed' be applied to the men behind all this?" And the answer came, ignorance of the great science of agriculture—the "Master Science" as it has been aptly termed by one of our leaders in the great work. But after all a "hayseed" is not by any means an insignificant thing. Think of the great fields of waving grass, the huge barns packed with the fragrant hay, and some conception of the greatness of a "hayseed" may be formed. And so in passing through this great collection of animals, products of the fields and implements, one may form a high idea of the farmer's occupation.

What other occupation can offer so many attractions to the man seeking a life study? See the different lines of farming, the varied and vast fields for work and study. Take first the raising of crops. Watch how they grow; from the tiny seed that supplies the tender shoot with its first nourishment, on to the fully matured growth, with its roots and leaves or blades, the one to draw food from the earth, the other life from the air and sun. Here again opens up the study of food supply from the chemical point of view, a field of study rich enough in itself to fill a man's life. Add soil physics, methods of cultivation, and I ask again what other occupation can unfold such wealth of material for study than even this one branch of farming? Pass on to the work of stock raising and feeding; see the interesting nature of this work, the various animals, their habits and uses. Apply again the discoveries of science to the production and development of the best. Thus in every department there is ever present the opportunity for the study of nature; in every part of the farm, at your feet, by your side, all around, wherever you lift your eyes a marvel is spread before you. See the beautiful hues and shades of color in the woods these glorious autumn days. What causes this varied coloring? Let chemistry come to your aid and unfold this mystery, tell you of the different substances and elements working to these wonderful effects. Learn the cause and effect of all that surround you and the country has charms that no city can offer.

With such a field before them why should we see young men leaving the farm? It can only be from want of the true knowledge of the hidden treasures they leave behind. Doubtless our agricultural experiment stations and lecturers are doing much to dispel the darkness, also our agricultural papers are spreading knowledge broadcast over the land, and in time we may hope for a return to the farm. There is room for all that take

up this work in earnest and give their best endeavors to the study of
the great science. New fields for enterprise will open up. Yet undeveloped lands of new countries, even the older countries of Europe
and Asia, must feel the spell of new-found knowledge, and in time will
come the call for educated and capable men to show the way. Already
Australia has sounded the trumpet call for advanced agricultural education and looked to this country for men to start the work. And what
other land shall be more fitted to supply the materials than this, we may
say, the cradle of scientific farming?

Such were some of "Hayseed's" thoughts strolling through a fair
ground. As one thought suggests another, so on "*ad infinitum*" over the
ever expanding field of agricultural life. As I pass out again into the busy
city with its crowds of men rushing to and fro one may well ask, "What
is the real end of all this?" Primarily and almost entirely in most cases
the rush is after sustenance of life; and here again one's thoughts revert
to the farm, the source of all sustenance. See these long rows of cars
loaded with the products of the farm, bringing food to the teeming millions of the cities. Take them away, cut off the food supply and the
most beautiful city on earth would become an appalling spectacle of
famine and misery. With so much resting on the products of the farm,
surely agriculture is a study for the highest intellect and the noblest
calling that man can follow. As time goes on bringing year after year
new knowledge and applying other scientific means for the working
out to the full of all the opportunities in agriculture then indeed shall
it become the "Master Science."

THE MANURE SPREADER ON GRASS LANDS.

Breeders' Gazette.

To The Gazette: It may be of timely interest to the readers of the
Gazette to read the record of our attempts to build up worn-out pastures.
A few suggestions as to the treatment of pastures during the critical
early spring months of March and April may be also of value. During
the severe drouth of last summer and fall nearly all the pasture grasses
on knolls and thin soil were killed out. In spite of some advice to the
contrary our manure spreader was kept at work. Besides the daily
stable cleanings which are dumped directly from the stable door into the
spreader standing beneath a trap door, every pile of manure about the
sheds and feed lots was scattered thinly and evenly over the burned
pastures. Not a load was allowed to start out without a peck or more of
seed, gathered from loft floors or mangers, being thoroughly mixed with
the manure. A few light showers during August and later produced a
magic effect upon all these fertilized spots. During all the fall months
they remained green and were almost the only grass-producing tracts on
the farm aside from the well-shaded areas and a few acres of pasture
upon which stock had not been turned until late. The covering of grass
on this piece served to retain sufficient moisture to keep it alive.

A valuable lesson can be learned from this and every farmer knows it but fails to heed it. Do not turn the stock on pasture too early. I know of many who declared they would not pasture until May 1st, but no doubt the scarcity and high price of feed made the few green blades brought out by the recent rain and warm spell too great a temptation, for on a trip through the country last week I saw the cattle of these same men gnawing the tender grass down to the very roots. It would be wiser and cheaper to buy feed for a few more weeks, as that sparse and washy diet which they are getting is of no value to the poor beasts and the pastures will also suffer for an entire season. The rich, ankle-deep growth that would have accumulated by the first or fifteenth of May would, in addition to filling the stomachs of stock with good fat and flesh-forming food, serve to retain the moisture and keep the pastures in a healthy and productive condition all through the dry months.

As a result of our last summer's fertilizing and seed-scattering the pastures so treated are already showing a heavy growth of early grass and where last spring one green blade appeared ten are now growing, and the manure spreader is still at work. We consider it not only the most economical and satisfactory distributor of manure but an excellent broadcast seeder, sowing and covering at one operation the seed which is usually left to rot or provide a breeding place for rats, mice, vermin and disease germs. It is our theory that every inch of soil on the farm should pay its share of the taxes and produce its proportion of the profits. The manure spreader is making a realization of our theory. Another and most important step toward the attainment of the same result is to allow the soil to provide itself with a heavy covering of grass to protect its supply of moisture from the burning rays of the sun. Give your pastures a fair chance for life and they will return you a grand reward for your patience.   *S. L. Brock, Macon county, Mo.*

DIFFERENT METHODS OF FARMING FOR A SHARE OF THE CROP.

Wallaces' Farmer.

We are having so many letters asking for advice on making leases for a share of the stock, that it seems worth while to give the subject a rather full discussion. As stated heretofore, the variation in contracts for a share of the stock is almost endless, owing to the various circumstances and conditions of the farm. For example, a young farmer writes us that he is farming 114 acres of his father's land, and is in partnership on grain, stock, etc. The land is fair, but needs to be seeded down. There is seventy-five acres of farm land and the rest in lots except about twenty-three acres in blue-grass pasture. He wishes to know if it would pay to seed it all to grass and feed cattle and hogs, buying the grain; or whether it would pay to buy cows in the spring half-fat, run them on grass, fatten and ship; or to buy cows that will have calves, let the calves run with the cows during the summer and fatten and sell both.

On a farm of this kind we have no hesitation in saying that a large place should be given to dairying. We would not buy cows half-fat and finish out on grass, for the reason that the price of this kind of stock per pound is liable to be low at any season of the year; nor would we buy cows and calves and aim to fatten both calves and cows. The farm is not large enough for that kind of business, and while there might be some money made by it, we do not think it is the best way of making money on that kind of a farm. Much of course depends upon the tenant himself, and something on the kind of buildings.

A farmer on this kind of farm can keep twenty cows either dual purpose or special purpose dairy cows, according to his fancy. He can afford to keep a hand separator. These cows, if worth keeping, will furnish enough milk for twenty calves and fifty pigs. The calves can be sold in the fall of the year at from $12 to $20, depending on the market. The butter sales per cow would range from $30 to $50 per year, depending mainly on the cows and skill with which they are handled. The cattle and horses necessary to manage the farm will consume the major portion, if not all of the roughness. By using a silo and converting part of the corn crop into ensilage and some of it kept during the summer if necessary, there will be an insurance against either a dry or a wet season. By using fodder corn or peas and oats, there will be further insurance against a summer's drouth, which tells so seriously upon the production of milk during that season of the year.

The number of cattle can be increased or diminished according to the requirements of the farm and after three or four years, when the farm is brought into good condition, it will be possible to keep the calves, selling them as yearlings or two-year-olds. In southern Iowa winter wheat can form a part of the rotation and thus furnish an additional cash crop. Farming in this way, the nearness to a creamery is not an important matter. Any bright young fellow can acquire the art of making butter, for which he can have permanent customers in any of the large towns or cities.

On the majority of farms of this size, we believe this method will give better returns than any other that can be devised, except, perhaps where they are very close to large cities. There is absolutely no waste. The cow is made the center around which everything revolves. Swine growing under these conditions can be conducted with the greatest profit because half of the skim-milk is sufficient for the support of the calves, and the other half will insure thrifty, profitable pigs with the least risk of cholera, small litters and unthrift which is usually found on farms where hogs are kept in large numbers, and fed almost exclusively on corn.

This system involves work and close confinement, especially morning and evening; but if there is any system of farming that does not involve work and careful thought as a condition of success, we have never yet found it, nor have we ever head of it. Farms of this size are not adapted to beef growers. They do not permit the raising of a very large amount of corn. If the land is in corn every year, it invariably runs down. If a rotation of crops is adopted, there is not room enough to grow enough corn. Where a man keeps all his land in grass and buys his corn, using it to feed cattle, he is liable some years to feed at a loss; and in any case should be sufficiently forehanded to keep at least a part of a year's supply in the crib. This again involves shrinkage and ratage. There are many ways when it seems cheaper to buy corn than to grow it. There are many farms on which it actually is cheaper, but in the long run it always pays the farmer on any kind of decent corn land to grow a very considerable part of this crop.

Courtesy of Wallaces' Farmer.
A couple of prize winners at the Iowa State Fair, 1902.

PART VII.

IOWA SWINE BREEDERS.

ANNUAL SUMMER SESSION OF THE STATE ASSOCIA-
TION CONVENED AT THE IOWA STATE COLLEGE
FARM AT AMES, IOWA, JUNE 3, 1902.

VARIOUS PHASES OF THE SWINE BREEDING DISCUSSED.

As reported by the Twentieth Century Farmer.

The annual meeting of the Iowa Swine Breeders' association, held June 3rd at the State Agicultural college farm at Ames, while perhaps not so well attended as some previous June sessions, was one of intense interest and was the occasion for the presentation of an unusual number of papers on subjects of particular importance, bearing evidence of wide experience, deep thought and scholarly preparation. The excellence of the programme, the beauty of the farm, with its wealth of valuable information to the man of observant habit, and the cordial reception and courteous treatment at the hands of the college people, combined to make the occasion enjoyable in every particular. President Harvey Johnson of Logan, Iowa, proved a most efficient presiding officer. Secretary George S. Prine of Oskaloosa, Iowa, has proved his value by filling his office since the organization of the association. Aside from Secretary Prine, but four of the old-time members were present. These were W. Z. Swallow of Waukee, Iowa; Alonzo Baker of Colo, Iowa; D. L. Howard of Jefferson, Iowa, and J. V. Wolfe of Lincoln, Nebraska.

President Beardshear welcomed the association in a few brief and well chosen words, to which Mr. McFadden responded. President Johnson followed with his address.

ADDRESS OF PRESIDENT.

—

Harvey Johnson, Logan, Iowa.

Another year has passed and we are assembled in our annual meeting. We should be grateful that our lives have been spared during another year; that we are permitted to meet at this time and place, and that we come under such favorable conditions.

The past year brought to us unexpected conditions and results, but on the whole it was a profitable season. While there was a shortage of crops, the high price of pork stimulated the demand for our stock, and our trade proved much better than we anticipated earlier in the season. There was also a shortage in the crop of swine diseases, a shortage that is always welcomed by swine breeders. At no time during the past fifteen years do I recall a season in which our percentage of loss by disease was as small as during the past year.

Through the peculiarities of the past season careful, observing farmers and stockmen have learned lessons that will prove beneficial in coming years. But it is a characteristic of this day and age that we look at the past only long enough to recall the lessons it has taught us, and then we turn our faces toward the future and enter upon its duties with that intensity of purpose that has always been a characteristic of Americanism, and in no class of men can this be found more fully developed than in the swine breeders of our state.

We are now about to enter upon another season, and it is only natural that we should be anxious about what it has in store for each one of us individually. It was a wise precaution that closed the future to our view, and yet conditions are constantly being given that indicate what is to follow. Judging by present conditions the outlook for a good trade the coming season is most encouraging. The pig crop throughout the state is reasonably good and in good condition; pork is high and will probably continue so for some time; the prospects for a grain crop are very flattering, and if a good corn crop should be raised, next fall and winter will bring a greater demand for breeding stock than we have known for years. We stand united in the hope that this may be the result. The swine breeders of our state are a careful, conservative set of men, and are worthy of the prosperity that may come to them.

NO NEW POLICIES TO OUTLINE.

As president of our organization I have no new or radical policies mapped out for us. I fully believe in organization and realize most fully the good that is accomplished through it, but this organization can in only a very small measure affect our success or failure as individuals; that rests with us, and with us alone. There is one policy, however, that I would advocate most strongly, not so much for the older breeders, whose reputations have been established, but for the large number of young men who are now entering upon this line of work and who hope to succeed, and it is this: That as we work in our own individual circles, whether they be large or small, that all of our business relations may show forth the principles of honesty, integrity and uprightness; that these

29

principles may be so incorporated in our lives and business that all who deal with us may feel that they have dealt with a man who is a man in deed and in truth, and he who ignores these principles takes failure as a partner, although his stock may be of the very best.

I do not hesitate in saying that I know of no business in which confidence in man plays a more important part than it does in the business in which we are engaged. It is in reality our capital stock more truly than the number and quality of the hogs we may own, and he who would establish a permanent business must build on this foundation. May we in all our dealings remember the teaching of the golden rule and may we so conduct our business relations that we will bring honor to ourselves and be a credit to this organization and to the business in which we are engaged.

I am glad that our annual meeting is held at this place, a place in which every farmer and stockman of our state should have a deep interest, and ι hope that everyone of us will use this visit to the best possible advantage and that we can go back with ideas gathered from hearing and observation while here that will make us more proficient in our work. Enthusiasm, like contageous diseases, is catching, but, like all those diseases, it does not affect all alike. Some have only a light touch—it is soon over and is forgotten—while others are affected more deeply and the results can always be seen.

This institution has inspired not only individuals, but states, to higher aims and greater efforts and we swine breeders will be dull indeed if we can come here, look over this institution, understand the character and extent of the work being done, see the quality of the stock, know the standing of the men at the head of it and not go home feeling proud of the institution and filled with a greater enthusiasm for our own work.

It is not always wise to publicly proclaim that we have the best there is, and especially is this true of stockmen, but there are times and conditions when we are justified in so doing. When we have something that is universally recognized as being the best there is it does not bring contempt upon us to make a statement of that fact and it will be regarded as enthusiasm and not egotism that prompts us to do it. In this relation we want to speak, not of our stock as individuals, but of our own state of Iowa. Our swinemen as a rule are a quiet set of men, but this does not lessen the love we have for our state, nor our pride because of the position it holds among our sister states.

The enumeration of all the things in which our state stands at the head would make a long list and, while we would not forget any of them, there are a few in which we farmers and stockmen take special pride. Iowa is the leading corn state, it leads in the value of its cattle and stands second only to the state of Texas in the number of its cattle. At the last report it had almost 10,000,000 head of hogs, leading any of the other states by about 4,000,000 head, and, while we would not say it, we swinemen can think it, that some of the very best animals known to the breed can be found in this number.

No other state in the union has been able to send a James Wilson into the cabinet, no other state has an Ames Agricultural college and no other state has a Beardshear nor a Curtiss.

May we all love the business in which we are engaged, may we be proud of our state and may we never dishonor nor forsake either one

---

SWINE BREEDING AS A PROFESSION.

W. M. McFadden, West Liberty, Iowa.

To have spoken of swine breeding a few years ago as a profession would have caused something more than a smile of derision. Not so very long ago the opinion prevailed that any man could be a farmer or stock raiser and that those who had failed in other lines of work or business might be depended upon to make more or less of a success at farming. But ideas along this line have changed materially, brought about largely by the agricultural colleges of the middle west. It has been demonstrated that while it may not be quite so absolutely essential that a farmer or stock raiser have a course of instruction as is required in some of the professions, yet whatever measure of success an individual might be able to obtain in conducting a farm. the success will be made much greater if it is fortified by a proper course of instruction, now so easily obtained.

So it happens that to speak of swine breeding as a profession sounds much more appropriate than would have been the case some time ago. The necessity for the most up-to-date ideas is recognized by the hundreds of breeders who attend the various judging schools. Such meetings as this of the Iowa swine breeders are only kept alive by the recognized need for interchange of ideas as a means of posting up along the lines in "hogology."

There are two branches of the hog breeding business in which a person must be well posted in order to be successful. The first and most important is that of form. The score card has a great many sins to answer for, and because some blunders and some things that might be called by worse names have been made in the name of the score card, a great many are inclined to say that it has done more harm than good. It has become a generally admitted fact that there is a certain point in the use of the score card by a breeder beyond which it is not wise to go, but nothing that has yet been devised will so readily fix the proper type in the mind of the breeder as the score card. There are a great many breeders who do not know and never will know a really good hog when they see it. There are those breeders that you can visit year after year and note little or no improvement. They are usually a long ways from the best standard of the breed they handle and do not realize how far from the right standard they really are. This class of breeders frequently breed a herd that has in it great uniformity, but uniformly poor ones is not the best uniformity for a successful business. Unless a man can get a fixed and definite idea of what the proper standard of the breed should be, he can not make a success as a breeder. The class of breeders above referred to are those who are outside the premium awards of our good fairs and are pretty liable to be in that class who are obliged to explain "how it happened" when the premiums are passed around. A wonderful amount of misdirected energy results from the failure on the part of a large proportion of hog breeders to properly recognize the right standard of excellence. While it is not possible for us to attain our ideal, yet it is only the breeders with the proper ideal of a hog in their minds who can make a success in breeding them, so I would set down as the most important essential to success a thorough knowledge of the ideal standard of the breed, and while I am not an advocate of the score card, I believe that in no way can this knowledge be secured as readily and as correctly as by a thorough study of the score card. Some years ago we had a number of breeders who carried the score card with them constantly and set it up as a sort of god to worship. The failures they made by this course prejudiced a great many against the use of the card in any way. It is a self-evident fact that unless we have a clear idea of what we are trying to do that we can not obtain success in the hog business any more than in any other line of endeavor.

Next in importance would come the proper appreciation of the value and knowledge of pedigrees. I would suggest that the man who wishes to fill a long-felt want might write a volume on the subject: "The Pedigree, Its Uses and Abuses." Only by the diligent use of the knowledge of pedigree have the best results in breeding been obtained, and yet nothing has been attended with such disastrous results as the pedigree craze. It seems quite impossible for the average breeder to know just how far to go with the use of the pedigree. He learns to study pedigree so as to derive the information he wants in regard to what it means and to note the effect of the blood lines in crossing and to determine what might reasonably be expected from an animal after the proper study of its ancestors. Having attained some little success along this line, a breeder is almost sure to become intoxicated with the pedigree craze, and then comes the disaster, both in a financial way and in the breeding results. No man ever yet made a s ccess who bred for pedigree alone, and, on the other hand, no man has ev r made a permanent success who disregarded pedigree. A pedigree should be valuable for the purpose of showing commingly of blood which produces certain results. A well posted breeder soon learns that certain families have peculiar characteristics and he may want just those certain characteristics or he may wish equally as much to avoid them. It is unfortunate, however, that the study of pedigree frequently leads to the use of an animal simply because it is well bred. In no way is it more possible to perpetuate a certain undesirable quality than by the use of a well bred, or so-called well bred scrub. A thorough knowledge of families will enable a breeder to foresee certain results of development in an animal that is of great advantage in determining its value.

The study of form, or standard of excellence, and that of pedigree constitutes the theoretical part of swine breeding as a profession. Their importance is becoming recognized more and more, and every opportunity is being taken by the up-to-date breeder to improve himself in knowldege of them. As has been indicated, some attain a large measure of success without formal instruction along these lines, and yet there can be no question but what their success would be greater and more readily attained with such instruction. Ideas and methods have radically changed in the last few years as to the necessity for being posted in them, and it is probable that there will be still greater and still more pronounced reasons for the necessity of such knowledge for the conduct of the breeding in the future.

But underlying all these is the more practical question of feed and care. Feeders are born, not made, and if a person is not satisfied that he is a success as a feeder and as a caretaker he had better try something else. Visit a model farm and note how the litters are divided and cared for separately and watch with what regularity the feed is given. Careful attention to these matters is absolutely necessary where hogs are raised in large numbers. A few on a farm can be cared for with some degree of success without so much attention to these details, but where a farm is given over almost exclusively to hogs and that is made the main product of the farm the success or failure of the venture depends more on the manner of their care and methods of feeding than on any other feature of the business.

Swine breeding as a profession will become more and more of an exact science and many of the methods of feeding and breeding which have heretofore yilded fairly good results must soon be discarded for better ones. There seems to be some difference of opinion as to what the great American hog is. Some would have us believe that he is of a bacon type. But I am convinced that the bacon type of hogs, for this section, is a long ways in the future. It is remarkable to how near the same standard all the breeds of hogs are working today. It would seem hardly probable that such a practically unanimous opinion as is evidenced by the results sought to be secured could be entirely wrong. Our Canadian brethren are convinced that we are chasing after false gods and could make a great deal more money if we were careful to produce a little different type of hog and market it at 200 pounds weight. They point to the fact that they get over $1 per hundredweight more for hogs than we do, making allowance for the difference in freight rates, but I think the much talked of bacon demand would fade into insignificance if it was supplied at the rate of 200,000 hogs per week of this type going into the Chicago market. So I am convinced that our type and our methods as recognized by the most up-to-date breeders are the proper ones for the country in which we live and that a thorough study and improvement of them will result in the most profit and best advancement of swine growing as a profession.

JUDGING BY SCORE CARD—ITS BENEFITS.

W. J. Kennedy, Ames, Iowa.

I am pleased to have this opportunity to appear before the Iowa swine breeders on this occasion. I am glad to have this privilege of forming your acquaintance and learning your methods of breeding, feeding, etc. We can justly pride ourselves on Iowa as a state. as an agricultural state, and especially as a swine producing state.

The subject assigned to me by your worthy secretary for presentation at this time is one in which I am deeply interested. No man can be successful as a swine breeder who is not a critical student of animal form. More than 100 years ago Robert Bakewell, one of the greatest live stock improvers the world ever saw. said that it was easier to find twelve men for cabinet positions than one good judge of live stock. We are a progressive people and have made great strides along many lines, but if Bakewell were to return at the present day he would not find things very much different from what they were in his day. Has it ever occurred to you that the ability to judge live stock correctly and well is of a rarer degree if not of a higher order than that which interprets the laws of the nation? The men who pass judgment on the stock which goes to our large markets, men who are required to know one thing only, command higher salaries than the judges at the bar of justice in the highest courts of our land. This is due to the fact that there are one hundred men qualified to preside at the bar of justice for one that is qualified to be head buyer for Swift & Company or Armour & Co.

A famous artist was once asked what was the first essential to success in his work. He replied, "To see right." Just so in the judging of live stock. The man who does not see right can never be a good judge. In the judging of stock observation and judgment are the factors which determine whether or not the man is successful. The man must be a close observer in order that he may detect at a glance the desirable and the undesirable points in an animal. He must always see the animal as it is. Too many would-be good judges see things that are not there and fail to see things that are before them. Good judgment is indispensable, as in exposition judging the decisions are nearly always made by the balancing of points. Seldom it is that any animal excels all the others in every respect. Right here is where skill is required. Most men can pick a good hog over a poor one, but it takes a critical judge to select the winner in good company.

Much has been said in favor of and against the score card. Some men condemn the score card and claim that is has no place. Others idolize the score card to such an extent that it is always to be found in their hand or inside coat pocket. I am firmly convinced that the score has done a great deal for the improvement of our domestic animals. Perhaps no other factor has been so instrumental in the perfecting of our swine. That is has a place no man can very well dispute, but like all other good things, it should be kept in its proper sphere, else it will be looked upon with disfavor.

The score card is supposed to describe the ideal animal, thus every man should have the score card definitely fixed in his eye, not in his hand or his coat pocket. It teaches the man to analyze and look for the little things which are so essential to success. It emphasizes the fact that some parts are more valuable than others, as indicated by the higher score given for the same. The score card, however, as an educator, is simply a means to an end, which is the fixing of a distinct model in the mind of the user of the same. In our class of work we use the score but for a few days, as the continued use of the same makes the student too dependent. He always has the description of each and every part before him at all times. Instead of requiring him to work down his score or the amount he cuts the animal under the various heads, we require him to fill out a blank form, giving reasons for each and every step. This is soon followed up by comparison work where the score is not used, but blank forms are where the student must place the animals first, second, third and fourth and write full reasons for doing so. This work is more practical and makes the student much more independent. The score card should never be used in the judging ring, as it is not reliable enough. Different men of equal ability will mark differently on the same animal, while the same judge has been known to vary from four to six points on the same animal at different times. They may all see the same weakness, but the variation comes in the amount to cut—that is, whether half a point, a point or a point and a half, etc. We can educate people to detect defects in animal form, but it is a most difficult task to train men to score these defects the same. The first is all important, the latter is not necessary.

In concluding I must say that the score card has done a great work and should be credited with such, but it is only a means to an end and has no place in an exhibition ring.

Mr. Wolfe, in a further discussion of the subject, said the score card had done more for the hog than any other one thing, that it was introduced as a means of education, like text-books in schools. It gave an ideal or model to go by in the production of better animals. He said a long time ago he used to wonder if hogs ever equalled the pictures the artists made of them, but that he had lived long enough to see them even excel. The ideal of today is higher than that of a few years ago. It is the breeders' duty to establish a high ideal and breed to it. More definite knowledge and real benefit come from the score card than from any other source. He said the judge in the ring had no use for the score card, but he could not be a capable judge unless he had the exact principles of the score card firmly impressed on his mind. He said the card was faulty in that it did not recognize difference of sex characteristics.

HEREDITARY PRECAUTIONS.

—

D. L. Howard, Jefferson, Iowa.

Not many days ago a street fakir who appeared in our town made the statement that men "were but reproducers," and as an illustration cited a grain of wheat being placed in the ground that sprouted and reproduced itself. Of course this gentleman had a point in view, and that was to sell a panacea for all the ailments and troubles of mankind, some secret compound, the formula of which had been buried ages ago with some of the mummies in Egypt and by some accident had fallen into his hands. And as a sort of an advertisement he was letting the people have it at $1 a pint. He was a smooth talker. He accomplished what he wanted. He sold his goods and I suppose that ere long the undertakers of our city will have to take up some other occupation on account of the long lives our people will live.

I listened to this gentleman for some time because he was an interesting speaker, and while I did not agree with him in his position that man was but a reproducer in the sense only that a grain of seed reproduces, he advanced one proposition that was a proven fact, towit: That the ailments and deformities. the weaknesses and idiocies of man sometimes seemed to be the most prominent in reproduction.

I had but just received a letter from Brother Prine, with a copy of the program of this meeting, and with it the first notice that I was on the list. The subject assigned me, "Hereditary Precautions," seemed to me to be of so much importance and of so wide a range that my mind was in a sort of a mixup as to how to approach it. So while in this condition of mind the speaker just referred to attracted my attention. The statement that in the reproduction of mankind the ailments of man seemed to be the easier fruit to produce started me into the channel of thought which I now take up. The street speaker said nothing regarding the evolution of mind and matter. He did not have to in order to sell to suckers this hidden mystery of prolonged life that had been revealed to him in some way from ancient civilization.

We read that in the beginning God created the heavens, the sea and the dry land. He created the beasts of the field. the birds of the air, the fish in the sea and all creeping things; the grass that covers the earth, the trees of the forest and all verdure. And. last of all, created He man— male and female created He them. He pronounced all His works good. From this we take it that every animal and beast. bird. fish and creeping thing was a perfect one of its species. Man He created in His own image. What the lower animals must have looked like, if the theories of some evolutionists are to be believed. we know not. For if, according to Darwin, man sprang from a monkey. the beasts below him in the animal scale must have been frightful looking objects. We will, however, not quarrel with those who wish to think their first father a monkey, but will be content to believe our Adam and Eve to have been in the image of the Creator and second only to the angels themselves. We will admit, though, that there may have been a monkey Adam and Eve and some room foi an argument in its favor, for the actions of some people surely show evidence of some connection to a long-tailed daddy. But we prefer to hold to our belief of having been better created, proof of which we seem to have in the clase proximity such a large proportion of the Eve part of man now take to the angel creation.

EVOLUTION OF ANIMAL KINGDOM.

The earliest secular history we have places man but little above the beasts. In other words, an animal with a little more intelligence than some of the other species so that the evolution of the animal kingdom began only after there had been some progress in the evolution of the mind of man himself. The years have come and gone and centuries have gone by. Gradually has there been revealed to man many of the hidden mysteries of nature, created by nature's God in the beginning of time, and only brought to the mind of man at the close of the nineteenth century and the beginning of the twentieth century.

The street fakir said, "We are only reproducers. Is that all? Spurn the thought. Someone says we are born this or that—this man a born cattleman, that man a born bogman, this man a born banker, that man a born merchant. How much of this is so? What is a born hogman? Is it one whose antecedents have been hogmen for years? Or a born shepherd one whose parents for generations have been sheepmen? Nothing of the kind, for the banker's son, if raised on the hog farm and he is intelligent and industrious, can become a successful hogman, and the hogman's son, if educated in a bank and he is intelligent and industrious, can become the successful banker.

The hereditary precaution necessary here is simply natural intelligence. Environment and training does the balance. That heredity is the foundation stone upon which we must base our improvement in our animals is a proposition well established. More modern history informs us of the different breeds of animals. The horse, descending from the Arabian stock of centuries back until we have the draft horse, the road horse, the trotter, the pacer and the runner, all having been evolved by man's intelligence and care until today we have the breeding of the horse brought to a science. The draft, the road, the runner, the trotting and the pacing horse can be reproduced with just about as sure results as that a potato can be made to reproduce potatoes. Cattle and sheep have been herded and bred and cared for for centuries, and bred and cross-bred with such care that today we have the distinctive breeds of cattle and the distinctive breeds of sheep, and the respective breeds being so improved upon by the intelligence of man until today can be. seen the splendid individuals of the different types of cattle scattered all over our land. And the numerous flocks of sheep for mutton and wool scattered all over two great continents. We are told that Abram was called and that his name was changed to Abraham, and that he and his descendants were herders of cattle and flocks. They had their horses! for some of them rode in their chariots. They even had the ass, for you know that Balsam's ass gave him a piece of his mind when he was permitted to speak. But the poor hog—he was ostracised just as effectually as any poor heretic who has been excommunicated by his majesty the pope. And when the law was given the Israelite was commanded to look upon anything as unclean that was cloven at the hoof and that chewed not the cud. And that was the hog. So the hog seemed to be looked upon with disfavor by even his Creator, for we have no account of any other created thing being able to take with them into the sea a pack of the devils of the evil one and drown them, teeth and toe nail. Since that time, however, history has shown us there has been considerable of improvement in the hog. We have many different breeds. But history does not carry us back so far in the hog world as in other domestic animals. That is, the time in which man has taken an interest in the breeding of the hog is not of so long duration. But how vast has been the progress! And what has been the main essential in this improvement? Hereditary precaution. This, coupled with intelligent mating, good feed and care brings not only reproduction but an improvement in the animal reproduced. Our text would imply that it is harder to bring about improvements than it is to reproduce defects, which I believe you will not question. The mating of animals to bring certain results more often disappoints us than produces what we are seeking. Every intelligent and honest breeder of hogs is very particular in keeping his litters marked so there will be no question of its ancestry. There are but a few families in the different breeds of swine that have been of any particular value in assisting their owners in raising the standard of excellence in the breed; occasionally merit shows up unexpectedly, and from a quarter where we expected a phenomena we get just a common hog. In my opinion, if the breeders, of swine would pork one-half to two-thirds of their crop of pigs each year that is now being sold for breeding purposes, for the next ten years, the advance in the value of the hog as a reliable and scientific reproducer of increased merit would be greatly enhanced. The breeder would get more for his crop of hogs if this were done. Instead of selling pigs for breeding purposes for from $10 to $20 each, he could have $25 to $40. The trouble is, too many hogs are offered for breeding purposes. Cut down the number offered, raise the standard of those sold, sell no man a animal for breeding purposes that you do not consider a good animal, make him pay its value or leave it. The purchaser, on the other hand, whether raising for breeding purposes or pork, had better pay $50 for an animal of merit than to use a poor individual or a scrub that cost him nothing. The time would not be so long in coming then when the breeding of the hog would become as close a science as is the breeding of the horse or the beef animal. Every hog breeder knows how easy it is to reproduce the defects in the sire or dam or both. Every breeder also knows that you can take a sire and dam of almost faultless individual merits and produce a litter. He also knows that he is foolish to expect each pig in the litter an equal or improved excellence over the sire and dam. He is almost sure that a part of that litter will show defects that were prominent in some of its ancestry. It may have been some ways back also. Is it not resonable to believe that by porking the defective part of the litter and using only the individuals that are as good or better than the sire and dam that the chances of reproducing defects will be greatly reduced? There is no animal that will respond to good care any quicker than the hog. There is also no animal that will degenerate into a scrub any quicker than the hog when in the hands of the scrub feeder. So, then, gentlemen, when studying the hereditary of the animals you may expect to couple and are carefully looking to their breeding lines and individuality, do not forget that it is easier to reproduce defects than it is merit; that an animal with the right kind of ancestry is essential. This, with individuality, gives you the foundation. Then environment does the rest. The boy with intelligence can become the banker if properly cultivated, no matter if he is born of farmers. The banker's son can become the hog man, likewise. The man that watches his feed pile diminishing instead of watching his hogs eat and grow and develop will never be a success. While trying to eradicate fro mthe hog what may be a defect, do not forget that it must be done by increased care on your part and that the feed cross is a most important one in the development of excellence.

We are not accountable for our own parentage or for the environment of our birth. But we are accountable for the parentage of our domestic animals and for the surroundings that go to aid their development and we owe it to ourselves and our children that the increase in value of our domestic animals should keep pace with the rapidly improving methods of farming and all other business enterprises.

Prof. Curtiss said the character of the animal became, in a measure, the capital of the breeder. The names of some breeders add value to animals, while the reverse was also sometimes true. The difference is due to the different judgment of breeders. Pedigree is valuable, in that it gives a full history of an animal and indicates its probable characteristics. Buyers are willing to pay higher prices for animals of assured value.

Mr. Wolfe concurred in opinion with most of the statements made in the paper, but wished to still further emphasize the fact that ailments and defects are more easily reproduced than excellence. He advises a more careful culling the number of animals sold for breeding purposes. He thinks not half of the pigs raised are good enough to be reserved as breeders and that in too many cases the best pigs are used as a pry to sell the poor ones. He believes the time of better things is coming.

ARE PUBLIC SALES A BENEFIT.

William D. McTavish, Coggan, Iowa.

With a view to opening up this subject for discussion by those present I will make a few statements of my own views and observations, hoping that every member will do the same. Without any preamble I will go right to the point.

In order to be of real benefit to the breed a public sale should be a benefit to the breeder, because the breed of necessity receives its improvement at the hands of the breeder. A man who is spending his life in breeding swine, if he improves his financial condition, must do so from the proceeds of the animal sold. By the improvement in his financial condition he is the better enabled to make improvement in the breeding and care of his stock than could otherwise be accomplished. So it is safe to say that, as a general rule, what benefits the breeder will benefit the breed and *vice versa*.

This being the case, a public sale, in order to be beneficial to a breed must be the means of causing the animal to bring as much if not more net income to the breeder than could otherwise be realized. I have no patience with the idea exploited by some promoters of public sales that a breeder is doing a breed such a wonderful lot of good by scattering his choicest sale stock among buyers who do not appreciate them enough to bid more than pork prices. Animals thus obtained are usually given scrub care and afterward valued accordingly. Such a sale, with such patrons, will do any breed or breeder more harm than good. Far better sell at private sale to parties who are willing to pay what the animals are worth, as such buyers will invariably give them good care and they will develop into more valuable animals and be more highly prized by their owners in the future. I dare say such sales will ultimately do a breed the more good.

A public sale has many advantages, such as meeting and exchanging ideas with men engaged in the same occupation, men who have spent their lives in the business and are posted in every phase of it. The old breeder becomes acquainted with the new man and the class of animals he buys. The stockman and the farmer in attendance will unconsciously receive impressions regarding pure bred stock that will cause them to improve their herds, if not to turn the leaf clear over and raise nothing but pure breds. Thus the public sale, under favorable circumstances, may be a great educator and a benefit to the breed.

Some very successful breeders will sell their stocks in the other way, while others equally as prosperous, sell entirely at private sale. It is, therefore, very evident that the manner of selling is really not of so much importance as the quality of the stock offered and the kind of buyers you have.

With these slight rumblings and the heaving of the surface in the territory of the public sale region do not expect an eruption to break forth with a fury for which you wholly unprepared. This is an old crater, which in days gone by has vomited forth great quantities of steam, smoke, black mud and considerable dust, but no burning lava nor deadly gasses. Of course we all know this old crater is quite active at times and there are those who, thinking discretion the better part of valor, have shunned the region.

We will be glad to hear the experience of those, however, who have had the nerve to explore. I have not tried to cover the ground fully, because I promised the secretary when he assigned this subject to me that I would merely open the subject up for the discussion of others.

ARE LOCATIONS HEREDITARY TO DISEASE?

G. H. Moore, Kansas City, Mo.

All things are created for decay. Wherever animal or vegatable life has existed or exists today the seeds of death are there, the one warring against the other. But here is a rule without an exception. Death conquers and all flesh must bow submissive to his sway. We read from ancient mythology when a plague was visited upon the people by some imaginary god the inhabitants would scatter and flee to the hills and remain in hiding until a messenger informed them that the plague had passed and all victims had died or been killed and burned, and recently a writer and explorer commented upon the gods as well as the plagues, saying: "The plagues were malignant fevers, cholera, smallpox and death.

As the world advanced in learning, experiments and the knowledge of nature's laws a higher civilization supplanted the old or superstitious and advancement was made as rapidly as men realized that natural causes produced natural results. When plagues or fevers visited the valleys and plains those wise in the councils of their people advised the followers to flee to the hills and scatter over a large area, remaining until the disease had disappeared. The same was true in densely populated cities, demonstrating the fact that these diseases originated in the lower sections of both · country and city. This is true today in Asia, India, Australia and other places that we might mention, proving that locations are hereditary to diseases.

As this is a meeting of men engaged in the culture, developement and improvement in swine, the animal that has and always will add to the bank account of the man who handles him wisely and well, who studies every common sense method of keeping their droves in a healthy and growing condition, the question is asked: Are locations hereditary to disease

If hogs are housed in a damp, dark, dirty barn, shed or hog house there is but one answer to the question; such locations are hereditary to disease, as it is only a matter of time when disease germs will devel · in these quarters. If hogs are allowed to sleep in old straw stacks, in manure piles, grovel in continuous dust and drink from stagnant pools or ponds there is but one answer to the question, locations are hereditary to. disease. As long as man continues to house, feed, develop and fatten 300 hogs, pigs and brood sows in a thirty-acre field he will satisfy himself that this exact location is hereditary to disease, but the wise breeder and feeder of hogs is not caught in this thirty-acre trap.

I now wish to call your attention briefly to a matter which, in my opinion, should receive your careful consideration, and that is the misunderstanding that sometimes arises between you and your customers as to the health of the animal you sell and ship.

That you are sometimes imposed upon by dishonest men is doubtless true, but that there is more often a combination of ignorance and carelessness on the part of your customers there can be but little doubt.

There are doubtless men before me, who have shipped on order, a hog in the most perfect health. In the course of a few weeks a letter is received from the purchaser, saying the hog appeared to be all right when he was received, but had since died of cholera. And he would expect to have the animal replaced or receive his money back. While as a matter of fact he was not justly entitled to either, as the animal was in perfect health when shipped, the purchaser being responsible for his death, largely through lack of experience and knowledge in administering to his needs.

Much misunderstanding and many bickerings may be avoided by the exercise of care on your part in having the crates in which you ship your animals thoroughly cleaned and carefully disinfected, and when possible, similar precautions should be exercised regarding the car. In your letter notifying purchaser of shipment, it would be well to suggest that the animal be kept on half ration for ten days or two weeks, or until such time as its system becomes thoroughly harmonized to the change of food, water and environment.

Many young men are engaging yearly in this great enterprise, who lack the knowledge and experience that has been acquired by the veterans here assembled, and I would suggest to every breeder when he ships an order that printed instructions be given to every purchaser, urging the absolute necessity of thorough acclimation and conditioning the animal, and I believe by adopting this simple plan mutual confidence would soon be firmly established between purchaser and seller, and the death rate reduced to the minimum.

Experience has taught me that it is wise to consult with and follow the advice of the successful man. After you have done all this, however, there is an experience in this field which every man must purchase, and ofttimes pay the highest price.

Where lice, mange, filth, worms and indigestion exist you will find a "location hereditary to disease." Where ignorance, neglect and carelessness hold sway will be found another location which is hereditary to disease.

As this paper is addressed principally to breeders, I feel that a word to the wise is sufficient. The industrious and intelligent breeder or feeder who avoids the locations I have briefly called your attention to and avails himself of the proverbial "ounce of prevention," will certainly have his efforts crowned with success, the goal we are all striving for.

F. F. Failor of Newton, Iowa, said Mr. Moore touched a vital point in referring to shipment of breeding stock. In his experience in the sale of breeding animals he had found more trouble to result from improper care by the buyer after purchase than from all other causes. Breeders, he said, must, in order to preserve prepotency and breeding propensities, feed other than a corn ration. He must provide a growing, cooling food, such as is best adapted to a vigorous and healthy growth. The novice feeding only corn and water, impairs digestion, induces ill condition and enters complaint against the seller for that which his own ignorance or carlessness is alone responsible for. He considered it important and necessary to send with each hog sold printed instructions stating how the hog had been fed and what his later feed and care should be. Breeders might not need these instructions, but those not breeders ought to know them. Ounces of precaution are worth pounds of cure.

Mr. Wolfe thought the paper suggestive and the discussion good.

It is quite a satisfactory indication of the prevailing healthful condition of herds of the state that no questions were at any time asked concerning treatment for disease.

———

Prof. C. F. Curtiss read a highly intertaining paper on modern pork production, in the course of which he exhibited several pictures of the different breeds of hogs as they existed half a century ago. His paper is as follows:

MODERN PORK PRODUCTION.

—'

C. F. Curtiss, Ames. Iowa.

Prof. C. F. Curtiss read a highly entertaining paper on this subject. in the course of which he exhibited several pictures of the different breeds of hogs as they existed half a century ago. His paper is as follows:

The archaeologists tell us that swine have been domesticated over 4,900 years. They are now more widely distributed than any other domestic animal, inhabiting nearly every part of the globe outside of the polar circles. All modern breeds and types have doubtless originated from the wild hog of Europe, Asia and Africa. No animal under domestication undergoes changes more readily or is susceptible of more rapid modification and improvement. No domestic animal multiplies so rapidly, with the single exception of the rabbit. The possible produce from a single sow in ten generations is estimated by a French mathematician at 6,000,000, not including the male offspring. No other domestic animal is capable of converting the feed stuffs of the farm into finished meat products so economically. The ability of the hog to render the highest returns for feed consumed has given him the well deserved appellation of mortgage lifter of all nations, and civilized man's chief reliance in the arts of peace and war, for no nation can now engage in a prolonged struggle of any consequence without first carefully calculating the potentiality of American pork products in sustaining the soldier. The modern hog is capable of making from every bushel of corn consumed from twelve to fifteen pounds of pork of a superior quality. The choicer parts of this pork, finished in its best form are worth from twenty to thirty cents per pound at retail.

The hog has some well marked peculiarities. Like the thick-skinned animals, the elephant, rhinoceros and hippopatamus, to which it is allied, the hog thrives best in mild climates and has a decided preference for humid and shadowy places. No animal is more sensible to climatic changes or suffers more from exposure to the extremes of a severe climate. The senses of smell and hearing are very acute, espcially in the wild state, and the hog is always the first to detect the signs of approaching storm. This peculiarity gave rise to the saying of the ancients that the "pigs see the wind."

HOG CHANGES UNDER DOMESTICATIONS.

Under domestication the hog undergoes many changes, first among which are the enlargement of the digestive organs, giving greater capacity and depth and length of body, accompanied by diminution in the size of the tusks and the muscles of the neck and shoudler. Increased digestive capacity gives earlier maturity and propensity to fatten. It is not long since even the so-called improved breeds were very slow in maturing. In 1842 the Woburn hog which was one of the popular strains of the day, was described as a very large hog requiring from eighteen months to three years to reach maturity. Their extreme size is indicated by the following record of six hogs purchased of Dr. Martin by a Mr. Savery: The six hogs yielded 600 pounds of lard, eight barrels of pickled pork and 600 pounds of ham, one of the hogs dressing 718 pounds.

The same author speaks of the White Chinas, another improved breed, being capable of making 150 to 200 pounds at eight to twelve months. In the refinement and improvement of these early types, the Siamese breed was largely used. According to Prof. Low, an eminent authority, it is to this breed that the Berkshire and other modern breeds of England owe their improvement. The need of regeneration and improvement is apparent from an examination of illustrations said to be reproduced from life representing the old English and Berkshire breeds in domestic animals, by Low, in 1842. The Siamese was the opposite of the prevailing type of hog of that day. He was described and illustrated as a small, short-legged, compact, round-bellied, erect-eared pig, weighing at "about one year not quite sixty pounds, most perfect in form, with soft black hair, sometimes presenting a coppery tinge, all feet white and a blaze on his face." In this connection it is interesting to note that two Berkshire pigs farrowed on the college farm in separate litters, but from the same sire this season, exhibit a decided tendency toward the copper tinge color.

MOST PROFITABLE ANIMAL.

The hog's superior capabilities of converting farm feeds into meat products renders it the most profitable animal domesticated on our farms and pork production the most profitable industry of American agriculture in spite of the ravages of hog cholera. This dreaded scourge gives no evidence of yielding to any of the loudly proclaimed methods of treatment or inoculation, but to the man who gives his hogs the range of all or the greater part of a fair-sized farm and who applies vigorous measures of isolation, disinfection and eradication, the disease is largely robbed of its terrors. It is generally conceded that there is no certain specific against hog cholera, but the free and extensive use of good grass, roots and succulent feeds will do much to maintain a healthful condition that will afford a reasonable safeguard against many forms of disease. The hog in the wild state is naturally an herbivorous animal and under domestication it would be much more herbivorous in its appetite if it had a chance. The grazing characteristics of swine should by no means be allowed to become extinct, but cultivated and perpetuated as a most useful quality. It will be conducive to hardier hogs, cheaper production and better pork products.

The American people are particularly fond of pork as an article of diet and the American farmer is eminently successful as a pork producer. The two conspicuous and most successful features of American agriculture are corn and pork production. Our resources in this field, however, have scarcely begun to develop and the quality of our products has not yet approached the standard of perfection. One has but to sit at an English breakfast table and partake of the celebrated Westphalia ham or delicious Wiltshire bacon to realize that our American pork products have not yet reached the standard of excellence demanded by the most exacting foreign markets. We produce a larger supply of pork products than any other country, but it must be admitted that American pork is the cheapest product in the leading markets of the world. There is no good reason for this, even though the American farms are capable of producing pork more economically. Corn is primarily the hog feed of the greatest hog producing states and no other feed will displace it as an economical and practical ration for pork production. The inferior quality of American pork cannot be properly attributed to the corn ration, as is frequently claimed. Recent investigations by the government experiment stations and by practical feeders in the United States, Canada, Great

30

Britian and Denmark have demonstrated that corn judiciously used in combination with other feeds to the extent of one-third or one-half the ration is not necessary injurious to the quality of the bacon produced, provided other conditions are right, and we are already producing some of the finest bacon products in the United States that can be found in any country, a large part of which finds its way abroad in the pickled or mild cured form and eventually reaches the consumer in Great Britian bearing the celebrated brand of Irish cured or Wiltshire bacon. The entire trend and effort of the American swine grower for about half a century has been in the direction of producing the broadest backed, thickest, fattest hog that science, skill and human ingenuity could evolve. This process set in and continued during the greater part of its progress under conditions of high priced lard when fat backs were a prime quotation in all of our leading markets. The tendency of late has been in a different direction. Cottonseed products and other substitutes have largely displaced lard and the tendency of the consumer, both at home and abroad, is decidedly in favor of leaner meat products of all kinds.

ESSENTIALS IN HIGH CLASS PORK.

The 1,800-pound bullock and 200-pound wether have disappeared from our markets and the overfattened hog, with his extreme weight and waste, no longer wanted. Theer are also many considerations besides the proportion of fat and lean. The tendency to push our hogs to early maturity by extreme forcing and selection for the form, giving excessive obesity. has also a tendency to softer tissues and a more flabby-sided carcass than can be combined with superior quality of the finished product. Fine grain, firmness of texture and a comparatively even distribution of fat and lean are the prime essentials in high-class pork products. These are the result, first, of hereditary and, second, of judicious feeding of wholesome, flesh-forming feed products, succulent feeds, grass and abundant exercise.

It is not to be expected that our country will in the near future, if ever, take rank with Denmark and Canada in the competition for the higher grades of bacon on the foreign markets, but the demand for better pork products of our home and foreign markets has already manifested itself in such a way as to command the attention of the farmer and producer. The change will undoubtedly come as a result of the modification of the type of our present popular breeds rather than through supplanting them with foreign breeds of the bacon type, although there is already a rapidly growing demand for hogs of greater activity, vitality and vigor and more prolific breeding qualities and a firm of packers in this state has recently imported several hundred head of an English bacon type and distributed it among their customers for breeding stock. Some of these foreign breeds, however, are not altogether adapted to Iowa conditions. It has been found that the Yorkshires, except as they are carefully selected, have too light a coat to withstand the summer suns and the intensity of our winter climate with the ordinary care given on the average Iowa farm. There is no question but what these breeds produce large litters. Three Tamworth sows on the college farm.

less than a year old, farrowed and are raising thirty-four pigs this season.

A WORD FOR THE BACON HOG.

The objection that the hogs of the bacon type are not as economical producers as the more compact corn belt type, represented by our popular breeds, is not well founded. The evidence of recent investigation, supported by practical experience where accurate observations have been made, indicate quite conclusively that the modifications of the hog under domestication have been in the line of increasing his stomach contents and digestive capacity without materially increasing his digestive efficiency. Domestication has increased the length of the intestinal canal of the improved hog; this enables him to consume, digest and assimilate a larger quantity of feed, but it has not been demonstrated that his modified digestive organs do the work any more thoroughly than those of his wild ancestors. The same principle holds true in comparing the bacon and corn belt types of hogs. The result of three years investigation in determining the cost of pork production and the relative value of the finished products with various breeds of hogs at the Iowa experiment station have been published in bulletin 48 and may be summarized in the statement that there is no material difference in the cost of a pound or pork in the feed yard by the different breeds. Of course the corn belt type fattens much more readily than the other, but they are not capable of making much, if any greater gains in a given period or from a given amount of feed. The difference is due chiefly to the kind of product made from the feed rather than any variation as to the amount. The market demands have also changed in reference to the valuation put upon the different cuts; while the American breeds of swine were in process of formation and development hams were the high priced products. Today they take second rank and the higher priced cuts are the sides which produce the bacon. The width of back and development of the ham are, therefore, subordinate to the length, depth, fineness and smoothness of side and I believe that our American breeds are certain to undergo a modification governed by these conditions in the near future. This modification will also be conducive to greater vitality and more prolific breeding qualities, which the farmer or producer for the block so much desires, and the breeder of pure bred stock and the expert judges should not lose sight of the demands of the producer and the consideration of practical utility and profit."

Mr. McTavish asked if the woven wire fence, in enlarging the pasture range and affording wider feed ration, were not making it possible for our popular breeds to fill the demand for bacon hogs. Prof. Curtiss replied that pasture itself changes type, improves product and induces a condition that wards off disease.

PART VIII.

EXTRACTS FROM THE DAIRY COMMISSIONER'S REPORT FOR 1902.

H. R. Wright, Dairy Commissioner.

ADULTERATED AND RENOVATED BUTTER.

LIST OF RENOVATED BUTTER FACTORIES.

COUNTY.	LOCATION.	FIRM NAME.	POSTOFFI E ADDRESS.
1 Calhoun	Rockwell City	Andrew Wood Co.	Rockwell City.
2 Clayton...	McGregor	The J.D Bicknell Produce Co	McGregor.
3 Dallas.............	Redfield	Smith Produce Co.	Redfield.
4 Des Moines.... ..	Burlington..........	Iowa Grain & Produce Co..	Burlington.
5 Dickinson	Spirit Lake.	Stevens Cold Storage Co....	Spirit Lake.
6 Johnson....	Oxford	H C. Brown.	Oxford.
7 Lee.	Keoku t.	Iowa Pure Butter Co	Keokuk.
8 Polk	'es Moines.	E. M. Ellingson Co	Des Moines.
9 Polk	Des Moines.	Schermerhorn-Shotwell Co	Des Moines.
10 Polk	Des Moines.	MacRae Bros.	Des Moines.
11 Wayne.............	Humeston	Jas. L. Humphrey, Jr.......	Humeston.
12 Washington..	Washington...... ..	Emery & Son...............	Washington.
13 Woodbury.........	Sioux City	E. J. Hathaway & Co.	Sioux City.

The foregoing list comprises all the process or renovated butter factories in this state which had been licensed up to November 1st under the new United States law. Of these, nine were in operation during the year ending May 1, 1902. A considerable number of small plants which were in operation before the law went into effect are now closed, so far as renovated butter is concerned; and several of the plants that were obstensibly operated as creameries have been obliged to go out of the creamery business. Statistics furnished by the nine plants in operation last year, and also in operation at present, show the following totals:

```
Pounds of renovated butter made.................4,530,388
Sold for consumption in Iowa....................  991,333
Shipped outside the state.......................3,539,055
Pounds of stock purchased in Iowa...............1,469,281
Pounds of stock purchased elsewhere.............3,061,107
```

The 3,539,055 pounds of renovated butter that was shipped out of the state went to the following markets:

New York	1,715,759
Boston	700,668
New Bedford, Mass.	514,807
The west	200,500
Chicago	171,572
Baltimore	120,000
Washington, D. C.	95,000
Buffalo	90,000
Ohio	29,749
Total	3,539,055

Almost one million pounds of process butter was sold in Iowa during the year ending May 1st, 1902. Nearly or quite all of it has been sold in the larger cities, especially Des Moines, and is uniformly sold in pound bricks, and has usually been sold as creamery butter; sometimes as "gathered cream butter;" but since July 1st these bricks of renovated butter have been branded in accordance with the new law, both on the butter itself and on the parchment paper containing it, with the words, "Renovated Butter."

The new oleomargarine law, so-called is an amendment of the original act of August 2, 1886, an act which defined butter and oleomargarine and imposed a tax of two cents per pound on oleomargarine and required certain license fees from manufacturers, wholesalers and retailers of oleomargarine. The new act amended these provisions, and also made new provisions governing the manufacture and sale of adulterated butter and renovated butter; so that the law contains definitions of oleomargarine and of three kinds of dairy products, butter, adulterated butter and renovated butter. Butter is defined as follows: "For the purpose of this act, the word 'butter' shall be understood to mean the food product usually known as butter, and which is made exclusively from milk or cream, or both, with or without common salt, and with or without additional coloring matter."

Adulterated butter is defined as follows: "'Adulterated' butter is hereby defined to mean a grade of butter produced by mixing, reworking, rechurning in milk or cream, refining, or in any way producing a uniform, purified or improved product from different lots or parcels of melted or unmelted butter or butter fat, in which any acid, alkali, chemical, or any substance whatever is introduced or used for the purpose or with the effect of deodorizing or removing therefrom rancidity; or any butter or butter fat with which there is mixed any substance foreign to butter as herein defined, with intent or effect of cheapening in cost the product; or any butter in the manufacture or manipulation of which any process or material is used with intent or effect of causing the absorption of abnormal quantities of water, milk or cream."

Renovated butter is defined as follows: "'Process butter' or 'renovated butter' is hereby defined to mean butter which has been sub-

jected to any process by which it is melted, clarified or refined and made
to resemble genuine butter, always excepting 'adulterated butter' as defined by this act."

From these definitions, it will be seen that any butter which does not
contain fat other than butter fat must come under one of these three
heads. Attention is called to the fact that the definitions are entirely
separate and distinct, and that the provisions in one of them do not
necessarily apply to either of the others. Also that adulterated butter
is, in general, butter in which "an acid, alkali, chemical or any substance
whatever is used for the purpose, or with the effect of deodorizing or
removing therefrom rancidity." It is also butter, "in the manufacture or
manipulation of which any process or material is used with intent or
effect of causing the absorption of abnormal quantities of water, milk or
cream." This last provision applies to manipulated or reworked butter
only and not to butter "made exclusively from milk or cream," without
the use of chemicals and which may possibly contain a slight excess over
the standard amount of water as established by the internal revenue department in defining the expression "abnormal quantities of water." The
department regulation is as follows: "Renovated butter having sixteen
per cent or more of moisture will be held to contain abnormal quantities
of water, milk or cream, and be therefore classed as 'adulterated butter.' "
Hence, no butter maker who is not using any chemicals to make his
butter contain an excess of moisture need fear that he will be classed
as a maker of adulterated butter, even if his product has more than
sixteen per cent of moisture, since the law will not apply to him, notwithstanding the reports to the contrary which at one time appeared in
the dairy press. Neither will the butter maker who uses a preservative
other than salt in his butter be classed as the maker of adulterated butter
because of any reference to "chemicals" in the definition of adulterated
butter, and the internal revenue department has so held. These provisions of the law are so stringent and the tax of ten cents per pound
upon adulterated butter so great that no licenses for the making of
adulterated butter, or for the sale of it, have been issued, and, therefore, none is being made at present in accordance with the law. It
will, no doubt, be the case that future amendments to this will establish
a standard for water in *pure* butter, and in case this is done the standard of sixteen per cent will no doubt be adopted.

The rules and regulations in regard to renovated butter formulated
by the secretary of the treasury and the secretary of agriculture in
accordance with the provisions of the law practically restrict the definition of renovated butter to that product made by the usual process of
melting, deodorizing by agitation and by blowing air through the melted
oil, and rechurning, with the usual additions of salt and coloring matter.
The manufacturer of renovated butter must pay a license fee of $50.00
per annum; must attach to each package tax-paid stamps to the amount
of a quarter of a cent a pound on the product made. He must display
on the side or end of the building in which the business is carried on a
conspicuous sign, giving his name followed by the words "Manufacturer
of renovated butter. Factory No. ———." He must also stamp upon
each print, brick or roll, or on top of the solid body of butter, if it be

packed in a tub or firkin the words "Renovated butter." In case he puts up his butter in bricks or rolls of not less than one pound, the successive papers or wrappers in which the print or roll is contained must also bear the words "Renovated butter." The outide of the original package, whether it be a tub containing a solid mass of butter, or a box of any kind containing a number of bricks or rolls, must also bear the words "Renovated butter." The manufacturer may also use a brand, giving his own name and words or marks descriptive of the quality of his product, provided the brands do not cover up the stamps or the other marks required by the law. From these provisions, it will be seen that, except in the case of butter packed in solid mass to be divided when retailed, the butter and all of its containers, or any of them, will always show the words "Renovated butter," unless the retailer removes the print or roll from its original package, erases the word "Renovated butter" pressed upon the butter itself, and re-wraps it. If he does this, he runs counter to the general provisions of internal revenue laws and the special rule of the secretaries of the treasury and agriculture, which provides that the butter must be retained in its "original package bearing the tax stamp and other prescribed marks until it is delivered to the consumer or purchaser in retail trade." The renovated butter, which may be packed in solid mass, must also be kept in its original package; but in this form might be easily sold to the purchaser for creamery butter. But when renovated butter is sold in bricks and in accordance with all the provisions of the law, the purchaser will invariably be informed as to the product he is buying. The difference in price between renovated butter and creamery butter is so small that scarcely any retailer would take the risk of violating the internal revenue law for the sake of the small additional profit he might make by so doing. The creamery man and the maker of dairy butter as well will find it to his interest to encourage the retail sale of butter in bricks and prints, instead of in other forms, so that the purchaser may know at any rate that they are not receiving renovated butter and paying for creamery butter.

Before this new law went into effect no retailer of butter in Iowa ever sold any renovated butter. He invariably sold creamery butter or dairy bricks, or butter with some other euphonious title. Even now some retailers attempt to sell renovated butter for creamery butter. These evident intentions to defraud by selling renovated butter in place of a better product, and at the price of a better product, can not always be excused on the theory of the ignorance of the retailer. Formerly he may himself have been deceived by the manufacturer who perhaps was running a creamery; but under the present United States law, he knows invariably what he is buying, and hence, has no possible excuse for attempted deception of his patrons. The new law has depressed the retail price of renovated butter in the city of Des Moines about four cents per pound, and probably has depressed the wholesale price to an equal extent, and naturally these decreases in price are visited upon the original makers of the butter from which the renovated butter has been made. It should be noted, however, that this difference in price of packing stock has been caused by the fact that this renovated butter must now be retailed for what it is and must sell on its own merits, and not on the merit of a better product, namely, creamery butter; so that, it is now selling for exactly what it is worth in comparison with creamery butter, whereas, under former conditions, it was fraudulently sold as creamery butter and for a creamery butter price. At any rate, these losses to the makers of this packing stock affects Iowa farmers to a very small degree, for the reason that only one and a half million pounds of the renovated butter made in Iowa originated in this state. Nearly seventy per cent of the renovated butter stock was purchased outside of Iowa. Practically, the farmer who makes the butter which eventually goes into the renovating factory loses the amount of the tax upon it, which is a quarter of a cent a pound, and any other difference in price of packing stock caused by the new law is accounted for by the fact that it eliminates the illegitimate profits that were obtained by selling the renovated butter for creamery butter; and this small loss may be easily changed into a considerable profit if, instead of making a cheap grade of butter, which must be renovated in order to be palatable, the farmers will patronize the creamery that is able to make the best and highest priced kind of butter.

SHOWING AVERAGE MONTHLY PRICE OF FANCY WESTERN CREAMERY BUTTER IN NEW YORK MARKET.

MONTH.	Twelve months ending Nov. 1, 1895.	Twelve months ending Nov. 1, 1896.	Twelve months ending Nov. 1, 1897.	Twelve months ending Nov. 1, 1898.	Twelve months ending Nov. 1, 1899.	Twelve months ending Nov. 1, 1900.	Twelve months ending Nov. 1, 1901.	Twelve months ending Nov. 1, 1902.
November.	$ 2510	$ .2330	$ .2112	$ .2325	$ 2337	$ .2600	$ .2487	$ .2412
December	.2440	.2500	.2250	.2290	.2160	.2720	.2540	.2510
January	.2519	.2266	.1900	.2040	.1975	.2650	.2262	.2425
February	.2394	.2000	.2050	.2042	.2100	.2500	.2250	.2362
March	.2670	.2185	.1900	.1937	.2075	.2550	.2212	.2340
April	.2000	.1650	.1880	.1980	.1962	.1960	.2099	.2825
May	.1785	.1572	.1530	.1580	.1790	.2012	.1910	.2275
June.	.1794	.1550	.1500	.1687	.1881	.1950	.1925	.2195
July	.1770	.1505	.1500	.1687	.1835	.1960	.1980	.2131
August	.1980	.1571	.1675	.1840	.2000	.2100	.2050	.1999
September	.2125	.1600	.1930	.2025	.2262	.2150	.2110	.2170
October	.2294	.1850	.2290	.2235	.2400	.2190	.2200	.2362
Av. val. per lb. for each yr.	$ .2190	$ .1882	$ .1885	$ 1971	$ .2065	$ .2278	$ 2165	$ .2416

The following shows the totals of butter shipped to the various markets of tne United States as reported by the creameries of the state. Not all the creameries reported the destination of butter shipments:

DESTINATION.	1901.		1902.	
	PER CENT.	POUNDS SHIPPED.	PER CENT.	POUNDS SHIPPED.
New York	67.4	35,703,374	70.8	38,264,280
Chicago	10.6	5,655,201	8.9	4,792,030
Philadelphia	3.5	1,855,910	3.5	1,929,308
Boston	5.4	2,899,063	3.3	1,824,050
New Orleans	3.1	1,604,978	3.1	1,696,606
Pacific coast	2.0	1,078,426	1.8	1,001,658
Illinois	.3	152,246	1.5	805,379
St. Louis	1.6	848,388	1.4	760,306
Cleveland	.7	405,049	.9	458.522
Buffalo	.5	246,452	.8	441,689
Baltimore			.5	269,345
Elgin	1.5	804,447	.25	138,559
Miscellaneous		1,617,252		1,430,615
Total		52,925.726		53,899,076

Iowa 1902

Farm Separator

Total number Farm Separator 8323

19 Farm Separator Creamerie.

LYON	8
OSCEOLA	38
DICKINSON	
EMMET	62
KOSSUTH	111
WINNEBAGO	33
WORTH	160
MITCHELL	394
HOWARD	284
WINNESHIEK	292
ALLAMAKEE	279
SIOUX	154
O'BRIEN	31
CLAY	28
PALO ALTO	25
HANCOCK	
CERRO GORDO	108
FLOYD	355
CHICKASAW	585
FAYETTE	6
CLAYTON	523
PLYMOUTH	47
CHEROKEE	2
BUENA VISTA	152
POCAHONTAS	409
HUMBOLDT	150
WRIGHT	373
FRANKLIN	102
BUTLER	33
BREMER	2
BUCHANAN	223
DELAWARE	209
DUBUQUE	2
WOODBURY	112
IDA	56
SAC	70
CALHOUN	44
WEBSTER	132
HAMILTON	27
HARDIN	126
GRUNDY	107
TAMA	10
BENTON	5
LINN	3
JONES	35
JACKSON	24
CLINTON	28
CEDAR	31
SCOTT	58
MUSCATINE	7
MONONA	
CRAWFORD	598
CARROLL	259
GREENE	
BOONE	
STORY	23
MARSHALL	148
HARRISON	65
SHELBY	218
AUDUBON	1
GUTHRIE	22
DALLAS	2
POLK	2
JASPER	3
POWESHIEK	30
IOWA	123
JOHNSON	72
POTTAWATTAMIE	460
CASS	5
ADAIR	34
MADISON	1
WARREN	1
MARION	5
MAHASKA	23
KEOKUK	16
WASHINGTON	20
JEFFERSON	
HENRY	20
LOUISA	
DES MOINES	
LEE	3
MILLS	6
MONTGOMERY	12
ADAMS	5
UNION	9
CLARKE	9
LUCAS	
MONROE	1
WAPELLO	1
VAN BUREN	3
FREMONT	12
PAGE	
TAYLOR	209
RINGGOLD	2
DECATUR	
WAYNE	1
APPANOOSE	1
DAVIS	1

FARM SEPARATORS.

There are eighty-three creameries of the state which receive cream from twenty-five or more farm separators, ranging in number from twenty-five up to 688 for a single creamery. These creameries have 15,500 patrons, of whom 6,250 have farm separators. The total number of creamery patrons of the state is 81,532, and the number of farm separators, so far as reported. is 8,323, and there are 334 creameries, more than two-fifths of the total number of creameries, which have one or more farm separator patrons. The total number of creamery patrons as given above is obtained by multiplying the average number of patrons of the creameries reported, by the total number of the creameries, and hence, is approximately correct. The number of separators is not so estimated, but it is the real number of farm separators actually reported by those creameries that make a report at all. Hence, the proportion of farm separator patrons may be a trifle higher than is shown by these figures. The number of farm separators is 10.2 per cent of the creamery patrons of the state. There are nineteen plants in the state that receive only farm separator cream.

There has been a great deal of discussion of the merits or demerits of the farm separator system, and some of the most extreme views advanced have been by men who knew nothing of the system and its results except the knowledge they may have gained from observation. Some of the views have been correct. and others have been erroneous. With the hope of getting together the ideas of men who have actually had experience of making butter from farm separator cream in the creameries of Iowa, the following blank was sent out to the butter makers of the state that had reported more than twenty-five separators among their patrons, and the tables following have been compiled from reports received from these creameries.

1. County in which your creamery is located..........................
2. Name of creamery...
3. Whole number of patrons........Number sending cream from hand separators...................Number sending milk............
4. What difference in price, if any, do you make between butter fat in milk and in cream?...
5. Have any of your patrons abandoned the use of the separator after using it a reasonable time? ....How many? ....And for what reason?................. ....
6. Is the use of the hand separator in your vicinity increasing?.........
7. Is the quality of the butter made at your creamery poorer on account of the hand separator cream you receive?......................
8. Have you had any complaint of the quality of the butter by your commission man? ....
9. Do your cream patrons receive more net returns for their butter fat than the whole milk patrons of your creamery or of neighboring creameries?.......... ....
10. Do you consider the hand separator system a satisfactory one?......

11. Do your patrons take better care of their cream than they did when they first began to use the separator? ....

12 The dairy commisioner will be glad to know your views on the hand separator system as fully as you may desire to write them.

The following tables are the answers received from three classes of creameries: First, from those receiving hand separator cream and whole milk; second, from those receiving hand separator cream and gravity cream and no milk; third, from creameries receiving hand separator cream only. These tables represent forty-two creameries of the state having 6,766 patrons, of whom 3,728 send cream from farm separators.

REPORTS FROM CREAMERIES RECEIVING HAND SEPARATOR CREAM AND WHOLE MILK.

Whole number of patrons.	Number sending cream from hand separators.	Number sending milk.	What difference in price, if any, do you make between butter fat in milk and in cream?	Have any of your patrons abandoned the use of the separator after using it a reasonable time?	Is the use of the hand separator in your vicinity increasing?	Is the quality of the butter made at your creamery poorer on account of the hand separator cream you receive?	Have you had any complaint of the quality of the butter by your commission man?	Do your cream patrons receive more net returns for their butter fat than the whole milk patrons of your creamery or of neighboring creameries?	Do you consider the hand separator system a satisfactory one?	Do your patrons take better care of their cream than they did when they first began to use the separator?
120	42	78	None..	6	....	Yes	No	No	Yes...	No.
360	160	200	1cmore	8	Yes ..	No	No	Yes.....	Yes...	Yes.
69	33	36	None.	No ..	No ..	Yes.....	Yes.....	No ....-	Yes...	Yes.
115	80	35	None..	No	No ...	....	Yes.	No ..	....	Yes.
75	26	49	None	5	No ...	Yes ..	Once .	No	No	Yes.
138	25	113	None..	No	Yes....	No ..	No .	Yes......	Yes...	Yes.
172	54	118	None..	2	Yes	No	No ...	No	No ...	Yes.
165	29	136	None..	2	Yes....	Yes....	Yes.....	No	Yes ..	No.
230	90	140	None..	No	Yes....	Yes....	No	No	No ...	Yes.
45	28	17	None..	No ..	Yes....	Yes....	No	Yes	Yes .	Yes.
160	30	130	None..	5	Yes....	Yes....	Yes.....	No	No ...	Yes
193	63	130	None	No	Yes ...	....	No	Yes	No ...	Yes.
220	150	70	None .	No	Yes ..	Yes ..	Once ..	No	Yes...	No.
96	41	55	None	No	Yes..	No	No	Yes.....	No ...	Yes.
70	35	35	None	7	No	Yes......	Yes.....	No	No ...	No.
120	25	95	None..	No	No ..	No ..	No	No	No ...	No.
210	25	185	None..	9	No	No ..	No	No	No ...	Yes.
278	38	240	None..	No .	No	No	No	No	Yes...	Yes.
100	70	30	None	No ..	Yes..	No ..	No	Yes......	Yes .	No.
281	264	17	2cmore	No .	Yes....	No	No	Yes.....	Yes .	Yes.
80	47	33	None..	No	Yes....	Yes..	Yes.....	Yes.....	Yes...	Yes.
3,297	1,355	1,942	....		....		.....	....	..	

REPORTS FROM CREAMERIES RECEIVING HAND SEPARATOR CREAM AND GRAVITY CREAM BUT NO MILK.

90	26	.....	....	Yes	Yes.. ..	Yes......	None......	Yes...	No.
15	20	.....	....	No	Yes ..	No	No	Yes........	Yes...	Yes.
150	20	.....	....	No	Yes....	No	No	Yes	Yes...	Yes.
287	30	.....	....	Yes	No	No	No ..	Yes	Yes...	Yes.
110	60	.....	.....	No	Yes	No	No	Yes........	Yes...	Yes.
70	15	.....	....	No	No ...No ...	Yes.....	....	No ...	No.
77	50	.....	... ...	No	Yes ...	No	o	Yes.... .	Yes...	Yes.
150	20	.....	... ...	No .	Yes ..	No ..	No	....	Yes .	Yes.
200	32	.....	..	No	Yes....	No	Yes.....	Yes	No ...	
120	60	.....	.....	No ..	Yes .	Yes........	Yes.....	No	No .	No.
162	30	...	.. ..	No	Yes .	No	No	Yes........	Yes ..	Yes.
1,459	363		....	....	....		...		....	....

REPORTS FROM CREAMERIES RECEIVING HAND SEPARATOR CREAM ONLY.

Whole number of patrons.	Number sending cream from hand separators.	Number sending milk.	What difference in price, if any, do you make between butter fat in milk and in cream?	Have any of your patrons abandoned the use of the separator after using it a reasonable time?	Is the use of the hand separator in your vicinity increasing?	Is the quality of the butter made at your creamery poorer on account of the hand separator cream you receive?	Have you had any complaint of the quality of the butter by your commission man?	Do your cream patrons receive more net return's for their butter fat than the whole milk patrons of your creamery or of neighboring creameries?	Do you consider the hand separator system a satisfactory one?	Do your patrons take better care of their cream than they did when they first began to use the separator?
80	80	....	....	No	Yes...	Yes........	No	Ye..	Yes	
130	130		....	No	Yes....	No	No	Yes..	Yes ...	Yes.
57	57	....	....	No	Yes ..	Yes	Yes......	No	No	No.
200	200		.. ....	No	Yes ..	No ..	Yes	Yes	Ye.. ..	Yes.
688	688	....	.. ..	No	Yes ..	No ..	No	Yes........	Yes....	Yes.
80	80		....	No	Yes....	Yes..	No	Yes........	Yes	Yes.
250	250	....	....	No	Yes ..	No ..	No	Yes........	Yes....	Yes.
25	25	....	.. ..	No	Yes...	No	No	Yes	Yes .	Yes.
300	300	....	....	No	Yes...	No	No	Yes..	Yes....	Yes.
200	200	..	....	No	Yes	Yes......	Yes	No	....	No.
2,010	2,010	.....	....	.....,..	....	....	.....	....	....	
6,706	3,728	1,942	Grand totals.							

The first table shows very conclusively that scarcely any creameries are paying more for butter fat in cream than for butter fat in milk. Theoretically, the cream costs less money to make into butter than the milk, but the difference in quality more than compensates for this difference in the cost of manufacture, so that the usual practice is to receive the cream and milk by weight and test and pay for them on the same basis.

From time to time reports have been circulated that in different localities the hand separator was being discarded by its former users. The reports given here in answer to the question: "Have any of your patrons abandoned the use of the separator after using it a reasonable time?" do not bear out the thought that the users of hand separators are generally disappointed in them. The hand separator in Iowa is no longer an experiment, and if the owners of hand separators in general were not reasonably satisfied with the use of the separator, much larger numbers of the machines would have long since been discarded. Such not being the case, it would seem very certain that the hand separator patrons of the creameries reported in the foregoing tables are well satisfied with the use of the separator and prefer the hand separator system to the whole milk system. If this be true, then the increase in the number of hand separator patrons in Iowa in the future will be equal to the increase in the hand separators during the last several years because the satisfied patron is the best possible advertising medium for the sale of other machines. That this is true is further shown by the almost uniform answer that the use of the hand separator is now increasing. The number of hand separators reported in 1898 was 904; in 1899, 1,762; in 1900, 3,332; in 1901, 5,231; in 1902, 8,323, so that the increase for the last year has been nearly sixty per cent, a result which could not have been achieved if former users of hand separators were dissatisfied with them and were discarding them, as alleged.

The ideas of the creameryman in regard to the hand separator system are not quite the same as those of his patron. The question in regard to the quality of butter brings forth answers which seem to indicate very clearly a majority opinion that butter makers have found themselves unable to make from hand separator cream a quality of butter equal to that which they are able to make from whole milk. However, most of the butter makers who confess to making a poor quality of butter from hand separator cream assert that they are still getting a "half cent above" and a uniform score of extras or better on the market to which they ship, and that it is only occasionally, usually during the warmest weather, that their butter is off flavor by reason of their hand separator cream. They further assert that complaints of the quality of the butter by the commission man are very rare, and yet, they freely admit that the butter is not so good as it ought to be. Several of the larger hand separator creameries are selling their butter on a contract which requires them to produce extras, and a number of the creameries of the state are making an excellent quality of butter from hand separator cream, but the majority of creameries receiving hand separator cream are not making so good a quality of butter as they did under the whole milk system. A good quality of butter can be made from hand separator cream, but most butter makers are unable to accomplish this result. This is the difference between theory and fact, and the small quantity of first-class butter made from hand separator cream proves only that the theory is correct as a theory, while the larger quantities of lower grade butter made from hand separator cream prove that the theory is not easy to put into practice.

If the creamery patron could be induced or compelled to take better care of his cream and deliver it to the creamery every day, the butter maker would be able to make from it a first-class product, but in the majority of cases it is seemingly impossible to get the cream to the creamery in a reasonably good condition.

Naturally the operators of hand separator creameries think that their patrons receive more net returns for their butter fat than the patrons of the whole milk creameries receive, and even some of the butter makers in the whole milk creameries also assert this fact. They add as an explanation the statement that they pay the same price per pound for their butter fat to their milk and cream patrons and that the cream patron has less expense in getting his product to the factory. They assert that it costs two and one-half cents per pound of butter fat to haul the whole milk to the creamery, while the cost per pound of butter fat for hauling cream is about one cent, and that this is the only saving that the hand separator patron makes. Some of them suggest, on the other hand, that there are losses in the skimmed milk from the farm separator which more than equals the difference in the cost of hauling. All of the butter makers, however, who express an opinion on this point, suggest that the skimmed milk from the farm separator has more value than the skimmed milk from the creamery. Generally speaking, this must be true, because the skimmed milk from the farm separator is fed usually before it has time to sour or become contaminated, while the skimmed milk from the creamery is from twelve to twenty-four hours old. This fact is one of the chief reasons why the owners and users of farm separators are so uniformly satisfied with their machines, notwithstanding the allegations of losses of butter fat in the skimmed milk and of losses at the creamery because of poorer quality of butter made. The fact that the farmer reckons the value of his skimmed milk more carefully than he did several years ago is one of the good signs in the present dairy situation. Another is that nearly all the butter makers report that their patrons take better care of their cream than they did when they first began to use a separator.

There seems to be no question but that the hand separator has come to stay. The average number of cows per patron for the state is about seven, and a moment's thought will show that the number of creamery patrons who have a number of cows sufficiently large to warrant the expense of a hand separator is very much less than the total number of creamery patrons; hence, the number of farm separators now in use, which is about ten per cent of all the creamery patrons, is probably twenty per cent, possibly thirty per cent, of the creamery patrons of Iowa who have twelve or more cows. The rapid increase in the number of farm separator creameries is also an indication of the faith in the system which the builders of these creameries have. Considerable sums of money have been invested in central plants, to which it is expected the hand separator cream and other cream will be shipped by rail, and the success such an enterprise depends upon the continuance of the hand separator system. Certainly these investments would not have been made unless the investors are reasonably sure that their system will continue. Despite all reports to the contrary, there is no locality in the state where any large number of farm separators have been abandoned; and on the other hand, there is no locality in this state where any reasonable number of separators have ever been owned and operated in which the separator system is not increasing with great rapidity. It is also true that manufacturers of hand separators are enlarging their plants and making every effort to produce enough separators to fill their orders. All of these facts indicate a future increase in the number of hand separators used in Iowa corresponding with the respective increases for the last four years. It is, therefore, a waste of energy to spend our time only in condemning the hand separator system and not making proper efforts toward educating the users of the separator system so that they shall send to the creamery a proper product. The butter maker is equally to blame with the farmer when he receives cream that is too old, or that has been contaminated by a filthy separator, or by being kept under improper conditions. For business reasons he may not be able to refuse outright to accept such cream, but he ought to insist that the cream be better in the future, and he ought to point out to the farmer the way to make it better. The hand separator system will certainly continue, and it is folly not to make every effort to improve the quality of the cream brought to the creamery, and consequently the quality of the butter made from the cream. It is certain that the hand separator system has a great many faults. It is equally certain that its advantages appeal to the farmer much more than its disadvantages, and this being the case, the farmers will continue to buy and use hand separators and the butter makers and creamery operators will be compelled to make the best of the situation; and the best of the situation will not be obtained by attempting to induce the farmers to discard the separators.

A number of butter makers complain that the agents for hand separators have been asserting that their particular machine does not need washing more than once a week. The dairy commissioner will be very glad to assist in combating this statement wherever it is made. The laws of this state require that the patron shall not send to the creamery "any unclean, impure, unhealthy milk or cream" (section 4989), and certainly cream from a separator that is not washed after each time it is used, could not, by any stretch of the imagination, be called either clean, or pure, or healthy. The dairy commissioner does not believe that any manufacturer of separators desires to have his agents use this kind of an argument in order to sell the machines, and if creamerymen will report such cases to the dairy commissioner's office, the matter will be taken up with the employers of these agents with the belief that the offending agent will be better controlled by his employer thereafter. Another fault of the hand separator system, which ought to be easily remedied, is the fact that most of the hand separator cream is not so rich as it should be. The reports made to this office indicate that hand separator cream ranges all the way from twelve per cent up. The butter maker should insist that the hand separator cream which comes to him should test above thirty-five per cent. There will be no disadvantage in this to the farmer, because his machine will skim as closely when skimming a heavy cream as it will when skimming a lighter cream. He will also save in transportation and have more of his product left at home. The butter maker will have an advantage with the heavier cream, for the reason, that the acid in the cream is found in the milk serum and not in the butter fat; hence, there will be less of an "undesirable starter" in a forty per cent cream than in a twenty per cent cream, and he will be able to dilute the heavier cream with his own better starter and the result will be a better grade of butter.

The butter maker should insist that the farmer wash his separator after each time it is used, because otherwise the cream will become inoculated with bacteria from the slime which is found in every separator.

The butter maker should insist, where it is at all possible, that the cream be delivered to the factory every day, for the reason that under the best possible farm conditions, the cream necessarily deteriorates in quality from the time it is separated from the milk.

The butter maker should insist that the farmer skim thirty-five or forty per cent cream, for the reason that he will be able to use his prepared starter to the best advantage.

The farmer should then insist that the butter maker make an accurate test of his cream and that he make a quality of butter which will bring the highest quotations.

CHEESE MAKING IN IOWA.

The number of cheese factories in Iowa has never been very large, nor the amount of cheese made enough to make a beginning toward supplying the demands of our own people. The number of cheese factories as shown by the dairy commissioners' reports are as follows:

1894, 64; 1895, 81; 1896, 71; 1897, 76; 1898, 67; 1899, 69; 1900, 73; 1901, 59; 1902. 59.

In 1894 there were 780 creameries and skim stations, which made 54,572,902 pounds of butter, an average of 70,000 pounds. In 1902, there are 920 creameries and skim stations, which made 77,885,696 pounds of butter, an average of 84,000 pounds of butter. From these figures, it will be seen that the number of creameries has increased one-sixth and their butter product has increased nearly one-half. and yet, the number of cheese factories of the state has not shown any perceptible increase during these eight years.

A study of the following table will in some degree make plain the reasons why butter making and creamery operation has increased much more rapidly than cheese making. The average amount of butter made by the creamery from each cow is 135 pounds, which has a value of about $27.00. The value of the skimmed milk from each cow is variously estimated at from $3.00 to $5.00 so that the total value of the product of the cow in the form of butter is not far from $30.00.

The average number of pounds of cheese, per cow, as shown by the following table. is only 200 pounds, and has a value at ten cents a pound of $20.00. The by-product, whey, can not exceed in value a dollar, so that the total value of the product of the cow, when made into cheese, under existing Iowa conditions, in existing Iowa cheese factories. is $21.00.

The cheese factories report that the expense of cheese making varies from one cent a pound to one and four-tenths cents. It takes approximately ten pounds of milk to make a pound of cheese and twenty-three pounds of milk to make a pound of butter. The cost of making a pound of butter is about 2.25 cents. From this, it will be seen that the expense of making milk into butter is practically the same as the expense of making cheese. The expense of hauling the milk will be the same in either case, so that under existing conditions. the income from the cow whose product is sent to the creamery is about fifty per cent more than the income from the cow whose milk is sent to the cheese factory.

There are about a dozen cheese factories in the state that are operated on a scale sufficiently large to make them profitable, and they are making a product that will compare favorably with the cheese from other states. These factories, without exception, were established, either before cream.

eries became so general, or in localities where conditions are much different from the average farm conditions in Iowa.

The plain fact of the matter is that cheese factories are not now, and never have been, popular in Iowa, for the reason that the operation of the cheese factory does not fit into the usual farmer's plans of raising hogs and cattle. If our farms were forty or eighty acres, instead of 160 or more acres, the plan of our agricultural operations would have to be different from what it is, and the making of cheese would no doubt be a popular and profitable industry. The man who sends his milk to a creamery has left in his skimmed milk the very thing that he needs to raise the pigs and the calves, to which he will later feed his corn and grass and hay. The man who sends his milk to a cheese factory has no such valuable by-product, and is almost as restricted in the raising of pigs and calves as the man who milks no cows at all, with the additional disadvantage that he must raise his claves by hand, while the man who milks no cows at all can let his calves run with the cows. Cheese factories in Iowa might be made profitable if they could secure the patronage of a reasonable number of cows, but experience shows that in most cases they cannot secure such patronage, and that the creameries can secure the patronage, and hence, in the competition, the creamery has the advantage over the cheese factory.

	Number reporting.	Value of factory.	Aggregate number of months run.	Pounds of milk received.	Pounds of cheese made.	Number of patrons.	Number of cows.
Adams	1	$ 1,000	5	144,000	1 ,	20	100
Appanoose.................	3	1,700	24	588,426	6 ,	55	255
Benton.....................	2	7,000	24	2,413,829	192,	110	1,100
Black Hawk...	2	....	24	2,947,697	290,	229	......
Carroll.....................	1	2,000	8	318,583		48	....
Cerro Gordo.	2	2,200	20	1,109,637	1 ,	50	360
Crawford	1	1,200	11	500,000	,	18	200
Clarke........	1	1,250	10	600,000		33	......
Decatur.....................	1	500	3	13,000	28,680	10	40
Floyd.........................	1	5,000	12	850,000	,680	40	
Greene.	1	5,000	12	2,739,000	2 ,710	94	1,200
Guthrie	1	2,000	9	900,000	90,000	50	300
Hardin.	1	2,000	12	750,000	75,000	54	250
Howard	2	2,500	22	1,146,2.8	112,620	85	500
Humboldt	1	1,000	8	335,000	33,000	....	100
Jefferson...................	3	3,700	33	1,738,750	166,375	162	500
Johnson	1	3,000	9	176,000	15,000	......	......
Keokuk....	1	2,500	2	11,000	1,100	10	......
Marshall	1	4,000	5	1,210,000	124,066	128	800
Monroe......................	3	750	30	262,980	27,000	15	100
Muscatine..................	1	1,500	12	350,000	35,000	25	150
Page......	1	1,600	12	980,000	93,000	80	500
Poweshiek.	2	4,000	24	1,669,000	154,912	55	600
Story	1	4,000	12	1,061,866	10,600	120	....
Taylor	3	3,500	36	1,950,000	182,000	160	1,300
Washington	2	3,500	20	1,503,617	141,616	0	525
Wayne........	4	5,400	16	658,374	64,634	200	1,140
Totals	44	....	415	26,926,967	2,499,960	1,931	10,020
Averages.	.....	1,708	9.2	641,118	59,522	46	286

Average number of pounds of cheese per cow, 200. Fifty-nine cheese factories must make 3,511,798 pounds of cheese worth approximately $350,000.

31

NET BUTTER SHIPMENTS BY COUNTIES AND RANK—AREA OF COUNTIES.

Showing pounds of butter shipped per square mile and rank of counties; also total net butter shipments for the state and net pounds per square mile, for the year ending September 30, 1902.

COUNTIES.	Total net shipments of butter for the year.	Rank by total lbs. shipped.	Area of square miles in counties.	Pounds per square mile.	Rank by lbs. per square mile.
The state....................................	72,714,584	......	56,025	....	...
Adair.....	710,983	36	576	1,234	38
Adams....................................	373,301	60	432	864	50
Allamakee............................	1,096,047	21	658	1,666	26
Appanoose..............................	59,419	86	516	115	86
Audubon..................................	915,602	28	443	2,066	18
Benton	504,081	54	720	700	54
Black Hawk.	1,552,136	14	576	2,712	11
Boone............................	93,313	80	576	162	81
Bremer	2,417,627	5	432	5,596	2
Buchanan	2,680,811	3	576	4,654	3
Buena Vista............................	862,506	30	576	1,497	30
Butler	1,947,837	10	576	3,381	7
Calhoun	1,190,589	29	576	2,067	17
Carroll	1,003.265	25	576	1,741	22
Cass	310,992	65	576	539	62
Cedar....................................	372 285	61	576	646	56
Cerro Gordo............................	662,009	39	576	1,149	40
Cherokee..................................	108,568	78	576	188	....
Chickasaw............................	2,281,208	6	504	452	62
Clarke.........	14,380	93	432	33	92
Clay................................	590,399	43	576	1,025	43
Clayton	2,503,524	4	728	3,438	..
Clinton ...	991,368	26	698	1,406	31
Crawford..................................	906,360	29	720	1,258	36
Dallas....................................	736,914	34	538	1,253	37
Davis	112,237	77	503	223	77
Decatur	19,116	91	534	35	91
Delaware..................................	2,244,684	7	576	3,897	4
Des Moines............................	248,578	67	413	601	57
Dickinson	538,935	48	405	1,330	35
Dubuque.....................	1,950,853	9	601	3,246	8
Emmet	649,839	40	494	1,608	27
Fayette..................................	2,056,986	8	720	2,856	10
Floyd....................................	806,071	31	504	1,599	28
Franklin	448,698	58	576	796	52
Fremont	2,883	97	509	5	97
Greene	239,243	69	576	415	70
Grundy	567,466	45	504	1,125	41
Guthrie	1,023,269	23	593	1,725	24
Hamilton	9,833	94	576	17	94
Hancock	460,467	57	576	799	51
Hardin....................................	1,541,837	15	576	2,688	13
Harrison.	345,561	62	695	498	64
Henry	60,117	85	433	138	84
Howard	1,204,099	18	476	2,529	14
Humboldt	746,747	33	482	1,728	23
Ida	258,703	66	433	597	58
Iowa....................................	537,799	49	584	920	47
Jackson..................................	958,966	27	638	1,503	29
Jasper	214,802	72	730	294	74
Jefferson	82,267	82	432	190	78
Johnson................................	177,627	74	618	287	75
Jones	3,388,707	1	576	5,882	1
Keokuk..................................	246,113	68	576	427	69
Kossuth..................................	1,642,669	12	977	1,680	25
Lee....................................	685,686	37	512	1,339	34
Linn....................................	1,005,048	24	720	1,395	32
Louisa	53,684	87	407	131	85
Lucas....................................		......	432	....	......
Lyon	317,674	64	587	541	61
Madison	9,605	95	576	16	95
Mahaska..................................	83,428	81	576	144	82
Marion	61,203	84	576	106	87

NET BUTTER SHIPMENTS—Continued.

COUNTIES.	Total net shipments of butter for the year.	Rank by lbs. shipped.	Area of square miles in counties.	Pounds per square mile.	Rank by lbs. per square mile.
Marshall..........................	508,385	53	576	882	49
Mills	5,300	96	444	11	96
Mitchell	1,582,612	13	473	2,346	16
Monona...........................	37,688	8	556	67	89
Monroe...	35,040	89	432	81	88
Montgomery	97,271	79	432	225	76
Muscatine	74,439	83	437	170	80
O'Brien...........................	526,290	51	576	913	48
Osceola	194,174	73	400	485	67
Page.............................	541,286	47	557	971	46
Palo Alto	1,401,448	16	576	2,433	15
Plymouth	466,905	56	860	519	63
Pocahontas	673,700	38	576	1,169	39
Polk	1,741,626	11	585	2,978	9
Pottawattamie....................	474,062	57	960	493	65
Poweshiek........................	341,321	63	582	586	59
Ringgold	17,233	92	542	31	93
Sac	713,558	35	576	138	83
Scott.............................	218,308	71	455	481	66
Shelby............................	595,938	42	590	1,010	45
Sioux.............................	516,148	52	769	671	55
Story	1,138,580	20	576	1,977	20
Tama	553,732	46	720	769	53
Taylor	168,171	15	548	306	73
Union.	593,898	44	432	1,850	33
Van Buren........................	30,534	90	484	63	90
Wapello	148,982	76	432	344	72
Warren	112	98	569	19	98
Washington.......................	233,323	70	566	412	71
Wayne	532,352	50	523	1,017	44
Webster	414,441	59	720	575	60
Winnebago	1,090,572	22	403	2,706	12
Winneshiek	1,267,195	17	694	1,825	21
Woodbury.........................	3,355,487	2	873	3,843	5
Worth	804,933	32	402	2,000	19
Wright	612,084	41	576	1,062	42

PART IX.

TWENTY-SIXTH ANNUAL REPORT OF THE IOWA STATE DAIRY CONVENTION.

CEDAR RAPIDS, TUESDAY, WEDNESDAY AND THURS-
DAY, FEBRUARY 3, 4 AND 5, 1903.

OFFICERS FOR 1904.

S. B. SHILLING, *President*, - - - - - -	Mason City
W. B. BARNEY, *Vice-President*, - - - - - - -	Hampton.
P. H. KIEFFER, *Secretary*, - .- - - - -	Strawberry Point
F. A. LEIGHTON, *Treasurer*, - - - - - -	New Hampton.

The Twenty-sixth Annual Convention of the Iowa State Dairy Association was called to order at 8:00 P. M., Tuesday evening, February 3, 1903, in the Auditorium building, Cedar Rapids, Iowa, by S. B. Shilling, president.

Rev. **Dr.** Green, rector of Grace church, delivered the invocation as follows:

Almighty Lord, our heavenly God, unto whom are hearts are open, and to whom we turn for inspriration. Grant that we may always serve Thee and magnify Thy name in our lives, that in times of trouble we may turn to Thee for aid, and that in the hour of success we may not forget that we owe all to Thee. May the beneficence of Thy spirit so envelop us that we may live and act for the good of the world and the uplifting of humanity and the glory of God. Grant the favor of Thy blessing upon the people here assembled. Prosper them in their enterprises; give them wisdom in their deliberations while here and in their individual business life give them a strong regard for righteousness, for purity, for manly honor, and a deserved contempt for trickery, chicanery, dishonesty and injustice. Through their influence and their acts bring the time to pass when among men there shall be peace and good will, when righteousness shall characterize our lives and enter into our business dealings, when we may be free from the sin of selfishness and uncharitable disregard for others. Bless our country we beseech Thee; guard and prosper our commonwealth; bless our towns and cities, fill them with the influence that shall be elements of culture and spiritual advancement, and grant that the time may not be far distant when Thy will shall be done in the hearts of men. Grant Thy blessing we beseech Thee, upon the exercises of the hour; give us that spirit of fraternity and mutual love which tends to accomplish the best results, and guard and bless all who participate, we ask it for Jesus' sake. Amen.

PRESIDENT : The next will be the address of welcome by Mayor Huston of Cedar Rapids.

ADDRESS OF WELCOME.

Mayor Huston.

Mr. Chairman, Ladies and Gentlemen: It is a great pleasure to me to say that the city of Cedar Rapids feels highly honored by the presence of the members of the Iowa State Dairy association. And it is a further pleasure to know that some of you—and I hope all of you—have brought your wives and daughters with you to attend the business meetings as well as the social sessions. As I look into your faces I wonder if there are any more at home like you. I do not doubt that you have the same high standing in your respective communities as have those who are members of your association in Cedar Rapids and in Linn county. In Cedar Rapids whenever a ward desires to be well and faithfully and honestly represented in the city council they look around for a member of the Iowa State Dairy association, and in two instances to my knowledge have been represented from the same ward by members of your association; the members have been Mr. Harwood and Mr. Cherry. I might also state that the people of Linn county have honored your members. I have one in mind at the present time. When the people of this county were looking around for a good representative in the state legislature they chose Mr. Nietert of Walker, who has been an honored member of your association for years. And speaking of members of the legislature reminds me of a little anecdote I heard a while ago about a member from Linn county. The legislature had convened, a speaker had been elected and the usual committees appointed. Among the various committees appointed was one to visit the state penitentiary and inspect it. However, no appropriation had been made for the payment of the expenses of that committee. A rural member observed the omission and thought seriously during the night, and on the following day addressed the speaker as follows: Mr. Speaker, on yesterday when a committee was appointed to visit the state penitiary I noticed that no appropriation was made for paying the expenses of these committee men. I, therefore, move you that the following resolution be adopted: "Be it resloved that the sum of $300.00 be and is hereby appropriated for the purpose of paying the expenses of the committee to the penitentiary and return." The member from Linn county couldn't let an opportunity like that pass and so he arose and said: "Mr. Speaker, I move to amend the resolution by striking out the words "and return."

It is safe to be assumed that no member of the Iowa State Dairy association was on that committee because they were needed in the legislature and they would have been glad to have them return.

Now, my friends, we have long known where our bread comes from. All that was necessary for us to do was to look out of our windows and observe our great mills situated within our borders, but never until tonight have I looked upon the faces of those who told us where our butter came from. Very few of our citizens are proficient in the art of butter making, but all of us are proficient in making the butter fly. So that is why Cedar Rapids is a good butter market.

My friends, you are indeed welcome to our city. I hope your meeting will be one of pleasure, as well as profit, and when you have finished your work here and returned to your respective homes we hope that it will be with pleasant recollections of the city of Cedar Rapids and her people who bid you welcome. I thank you.

PRESIDENT: We are honored by the presence of an ex-member of the legislature from Walker, Hon. H. J. Nietert, who will respond to the address of welcome.

RESPONSE TO ADDRESS OF WELCOME.

H. J. Nietert, Walker, Iowa.

Ladies and Gentlemen: I presume the president has tried to punish me a little bit by his slight reference to the uncomfortable position I at one time held in this state, but he doesn't know all of my history or he wouldn't refer to that.

I am sure we have all listened with much interest to the address of the honored mayor of Cedar Rapids. He has warmed the cords of friendship and fratenity in the hearts of the members of this association by the most cordial welcome through him from the citizens of Cedar Rapids, and on behalf of the members of the Iowa State Dairy association I wish to thank him and the citizens of Cedar Rapids through him for this welcome. This certainly is a city that all should be proud to visit. It is a young city but its growth has been marvellous in the last decade. It has grown from a small town in the 80's to its present population of over 30,000, and I dare say there is not a city of the same population in the country, whose inhabitants are so greatly marked for their good citizenship, integrity, industry and good morals. By a man's acts we judge him, and by the acts of the inhabitants we judge the community. When we for a moment stop to view the surroundings, we observe that this city was set in beautiful environments and situated most happily. We find that it is a most energetic and progressive class of people that populate it. You will observe that they have most beautiful structures here, both in their many large and substantial churches where all the religions of modern denominations are represented, where God is honored and revered by the citizens, and in the many monuments of education, its public schools, high schools and colleges, which disseminate and spread knowledge in the young minds and teach our boys and girls to make good citizens. By our system of education the perpetuity of this country is assured, because no country can under our form of government succeed in ignorance. We go further and observe their manufactories. The mayor was a little modest when he spoke about it. The greatest oat meal mill in the United States is situated here. They have one of the greatest beef and pork packing companies in this country. Its meats are so fine and palatable that they are known all over the world. Their reputation for fair and honorable dealing is known to all the farmers of Iowa and beyond the borders of the state. They have here three of the largest pump manufactories in the state of Iowa— larger than many of the neighboring states have—which sell their wares not only in this state but in all the other states and territories, bringing in wealth to this city's coffers. They have foundries and machine shops, employing large numbers of men. Their beautiful paved streets, improved street railways, up-to-date civic improvements, the enterprise of their citizens and energy and push of their business men certainly appeals to the spirit of every man interested in the progress and advancement of every business enterprise and the betterment of the condition of man. The fame of this city is not only known to the members who reside in Linn county; its fame is not confined to the borders of the state, and for its future I promise more wonderful advancement and improvement than it has known in the past. It is known all over the United States, even across the sea the people read of this beautiful city of Iowa, not only for its schools, colleges and manufactories, but for its thousands and thousands of happy homes, for I dare say there is no city on the face of the earth where more of the citizens own their homes than in this city, and I can imagine nothing that is more conducive to building up a community than where the people build and own their own homes. I appeal as a citizen of Linn county to take up the work where the founders have left it and this city will grow to greater popualtion and greater glory to the state of Iowa. Now what I have said has been said in a rambling manner, but it has been the truth. But we are essentially here to consider the dairy interests of Iowa. You may wonder why we come to a city of this size instead of going into the country. We come here because your people invite us; you have heard your mayor promise us everything. Now if any of the members of the association find themselves short of money, and bills are presented which must be paid before they can leave, why take them to the mayor. He's a good fellow and he will doubtless pay them for you. We come here also because we want you to know what good butter is and how it is made. We don't want the dairymen to know all about it. You might get to eating oleomargarine if you weren't educated and taught what we are doing. Now you know the ancient Romans and Greeks used butter simply as an ointment when they took their baths—I suppose something like Cuticura. Today in the country districts of Portugal and Spain and in southern Italy and France you will still find butter put up in small bottles and sold as salve at the drug stores as a remedy for certain things. Not until 1860 did the new era of the dairy industry begin to take its present aspect. Up to that time the women and children in happy go lucky fashion made the butter in wasteful and careless manner. They were strangers to some of the bacteria which trouble the butter makers of the present day. Our state has been lauded on account of its dairy interests. I will not take up much of your time because Mr. Wright is going to tell you all about it. People in the cities too often lose sight of the importance of the dairy industry. Now in the farm districts they hold their farmers' institutes, and these matters are all talked over and education in butter making is going on every year. But usually in the larger towns and cities they do not have that interest in it. I know in some places they are getting for butter what they call butter, but the Lord save the butter makers that made it, for they couldn't save themselves. I wish to impress upon you that the dairy industry is one of the greatest factors in producing wealth in the state. The cow does not only produce the cream to make butter, but she produces the young beef which supplies the tables of the land with steak. We have in this state nearly 4,000,000 cattle, 1,500,000 cows. The cows are valued at $30.00 per head, which makes $45,000,000 worth of cows. We produce in this state 150,-000,000 pounds of butter per year. We produce twenty-five per cent of all the creamery butter made in the United States, and ten per cent of all the butter made in this country. I am not here before you to praise you. I am here to tell you the conditions. That is why the dairy association meets in this city; that is why it meets in other cities each year, to try and spread this knowledge among the people of Iowa. We are not perfect. I have not found a business yet in the state of Iowa, or any calling which I consider perfect, and when we do think we are near the point of perfection and load our minds with that thought, then we are treading on thin ice and do not understand ourselves. We manufacture millions of pounds of butter, but there is a possibility of greatly improving the quality of that butter and it is the duty of every dairyman in this state to improve, from the cow on up through all the various stages of converting cream into butter, to make still better butter. Now then we can never be successful unless we keep hammering at this proposition all the time. We take it up voluntarily because it is a pleasant task. We are all interested in the advancement of the dairy industry in the state of Iowa, and we want to see Iowa butter take front rank and be at the head of the procession of the states. It has been made possible for the Dakotas to blossom like a rose. Minnesota, Kansas and Missouri have learned their tricks from our state. They learned how our progressive men have conducted profitable dairies and made butter. Why, it has made the Dakotas rich. They have made a bid for the national convention. They are ready to come down with thousands to help pay premiums on the butter the men may bring. Now I trust I have not bored you with these remarks. But it is a great industry; it represents many millions of dollars in butter and cheese; it does not impoverish the land; it eats up your roughage and builds up your land at the same time. These men who have exhibits in this hall display their improved creamery appliances. We recognize them. We are not back in the ages when men put their milk in a goat skin and put it on the back of a camel and churned it. I trust this meeting may be a success ful one. We have many good and instructive papers to be read which will be of interest to all of you. I thank you for your attention.

PRESIDENT: In one thing, if in nothing more, I expect my address will please you and that is in its briefness. We have a programme of some length and much interest to follow.

PRESIDENT'S ADDRESS.

S. B. Shilling, Mason City, Iowa.

Mr. Chairman, Ladies and Gentlemen: When you elected me one year ago as the president of this association I realized the fact at that time that you had conferred an honor upon me, and since serving you a year I have come to realize that it is not only an honor but it has been a great pleasure as well. While the results have not been as great as I would have liked to bring about, while some of the plans I have had for the advancement of the dairy interests of the state have fallen short, yet I believe we can congratulate ourselves that in the past year something has been done to elevate the standard of Iowa butter.

The year just past has been a notable one for several reasons; for the number of successes and the number of failures, more particularly the failures that attended the business. But the failures have taught us some lessons that may profit us ultimately. One thing it has taught us is that we must not start creameries where there is nothing to support them. Of all the creameries, either individual or corporation, that have failed during the past year, nearly every case was the result of weak patronage or close proximity to stronger creameries who were able to out pay them.

The year has been notable for another reason, the inauguration of the oleomargarine law, and now we can safely say for the first time in ten years butter has had a fair show.

Iowa does not hold a very enviable position in the point of excellence of manufacture of butter today. This fact has just been referred to by the honorable gentleman who preceded me. It is with feelings of humiliation that I have to say to you that at the recent convention held in Milwaukee we occupied the very lowest position in the scale of excellence of butter, receiving the lowest average score of any state exhibiting butter. There are several reasons for this and I do not care to take them all up at the present time. I wish to say this, and I say it without any intention of reflecting upon any system. It is a well known fact that Iowa being the oldest dairy state in the union has been the most fertile field for the various separators. They have come into our state and the system has been very widely introduced, and now whether we are on the threshold of one of the greatest advances in the line of progress, or whether it means further deterioration of the quality of our butter I am unprepared to say. I believe there are arguments on both sides, but the fact of the matter remains at the present time that wherever they have been introduced it has had the effect of lowering the standard of the butter. I do not wish to find fault with them. I can see no fault in the system, or no reason why the cream should not be separated on the farm and with proper care the same quality of butter produced as where it is separated at the creamery. To me it looks as though it was a matter of education, and whether we can educate the people up to a standard to enable them to do this is a question and considerable of a question in my mind. But we may be on the threshold of the greatest progress we have made.

Another reason for the lowering of our grade is this. Iowa is the first state in the Union which engaged in the manufacture of butter to any extent. It is the home of the creamery industry. When John Stewart hauled that load of lumber and built the first creamery over near Manchester he little thought he was laying the foundation of a system which would extend to every country in the universe. If the name of John Stewart occupied today the place it should in the history of the country it would be among the benefactors of the human race. And I hope to see the day when his memory will be honored in the way it deserves, when instead of sleeping over in Anamosa in an unmarked and almost unknown grave, the dairymen of the country will build him a monument, and they can never build the foundation too broad nor the monument too high to be commensurate with the good done by John Stewart to the dairy industry.

But the reason I had started to give was this. We were engaged in this dairy business before any other state and our creameries are older than those of any other state. They were built with a limited knowledge of sanitary conditions and surroundings and today they have grown old, and in many of them it is impossible to get the best results. I am happy to say that all the new creameries have been built with a view of sanitary surroundings, and I predict this, so far as the other states are concerned; that when their creameries are as old as ours they will be reaping the same results.

Another reason is the lack of interest taken by our state legislature. We have certainly been handicapped in a degree no other state has been. For instance, over at the institute held at Tripoli last week I met Prof. Haecker of Minnesota, and he told me that Minnesota, with less than 600 creameries, has eight creamery inspectors. Iowa has over 900 creameries and only one inspector. The Iowa legislature has ignored the dairy interests and we as a consequence are suffering. I asked Prof. Haecker what the Minnesota state dairy association received and he said $2,000.00. One year ago you appointed a committee to go to Des Moines and ask for $1,000.00. We have not yet received it. Prof. Haecker made the statement that when the Minnesota association asked the legislature for $1,000.00 the latter asked if they couldn't use $2,000.00, with the result that Minnesota occupies today the position to which we entitled. Wisconsin gets $1,000.00, and little Nebraska with less than 300 creameries gets $1,000.00. I wish to urge this association to make some strong resolution, that the matter be taken up again and that it be taken up in time. The trouble was the last time the committee didn't get to Des Moines as early as it should have. I would recommend that a strong resolution be passed at this convention, asking our legislature for the aid we are justly entitled to in this connection.

Among the first work I did as president of your organization, to improve conditions was calling upon the butter makers to form into organizations for the purpose of bettering their knowledge of butter making by engaging in educational tests. The results have far exceeded our expectations. Without a single exception there has not been a backward step in the score at any of these meetings. Every organization has made a score in advance of the one preceding. The butter makers responded almost to a man where it was possible for them to come into contact with these organizations. The traveling men have helped willingly and without them it would have been impossible to have carried on the work. We have had the hearty co-operation of our state dairy commissioner who has never failed to attend a meeting and have his deputy there. We have had the hearty co-operation of Ames. They have explained everything we have asked them to, and all they have asked is that we pay the expenses of the men they sent to score the butter and tell us how to remedy it. The progress made has been so gratifying I would urge the importance of maintaining these organizations, and I would tell the creamerymen, as I have told the farmers' institutes, the necessity of uniting with one of these organizations. They should see that their butter makers do this. It was our intention when we started out to make these for the butter makers as well as the patrons and get them together and have a better understanding, and we have been very successful, especially at the late meetings. I believe there is another way in which we can get hold of the patron, and that is by holding joint picnics. One or two creameries or two or three, get together and have a picnic every year and have a speaker there and entertain them. .The ground work of the whole thing is the farmer and we have to get him.

One thing particularly gratifying to me is this: The importance of improving the standard of our butter is so manifest that I do not think today we have a traveling man in the state of Iowa, whether he is selling creamery supplies, salt, or is a railroad agent, but is lending his best influence to help along the improvement of butter.

Now one thing more I believe would add greatly to the raising of the standard of Iowa butter, and you may think me radical; it may be something you will not bear me out in, but I believe we should have a license law in the state of Iowa. Out of our butter makers only one-fourth of them I believe are members of this association; there is a class we have been unable to reach as yet. I believe if we had a license law in the state in which a first certificate, second and third, were awarded that the tendency would be for each butter maker to stand as high as possible. I have in mind a creamery in Iowa which sells three or four cents below western extras, and the state officers have no hold upon this class of butter makers, and the creamery patrons have no protection against them. If we had a license law founded as I have just mentioned the incentive would be for every butter maker to strive to obtain a first grade license, and in case they made no progress along this line the state officers would have the right to revoke the certificate already held. I would recommend that this matter be taken up in one of our meetings and resolutions passed, if it meets with the judgment of the association, that the matter be placed with the state dairy commissioner the members of the dairy school and the officers of this association to grant the licenses, and we would weed out some of the butter makers of the state, and raise the wages of those who are trying to do their best correspondingly.

There is another thing, and I do not wish to find fault about it as I don't see how we can avoid it. It is the practice of commission men in giving a premium, and just so long as the butter makers can say "I am getting ½ above New York and I do not care to do any better" what can we do about it? I do not wish to stand up and say this with a spirit of criticism, but it looks as though something was wrong. I can see no reason why they should keep this practice up so much to the detriment of our butter makers of the west.

We want a spirit of reformation to sweep over Iowa again. We want it to start in with the patron and end with the commission merchant I have been talking about. As far as the intelligence of the butter maker of Iowa today is concerned they stand equal with the butter makers of any state; we only want the same chance the butter makers of other states have. We want to inaugurate a movement of reform not only with the patron, but with the butter maker, the supply men and the commission men, and with the united effort of all, and with the license law we can bring Iowa again back to the proud position she held once before. I thank you.

Mr. Raines of Independence, whose name appeared on the programme not being present, the convention was favered with a vocal selection by Mr. Farr of Cedar Rapids.

PRESIDENT: Iowa is favored with a real live dairy commissioner. He is alive. And the worst hardship I have endured the past year has been trying to keep up with him in his travels around the state in the interest of butter making. The only way I have ever had opportunity to get even with him is that I have borrowed money of him a few times. We have this gentleman with us this evening and I have the honor of introducing Commissioner Wright.

ADDRESS.

H. R. Wright, Dairy Commissioner, Des Moines.

Mr. President: A great deal has been said about the decline of dairying in Iowa, and a number of people have gone so far as to suggest that dairying was not suitable for Iowa conditions, and hence, not at all profitable, and that these were the reasons for the falling off in our product of butter for the last several years. Without discussing the reasons why we do not make quite so much butter as we did in the hard times of '96 and '97, we may, with profit to ourselves, consider the question of the suitability of dairying to Iowa's conditions and the profitableness of the business in this state.

This is primarily a corn state. We must raise corn on our farms because nature has especially adapted the soil and climate of this state for the product of the king of cereals. And having raised corn we must feed it to hogs and cattle and other stock in order to get the greatest value from the grain. We ought not then to adopt any addition to corn and hog and cattle growing in Iowa that will render less profitable these lines of effort. But dairying does not so interfere because the by-product of the dairy, skimmed milk, is the ideal feed on which to raise pigs, and the farmer who milks his cows and raises his calves on skimmed milk and corn may have just as good calves as does the man who allows the calves to run with the cow. Dairying is eminently suitable as an addition to our growing of hogs and cattle, and indeed, is almost a necessary part of stock growing in Iowa. The fact that for a quarter of a century Iowa has made more butter than any other state, or any equal area in the United States, seems to prove that dairying is not only a suitable addition to our system of agriculture, but that it is also a profitable addition.

Dairying is a profitable business because it takes nothing from the soil. Dairying tends to the maintenance of the fertility of the land upon which it is carried on. All the products of the farm come primarily from the soil, or the air. If a man sells those products the substance of which comes from the soil, he is selling his farm piece-meal. This is exactly what the grain seller does. The stockman and stock feeder do the same thing to a much less degree. A dairyman sells absolutely nothing from his farm which would be of any value if left in the soil. The carbon hydrogen and oxygen which make up butter come altogether from the atmosphere, and the man who carries on dairying sells from his farm a manufactured product and he has left in his soil all the fertility that it originally contained.

Dairying is profitable because the dairyman has little or nothing invested. This is a hog and cattle state. We must raise cattle, whether we wish to do so or not, and so we may say that the farmer keeps the cow for the purpose of producing the calf; and hence the cow, in a sense, is not a part of his investment in the dairy business. All that is invested is the small amount of feed which she eats in a month or six weeks at the end of which time, he gets his return from the creamery. On the other hand, the man who raises and fats a carload of steers, or who raises a drove of hogs invests more and more in them every day for a year, or two years, or longer. His investment is subject to the change of prices, the disease peculiar to the animals, and other disasters. The dairyman has little invested; he has an almost immediate return from his feeds and there is little or no probability of loss in the business.

Dairying is profitable because it enables the farmer to get two returns from his cows instead of one. The farmer expects two returns every year from every kind of live stock usually kept on Iowa farms, except cows. A man could not afford to keep sheep in Iowa, if he did not get a crop of wool and a crop of lambs each year. A farmer could not afford to keep a mare a whole year for the single purpose of raising a colt; he makes her work to pay her board. We could not even afford to raise hogs in Iowa, if they reproduced themselves only in the ratio of one to one, as cattle do, and yet there are hundreds of farmers in this state who are attempting the impossible task of getting rich from the profit arising from keeping a cow a whole year for the single purpose of producing a calf. The dairy business enables the farmer to raise just as good calves, and also to get $25 to $50 worth of butter from the cow each year.

Dairying is profitable because it brings the farmer the largest return for his labor and the products of his farm. It enables him to get a larger gross and net income from his farm than he can obtain without it. The feed that will make two pounds of beef will make a pound of butter, and the value of a pound of butter is always more than the value of two pounds of beef, even during the last few years of relatively high prices of beef and low prices of butter. All the arguments in support of diversified and intensive farming may be used to prove that dairying is necessary to the profitable operation of our farms. When our farmers raised wheat they became bankrupt and their farms were worth but a few dollars per acre. When they turned to stock raising and to dairying their farms advanced in value to nearly a hundred dollars, their prosperity became almost unlimited, and their bank accounts and their credit have increased accordingly, because they contained a larger gross and net return from their farms.

Dairying is profitable because it is a cash business. The dairyman gets his returns at the end of the month, is able to pay for his groceries and dry goods and he keeps out of debt. When he does sell a drove of hogs or a bunch of cattle, he applies the larger sum on his indebtedness or his bank account.

The sections of this state and of others where dairying is practiced, have never known hard times in the same sense that other sections have, for the reason that the dairymen always have a reasonable amount of ready money from the sale of their dairy products and this money going into the retail channels of trade, relieves the stringency in the periods of hard times.

Dairying is profitable because the butter that is produced is a net profit. The farmer must have the cow in order to raise the calf. The cost of keeping the cow must be charged against the value of the calf, and if there is profit in that, as our beef growers assert, then any other product that can be obtained from the cow must be nearly or quite a net profit, against which may be charged the extra labor necessary to obtain the other product. Suppose two farms of equal size and productiveness managed by two farmers of equal skill and ability and operated on the same lines, except that one milks his cows and the other does not. The dairyman will raise more pigs than his neighbor does because he will have skimmed milk and his neighbor will have none. He will raise just as many and just as good calves from the same number of cows. He will have exactly the same products, and of the same value as his neighbor who has not milked any cows and he will have from $25 to $50 worth of butter from each cow. The butter fat is a net profit to that farmer. The census returns will show the same thing for the various counties of the state. Counties of equal area, equal farm population, and of equal productiveness presumably ought to sell out of the state each year the same number of dollars' worth of farm products; but the fact is that in comparing such counties, the records show that the dairy county ships just as many dollars' worth of horses and hogs and cattle and poultry and other farm products as the county where no dairying is carried on, and a quarter or a half million dollars' worth of butter besides. The butter is a net profit to the individual. the county and to the state, and in the last ten years this net profit to Iowa's dairy farmers has amounted to a hundred and fifty million dollars.

Dairying is a profitable business because it is a sure thing. In a wet year or a dry year a dairyman can raise feed for his cows. When prices are high, or prices are low, the dairyman has money in his pocket. The price of butter is more uniform than that of any other farm product. Last summer cattle sold in Chicago for about eight cents. Now they are selling for a little more than five cents. Just now hogs are selling for a very high price. One does not have to think back very far to remember when they sold for about half of present prices. There have never been any such sudden or violent fluctuations in the price of butter. Many a man has lost the profits of several years by one visitation of hog cholera. Many a man has lost largely in feeding cattle on a declining market, but the man who produces butter is sure of success and is sure of a uniform price. The price varies from summer to winter, but the average yearly price of butter is by far the most uniform and stable and certain of all the prices of farm products.

These are the reasons why the dairy districts are the most prosperons portions of this state; the reasons why the wealth of the dairy counties is generally distributed; the reasons why their farmers are uniformly well to do; the reason why their lands sell for a higher price than other lands; the reason why their banks have more money; the reasons why hard times do not affect their farmers disastrously and the reasons in large part, for the extraordinary and continued prosperity of the large part of the state of Iowa.

Corn is king in Iowa, but the dairy cow is queen, and the dollars of the Iowa farmers are the product of this royal pair.

PRESIDENT: We are favored tonight with the presence of J. S. Trigg of Rockford, Iowa, to whom I have to the pleasure of introducing you.

THE KICKING HEIFER IN FLY TIME.

—

J. S. Trigg, Rockford, Iowa.

The limitations placed upon me by the president and secretary of this association, in the matter of briefly addressing you this evening, on a topic of my own selection suitable for this occasion, are extremely rigid and arbitrary. I am requested to carefully avoid any reference to the scientific, commercial, financial, practical and statistical phases of the dairy industry, and confine my remarks exclusively to such esthetic, poetic, sentimental and humorous facts and fancies, as I can evolve, associated with the cow and her belongings.

In the mad rush for the dollar in the present very materialistic age, I feel that I am simply turned loose in a barren field—asked to make bricks without straw, or finding some trace of the esthetic and poetic left will bring my treasure to unresponsive souls and unappreciative ears. Modern inventive American enterprise and the almighty dollar have so completely invested the cow and her beneficient mission, that a modern poet would find in a corn sheller or washing machine, as fit a subject for his muse. However, it was not always thus. In days past some pleasing and very gracious things have been written upon this theme. The mystery of milk, its secretion and production, the conversion of the nutriment and fragrance of the rich herbage of pasture and meadow into a delightful aromatic delicacy, coupled with all the peaceful and fascinating environment of rural life has often been touched upon by the poets.

Jean Ingelow in her beautiful poem "The High Tide on the Coast of Lincolnshire," says:

> She moved where Lindis wandereth
> My sonne's faire wife, Elizabeth.
> "Cusha! Cusha! Cusha!'" calling,
> Ere the early dews were falling,
> Farre away I heard her song;
> "Cusha! Cusha! all along;
> Where the reedy Lindis floweth.
>
> Floweth, floweth,
> From the meads where melick groweth
> Faintly came her milking song:
> "Cusha! Cusha! Cusha!" calling,
> "For the dews will soon be falling;
> Leave your meadow grasses mellow,
> Mellow, mellow,
> Quit your cowslips yellow, yellow;

Then the pitiful tragedy—the bells of the village church playing the danger signal for the simple folk who dwelt in the valley of the Lindis, while the angry high tide from the great North sea overwhemled the peaceful plain, its roar mingling with "The Brides of Enderby" from the church bells.

> "The waters laid her at his doore
> Ere yet the early morn was clear
> The pretty bairns in fast embrace
> *   *   *   *   *   *   *   *   *
>
> And sweeter woman ne'er drew breath,
> Than my sonne's wife, Elizabeth.

Longfellow in his immortal poem—Evangeline, describing the simple pastoral life of the Acadian farmers says:

> Now recommenced the reign of rest
>   And affection and stillness.
> Day with its burden and heat had departed,
>   And twilght descending
> Brought back the evening star to the sky
>   And the herds to the homestead.
> Pawing the ground they came, and resting
>   Their necks on each other.
> And with their nostrils distended inhaling
>   The freshness of the evening.
> Foremost, bearing the bell, Evangeline's
>   beautiful heifer.
> Proud of her snow white hide and the
>   Ribbon which waved from her collar.
>
> * * * * * * * * *
>
> Patiently stood the cows meanwhile, and
>   Yielded their udders
> Unto the milkmaid's hand; whilst loud and
>   In regular cadence
> Into the sounding pails the foaming
>   Streamlets descended.

And again in his story of the Courtship of Miles Standish, the poet pays a gracious tribute to the head of the herd as follows:

> "Then from a stall near at hand, amid
>   Exclamations of wonder
> Alden, the thoughful ,the careful, so happy,
>   So proud of Priscilla
> Brought out his snow white bull, obeying
>   The hand of his master.
> Led by a cord that was tied to an iron ring
>   In its nostrils.
> Covered with a crimson cloth, and a cushion
>   Placed for a saddle.
> She should not walk, he said, through the dust
>   And heat of the noonday;
> Nay, she should ride like a queen, not plod
>   Along like a peasant.

B. F. Taylor also pays a pretty tribute to the cow and her mission. Of the old time milk house he says:

> At the foot of the hill the milk house stands,
> Where the Balm of Gilead spreads his hands,
> And the willow trails at each pendent tip
>   The lazy lash of a golden whip,

And an ice cold spring with a tinkling sound
Makes a bright green edge for the dark green ground.
Cool as a cave is the air within.
Brave are the shelves with the burnished tin
Of the curving shores, and the seas of white
That turn to gold in a single night,
As if the disc of a winter noon
Should take the tint of a new dubloon.
Besides the churn a maiden stands
Nimble and naked her arms and hands—
Another Ruth when the reapers reap.
Her dress as limp as a flag asleep
Is faced in front with a puzzling check;
Her feet as bare as her sun-browned neck
Her hair rays out like a lady fern
With a single hand she starts the churn.

The poet Shelley also had this same business in mind when he wrote in his "Hymn to the Earth."

"Happy are they whom thy mild favors nourish
All things unstinted round them grow and flourish.
For them endured the life sustaining field
Its load of harvest, and their cattle yield
Large increase, and their house with wealth is filled.

But these are visions of the past, for but few women today would or could say of their son's wives, what was said of Elizabeth, while our modern Evangeline belongs to the smart set and is afraid of a cow; and, hard up as many of our modern Priscillas are for a John Alden, not one could be found who to get him would be willing to ride a snow white bull in a bridal procession. Times have changed, in one sense for the better. In a sentimental way for the worse. Machinery has knocked about all the poetry out of living anyway, and particularly out of the dairy business. Instead of the sweet girl calling the cows home at eventide, "Co boss, Co boss," gently echoing down the pasture lane, and over the quiet meadows, blending with the last song of the birds—a call not unlikely heard by a lover as well as the cows, who will meet her at the pasture bars and steal a vesper kiss,—we have a barefooted young cowboy mounted on a broncho, racing down to the pasture to hustle the cows home; instead of the old milk house at the spring, with its clear, cold, bubbling water, the pans coated with thick blankets of rich cream, and a barefooted Venus churning the butter, while she

"Closes her eyes and, side by side
Sees, he the bridegroom, and she the bride."

We have the whirl and racket of an old separator, the cough of a fretting, fuming engine, a gang of coarse men in wamuses, overalls or fur coats impatiently waiting their turn to unload their cans, busy cussing the butter maker for their short tests, and ready to steal their neighbor's share from the skimmed milk tank. We have a ponderous combined churn and butter worker, a damp, noisy place where coloring, pasteurizing and testing are praticed, and bacteria, starters and over runs are talked. We have a hairy-armed, rubber-booted athlete weighing milk, stoking the engine, operating the machinery and shoveling butter into tubs, with as little grace and refinement of manner as Pat shoveling gravel onto a flat car—a strictly business like, matter of fact way of doing things, that knocks all the poetry and sentiment out of the business.

We came across one of those old time spring milk houses this summer, up among the hills of northeastern Iowa. Its glory was departed. It was no longer used. Nestling close up to a rocky bank, a Virginia Creeper was doing its best in nature's kindly way to hide the dismantled roof and crumbling walls ,and where the water, clear and sweet as of old, welled up from the rocky depths, a flock of gabbling dirty ducks befouled its purity. The good wife who used to set the milk, skim off the rich cream and work the old dash churn to the music of the babbling spring and the orioles in the over arching elm, now rests from her labors, while her daughter buys her butter from the creamery, reads the Ladies Home Journal, and does not know the name of a cow in the farm herd. The justification for all this lies in the fact. that more and better butter is made with far less labor than in the old poetic days, and that no boy is now required to work an old dash churn on a lot of balky winter cream while he studies his next Sunday school lesson. The best butter maker in the neighborhood has also dissappeared—the dear good woman, who regardless of tests, coloring, starters, bacteria, temperature and age of cream, could somehow make that brand of good old dairy butter with that nutty flavor, which just melted in your mouth, and which drew first prizes at the county fairs, even if there was a hair in it once and a while. None of this kind of butter could be had now for love or money.

When we look at it there is something remarkable about the amount of fraud and cussedness man has been able to develop in connection with so common and indispensible an article as the milk of the cow. Every class which handles either it or its products having invented some fraud or counterfeit in connection with it. The solemn old deacon has been caught watering his milk, and selling the second milking to the factory; the good wife has been tempted to sell rolls of poor butter coated over with good; schemes without number to substitute coloring matter for cream, to mix casine and water with butter, to steal the cream and substitute cheap fats in cheese, and last but not least the champion fraud of all to try to run a dairy with steers instead of cows, and with drugs and tallow palm off upon a confiding public a product labeled as the finest creamery goods. Fortunately the test has eradicated most of the old time petty frauds and now men have to be honest whether they want to or not, while congressman who realized that farmers were after them wiped out the oleo fraud and gave the cow and her owner their legal rights.

All honor to the men who made this fight in the interest of pure food, and a fair show for one of the country's most important industries.

With all truth it may be said of Charlie Knight, that he is indeed a Knight of the Golden Circle—the sixty pound tub of genuine western extra creamery butter.

Alone for the man who keeps a family cow. Is there any of the old sentiment left, and this cow should be a Jersey, a dainty matron with soulful brown eyes, a golden skin, little incurved horns, of fawn color, and always and ever the family pet. With her well fed and cared for follows good living for all—cream for the coffee and oatmeal, pudding and milk for supper, rolls of nice butter, pats of cottage cheese, and pitchers of buttermilk, a drink fit for the gods; and then as the strawberries get ripe, you go out and pick a heaping panful, and getting the Jersey cow, the berries and the sugar bowl into happy conjunction you return thanks that verily life is worth the living after all, and realize some of the sentiment which inspired the poets of old.

We once heard Artemus Ward deliver a lecture in St. Louis upon the Mormons, during the whole of which he never once referred to the polygamous crowd. I see that I have been following his example, ignoring the topic of this address, and so I will close by saying that milking is the fly in the ointment of even modernized dairying. While far enough advanced to raise our babies on a bottle, we still have no machine which will milk a cow. It is best that this should be so, else the small dairyman would have no show in the business. So long as this work is done by hand, just so long will the emergency arise which forms the title of his address—that of having to milk a kicking heifer in fly time. A good man should not attempt this job, unless he is out in the pasture or away back behind the barn. It is an experience destructive alike of dignity, good morals and church standing, and a man should always let his wife, or the hired man with no soul to save, do this job.

I speak of a cosmopolitan audience—the man who keeps the cow, the creamery operator who makes the butter, the sharp New York and Chicago men who buy and sell it, the makers and sellers of creamery supplies, and the people who eat the butter, the product of these joint labors.

While the poetry and sentiment may be and probably is, pretty much obliterated by the use of modern methods and machines, it still remains a fact that no product requires more intelligence and skill than the pound of creamery butter, score 97, the production of which forms the special business of this meeting of the Iowa State Dairy Association.

PRESIDENT: This closes the programme for the evening. I would ask all holding railroad certificates to please hand them to the secretary this evening. You stand adjourned until tomorow afternoon at 2:00 o'clock.

WEDNESDAY AFTERNOON.

PRESIDENT: It is nearly a half hour past the time set on the programme for us to begin, you will, therefore, please come to order at once, and Mr. W. B. Barney of Hampton, will speak about "Silos for Iowa Dairymen."

THE SILO FOR THE IOWA DAIRYMAN.

W. B. Barney, Hampton, Iowa.

It was with reluctance that I permitted the use of my name on your programme after having recently addressed the State Farmers' Institute on the same subject. However, I appreciate the honor conferred and as my interests are all identified with those of the dairymen of our state, I felt I could not refuse to comply with the wishes of your executive committee.

A silo is a cheap means of canning green feed on a large scale. After using one for the last seven years on my dairy and breeding farm, I must say that I would hardly know how to do without it.

I can hardly conceive of conditions such as would make a silo on a dairy farm an unprofitable investment. As to the kind each must choose for himself that which is best suited to his wants, and the means at his command for its construction.

Like all other farm buildings I think it pays to use good material and make it substantial. The location of the silo should be such as to be accessible to the feed alleys in the barn. The man is fortunate who has a bank barn, and can build his silo on the up hill side with bottom not more than three or four feet below the feeding floor, using stone laid in cement for the lower section or part that is in the ground twelve or fourteen feet. There is a great saving of power in filling, as the length of the elevator will be lessened fifteen or twenty feet. Where stone or brick is cheap either of these materials make a most excellent silo.

In the dairy districts of Wisconsin where silos have been in general use for some years, they are nearly all round and built of wood with a five or six foot wall under them. About three or four feet of this wall is in the ground, on top of the wall 2x4's are set twelve inches apart center to center of proper length. The inside lining is of No. 1 fencing resawed and dressed at the mill. Two layers are used, with P. & B. acid and water proof paper between.

For outside rabbeted house siding is used. If silo is more than twenty feet in diameter, a layer of same material as is used for inner lining is put under this siding to give additional strength on account of the pressure which is increased as the diameter grows larger.

The last silo I built is of this pattern and it is entirely satisfactory. Some are lathing this kind of a silo and plastering with a coat of cement. I can do this at any time when the inner wall shows signs of decay, as all wood walls will do in time, on account of the action of the juices of the corn. After using both the square and round silo, I unhesitatingly recommend the round form as being the most practical and modern. One of the most important things is to get a silo as deep as possible in proportion to the diameter. This lessens the feeding surface exposed and prevents molding that may set in after a few days. We feed one-half of the top surface one day, and the other half the following day. This gives us silage every day that has not been exposed long enough to be effected by the air.

A silo thirty-six feet deep will hold nearly five times as much as one twelve feet deep. The weight of the silage per cubic foot at thirty-five feet deep will be close to sixty pounds, within two feets of the top it will weigh about twenty pounds. The mean weight will be forty pounds in a silo of this depth. Too much attention cannot be given at time of filling to see that corn is well mixed, well spread and thoroughly tramped at the edges. I think that poor work in the silo has had more to do with people abandoning their use after they have been built, than any other one thing. All the conditions this year were aginst the making of good silage in northern Iowa. The heavy frosts early in September caught our corn before time for filling. We made up our mind that if there ever was a time when careful work was necessary it was this year.

The corn was quite dry when it went in. By the use of about fifty pails of water per day and six or eight barrels put on top when we had finished, we are now feeding some of the best silage we have ever used. Water cannot take the place of the natural juices but it helps to soften the tissues and the silage packs more firmly. Four or five inches on top was of little value. The indications are that there will not be ten bushels in the 350 tons, aside from the top that will be wasted. As to the value of silage for dairy cows and young stock it is in my opinion hard to over estimate it.

For the economical production of milk there is nothing its equal. The silo is, we believe, the best safeguard against summer drouth. It is very difficult to have a soiling crop ready to feed when pastures fail, as this varies from year to year. Many of the most prosperous dairymen now have one ready to open at any time in summer.

If your field is not more than one-third of a mile from your silo, the cost of labor and machinery for putting in a ton will be close to fifty-five cents, while the cost of the silage put in is estimated at from $1.25 to $1.50.

We had some silage left last summer and were quite surprised to find that our cows prefered it to the green corn. We opened our silo this winter about December 26. Our reason for not opening earlier was that we had an abundance of other feed. Our cows are now giving about twenty per cent more milk than before feeding silage. My experience is that they assimilate and digest the other feeds much better when fed silage than without it, and that they prefer it to any other kind of feed.

Hoard's Dairyman of recent date gives the following ration for Holstein Friesian cows weighing about 1,350 pounds:

40 lbs. Silage,
10 " Mixed clover and timothy hay,
4 " Bran,
4 " Oats,
1 lb. Oil meal.

As part of the winter ration for domestic animals it is the best substitute for roots we have ever tried. It is only within recent years that canned fruits and vegetables have become so great a part of our table diet. It is a misfortune to the dairymen of our state that so few realize the advantage of succulent food for winter use.

The objection formerly offered to silage as a feed for dairy cows on account of tainting the milk is practically a thing of the past. At the test made at the Illinois Experiment Station it was shown that out of 220 persons who were given silage and non-silage milk 118 prefered silage, sixty-five non-silage, and thirty-seven had no choice.

Experiments show that the use of any feed that is apt to taint the milk is much more liable to do so if fed an hour before milking than several hours after. Spoiled ensilage had better be fed to hogs or young stock. Freezing does not seriously damage silage but it is not well to feed it while frozen. Silage may be carried from one year to another without loss. If we discontinue its use in the spring, the top becomes covered with mold for a few inches until the air is excluded. In case this is left until filling time the next fall the top should be taken off. It is not often that the conditions are such about a well kept dairy farm that any degree of cleanliness can be maintained in feeding shocked corn to the cows and permitting hogs to follow them. Even if shocked corn were as good a feed for the cow as ensilage there would be a loss of sixteen per cent in feeding it without the hog, while the loss is reduced to two per cent by the use of ensilage.

This is accounted for from the fact that silage is a pre-digested food. We are told that about 200 creameries have been closed in Iowa within the last year for lack of patronage.

Had silos been more numerous among our dairymen and farmers this would not have been the case. Another reason for this, is the poor class of dairy cows in Iowa. The steer question has had too much consideration in the dairy, and too many cows are kept that are not in any sense of the term profitable dairy cows.

We can all profit by the more intelligent use of the feeds at our command. There are many of us who would not think of getting the best results without feeding a lot of steers about all they can eat.

How many of us treat our cows that way? They should be fed up to their full capacity. A silo will help cheapen the cows ration and make her so profitable that even the hired hand may be induced to milk her. I put in ten acres of alfalfa last year and have a most excellent prospect. If this can be successfully grown in central and northern Iowa, we shall be able to produce milk at a minimum cost.

As our lands advance in price our farms are sure to grow smaller. More cattle can be kept on a given area with a silo than is otherwise the case.

Pasturing is an expensive method of feeding cattle and the summer silo is sure to come into very general use. The cost of our barns may be very much reduced if the silo is built in connection, as there will not be the necessity for large hay mows.

The haying season is cut short, the time of husking much reduced, the feed is all under cover.

The advantages of a silo so far out number the disadvantages that I will not try to enumerate them here.

PRESIDENT: This question of silage is one of very great importance to the average dairy farmer and we have about ten minutes in which to discuss it. If anyone has questions, Mr. Barney will be glad to answer them.

MR. HUBBARD: How many tons of silage can you get from an acre of corn?

BARNEY: An average year about twelve tons.

HUBBARD: How much silage do you feed a day?

BARNEY: About forty pounds.

ANDERSON: That is to a cow?

BARNEY: Yes, sir.

MR. WRIGHT: I would like to know what proportion of the ration is ensilage?

BARNEY: It depends somewhat on the cow you are feeding to. I feed with about forty pounds of silage, ten pounds of timothy or clover, about four pounds of oats and four of bran, and if I have oil meal I feed a little of that—something near a pound.

WRIGHT: Then according to your figures an acre of ensilage is worth about four acres of the corn.

BARNEY: I think so for dairy cows, especially as far as young stock is concerned; I use it in the place of corn, and I find they do as well on it as they do on whole oats or oats and corn, and I think for dairy stock it is preferable to any other feed. Their coats will look smoother. I have heard the objection that when cattle fed on it were turned out they were more subject to the chill winds than if fed some other food. I differ. I think the average dairyman has a pretty warm barn and when you turn the cattle out they are naturally chilly because they have been in a warm place instead of on account of the feed they have been fed on.

Mr. Wentworth: I would like to ask Mr. Barney how he plants his corn for silage, how much he plants and how much work there is in taking care of it compared to field corn.

Barney: There is not necessarily any difference. There is another advantage I claim for the silo. If I find my field corn is not going to mature for husking I put it in my silo. This is a saving for of course there is a loss on corn that does not mature unless you can convert it into silage. Now in planting corn for silage the only difference I would make would be that I would plant it a little thicker, more stalks in a hill. My experience has shown me that I can do just as well by taking a chance on a field that may not be fully matured as to plant it for silage alone. I do not usually make any difference in planting for the silo.

Wentworth: Isn't it a fact that you can plant certain kinds of corn especially adapted for the purpose and get much larger yield per acre?

Barney: You will get a larger yield, but I do not think it is quite as good as from common corn. You will get more leaves, but I think you will get better results by using ordinary corn than from this B. W. & S. corn, and I presume it is that to which you refer.

Anderson: You say you think so. Do you know it to be a fact?

Barney: Yes.

President: On account of the early frost did you manage your silage any different this year from other years?

Barney: Yes, I learned from a trip I made to Wisconsin a year ago that frosted corn could be made into very good silage. You take ordinary years and I take the corn about a week before you would cut it to shock, but this year I was caught like everybody else. The reason you cut it earlier is because you have to have a certain amount of moisture. Now after corn has been frosted I use water to get the proper moisture, and while I do not think my silage is as good this year as some years where I have cut early, yet it is all right. After my silo was filled at noon I would pour about twenty-five pails of water over the top, and about twenty-five more pails at night and then afterwards I put on about eight or nine barrels. I don't think it is quite as strong as some years, but it is good. If I thought the corn was a little bit dry, even if not frozen I would put the water on. One of the greatest mistakes is in not getting it into the silo right. You can't put your material in anyway and think you are going to have good silage.

PRESIDENT: That occupies all the time. It is too bad, because today I think it is one of the most important questions before the dairy people. The next on the program is "The Profitable Dairy Cow," by J. N. Munsey of Jesup, Iowa.

THE PROFITABLE COW.

J. N. Munsey, Jesup, Iowa.

If I was president of the United States and was writing an inaugural or message to congress, both of which are synonymous, as you can readily determine by placing the broad generalization in juxtaposition, after I got through writing about rivers and harbors, Indian reservation, negro slavery, trusts, and hard vs. soft coal for live people, I would take up the American cow. That paragraph devoted to this part of national affairs would read: "Uncle Sam milked 25,090,000 cows last year and fed 80,000,-000 of people on butter and oleomargarine. The cow bureau reports wonderful progress in the dairy industry of the United States. If it had not been for the American cow industry thousands of our principal rivers and lakes would have overflowed their banks and millions of pigs would have squealed themselves to death annually. I would call special attention of congress to the large annual production of 150 pounds of butter per cow as something remarkable in the history of our infant nation. The committee appointed to investigate whether in any locality dairymen were delayed with their spring work by being unable to find the udders in the evening without the aid of lanterns is true in but thirty per cent of the herds examined. Ten thousand editorials written by Latin and Sanskrit scholars would appear the following day commenting on the phenomenal progress of the dairy industry, and congratulating the rural population for possessing cows that secrete such enormous quanties of milk, butter fat, cheese and water. Nine-eighths of the readers of these editorials would say what powerful udders these cows must have to give 150 pounds of butter annually. Everywhere the farming population is beginning to have a just realization of just how hard a cow must have to exert her gizzard and other secretory ducts to give the enormous amount of 150 pounds of butter annually. If I was on the agricultural committee in congress I would introduce a bill providing for the systematic extermination of all cows not reaching 350 pounds of butter annually. If the bill passed I would start President Roosevelt and other rough riders up and down the Mississippi with instructions to scare all the poor cows east and west so that they would not stop running until they jumped into the Atlantic and Pacific. I have estimated by careful trigonometrical and rhetorical formulas that the waters in these oceans would be raised six feet six and nine-eighths inches. This cow movement would start a wave of prosperity or water the like of which the world had never seen since the days of Eve'n Adam or Noah. Any man who doth not agree with me thus far is not a fit subject to enter the narrow gate that leadeth to a good cow.

DECLINE IN DAIRYING

Without doubt I think the interest throughout Iowa and the United States is on the decline. I base this generalization on reasons gathered from many sources. Butter makers in different and widely separated localities concede this point. At the recent farmers' short course at Ames there seemed to be unusual interest manifested in pork and beef, and a lack of interest in the dairy cow. In a recent review of the prominent agricultural papers I find a remarkable decrease in the amount of advertising of the dairy breeds as compared with that of ten and fifteen years ago. In one paper there are but two advertisements of dairy cattle in about twenty pages. In another, nine in fifty-three pages; in another and special dairy paper but fifty ads, covering only four columns. In Iowa there has been in the recent years of 1898, 1899 and 1900 a decrease of five to six million pounds of butter sent out of Iowa. This decline is due to not one but to a number of causes. The mismanagement of creameries through neglect to improve the quality of our butter and hence increase its consumption, the reckless and indifferent breeding of dairy cows; the average inferiority of cows; the uniformly low prices for eight years; inability and indifference in feeding the cow. The majority of farmers perhaps at the leading live stock exhibitions are found admiring the plump, well rounded, symmetrical beef animal. Less number are showing interest in the dairy type of cattle. Of course, Jones likes to have a car of steers that reach seven and one-half to eight cents. His neighbor though may make just as much money by keeping a car of inferior looking cows. You may get $100.00 for a two-year-old steer; you could get $100.00 for one year's milk from a good cow.

We consume butter in Iowa to the amount of about 138,000,000 pounds annually. Much of the butter made and consumed on farms is made in a very wasteful manner. It would be much better and more enconomical for thousands to purchase their butter of the creamery and sell all the milk produced than to undertake to make their own butter. In the United States we have today probably 80,000,000 people. Basing my estimate on the actual quantity we consume on the farm I conclude we must eat on our tables in the United States and for cooking 5,018,000,000 pounds annually. I have assigned only two and one-half ounces per person a day for the urban population and thee ounces per person a day for the rural population. This represents, at twenty cents per pound $1,003,600,-000. Piled up in sixty pound tubs in a pyramid one rod square it would reach upward seventy-seven miles. At 200 pounds butter per cow it would require 25,090,000 cows. Load these cows twenty in a car and you have ten parallel tracks covered for 995 miles.

My experience in dairying covers a period of fifteen years with Holsteins, their grades, natives and grade Short-Horns. During this time I have kept many monthly milk records of cows for a year, not with a view to publication, however. I have also made many periodic tests of their butter fat capacity. During these years I have retained cows that were absolutely unprofitable for dairy purposes. Eastern buyers nearly always shun the ideal dairy cow, one of mean outline and carrying a limited amount of flesh. Almost invariably they would select the beef type of Holstein. This shows conclusively that their purchasers have demanded of them what they demanded of me. Many purchasers reason by their many failures in selection that it would be wise to select a fleshy carcass which could be disposed of in a year in case of marked inferiority than to select "raw boned cows." The purchasers may have made and lost money by this procedure, but in my opinion they would have made more and lost less by more judicious selection. Here and there throughout the states reformation in selection and feeding is going on and only the wide awake up-to-date feeders and readers are making money. During my experience I had one cow that gave upwards of 12,000, two or three 10,000 pounds of milk in a year. I sold one to a patron of the creamery. He said she gave 10,000 pounds. This man after listening to Prof. Haecker's talk in our vicinity became so convinced of the errors of his way that he began testing and feeding balanced rations and rejecting worthless cows. Speaking approximately, he quadrupled his cream checks in less than a year, from the same number of cows.

The statement of the writer fifteen years ago that a three-year-old heifer had given sixty pounds of milk in twenty-four hours created wide local comment. It was pronounced an advertisement, untrue and impossible. The following year I took the same cow to the village and invited those interested to see her milked. She gave an average of seventy-eight pounds of milk per day for seven days and for forty-eight hours she gave six pounds four ounces unsalted butter. I have a record of some twenty visitors on my book. The widespread unbelief then existing has not entirely disappeared. It is, however, disappearing among the better class of dairymen. This cow was fed thirty pounds of ground feed per day, consisting of corn, oats and bran mixed in the ratio of two bushels of oats to one of corn and fifty pounds of bran. She weighed 1,300 imported as a yearling, was a long bodied, wedge shaped cow, a hearty eater; she had long, large, irregular milk veins. She carried little flesh. Her feed you will see was mixed in the ratio of one to six and two-tenths.

There has been slow but sure progress in ideas as to what constitutes a good cow since 1875. In 118 tests of two leading breeds at the various United States fairs, extending from 1886 to 1897, and covering a period of from one to seven days, the average daily butter fat record was 1.82 pounds, or butter record of two pounds two ounces. These tests were honestly made under widely varying conditions and with cows of different ages, but usually they were in the early days of a lactation period. During these twenty-five year the breeders and feeders of beef types of cattle have rarely or ever I think exhibited for competitive milk tests the beef type cow. They have rarely or never shown photographs or wood cuts of cows with

Scene on the farm of W. P. Adams, Odebolt, Iowa.

commendable udder development. Organizations of representative breeders of dairy cattle have themselves modified their low ideals in dairy cows for the past twenty-five years. I find a leading Ayrshire breeder quoting a record of 7,500 for Ayrshire and 4,366 for Jerseys, the cattle being owned by the same man in Maine. A leading Illinois dairyman at a State Dairy association says: "I have so improved my herd that my present average is 266 pounds of butter. Alvord in early days mentions Jerseys giving 4,700, and a Native 5,300 pounds of milk. Another prominent reader and dairyman has said: "I would not keep a cow that gave less than 5,000 pounds of milk." Examples like these could be multiplied. I wish thus to emphasize the fact that our average ideal cow of twenty-five years ago is the average outcast of today, at least among the more wide awake men. I doubt very much if any country in the world has made as rapid improvement in dairy breeds as has the United States. The systems of advanced registry of registered cows, as adopted by the breeders of dairy cattle is certainly commendable. No one can question the accuracy of their tests. Experiment station representatives are required to see the cows milked. I find for the month of December, 1902, 22 cows 7 years old averaged 422 pounds of milk and 14.53 pounds of fat one week, 24 two-year-olds averaged 286 pounds of milk and 9.21 pounds fat, and 70 averaged a fat test of 3.35, and an average of 54 pounds of milk per day; 633 cows, made up of 165 two-year-olds, 65 two and three-fourths year olds, 117 three-year-olds, 95 four-year olds and 191 seven-year-olds averaged 14.15 pounds of butter per week on an average fat test of 3.38. These are Advanced Registry Holstein Frisian cows.

It is indeed to be regretted that any experiment station in the United States, and there are sevaral should have ever started to teach the cost of production of milk and butter for a period of one or five years, with a large number of cows of small productive capacity, uncertain breeding and inferior conformation. The same valuable lessons, with a smaller number of inferior cows and a larger number of well bred representative animals would in five or ten years time have proved an object lesson worth ten times the money to the rural population and the station itself. You may say that this statement is biased and made in the interest of the representative breeders of dairy cattle. I believe I speak without bias, for I have no interest in any way in any breed. Surely, directly and indirectly the Jersey, Guernsey and Holstein breeders have been more influential than all other forces combined in improving our ideals of a cow. We want no 5,000 five per cent fat cows. We want today 8,000 pound five per cent fat cows, 10,000 four per cent, and 15,000 3.25 per cent cows in our dairies. Get them if you want to. They are probably worth $100 to $150.

The majority of the business transactions made in the purchase of dairy cows is made on the assumption that but little dependence is to be placed on the so-called good points of a cow. They want size, short tail and long teats. Size, because they warm up the barn, short tail for fly time convenience and long teats so that in case the milk hauler is but a block away they can hurry business by putting the two youngest on the same teat. "If dat cow make me von calf and I sell dot calf for fler and swansy dollar den dot vos britty good." The Dutchman is not the only one guilty of such logic.

A good illustration of agreement in selecting a cow is here given to show that outward signs and appearances may probably be, and in my mind surely is worth a great deal in making selections. My neighbor, a man of limited dairy education, a stingy reader, but a man of thirty years' practical experience feeding cows, was in attendance at a farm sale where twenty-five cows were to be sold. The writer and one, R. S. Wooster, a dairyman of scholarly attainments were present. Wooster desired to determine to his satisfaction whether my neighbor and myself would select the same cow as the best one in the twenty-five. Accordingly he detailed one man to take my neighbor away and get his decision. Mr. Wooster treated the writer likewise. The same cow was selected. The sale was genuine. All cows were sold but this one and the reason given was "that is the woman's cow." Here then you have agreement between two men and the woman who did the milking. It is highly probable, therefore, that this was the best cow in the twenty-five. A wide awake, money making German in our locality had observed our selections of cows for several years and told me but two years ago that he had always wondered how it was I could pay $45 to $50 for a cow when the average were selling at $30 to $35. He says: "I discovered your ideas. Accordingly my selections were made principally on the point that the cow should have no disposition to carry beef." This German actually received $20 to $25 per month more for the same number of cows than his neighbors. His ideas of selection were only moderately good, but he had wonderfully improved his former conditions.

I always have been and am at present an exponent for the large dairy cow. When I say large I mean a cow weighing 1,000 to 1,300. Of course, size alone would not govern my selection. I want size coupled with individual excellence in other more important characteristics. Those of you who saw the twenty-five World's Fair Jerseys will agree with me that they were uniformly large for the breed. That lesson must have aroused enthusiastic dairymen to some of the possibilities in dairying. It has always seemed to me that animals require maintenance somewhat in proportion to surface exposure. The cost of producing a pound of beef if known to increase as the weight of the animal increases. May that not be due to variation in the per cent of food digested in different stages of growth and not to the amount actually needed for bodily maintenance. Compare two cubical blocks two and three feet on a side respectively. One has eight, the other twenty-seven cubic feet. One has fifty-four, the other fifty-four square feet of exposed surface. The large block has three times as many cubic feet and about twice as many exposed surface feet. What is true of these blocks is true of cows, so far as surface exposure is concerned. Take for example W. L. Carlyle's of Madison, Wisconsin, Rose, a grade Short-Horn, weighing 1,550 ate $33.93, and butter costs 7.7 cents. Here butter for 6.9 cents. While Daisy, a Guernsey grade, weighing 980 consumed $31.86 in feed and produced butter for 7.1 cents. Another grade Short-Horn, weighing 1.550 ate $33.93, and butter cost 7.7 cents. Here is a case of a cow weighing 570 more than Daisy, eating but $1.97 worth more of feed and producing a total of skim milk and butter of but 97 cents less for the year. Rose made a profit of $11.82 for the year in excess of Daisy. Surely nothing here to show that the large cow is the expensive producer. Butter is estimated at twenty cents and skim milk at one-fourth cents per pound.

Comparison of two cows with one cow for eight weeks at two stations:

NAMES.	Weight of corn.	Pounds of butter in eight weeks.	Milk in eight weeks.	Cost of feed.	Value product butter 20, skim milk 25 per 100.	Net
Houston	967	206	3810	$ 17.82	$ 50.20	$ 32.38
Fortune..........	935					
Rosa Bonheur.........................	1750	169	5146	22.44	46.24	23.80

The feed of the two smaller cows was grain 28, hay 16, ensilage 40. The feed of the larger cow was grain 27.29, mangel 29.6, ensilage 81.6. The price of feed is not given by the Minnesota station, but rather as the Michigan station figures, viz.: Hay $6.00, ensilage $2.00, oil meal $22.75, oats $16, corn meal $19, bran $14, barley $19 per ton. All came in about the same time. Rosa Bonheur was fed in Michigan, Houston and Fortune in Minnesota. Rosa at this time had a box stall, one side of which was but one thickness of boards unevenly battened, the weather at zero and below for several successive nights. I know nothing about the barns of Houston and Fortune. Again Houston is reported to have eaten 20.16 pounds dry matter to make one pound of butter fat in winter of '93· while Rosa Bonheur made on pound of fat from 19.7 dry matter. I see no reason from these data to conclude that of two equally thrifty persistent milkers, one weighing 800, the other 1,600, the former should produce a pound of milk and butter at the lesser cost. If we could find two cows having productive capacity exactly proportionate to weight, being equal in thrift, appetite and ability to digest and convert food into milk and butter, I should expect the larger cow to prduce at the lower cost.

The size of the udder is not necessarily an indication of relative value. The largest udder on a Short-Horn type of Holstein cow that I ever saw proved to have unusually large, fleshy and small glandular development. This cow never made a record worth publishing. The skin covering the udder should be soft, flexible and elastic, not thick, harsh and rigid. After milking it should collapse and hang in folds. The greater the dimunition in the size of the udder before and after milking the greater the indication of milk secreting development. If the teats hang close together you must expect inferiority. I am not prepared to reject the Guenon Escutcheon theory. In fact, as far as my unrecorded observations go, it seems to me good cows have usually had large escutcheon development. It may be finally determined that the escutcheon will be an indication of quality, though not propotionate to the claims of its advocates. Proper care and feed and sixty days dry a year will produce development.

The size of veins are prominent indications of a good cow. The Short-Horn cow, College Moore, at Ames, Iowa, has quite large, not long and slightly irregular milk veins. Not a remarkable development in this direction, but of course superior to tens of thousands of the same breed.

Briefly, I want a long bodied cow, having bright, large active eyes, indicating motherly affection. She must have neat shapely head, small downward curved horns, mild disposition, not a lazy indifferent look, slim neck, narrow foreparts, broad hind parts, and showing a disposition to carry minimum amount of flesh. I want indications of large digestive capacity. Like selecting steers for feeding if there is any indication of a daintiness in feeding you don't want the cow. The greatest eaters are probably nearly always the cheapest producers of milk or beef.

The profitable cow in the hands of a feeder who knows that dried up corn stalks and late-cut two days dried timothy hay and plenty of bedding will produce profitable returns, is a failure. The profitable cow must have some friend and that friend is the profitable feeder. Early cut tame or wild hay put up after a very little curing is as welcomed by the good cow as a dish of fruit salad is by the hired girl. Build a silo? Yes. Some one has aptly said that the motto of too many reads: "Stuff the steer and starve the cow." In some cases I would change it to read, stuff the cow and starve the steer, in others "starve the steer and starve the cow." But if you want to be a Christian you will "stuff the steer and stuff the cow," if they are worth it; it not, consign them to the sausage mill. Don't feed a cow dried bread nor all pie and cake. Give her a variety. It will be difficult in a few years more to find any dairymen who ever poked fun at the practical experiments with balanced rations. You can't find a man today who ever said, for example, that the United States Department of Agriculture was wild when it called Dr. E. Lewis Sturtevant to investigate the merits of the first Danish Weston Milk Separator, and yet there were hundreds. Do not turn cows out too early in the spring. Do not allow them to eat much grass the first few days. Continue the grain feeding for a week or more, after which if you have pasture in abundance, stop. We must now concede that liberal pasture will produce as much and as rich milk as can be produced by additional grain feeding. If you can have your pasture lots divided so that you can alternate occasionally it will be a marked benefit I firmly believe. The rains wash off the bad odors and foreign matter which has adhered to the blades of grass as the cows walk round. Have your barn warm. It ought at least to be 34 degrees Farenheit, better at 44 degrees ,and very doubtful about having a temperature of 60. Let the cows have a limited amount of exercise when the weather is favorable in winter. Keep them in when the weather is 10 below and shut the barn doors. This is just as important as it is to shut the kitchen door. You scolded your wife because she was using wood to warm up other peoples' back yards and you are trying to warm up 160 acre farm with ten cents worth of feeds.

BURNING OUT COWS.

This theory is quite firmly interwoven in the popular conversation of average farmers, even today. By this is meant that a cow is short lived for dairy purposes if liberally fed. These men have no doubt fed very liberally on clear corn meal and hay. Others have fed the same food on a starvation basis. Naturally they have inferred that too much feed will "burn out the cow." Arthur Brigham of the Rhode Island Experiment Station mentions a herd of Holsteins that were "almost ruined by their owners feeding silage, corn meal and gluten." Think, my friend, Geneva S., a Jersey gave as a result of a liberally fed balanced ration for six years an average of 509 pounds of butter. The writer's best cow was in the herd for eleven years. Her average production I can't give, but to me it was wonderful. Three cows gave 400 to 453 pounds of butter for an average for five years. Briefly then, drop this eroneous notion. If a cow was actually "burned out" every five years, it would be better for the farmer if he got such results as here mentioned.

About thirteen years ago I said that in my estimation from my milk records of four or five cows that it was highly probable that November was about the best month in the year to have cows drop their calves. I see no reason to change that opinion, at least as to quantity of milk produced. It seems reasonable that a cow giving milk from December to May 10, inclusive on dry feed should respond and increase in flow or at least maintain her flow for a longer time. Linfield of Utah station in 1900 made observations on the increase in milk flow by dividing the herd into two lots, one lot calving March to May, the other September to February. The former lot increased in a given time sixty-six, and the latter fifty-four pounds of milk. This is strongly in harmony with my opinion. A cow ought to calve once each year. This improves and develops her milking qualities, develops the udder and retains femininty. I cheerfully and emphatically differ with a prominent dairy writer who has said that four weeks is a sufficient time for a cow to go dry. My rule is sixty days. I would not think of undertaking to dry up a cow four weeks before calving. The rate of growth of the foetus the last sixty days must be very rapid compared with the previous sixty days, or previous seven months. I do not think four weeks is at all sufficient time to get a full and normal distension of the udder before calving. Undoubtedly the same cow calving once a year will produce a greater total profit than she would by calving say every 500 days. I believe that. A cow ought to be in high condition at calving time. She must not be fat but she could carry her normal flesh or a little more.

PARTURIENT APOPLEXY.

In my experience I had only three cases. Lost two, saved one. These three cows came into my possession from a feeder in 1884 who had fed too liberally of a fat producing food. They were in very high condition at time of calving. In fourteen years I never lost another from this quite incurable disease. I certainly have reason to infer that more judicious feeding diminished my losses in this direction.

33

W. B. Smith & Sons of Columbus, Ohio, in a recent reply (January 27, 1903) to my question asking cost of production, said:

We looked the herd over the other day. They are fed 30 pounds ensilage, 13½ pounds grain as follows: 4 pounds bran, 4 pounds malt sprouts, 3 pounds corn, oats and barley, 2½ pounds distillery gluten, and about 15 pounds corn stover from which they will get probably 4 pounds and about 5 pounds hay, mixed timothy and clover.

The cost is 23⅞ cents per cow per day, and our milk cost us per gallon, of 8¼ pounds 7.31 cents.

We get 16 cents, but the cost of men cuts profits all to pieces, we find the cost to run the dairy in a good sanitary shape cost us 5¼ cents per gallon, we use nothing but pure bred Holsteins, I figured out for a neighbor who had just gone to the wall, he was using Jerseys and Grades, that his feed was costing per cow, 21 cents, his milk was costing him per gallon, 11 cents and he trying to sell it for 10 cents, or he was doing all the work and loosing one cent per gallon.

What the people need more than anything else is figures, figures, figures, so that they will know what they are doing.

Encourage the consumption of our butter and milk in every way possible. The average butter making quality of our milk in Iowa is remarkably below that delivered in the Elgin district. The average milk delivered is not clean and will not make good butter. It might be well for our legislature to still further encourage our dairy industry by giving the dairy commissioner more helpers. Prof. McKay is doing a great deal. If the directors of these co-operative creameries would establish and enforce as rigid rules as condensers have they would without doubt improve the quality of butter two cents a pound. It can be done. Our dairy commissioner is investigating the per cent of fat in the various milks delivered in the cities in Iowa. We need improvement here also as to cleanliness. And when consumers have as much confidence in the cleanliness of Iowa milk as the people of DeKalb, Illinois do of Gurler's milk, there will be more consumed on our tables. Improve our quality and the demand will increase. Improve the dairy herds and encourage liberal feeding and our profits will increase. The country is ready now for this reformation.

PRESIDENT: If there are no questions we will pass on to the next paper, "Creamery Centralization," by C. B. Hubbard of Independence. Mr. Hubbard finds himself the victim of such a severe cold that he has asked Mr. Carpenter to read the paper for him.

MR. CARPENTER: It gives me pleasure to stand before this body of men, and some ladies to read this paper, even if I can not give you something of my own production. There is one distinctive feature in looking into the faces of an Iowa audience different from the Minnesota convention. Up there they all bring their wives and we have a very profitable and pleasant time.

CREAMERY CENTRALIZATION.

—

C. H. Hubbard, Independence, Iowa.

In the discussion of the subject of centralization, or, one might say, conforming with the demands of the age, or the times in which we live, It is worth our while to take a retrospective view, recall the past, and consider for a few moments the evolution of the dairy industry.

Little more than a quarter of a century ago the environment surrounding the industry that today has grown to marvelous proportions and the conditions under which butter was made, were decidedly unfavorable. Cream was raised in shallow tin pans and churned by the weary overworked farmer's wife and sold at the country store at prices hardly possible to pay the cost of production, not considering the labor involved in manufacturing the product.

Later it was discovered that milk might be creamed by the gravity process in long, narrow cans submerged in cold water. This was a step forward and four cans did away with the labor of washing sixteen tin pans and the labor of churning in 100 or more farm was reduced to the labor of two men at the creamery, removing the burden of one hundred churning on the farm, and this was not all. Instead of one hundred different lots of butter flavored with the odors of cabbage, onions, turnips, pancakes, catnip tea for the baby, and various other things too numerous to mention. The butter was greatly improved and sold at prices ranging from six to ten cents per pound higher, because of a more uniform product, and although not the best that could be procured, it was so much better than a hundred different lots made under more unfavorable conditions that the results were quite gratifying, and the number of cows increased and the industry began to grow.

Not enough, however, had yet been accomplished. In the onward march of progress, in the great inventive genius of the world, the art of creaming milk with centrifugal separators was discovered, and again in the evolution of the dairy industry the slow process requiring thirty-six hours to cream milk in five gallon cans, poorly and incompletely, must give way to the centrifugal separator, in the creamery, extracting the cream from 3,000 pounds of milk per hour, and again by reason of the butter maker receiving his cream sweet, enabling him to introduce favorable germs of bacteria, the growth and vegetation of which produces distinct and desirable flavors, the market price was again advanced. The introduction of the hand separator upon the farm is still another step in the onward march of progress which enables the dairyman to separate his milk at home (from the cream) and feed the milk to the calves and pigs, and instead of hauling 1,000 pounds of milk every day to the creamery the farmers takes 150 pounds of cream.

In the evolution of all these changes in the dairy industry, not one of which has not proved most satisfactory and profitable to the dairyman, and yet each step has been greeted with opposition and looked upon with grave suspicion. However, the law is an inexorable as the law of death.

The survival of the fittest has settled the difficulties and removed suspicions and as it ever has been, so it ever will be. The best and greatest good for the greatest number only will be permanent.

In the rehearsal of the foregoing facts and the evolution through which we have passed, the writer has endeavored to prepare your minds for the next evolution, cheaper production, which involves centralization, and again the unchangeable law, the survival of the fittest, will decide whether it will be permanent or temporary.

One central creamery plant manufacturing a carload of butter per day will extinguish the fires under forty boilers at 10 o'clock a. m. which otherswise would consume fuel several hours longer, if the butter is manufactured at the forty different points. The economy of labor requiring at least one man less in each of the forty creameries, is an item the magnitude of which cannot be ignored. A carload of butter all manufactured under one roof where one expert superintends ripening the cream, securing superior aromatic flavor, one shade of color, all uniformly salted, will command one-half to one and a half cents per pound higher than a carload of butter manufactured in forty different creameries of various shades of color, salt and flavor.

It is a difficult matter, indeed hardly possible to secure a carload of butter from forty creameries without great variation in quality, which secures the fancy brand and commands a premium. The extra price possible to secure on a carload of butter uniform in quality, of superior merit, would go far toward paying the operating expenses. Purchasing tubs, salt, and coal in carload consignments would secure the minimum price at which these supplies could be procured, which would be equally true of butter color, tub liners and other minor supplies. Another very important matter, the value and results of which could hardly be overestimated: The employment of a food instructor in the field to instruct the milk producer in scientific feeding and the importance of better care and breeding.

The writer not long ago was the observer at one station in Wisconsin that received in one day 6,330 pounds of milk from 238 cows, an average of 26 59-100 pounds per cow. On the same territory one company receiving milk from 18,328 cows the average was only 17 58-100 pounds, 9 1-100 pounds less than the average of the cows of the dairyman that had adopted better care and feeding a balanced ration. The loss from the 18,328 cows to the dairyman amounted to 165.135 pounds of milk, over 82½ tons worth at 70 cents per hundred, $1,155.94 in one day.

Iowa is the greatest butter producing state in the Union, and the one in which the greater proportion is made on the factory plan. Iowa has 780 creameries, only two counties being without them. In these creameries about 88,000,000 pounds of butter are annually manufactured from

624,000 cows. It is estimated that 50,000,000 pounds of butter in addition are made from farm dairies. The total butter product of this state is one-tenth of all made in the United States. Iowa sends over 80,000,000 pounds of butter annually into other states. New York is next in importance as a butter producing state, and then come in order Pennsylvania, Illinois, Wisconsin, Minnesota. Ohio and Kansas. If the Iowa dairymen would adopt a system of scientific feeding and give their herds better care and provide for their comfort in winter, conservatively speaking the 80,000,000 pounds of butter shipped annually might be increased 50 per cent, increasing the revenue of the commonwealth $8,000,000.

Centralization would enable a large central organization to have a food instructor delivering lectures in school rooms or halls, on the proper combinations of the farm grown grains and roughage, concentrates and mill feeds when necessary to secure the best results from their herds. The departure from the present system of manufacturing butter will be centralization. It is as sure to come as the rising and setting of the sun or the revolution of the old world on its axis. The only thing that will hinder the desirable and should be coveted condition, that will increase the profits of the dairymen, will be the unwarranted prejudice of men who do not investigate sound business principles. The bugaboo is the oft-repeated old, old story—monopoly, absorbing the profits or usurping the rights of others. This in itself would be a menace to the perpetuity and welfare of the organization.

In a country where capital is seeking employment to so plentiful as in our country, creating freedom of competition, any creamery organizations that attempt to exact from the milk producer more than a legitimate return upon capital and service, write the charter of their own defeat. We have many proofs that this great law does not sleep and that it will not be suppressed. There can be no permanent extortion of profits beyond the average return from capital in any manufacturing or transportation. Any attempt to maintain either must end in failure, and failure ultimately disastrous, just in proportion to the temporary success of the foolish effort.

It is simply ridiculous for a party of men to meet in a room and attempt by passing resolutions to change the great laws which govern human affairs in the business world. These words are from one of the greatest political economists of the age. Permanent success is not obtainable except by fair, honorable dealing, by irreproachable habits and correct living, by displaying of good sense and rare judgment in all the relations of human life, for credit and confidence fly from the business man, foolish in word and deed, or irregular in habits, or even suspected of sharp practice. The creamery organization depends for its existence on the product of the cow. It has no other source of life. Individuals may come and go, we will all sooner or later pass from active life, but the land, the country, its resources will be here permanently; the herds and the creameries, and they either will prosper together, or be poor together. Unprincipled men may engage in the business and flourish for a time and fail, however, the law is positive as the law of gravitation, will soon do away with all such illegitimate competition, and only the survival of the fittest will permanently exist,

they and their generations that follow with the priceless heritage, as benefactors of the human race.

The cows of the United States were not counted until 1840. They have
been enumerated since, however, for every decennial census. With the
closing years of the century, it is essential that there is one milch cow in
the United States for every four persons. This makes the total number
of cows about 17,500,000. They are unevenly distributed over the country,
being largely concentrated in the great dairy states. Iowa leads with
1,500,000, followed by New York with almost as many, then Illinois and
Pennsylvania with about 1,000,000 each. The states having over 500,000
each are Wisconsin, Ohio, Kansas, Missouri, Minnesota, Nebraska and
Indiana. Texas is credited with 700,000 cows. Very few of them, however,
are dairy animals.

In the middle and eastern states, the milk produced goes very largely
to the supply of numerous large towns and cities. In the central west and
northwest butter is the principal dairy product. The value of the dairy
product of the United States in the year 1899 was approximately as follows,
in quantity and values: Butter was produced from 11,000,000 cows; rate
of production per cow, 130 pounds; total 1,430,000,000 at 18 cents; total
value, $257,400,000.

Cheese from 1,000,000 cows 300 pounds per cow, 300,000,000 pounds
total product; at 9 cents per pound, total value $27,000,000.

Milk from 5,500,000 cows, rate of milk per cow, 380 gallons, 2,090,000,-
000 gallons at 8 cents, $167,200,000.

"This gives a total of the dairy products of the country a value of $451,-
600,000. If to this be added the by products at their proper feeding value
and the calves dropped yearly, the annual value of the product of the dairy
cows exceeds $500,000,000.

Accepting these estimates as conservative, they show the commercial
importance of the dairy industry of the United States is such as to demand
attention and justify all reasonable provisions for guarding its interests."

PRESIDENT: We have with us this afternoon Mr. F. W. Taylor
of St. Louis, chief of the agricultural and horticultural departments of the Louisiana Purchase Exposition, who has kindly consented to talk to us.

THE AGRICULTURAL AND HORTICULTURAL DEPARTMENTS OF THE LOUISIANA PURCHASE EXPOSITION.

F. W. Taylor, St. Louis, Mo.

It is always a great pleasure to me to report back to the people whose
interests I represent. It has happened that for the last six years I have
been devoting my time to exposition work, and I have come to look upon
the people who come to these organizations as the people who employ me.
Incidentally a city gets ready and prepares to hold an exposition. All they

do is to get together and build the buildings, provide the houses for the exhibitors and invite them to come and exhibit in them.

I think that in all recent expositions there has been just cause for complaint on the part of the dairy men that their interests have not been cared for. I think half of that has been the fault of the exposition people and the other half the fault of the dairy people. In the last three expositions in which I have taken part the dairy people have demanded a separate building for their products. This is the worst mistake they could make. On the other hand, the exposition commissioners have demanded that the dairy interests be placed on two floors. I never like to make comparisons, but you can never tell what progress we are making unless we compare, so I shall take the liberty of speaking of the area we have in comparison with Chicago.

In Chicago there was a building devoted to agriculture and agricultural implements, and one building for dairy interests and implements. Both of these buildings had galleries. All of the agricultural implements were exhibited in galleries. In the St. Louis exposition there has been provided a single building to hold all the products I have mentioned, there being no galleries. It has a ground area of 1600x500 ft. That building will contain four classes of exhibits, all of them agricultural. The first will be the agricultural resources of all the countries of the world; the second food products; the next will be dairy products and dairy implements, and the fourth agricultural implements. All of these will be under one roof and on one floor. This provision has been made because it is believed that everyone who has had experience will agree that this will bring past a single exhibit more people than any other arrangement which can be made. This is what we have done for you, and after providing the housing, classification and facilities, the rest of it—to use a slightly vulgar but very applicable expression—is up to you. You have just heard it stated that Iowa is the greatest dairy state in the Union. Have you ever stopped for a moment to think what that means. The youngest person in the audience can remember when that was not so. and I have lived in Iowa for twenty-five years and know something of the condition as they apply here. When you think of the wonderful progress made in so short a period should it not be taken as meaning that little has been done compared with what can be done? Is there any better way to set before ourselves, before you as well as before those who live elsewhere than in this state, what can be done here? Before I was connected with this work I was in the educational business. And I think expositions are as truly educators as anything can be. I believe that when we lay out these plans and ask you to be guided by them, because these exhibits are to be placed before people some of whom will never have any broad educational advantages in the sense we mean them. ·This is what we do at St. Louis. We wish every phase to be educational, so that there will be no question but what opportunity has been given for study and that they will have studied. As to the exact thing this one state should do and can do—it is this: In the first place—having already, I presume, a considerable appropriation, I would suggest that this organization ask, if it has not already asked, that there be a certain amount set aside specifically for the dairy exhibit of this state. The next thing is to select a man whom all of you believe to be the best man to represent the state there. Urge that he be appointed in ample time to make the many and varied preparations he must make to install that exhibit and keep it until the closing day. I have found that local societies do not quite realize what they might do by urging the necessity of having their own interests cared for, until it is too late. I don't know of anything else you need to have said to you. I don't believe you need to have this said to you, but it is something I always say in order to have my conscience clear. What I have said with regard to the placing of the dairy exhibit on the first floor of the building means that it will have good space and as much of it as it needs; that there is a greater amount of ground space than in Chicago, and if the state will make the necessary appropriation to show that they will carry out an exhibit they can have the proper space. I have no doubt you will do your part to bring the exhibit there. I know of no industry which has made more progress since the last exposition than has dairying, and I know of but one that has made as much. I refer to horticulture, the growing of fruit and particularly of apples. Part of the growth of these industries has been in instilling into people's minds better ideas in regard to packing, and part to better facilities in shipping—cold storage for instance.

We expect within sixty days to have the final plans of this building sent out and we expect to have appointed a superintendent of dairy exhibits. I don't know yet who it will be, but I am sure you will be satisfied. As soon as we are ready to send out the name of the superintendent it will be your duty to respond. And if there is any way in the world in which my department can help I know it will be glad to do it.

PRESIDENT: The next question before you is a question which today is probably the most important of any before the dairymen of the state. And I am going to request that in the discussion of it you refrain from all personalities, that you will not take the opportunity to do any advertising. We will now have a discussion of the hand separator question. Mr. N. H. Trimble of Alden is first.

ADDRESS.

———

N. H. Trimble, Alden, Iowa.

When I came into the auditorium last night and saw all the hand separators on exhibition, and looked around and saw all the hand separator agents I was a little sorry I had come. Two weeks ago today I was put on the program at a Farmers' Institute without my consent. They had me on to talk on the hand separator. I said some things about the hand separator then and when I saw that some of the hand separator men were in the audience I didn't know but what I was going to get the worst of it.

But one of them came to me afterwards and said I had been quite fair in my talk and hadn't said much against them. I had made the assertion that we only had two separators which would skim a 30 per cent cream.

Up to a year ago last June I hardly knew what a hand separator was. I was up in Palo Alto county then, and while they would not object to taking hand separator cream no person in the district had a separator. The manager and secretary of the Alden creamery came to Ayrshire and wanted to hire me. I asked about the conditions over there and they told me things were in bad shape. They had a skim station. I hired to them and came there on the 25th day of June, and if I had been back in Ayrshire on the 1st day of July I would have been there yet. The second day I was there a great big Irishman came in. Now I'm Irish myself, but I wasn't as big as this man. His milk was sour; it was bad. Now I had guaranteed the company to make western extras. I said, "I can't take that cream." He said, "You will have to take it; I am one of the stockholders." I said, "Mr., I am afraid I can't." He said, "I will see the president." I said, "All right, but he told me not to take anything that wasn't fit and this certainly isn't fit." Now I am going to say something about the hand separator agents. One of the agents had been through there selling separators and had told the buyers that if they separated at home they wouldn't have to bring their cream but once a week and it would be all right. That is what the agent had told this man. He didn't care; he was making his $25 or $30. I don't know just what they do make. This man told me what the separator agent had told him, that he could bring his cream once a week. Well, I didn't take his cream and that man got real angry. He didn't come again for about four weeks, and finally he quit me altogether. He tried making butter at home and made a complete failure of it. His neighbors all came to me and he had to go to Williams all alone. He hardly speaks to me now. I tried to get the board to pass a resolution to compel them to bring their cream every other day in the summer time and three times a week in the winter. I had guaranteed to make Western Extras. I had been getting a good price for my butter where I came from, and they wanted me to get the same price here. I told them I couldn't do it unless they restricted the hand separator business, but I finally got them to bringing good cream. A week after I got there we got three-fourths of a cent below. We had forty hand separators when I went in; we have forty-seven now and I think we will have more. We are taking in milk also. We are improving in the quality of the butter, although some of them insist on coming only twice a week. We hadn't a starter can and I ordered one the first day. I commenced getting after the patrons too and finally they got to bringing pretty good cream. The cream they brought tested from 10 to 25. Our dairy commissioner says we ought not to take less than 30 per cent cream and ought to insist on 35 per cent. Now I am not going to mention any separators, but the average separator doesn't skim that way. A separator man came to me and said that his separator would skim all right if the farmers knew how to use it. I asked him why he didn't educate them to it. He says the farmers won't do it. He had sold one of our patrons a separator and that patron was bringing 16 per cent cream. I told him to bring in the skim milk and I would test it, and I found he was leaving eight-tenths of one per cent in the milk. He said it was good enough for him. He was stuck on his separator. He ran it for three months and then he broke a wheel and notified the agent about it; but it hasn't been fixed yet and he is bringing his milk today and he says he is losing money by doing it. The farmers up there say they are getting a dollar a month more out of their cows with the separators. The farmer who had been bringing his milk quit and I asked him if he was going back to the seperator. He told me he had young calves and they did so much better on the milk right on the farm than they did on that brought back from the creamery and then he went out and told some of his neighbors that he had lost $10.00 that month by quitting his separator and sending his milk, which he had done just to please a neighbor.

When our dairy commissioner gave out his report this year, he had sent out letters with questions like this: "Is the use of the hand separator in your district increasing?" Of 20 answers, 13 said yes, 7 said no. The next questions was, "Is the quality of the butter made at the creamery poor?" Eleven answered yes and 9 answered no. The next was, "Have you had any complaint of the quality of your butter from your commission men?" Seven answered yes, 13 answered no. I said "No" then; three weeks later I would have said, "Yes." Of course it is natural for the butter-makers to think that we are never to blame for anything. Well my commission house wired me that the butter was off, to look out. The next morning I received a letter stating that an inch of butter on the top was tainted. Of course I thought at once that it was the hand separator. So I took my hand separator cream and kept it by itself and churned it and I took the milk and kept the cream off it by itself and churned it. Used the same starter and everything in each case. I sent it into the commission house marked, and they answered that they couldn't see any difference. So I made up my mind the fault must be with the buttermaker, but of course I didn't tell the directors. The butter has come around all right now. But about six weeks after I had tried to find out what the trouble with this butter was and had failed, we one day opened a barrel of salt that had a peculiar odor. I said I am not going to use that salt except on four tubs. I did and sent it to the commission men and next week received a telegram, 'Four tubs tainted." Now I had a little experience with a commission house which calls to mind what our president said last night, that he hoped the day would come when butter would be sold on its merits. The last year I was at the other creamery we were shipping to New York and I had my butter scored by Healey every month. One day when I was busy at the creamer the secretary came down and handed me my returns, butter scoring 85. I threw the thing on the floor, but on second thought I picked it up and looked at it again and saw that it was not mine. It was returns from a commission house in New York I had never shipped to. The name of the creamery was the same, but some mistake had been made. We went up town and there found my returns, and I had scored 96, and that man whose butter had scored 85 was getting just the same price that I was for mine. We were selling on the same basis too. Now the sooner we can get to a point where we sell butter on its own merits the better.

The hand separator people claim there is much saved in hauling. That may be true. We lost a great deal of milk last summer because it was so muddy we couldn't get the milk through. We had in our district a man who bought a separator last fall and he had always raised good calves. This last year he lost all his calves. That man was at the depot yesterday when I came away, and I said, "You have lost all your calves this winter?" He said, "Yes, but I don't blame the hand separator." I don't think we can do as our dairy commissioner tells us, make them skim a 35 per cent cream, but I believe we can make pretty good butter out of hand separator cream. The hand separators are here and I think they are going to stay. I have heard the remark made that they will get tired of them after awhile and set them aside. Now we have lots of men who have bought their second separator and I think they are going to use them. I think a buttermaker should insist on their getting a separator which will skim a good cream, and insist on the separators being kept clean. An agent came to Alden once last fall and told all the farmers that it wasn't necessary to wash the separators more than once a week. And I think this class of separator agents have done more to injure the quality of Iowa butter than anything else. But there are some good agents and occasionally they tell a buyer to go to his buttermaker and find out how to take care of his separator. That is all I have to say.

HAND SEPARATOR VERSUS WHOLE MILK.

E. Pufahl, Nora Springs, Iowa.

I came up here to discuss the question from the hand separator standpoint. In the first place I would say that Mr. Trimble said he was only getting one-half cent above when he started in, and had to learn how to handle hand separator cream, and now he has worked it up so that he is getting one cent above. When he told about his commission merchant telling him that his butter was a little bit off I thought the hand seperator was going to catch it, but it seems he kept his hand separator cream and other cream separate and made butter from both and the commission merchant couldn't tell the difference. I have prepared a paper on the subject, which I will read:

Five years ago it would have been a hard task for a person to discuss the advantages of the hand separator over the whole milk system because he would have been compelled to talk mostly from a theoretical standpoint; today he can say, it has been tried and successfully stood the test. To begin with I will say where a whole milk creamery is running successfully, the admitting of hand separator cream causes confusion because it cuts up the milk routes. If the farmer sending in hand separator cream is compelled to pay as much for the hauling of it as for the milk, he will become dissatisfied and he stirs up agitation and either forces the company to haul his cream cheaper or else he takes it to the nearest railway station and ships it.

If the creamery company hauls it for less than his milk he receives more per pound butter fat than his neighbor who sends whole milk, and then of course his neighbor is the one that kicks, but the result generally is that he also will get a hand separator as he sees that he will get more money out of his cows and by and by there are so many farmers with hand separators that a meeting is called and it is generally decided to take cream only if the hauling of the milk becomes too great an expense, and after that things again run harmoniously. I admit that during this change is the critical point of the welfare of the creamery.

I probably have fought the hand separator as hard as any man in the state of Iowa. This was during the six years while I was secretary and manager of one of the largest whole milk plants in the state. I remember about five years ago we had a stockholders meeting as a few of the farmers (probably a half dozen) wanted to buy hand machines. The result was that these few were the only ones who voted for the adoption of admitting hand separator cream, and so were overwhelmingly defeated. I was one of the majority who fought them hard, as I thought then it was but another new fad, but in time I changed my mind.

The general feeling of the stockholders at this meeting was such that it would have been dangerous for any hand separator agent to have been in reach as he certainly would not have been handled gently. Today these same farmers all have hand machines. The few who wanted hand machines at that time continued to send their milk to our creamery but still felt that they had not been treated fairly, but we paid no attention to them, rather felt jubilant over our success to think that we had compelled them to continue sending milk.

But in a year or two a certain creamery man thought he saw a good opening for a hand separator creamery in our territory—started one, and of course these parties at once bought hand machines and delivered their cream to him and received good results. And you may bet they were not slow in trying to convince their neighbors of the advantages of the hand separator. This of course compelled us to change front very suddenly and we also accepted hand separated cream and handled it very successfully I think.

The hauler brought in the cream the same as the milk, poured it into the weighing can where it was weighed and a sample taken. The cream was then allowed to run into the receiving vat which mixed it with the milk and was again separated. Our object in doing this was three fold. First, this method made the least amount of extra work. Second, the average cream ran about 25 per cent test, while we skimmed a 50 per cent cream. This thin cream would have taken too much additional vat room. The third and main reason was that by again skimming it we took out considerable of the bad odor it might have attained. The result was that we made as good butter as we did before we handled hand separator cream. The farmers continued to buy more machines and today the plant takes in no whole milk whatever. The hauling of the milk cost all the way from 2½ to 4 cents per pound butter, while I understand it now costs about 1½ cents or less on an average. Then again the running of a creamery is considerable less than it was before. By this experience I saw that a hand separator meant more dollars and cents into the pockets of the farmers.

When the farmer has finished separating his milk he feeds his calves the nice fresh skimmed milk, pours what he has left into the swill barrel. His wife washes the cans and separator, which is done in short order as the dirt has no time to stick to sides of the cans and separator. Our opponents may say that the washing of the separator is quite an item, but I have some of the farmers' wives tell me that by long odds they would sooner wash the separator than the milk cans in the condition they are when they come back from the creamery. It certainly is easier to cool the cream than the milk, for even though cream does not cool as quick as milk the amount is so much less that the advantage is decidedly in favor of the cream., Our opponents will most likely say again, "But the farmer does not give his cream the same care and attention as the milk, and besides will try and keep it two or three days, as the amount looks too small to him to send to the creamery." It is true the farmer will at first have a tendency to do this very thing, but if the butter maker or weigher insists upon him sending good cream and points out to him the bad results of this practice the farmer will take better care of his cream. At least that was my experience. Another strong point in favor of separators is that the farmer is not compelled to send his cream to his home plant, if at any time he thinks he is not getting fair treatment, or if the creamery is for some reason or another compelled to shut down. In either case he can take his cream to the nearest railway station and ship it to where he can obtain good results.

Briefly stated the advantages of hand separator cream over whole milk are: Better feed for the calves; no danger of having sent back impure milk from another patron's herd; less expense in hauling and running of creamery, which means more money into the pockets of the farmer from the creamery, and the doing away of the running of the creamery on Sundays which a great many whole milk plants insist upon. This last advantage created a better moral effect on the community in which the creamery is located.

Gentlemen: If any of you want a good, thorough discussionn the farm separator as based upon observation and information obtained from those having had experience with the same, just read our dairy commissioner's report on farm separators and I think you will concede that the advantages of the farm machine more than offset the disadvantages and that the hand separator is here to stay.

PRESIDENT: The next part in this discussion was to have been taken by Mr. Leighton, but it is impossible for him to be present at this hour, so we will listen to Mr. A. O. Elvidge of Elkader.

HAND SEPARATORS.

A. O. Elvidge, Elkader, Iowa.

They have me down on the program for a little talk on the hand separator, but as I am no orator you will have to put up with anything I have to say. I am at a loss to suggest anything new on the subject. My position is purely a selfish and mercenary one, as by the use of the hand separator I can cover a larger territory and get the milk to the creamery at a saving of from one-third to one-half, and thus saves the farmers what in some localities amounts to a good deal. Then again the milk on the farm warm and sweet is worth twice as much to the farmer for feed as it would be if it had been hauled ten to fifteen miles to the creamery in the heat. Then the cost of running the creamery is much less. Our opponents will tell you that what we gain in this way will be lost in the quality of product. Now where there may be a shade of truth in this in some localities, especially where the proper use of the separator is not yet understood, in my case it is not so. We have factories operated on the whole milk plan and on the hand separator plan, and the butter from the hand separator factories sells for as much as that from the milk factories. I will admit that the chances for loss are greater under the hand separator system than under the whole milk, but in both cases we reject if it is not. In conclusion, the hand separator must have some merits or the system would not have grown to the proportion it has.

PRESIDENT: Mr. M. O. Wheelock of Independence will make the closing remarks.

M. O. WHEELOCK: There is nothing left for me to say. Everything has been thoroughly gone over and it all seems to be in favor of the hand separator.

PRESIDENT: Now we have about ten minutes left and you can ask these gentlemen questions.

MR. ANDERSON: I would like to ask Mr. Pufahl under which system his Luena creamery has been most successful.

PUFAHL: Of course I would naturally talk from a selfish standpoint. While I was running the creamery at Luena it was running, good, both while I was handling whole milk and while I was handling cream. But I will say that at the last the cost of hauling the milk was so much that we could not pay the patrons so much as when we bought cream. As I said, it was a critical point in the welfare of the creamery. Part of them had separators and part were bringing whole milk.

ANDERSON: Under which system did you ship the greatest amount of butter?

PUFAHL: During the first year I was in business we shipped the most. We handled it for two years without any hand separator, but we were dropping off because the farmers were not milking so heavily. I will venture to say that this summer the patrons got more dollars and cents out of their cows in proportion.

MR. ROSS: I would like to ask the same gentleman about receiving cream when they were running and mixing the cream with the milk and re-skimming, would you advise that as a safe method of getting a heavy cream?

PUFAHL: I certainly would advise that method if I was running a plant and had milk and cream both. I would skim the cream again and get a heavier cream.

MR. NIETERT: I would ask if the object of that was not to improve the quality of the hand separator cream?

PUFAHL: I said it was to take out the bad odors it might have attained.

NIETERT: That was the purpose you had in view?

PUFAHL: Yes, that was the purpose.

MR. KIEFFER: I would like to ask Mr. Pufahl if he can tell us whether the quality of butter at Luena creamery is the same now as it was when the whole milk was delivered to the plant?

PUFAHL: That of course I can't tell, because I am not there.

KIEFFER: Then the only object you had in changing to the hand separator was the enormous expense in hauling to the creamery?

PUFAHL: That was one of them.

KIEFFER: That was the main reason?

PUFAHL: We have lots of main reasons.

KIEFFER: Hasn't the amount of butter production fallen off at that creamery?

PUFAHL: Why, you can't give that a fair show, because there has been mis-management there.

KIEFFER: Isn't it a fact that one of the causes of the change to the hand separator system was because they were paying as high as six or seven cents on a pound of butter for the hauling of milk. Didn't it run up to nearly that at Luena before you made the change?

PUFAHL: Yes, certainly; that was one of the causes that forced us to change.

KIEFFER: That being the case, it was the main cause for the change, wasn't it?

PUFAHL: It would be a good cause I think.

MR. HUBBELL: Isn't it a fact that the territory has been cut down by the establishment of a new creamery on the territory.

PUFAHL: There were several reasons the patronage fell off. They didn't milk as heavy and the territory was cut down some last summer.

MR. CARPENTER: Did I understand that you took that new milk in to redeem the cream?

PUFAHL: No, I took it and mixed it for the reason that I thought it took out the bad odors.

CARPENTER: Now the audience seem to think that you took in that milk in order to redeem that hand separator cream.

NIETERT: I wish to set myself right. That is the reason I am asking these question. I am not informed about hand separators, and I am here to get information, and the best suggestion I have heard about improving the cream was what this gentleman told me about putting in the new milk. That is the reason I put the question the way I did. I believe he is an honest butter maker and I am a creameryman interested in any method that will improve the quality of Iowa butter. The grade of Iowa butter has not been kept up as it should have been. I am not here to irritate anybody but to find out about it.

PUFAHL: I still maintain the very point. If I was running a creamery I would still try to run the cream through the milk and skim over.

MR. ROSS: I have forty-seven hand separators on my territory and I have been following that method myself. I have fought the hand separator question to a finish in my territory, but lately I have taken up the system. I will say that I do not believe I am making quite so good butter, as I did before I went into this system, but if you will insist on good cream I think as good butter can be made. I had one patron who had bothered me for a year. I had talked, scolded, and sworn a little, I think. One morning I was sitting in my office and my helper called me out and this patron who had been bothering me had thirty gallons of cream. He said it was cream. It looked like Dutch cheese. My helper asked me what I was going to do with it, and I hardly knew, but we finally went to work and dumped the stuff out. And from that day to this we have not had one bit of trouble with the hand separator cream. I have come to the conclusion that we will have the hand separators, like the poor, with us always. I have found it helps to mix it with the milk. I think that when the hand separator system is used throughout the state the quality of Iowa butter will be improved, but the butter maker will have to stay awake nights planning about it. It doesn't do any good to fight the agents. But I don't think there is a patron in my territory who doesn't fetch his tale of woe to me, and I don't hear any complaints about the agents.

PRESIDENT: We have only five minutes left and we will give that to Mr. Barney.

MR. BARNEY: This seems to be a one-sided discussion, but I want to say this: That if there are any farmers here who want to raise good calves if they have the same experience I have had they will have to have separators. I have had one about six years, and one of the most important things in my business is the raising of good calves. I can say I raise just as good calves with a little feed and the separator milk as I ever did. I am using it today and the creamery man is coming my way, and when he doesn't I am going to use my hand separator and churn my own milk, because I couldn't get along without it.

MR. CARPENTER: Returning to the matter under discussion a moment ago. There is no question but that the new milk did probably relieve the cream, but what is there about a hand separator that spoils that cream. It keeps it way beyond the time

34

when it should have been churned. This sweet milk arrests the fermentation for a time.

NIETERT: I think the gentleman misconstrued my language. I didn't mean to insinuate that the separator spoiled any cream.

MR. HUBBELL: There was a farmer some six or eight weeks ago bought a separator. He was a gentleman of Swedish extraction and a good butter maker. I met him and asked him how he was getting along. He said: "I am making better butter than the creamery." I said: "Of course you are a good butter maker, but how do you make better butter than the creamery?" He said: "Why, I tell you. Those scientific gentlemen tell you about something that be in the milk that be not pure, and when you leave that in the milk it makes a bad smell, and when you take and keep it one day or two days and send it to the creamery it have a bad smell, and you know that is the part of the animal that does not give out a good smell. Now that which is taken to the creamery is not separated the right way. Now in my separator I separate it the right way." He takes it out and has it perfectly pure and has extracted all the impurities of the milk as it came from the cow.

PRESIDENT: The next on the programme is the report of the secretary and treasurer. I would say that Mr. Ashby, the treasurer, is not here, and did not get the books here until noon, and the auditing committee has not had time to go go over them as yet, so have delayed the reports until this evening.

I wish at this time to appoint the committee on resolutions, so that they may go to work at once. I will appoint H. J. Nietert, Fred Kimball and M. O. Wheelock.

I wish to state that the National Dairy Union have placed on sale here their book, and I hope you will give the Dairy Union the support of purchasing one of their books. You now stand adjourned until 7:30 this evening.

EVENING SESSION.

Meeting called to order by president at 8:00 P. M. The Cedar Rapids orchestra were present and furnished music.

PRESIDENT: For the past two years almost the entire agricultural world has turned its eyes Iowaward. The Ames Agricultural College, of which every man who lives in Iowa is proud, has achieved such success that it has directed universal attention to it. We have with us tonight the man whom largely the credit is due, Prof. Curtiss of Ames.

MODERN DAIRYING.

Prof. C. F. Curtiss, Ames, Iowa.

I am glad indeed to have the privilege of meeting with this association in the good old dairy stronghold of Linn county, and while it may not make as many pounds of butter per square mile as some others, yet I know of no other city which dispenses more genuine hospitality to the square inch than Cedar Rapids, and the calling of a meeting in this city always insures a good convention.

A few years ago when it was believed that the dairy belt of the United States would always lie east of the Alleghany Mountains, a pertinent question asked was, "Can anything good in the way of dairying ever come out of the west?" About that time Iowa concluded to go into the dairy business. She made her first appearance in a national contest at the Centennial Exposition in 1876 and when the contest was over Iowa butter carried off the gold medal and the highest honors. The old stone creamery in which this butter was made remained for many years as a landmark by the side of a little spring in the edge of Manchester, the county seat of Delaware, the pioneer dairy county of Iowa. Since that time our dairy interests have grown until Iowa occupies the proud position of producing more creamery butter than any other state in the Union and about one-fifth of all the dairy butter made in the United States. If the Iowa cows were to go out on a strike for sixty days, there is scarcely a family table in America that would not feel its effect. Nor is that all but for five years past the Iowa State College Creamery has each winter sent an Iowa born, bred and educated boy to Amherst to teach the sons of old Massachusetts to make strictly first-class, prize-winning, market-topping butter. And more than that, Iowa boys have made butter that has taken the highest rank in national contests in competition with eight hundred exhibitors from every dairy state in the Union; and Iowa trained boys are today making butter in practically every dairy section in the United States. Gentlemen, I take no stock in the doctrine that the dairy interests of Iowa have permanently declined or that Iowa butter has deteriorated even if our buttermakers have fallen out of the first ranks in a recent national contest. The Iowa butter makers are not quitters. They are not made of that kind of stuff. This experience will only stimulate them to higher and better efforts and the dairy industry is destined to become a more important factor in Iowa agriculture than ever before.

In the panorama of agricultural progress no branch or phase of agriculture has presented more striking change nor more rapid development than the field of dairying. Modern methods have revolutionized the industry. The process of butter making has recently emerged from methods that were crude and ignorant, and in the brief space of a few years attained the rank of an educated profession. We are indebted to the creameries and the creamery butter makers for most of this progress. The good home dairy butter is a standard article today, unexcelled by any other product on the market, but there is comparatively little of it, and without the creamery system nothing like general progress could have been practicable or possible. The cardinal principles of success with the creamery today, as in all times, is economy of production and excellence of finished product. This principle lies at the very foundation of American agriculture, and indeed of every American industry. The records of the last census show that the productive capacity of the average American farmer has increased 33 1-3 per cent during the last two decades, and furthermore that the productive capacity of the Iowa farmer is greater per capita than that of any other farmer in America. Iowa's agricultural products foot up to the neat sum of over a million dollars for every day of the year. The results that have been attained by the Iowa creameries and the Iowa dairy interests have been no small factor in this most creditable showing.

The past decade has wrought changes of far reaching importance in the agricultural industry of America. We have been undergoing a period of transformation of deep significance. A short time ago at a meeting of the live stock agents of the leading lines of railroad centering at Chicago, a representative of an eastern road called attention to the striking fact that twenty years ago the richest and most valuable agricultural lands of America were in the valleys of the Ohio and Miami Rivers and eastward. Since then these lands have declined from fifty to one hundred per cent in value and the richest, most productive and most valuable agricultural lands lie today in the Mississippi Valley and westward. This confirms the judgment of Horace Greeley and substantiates the statement that "westward the star of empire takes its way." But it does more than that, and it is a condition that is worthy of more than a passing thought. It means more than merely the westward course of the star of empire, and the unlocking of virgin fertility. It means that we who occupy these fertile fields and productive lands have come into possession of the richest heritage of the agricultural world; a region which is today and must continue to be, a prime factor in the world's food supply and a vital force in the center of the world's greatest activity and progress. We may well pause to reflect on the magnitude of our inheritance. It means new and more exacting conditions, larger obligations and greater responsibilities. If the lands that are today the most valuable and productive are to yield returns commensurate to the value put upon them, and be maintained in their present state of productiveness, it means that those who occupy them must

wisely conserve their resources, and apply the most intelligent and skillful methods of modern agriculture. It means that the methods of agriculture that have impoverished virgin soils and fertile valleys in other regions
will eventually and inevitably impoverish these if we are so short sighted
as to follow them. It means, if it means anything, a better system of farming, a higher type of agriculture and a better civilization. Civilization and
agriculture are inseparably connected. No civilization of a high standard
in any land has ever endured apart from a successful agriculture. Twenty-
five years ago the farmers of the older parts of Iowa awoke to a realization
of the fact that their lands would no longer produce wheat profitably under
existing conditions. It was then that they turned their attention to dairying and they have in the meantime not only placed Iowa in the foremost
rank of dairy states, and advanced our rank in all other agricultural
products but our farms will also produce more wheat and better wheat
per acre today than ever before in the history of the state.

In selling $1,000 worth of wheat from an Iowa farm at present prices,
we sell with it about $350 worth of fertility. In selling $1,000 worth of
corn, we sell about $250 worth of fertility—or constituents which would cost
the farmer this amount if he were obliged to buy commercial fertilizers
to maintain the fertility of the farm. But we can convert $1,000 worth
of corn into beef, pork or mutton and sell it in that form and not remove
over $25 worth of fertility from the farm, or we can convert $1,000 worth
of feed into butter and not remove a single dollars worth of fertility with
it. Butter is almost wholly pure fat or carbon and it adds nothing to the
value or productive capacity of the soil. We probably shall never be
obliged to pay out much money for commercial fertilizers in Iowa if we
farm intelligently but we have already learned that we can not grow wheat
indefinitely, or constantly draw upon even a bountiful store of plant food
without diminished returns. The fact that this lesson has been learned
and is coming to be universally recognized is the main safeguard and the
strongest feature of Iowa agriculture. We not only produce an average
of a million dollars worth of agricultural products for every day of the
year, but we know enough to feed over one-fourth of a million dollars'
worth of produce on the farms every day. No other state in the Union
approaches this amount and there are only five other states that feed even
half as much. By this means Iowa not only leads in agricultural products
but conserves her resources.

The manifest tendency of modern times is toward specialization and
concentration. The creamery system is the outgrowth of this movement.
It puts under the control of one man what was originally the work of forty
men and women. The conditions surrounding the work and the results
achieved are decidedly favorable to the one-man system. This process
is going still further and the creamery system of a few years hence will put
into one plant what was originally the work of not less than 500 different
individuals. It is already impossible for the small creameries to maintain
a profitable existence. The losses which attended butter making a few
years ago would be absolutely ruinous today and some of the losses now
existing will a few years hence put the creamery management which tol-

erates them out of existence. And whether we like innovations or **not,** gentlemen, they are coming because they must come—because they are inevitable. I can appreciate the complications and the difficulties which the hand separator has in store for the butter maker, but I have but little sympathy for the butter maker who feels called upon to put obstructions in the way of this or any other improvement of real merit. The hand separator system is right in principle and it can be right in practice, and it is the butter makers' duty to help to make it right. If its use presents new problems to the creamery and patrons, these problems should be solved in the best spirit and for the best interests of all. The total skim milk product of the United States amounts to about thirty-one billion pounds. A conservative estimate of the feeding value of this product in good condition, based upon the prices of feed stuffs prevailing during the past year, would reach $75,000,000. This value can easily depreciate one-third by the losses which ordinarily take place in putting the skim milk through the creamery separators and hauling it back to the farms. The skim milk product of Iowa alone has a feeding value of about nine million dollars annually. There are doubtless abuses and misrepresentations growing out of the hand separator system and it is not my purpose to defend them. These abuses must be remedied and they will be. There is but one source of relief for the butter maker. He must rise to the occasion and master these and other new problems.

A few years ago a modest young butter maker had charge of a small creamery in Iowa. This young man sent a tub of butter to a state contest and took first prize. He attended a state dairy convention held at Ames and concluded he wanted to know more about the science and practice of butter making. When he resigned his position and started for Ames some of his friends told him he was a fool to think of wasting his time and money up there. They told him he was already the best butter maker in the state. But he knew that he could improve, and today that man is in charge of a plant that handles the cream of fifty creameries and its products have established a high reputation in several hundred cities and towns of the United States extending from one side of the continent to the other. That is what comes from a determination to excel. The great millionaire, John D. Rockefeller, says that "success in life comes from knowing how to do common things in an uncommon manner."

A few years ago the late Senator Davis who ranked as one of the ablest lawyers and most prominent men in public life said in addressing a class of college graduates: "Young men, you are leaving an academy to enter the university of life. About all you have learned up to this time is how to learn more. Those of you who ever amount to anything in this world will go on studying. You will sit up nights with your books. The first ten years of your life will be hard, grubbing for bread and butter, and wondering why the old fellows don't die off and give the young men a chance. But upon the use you make of these ten years depends your future fate. Only one man out of twenty studies after leaving college; nineteen out of twenty fail to attain success." I know of no sounder, more appropriate advice for butter makers. The young man to whom I have referred sat up many a night with his books and with a vat of cream. So has every other butter maker who has amounted to anything. And in conclusion, gentlemen, I beg to remind you that the real source of wealth of Iowa does not lie in her corn, her cows, her creameries, or her golden butter, magnificent as are these possessions in the present days of prosperity; but that the richest, most potent and lasting heritage lies in the brain power that is back of, and directs and controls, the making of the finished products of American agriculture, and if Iowa maintains her advanced rank it will be by reason of the intelligence and skill brought to bear on these problems that underlie successful agriculture.

Mr. James H. Hughes of Cedar Rapids favored the audience with a vocal solo, which was heartily applauded and Mr. Hughes was obliged to respond with another number.

PRESIDENT: I am sorry to be forced to tell you that Governor Cummins can not be with us. The fact of the matter is that the Governor's energies are more than his physical strength, and he finds himself too ill to be here this evening. We have several interesting numbers on the program and hope you will not be disappointed at the Governor's inability to be here.

We have with us Mr. Ericson of Boone, chairman of the committee on dairy products for the St. Louis exposition. He has kindly consented to talk to you for a few moments.

ADDRESS.
—

C. J. A. Ericson, Boone, Iowa.

I am a little afraid that I cannot make myself heard very well on account of the condition my throat is in, but I will do the best I can. I am glad of this opportunity of meeting you gentlemen who are engaged in this industry. I am not able to instruct you in the way of making butter according to the modern methods, but I am here as a representative of the Iowa Commissioners to say to you that we are interested in your product very much and wish to become in touch with you as an association and as individuals, and to interest you in the World's Fair that is to come. The commission have been organized and the preliminary work has been done to some extent, yet we have not got down to details. But I want to say this to you. The commissioners will aid you in every way possible according to the means at our command. I am sorry I was not here when Mr. Taylor addressed you, for I do not know what he said to you in regard to this department. I simply met him this evening and asked him one question. I said, "Can you give us as much space as our association had in Chicago?" and he assured me that he could and would. At the Columbian Exposition I find by the reports that there were 120 exhibitors of butter from Iowa. The butter was of course disposed of each month and a new product put on exhibition. Seventy-eight of the exhibitors at the World's Fair received medals accompanied by a diploma which recites the points of excellence in the exhibits, and to those companies and creameries, 128 awards were given in all, so you see Iowa made an excellent showing. Iowa showed higher score of points in the four consecutive tests than any other state. The space allotted to us in the exposition was 50 lineal feet of glass cases, and this space held about 100 tubs of butter, and no other state had more space than Iowa. I have a personal pride and interest with you in maintaining this excellent record at the new World's Fair, and thereby extending the reputation and gaining more extensive markets for the dairy products of Iowa. The honor of having butter on exhibit at the World's Fair is an opportunity which does not come in the lifetime of many. To be enrolled in the catalogues and have the privilege of competing is a mark of merit in itself. Iowa must sustain its reputation as the banner dairy state when it comes to winning universal honors. It is the desire not only of the Iowa commissioners, but of the St. Louis World's Fair people that space should be applied for as early as possible. You know the catalogues will have to be printed long before the exposition opens, and unless application is made and names and residences given your names will not appear in the catalogues, therefore this is of importance. There are many gentlemen here no doubt who participated in the exhibit at the Columbian Exposition, and the Iowa Commissioners look to you for help in this matter. I don't know what you think would be best in the matter. Whether the commissioners should correspond with your executive committee, or whether you think favorably of appointing a special committee for this purpose. Circulars will no doubt be printed and circulated among you later with reference to exhibits in this department. I hope to enlist the co-operation of Mr. Wright, the state dairy commissioner, and with your co-operation too, we shall undoubtedly make it a success. We have the pastures and cows, the creameries and butter makers, and the men with ability, push and capital to carry this through, and who shall say we cannot make a success of it.

I stated at the outset that I didn't know anything about making butter under the processes of today, but I have half a notion to take it back. I used to know something about making butter and selling it in the pioneer days, and I don't know but what I will relate it for your amusement, not instruction.

I came to Boone county in 1859, and set up a country store at the corners, with a blacksmith shop and postoffice. In those days there was no money in the country, and there were half a dozen things at the store which were current exchange, beeswax, honey, muskrat skins, coon and mink skins, dry hides and maple sugar. Going into a new country like that I was studying what could be done to have something produced which could be exchanged for merchandise and used for money. Every man in the country had one or more cows and made butter for his own use, but there was no one to buy it, and the nearest railroad was Iowa City. After I had been there I got to thinking about butter and handling it, providing I could dispose of it. So I wrote to a commission merchant in Chicago and asked him about butter and he said it could be sold at some price, and so I undertook to have the farmers make butter. We didn't have butter tubs like we have now. We had to have firkins or kegs made. There was no cooper in the county, so I sent some men to the timber to cut it, and sent east for a cooper. Well the time came when the farmers commenced to bring in their butter and I set up a row of those firkins opened and one big barrel at the end. The butter began to come in. I didn't have the tests then that you have now. We only had three tests. They were see-ing, tasting and smelling. So when a woman came in with butter we used the tests we had, and if the butter proved to be No. 1 it was put in the first keg. The next lady might have good butter, but the color might not be the same, and so it was put in the second keg, and the next lady might have good butter, but still lighter, and that would go in the third keg, and the next lady might have stronger butter and that would go in the fourth keg. And once in a while some butter would come in that could hardly be recognized as butter, and that would go into the big barrel. That was the soap grease barrel. It was a new country and half the women didn't even have cellars, let alone milk houses, and many of them were inex-perienced too. It didn't cost very much to go into the dairy business then. I think the total amounted to about $2.50; it consisted of milk crocks and a stone churn and a large wooden bowl and ladle, and the store furnished these on credit and the butter was to be brought in to pay for it. Pretty soon the butter business increased. I was going to say also that sometimes the women got unpardonably provoked when they came in and saw their butter go into the soap barrel and another woman's go into the first keg. But this was the only place in the country that would buy butter, so they couldn't go any place else. Sometimes there would be a ton of butter come in in pails and batches. This butter had to be hauled to Iowa City by wagon, 150 miles, and we had no con-veniences of refrigeration. The commission merchants in Chicago had only one additional test to those we made at home. They had a steel rod made sharp at the ends so that it would act as an augur. They would run it down to the bottom of the keg and cut out a sample, and then they would smell it and if they could they would taste it. And after a while the people improved in making butter and the demand increased. The war came on and the army needed butter, and we helped to supply the demand all we could. This is the way the dairy business commenced in my county. And if you are making butter under the new processes you needn't ask me any questions.

Now I hope gentlemen you will remember that the Iowa commissioners will aid you in any way they can when the time comes. I thank you for your kind attention.

PRESIDENT: The orchestra have kindly promised to stay with us and give us one more selection if they can come on now, as they have another engagement.

The number was greeted with applause and the orchestra responded to encore.

PRESIDENT: We have with us tonight a man who is probably more widely known than any man who is interested in the same way in the United States, and a man who has probably by his work for the dairy interests placed more money in the pockets of the dairymen than any one else in the United States; Mr. Charles Y. Knight will address you.

ADDRESS.

—

Chas. Y. Knight, Chicago.

Mr. President, Ladies and Gentlemen of the Convention: For a number of years I have been working to prevent imitations and substitutes. Tonight I feel that I am somewhat inconsistent in that I have been substituted for a very brilliant Iowa statesman of whom I am a very poor imitation. It seems to me you people will feel as though you had been invited to a champagne dinner and served with soup. In other words, where the program says "pure butter" olemargarine has been substituted.

You can not always expect to meet good Iowa people. I know you meet them everywhere. It is almost impossible to do anything in the United States without consulting Iowa. When we go to Washintgon to talk legislation the first man who has to be consulted is an Iowa man. He occupies the position of speaker of the house, the second man in power and authority in the United States. After we have run—if we do successfully—the gauntlet of the house under the supervision of an Iowa speaker, we come to the senate and an Iowa man stands in the door there. Senator Allison is chairman of the republican steering committee of the senate, and has more influence on legislation to be acted on there than any man in the United States. When it comes to the matter of breaking into Uncle Sam's treasury we find Iowa at every door. The first man we have to deal with in that case is also Senator Allison, also chairman of the committee on appropriations, the most powerful man in the United States. No appropriation of any kind can be made without his approval. Then when we get the appropriation it is necessary for us to consult another man, ex-Governor Shaw, who is at the head of the treasury department, and of whom we are all proud. And after you have seen him and arranged with him for whatever is to be done in the way of getting into the treasury you will have to go to another Iowa man. I refer to Mr. Roberts, superintendent of the United States mints. And yet Iowa's authority does not end there. You can't get into the United States, if you come in at the port people usually come in at—New York—without consulting another Iowa man. When you come up New York harbor and prepare to get off the steamship you have to consult Collector of the Port Clarkson of Iowa. So when I address an Iowa audience I think I am pretty near to the center of the hub. And I am glad to say that it is generally regarded and accepted in Washington that the representatives which Iowa send to Washington, that the position which they hold there is the result merely of their being representative Iowa people. And Iowa is to be congratulated on the position it holds politically in this country. There is little use for me to say anything about the position she holds in dairy matters, in agricultural matters. I believe and understand that it is generally conceded that the state of Iowa has the best average class of people of any state in the United States, fewer paupers, fewer millionaires; no immense cities, but medium sized cities. And it always gives me pleasure to come before an Iowa audience, although it is embarrassing to step into an Iowa man's shoes when you are so incapable of filling them.

I am on the program for a talk on the oleomargarine subject. The subject for me is difficult to handle, difficult for the reason that there is so much of it. I have been up against it to such an extent during the past two years that it is difficult to make a satisfactory exposition of the question in a short time, and I believe in short talks. The first address I ever made in my life was made on this question at New Orleans some years ago before the League of National Commission Merchants. The subject was new at that time. They told me they were very busy and asked me to make my address as short as possible. After the meeting was adjourned the president said to me, "Mr. Knight I want to congratulate you on the address you made." I thanked him profusely. I was proud of my maiden effort. "Yes," he said when I thanked him, "some people never know when to stop."

We have worked upon this recent law for four years. We passed the law and it was signed by the president the 9th of last May and went into effect the 1st day of July. Well, they say that when a man gets married his troubles begin. Sometimes he thinks the trouble is at its height when he is trying to get the girl, but I will assure you that our troubles began when the law went into effect. Now it would be a nice thing, if possible, for the dairymen of the United States to go to congress and write out a bill and present it to the chairman of the committee and say: "Here is a bill we wish to have passed and we will be back to get it at 3:00 o'clock." Probably we would get what we wanted if it could be done in that way. But when you go to congress for a measure the first thing you have to do is to get it prepared the way you want it. Get some man of influence on the majority side to introduce it and select the committee to handle it. Size up the committee and see how it stands and then endeavor to prevail upon that committee to report the bill. You understand that when you hand in a bill it is merely a suggestion of what you would like; they give you that privilege. The committee meets, seventeen members as a rule. The committee calls in all of the conflicting interests throughout the country; lawyers come in from all the states; all kinds of propositions are suggested, and then the committee proceeds to tear this measure to pieces and build it up to suit themselves. I assure you that very frequently it is exasperating to sit by and see how they will cut out the points you think most important. If the committee sees fit to report your bill to the house you have then to go before another committee, known as the committee on rules and ask them if you can get a day for consideration. When you consider the fact that in an ordinary session of congress there are 15,000 measures introduced and not over 7,000 acted upon you see it means that only a small proportion of those introduced ever see the light of day from the committee. When you get a favorable report from the committee they decide to let you come onto the floor. Then you are dealing with 357 members of the house, and at the next session, with the increased membership, there will be 387 members to look after. You have got to have a majority of that 387 members. After you have secured this majority and the favorable action of the house, after every trap has been avoided and you have the bill through the house, you have to take it to the senate and ask to have it referred to the senate committee. If you are fortunate enough to have it referred to this committee then you have the same work to do you had in the house, going before the senate committee. You must bring your evidence before that committee and convince a majority of them that your cause is just. If they decide to report your measure and it is reported, you must see the members of the senate objects to that bill being disposed of, it can not be disposed to have it brought before the senate, and when it is brought before the senate at last you must have the consent of every member of that senate to have the bill voted upon. So long as a single one of the ninety members of the senate objects to that bill being disposed of it can not be disposed of. So you see the manner of making laws down at Washington is complicated and long drawn out. And after a measure has passed through the gauntlet of all of these committees it gets kind of out of shape. If the senate happens to make an amendment to the measure you have to have the thing go back to the house again, concurred in there, then sent to a committee on conference from the two bodies and have them agree on the new measure.

When we went to Washington in 1899 we had a bill formed, the vital part of which was a ten per cent tax on all oleomargarine containing any shade of yellow and sold in imitation of butter. There was a great deal of discussion over the matter as to whether oleomargarine could be made without some shade of yellow. Now yellow is a color pretty close to white. Snow is white, and as a rule when you look at white paper you would say it was white, but put it aside of the snow and you would see it showed some shade of yellow. The opponents of the measure contended that all oleomargarine contained a shade of yellow, because part of the materials from which it was made, viz.: cotton seed oil and oleo, gave it a shade of yellow. We experimented in the committee room of the United States senate, and the friends of this measure were obliged to admit that when this mixture was compared with a piece of paper or snow or your shirt front, it showed a shade of yellow. There were some members who claimed to be with us but who decided that they could not go to the extent of placing a tax on all oleomargarine that had a shade of yellow. But they were willing to vote for a tax of ten cents a pound on all oleomargarine that contained artificial coloring of yellow. This made it possible for the oleomargarine men to produce their product from the natural oils and fats. We accepted this amendment because it was brought up at a late hour and we say that it was the only way of getting the measure through. The leaders of this movement, the dairy commissioners, and those expert in dairy legislation were called in consultation and we asked them whether we should accept it as it was, or whether we should go back to the senate and fight it out and either get the whole bill turned down or passed as it was. The result was that they decided to let it go through as it was and find out whether it was possible for them to get any coloring which would make oleomargarine yellow without artificially coloring it. The law was passed with the amendment. Now our trouble commenced. When the first of July came the oleomargarine manufacturers were just as much at sea as we had been. They knew no more what they could do to get around the law than we did. They put all their men out and endeavored to sell the white oleomargarine, and they did sell it in the month of July. But no sooner had this white oleomargarine got out than it began to come back. The public would not have it. The next month their product fell off sixty-six per cent. They only put out 17,000 packages. Then after seeing that the public would not take their goods in the shape they were being produced; after learning that the people when they knew the character of the ingredients would not use it, they began to scheme to get around the law. The first thing they used was palm oil, an oil produced from the Olive Palm of Africa. It is what Frazer's Axle Grease is made from. That oil is so red it is brown. It is one-third the strength of the best analine butter colors. We made a test and found that one-half of one per cent introduced into a pound of oleomargarine would make a pretty good imitation of June butter, but also that the qualities in the oil were so pronounced that even one-half per cent would spoil the quality of the oleomargarine. Then they began to neutralize the taste and smell of this oil and put in much time at it. Then we made complaint that the use of this oil in such quantities was an artificial coloring in imitation of butter. The matter was argueed before the commissioner of internal revenue and he decided that the use of palm oil was an artificial coloring, and that oleomargarine so colored would have to be taxed ten cents per pound. And then we ran up against this kind of a proposition. There is great similarity between all kinds of vegetable oils. Cotton seed oil has always been a component part of oleomargarine. A manufacturer in the south bethought himself of mixing a small quantity of de-odorous palm oil with cotton seed oil, and selling it to be used as a coloring under the name of cotton seed oil. A sample was sent to Washington to be examined, and while they found that the cotton seed oil which this firm was turning out contained palm oil, there was absolutely no test that would prove it. Now while they found an ingredient which would impart a color that the internal revenue department could not say was artificial coloring because the government chemist could not detect it, yet they found that the use of this oil depreciated the value of their product. They have been making a low grade of goods and so greatly damaged their business. Up to the first of January of this year the oleomragarine factories of Chicago turned out 140,000 fifty-pound tubs less of oleomargarine than in the previous year, a decrease of thirty-three per cent. And creamery butter showed an advance of three cents per pound. Always in the past the make of oleomargarine has increased with the advance of butter in price. The oleomargarine people admit this and say that if it had not been for the passage of this law they would have increased their production thirty-three per cent instead of decreasing thirty-three per cent. Their falling off for the six months ending January 1, amounted, as I have said to 140,000 tubs. Therefore, the falling off in the United States was 280,000 tubs. This amounts to 560 cars, or a train about six miles long. There is no question but what the oleogargarine law had an immediate effect as soon as it was passed, upon the price of butter. Speculators come into the market in the anticipation of the rise and paid an almost unprecedented price for June butter, from three to four cents per pound higher than the year before. The price of creamery butter during the year 1902 averaged 3.2 higher than in the year before. The butter of the United States amounts in one year to 1,500,000,000 pounds. The increased price of the produce in the United States therefore at three cents per pound is $45,000,000. Now if we have just the amount of butter needed for the trade you can get almost your own price for it, but if there is a supply coming in all the time the prices invariably run down, so taking 560 cars of butter out of the market has had the effect of giving us, I think, the best butter market we have ever known.

Now in connection with our work it is my duty to say to you some things which may not find the audience altogether in harmony. We have fought in congress for four years to get a measure through. We have had the entire support of the butter interests of the United States. When we came to the test vote we only had one vote to spare. It is going to be absolutely necessary for us to have the law of 1902 amended to stop up the loop holes the oleomargarine manufacturers will escape through. In handling national affairs we must look to those people who are accustomed to managing large things, and follow to a certain extent their example. For instance, I had the pleasure a couple of years ago of meeting William J. Bryan on my way to Washington. And he said he had been taught a lesson regarding the dairy business which would make him careful of what he did in the future. He said he was at a convention one time in Missouri and the convention was torn up on the question of breeds. The question of Jersey cows was under consideration, and a man, a Holstein breeder, got up and said: "Yes, you take a pail and go out to milk and you put a silver dollar in the pail and start to milk, and when you get done milking and have just enough milk to cover the silver dollar you may know it is a Jersey." And a man, a breeder of Jersey cattle, got up and said: "You take a pail and put a silver dollar in the bottom and go out to milk, and when you have milked the pail brim full and you look down and see the silver dollar in the bottom, then you may know you have been milking a Holstein." Mr. Bryan said when he went to farming, knowing the wrangle about the different breeds, he went around and selected a couple from every bred. He said he had all kinds of cattle in his herd and was not discriminating against any breed.

We have many breeds of butter in this country. If you run over the current breeds you will find we have seven or eight classes of butter. Some of them are pretty sure they are the whole thing, and the public is inclined to accept their judgment. Everybody except the owner of the private dairy admits that finished creamery butter is about the best thing today. The production of butter last year, as I told you was 1,500,000,000 pounds of butter. But 400,000,000 was creamery butter, 1,030,000,000 was produced on the farm. We who are interested in the welfare of the butter business in the United States do not believe it is the proper thing to sell a laddle butter for creamey butter or creamery butter for dairy butter, and we do not feel it is right to sell process butter for creamery butter, but we must take into consideration that all of these grades of butter are produced by the farmer. He is looking for the best possible market for his goods. He has the right to get the very best price he can for that butter. While I believe that renovated butter and process butter should be designated and branded so it can be sold as creamery butter, my experience in the markets, my general overlooking of this question from one end of the country to the other, leads me to believe that we, representing the creamery interests, can not afford to prosecute any other brand of butter. I do not think we can afford to stand up and say to these people whose butter is made over at central factories that they must put a brand on it which will make it repugnant to the public, so that it can not be sold. I think it is a mistake for us to approach that sort of business from any stand point or direction, because it has been my observations in the last two years that wherever renovated butter is driven out of the market through the repugnance the public has to anything renovate that oleomargarine comes on the market. Let this butter go out, not as creamery butter, but let it go and seek its outlet, so it will not block the channels of trade for creamery butter. Now this question must come up in Washington at the next session of congress. The butter interestes of the United States as a whole are solid for our legislation. The renovated butter manufacturers, representing the production of prob-ably $100,000,000 per year, while we had provisions in our bills putting a $50 a year license on these manufacturers, requiring their goods to be inspected and taxed one-fourth cent per pound, and putting in provisions requiring them to brand their goods according to the laws of the state in which they were manufactured, these manufacturers came in and helped us in the fight. If they had opposed we never could have made it. The code of 1902 says that "renovated butter shall be marked with the words 'Renovated or Process' butter." The dairy division of the bureau of ani-mal industry has ruled that it must be marked "Renovated butter" re-gardless of what state it goes into or what state it is manufactured in. They are in that way working up trouble for us, because the renovated butter people have got to a point where they are ready to go with us or with the oleomargarine people to knock out creamery butter. I believe the law should be enforced as it is on the statute books and marked renovated butter when it is going into a state whose laws demand that it shall be so marked, but that when it goes into a state which does not have such laws that the manufacturer should have the option of marking it "process butter" if he so desires.

We expect to go before congress next session to ask for amendments to the law of 1902 covering all the weak points. A law is like a boat; you can never tell where the leaks are until you put it in the water. We will have had two years' trial by the time the next congress comes around and we expect to go before them then with the perfected bill. I thank you.

PRESIDENT: We have with us Mr. Brigham, state labor commissioner, who will address you.

ADDRESS.

E. D. Brigham, Des Moines, Iowa.

Mr. Chairman, Ladies and Gentlemen of the Convention: When your secretary extended an invitation to me to be present here to say something to you, I assure you I accepted with pleasure, and while it may not be clear to you where any affinity exists between the bureau I have the honor to represent and the dairy interests of this great state, I believe you will all agree with me that labor is an essential element to the conduct of the dairy industry. The able speakers who have preceded me have called your attention to the necessity of a proper exhibit at the St. Louis Exposition, and have covered the ground quite thoroughly I believe, and yet I have something to add, which I believe will be of interest to you. Iowa land at $100 per acre and going up, to be successfully tilled, needs the assistance of the dairy industry. The dairy industry in Iowa we know to be in the front ranks as compared with other states. It seems to me that it is neccessary in order to maintain our position in the front ranks to put up at St. Louis a splendid exhibit of the dairy products of Iowa, and in connection with that it seems to me that the dairy appliances and dairy machinery that is manufactured in Iowa ought also to be represented in the best possible manner. By getting together and getting a close interchange of ideas it will be an easy matter to accomplish a result I have started out to accomplish, namely the establishing of a Reciprocal League among the manufacturers of Iowa to patronize each other; and all of this means of course added employment for our labor. Now you can begin to see where I am at. If our labor is all well employed we will have a good home market. If we have a good home market you get the largest possible price for the product you make. I am endeavoring to furnish every manufacturer, every person who uses a manufactured article in Iowa, the names of the firms who manfacture any line of goods they want. In a few days I will have the names of all the manufacturers who employ over five men. I believe it is an important thing and that this work will be very beneficial to the people of Iowa, and especially to the labor they employ, to put them in close touch with each other. And while labor is fully employed, as it is at the present time, under very satisfactory conditions, we are giving much attention to it. The principal object of my address was to make this plan clear to the people who assembled here to consider matters pertinent to the dairy industry. I think you will all agree with me that this matter of an exhibit at St. Louis is a very important one when you come to consider the splendid advantages offered by the management in the matter of free space. When you come to consider the immense amount of money that has been appropriated, when you come to consider what a colossal affair it is going to be, you begin to realize that it will probably out class any exposition the world has ever seen. The St. Louis exposition has an appropriation of $5,000,000, and in addition to that other appropriations have been added, making a total at the present time of $17,000,000. It is going to be a wonderful advertising medium for everyone who participates. We have a great many things to bring to the attention of the world. The splendid water power which can be obtained from the Mississippi, the most powerful in the world. I refer of course to the proposed dam at Keokuk, which is of national interest. There is also a splendid opportunity at Muscatine, or a point opposite, where a canal can be cut from the Cedar river to the Mississippi, a distance of seven miles, and a 100 foot head of water power can be secured. There is also another opportunity at the bend of the Des Moines river at Keosauqua, and I am assured by the business men of Keosauqua that that water power is to be soon developed. Now think of the opportunities we can offer the manufacturers in the east who are desirous of coming west.

I will simply mention in connection with the work of the labor bureau that the first six months we are sending out blanks to the employers and I hope if you receive one that you will give it careful attention and reply at an early date. We are going to try and give you a report that is worth all its costs, and as much more as we can possible make it. I hope that representatives of the dairy industry in Iowa will not forget what I said about patronizing home industries, those manufacturers in Iowa who manufacture what you can use. At the same time I do not wish to offend any firm making an exhibit here. Now the hour is late. I believe I have outlined all that is necessary. I thank you very kindly.

PRESIDENT: I wish to announce the names of the committee on Legislation. I have selected them with a view of securing from the state legislature the concessions we should have had long ago, rather than for the purpose of recognizing any particular branch of the dairy industry:

E. M. Wentworth, G. L. McKay, Joe Mattes, C. F. Curtiss, H. J. Nietert.

I will also appoint an Auditing Committee of Mr. Anderson of Oelwein, Mr. Pufahl of Nora Springs, and Mr. Reed of Des Moines.

I wish to again call to your attention the fact that the Iowa State Dairy Association is supported by its members. All we

35

have is the membership fees and the butter contributed by the exhibitors, and the subscriptions, which we are trying to leave out as much as we can. The membership fee is only a dollar and we hope you will all take out meberships before you leave. You stand adjourned until 9:00 o'clock tomorrow morning, when the butter sale opens. The business meeting will be at 11:00 o'clock tomorrow morning.

The first, second and third highest scores were announced in butter hall as follows:

CREAMERY CLASS.

First—Highest score was won by No. 12, H. J. Evans, Strawberry Point. He used Alpha separator, Victor churn, Alderney butter color, Genessee salt, Keith's culture. Score, 97½.

Second—No. 22, S. Peterson, New Hampton. Used Alpha separator, Simplex churn, W. & R. color, Genessee salt. Score, 97¼.

Third—No. 19, P. M. Jenn, Toronto. Used Alpha separator, Victor churn, Alderney butter color, D. C. salt. Score, 96½.

DAIRY CLASS.

First—No. 87, M. S. Barber, Marion, used American separator, Box churn, W. & R. color and D. C. salt. Score, 90.

Second—No. 23, D. J. De Hough, Boyden. Used Alpha separator, combined churn, Alderney butter color, D. C. salt.

Butter was then sold to Gude Bros. of New York for 26 cents delivered in butter hall.

DETAILED SCORE.

Number.	NAME.	ADDRESS.	Flavor.	Grain.	Color.	Salt.	General appearance.	Score.
1	Caledonia Creamery Co..	Paullina	38.5	25	14.5	10	5	93
2	L. C. Peterson	Rosendale	38.5	24.5	15	10	5	93
3	H. W. Pettibone	Fenton	37	25	9.5	5	5	91.5
4	Fred Janes	Charles City	33	24.5	14.5	10	5	87
5	T. M. Borglum	Rutland	36.5	25	15	10	5	91.5
6	Fred Schreiber	North Washington	35.5	25	15	9.5	5	90
7	Jensen & Krause	Eldora	37.5	24	15	9.75	5	91.25
8	R. J. Erb	Arbor Hill	38.5	24.5	15	10	5	93
9	P. O. Knutson	Thor	34	25	15	9.5	5	88.5
10	J. A. Barker	Luana	33.5	25	15	10	5	88.5
11	W. S. Smarzo	Masonville	37	25	15	10	5	92
12	H. J. Evans	Strawberry Point	42	25	15	10	5	97.5
13	R. Stalbyerg	Pioneer	33	25	15	10	5	88
14	J. F Dawson	Iowa Falls	37	25	14.5	10	5	91.5
15	John Baitinger	Ladora	38	23	15	10	5	93
16	G. F. Scott	Magnolia	35	25	15	9	5	89
17	L. T. Fosse	Ridgeway	35.5	24.5	15	9.75	....	89.25
18	L. J. Spohn	Teed's Grove	37.5	25	15	10	5	92.5
19	P. M. Jenn	Toronto	42.5	25.25	14	10	5	96.5
20	George Strait	Marengo	37	25	15	10	5	92
21	S. W. Laird	Walker	38.5	25	15	10	5	93.5
22	S. Peterson	New Hampton	42.5	25	14.75	10	5	97.25
23	D. J. DeHoogh	Boyden	30.5	25	14.5	10	5	85
24	A. Erickson	Clermont	38.5	25	15	10	5	93.5

DETAILED SCORE—Continued.

Number.	NAME.	ADDRESS.	Flavor.	Grain.	Color.	Salt.	General appearance.	Score.
25	J. P. Neilson	Brayton	33	25	15	10	5	93
26	A. E. Hookman	Chester	30.5	25	14.5	10	5	85
27	Herbert Brokaw	Rowley	33.5	25	11	9.5	5	87
28	W. H. Woodstock	Conroy	37	25	15	10	5	92
29	Peter J. Peterson	Montezuma	33	25	15	10	5	93
30	L. C. Adams	Lone Rock	36.5	25	15	10	5	91.5
31	H. C. Kooneke	Artesian	37.75	25	15	10	5	92.75
32	M. J. Donovan	Jericho	33	25	14.75	10	5	92.75
33	J. E. Swanson	Colo	35.5	25	15	10	5	90.5
34	John F. Shultz	Arnold	36.5	25	1'.5	10	5	91
35	W. Peterson	Steamboat Rock	35.5	25	15	9.5	5	90
36	Louis Richards	Forest City	36	25	15	10	5	91
37	John B Deitring	Bancroft	37.5	25	11.5	10	5	89
38	M. J. Mansager	Ellsworth	38.5	25	14.5	10	5	92.5
39	J. J. Bruner	Charles City	35	25	15	10	5	90
40	G. Y. Ross	Fairfield	35.5	25	15	10	5	90.5
41	Wm. Evans	Bradgate	36.25	25	15	10	5	91.25
42	Chris Morck	Swea City	37.5	25	13.5	10	4	90.5
43	Cecil E. Carr	Frederika	41	25	14	10	5	95
44	Wm. Strampe	Paullina	39 5	25	15	10	5	94.5
45	M. J. Johnson	Shell Rock	31	25	15	10	5	86
46	J. H. Griffith	Hopkinton	34	24.5	15	10	5	88.5
47	Frank Larson	Dows	38 5	25	15	9.5	5	93
48	H. S Wood	Salina	31.5	25	14	10	5	85
49	Ivan Barlow	Calmar	37.5	25	15	10	5	92.5
50	T. A. Storvick	Silver Lake	37	25	15	10	5	92
51	A. J Dowlschal	Duncan	36.5	25	15	10	5	91 5
52	C. E Brant	Fairbank	32	25	15	10	5	87
53	F. L. Odell	Greenfield	37.5	25	14	10	5	91.5
54	E. G. Herring	Dexter	37	25	14.5	10	5	91.5
55	W. J. Nagle	Scarville	37.5	25	14.5	10	5	92
56	N. H. Knudeen	Emmetsburg	41	25	14.5	10	5	95.5
57	C. H. Abbott	Hazel Green	33	25	15	10	5	93
58	H. L. cNary	Britt	36.5	25	15	10	5	91.5
59	A. D. Gimer	Clives	38	25	14.5	9.5	5	92
60	Geo. Williams	Spirit Lake	33	25	14	10	4	80
61	M. E. Enooldson	Gilbertsville	33.5	25	15	10	5	91.5
62	Charles A. Allison	Newell	35	25	15	10	5	90
63	F. W. Stephenson	Dundee	36.5	25	15	10	5	91.5
64	Peter Larson	New Hartford	38.5	25	15	10	5	93 5
65	Fred Heilman	Hamlin	37.5	25	15	9.5	4	91.75
66	N. H Trimble	Alden	39	25	15	10	5	94
67	Frank Barnes	Schley	38	25	15	10	5	93
68	F. H. Finish	Waverly	37.5	25	15	10	5	92.5
69	Wm. Gallenbach	Bremer	36	25	15	9.5	5	90.5
70	H. J. Kiepert	Alexander	37	25	15	10	5	92
71	Geo. Wick	Story City	37	25	15	10	5	92
72	J J. Hockreavey	Coggon	35	24	15	10	5	89
73	A. Kindberg	Dyke	33	25	14.5	10	5	87.5
74	F. S. Kleckner	Lamont	39	25	14.5	10	5	93.5
75	H. N. Miller	Randall	38	25	15	10	5	93
76	Bertel Jensen	Ross	31	25	13.5	10	5	84.5
77	P C. Flaskegaard	Storm Lake	37	25	15	10	5	92
78	H. E. Forrester	Fredericksburg	36.5	25	15	10	5	91.5
79	John B Keachie	Estherville	39	25	15	10	5	94
80	J. E. McCaffery	Earlville	37.5	25	15	10	5	92.5
81	W. H. Anderson	Ruthven	36	25	14.5	10	5	90.5
82	Peter Peterson	Elkhorn	33	25	15	10	5	93
83	T. B. Russell	Roland	37.5	25	14	10	5	91.5
84	B. C. Iliff	Ossian	37	25	15	10	5	92
85	J. A. Stamen	Carroll	36	25	15	9.5	5	90.5
86	J. B. Feldman	Dyersville	34.5	25	15	10	5	89.5
87	M. L Barber	Marion	33	25	15	10	5	90
88	C. D. Elder	Manchester	37.5	25	15	10	5	92.5
89	H. K. Gronbeck	Jewell	36	25	15	10	5	91
90	A. A. Palmer	Manchester	38	25	15	10	5	93
91	Theo. Winter	Williamsburg	37.5	25	14.5	10	5	92
92	L. Nielson	Salem	38.5	25	15	10	4	93
93	C. N. Beach	Alpha	30	25	15	10	5	85
94	B. Loming	Huntington	37	25	15	10	5	92
95	A. J. Frees	Cedar Falls	35	25	15	10	5	90
96	W. B. Johnson	Westgate	36.5	25	15	10	5	91.5
97	J. P. Whalen	Elma	35.5	25	14	10	5	89.5
105	H. C. Dauchey	Van Horn	37	25	15	10	5	92

PRESIDENT: Now gentlemen, I will have to again ask you to close your booths and come down and occupy seats in the audience and the meeting will be called to order. We would like to have it as quiet as possible before we proceed. According to the by-laws of our Association, the officers of this association must be elected at 11 o'clock, the hour set on our program. We will therefore proceed to the election of officers.

MR. WENTWORTH: Before we proceed to the election of officers I wish to say a few words of a man who has been more closely identified with the work of this association than any member present. He made an unparalleled record as dairy commissioner, but for the past nine months he has been confined to his bed and room, practically without a day's exception. And I now move that we all rise and join in singing Auld Lang Syne in honor of Hon. W. K. Boardman, president of this association during its twenty-second and twenty-third sessions, and dairy commissioner for six years. I don't think anything could do his heart more good in that sick room one hundred miles west than to know that we thought of him and missed him at our convention. Mr. Moody has kindly consented to lead us in singing.

PRESIDENT: I don't think it is necessary to entertain a motion on a matter of that kind, for I am sure it is the universal wish of this association, so I will simply call upon you all to rise.

The audience rose, and Mr. Moody leading, sang Auld Lang Syne.

MR. WENTWORTH: And as a further token of our appreciation and respect for that good man I move you that you, as president of this association, sent him a telegram. And I am proud to say that Mr. Broadman is now in a condition so that when that telegram reaches him and is read to him, he will understand its meaning. Six weeks ago this would not have been the case, but he has improved. And I move you that we telegraph our congratulations to Mr. Broadman, and would also suggest that this association send to that sick room a bouquet of cut flowers.

Motion seconded.

MR. LEIGHTON: I would like to offer as an amendment that there is another man, also a member of this association, who is detained at home by sickness. I refer to Jules Lombard, whose songs we have missed at this convention, and I would like to amend the motion to include Mr. Lombard also.

MR. WENTWORTH: I accept the amendment to my motion.

Motion as amended, seconded and carried.

Mr. Sherwood was called to the chair and declared that the association would proceed with the election of officers and that nominations for president were in order.

MR. WRIGHT: I nominate Mr. S. B. Shilling to succeed himself.

MR. NIETERT: I would be pleased to second the nomination.

It was moved and seconded that the rules be suspended and the secretary be instructed to cast the ballot of the association for Mr. Shilling for president. Motion carried.

MR. DALY: It gives me great pleasure to cast the entire ballot of this association for Mr. S. B. Shilling for president for another year.

MR. SHILLING: Gentlemen, I appreciate the honor from the bottom of my heart, and I know it is no small honor. I stand ready to promise you that in the year to come the very best that is in me shall be devoted to the dairy interests of the state of Iowa, as I have tried to do in the past. I want to ask the cooperation of everbody in the future, as I feel I have had it in the past. One thing I am pleased to say. I do not believe we have ever had in the history of dairying in Iowa a time when this organization, the state dairy commissioners and the dairy schools have worked in such harmony as they are doing at the present time. And I want to thank the travelling men of the state for the strong help they have given me. I believe what has been done the past year has been largely owing to the assistance of the state dairy school, the dairy commissioner and the travelling men, rather than anything I have done myself. I hope the ensuing year may see Iowa make rapid advancement in the dairy industry With the measures we have taken and the committees we have this year we ought to be able to accomplish much. And when you go home, remember that we are going to commence with the election of the members of the legislature to get the assistance and co-opration Iowa deserves. Gentlemen, I thank you.

MR. P. G. HENDERSON: In view of the fact that we want the dairymen of this state closely identified with this association, and in fact more closely associated with it than they have been, I wish to nominate Mr. W. B. Barney of Hampton for vice-president.

Motion seconded.

MR. NIETERT: I move that in this and the following nominations the rules be suspended and the secretary be instructed to cast the ballot of the association for the candidate where there is no contest.

Motion duly seconded, put to vote and carried.

MR. DALY: It gives me pleasure to cast the entire vote of this association for Mr. W. B. Barney of Hampton, for vice-president.

MR. BARNEY: Mr. President, and gentlemen of the convention. In giving me this office I recognize the fact that it is given me as the representative of the men who are conspicuous by their absence. This should not be. It is in name the Dairymen's convention of Iowa, and our greatest trouble is that we do not get out the men who have the cows. We do not get out the dairymen of the state. I am glad to see many of the creamery men and butter makers here, and I am satisfied that the interest of the owners of the cows will soon be secured, and that we may have them at our future conventions. I thank you.

PRESIDENT: The next in order is nominations for secretary.

MR. WENTWORTH: I think it was seven years ago when we arrived at this point in the order of business there were two or more candidates presented for the office of secretary with the attendant labors. After a warm contest the man who has so efficiently performed the duties of that office at Waterloo, Charles City, Mason City, Storm Lake, Dubuque, and still here at Cedar Rapids, was elected. He has served as your official as long as Jacob served for Leah. He has declined to serve again. And on behalf of the men who make the butter, on behalf of the men who eat the butter, and on behalf of those who came back from Milwaukee with a lower figure on their scores than any other state and an intelligent criticism in connection with their tests, I have the pleasure and honor of presenting the name of P. H. Kieffer, assistant state dairy commissioner, as secretary for the ensuing year.

PROF. McKAY: It gives me pleasure to second the nomination. He has not only made a reputation for himself as a dairyman, but by his honesty and integrity. While Mr. Daly has performed his work well and is a hard man to follow, still I am sure Mr. Kieffer will perform the work equally well.

Motion seconded and carried that the secretary cast the ballot of the association for Mr. Kieffer, for secretary.

MR. DALY: It gives me a great deal of pleasure to cast the vote of this association for Mr. Kieffer. I know that he will carry on the work that we have endeavored to perform in the past few years, and with the assistance of the other officers he will endeavor to keep the Iowa State Dairymen's Association in the front ranks of the state dairy associations of the country.

PRESIDENT: If Mr. Kieffer is in the room he will please come forward and occupy a seat on the platform.

MR. KIEFFER: Mr. President, and members of the Iowa State Dairy Association. My breath was so taken away that it is almost impossible for me to make a speech after listening to the flattering remarks made by Mr. Wentworth and Prof. McKay and Mr. Daly. I don't know that I am deserving of them, but I will make an effort to serve you well. I will make an effort to follow in the footsteps of my predecessor. I thank you for the high honor you have bestowed upon me.

MR. NIETERT: I wish to place in nomination for treasurer a gentleman with whom we are all acquainted. He has been identified with the dairy interests in this state for many years. He has a thorough knowledge of the dairy business and of the creamery business as well. He at one time had charge of the dairy department of the State Agricultural School at Ames, and was efficient and proved faithful to the trust. And while he was dairy commissioner if he had an enemy among the creamery men or dairy men of the state I would like to see him, for I never heard of one. I wish to nominate Mr. F. A. Leighton of Hampton for treasurer. I know he will be a thorough worker, and the funds will be safe in his hands and will not be lost if he will keep some of the rabble like myself away from him.

MR. ANDERSON: I rise to second the nomination of Mr. Leighton.

Nominations were declared closed and the secretary instructed to cast the ballot of the association for F. A. Leighton for treasurer.

MR. LEIGHTON: Gentlemen of the dairy association, I thank you very cordially for this honor you have conferred upon me. I assure you I shall take pleasure in working with the officers you have elected and I will do all I can to further the interests of Iowa butter makers and Iowa dairymen. I thank you.

PRESIDENT: We left over two reports from our program of yesterday afternoon. We will listen to them now. I will say that our treasurer, Mr. Ashby, failed to come, but sent his books, and your secretary, Mr. Daly, will read the report of the treasurer as well as the secretary's report.

TREASURER'S REPORT.

———

GENERAL FUND.
Receipts.

By membership fees	$297.00	
By sale of butter	832.60	
By sale of butter tubs	5.00	$1,134.60

Disbursements.

Balance overdrawn last report	$ 78.33
Bill of C. Renner	35.54
Hotel bill Jules Lombard	9.00
Express on butter	82.08
Henrietta Boyce	5.00
Bill, F. M. Brown	17.00
Bill, Mary McGinniss	1.75
Bill, Zeiner Bros.	21.60
Balance on butter to exhibitors	76.13
Harriet Strelau, stenographer	78.00
Bill, Creamery Journal	30.00
Bill, New York Produce Review	18.00

Bill, Chicago Dairy Produce	22.50	
B. F. Wright, printing	9.00	
Joint R. R. Agent	17.00	
J. C. Daly, salary	150.00	
S. G. Sloane, printing	37.00	
T. L. Haecker, expenses	15.50	
Bill, J. C. Daly	30.45	
S. B. Shilling, expenses	11.00	
J. C. Daly, postage	16.00	
Western Passenger Association	17.00	
Louis A. Fisher, stenographer	18.00	
Balance on hand	338.72	$1,134.60

Respectfully submitted,

M. W. ASHBY, *Treasurer.*

SECRETARY'S REPORT.

PREMIUM FUND.

Receipts.

Balance on hand last report	$ 1.99	
Contributions to fund	645.00	
City of Dubuque	200.00	$846.99

Disbursements.

Telephone	$ 1.25	
Frank Shroder	.40	
James Levi & Co	2.50	
Express	1.40	
L. E. Gerbig	2.00	
Creamery Journal, printing	10.00	
R. McGinniss, labor	12.00	
G. C. Ray	.50	
Bill, J. C. Daly	45.08	
Hotel Julien, labor	3.00	
Hotel Julien, labor	5.00	
S. Edward Davis, butter judge	50.00	
J. P. Walsh, labor	6.00	
Jurgens & Anderson, medals	44.50	
Wm. Cazatt, labor	7.00	
B. F. Wright, printing	15.50	
Paid butter makers on pro rata	619.21	
Balance on hand	21.65	846.99

Receipts.

Collected from firms exhibiting in hall.........................$ 59.50

Disbursements.

Fund overdrawn last report.........................$ 3.66
F. M. Brown. bill...................................   13.50
Ulrich Willy 45.00 $62.16

Fund overdrawn 2.66

Respectfully submitted,

J. C. DALY, *Secretary.*

REPORT OF AUDITING COMMITTEE.

We, the Auditing Committee, would respectfully report that we have examined the reports of M. W. Ashby, Treasurer, and J. C. Daly, Secretary, and checked same with bills and vouchers attached thereto and find the same to be correct as reported.

F. M. BROWN,
A. E. ANDERSON,
N. H. TRIMBLE,
Auditing Committee.

It was moved, seconded and carried that the report of the secretary be accepted. ·Moved, seconded and carried that report of treasurer be accepted.

PRESIDENT: That ends our business meeting, but in view of the fact that we have a long program for the afternoon and that "unfinished business" appears on that program, I will take the liberty of taking up the "unfinished business" at this time.

MR. WRIGHT: *Mr. Chairman,* I will make a few remarks. As everyone knows I am very much interested in having the next legislature increase the number of assistants. Now the committee just appointed will be absolutely powerless unless you fellows will help. When they go to Des Moines and bring the matter before the legislature and tell them what we want the representative will say, "Yes, yes, that will be all right," but the son of a gun won't do a thing. But when you people who elect him go to him and ask him to do anything he steps side-ways to do it. That is what you people have to do. The committee will engineer the thing, but you fellows will have to be back of it. What I want to urge upon you is to get acquainted with the members of the legislature from your county and tell them what you want and that you have got to have it.

PRESIDENT: Mr. Nietert informs me that he has to go away at 3:00 o'clock this afternoon. He is chairman of the committee on resolutions, and properly these resolutions should be read this afternoon, but he has asked that he be allowed to read them now if there is no objection.

MR. WRIGHT: I move that we have the report of the committee on resolutions at this time. Motion seconded and carried.

Mr. Nietert reported the following which was adopted.

RESOLUTIONS.

We, your committee on resolutions, beg leave to submit the following resolutions, and respectfully recommend their adoption:

WHEREAS, We desire to express our appreciation of the loyalty and co-operation of our efficient secretary of agriculture, Hon. James Wilson, who has ever been the faithful friend and defender of the dairy interests, and,

WHEREAS, we realize with regret that the present chief of the dairy division of the bureau of animal industry of the agricultural department of the United States is not in sympathy with the dairy sentiment of this country upon important amtters, and such lack of sympathy is the cause of friction which has practically nullified his usefulness in that capacity; therefore be it

Resolved, That we urgently request the appointment of some competent man to fill this position at as early a date as possible; and be it further

Resolved, That the secretary of this association be instructed to send a copy of these resolutions to the secretary of agriculture, as an expression of the desires of the dairymen of Iowa.

Resolved, That we return many thanks to the officers of the National Dairy Union as a partial expression of our appreciation of their untiring and able efforts in behalf of the dairymen and honest butter in securing the passage by congress of the oleomargarine law of 1902.

Resolved, That we also extend our thanks to Senators Allison and Dolliver, and our representatives in congress for their loyalty to the dairymen and honest butter, and their valuable assistance in securing the enactment of our present oleomargarine law.

Resolved, That the Iowa State Dairy Association extends cordial greetings to the dairymen of the eastern states, and we hereby express the hope that the western contingent may meet them in their own country in joint convntion in the near future.

Resolved, That the Iowa State Dairy Association urges upon the Iowa World's Fair commission the importance of setting aside a fund sufficient to make a creditable exhibit of the dairy interests of this state at the Louisiana Purchase Exposition.

Resolved, That the Iowa State Dairy Association expresses its profound gratitude for the generous treatment and cordial hospitality accorded us by the Cedar Rapids Hotel Men's Association and the citizens of Cedar Rapids generally.

Resolved, That we thank the railroads leading into this city for courtesies shown, and the granting of low rates for the delegates.

WHEREAS, John C. Daly has retired from the secretaryship of this association, be it

Resolved, That for his many years of faithful service, and his zealous work in behalf of the association and the dairy interests of the state at large he is entitled to the sincere and hearty thanks of every member of this association.

Resolved, That this association appreciates the good results already obtained and to be secured through the work of expert instructors of dairymen and butter makers; and that the magnitude of the dairy industry of this state warrants us in asking that the next session of the legislature give authority for the appointment of five additional assistant dairy commissioners, to the end that the profits of the dairy people of the state may be increased, and the industry further developed.

Resolved, That we most heartily endorse and recommend the appointment of Mr. Edward Sudendorf as superintendent of the dairy exhibit at the Louisiana Purchase dairy exhibition, whose peculiar fitness for the place is everywhere recognized.

Resolved, That the Iowa State Dairy Association give their hearty endorsement to the great exposition to be held in St. Louis, in 1904, commemorating the Louisiana Purchase of which Iowa was a part.

Resolved, That this association tender to the Iowa commission to this exposition their hearty co-operation in providing a display of the dairy products of the state, that the great industry may be creditably represented, and Iowa maintain her position in the world as the greatest of all dairy producing states.

Resolved, That the thanks of this association are hereby tendered to Chief F. W. TAYLOR of the exposition, for his address and for the interest shown by his special visit to this meeting; to Hon. C. J. A. ERICSON, Chairman of the committee of the state dairy exhibits from Iowa, and for his able presentation of the matter; to MR. EDWARD D. BRIGHAM, State Labor Commissioner, for his address during the co-operation of all Iowa industries in advancing the sale in Iowa of Iowa products and the building up of Iowa's enterprises.

H. J. NIETERT,
F. L. KIMBALL,
Committee.

Mr. Ross: I move the adoption of the resolutions as read. Motion seconded and carried.

Mr. Wentworth: I would suggest that it might be well to appoint a committee to have charge of whatever may be necessary to be done in regard to the exhibit at the Louisiana Purchase Exposition. I would move that a committee of three be appointed, of which the president of this association will be chairman.

Motion, seconded, put to vote and carried.

President: We have an afternoon session—the last. We have provided a program of unusual interest to butter makers. We had yesterday one of the liveliest discussions that was ever held at any dairy meeting, and I assure you we are going to have just as interesting a time this afternoon, and we hope you will all stay over and we may have a full audience for the last meeting.

President: This convention is adjourned until 2:00 this afternoon.

AFTERNOON SESSION.

President: The meeting will now come to order. The first on the program is "Receiving and Sampling of Milk," by C. A. Larson of the Ames Iowa Agricultural College.

RECEIVING AND SAMPLING OF MILK.

C. A Larson, Ames, Iowa.

Old as this subject may seem it is nevertheless as important now as it was years ago, for the success and welfare of a creamery is almost wholly wrapped up within those two words "receiving" and "sampling." The amount and quality of milk taken in depends to a great extent upon the manner in which the receiving and sampling is done, and without milk no creamery can succeed. So much attention has recently been given to such subjects as "The Preparation of Starters," "Ripening of Cream" and "Churning of the Butter" that the work connected with the receiving and sampling of milk has been crowded into the background. It is exceedingly important to know how to do this work, but it must not be to the neglect of receiving and sampling of milk. It is a fact that in many creameries where division of labor occurs, the head butter maker, or the man with the most practical experience and with the most mature judgment is chosen to look after the ripening and churning. A second man, or usually a boy, is delegated to look after all the important details involved in the receiving and sampling of milk. There is no place in a creamery where all the different qualifications of a man are put into use as they are in the weigh-

ing room. To prepare starters and to ripen cream are subjects that most
any man with average ability can be taught how to do. It is more of a
manual or mechanical proceedure where skill is the chief requisite qualification. But to receive and sample milk rightly one must be endowed
with skill, ability to handle details, accuracy and quickness in handling
figures and making computations, ability to grade and select milk, ability
to stimulate interest in the production of good milk, and ability to reconcile and satisfy unsatisfied patrons. In order to accomplish these latter
results one must have some judgment of human nature, and as some one
has termed it, "a liberal sprinkling of business principles."

To many dairymen the term receiving of milk is limited to simply
pouring the milk out of the patron's can into the weighing tank, recording
the number of pounds of milk, and then lifting the valve so that it can
escape into the receiving vat. Such a conception of receiving milk is easily satisfied. Any boy or man without mature judgment or special training can do this. But when we give the term "receiving of milk" its broad
and comprehensive interpretation we must include first the selection of
milk. This can be properly done only when a man's senses of smell, taste
and sight have been cultivated, and are made use of, together with the
power of observation. How to select milk depends upon the acuteness of
the senses, but how to dispose of these different qualities of milk in the
most economical way depends upon the knowledge the receiver has of the
effect of these different defects of milk upon the ultimate product, and
also upon the amount of common sense and judgment he is able to consult.
Because a can full of milk is sour, if otherwise clean, does not necessarily
indicate that it is unfit for the production of a first class quality of butter;
of course it should not be mixed with the sweet milk, as it might coagulate
it all or clog up the separators, but if retained until after the sweet milk
has been skimmed it might be run through the separator successfully.
However, it is more safe to class it as defective milk, and keep it together
with the rest of the poor milk in a small vat by itself. Dirty, putrid and
bitter milk is the kind of milk that is specially conducive to a poor quality
of butter. One can full of such milk if mixed with the rest of the milk
may lower the grade of all of the butter made during that day one or even
two cents per pound.

To keep this poor quality of milk by itself in the receiving vat is of
utmost importance, but it is equally important to keep the weight of it
by itself on the milk sheet. When a patron delivers a can of poor milk
to the creamery he should not receive as much for it as does the man who
delivers a first class quality of milk, for it is an established fact that as
good butter cannot be made from the poorer milk. The quality of milk
delivered can be designated on the milk sheet by marking the good milk
"A" and the poor quality "B" milk. Thus, at the end of the month each
patron can be paid according to the quality of the milk he delivered without much trouble to the creamery operator and with justice to the patrons.
This is one of the best means of bringing about a reform in the methods
of caring for milk or cream on the farm. There are dairy farmers to whom
explanations and teaching concerning the care of milk should be admin-

istered until doomsday without any effect but who could be brought to a realization of the importance of giving milk proper care before it reaches the creamery if they were taught by receiving less pay for the milk of poorer quality, and also through teaching and explanation, the former acting as a cure and the latter as a preventive. Thereby the best possible results ought to be obtained. It is true if such a method is pursued another point of complexity has been added, and another source of dissatisfaction to the patrons has been introduced, yet it is the only right way to pursue, and in the dairy industry as well as in any other industry, "right makes might."

Enough has been said of the importance of knowing how to judge milk and cream, but there is still another field of judgment even more important financially speaking than the first one mentioned. viz., that of judging human nature. The receiver of milk should know each of the patrons thoroughly, and be able to control and govern his actions accordingly. It is a known fact that some butter makers can make suggestions to farmers concerning the care of milk without creating any offense, can even reject milk without being censured in the least. He can make money, build new creameries and prosper without losing the confidence of the patrons, while if some other man should attempt to do the same thing he would receive as a reply, "You don't have to take my milk. I can sell it somewhere else or feed it to my calves." This difference simply lies in the fact that one is able to judge the nature and disposition of his patrons and then control and govern himself accordingly, while the other one is not. Self control is one of the qualifications essential to the receiver of milk. He is one who is bombarded with criticisms and complaints concerning the test. He is the one who is openly accused of cheating the patrons on the scale. He is the one who must listen to the grumbling and growling because the neighboring creamery paid one-fourth of a cent more per pound of butter fat during the last month. He is the one who must face the consequences resulting from a rejected can full of milk, and unless there is self control something of a serious nature is likely to happen. If a set of patrons once gets dissatisfied it is about as hopeless and useless for one to reconcile them as it is for an intruder to make a disturbed nest of hornets settle. The more they are fought, the worse they will sting. If they are treated gently and judiciously perhaps only a few of them will light and do any harm. Congenial and conciliatory measures are usually to be chosen in preference to uncongenial, sarcastic and radical decisions. To habitually reject milk is a dangerous method to pursue. It irritates any man to haul his milk to the creamery and back again for nothing. He would rather leave his milk at the creamery and take less money for it. The receiver of milk who has the ability and judgment to govern his conduct according to the different patrons and different conditions arising is wise. He is like the willow tree and the radical and decisive milk receiver is like the hard wood tree. The willow bends and gives to the storms and comes up again smiling when the storms are over. The hardwood tree defies the storm, refuses to give or bend and as a consequence is blown down. The milk receiver must in many cases suffer wrongs quietly, but he should learn to suffer injustice for he will thereby be the stronger in his position afterward.

Concerning the details connected with the sampling of milk little need to be said. Suffice it to say that in order to get a fair and correct composite sample from each patron's milk, a sample which represents the quality and forming a certain proportionate part thereof must be taken. This can not be accomplished by the use of a dipper, but a milk thief, or a sampling tube must be used instead. To illustrate If a patron should deliver 200 pounds of milk testing 3 per cent fat one day. Another day he delivers 100 pounds of milk testing 5 per cent. If a dipper full is taken from each for a composite sample the test of that sample will be 3 plus 5 divided by 2, or 4 per cent. According to the composite sample taken those 300 pounds of milk delivered will contain 12 pounds of butter fat. In reality 6 pounds were delivered in the 200 pounds of milk and 5 pounds of fat in the 100 pounds of milk, making a total of 11 pounds of fat. Thus we see that the "dipper system" is not reliable, and in this case the patron was paid for 1 pound of butter fat too much for two days delivery, and only 300 pounds of milk; and as there are more reliable methods of sampling milk, which will give an accurate test when the quality of milk varies, it is wise to abolish the system which is likely to give erroneous results.

There are other points which might be dwelt upon, such as how to preserve composite samples in the best condition, how large a sample to take each day, how much preservative to use, how often to test the sample and how best to sample frozen, churned and coagulated milk. Such details in the receiving and sampling of milk are many, and it requires presence of mind, judgment and skill in order to accomplish them all well. Even with those requisites, interest in the business and a firm purpose of success in view are necessary perquisites in order to perform them all well.

PRESIDENT: We have about eight minutes left to fire questions at him. Now ask him any questions you want to.

MR. SAWYER: In sampling milk and using the dipper—I believe that is the general practice now—in using the dipper is there liable to be enough inaccuracy to warrant the use of the milk sampling tube? Is there any inaccuracy to amount to anything in using the dipper?

MR. LARSEN: Yes, as a general thing. There may not be in every case, but if a patron finds out about it he may deliver cream one day and skimmilk the next and it might amount to a great many hundred dollars. So long as the quality of the milk is the same every day it would not make any difference what kind of a sample you used.

MR. ANDERSON: In the illustration which you gave—which was a very good one—illustrating that the samples tested a little less, has there been any actual test at your station, or elsewhere that you know of where during the period of 30 days there has been any great injustice done to the patrons by the composite test.

MR. LARSEN : No sir, so far as experiment goes I don't know. We have never experimented. Such injustices may exist as a matter of fact.

MR. ANDERSON : Is that theory or practice?

MR. LARSEN : It is certainly both.

MR. ANDERSON : Would you advocate the abolition of the composite test then, that is what I would ask?

MR. LARSEN : No sir, I would advise sampling every day and testing every two weeks.

MR. ANDERSON : Then you would mix the samples taken every day?

MR. LARSEN : Yes, I would mix them.

MR. ANDERSON : That would be a composite test wouldn't it?

MR. LARSEN : Yes, but it would be taken with a milk thief.

MR. ANDERSON : You don't catch my idea. You said if a cow's milk tested 3 per cent today and 4 per cent tomorrow, for instance, the man was being paid more than he ought to be paid.

MR. LARSEN : If you took a dipperful from each of the two samples, yes.

MR. ANDERSON : Now, would you advocate thirty tests a month, one daily?

MR. LARSEN : No, I would advocate taking a good sample from the milk each day with a milk thief, use a preservative and test about every two weeks.

MR. ANDERSON : Isn't that what they are doing now mostly?

MR. LARSEN : No, I don't think it is.

MR. BANCROFT : The way I understand it is that one day they received 300 and another day 100, and the first day they should have taken out three times what they did when they received only 100.

MR. LARSEN : Yes, sir.

MR. BANCROFT : Therefore the composite test would be correct?

MR. LARSEN : Yes.

36

PRESIDENT: The next on the program is "Buttermaking as a Profession," by Prof. McKay, of Ames. I want to say right now that Prof. McKay is feeling extraordinarily good. He said he never felt better at a convention. I presume it is because all the highest scores were taken by former Ames students.

THE BUTTER MAKER'S PROFESSION.

Prof. G. L. McKay, Ames, Iowa.

Within recent years many changes have taken place in buttter making. It was formerly supposed that most any one who was neat and tidy could make good butter. Since investigations have been pursued along scientific lines, we find that it requires skilled labor.

The men who are pursuing dairying at our school now are possibly twenty-five per cent in advance both in education and skill of the students who took dairy work seven or eight years ago. As we look the country over, we find the people who have become famous in the dairy world are men of unusual intelligence, who would undoubtedly have made a success in most any other line of business. I like self esteem in a young man. I like to see the young man with the "git there" spirit in him, no matter what line of work he is pursuing. I believe every young man has enough natural ability to acquire an education providing he has the will power to assert himself. It is the lack of self conceit that keeps a man from rising to the level that it is possible for him to attain. We complain frequently about people being egotistical. I admire a certain amount of this quality in any person. This is an age of combinations and concentration of capital. It is also an age of specialists. The general purpose man must necessarily fall to the rear. Every man should be educated along some line of business. While I am a strong believer in adaptability, I cannot think that a man who has made a success as a specialist would have been a failure in some other business, if he had applied the same energy and thought to it.

Success in any business never comes by chance or luck. Chauncey Depew, being asked by a young man to give the secret of success, replied, "My boy, there is no secret to it. It is just dig, dig, dig." Edison being asked to give the definition of genius, answered, "Two per cent is genius, ninety-eight per cent is hard work." On another occasion when this great inventor was asked if he did not believe that genius was simply inspiration, he replied, "No, genius is perspiration." The editor of a western newspaper sent to all the successful men in the city this question, "Why is it that not more of our young men succeed?" And one answer came back in this laconic phrase, "Because too many of them are looking for white shirt jobs." Possibly this was a homely way of saying it but it is true in many cases, especially with many of our college graduates. Some imagine because they have a college education they must necessarily get an easy, high salaried position. It is well to have a technical education but it is

Scene on the farm of **H. B. Smith**, Odebolt, Iowa.

also well to have a manual training. Lord Bacon used to say, "Learning should be made subservient to action. We need a knowledge more of how to do things than how to explain things." The world today is looking for men and women who can turn out the finished product. The time we hope is past when it will be considered a disgrace for a man or a woman to work with their hands. No man would be so irreverent as to say, "That the man Christ was lacking in brain power or manliness," yet we find Him a carpenter, toiling with His hands. Study the lives of all successful men and the story will be foundd in each case exactly the same. The methods varying as they must but the actual basis of every successful life is the persistent, hard, hard work of years and many a personal sacrifice. This is not always apparent simply because we are all apt to look at a man when he has achieved his success, but there was a struggling period nevertheless. Thoroughness in everything is the key note of success. As Mr. Bok, the distinguished editor of the Ladies Home Journal, says, "A thorough workman never says, 'There that will do,' but 'there, that's it.'' and this is what every young man in business should learn—that absolutely nothing is good enough if it can be made better. And better is never good enough if it can be made best. We frequently hear men complain that there is no us in doing extra work, that their employers do not appreciate it. They work merely like an automatic machine with no interest or heart in their work. As a rule the fault is more often with the employed than with the employer. There are exceptions to this as to any rule but as a general thing the man gets paid about what he is worth. The man who most loudly complains of being underpaid is frequently the man who is overpaid. I find it much more difficult to get men to fill the best positions than it is to get men for the ordinary positions. A. T. Stewart used to say that he always had plenty of vacancies in his store which he could not fill, although he wanted to, for ten thousand-dollar employees. The same condition exists today in many other branches. Let an important position open up in any branch of business and it is very difficult to find a competent man to fill it. A universal precept and rule of success which was spoken long before universities were thought of, applies to academic studies as it does to every action and decision of human life. "Whatsoever the hand findeth to do, do it with thy might." No work is worth doing badly and he who puts his best into ever task that comes to him will surely outstrip the man who waits for some great opportunity before he condescends to exert himself. We are not all adapted by nature to be physicians or lawyers so it is well for the young man to find the line of work for which he is best adapted and then use all his energies to make it a success. The creamery business of today opens up a large field for intelligent young men who are not afraid to work, who are willing to work with their hands as well as with their heads. In fact the man who successfully operates a creamery must be an all-around good fellow. The dairy business is practically in its infancy. We know very little about milk or its production. I think it was ex-Governor Hoard who said that the "laboratory of a cow was one of the darkest places in the universe," which is quite true. The success of the creamery depends more on the butter maker than any one else. Many things that to the careless maker seems of little importance, to the intelligent maker are of the greatest importance. This condition is quite evident to any one who has visited a large number of creameries. In some creameries, we find every evidence of prosperity. The maker meets the patrons with a "Good morning" and a pleasant smile, and weighs and samples the milk as it should be done. The creamery is in first-class order and there is a pleasant atmosphere everywhere. It is a pleasure to visit such a plant. Contrast this with a creamery where we find everything in a dilapidated condition, with an untidy maker at the head of it, patrons dissatisfied and the complaint is made on every side that the creamery business does not pay. In fact some of the patrons think that the creamery men are the greatest rascals in existence. That is what is preventing the creamery business from progressing as it should. Jealousy among farmers has destroyed more creameries than all other things combined. More faith in mankind is needed. I believe there are very few dishonest men in the creamery business. If one-fourth of the dishonesty that is printed in the sensational papers is true, the business of the world would be seriously affected. When we consider that only five per cent of the world's business is done on a cash basis, we find that business men have faith in mankind. We frequently hear farmers in a community find fault with the creamery in their section and do everything they can to injure the operator's business, when in reality the very presence of a creamery in their neighborhood is advancing the price of land possibly from three to five dollars per acre. With your permission I will review the butter business from the time the milk is received up to the finished product. The weighing of milk which seems of little consequence to some makers is a very important place in a creamery, and a place where the head maker should always be found in the morning. Here is the opportunity of coming in contact with the patrons and doing missionary work that will educate him to furnish a better product. It also gives the maker a knowledge of the condition of the milk that he is to handle that day. The importance of taking a correct sample of milk is quite an item in keeping the patrons satisfied. More dissatisfaction exists over the testing than any other business in connection with the creamery. If milk is allowed to stand only a few moments in the weighing can and a sample is taken without carefully stirring the cream, the result will be an inaccurate test which may defraud the patron or the creamery. The leaving open of milk jars as frequently happens after samples are taken, will not give accurate results, as evaporation of moisture is taking place all the time. I have known samples of this kind to cause a variation of two per cent. Take up the question of testing milk. Testing machines must run perfectly smooth and at a certain speed to insure correct results. Sulphuric acid should also be of a certain specific gravity. These things require skill. The heating of milk for separation is not receiving the attention it should. It was my privilege at a great national convention to try and point out the defects in the butter exhibited. I found possibly thirty to forty per cent of the flavor was injured more or less by the use of live steam for heating the milk. It was an easy matter in most cases to select the butter where live steam had been used before reading the methods of making it, many using the exhaust steam from the engine to heat the feed water for boiler. Here we found the cylinder oil transmitted to the milk from the boiler, thus giving a decided oily flavor to the butter. The use of boiler compounds showed their injurious effects also. Why live steam should be used for heating milk at the present time is a mystery to me. Many of the live steam heaters not only injure the flavor by transmitting impurities from the boiler but the heating is not sufficient to give the best, or the desired results. The heating of milk is supposed to help the fluidity of the fat globules. The quick, flashy heating of milk has very little effect on the fat globules, therefore the separation is not as perfect. Milk should be heated for some time before separation to get the best results. The centrifugal separation of milk is a wonderful process. Think of a separator bowl making from six to twenty thousand revolutions per minute. Here we see sweet milk put into the machine and skim milk and cream immediately separated. Most any separator will skim clean to a certain limit if the machine is run perfectly smooth and at the proper speed. A little vibration of the machine causes a remixing of the cream and no separator will skim thoroughly clean that vibrates. This is where some makers in large creameries lose possibly more than their wages. The next thing is cream ripening which is possibly the most important step in the whole process as this is a factor that largely controls the flavor, and flavor is the quality that distinguishes butter from lard, tallow or any of the other fats. Flavor does not come by chance. Every intelligent butter maker is fully aware of the uncertainty and difficulty of producing a uniform high flavor. Experience has taught us that when certain processes are followed, the resulting product is usually of at least fair quality. But even under the best sanitary conditions the product is often strikingly variable in flavor from day to day. The cause of these variations and difficulties open up an important field for future investigation. The subject is of great scientific interest as well as of practical value. Butter fat in itself is supposed to have little or no flavor. It was formerly supposed that the flavor was largely due to the volatile fatty acids. The flavor substances are possibly absorbed by the fat or are associated with the other constituents which compose a portion of the butter. The chemical nature of the substance which give the delicate flavor and aroma are not known. I think I am safe in saying that it is generally accepted now that the flavor substance whatever they may be are the products resulting from the breaking down of the milk solids. It was shown by Professor Storch that they are the result of the growth of bacteria. Professor Storch tells that the flavor of good butter comes from the decomposition of milk sugar. I might say that Dr. Weigmann, the noted German bacteriologist, held the same view when I visited his labaratory a little over a year ago. Dr. Conn, on the other hand, thinks that the nitrogenous material in milk as the casein and albumen, furnish the product which gives the flavor. The feed consumed by the animal no doubt has an influence on the flavor as well as on the color and the hardness of the butter. But in general this influence is much less than the effect of fermentation which has taken place in the milk and cream. In cases where feeds, such as turnips or wild onions and weeds are consumed by the cows, the flavor will undoubtedly be imparted to the milk, butter or cheese, unless the milk or cream has been pasteurized, when these volatil products pass off. The effect of differnt kinds of ferments is not as easily removed, not even by pasteurization. This is the principal reason why we get much different flavor in the winter than in the summer months, as the cows are usually milked in the stable and the germs that get into the milk are mostly of the putrefactive groups—those which cause ordinary decay. We found from investigation at our school that about seventy-five per cent of the bacteria in milk were of the undesirable kind during the winter months, while in the best periods of the summer months we found as high as ninety per cent of the desirable kind. The thorough brushing and dampening of the udders before milking and the removal of the milk from the stable as soon as drawn would greatly diminish these effects. In our best cream, we found from ninety-two to ninety-eight per cent of the bacteria present to be of the acid producing species. A maker can more readily control the flavor by the use of a starter. An example of this kind was shown at the national contest. We find that one maker got an average score of 98.12. This was not brought about by chance nor entirely by the good milk furnished by the patrons. This maker informed me that he carried twelve or fifteen starters during the entire contest. Here we find him selecting the kind of bacteria that produces the best flavor. A starter of any kind is only adding enormous quantity of a species of bacteria that we expect to predominate in the final product. This takes skill and hard work on the part of the maker. Starters of any kind are quite difficult to carry forward as every detail must be attended to punctually. The maker must have smell and taste well cultivated so that he will be able to detect the slightest change or off-flavor. He must also have some knowledge of the principles of bacteriology. A few years ago, it was largely chance work for a maker to win two high scores in succession. Now we find makers who use pure cultures and have a knowledge of the scientific principles of cream ripening scoring high in most every contest. It is asked—does all this care and trouble pay? I would say yes. As the value of butter may be enhanced as much as five cents a pound. The churning and working of butter is another important factor that does not receive the attention it should from the creamerymen of the country. We have a law limiting the per cent of water in butter to sixteen per cent, yet we find in the chemical analysis of butter in the six-month contest is something less than twelve per cent. The maker who is able to incorporate between fifteen and sixteen per cent of water in his butter will increase his yield nearly four pounds to the hundred. Take an ordinary make of five hundred pounds per day and we will have a difference of twenty pounds. Twenty pounds at twenty cents a pound will give us four dollars, quite an item on a man's wages. Here is where skill comes in. The dry butter or that containing a low per cent of water does not sell any higher than the medium and in some cases not as high. I tested butter in the London market and found the French Rolls and Danish Selected which sold the highest in the English market to contain about five per cent more water than the New Zealand butter which brought three or four cents less per pound. In this case, the New Zealander would lose four or five pounds of butter per hundred and was also losing in price. I asked the late Prof. Siegleke why the Danes incorporate so much water in their butter and he answered that butter was supposed to be plastic. It was intended to spread on bread and this could not be done if the butter contained all fat. While I do not like to see slushy butter I think that from fourteen to fifteen per cent of water can be incorporated with good results. It is almost impossible to form any conclusion of the amount of water butter contains by looking at it. Frequently butter that seems slushy will contain very little water under chemical analysis. Professor Storch has been working on this subject for a number of years and he has been unable to fully explain why some samples of butter have a very dry appearance and at the same time contain a very high per cent of water, some samples testing as high as eighteen or nineteen per cent. We do know that when a lot of cream is churned at a time that the overrun will be much greater than when a small quantity is churned. This is possibly due to the fact that when a small quantity of cream is used the fat globules are thrown together more compactly and do not hold the same amount of water as when a large quantity is churned. There are several other conditions that influence the yield which the skilled maker understands and some conditions which I would not care to explain here.

The washing of butter is a far more important factor in butter making than is generally supposed. The keeping qualities as well as the flavor can be seriously affected by undesirable bacteria being transmitted through the wash water. C. Larson, one of my assistants, has been carrying on experiments during the past year along this line, and he has had some startling results from butter washed with seemingly pure water as compared with butter washed with water that had been pasteurized and cooled. I believe the time is not far distant when all wash water will be pasteurized or sterilized. Take the question of color or mottles, thousands of dollars are lost annually by butter being mottled. This defect is caused by an uneven distribution of salt as many of you know. Take three lots of butter from the same churning even where no artificial coloring has been added, salt one lot at the rate of a half ounce per pound, the second lot at an ounce and the third lot at one and one-half ounces, and the color will be so strikingly high in the last lot that it could not be mixed with the other lots without showing streaks. This is no doubt due to the fact that salt has an affinity for water. The tendency is for them to run together and form a solution. When salt is used, the water collects in large beads thus giving the butter a darker shade of color. Whenever you find light streaks in butter you will invariably find no salt, therefore the first consideration in salting butter is to get good salt that will dissolve readily. The butter should not be drained very dry. It is better to use a little more salt if it is inclined to wash off some. Salt should always be put on the butter in the churn and churn revolved a few times to thoroughly incorporate salt and butter before putting rollers in gear, thus retaining as much moisture in the butter as possible. Allow butter to stand from fifteen to twenty minutes before working in this condition and then work until butter has become waxy in appearance and salt ceases to be gritty. If these precautions are observed, there will be no danger of mottles. In the preparation of the package, tubs should be thoroughly steamed then soaked for a few hours in a weak brine solution when they are ready for a coat of paraffine. Parchment paper should be used of the best grade, after it has been soaked for ten or fifteen minutes in boiling water. It should then be immersed in cold water and left until used. If paraffine is not used, the tubs should be soaked for a longer period. Parchment paper should be allowed to project about an inch over the top of the butter and neatly folded. The tub should be filled full and stroked off level. This gives a nicer finish. As a general thing, not enough precaution is taken in packing the butter in firmly in the tub. Nothing looks worse in a strip tub than to see holes in the side of the package. The appearance is not only bad but the imprisoned air makes the conditions favorable for the growth of mold. A nice, clean appearance and good finish go a long way in fixing the price. It is almost impossible for a creamery owner to place an intelligent estimate on the service of a good maker. We have one or two large creameries in Iowa that are getting one and a half cents a pound above western extras. These creameries could pay their makers three thousand dollars a year and still have one cent above left. If you have a good maker, do not hesitate to pay him a good salary. Five dollars a month given unsolicited would be more appreciated by a maker than ten dollars given on demand.

The opportunities were never better for first-class men in a creamery than they are today. College men need not hesitate to take up this line of work if they have a liking for it.

MR. LAIRD: The professor spoke about having a good over run. What is considered a good reasonable over run under favorable circumstances where everything is conducted in an honest manner.

MR. McKAY: About 16 to 18 per cent. There are some makers who will be able to incorporate a little more water than that. Now I want to tell you what a difference a butter maker can make in a large creamery. I know of one large creamery in this state where the butter maker made a difference of 31,000 pounds of butter per year, giving the patrons about the same test.

MR. WRIGHT: I would like to have Prof. McKay make some statements in regard to the contest he is preparing.

MR. McKAY: The contest is purely an educational contest which we are giving. A great many butter makers did not seem to understand the National Educational contest. I might state what we are offering to the public. The first 20 lbs. of butter sent to the contest we demand to pay the expense of cartage from the school to the station, and the postage sent out. If there is any money left after paying these expenses it will be returned to the butter maker. The butter will be scored at the school and a chemical analysis made. The butter will be scored two weeks later in New York by Mr. Healey to ascertain its keeping qualities.

If any creamery in the state seems to be having difficulty in making good butter and will notify Mr. Wright he will have Mr. Kieffer go there. Those who are having extremely poor butter can have Mr. Kieffer come to the creamery and spend a day or two and try to find out what is the matter, whether it is the fault of the creamery or the patrons. Mr. Wright spoke this morning of the good feeling existing between the dairy schools, the dairy commissioners and this organization. We are all aware of this harmony and it is as it should be. Mr. Wright is on the road night and day travelling over the country. The president is on the road all the time. We have organized this year and appointed some strong committees and we want to go to the next national contest and place Iowa butter at the head where it belongs—should belong.

PRESIDENT: You will be favored with an address by a professor with whom you all feel acquainted, one who has done much to help you in your knowledge of butter making, Prof. Farrington, may I call you a pupil of Dr. Babcock?

PROF. FARRINGTON: You may, I am proud to be so designated. I only wish it was possible to get Dr. Babcock to attend these meetings more. But he has a strong dislike to leaving his own home. It is impossible to get him out of Wisconsin.

TESTING MILK AND HAND SEPARATOR CREAM.

E. H. Farrington, Madison, Wis.

About ten years ago the dairy industry was presented with the Babcock milk test. This test was rather cautiously received in some localities at first but after those interested had passed through an educational period the test became permanent and a prominent factor in every branch of dairying. Ever since the practical value of the test was well understood there has been a wide spread interest in the subject of milk testing and people have become so well informed about it that a general description of the method or of the apparatus is unnecessary at this time. Butter makers and dairymen are now so familiar with the method that I will confine what I have to say to a few suggestions regarding some points in testing that have given more or less trouble.

The first persons that became acquainted with the test were the creamery butter makers; they soon learned how to operate it and I think that after using the test a while, every competent butter maker feels as if he is able to test milk accurately, although he connot always give a satisfactory explanation for some of the results he gets. His experience soon shows him that the cause for what may seem to be an abnormal test or result must be sought for in the sample instead of being the result of a faulty method of testing. This confidence which the butter maker has in the method is not always shared in by everyone who is interested in the test. It often happens that dairymen or creamery patrons from their lack of familiarity with the subject are sometimes suspicious and inclined to condemn the method whenever the results obtained do not correspond with their idea of what the tests ought to be.

It is occasionally hard for a patron to understand why the tests of his cow's milk will vary as is sometimes the case. He naturally thinks that so long as he feeds the same cows the same feed that the tests of their milk ought to be uniform from week to week. This undoubtedly ought to be true and is in many cases, but observations made by testing the milk of each cow in a herd at every milking for a full period of lactation have shown that any kind of excitement, such as hurrying the cows, roughly treating them or exposing them to cold, wet weather will very often have an immediate effect on the milk test. It has also been noticed that indigestion will also effect the test of a cow's milk. This was very strikingly illustrated in the dairy tests at the World's Fair. The superintendents of the different herds at that time kept a careful watch of the daily tests of each cow's milk and I well remember that any sudden rise or fall in the tests would direct the herdsman's attention to such cows and a careful examination of them would be made at once.

There are many other ways of varying the test of milk and we recently had an illustration of a variation in a patron's milk test at the Wisconsin Dairy School that may be of interest to others. A sudden drop was noticed in the test of the weekly composite sample of a certain patron's milk and he at once came to the creamery to see what was the matter. We discussed the subject a while and I tried to suggest all the things I had ever heard of as the possible cause of the drop in test. I did not seem to make much impression on him for he said he "had no new cows and no fresh ones." He was feeding corn and every part of the feeding and milking was being done in the same routine way each day. He knew this to be true because he was doing the work himself. He suggested that either our sampling or our testing was incorrect and that the creamery should pay for his milk on the basis of the tests obtained before the sudden drop. The creamery manager could not find a good reason for accepting this proposition and explained to the patron how the milk samples were taken and how the testing was done at the creamery. This did not convince the patron who insisted that there must have been some mistake at the creamery and that he was the loser on account of another man's error. The manager was not convinced that such was the case because of his confidence in the Babcock test. He was, however, anxious to have the patron satisfied with his tests and he suggested that the patron should send him a sample of the milk from each cow in the herd. He explained how the sample should be taken by milking each cow dry, an then filling a bottle with the thoroughly mixed milk from each cow. The patron did as requested and after awhile brought such samples to the creamery where they were tested. These tests turned out to be nearly all higher than those which this patron had been receiving at the creamery. He was naturally pleased by this showing but the manager was inclined to think that either the cream had been allowed to rise somewhat before the farm samples were taken or that the sample bottles had been filled by milking directly into them. Such samples are never a fair representative of the entire amount of milk a cow produces and great care must be used in taking test samples in order to have them tell a true story. The question of sampling milk was again discussed at some length and the patron was finally induced to take another lot of samples from his cows. He returned a few days later without bringing the samples with him but explained that he had discovered the cause of the drop in his test. He had found that there was a small hole in one of his milk cans and that when he set this can of milk into the water tank after milking, that the milk and water changed places. The water which leaked into the milk had diluted and lowered the test.

The experience converted the patron from suspicion of the test to confidence in it and he talked about the incident so much among the other patrons that they were also helped to believe in the Babcock test.

There are probably many butter makers who could relate similar experiences with their patrons but the present indications are that milk testing is being done more and more at the farms and where this is the case the patrons are learning many valuable points about their cows and also about milk testing.

The creamery butter maker may be of a great deal of assistance to his patrons by giving them the benefit of his longer experience in milk testing and in aiding them to overcome any difficulty they may have with a new tester.

The butter maker will find that testers at the farms of his patrons will be a great benefit to profitable dairying and will be a great help to the creamery industry. He should therefore do everything possible to encourage his patrons to own milk testers.

Another experience which came to my notice during the past year shows the value of milk testing at the farm.

Two dairymen each supplied a creamery with about 500 pounds of milk daily from a herd of cows which each man was justly proud of. For some unknown reason the test of one patron's milk was uniformly about one-half per cent higher than the other. This difference occasioned some good natured discussion between the two men but as they both had prefect confidence in the Babcock test and were not suspicious of either the butter maker who did the testing or the manager of the factory who did the figuring, the tests were accepted as showing the superiority of one herd over the other so far as the test of the milk was concerned.

In the course of time it so happened that a student of the Wisconsin Agricultural College visited one of these farms and tested some of the cows. While engaged in this work one morning he needed one more test to make the tester balance and as the can of milk to be sent to the creamery was near he took a test out of that milk and ran it with the others from the single cows. The owner of the herd chanced to come around as the completed tests were being read and he noticed that the test of the milk going to the creamery was about one-half a per cent higher than he had been in the habit of getting at that place; he therefore asked the student to test the can of herd milk each day just before it was sent to the creamery. This was done and the farm test was always higher than had been received at the factory for several months. Neither the student nor the owner of the herd could explain the difference so the matter was taken to the creamery for investigation.

A search for an explanation was diligently and honestly made by all parties concerned, many arguments and experiments were proposed but without going into details about them we will give the final result of the evidence obtained. It seems that the custom of this butter maker was to test each patron's milk in the same test bottle every week. The creamery was so steady going that there were few changes in the number of patrons and few test bottles were broken so this practice could easily be carried out without any disturbance in the routine work. Such a system of doing the work, however, proved to be the cause of the low test always coming on one man; the investigation showed that the test bottle which had been used constantly to test the milk coming from the farm where the student was testing, was not correctly graduated and the results it gave were always aboue one-half a per cent too low. The unusual practice of the butter maker to test each patron's milk in the same test bottle was therefore the cause of all the trouble; the defective bottle always cheated the same man.

After making this discovery the patron began to figure how much he had lost by this deal as it was a clear case of failure to get pay for one-half pound of fat for every hundred pounds of milk which had been tested by that bottle. A few calculations were made and the damage done by the defective bottle was settled for $25.00 by the owner of the creamery.

This little experience shows three things: first, that all test bottles ought to be carefully examined and the graduations tested before the bottle is used; second, that although tests may be incorrect the maker of them is sometimes innocent of his error; and third, and every man who sells milk ought to have a Babcock tester and he ought to use it.

FARM SEPARATORS.

There is another machine that is now being extensively bought by farmers who own cows. The hand separator is just now having a marked effect on dairying and in some localities it is the cause of radical changes in the equipment and in the product of many creameries. This change in dairy is being enthusiastically promoted by some parties and uncompromisingly condemned by others.

There seem to be at least three sides to the question, or three important interests involved; those of the farmer, the butter maker and the consumer. First. There are farmers who claim that hand separators give them the best possible skim milk to feed to their stock; such skim milk, they say, protects them from the danger of contagious disease being brought to the farm by the creamery skim milk and they also claim that the saving of time required to draw the milk daily to the factory is an important matter with them.

On the other hand they must invest considerable money, not only in the separator but in some sort of a power to run it, as the necessity of having something besides man power to run a farm separator is admitted by all dairymen who have attempted to turn the crank themselves. The loss in skimming at the farms where one hundred or more separators take the place of one factory machine is another important item, as is also the diminished price of the butter which is often of a lower grade than that made by skimming the whole milk at a factory.

The next group of individuals that feels the effect of this radical change in the creamery industry are the creamery owners and the butter makers? Some of these feel keenly the loss on the quality of butter made from gathered cream. The experience of many factories with farm gravity cream in the past has been such as to cause butter makers to doubt the practicability of making so fine a quality of butter from farm separator cream as they formerly have made from whole milk.

It will take a long time to overcome this prejudice but we should remember that gravity cream is not hand separator cream. The standard quality of butter certainly should not be lowered by farm separator cream and when it is skimmed from milk which is twelve or more hours old. condition than that skimmed from milk which is twelve or more hours old. The sooner cream is separated from the milk after milking the better the cream for any purpose and this being true any faults in the butter made from such cream can not be charged to the farm separator. The defects found in gathered cream butter usually arise from improper care of the cream before it is delivered to the factory. These defects develop or are introduced into the cream either by the method of caring for it at the farm or by the way in which it is transported to the creamery.

In order to get farm cream to the factory in a condition so that it is possible to make an extra quality of butter from it, the farm separator should be placed where there are no barn or other bad odors. It must be thoroughly clean, the bowl and all tinware scalded and put in a clean place out of the reach of dust. Under no circumstances should the separator bowl be left until it has been used a second time before the cleaning is done. The bowl slime and rinsings left in the separator after skimming, begin to sour and decay in a very short time, and if the cleaning is not done immediately after skimming the taints of sour milk are hard to remove.

CARE OF CREAM.

The ideal way of cooling separator cream is to have it run from the cream spout of the separator directly over a water cooler. This should reduce the temperature to as near 50 degrees Fahrenheit as possible. The cream must then be kept at a temperature below 60 degrees Fahrenheit by setting the clean cans in cold water. It should be gathered for delivery to the factory as often as every other day in the hot summer weather. When a cream cooler is not used the cream cans should not be over six inches in diameter and by setting these cans in cold water the temperature should be reduced to 60 degrees Fahrenheit or below. This must be done at once and in order to hasten the cooling, the cream should be frequently stirred. A tin disc to which is attached a strong wire handle two feet long makes an efficient agitator for this purpose.

THE CREAM HAULING.

It often happens that cream which has been well cared for at the farm is damaged during transportation to the creamery. The cream gathering wagon starts out early in the morning and the first cream which it collects must remain on the wagon until it returns at night. This trip when taken in the hot days of summer or cold days of winter is apt to be injurious to the quality of the cream and its protection from these extreme temperatures is a problem which must be solved if the butter made from it is to grade as extras in quality. The cream-carrying receptacle whatever it is should be well insulated and provided with a float to prevent churning during transportation. Different styles of cans, barrels and tanks are now used for this purpose. The creamery should make every provision possible for keeping the cream in a sweet condition until it is received at the factory.

When patrons fail to take good care of their cream at the farm, some creameries adopt the practice of grading it and keeping the tainted, sour cream separate from that of good quality; two grades of butter are made and the farmers are paid for the kind of butter which their cream makes.

These problems in regard to farm separator cream are important ones. The creamery owner and the butter maker together with the farmer, will have to shoulder his share of the responsibility of upholding the standard of American butter and the condition of the creamery industry five years from now will show how well this work has been done.

RUNNING THE FARM SEPARATOR.

In localities where the hand separator has been used for a while and seems to have obtained at least a temporary foothold, it has been found that many of the operators of these machines are more or less puzzled by the variation in the test of the cream as reported by the factory to which it is sold. They do not understand why it is that cream from their separator does not have a uniform test from day to day. It is perhaps natural for them to expect that since the separation of cream is a mechanical process the product should be fairly uniform in composition. There are, however, several things which influence the test of separator cream and they should be well understood by the owners of hand separators.

First—The temperature of the milk when separated ought to be uniform. If there is a variation of ten or more degrees when the milk is run through the separator at different times, the richness of the cream will vary with the temperature. In some cases the milk may not be separated as soon after milking as at other times, on account of some delay at the farm, and when the separator is finally started the milk has cooled off considerably below the proper temperature of separation and the test of the cream is thereby changed.

Second—The speed of the bowl has considerable influence on the richness of the cream and if for any reason this speed is not uniform, or is different at one separation than at another, the test of the cream will be changed by this irregularity.

Third—Cream changes in richness with the amount of milk separated per hour. If at any time the separation is hurried by crowding more milk through the bowl than it is customary to separate, the test of the cream will be changed.

Fourth—The cream screw in the separator bowl is placed there for the purpose of changing the thickness of the cream when desired. This screw can be regulated so as to make a thick or a thin cream and it will perform its work if all the other factors of separation are uniform.

Fifth—The amount of skim milk or water run through the bowl when the separation is about finished will influence the test of the cream, depending upon whether the bowl is flushed out with a little water or if a large quantity is used.

After the operator of a hand separator becomes aware of the effect which each one of these things has on the test of the cream, he can, if he wishes to do so, run the separator each time so that his cream will have a uniform test. Now, it so happens that when milk is separated at the farm there are a great many things that interfere with the regularity with which the separator is operated. At some farms the separator is started up when the dairyman begins to milk and it is allowed to run from the beginning to the end of milking. Each cow's milk is poured into the receiving can on the separator and the milk is separated by the pailful. In such cases the separator skims for a few minutes and then runs empty. This alternation of skimming and not skimming has considerable effect on the cream separated, and a cream more nearly uniform in composition can be obtained by arranging the milking so that the separator will be running at full capacity until the milk has all been through it. In other cases the dairyman gets rushed and tries to hurry a lot of milk through the separator in a short time, thus changing the rate at which the milk is skimmed, and the effect of this fluctuation will be noticed in the test of the cream.

If the users of hand separators are careful to regulate the skimming each time so that it is done in the same uniform manner they can depend upon getting cream that will be uniform in test. The points which need to be especially watched are the speed of the bowl, the temperature of the milk, and the amount of milk skimmed per hour.

CREAM TESTING.

The testing of cream is a subject in which many people now take a lively interest. A great deal more of it is done now than was the case two years ago and I think the universal experience of all those who have carried on this work, is that cream testing is far more difficult than milk testing. The ordinary manipulations of the test are generally understood and there are only a few points connected with the subject that I wish to mention.

THE SAMPLING OF CREAM.

When cream haulers sample cream at different farms, a box of one-half pint sample bottles should be taken along and this box of samples ought to be iced in summer and kept from freezing in the winter just as carefully as the cream-carrying cans are protected. These half pint bottles filled to the cover will furnish a good sized sample of each lot of cream and when no preservative is used in them the butter maker has a chance to inspect the condition of each lot of cream which was poured into the large cans. This will help him to locate any trouble he may be having with his butter. If these samples get sour and lumpy there is some defect in the method of caring for them during transportation, but I think on the whole, such a large sample as this without using a preservative until it arrives at the creamery, is the most satisfactory one to take and after it has been thoroughly mixed and tested that which is left may be emptied into the cream vat.

WEIGHING SAMPLE AND CLEARING FAT.

When it comes to testing the cream I presume that every butter maker knows that it should be weighed and not measured into the test bottle. The scales made with agate bearings and knife edges are most easily kept in good condition for this purpose than those having metal bearings which will easily tarnish and rust. Another thing that will be of great aid in obtaining accurate readings of the cream fat is to allow the test bottle to cool and the fat in the necks to solidify or crystalize after the last whirling in the centrifuge. This cooling helps to separate the water from the fat which in many cases has not been accomplished by the whirling alone. When re-melted and warmed to about 120 degrees Fahrenheit the fat will be clear, oily, water-free, and in the best condition possible for measuring.

THE CREAM TEST BOTTLE.

A new idea regarding the cream test bottle has been proposed and used somewhat in recent times. This is designed for the purpose of testing very rich cream. The commonly used cream bottles are graduated to measure thirty per cent of fat when eighteen grams of cream are taken, but the new bottle is made with a longer neck and is whirled in a larger tester than those formerly made. My experience with these test bottles is rather limited and I am consequently not able to discuss them, but I have always felt that so long a column of fat as would be separated from a forty to fifty per cent cream, was hard to measure accurately, on account of the careful work needed in regulating the temperature of so much fat. The expansion and contraction of so long a column of fat effects the readings so much that it has always seemed to me to be safer to use less cream, say nine grams, in a test bottle that will measure thirty per cent fat, than to try to test eighteen grams in a bottle that will measure sixty per cent fat. This use of the thirty per cent cream bottle will also make it possible to test all kinds of liquid dairy products in one tester or centrifuge.

The thirty per cent cream test bottles, however, need some attention. They have been made in the past of the same length as the milk test bottls but the diameter of the neck is increased in order to hold the larger quantity of fat that is separated from cream than from milk. For some unknown reason the manufacturers have been gradually increasing the diameter of the neck and contracting the length of the scale on the cream test bottles so that in some cases the entire graduation from zero to thirty per cent occupies a space of only two inches in length. This brings the lines of the scale very closely together so that the graduations which represent one-half per cent of fat are not much father apart than the width of an ordinary pencil mark.

With such test bottles it is almost impossible to read a test accurately to much less than one per cent fat. This is a serious mistake and when there are so many other difficulties in the way of testing cream accurately, an effort should be made to increase the length of the graduated scale rather than to diminish it.

Realizing the necessity of this I have had a cream test bottle made of the usual length of a milk test bottle, but in order to give it a longer neck than cream test bottles generally have, I had the bulb of the bottle cut down so that it has a capacity of about 45 c. c. up to the zero mark of the scale instead of 55 c. c., which is the capacity of the bulb of the old cream test bottle. This size of bottle 40 to 55 c. c., I find is plenty large enough for mixing the cream and acid before whirling the test bottles in the centrifuge, and by cutting it down the neck of the test bottle can be made longer. The necks of many cream test bottles on the market are only about three inches long; that of the new cream bottle is at least four inches long and by making the diameter less the graduations of the neck are placed so far apart that it is easy to read so fine as one-fourth per cent fat instead of one per cent as was only possible in the old style of cream test bottle. In fact, the scale representing one per cent on the new cream test bottle is as long as that of two per cent in the old bottles. This elongation of the neck is a great help in reading the test accurately and to smaller fractions of one per cent than one is able to read with the old cream test bottle.

CALCULATING CREAM DIVIDENDS.

When cream only is received at a factory, the payment of patrons by the Babcock test is made on the same general plan as at whole milk factories. There are, however, at the present time, many creameries which receive both milk and cream from the patrons. When such is the case the cream patron should receive pay for the fat in the skim milk left at the farm as well as for that in the cream he delivered. If this is done he will be paid on the same basis as the whole milk patron who has his dividend calculated on the total fat in his milk. In order to carry out this system

37

of payment it is necessary to assume some constant figure as representing an average test of separator skim milk and credit all cream patrons with this uniform loss. A fair figure seems to be three per cent which is assuming that the skim milk tests 0.12 per cent and the whole milk 4 per cent fat. This 0.12 is three per cent of the 4.0 pounds of fat. All that is necessary now is to add three per cent to the weight of the fat brought to the factory by each cream patron for a given period and the sum will be very nearly the fat in such patron's whole milk. An illustration may help to make these calculations clearer:

Suppose 125 pounds of butter are sold by a factory for thirty dollars, and that the factory receives four cents per pound for making the butter, which will amount to five dollars; this leaves twenty-five dollars to be paid to the patrons A. B. C, who supplied the following weights of milk and cream:

Patron.	Milk.	Test.	Butter fat.	Corrected weight.
	Lbs.		Lbs.	Lbs.
A............	1,000	4.0	40.0	40.0
B...........	1,200	3.8	43.2	43.2
	Cream			
C......	400	16 8	16.3	16.8

In order to pay the cream patron for his milk fat, his weight of butter fat should be increased by three per cent, and patron C who delivered 16.3 pounds butter fat as cream, should accordingly have this 16.3 multiplied by 1.03, which is equal to 16.8 pounds.

The weights of fat from each patron's share of the receipts are calculated will be: A 40 pounds, B 43.2 pounds, C 16.8 pounds, or a total of 100 pounds fat, for which twenty-five dollars was received. From this we find that one pound of fat is worthy twenty-five cents.

The amount due each patron is then found by multiplying his weight of fat by this price per pound:

A 40 lbs. at 25 cents......$10.00
B 43.2 lbs at 25 cents...... 10.80
C 16.8 lbs. at 25 cents...... 4.20 $25.00

In calculating the dividends of cream patrons when both milk and cream patrons come to one factory, the weight of butter fat (found by testing the cream) is, therefore, multiplied by 1.03 and this result is taken as the total amount of fat that would have been delivered by the cream patron if he had sent his milk to the factory.

MR. MUNSEY: Supposing a farmer gets the idea into his head to know absolutely whether he is getting a correct test of his cream. He purchases a hand separator and takes it to his farm. And by the end of the month has found out that we are giving him 4 per cent more than belongs to him. We hear it in an indirect way. His neighbor gets suspicious. It looks as though our test wasn't accurate. Let me say that the creamery test is exactly correct. Now would you advise these farmers to have these machines on the farms and test their own cream? He tells his neighbor about the discrepancy and they are both suspicious. Supposing of course the creamery tests correctly.

MR. FARRINGTON: Then I would advise the creamery man to go out and teach him how to run his tests correctly.

PRESIDENT: The next is "Pasteurization," by M. Mortensen.

PASTEURIZATION.

M. Mortensen, Sioux City, Iowa.

It is the desire of every butter maker at the present day to make himself familiar with the subject of pasteurization. We pasteurize our milk for starters so as to acquire control of the fermentation. We pasteurize the skimmed mild in order that the farmer may have a better article for feeding purposes, yet pasteurization of cream for butter making is only practiced at a few creameries.

By pasteurization we understand the application of heat to such a degree that most of the bacteria are destroyed; the temperature generally made use of ranges between 140-185 degrees Fahrenheit. This should not be confused with sterilization, by which we understand complete destruction of bacterial; this may be accomplished either by application of heat or by use of chemicals.

Every butter maker at present has become so familiar with pasteurization that he can without difficulty pasteurize milk for starters, but pasteurization of milk and cream for city supply, and especially cream for butter making requires more experience and very careful work. The cooked flavor which milk acquires after it has been heated to a temperature of 150 degrees Fahrenheit must be prevented when milk is to be sold for direct consumption. The consumer generally objects to the cooked flavor; only a few understand that the flavor serves as a guarantee that this milk is a pure, healthy food.

The Wisconsin Experiment Station recommends that the milk be heated to 140 degrees Fahrenheit, for 30 minutes; that does not produce the cooked flavor and does not affect the rising of the cream as do higher temperatures.

Pasteurization of milk and cream for direct consumption is continually growing in favor. As to the digestibility of pasteurized milk compared with raw milk, opinions are divided. Experiments along that line of work have been conducted at the Maryland Experiment Station, where they arrived at the conclusion that raw milk is more easily digested when fed to calves than either pasteurized or cooked milk; they also corresponded with physicians in charge of children's hospitals, and the majority of them favored the use of raw milk for infants, when the milk was known to be in perfect condition, but favored pasteurized milk under ordinary conditions.

Dr. Fleischmann, together with Dr. August Morgen, and other European scientists conducted experiments which lead to the conclusion that the nitrogenous matter in milk which has been submitted to a high temperature is somewhat more digestible than in fresh milk.

Pasteurization of milk is done very satisfactorily by intermittent pasteurization, whereas for cream it is necessary to use a continuous pasteurizer. It is a mistake when people conceive the idea that they will start to make pasteurized butter, and first experiment awhile before they go to the expense of buying a pasteurizer. The result is they start to pasteurize their cream in cans. If cream, especially that cream which is rich in butter fat is exposed to high temperature for any length of time the body will be injured and butter made from such cream will acquire a body similar to that of renovated butter. That kind of butter will sell below quotation, and the operator is apt to decide that pasteurized butter will not be a success. It must be fully understood that whenever we want to pasteurize cream for butter making we must invest money in a pasteurizer, as the can system will always be a failure.

All manufacturers of pasteurizers use every effort to make the best on the market and one that can be operated with the greatest possible degree of economy. They are fitting them with stirrers of various construction. These are to make the milk move rapidly over the hot surface with the object of having it thoroughly mixed, and to prevent it from burning on the sides of the machine. They also aim to have the cream exposed to the high temperature only a short time and then cooled immediately so as to prevent any injury to the body.

Experiments conducted at the Royal Experiment Station at Copenhagen prove that if a pasteurizer is properly constructed and properly operated it will require about ninety pounds of steam for heating 1,000 pounds of milk from 90 to 185 degrees Fahrenheit. If we figure that it takes one pound of coal to produce four pounds of steam, to produce ninety pounds of steam will then require twenty-three pounds of coal. Figuring coal at $4.00 per ton, and our butter yield four and one-half pounds of butter to 100 pounds of milk, makes the cost of pasteurizing one pound of butter about one-tenth of a cent. This expense however is reduced considerably by pasteurizing the cream and skimmed milk separately. The cream is reduced to such a small amount that the expense per pound will be very little. For pasteurization of skimmed milk the exhaust steam can be used. This is also more satisfactory to the patrons as milk when pasteurized after skimming is warm enough to scald the cans and the milk keeps sweet longer.

Regarding the efficiency of continuous pasteurizers Mr. Monrad in his book on "Pasteurization" quotes the following from Dr. Eaton. "The efficiency of the continuous pasteurizer is very likely due to the extremes in temperature, to the rapidity with which the heat is applied and to the sudden cooling of the milk." The same author quotes from Dr. Stohman: "The killing of the bacteria will be promoted through the sudden change of temperature." Actual experiments have been conducted by the experiment station at Geneva, New York. Results there obtained with temperatures from 175 to 185 degrees Fahrenheit were very satisfactory. According to Dr. Bang of the Danish Experiment Station, the danger from the germs of tuberculosis in the milk is removed by immediately heating the milk to 185 degrees Fahrenheit, followed by immediate cooling.

We are frequently asked is it advisable for a small creamery to make pasteurized butter? The only one who can answer that question to any satisfaction is the man who is buying the butter. If he wants to have the product pasteurized and is willing to pay the extra cost, then it will pay to pasteurize because the butter will always give better satisfaction. It is a fact that the butter maker who is pasteurizing the cream has several advantages over the one who has not. By pasteurizing the cream and adding a starter he secures perfect control of fermentations, and he will be enabled to make a uniform grade of butter. Of course it is neccesary that he keep a good starter on hand all the time; he can never depend on luck the way he often does when he is handling the raw cream.

By pasteurization it is also possible to remove taints caused by the foods consumed by the animal; also taints that have been absorbed by the milk with unfavorable surroundings. Flavors or taints caused by bacteria however can not be removed by heating.

One point strongly in favor of this system is the keeping qaulity which pasteurized butter possesses. If we desire to compete for the foreign trade we must make pasteurized butter. A dealer in Montreal informed me that he would willingly pay one cent more a pound for pasteurized than raw cream butter. Another in Manchester, England, when showing me one of his best makes of Danish butter said: "This is nearly perfeet butter. You would probably want higher flavor, but we are a little inclined to call that butter strong which the Americans pronounce high on flavor."

The requirements are gradually changing in this country. People seem to like pasteurized butter very well after they have once tasted it. One thing is evident, the American people, as well as the English, want butter with keeping qualities, and no other kind meets the requirements as well as pasteurized butter.

PRESIDENT: Prof. Eckles not being present we will pass on to the next paper, "The Creamery Patron," by our assistant dairy commissioner, P. H. Kieffer, of Strawberry Point.

THE CREAMERY PATRON.

P. H. Kieffer, Strawberry Point, Iowa.

Mr. President, Members of the Iowa Dairy Association, Ladies and Gentlemen: Owing to the important subject assigned me, and I believe the most important subject of all, the creamery patron, I will, with your patient attention. try to partially discuss it. I wish I were able to impress upon the mind of all the importance of the proper consideration of the creamery patron.

The creamery patron is the foundation and support of the creamery, for without him there would not be any creameries. The creamery patron is one of the best citizens of this country, pays as much, if not more taxes, in proportion, than any other branch of industry, and is deserving of the proper consideration by our legislative body, and should be provided with the proper protection for his production and also furnished with the best methods by competent instructors of how best to feed the cows, their care, the handling of cream and milk, etc., in order to obtain the most profitable result from the business.

The output of butter in this great dairy state, which has all the natural resources for milk production, has been, according to our state dairy commissioner's report, decreased yearly for the past five years, the largest decrease according to the last dairy report, was during the past year, which is as follows: In 1901, there were 89,376 creamery patrons; in 1902, there were only 81,532, over 8,000 less patrons. In 1901, there were 627,948 cows; in 1902, there were 579,070 cows, a falling off of 48,678. The production of butter in 1901 from all the creameries was 82,704,944 pounds; in 1902, it was 77,885,696, a falling off in the manufacture of butter at the creameries of 4,819,248 pounds.

A business that is as profitable as the dairy industry when conducted in an intelligent way in a dairying state like ours, should be on the increase in the place of decrease. The decrease in the manufacture of butter in this state has been more harmful than is generally considered. Thousands of dollars have been invested in buildings and machinery, which, when caused to cease operation, on account of the shrinkage in patronage, is indeed a great and serious loss. When we consider the shrinkage of the patronage, and the loss of the capital invested in creameries and machinery in this state, it sets one to studying what the causes of the shrinkage and losses are, and its remedies. It has been proven that a pound of butter can be produced at about the same cost that two pounds of beef are produced, providing one possesses the right kind of cows, and feed the proper ratio, and receive the right care. In order to get the best method of handling our dairy cows by practical dairymen to obtain the best results, I would suggest that we interest the creamery patrons in a contest, something about as follows: The methods of the winners be placed on record and extensively advertised. The plan is this: For the Iowa State Dairy Association to give a prize, either in money, or a gold medal, to the creamery patron, or patron of a cheese factory that can show the best record for one year from his cows by presenting the statement of the secretary of the creamery or cheese factory, number of cows, pounds of milk and test. The one showing the greatest amount of butter fat from his herd for a year to receive first prize, and the next one in order, to receive the second prize, which would, to some extent, have an affect of interesting our patrons more in our association. The creamery patron should become a member of this great dairy association and take the advantages of this great organization, which is now largely composed of members, who are not producing the milk.

Our honored president, Mr. Shilling, seeing the necessity of getting the patrons interested in this great work, has organized in the past year several district butter makers' and dairymen's associations which, so far, have accomplished better results than was expected in so short a time. It is the getting together of the butter makers, creamery patrons, and others that are deeply interested in the success and welfare of the greatest and most profitable industry of the state, the discussions of the different subjects along this line of our actual conditions and how to better the same.

In conclusion I wish to say that the most important thing for the creamery patron to observe is to immediately after milking cool his milk or cream to about fifty-five degrees, or colder, so as to check the development of bacteria. A better grade of butter can be made and the patron profit thereby, and I believe that it would not be necessary to operate the creameries on Sunday, thereby giving the butter makers and milk haulers an opportunity to better fit themselves for the week's work.

PRESIDENT: In accordance with the motion made this morning to appoint a committee to look after the World's Fair Exhibit at St. Louis, I will appoint to assist me in this work State Dairy Commissioner Wright and Mr. M. Mortensen of Sioux City.

The auditing committee have reported as follows:

We, the auditing committee have examined and checked the secretary's report with vouchers and bills attached, and find the same correct.

We have also checked over the books of the treasurer and the report as given is correct.

Moved and carried that the report of auditing committee be adopted.

PRESIDENT: The following telegram was sent to Messrs. W. K. Boardman and Jules Lombard.

"The Iowa State Dairy association in convention assembled send congratulations on your improved health and deplore your inability to be with us. All stood and sang Auld Lang Syne in your honor.

J. C. DALY, *Sec.*

PRESIDENT: I do not believe we have ever held a convention in which the machinery men who have exhibits here have cooperated as they have at this convention, and I wish to thank them.

The business of this convention is now at end, and you stand adjourned *sine die.*

LIST OF MEMBERS.

NAME.	PLACE.	NAME.	PLACE.
Allen, A. R	Dubuque.	Finch, Ira	Fairbanks.
Anderson, A. E	Oelwein.	Fridley, A. E	Sumner.
Adkins, F. J	Ely.	Fosse, L. T	Ridgeway.
Andrews A. J	Goldman.	Finch, F. H	Waverly.
Adams, L. C	Lone Rock.	Flaskegard, P. C	Storm Lake.
Abbott, C. H	Hazel Green.	Forester, H. E	Fredericksburg.
Allison, Chas. A	Newell.	Feldman, J. B	Dyersville.
Anderson, W. H	Ruthven.	Frees, A. J	Cedar Falls.
Bee, William	Fredericksburg.	Guptile, F. E	Cedar Falls.
Barney, W. B	Hampton.	Gordon, J. A	Postville.
Benton Co. Creamery Co.	Vinton.	Gurler, Charles	DeKalb, Ill.
Bowen, Geo. B	Mason City.	Graham, E. J	Nashua.
Bates, J. W	Waubeek.	Green, S. F	Chicago.
Bates, E. J	Waubeek.	Gallagher, T. F. 191 S.	
Barnum, R. Duke, 156		Water street	Chicago.
Reed street.	New York..	Goodrich, A. M	Fayette.
Benson, M. E	Brandon.	Griffith, J. H	Hopkinton.
Baker, E. M	Monticello.	Gimer, A. D	Cleves.
Beyer, H. F	Edgwood.	Gullenbach, Wm	Bremer.
Byrne, Geo. P	Genoa Bluff.	Gronbeck, H. K	Jewell.
Bracey, C. B	Maynard.	Hoppenworth, A	R. D. I., Waverly.
Brown, H. C	Oxford.	Hoppenworth, A. D	R. D. I., Waverly.
Brown, David	Sioux City.	Hohnsbehn & Son, C	Waverly.
Borglum, P. N	Rutland.	Hippe, N. O	Nordness.
Barker, J. A	Luana.	Hubbell, G. L	Cedar Rapids.
Betinger, John	Lodora.	Hubbard, C. B	Independence.
Brokaw, Herbart	Rowley.	Heath, H. R	Mason City.
Brunner, J. J	Charles City.	Hall, E. G	Union.
Barlow, Ivan	Calmar.	Henrikson, J. N	I. A. C., Ames.
Brant, C. E	Fairbanks.	Hazlerigg, S. N	Anamosa.
Barnes, Frank	Schley.	Hemmingway, H. C	Waubeek.
Barber, M. L	Marion.	Henry, K. J.	Millersburg, Ill.
Beach, C. N	Alpha.	Hartinger, C. R	Alden.
Casey, W	Elgin, Ill.	Hoopman, A. E	Chester.
Cherry, W. T.	Cedar Rapids.	Herring, E. G	Dexter.
Cherry, W. R.	Walker.	Hillman, Fred	Hamlin.
Culp, P. C	Liscomb.	Itskin, R. E.	Waterloo.
Clausen, H	Randall.	Irwin, C. R	Lake View.
Clausen, L. J	Randall.	Iliff, B. C	Ossian.
Carpenter. H. C	Waterloo.	Jenon, W. F	Topeka, Kan.
Cooper, C. R	Chicago.	Jennings, A. L.	Chicago.
Colven, W. J	Omaha, Neb.	Johnson, P. W	Chicago.
Caven, Geo., 154 Lake St.	Chicago.	Jones, E. T	St. Joseph.
Carpenter, H. R	Elkader.	Jennings, C. R	Victor.
Cummings, J. S	Maynard.	Jones, J. R	Sigourney.
Clark, W. G	Dysart.	Janes, Fred	Charles City.
Clark, Tom	West Bend.	Jenn, P. N	Toronto.
Curtis, C. F., I. A. C	Ames.	Johnson, M. J	Shell Rock.
Condit, J. S	Monticello.	Jenson, Bertel	Ross.
Calkins, C. W	Iowa Falls.	Johnson, W. B.	Westgate.
Carr, Cecil E	Frederika.	Jenson, & Kraus.	Eldora.
Caledonia Creamery Co.	Paullina.	Kendall, W. L	Cedar Rapids.
Daly, J. C	Charles City.	Keachie, Jas. L	Dexter.
Drysdale, A. C	Dubuque.	Kelley, L	Waterloo.
Davis, W. H	Chicago.	Keiffer, P. H	Strawberry Pt.
Dean, H. L	Tipton.	Kimball F. L	Waterloo.
Deitring, J. B	Bancroft.	Kingsley, R. G	McGregor.
Dillon, O. W	Union.	Kroeger, W. H	Bennett.
Davis, W. J	Delaware.	Knutson, P. O	Thor.
Dawson, J. F	Iowa Falls.	Keoneke H. C	Artesian.
DeHoogh, D. J	Boyden.	Knudson N. H.	Emmetsburg.
Deitring, John B	Miller.	Kiepert H. J	Alexander.
Donovan, M. J	Jerico.	Kindberg, A	Dyke.
Dauchey, H. C		Kleckner, F. S	Lamont.
Elvidge, E. O	Elkader.	Keachie, John B	Estherville.
Elder, Geo. A., Tacoma		Little, C. H	Cedar Rapids.
Block.	Chicago.	Lukring, William	Waverly.
Edwards, L. S	Moulton.	Larson, John M.	Omaha.
Erb, R. J	Arbor Hill.	Larson, Henry	Dows.
Evans, H. J	Strawberry Point.	Logan, V. A.	Omaha.
Erickson, A	Clermont.	Leighton, F. A.	New Hampton.
Evans, Wm	Bradgate.	Laird, T. I	Lamont.
Encoldson	Gilbertsville.	Larson, J. E	Sioux City.
Elder, C. D	Manchester.	LaBarre, F	Owatona, Minn.
Farr, E. D	New York City.	Lauds, E. P	Dubuque.

LIST OF MEMBERS—Continued.

NAME.	PLACE.	NAME.	PLACE.
Laude, H. W.	Dubuque.	Russell, T. B.	Roland.
Laird, W. S.	Walker.	Shilling, S. B.	Ma-on City.
Larson, Frank	Dows.	Sudendorf, E	Clinton, Ill.
Larson, Peter.	New Hartford.	Stahhope, J. T	Sioux City.
Lonning, Ben.	Huntington,	Soenke, P. F.	Boone.
Meinhardt, F., 253 La-		Schermerhorn, D. S	Des Moines.
Salle street.	Chicago.	Symons, Fred.	Des Moines.
Mitchell, I.	Vinton.	Smith, W. E	Des Moines.
Mallard. Frank.	St. Clair, Mich.	Struther, E. Del	Waterloo.
Marsh, Charles	Jesup.	Scott, G. D.	Dubuque.
Milber, Jas.	Fairbanks.	Sayles, A. B.	Monticello.
Moody, W. E.	Davenport.	Sawyer, P. W.	Central City.
McVann, E. J., 258 Mich-		Sorenson, A. M.	Portsmouth.
igan street	Chicago.	Sallamarsh, W. S.	De Witt.
Miller Pasteurizing Co.	Canton, Ohio.	Screiber, F.	N. Washington.
Montgomery. E. E.	Williamsburg.	Smarzo, W S.	Masonville.
Mortensen, M.	Sioux City.	Scott, G. F.	Magnolia.
Murphy, D. E	Hartwick.	Spohn, L. J	Teeds' Grove.
Menzies, D. A.	Wilton Junction.	Strait, Geo	Marengo.
Mack, F. A	Waterloo.	Swanson. J. E.	Colo.
Minert, E. E.	Des Moines.	Schultz, John F.	Arnold.
Mansager, M. J.	Ellsworth.	Strampe, Wm	Paullina.
Morck, Christ.	Swea City.	Storvick, T. A.	Silver Lake.
McNarry, H. L	Britt.	Stevenson, F. W	Dundee.
Miller, H. N.	Randall.	Stamen, J. A.	Carroll.
McCaffery. J. E.	Earlville.	Stalbyerg, R.	Pioneer.
McAeravey, J. J.	Coggen.	Tabor, W. C.	New York City.
Neitert, H. J	Walker.	Taylor, B. G.	Rowley.
Nichols, S. B	Mason City.	Power, N. D.	Kansas City, Mo.
Nicholson, C. A.	Dows.	Thomas, Z. W.	Fort Dodge.
Newman, John & Co.	Elgin, Ill.	Thomas, J. A.	Ryan.
Nelson, Christian.	Dysart.	Trimble, N. H.	Alden.
Nielson, J. P.	Brayton,	Van Camp, J. E.	Muscatine.
Neilson, L.	Salem.	Van Auken. E. E.	Charles City.
Nagel, W. J.	Scarville.	Vorhees, J. A.	Monticello.
O'Dell, F. L.	Greenfield.	Wentworth, E. M.	State Center.
Pufahl, E.	Nora Springs.	Wilson, D. W	Elgin, Ill.
Palmer, V. A.	Monticello.	Wright, H. R., state house	Des Moines.
Plumb, H. B	Waterloo.	Woodring, I.	Waverly.
Petribone, F. G.	Chicago.	Whitmore, E. J.	Owatona, Minn.
Packer, Geo.	Ryan.	Wais, A. W.	Waterloo.
Peterson, L C	Rosendale.	White, E. A	Sioux City.
Pettibone, H. W.	Fenton.	Wheelock, M. O.	Waterloo.
Peterson, S.	New Hampton.	Woellert, J M.	Epworth.
Peterson, Peter J.	Montezuma.	Wright, Z. L	Ely.
Peterson, Peter.	Elkhorn.	Wheeler, F. P.	Sibley.
Palmer, A A.	Manchester.	Wright, St. Elmo.	Central City.
Peterson, W.	Steamboat Rock.	Wilcox, F. F.	Panora.
Reed, S. B	Des Moines.	Waele, H. H.	Ryan.
Russell, W. H	Luana.	Welsh, R. R.	Arlington.
Rehorst, J. H	Monticello.	Wetz, J. E., 381 Wells St.	Chicago.
Roe Brothers	Vinton.	Whitney, A. M.	Alden.
Ritter, C. A	Wall Lake.	Wiley Scott	Fulton.
Rundall, W. E	Cedar Rapids.	Woodstock, W. H	Conroy.
Ross, W. W.	Central City.	Wood, H. S.	Salina.
Rohdie, C. J.		Williams, Geo	Spirit Lake.
Royer, A. M	Waverly.	Wick, George.	Story City.
Richards, Louis.	Forest City.	Winter, Theo.	Williamsburg.
Ross, G. Y	Fairfield.	Whalan, J. P.	Elma.

PART X.

PROCEEDINGS OF THE IOWA PARK AND FORESTRY ASSOCIATION.

SECOND ANNUAL MEETING DES MOINES, DECEMBER 8, 9, AND 10, 1902.

OFFICERS OF THE ASSOCIATION.

President, - - - - - - PROF. T. H. MACBRIDE, Iowa City·
Vice-President, - - - - - WESLEY GREENE, Davenport.
Secretary, - - - - - - - - L. H. PAMMEL, Ames.
Treasurer, - - - - - - HON. SILAS WILSON, Atlantic.

Executive Board, - - { J. S. TRIGG, Rockford; PROF. H. C. PRICE· Ames; C. A. MOSIER, Des Moines.

Committee on Ways and Means, { WESLEY GREENE, Davenport; COL. W. A· BURNAP, Clear Lake; HON. EUGENE SECOR, Forest City.

Committee on Civic Improvement and Municipal Legislation, { PROF. A. T. ERWIN, Ames; PROF. B. SHIMEK. Iowa City; HON. SILAS WIL· SON, Atlantic.

To the Secretary of the Board of Agriculture:

I have the honor to transmit herewith the proceedings of the Iowa Park and Forestry Association, being the papers read at the Des Moines meeting, December 8, 9, 10, 1902.

Just at present there is a wide spread interest along the lines of civic improvement, and also along the line of protection of our forests. This interest is not merely local, but there are words of encouragement from all sections of the country.

When the lumber interest was at its height in Wisconsin and Minnesota the forests were removed without any thought of the future. The trees were cut down and after the lumber was cut fires were permitted to run through the denuded areas, thus destroying the chance of a future growth of timber. We have reached such a stage in the development of our country that it has become an imperative necessity to give some attention to the subject of the culture of timber, a question that received considerable attention during the early days of the agricultural society.

But a small share of Iowa is devoted to the culture of timber. There should be much larger areas in timber. The Iowa Park and Forestry Association desires to increase an interest in the growing of trees, and it has urged both national and state legislation to protect our forests for the future supply of timber. It has sought for the unification of the forest work of the United States government. It has urged that this work be transferred to the Department of Agriculture, where competent and able men can look after the interest of the reserves and timber supplies.

The Park and Forestry Association has in addition to this mission another one to fulfill, namely: the making of more beautiful homes by the planting of trees, not only in cities and villages, but in the country as well. It has urged that more time be given to the subject of parking; that we have state, county and city parks, which may be had without very much trouble or expense. The subject is well presented in this report by the admirable address of the president, Prof. T. H. Macbride.

Yours truly,

L. H. PAMMEL.

Professor Macbride, of the State University of Iowa, then delivered the president's address on the evening of December 8, as follows:

THE PRESENT STATUS OF IOWA PARKS.

T. H. Macbride, Iowa City, Iowa.

Gentlemen of the Iowa Park and Foresty Association: This society may this evening well congratulate itself on the success and enthusiasm of this its first anniversary. Our effort has certainly met a hearty response throughout the state, and we rejoice in a very general expression of public sympathy. In fact, the cause for which we stand is certain one day to appeal successfully to every intelligent citizen of the state, to every thoughtful man and woman who lives within its borders.

There are thousands of us who love nature for her own sake; who rejoice in the trees and streams because they are beautiful, because they attract us away from all that is sordid and petty and mean, and lead us to more quiet and peaceful thoughts to the love of living. It is the sign of the sound spiritual and intellectual health of our people that the number of those who thus use the natural world in esthetic fashion, for their individual good and uplift, is ever increasing; and the effort to establish parks, to maintain our native bits of woodland groves, the cleanness of our streams and fields, makes by no means unheeded appeal to these.

Again, there are very many among us who realize the value of pleasure grounds, play grounds, open air commons as institutions purely sanitary. Such may or may not have sympathy with those people just described who love beauty and life and nature for its own sake; but they know that

Railroad improvement along the Chicago & Northwestern Railroad at Ames.

such things are after all right, right for all the people. They know that a speedway, fifteen or twenty miles, along the Des Moines or Cedar river, a speedway, where the tired man of business may for an hour or two in the evening whirl along amid the trees, or past points overlooking the fertile fields, or may let his eye, as the sun goes down, rest upon the far flashing softened lights of the winding river—they know that this makes for the good health and consequent success of the man who is called upon to determine the fortunes not of himself and friends alone, but in large measure, also of the city, the community entire. Nor less do such people appreciate the value of such a roadway to the plain people; to the bicycler with his wheel; the clerk, the teacher, the boy with his pony cart, the mother and her children; the laborer who for a little sits on a bench by your provision placed, and smokes the pipe of rest as the sun goes down above the river, the field, the city.

The physician, the philanthropist, the officers of your city, all those who in any way have care of the public weal, are with us in our efforts to establish shade gardens and drives and roads for the people, for all, for their constant use and comfort and health. But we may go further yet. The people themselves ought to be with us, for it is largely their cause that we today are pleading; but thousands of them do not understand it yet; have not been brought to think about it. Bound by the interests of today, the cares and responsibilities of the present, men have no time to consider the future, even the near future, or to realize the wonderful possibilities of a state like ours. When you talk parks and trees and streets

Railroad improvement along the Chicago & Northwestern Railroad at Ames.
Hydrangea in foreground.

many men are indifferent; they are too busy. But the park builder has an argument which will catch the very busiest man in the community: *park building pays*—pays in profit—in increased value—in good money. Show people that, and the Iowa Park and Forestry association becomes at once a lodge of promoters, and may begin to issue literature and send out agents.

Now we, as here organized, are ready to deal with all these classes of people. We are sure of the help of the esthetic, poetic soul who loves nature for her own sake—he will applaud us, quote poetry for us, write to the newspapers, but is apt to be rather impractical when it comes to the down-right hard work that in every community remains yet to be done. But we need especially the aid of the physicians of the state, the naturally appointed guardians of intellectual and physical health. They are with us to the man. We may count on them in every town and city. Busy as the physician is, and liable to be called away at the very moment when his advice is needed, nevertheless he will prove an unfailing assistant and co-adjutor in all the work that lies before us. Business men, too, men of affairs, men of experience know what we seek and the commercial value of it. What street in your town shows at this moment highest real estate values? Outside the few blocks devoted to the direct purposes of trade, surely the valuable lots are along that street which has been laid out, best planted with growing trees, best paved it may be, or parked, or laid with walks, midway in grassy borders. Generally all these things go together; just as a man who is careful to wear a good hat or coat will generally see to it also that his boots are clean. Even one fine house or well kept place of residence renders more valuable every bit of real estate in the neighborhood. We all know this, and those who realize it best make most money out of the fact. People who lay out for commercial profit additions to our cities invariably plant their plats with trees, advertise parks and boulevards and all these things to prospective or possible purchasers; such men are smart enough for that; and we have the "Highland Park" addition and "Oak Park" and "Kenneth Square" and all sorts of devices of this kind—simply a recognition of the fact that business men appreciate in sensible Americans an innate love of that which is beautiful and orderly and clean and forever new. Is it conceivable that we Americans will allow promoters to do these things for us and pay them roundly for it, and yet are unwilling to do the same things for our own profits?

The time for our efforts is propitious. A wave of enthusiasm in the interest of all sorts of civic improvement and adornment is sweeping the country; we need only intelligent guidance, direction, and our land will soon be the fairest as well as the most splendid on the earth, the most beautiful the sun has ever witnessed in all of the fields of time. But this guiding of a good impulse, this direction we do need very badly. The past is full of mistakes, mistakes easily excusable in view of our peculiar, unexampled history. Our people have destroyed much beauty. It was a goodly land with its open groves, far-stretched flower-bedecked meadows, its clear pellucid perennial streams. Ask your pioneer about it; I may stop to tell it all tonight. I am not a very old man, but I have dipped oar in the Des Moines river away down near its mouth and seen the netted sunbeams on its gravel covered bottom all the way across. Who looking now upon the muddy channel would think of such thing possible? But our people have been careless; as the man, who, while his house is building, suffers the horses of the builders' to gnaw the bark from all the standing trees of his prospective lawn. We have had so much to do to provide shelter that we have not had time to consider beauty. We have been poor; we brought little to the state but willing hands and hearts courageous, and we have not, as the years of labor passed, found much to spend for anything that did not return in cash the interest on the investment and that promptly, for we had interest in cash to pay. We have planted trees, it is true, but they have been generally of the cheaper, more rapidly growing varieties which should most quickly respond to our need of shelter.

But today all these conditions have entirely changed. In the first place we are no longer destroying natural beauty; there is little of it left for our injury or desecration; the prairies are plowed almost to the last acre; the woodlands have been cleared away entirely or converted into pasture lands dry and destitute of all but starving representatives of our hardiest arboreal vegetation; the streams near the town are the dumping places of all uncleanness, and in the country are esteemed only as convenient places for watering domestic animals. The beauty, and the concomitant disadvantages, of human occupation have succeeded upon the wild freshness of primeval nature, and we are now left to manage the situation for ourselves.

In the second place we are no longer poor. The wealth of Iowa has easily doubled in six years, not in the sudden expanse of corporate property, or the accumulations of some enormous trust affecting the fortunes of a favored few, but in a widely disseminated prosperity affecting the fortunes of every property holder in the state. We are able to do what we please.

In the third place we are no longer careless. We are actually interested. In fact the plain people in their thousands have never wholly lost interest. Through all the years there has been unceasing constant effort. There is not a town in the state that has not made some effort toward outdoor adornment, civic beauty. There is probably not a free-holder in town or country who has not expended money in purchase of nursery stock for ornamental purposes only. And we are at this moment all interested in this thing, more interested by far than ever before, and with our increasing wealth more able than ever before to carry forward intelligent and wisely directed enterprise having for its end improvement in our artistic and esthetic living. In order to ascertain with some exactness just the condition of our Iowa towns in regard to parks and civic improvement generally I have written to the clerks of the principal towns and villages of Iowa asking certain questions relating to the present topic. Out of more than 150 replies, only six report no parks at all. There is everywhere some attempt. Seventy towns in Iowa have the old-fashioned square in the middle of the town and, of these, forty-two use the square for some public building, generally the court house. There are reported in say 150 Iowa towns altogether 1,300 acres devoted to park purposes. This, if equally distributed, might not be so bad; about nine acres on an average to each town—but Des Moines reports 465 acres of this amount, and Cedar Falls follows with 200; half the total acreage in connection with two cities. This reveals our situation. The greater number of the towns of Iowa have, as a matter of fact, no parks—simply in the majority of cases a square or two in the center of the town, and this too often given up to some special, or only semi-public purpose.

It is a singular circumstance, albeit perhaps a perfectly natural thing, that our cemeteries have in nearly all the counties received much more willing and liberal attention than our public squares and parks; although these, too, are generally far from what they ought to be. We have given more attention to the cities of the dead than to the cities of the living. One of my generous correspondents generously tells me in reply to my inquiry in reference to city parks, "We have no parks, but we have two nice grave yards!" It is also singular to learn that in a great many places the cemetery is used by the people as a park! Is not this a commentary upon our sociologic method, upon our carelessness and neglect of the interests of our people? The people need the park; they instinctively seek it—must have it, but in a great many of our cities, probably in all where the cemetery is contiguous to the town—there being no park provided, the people, the plain people, mind you, betake themselves to God's acre, and stroll back and forth among the tombstones and monumental marbles. This seems particularly the case, naturally enough, on Sundays. Sixteen of our larger cities report the cemetery made use of as a park, often to the great detriment of the cemetery, its paths, its lots, its shubbery, and, I regret to say, sometimes to the defacement of its marbles. I believe it will be found always the case where no park is provided for the people; if the cemetery is near by they will betake themselves thither and the incongruity of the habit will be never noted. However, on the other hand, one correspondent answers my query as to use of cemeteries as parks by this somewhat disdainful statement: "No. Cheerful people who like to read the inscriptions on tombstones do not live in this town." I learn also that "Cemetery Park down at Centerville is not used as a cemetery." All this is suggestive. The fact is the cemetery should indeed be laid out as a park, but after all it should be a cemetery-park, the tranquil, peaceful dwelling place, resting place of our beloved dead. The cemetery should be a park, but the park should not be a cemetery.

Brethren, does not this situation demand immediate and serious thought? It is all well enough to build churches for people that their religious longings may be satisfied or at least appeased; it is well to endow colleges and universities that means of intellectual satisfaction may be accessible on every side; it is well to spend millions in libraries that means may be had for popular entertainment; but shall we neglect all provision to meet that instinct of all our people, an instinct which confessedly means so much to our mental and moral soundness, that instinct which ever impels them to escape their houses, their shops, their darkened, smoke-stained streets, to go forth under the open sky, to the pure air, the refreshing greenness and coolness of the grass and trees, the beauty of God's pure and clean natural world! How long shall it be said of this prosperous and wealthy commonwealth that her weary sons and daughters of toil if they go forth to recreation—re-creation—mark you—must betake themselves to the cemetery? It is enough to breed anarchists and suicides, the situation as we see it now.

Another suggestive fact has come to light in this direct examination of our problem, and that is that in at least six instances the effort for city and park improvement has fallen to the hands of the women of the city.

The cares of this world and the deceitfulness of riches have so engrossed the attention of our men of affairs that opportunity for public service has not been found and the solution of this public problem has been left to the women whose hands are always free for every good endeavor. But what the women need, what we all need, what every community needs, is intelligent direction. There is every where demand for the landscape architect. The proper laying out and erection of a city park requires expert skill and intellectual gifts of no mean order. But we Iowans except in our largest cities have much yet to do before the landscape architect arrives.

In the first place we must have a place for our park proposed. It is just as necessary to have a location for your park before calling in the landscape man as it is to have a lot for your building before you seek the services of your architect. Now in the case of the greater number of Iowa towns and cities there is no trouble about appropriate and suitable convenient sites. Many of our cities are near streams and rivers whose banks and hills are all ready to our purpose. We must give up the idea of city squares; they perhaps have had their place in city building but we have outgrown them. I may not take time to discuss here the mistakes of Wm. Penn and their consequences; what the present day demands is a wider area set apart for public use, but under absolutely just regulations and thoroughly efficient control. We may have to have some special park legislation before we get far in our work, but that will be suggested as we go on. The first thing is to secure suitable location. Of course, in the smaller towns for outdoor assemblies and the like, the public square of a single block, or of two adjacent blocks, may sufficie; but what we should plan for is something very much larger, which shall afford opportunity for complete retirement from all the ordinary sights and sounds of life's routine and enable your people rich and poor alike a taste of nature's purity and sweetness.

I shall show you presently on the screen some of Iowa's possibilities in this direction. Nature, of course, does the work for us; in some places she has already for our people done much more than in others. There is often, right close to the city limits, or even within the corporate enclosure, just what we want. Perhaps it is a river with rough, rocky, or furrowed wooded shores; perhaps it is a hilltop commanding a wide view of a peaceful country rich in homes and farms; perhaps in the more distinctly prairie and level regions of our state it is a farmstead by its owner, now grown old, more richly planted than any farm in all the country. I have seen many such places, where hundreds, perhaps thousands, of trees were set out to decorate the home of some pioneer. If this property is to be sold it should go to the community; it must not be wasted by being divided up and stripped of the accumulated beauty of many years. But generally it will be found that the land which ought to go to parks in Iowa is otherwise nearly waste land. At any rate waste land about the town should go to parks. It often happens that park land may be had for the asking if the community will show a disposition rightly to use and govern. There is no reason why we should not have parks as bequests;

38

we shall have them, just as fast as we deserve them, and we shall not have to pledge ten per cent per annum for the endowment either.

But there is another side to our problem that is perfectly manageable without the landscape artist, and without very much expense. Much of the waste land about our towns is already grown up with native trees and vines. I have been arguing for years that a park in its planting need not be costly. We need to us only the vegetation which is native to Iowa to make our town park as beautiful as any in the land, indeed more beautiful than can be made in any other way. Our own vegetation, our oaks, our lindens, our hazels, our sumacs, our wild grapes and creeper did once clothe these hills and banks with summer beauty and autumn glory, and the plants will make all such locations splendid once again if we but afford them the chance. Minneapolis does not ask for tree ferns and palm trees to make the parks the pride of the town and of the Mississippi valley; she has used conditions as she found them with the results we see.

But once again; the beauty of a town lies not wholly in its parks, or lands set off as such. There is in a hundred instances no reason why the whole town should not be a park. Of course, in our Iowa villages, there must be the street for traffic, a few business blocks, but the larger part of the town is given over to the purpose of homes. Now there is no reason why these smaller towns of Iowa which are, by the way, her boast, should not be each in its own way a park. Blue-grass and elm trees will grow in every one of them, and with blue-grass and elms we can make any town a delight to all beholders. The prevailing use of cement for walks is doing a great deal to help the appearance of our cities; board walks are evil and that continually, and it requires concerted action along any given street to give regularity to the walks, regularity to the tree-line, the sidewalk line, the curb line. In our Quaker rectangular towns these lines must be respected and our only hope of ultimate beauty is in mathematical exactness.

Our Iowa towns are just now in transition state. They were built of wood. We all remember the little white painted store building with top-heavy white front and cornice. These are rapidly disappearing, in every town in Iowa, fast giving place to structures of brick and plate glass and steel. We are passing from the temporary and imperfect stage of poverty and uncertainty to that of permanence of substantial and abiding commercial and social life. How rapidly our railways are replacing the old box-like station houses of our early experience with more or less elaborate, but always tasty and substantial permanent structures; is there any reason why a similar policy should not now apply to our tree planting and the establishment of highway and street? The soft maple and box-elder have been useful trees; no one more ready than I to yield them appreciation, but the time is now at hand for the use of more graceful and permanent species.

As we are passing from wood to brick and stone and cement we should pass from boxelders to oak and elm.

A recent Japanese traveler in America has written in book form his impressions of America and especially American cities. We cannot complain of this; we are always doing it when we go to Japan. But our Japanese brother describes the style of architecture in our villages and towns as absolutely depressing, the buildings generally squatty, hideous looking things, devoid of taste, etc., but the streets, unpaved, dirty with filth of years, dusty and littered with rubbish. a heap of accumulation sloping up in front of each merchant's door. Now we are rapidly passing beyond such reproach. A few years more we shall have entirely passed. Our towns are becoming more beautiful, everyone of them, year by year. and wealth increases. and leisure comes more and more. With more fixed and settled habits of American life we may hope that the proverbial good sense of the American citizen will also make him master of civic and municipal problems in such fashion as at length to show to the world the exemplification of the philanthropist's highest hopes and the architect's fairest dreams.

REPORT OF LEGISLATIVE COMMITTEE.

Made by the Chairman, Prof. B. Shimek.

DES MOINES, IOWA, Dec. 9, 1902.

To the Iowa Park and Forestry Association: Your committee on legislation beg leave to present the following report:

In accordance with your instructions your committee took steps to present the question of the encouragement of tree planting by the Twenty-ninth General Assembly. The bill recommended by this association one year ago was taken in charge by Hon. Eugene Secor, who offered it in the house.

The Iowa Academy of Sciences in its December meeting in 1901, concurred in the approval of the Forestry bill, and likewise appointed a committee on legislation, consisting of Profs. L. H. Pammel, B. Shimek and M. F. Arey.

The chairman of these committees, with Mr. C. A. Mosier and Capt. C. L. Watrous, appeared before the house committee on horticulture, and, after consultation and a discussion of the details of the bill, the committee on horticulture, of which Mr. Secor was chairman, recommended the bill in the modified form in which it is appended to this report, and in which it has already been published in the proceedings, and it was passed by the house without a dissenting vote. In the senate, under Hon. J. J. Crossley's direction, with whom the chairman of your committee consulted, the bill was favorably reported by the committee on horticulture, and also finally on the last day of the session by the sifting committee, but failed of passage on the final vote.

Considering the fact that the question was brought up by this association so late that there was not time for public sentiment to crystalize, and in view of the further fact that any suggestion of exemption from taxation is always sure to be received with hesitation, your committee believe that the progress made by the Forestry bill was encouraging, and that the efforts of this association to secure forestry legislation should be re-doubled, because of the evident need of such legislation, and because our state is today wholly without forestry laws.

Aside from the hurry and confusion of the final session of the senate, in the opinion of your committee the chief cause of the ultimate failure of the bill is to be sought in the lack of unanimity of opinion among those who favor forestry legislation. To some our bill seemed to offer too little inducement, while on the other hand there were those who objected to any concession to tree planters. It is tre that the bill as submitted did not offer great pecuniary inducements to those who would cultivate trees, but it was a beginning which would have lead to better results. It will be difficult to secure more radical legislation for the encouragement of tree planting so long as the citizens of our state recall the abuses of former laws on this subject, and for that reason a moderate beginning was rec-ommended, chiefly in the hope that it might produce educational results.

Your committee believe that the bill as recommended a year ago should be strengthened somewhat in those features which are intended to serve as an inducement to tree planters, but rather than make a definite recommendation along this line at the present time, we recommend that steps be taken to place the whole question before the people of this state at agricultural and horticultural meetings, through the press and in such other manner as may bring about the discussion of questions of tree planting, and that the results of these discussions be collated in such manner that they may serve as the basis for recommendations to the Thirtieth General Assembly, and that either a committee, or the regular officers of this association, be entrusted with the direction of this work, to report at our next annual meeting, and that the discussion of this question be made a special order of business in that meeting.

Respectfully submitted,

B. SHIMEK, Iowa City,
ELMER REEVES, Waverly,
C. A. MOSIER, Des Moines,
Committee on Legislation.

Although this bill was published in the proceedings of the first annual meeting of the Park and Forest association, because of its importance it is printed again, and all persons interested in furthering the objects of the bill are earnestly requested to correspond with Prof B. Shimek on the desirability of passing some law favoring the planting of trees.

L. H. PAMMEL,
Secretary.

THE PROGRESS OF FORESTRY AND THE WORK OF THE BUREAU IN IOWA.

Wm. H. Mast of the Bureau of Forestry, Washington, D. C.

Many years before the woodsman had begun work in America's great timber area forestry in Germany had become a well known and diligently studied science. This thrifty people had learned the value of wood and had measured the available supply. Their waste lands had already been covered with forests and were yielding good returns. The wood crop received great care. That it was a thing of concern both for the present and the future could not be overlooked. The Germans had gained much knowledge by experience. They had solved and were still solving many important problems and their comprehension of forestry principles placed them foremost in this science, which position they still rightfully hold. We have much to learn from them and a great deal to find out for ourselves, though they may have solved the problems correctly, we realize at once that their results cannot always be accepted by us, because American conditions are vastly different from European. The size of our country, the distance lumber is transported, the kind and quality of material demanded, all differ from that of Germany. These and many other things make their methods unpractical for our use.

In this country the timber was once considered worse than worthless because it covered good ground and its removal meant much hard work. It was formerly thought that the supply was too great to be exhausted. We have only now begun to realize the necessity of reserving a wood supply for future generations, and awakening from our stupor we are brought face to face with immense problems which must be solved without delay.

For a great many years our forefathers thought *only* of *ridding* themselves of the timber which cumbered their land. But there began to appear such men as William Penn, who was thoughtful for the future, and thus the necessity of forest conservation became recognized. Public opinion was gradually changed and laws for regulating and prohibiting the cutting of timber were made. Among the earliest of these we note that in 1640 certain regulations as to the cutting of oak were established in Exter, New Hampshire. In 1662 Wm. Penn in his ordinance regulating the sale of land in Pennsylvania demanded that for every five acres cleared one should be reserved in timber growth. About fifty years after this the Provincial Assembly of New Hampshire prohibited the cutting of timber suitable for ship masts from ungranted lands, under a penalty of one hundred pounds (£100). At this early date New Hampshire had a surveyor general of forests who received his commission from the English crown.

Between the years 1785 and 1805 two French botanists, Andre Michaux and Andre Francois Michaux, in their study of American trees, did a great deal to enlist public sentiment in the belief of the necessity of rational treatment of our forest resources. During this time a New York society published a report on the "Best Method of Preserving and Increasing the Growth of Timber." In 1799 the federal government recognized the necessity and passed public laws dealing with the timber supply of the country. Congress also appropriated $200,000 for the purchase of standing timber, especially forest lands on which timber suitable for the navy was growing. The selection of these tracts was left to the president, and under this act 19,000 acres was reserved on islands off the coast of Louisiana and the Gulf states. In 1818 congress made another appropriation of $100,000 for the purchase of land on Santa Rosa Sound, Florida, where seeding and planting was first attempted. In 1831 provision was made for the punishment of anyone destroying live oak, cedar or any other tree growing on public lands of the United States. At this time 244,000 acres of land was reserved in Alabama, Florida, Louisiana and Mississippi. It was not the conception of a need of a national forestry policy that caused the enactment of these laws, but the real incentive was the saving of special kinds of timber necessary in the navy.

As late as 1840 lumbering operations such as we have today were never dreamed of. At this time the value of the total annual cut was about $13,000,000. Fifty years later it had increased to over thirty-one times that amount. The rapid consumption of forest supplies, coupled with wastefulness and destruction by fires with no attention paid to reproduction caused considerable agitation on the part of many citizens who gave vent to their opinions through the daily press. Two important publications that helped to shape public opinion were Dr. Warden's report on "Methods used Abroad in Forests," and Marsh's work "Earth as Modified by Human Action."

Only thirty-two years ago the first canvass of the United States forest reserves was made by Prof. Brewer of Yale. His report was published in the census of 1870. In 1873 the American Association for the Advancement of Science presented congress with a memorial and as an outcome three years later, August 15, 1876, an agency of forestry was established in the United States department of agriculture. This in a few years became a division, and in July, 1901, a bureau. Under the provision of the act which established an agency. In 1876 Franklin B. Hough of Lowville, New York, was appointed an agent to make a special report to congress of the forest resources of the United States. This act was the first to give the subject of forestry a place in the government departments and insure for it public recognition.

Prior to 1876 a number of states had begun forestry movements. In 1867 Wisconsin appointed a commissioner to report on the disastrous effect of forest destruction. Two years later Maine appointed a board of men to report on a forest policy for that state. Shortly after this laws encouraging timber planting either under bounty or exemption from taxes were passed in Iowa, Kansas, Nebraska, New York, Missouri, Minnesota, Illinois, North Dakota and Connecticut. The government then joined in the legislation and the timber culture act was passed March 3, 1873. By this act the planting of timber on forty acres of land in a treeless territory conferred title to 160 acres of public domain. Amendments to this were made in 1876 and 1877, but like the state laws it had little effect.

Therefore, on account of the crude provisions and lack of supervision it was repealed March 3, 1891. It had already been much abused and given rise to a great deal of fraud. The claims that were planted with trees never amounted to anything. During the first seven years after this act was passed 38,000,000 acres had been entered as tree claims.

The passing of these acts was an aid to forest culture, but the private interests of settlers in these treeless regions were a greater and more wholesome influencing factor. The establishment of Arbor day, which was originated by J. Sterling Morton in 1872, did much to awaken public interest especially in the treeless states. In the wooded states Arbor day has had little influence on tree planting, as it leads people to think that the forester's business is only to plant trees, while to a large extent it is to care for the existing forests.

The first association to advance forestry interests was started at St. Paul, Minnesota, in 1876 by Leonard B. Hodges. This organization published a tree planting manual. In 1882 a forestry congress met in Ohio, which laid the foundation for the present American Forestry association. This organization has been a great stimulus to forestry movements through its official organ, the "Forester," which has recently united with "Irrigation" and become "Forestry and Irrigation." The "Forestry and Irrigation" is now the foremost advocate for the development of the unclaimed west.

Forestry association have been formed in the following states: Maine, New Hampshire, Massachusetts, Connecticut, New York, Pennsylvania, New Jersey, North Carolina, South Carolina, Ohio, Wisconsin, North Dakota, Colorado, Washington and Iowa. In recent years a large number of states have appointedd forest commissioners. These officers inquire into and report on a proper forest policy. In certain states these commissioners have become permanent parts of the state organizations.

Laws regarding the protection of forest property have been enacted in nearly every state, but the efficient laws of this nature date from 1885. The inefficiency of the laws prior to this time arose chiefly from the lack of responsibility of carrying them out. New York was the first to recognize the need of official responsibility for the execution of the law, therefore a force of fire wardens were appointed throughout the state. Maine, New Hampshire, Pennsylvania, Wisconsin and Minnesota soon followed New York's example. At present Michigan, Maine, Wisconsin and Minnesota have the best fire laws, but the law of Minnesota is the most efficient law in the Union. The state auditor is the forest commissioner, and he appoints a deputy known as the chief fire warden who has charge of the fire warden service of the state. If the fire wardens are unable to suppress a fire, deputies may be appointed. Penalties are provided for wilful, malicious or careless setting of fires.

In 1888 the American Forestry association placed before congress a bill providing for the withdrawal, entry or sale of all public timber land unfit for agricultural use. This failed to pass, but modifications were made from year to year till in the Fifty-first congress the following section was passed calling for the withdrawal of the timber culture act; Sec. 24:

"The president of the United States may from time to time set apart and reserve in any state or territory having public lands bearing forests, any part of the public lands, wholly or in part covered with timber or undergrowth whether of commercial value or not, as public reservations, and the president shall by public proclamation declare the establishment of such reservations and the limits thereof."

Under this law, which was approved March 3, 1891, nearly 60 millions of acres of land have been set aside. When these reserves were being made it became evident that some system of protection and management must be inaugurated. In 1896 Secretary Smith of the Department of Interior realized this necessity and requested the National Academy of Sciences to investigate and report on a National Forest Policy for the forests belonging to the United States. He especially desired that they be managed in such a way as to exert the greatest influence on climate, soil, and the conservation of water. The committee gave a preliminary report in February, 1897, in which they recommended the creation of thirteen additional reserves. The whole number were proclaimed by President Cleveland. In May the committee submitted their complete report as Senate Document No. 10. A wide-spread discontent arose among cattle and sheep men on account of the curtailing of their grazing area. They then succeeded in getting a bill through Congress in June suspending all reservation made that year till March, 1898. This bill provided our first system of forest administration by setting aside $150,000 for the survey of the reserved land. Congress now appropriated $300,000 yearly for the care of the reserves.

The forestry work is now conducted under three sections of the government, namely: Division R, and the Geological Survey of the Department of Interior, and the Bureau of Forestry of the Department of Agriculture. It is probable that within a few years all the forestry work will come under the supervision of the Bureau of Forestry.

. The government has set aside nearly twice as much land for Indian Reservations, Military Reservations, reservoir sites, etc., as it owns in Forest Reserves. In 1898 there were about 159 million acres in reserves. Eighty-three and one-half millions of these were Indian Reservations, nearly three and one-half millions in national parks, and about one million in Military Reservations. The Indian Reservations are more or less in forests. The national parks are mostly wooded and probably will soon be managed under a forest system. The total reserved land in the United States is about 8 per cent of the total land excluding Alaska. In 1898 more than 30 per cent of the entire area was unreserved public land. Most of this is in the west where there is estimated to be 125,000,000 acres of forest in unreserved land.

Almost all of the best timber land of the country has passed from the government to private individuals. The private forests exceed in area both the state and federal government reserves combined. The enormous consumption of forest products has made rapid inroads upon the private forest supply of timber. Recognizing that the treatment of private forests usually tends to destroy rather than increase their productivity, the Division of Forestry in 1898 inaugurated the policy of co-operation with the owners of forest land. This was done in order to instruct owners in the best methods of handling their property. The two points considered in giving advice are first the present interest of the owner, and second the protection and improvement of the forest. It has been the aim in this co-operation to show that improved methods of handling timber land are advantageous both for the owner and the wood crop. It was thought that by assisting a few owners and publishing the results it would be beneficial to the public at large. In 1899 the co-operation between the owner and Bureau of Forestry was extended to that of *establishing* of forests. The reasons for this arose from the many failures of those attempting to start forest plantations. In this the plan of the government is to give expert advice and prepare planting plans. The growing of forest trees for economic purposes cannot be successfully undertaken without some knowledge of the habits of the species and their adaptability to the place where they are to be planted. The owner must know how and what to plant as well as how to give his trees proper care after they begin to grow. Therefore we can plainly see the need of expert advice in the establishment of forests.

Although forests that have a protective value concern the state rather than the individual, our government, unlike European countries, does not exercise any control over forest land, whether protective or not; after it has passed into private hands.

Trees require a long time to come to marketable size, and in this country they are very subject to fire and other injury. So it seems there is everywhere a strong inducement for the owner to cut all of this timber that is of any value. Even taxes are a great detriment to forestry because the assessment is not made on the yearly productive capacity of the land, but on the standing crop of timber. Thus the owner of timber land may pay a heavy tax for a number of years previous to harvesting a crop. This tax may amount to almost as much as the value of the increment of his forest during that period, and he has gained very little in allowing his timber to stand.

In trying to develop good methods for carrying out economic forestry principles, we have constantly met such obstacles, but American ingenuity has gradually and completely overcome many of these obstructions, and our progress in the last quarter of a century has been rapid.

The plan of co-operation with farmers in the planting of forest trees is explained in Circular 22 of the Bureau of Forestry. This plan has not appealed strongly to Iowa farmers because of the exceedingly low per cent of non-agricultural land in the state. However, since October, 1899, 1,859 acres of land has been examined by agents of the Bureau, and eight planting plans covering about 43 acres have been made. The largest area covered by any one of these plans is 19 acres on the farm of George O. Clinton near Mallard, Palo Alto county. The other areas are small and are scattered through Sioux, Johnson, Hancock, Pottawattamie, Howard and Iowa counties. Twenty-seven different species have been used in these plantations. From this fact alone we would at once infer that they have not been established on economic principles entirely. As there is little waste land in Iowa we can never expect to see large forests established on economic principles. The most of our planting must be confined to the small wood lot where much attention will be paid to the ornamental and protective value of the trees. This kind of planting we can do. Let us insist that more of it be done. We can add a great deal to the value of our farms. We can make our homes more attractive by surrounding them with trees. We can beautify our towns and villages by placing small plantations of forest trees within them. May we become more enthusiastic on these lines, but let us ever firmly adhere to our best knowledge of forestry principles when we attempt to grow trees.

The next quarter century will call for greater progress in forestry than we have made during the last quarter. There is little doubt but that our most sanguine hopes for such progress will be reached or even surpassed. We now have three well established schools of forestry, and a number of institutions over the entire country are adding forestry work to their curriculum. These will be largely attended and enthusiastic investigators and workers sent from them. The public will give more thought to the subject of forestry in the future than they have in the past and forward movements will receive steady support. Our most earnest efforts must go toward the diffusion of the best forestry principles, for mistakes in forestry are hard to rectify.

CIVIC IMPROVEMENT FOR SMALL CITIES.

De La Sheldon, Ames

The question of civic improvement for large and small cities is one with which the enlightened and progressive men and women of today are concerning themselves. The idea of beauty is inherent in us all; the savage of the jungle as well as the Indian of the plain have in their crude way endeavored to surround themselves with the beautiful by bedecking their person and steed with those trinkets and colors which appeal to their uneducated sense of the beautiful. But primeval or barbaric man concerned himself not with matters pertaining to public welfare; his spirit was one of selfishness, not doing good to all. And, in fact, we fail to find an enlightened idea of beauty till we come in contact with enlightened man. Here it exists in proportion to the educative influences that have enveloped his life. It is sad to think that in this day and age we have not all received alike and, as a consequence, are in universal possession of the same exalted ideas which have for their foundation the conversion of neglected areas— be it a city, town, or building lot—into a "Heaven here on earth."

Many of our "get-rich-quick" men imagine that life is too short to clean the back yard, the front yard, or improve the vacant building lot. This they leave to their more asthetic inclined brothers and as a result they are often caused to blush at things which are as they ought not to be. If a stranger or a speculator visits our little city we take pride in showing him the fine business blocks, imposing residences, orderly lawns, and well-kept parks, but we carefully avoid "Angel and Paradise" alley. These we know are a poor recommendation—they speak not of enterprise, progress, or an enlightened and desirable class of citizens. We measure a man at first sight by what he appears to be; we select a horse that is without blemish; we marry a woman who possesses a beauty that appeals to this sense; and we prefer to locate in towns that have this much desired qualification.

By considering carefully this thought many of us can easily reason why our city fails to attract a more desirable class of citizens; why it does not progress as we would have it; and, indeed, the fact forces itself upon us that we have sunk to our own level; that the inducements we can hold out to the waiting world have attracted only those who have been as neglectful and as careless of their door yards and streets as we, ourselves, have been. You never heard of an up-to-date, progressive, and enterprising man locating in a run-down, unkempt, and untidy appearing city—he goes elsewhere—while the inhabitants of this same city bewail the fact that they are not making the progressive stride which their little rival some few miles away is taking.

This suggestion is not an exaggerated one. Our small cities are far from being perfect, and I shall now endeavor to point out some few ways in which our sense of beauty is often jarred—conditions which caused us to speculate as to how they might be improved. To commence with, let us briefly consider the home with its door yards, outbuildings, etc. Not many of the properties of our small cities are all that we can desire, but because a few are so we should not rest content. but on the other hand ought to strive to make our municipality a "garden of Eden" from its border to its heart. We are all familiar with that portion of the town where the houses are one-storied, the sidewalks are dangerous as an Alpine mountain pass, the back door yards and alleys a garbage dumping ground, the flower beds and shrubs a minus quantity, and the trees and fences suggesting the recent passage of a mild cyclone. Here, generally, dwell a class of citizens whose esthetic sensibilities have become so dull that it is a Herculean task to sharpen them to the point where desired results can be obtained. But we can hope for a bettering of such conditions, and it only requires the initiation of the influential members of the city to work miracles here. I make this statement advisedly and would not do so had we not good examples of work accomplished along this line. I presume many of you are acquainted with the work of the National Cash Register Co. at Dayton, Ohio. Suffice to say that in this section of the city where this manufacturing establishment is located that such a condition prevailed as described above. It was the eyesore of the city and would probably be so today had it not been for the work of this same manufacturing company. The employes of the company were located here and were interested in the improvement of their dwellings and yards by this company, who set them a worthy example by beautifying the grounds and buildings of their manufacturing plant. As a result South Park in Dayton is one of the most beautiful sections of the city. It is not noted for its magnificent residences, but its door yards as well as the windows and porches of each and every home contribute a wealth of beauty in their floral and shrubbery offerings.

I will not go further into the details of what has been done there, but would say that great good can be accomplished by the influential and leading men of every small city, if they would first set the example and then call together certain portions of the city at a time and unfold to them plans whereby their homes and grounds might be beautified, furnishing them if necessary with the seed for this purpose, and also instructing them in the planting of it and the cultivation of the resultant flowers or shrubs. Lantern slides can be used advantageously in showing them how door yards, walks, and porches have been treated in a tasteful yet inexpensive way by those who know how. They further prove suggestive and will bear fruit if the efforts of these leading spirits are persistent instead of sporadic.

Now a word about the vacant building lot. It is familiar to us all for, "like a stranger from a strange land," it stamps itself indelibly upon our minds. With our mind's eye we can now see many of them, covered with weeds three to four feet in height; a "For Sale" sign struggling as hard to make itself seen as a four and one-half foot man in a crowd of six-footers; broken bottles, empty oyster cans, and many other such suggestions of rubbish peering out at the base of the stalks—the whole lot presenting such a sight that the buyer hesitates before purchasing it. These conditions lower the market value of these lots as well as the city's standard of beauty. Would they not look better neatly sodded or even being utilized as truck patches by the poor? Most assuredly, and city councils ought to take action remedying such esthetic defects. Further, the citizens should bring a not-to-be denied pressure upon their councils for the removal of bill boards. They are unsightly, never possessing a semblance to beauty, but on the other hand are often plastered with posters which are vicious in their nature and which tend to lower the moral standard of the young especially.

Our business streets may be paved with brick, asphalt, or macadam, and bordered with the best of cement sidewalks, yet these same sidewalks and streets are often worse than the farmer's barnyard for our wives and daughters to go wading through. It would be well if every city followed the example of St. Paul and Minneapolis by passing iron-clad ordinances forbidding the expectorating of tobacco, etc., upon the sidewalks, street cars and public building floors. Such movements result in not only improved appearances, but sanitary benefits of no small proportion, as well.

Further, we are aware that in almost every city the streets of its humbler parts are often littered with rubbish while its trees would never prove to be an inspiration to one passing either the most exalted or the most crude ideas of beauty. At a comparatively small expense every city may be made a park. Line its streets with broad elms or some hardy tree. If the streets are but little used for business traffic, narrow the paved portion and alongside each side in addition to a row of trees, there may be plots of green or, if the property owners prefer them, strips may be used as flower beds or in such way that beauty will be created. It is well also to remove all fences when park-like effects are desired, and if the privacy of the home is thus invaded it can be retained by the planting of shrubs or vines so that the porches and verandas remain screened.

In conclusion I would urge that we all take measures to improve our cities and towns. It pays when we stop to consider the matter. No man speaks lightly of an orderly, well kept, beautiful city. He would like to bring his family and live there; the moral atmosphere seems clearer and purer; health seems to surround one on every hand; high ideals are created in the minds of the young, their thoughts are elevated, their natures rendered more refined. In fact, most children are born with a love for flowers and trees, and we owe it to them to make their environment as nearly ideal as possible. We should guard against blasting their lives or dwarfing their natures for they are to carry on the work that we have begun; and if conscientious work is done, the city with its dreaded influences can be made to produce the same quality of manhood and womanhood as now comes forth from those regions where nature beams more kindly upon her children.

CITY PARKS.

J. T. D. Fulmer, Des Moines, Iowa.

We are once fairly started on our progressive march in this section of the country ,and as we advance we find more and more of our city property being built up with tenement rows and flats, thus crowding the people into closer and more confined quarters. Hence the growing demand is thus formed for a place to get relief in the natural, sweet, fresh air, and so we look for a place provided for that purpose, called a park, and the people are willing to tax themselves quite heavily to have such a place.

It is of these places, called city parks, that I speak. It is immaterial as to how large a park shall be—whether of few acres or many—the intent is the same, i. e., to afford a place for rest and enjoyment in nature's surroundings, amid beautiful foliage and songs of birds.

We will first take up the tree planting, which should be as natural as possible and done promiscuously—not in straight rows (unless along some park-like boulevard.) When we say promiscuously, we mean mixing the kinds, i. e., do not plant many of a kind together. Mass or group them, being careful to select varieties that look well near each other. And do not plant a tree unless you are convinced that that very tree will be an improvement to that particular place. I once asked the question, "What is the object in planting those trees" The answer 1 received was, "Oh, just to cover the ground." So, I would say, never plant trees merely to cover the ground, but have some object in view, and that of shade or ornament, or to help to carry out a view that may need some conifers, elm, pin oak or balm of Gilead. And, let me say while I advise the use of native trees for parks I would not be restricted wholly to them, for there are many trees that are not strictly native that do well and are almost indispensable in making parks look what I would call complete.

We think if the trees are not trimmed at all it adds to their beauty, especially conifers and elms. Even pin oaks are finer when their branches droop almost to the ground. So it follows that the pruning knife should be kept in experienced hands.

Now as to the shrubbery. It should be selected with an end of having some of it bloom or fruit all summer. It should be so planted as to have a natural, easy appearance and not look stiff and formal as though made by hand at the carpenter's bench.

Then, there is the green or lawn. This should be so arranged and kept as to have a dark green appearance! and we would recommend the use of commercial fertilizers instead of manure, on account of weed seeds. We must not forget the playground for athletic sports, or the outdoor kindergarten, or the public bathing and boating places. In fact, the aim should be to afford the maximum of outdoor recreation and enjoyment for those who are so much in need of pure air and sunshine amid flowers and trees.

The aquatics are also an eminently interesting and instructive feature and should not be omitted. Then as to the flowers, more commonly called greenhouse plants, these should be, as nearly as possible, in one garden or part of the park, and should consist of both sub-tropical and carpet bedding. I am aware that some of our best known landscape gardeners oppose carpet bedding, and with all due respect to these gardeners I will say that carpet bedding will be with us after they are gone. When this kind of planting is not overdone it is fine, is interesting and instructive, and it tends to refresh one's interest in nature and art combined.

The drives and walks should be as easy as possible, free from short curves and steep hills. At prominent places alongside of them should be pieces of statuary, so placed as to give a pleasing effect. There should also be drinking fountains or springs in abundance to accomodate all visitors.

We have now come to the management of parks which is by no means of the least importance. First, there should be a park board, which should consist of three or five men, and should be as far eliminated from politics as possible. They should have direct charge of all the finances and all improvements of the park. Next, under them, and selected by them, should be a superintendent of the entire park system of the city, or a superintendent for each park, as the board may see fit. In either case this suprintendent should be a park man of knowledge and ability, for what five men would think of forming a partnership and starting a flour mill without securing the services of a miller, or of starting a drug store without a pharmacist. So in a park it is just as essential to have a park man for superintendent; and do not put in a man who cannot tell a conifer from a quercus, or a deciduous from an herbaceous plant. Then next in order comes the gardener, who should be a gardener in fact, as well as a man to plant the garden. He should be a propagator as well as a grower, and, indeed, he must be an all-round florist. After him is the foreman, and under the latter the men do the general park work, such as keeping the drives and walks edged and rolled, the lawns mowed. All trimming of shrubbery and trees should be in the hands of the gardener.

All of the men about this ideal park should be gentlemen at all times and under all circumstances, for they are in a position where there will be ladies and children within sight and hearing distance at all times.

THE ELM AND OTHER SHADE TREES.

Albert Duebendorfer, Ames, Iowa.

The shade tree is a necessity on the prairies of this state and must be given a great deal of attention if we ever expect it to compare with eastern countries where avenues and streets in the large cities, as well as in the country towns, are lined most beautifully with a variety of good trees. In those eastern places many a tree has been tried and discarded, often because a reasonable amount of judgment in its care was lacking, but generally because it was not adapted to the climate. Many of the horticulturists who have laid the foundation of their profession in some foreign country have been disappointed in their favorites because the dry and hot summer air of their new home proved to be fatal to many trees which they expected to grow to perfection.

In a recent visit to Chicago and many of its subsurbs I noticed with great satisfaction that the elm is foremost everywhere, and its nearest rival is the soft maple. Along the lake front on the north side where the energetic Chicagoan has crowded the water line out farther into Lake Michigan so that he may build up a grand boulevard and give his fellow man a place where he may enjoy the brisk and refreshing lake air, he has deemed it wise to use the elm for a shade producer. The wind on that lake front sometimes has a fierce sweep and a silver maple, box elder, American linden or any other fast growing tree would not amount to much, while the elm continues its majestic growth.

Not only on Chicago's water front, but everywhere where trees have been planted—at least as far as my travels have taken me in the states—the elm is successfully grown where other shade treees are crippled by heavy wind playing in the tops of the trees with force enough to break down eight and ten inch limbs on the silver maple, box elder, poplar or linden, here you may observe that the grand ol delm, though its limbs might have pointed all in one direction and its leaves were whipped like the laundress would whip the fringes on the bureau-spread in order to straighten them, will come back to its own graceful shape and beauty. It was my misfortune to witness one of those seldom occurring storms that took buildings off their foundations and played havoc on all trees in its path but the elm. Apple, pear, cherry, hard and soft maple, beeches, birches, pine and spruce were uprooted where this storm crossed the beautiful Batenkill valley in the town of Manchester, Vermont, and left the elm to prove that its root system is not easily torn from the earth and its tops are too wiry and strong to be injured very much.

This New England village is located on about the highest point of the public road between New York and Montreal, and if approached from either side, the incline is just enough to permit the traveller to take a good look at the magnificent elms and sugar maples which line the especially wide street through the center of the town. In this line of trees we can find grand elms that spread 110 feet and their trunks will show a circumference of as high as 14 feet, 2 inches. These elms have good high trunks, and still the tips of their limbs droop most gracefully down into the road, almost low enough so that a carriage top might touch them. I know of no other street that will please the eye of the horticulturist as much as this one, and it is all to be credited to the American elm with its great, arching branches. One of those trees has, as already said, a circumference of 14 feet 2 inches, with a spread of 102 feet, and a second one is 14 feet in circumference, spreading over 110 feet of ground, and still another covers 95 feet of earth and it requires 10 feet 6 inches of the tape line to reach around it. All those gigantic elms are over 100 years old, and no care as to pruning and cultivation of soil has been bestowed upon them, and still I am fully convinced that the proper application of the knife with a loose and deep earth mulch will hasten the growth sufficiently to repay the busiest man for the time he may put into it.

I am not much in favor of heavy top trimming at the time of planting, but judging from the amount of root that has been cut off, I like to cut the leading branches back just enough so that the remaining roots will be strong enough to support a good growth of leaves. If the first year's growth is weak but every twig produced good leaves, I am satisfied, because I know that with a heavy pruning the second year I can produce a good and often an extra heavy growth because the young rootlets established in the previous season are strong enough to push the sap up to the top and open the tight bark, pushing the young bud to a vigorous branch. The pruning hereafter usually consists of thinning out only, unless a strong wind from one direction forces the growth all to one side, when the leader must be repeatedly cut back, sending an equally strong growth against the wind, which is easily done with the elm. Here again we find the elm the most obliging of all shade trees for the union of those limbs that have been forced out by pruning is so perfect that it is not easily disturbed, and the cut or wound is soon covered with young wood. There is no need of having any sprawling or one sided elm trees since it responds so well to the knife without sacrifice to its growth. I wish to emphasize that after each pruning of the young elm its roots are forced down into the earth where there is more moisture, acting the same as a night's rest on the daily toiler.

On the elm as well as the ash, and in fact on all deciduous trees, with perhaps the exception of the willow and tamarix, the renewal plan of pruning is far preferable, and all stump cutting should be avoided. Under the renewal plan I understand the method by which the operator in his desire to shorten an out of proportion, strong growing limb by carefully selecting a side branch—usually one on top of the main limb— for its future leader, exercises particular caution to make his selection so that the flow of sap to this section of the tree is not checked too much and the desired end diverted further than it was at the beginning and the tree more deformed than ever. The new leader must have sufficient vigor to cope with at least about half the sap that its predecessor had been drawing. In order to accomplish the largest possible amount of labor in the shortest time, the man with proper judgment in this work may find it necessary to shorten such side limbs on this main limb as seem to offer a danger of taking up the leadership in the wrong direction.

With the elm as the frontier pioneeer I believe we level the road of success for many other pets that we wish to grow in order to have variety and perhaps good autumn coloring. Touching on this I cannot help but say a few words about it as seen in New England.

The same town of Manchester in Vermont that can boast of th magnificent elms above spoken of has a point of attraction for autumn leaf coloring that is as perfect a picture as I have ever observed. I believe about 1800 feet up on the side of Mount Equinox, which reaches its summit of 4000 feet just west of Manchester, there is the so-called Table Rock, protruding proudly from the natural timber growth, affording a grand view up and down the valley. In the fall of the year when the soft and hard maples, the basswood, poplar, birch, oak, elm and many other trees are clad in their highest autumn glory, from the Batenkill river up to the higher ridges of the Green mountains backed with dark green spruce it makes a picture which never fails to inspire the longing for the possession of just such trees, and I wish I could impart such a longing to every listener here and so be instrumental in beautifying this state.

In closing my remarks I wish to say that I consider the nursery grown trees the best for transplanting because their roots are more fitted for that purpose, and I apply this to the elm as well as all other trees. However, natural trees may be readily fitted for transplanting so as to even make their success a certainty, but it is only economical on large trees, say from three inches to one foot in diameter. For example, if in our judgment we find it necessary to take a ball of dirt about five feet in diameter and 18 to 24 inches in depth, along with a certain tree in transplanting, we may any time between leaf dropping in the fall and starting in the spring dig a trench around this tree about six inches smaller all around and fill in again after all the detached roots have been cut smoothly with a knife from the bottom up and the tops previously shortened as above. These smoothly cut roots soon send out a mass of rootlets, clinging tightly to the soil that we had packed into the trench again, and in the coming transplanting season between fall and spring we again dig around this tree, leaving the ball as in our first judgment, and plant it only a few inches deeper in its new place. Such trees may safely be moved during fall and winter when time is not always as valuable as in the spring, while small trees should only be planted in the spring, which is and will remain the best time for all planting.

39

ONE OF IOWA'S BEAUTY SPOTS.

Euqene Secor, Forest City.

When the Almighty smoothed these prairies and laid the foundations for Iowa's present fertility and prosperity, it was wisely planned that a dead level of uniformity should not weary the eyes of generations destined to inhabit them.

He ground the primal rocks in the mills of the glaciers for the use of man. He shoved a generous product ahead of his giant ice plows and disturbed the material over wide areas, but beauty as well as utility was the result of his handiwork.

He made enough extra material to form the slight eminences which were left here and htere over the prairies to relieve the montony by glimpses of unexpected scenery.

Rivers have cut their sinuous courses through the pulverized drift of former geologic times and bluffs of rare beauty and interest are exposed to view.

Thus it is that go where you will in Iowa, the scenery is unlike any other place you can recall. All of it useful, all of it available for agriculture, for grazing or for tree-growing, yet the ever changing landscape is always interesting, always restful.

But there are a few spots in Iowa which appeal to the artist. They stand out in bold relief—prominent, beautiful, grand. One of these I will try to describe. It differs from any thing else in the state, or in this country, so far as I know. It is Pilot Knob, located about five miles east of Forest City. It is one of the highest points of land in Iowa, its elevation being fifteen hundred feet. It is supposed to be morainic in character, being near the eastern edge of the last glacial drift in Iowa, called the Wisconsin. Appearances indicate that one lobe of the vast ice-sheet melted near the southeastern corner of Winnebago county and left its debris of clay hills just as they were when moving ahead of the southbound ice-scrapers of prehistoric times. Numerous clay hills of varying heights, generally covered with timber and interspersed with small ponds, are clustered about the "Knob" as if waiting on that queen of beauty and supremacy. It might be styled the park region of north central Iowa.

In travelling toward that prominent elevation, one finds many surprises. Now up a smart declivity lined on either side by over-hanging branches of scarlet and bur-oak, wild cherry, linden and popular, with an undergrowth of sumac, prunus pennsylvanica, hazel, wild blackberry, western dogwood, spiraea, New Jersey tea and all the minor beautles that nestle among the sheltering growth of the northern woodland, and as one looks back toward the "Hill City" he left a few moments before, so plainly visible is the town and so entrancing the sight one feels sure he will see nothing further or more interesting.

But suddenly he finds himself at the top of a hill with new vistas opening before him, other hills still higher with a lovely valley between.

In the distance, bare and ancient, is seen the point which first beckons to the rising sun, and last bids him goodnight—the point of our destination. Pursuing our journey, we may, if it is an early autumn, discover a clump of scarlet-fruited sumac on the margin of an open meadow, with perhaps a foreground of Lilium superbum, that would capture the heart of a landscape gardener or enrapture the soul of an artist. And thus we delightfully wend our way toward higher attitudes. Within a half miles from the summit and perhaps a hundred feet lower is a small lake nestling among the surrounding hills, covering about two acres, with abrupt wooded margins on two sides, where three varieties of pond lilies greet the rising sun with smiling petals. This is called Dead Man's Lake, but no ghostly form rises from the surface to explain the ghastly name.

One more upward pull and the summit of the knob is reached. If one could only truthfully repeat the lines attributed to Alex. Selkirk on the Island of Juan Ferandez.

> "I am monarch of all I survey
> And my right there is none to dispute,"

then, indeed, would one be a "land-lord." Not less than fifty thousand acres of beautiful, undulating, fertile land may be seen with the naked eye from this point, and with a good glass, four times as many.

To the north into Minnesota, east into Cerro Gordo and Worth counties, south into Hancock county as far as the M. & St. P. R. R., and to the west with undulating prairies of Winnebago with Forest City sitting like a queen on the hills that have given her the appropriate name of "Hill City."

Lime creek, whose source is in Mennesota almost north of the point where we stand, winds its sinuous way through a rich and lovely valley, bearing west until it gets almost to Forest City where it broke through the morainic hills, and then turns toward the east till it passes Pilot Knob (about two miles south,) then bears north again into Worth county, have been thrown from its general course to the southeast by these huge piles of clay left by the plows of the infinite.

What a grand sight is before us! There was a time, perhaps, when scouts of the warlike tribes that preceded us may have climbed this prominence to sight a tawny-skinned enemy or to light their beacon fires, but today they are a memory only to the early pioneer, and to the younger generation as little known and understood as the natives of the Philippines.

Lime creek, timber-lined and valley-nestled, describes more than a half circle at our feet. Natural grove and open space succeed each other in delightful panorama. The protection from prairie fires which the stream affords has encouraged the growth of trees, and hundreds of acres that might otherwise have been as treeless as a prairie are adorned with the covering which nature chooses when she wants to make a country fit for a man to live in.

The owner of this park region has been advised to fence it in and stock it with goats. But there are some things a man ought not to do. If he has a spark of sentiment or a grain of love he could never bring himself to the thought of pasturing his mother's grave. And the gainful idea of denuding every tree-covered spot which God never intended for the base use of ordinary money-getting is a cropping out of the barbaric instinct to kill every living thing in sight and trample under foot the lofty sentiments of the soul. Hundreds of acres of Iowa's beautiful lands have been skinned by the tree-butchers to get a little indifferent pasture or a field marred by gullies after every heavy rain.

Perhaps there is little or no money in sentiment. It has little commercial value in the present rushing western life. The prevalent thought of today is to let the next generation take care of itself; and yet who shall say that some of the wasted timber resources of this country had not better been husbanded in a money point of view!

But there is a higher aim that ought to inspire the leaders of horticultural thought. This world is not always going to be dominated by the utilitarian idea. Culture is going to have its inning. The time is coming when a park will be more attractive than a goat-pasture.

I hope you will pray that the present owner of one of Iowa's beauty spots may not become so avaricious of present gain that he is ready to sacrifice the artistic for a little vulgar coin.

HISTORIC TREES OF IOWA.

Ida Grillett, Ames, Iowa.

In almost every country the world over, we find some majestic old tree preserved by the people as a historical relic. Perhaps the oldest of such trees that we have record of is the "cypress of Somma" in Lombardy. It is supposed by the inhabitants of the place to have been planted in the year of the birth of Christ, but an ancient chronicle of Milan proves that it was a tree in Caesar's time, 42 B. C. It was one hundred twenty-three feet high and twenty-three feet in circumference, measured one foot from the ground, the last time any account of its measurement was given.

The United States has many trees such as the "Washington Elm" and the "Charter Oak" woven into her history, and even Iowa has several of more or less importance that are being protected from ruthless destruction.

Being a prairie state, Iowa has many trees that were designated by the settlers of that section as "Lone Tree" which at present are surrounded by dozens of their progeny that have sprung up since the early history of the state. Among such trees is "Lone Tree" in Johnson county, an old elm from which the town in which it stands derived its name.

"Council Oak"

Near mouth of Big Sioux river. Made famous by an Indian council held under its branches at the time Lewis and Clark passed the mouth of the river on August 22, 1804.

This tree is estimated to be about one hundred twenty-five years old, and although its top has been broken off by storms, it is about sixty-five feet high at present with a crown sixty feet in diameter. It is now surrounded by a younger growth of trees, but at one time could be seen from a distance of fifteen miles. Another "Lone Tree" more or less widely known is found in Clay county. A photograph of it, taken by Professor T. H. Macbride, is given in the report of the "Geological Survey" of that county.

In Princeton, Scott county, there was a "Lone Tree," a box-elder, which was called by some the "Farriage Tree," presumably the mark to a ferry before the day of bridges. On Muscatine island there is a cotton wood known also as "Lone Tree."

There is a large cottonwood tree in Clinton that marked the old boundary line between Clinton and Lyons when these towns were separated. This tree is a survivor of a number of which were planted some fifty years ago to mark the boundary of a farm, and as this line corresponds to a section line, it was later made the city limit. The tree is now cared for as a historical relic.

But probably the best known and grandest old tree of the state is the "Council Oak" on the bank of the Big Sioux river about a mile from its mouth, made famous because of its connection with Iowa's Indian history. Although the tree has several stumps of dead branches ten or fifteen feet from the base, its top is still quite evenly developed; there being no other large trees around it to disturb its growth. It measures thirteen feet in circuference two feet from the ground, is about eighty feet high, and has a crown seventy feet in diameter at the broadest place. The bark is from three to five inches thick and the tree is supposed to be over a thousand years old. There are many traditions connected with it but probably the most authenticated are found in the following extract from the history of the northwest.

COUNCIL OR MEDICINE TREE.

"On the 22d day of August, 1804, Captains Lewis and Clark, with forty-two enlisted men, passed the mouth of the Big Sioux river about one miles to the south of this renowned tree. On the day before, viz.: August 21, 1804, while the command of Lewis and Clark laid over at a point about five miles below to pay their respects to Sergeant Charles Floyd, who was buried on the summit of a high bluff with the honors due a brave soldier, it is believed that the Sioux Indians, who inhabited this section and were known as the Yankton Sioux, were at the same time holding council by their chiefs and medicine men under this tree, and were excited beyond measure on account of the proceedings taking place five miles below them on the Missouri river, by what to them was an invasion of their country by the long hated yet never until now seen white man. If this noble tree could now communicate to us what took place there on that day and on the days following until the summer of 1848, when Wm. Thompson settled at the mouth of the Floyd river, history would then indeed be complete. In 1846 it is believed that Theophile

Brughier made choice of the land where this tree now stands, as he was a prominent man and acquired great influence with the Yankton Sioux, and became the firm and staunch friend of Hu-yan-e-ka (War Eagle), who was always the friend of the white men . Hu-yan-e-ka (War Eagle) being about 18 or 20 years old at the time Lewis and Clark passed up the river, August 21, 1804, was no doubt among the many who counseled on that day under this tree of what should be done with the invaders. The title of the Indians to this land became extinct in 1847, and in 1849 Mr. Brughier settled on it and became the owner. The evidence of burnt stone and bone under the grass and roots tell us much of what has taken place under the shadow of this great tree; and like the bird that comes home to die, so with Hu-yan-e-ka (War Eagle), when aged and feeble, he came and died near this historical tree, in 1851, and was buried, like Floyd, on the summit of a high bluff overlooking this now beautiful park, where the eye with one vision can scan a portion of the commonwealth of Iowa, Nebraska and Dakota, with Highland and the Corn City as a background. Perhaps the last council of a chief was held under this tree in 1854, when Smutty Bear, the successor of Hu-yan-e-ka, was surprised to find John K. Cook and Gen. Lyon, who fell at Wilson's creek, with others making a survey at the mouth of the now Perry creek, where Sioux City now is. Smutty Bear ordered Dr. Cook to cease his labor, but not succeeding, he is supposed to have repaired to the old council tree, and there, with chiefs and medicine men, decided to strike their teepees and departed to the northwest; ;and it is believed that this was the last council ever held under the ancient tree on the once famous camping ground of the Sioux, now the Riverside park.

"Waka-cha-sha, Pet of the Sioux."

BEAUTIFYING AND UTILIZING OF RAILROAD GROUNDS.

E. E. Little, Ames, Iowa.

· In this paper I not only wish to discuss the ornamentation of railroad station grounds but also the improvement and utilization of ground along the right of way.

Gardening and planting along railroads has been practiced for nearly a half century in some of the European countries. Foremost in this work is England, Denmark, Sweden, Germany and France. The large railroad systems of these countries have planted for both ornamentation and economic purposes.

In Sweden there are three distinctive purposes in mind when planting: First, the planting for decoration on the station grounds. Second, mixed planting along the right-of-way for economical purposes. Third, the planting on the borders of the right-of-way with hedges for protection from snow, and pleasing effect of plants over fences.

On the station grounds are planted trees, shrubs, perennial and annual flowering as well as bedding plants. Along the right-of-way, fruit trees, small fruits, a few ornamental shrubs, some of the flowering plants and small kitchen garden vegetables are used. On the line of the right-of-way, various hedges are planted—those adapted to the section in which they are planted.

As far back as 1870 in this country this movement was manifested. Several years later articles were now and then printed on this subject. In 1880 the movement gained rapidly in favor, and in 1889 a prominent writer said: "Railroad gardening has come to be considered a necessary part of construction and maintenance among prosperous and progressive companies seeking to develop local passenger business." Among

Scene at a railroad crossing along the Long Island Railway system. (Loaned by Floral Publishing Company.)

the first companies to improve their station grounds by decorative planting were the Central of New Jersey (1869), the Baltimore & Ohio; Boston and Albany (1880), New York Central (1880), and the Erie (1881). Other roads were greatly impressed by this work until now it has spread to every large system. All of the trunk lines of Iowa are doing considerable planting at present, and the future promises more effort in this direction.

Many systems in the United States and Canada have not only practiced ornamental planting about their grounds, but are engaged in large plantings along the right of way for economic purposes. Foremost among the lines planting in the latter direction is the Canadian Pacific of Canada and the Northern Pacific Railway of the United States. Only recently I noticed an article in one of the dailies that the Michigan Central Railway has decided to plant in the spring Catalpa trees along its right of way, and I am informed by their engineer that this work is well under way. When fully grown the trees are to be used to supply the company with material for ties. In Europe the planting of fruit trees and small fruits has been largely practiced with good success.

The planting for protection so far as I know has been but little practiced in this country. One system in the east has taken up this phase of the work. The object is two-fold—first, the hedges are planted to protect from snow and winds, and they also aid in land slides. Secondly, the covering of banks with vegetation prevents washing and erosion.

This planting is generally given over to the engineering department of the large systems. Wherever moderate sized ground are to be planted plans and specifications are drawn up the same as in the planting of large, private grounds. In this way the details of arrangement and the planting can be more satisfactorily carried out. **The principles**

underlying the planting of the ground about the station are simple. The important arrangements are for good approaches, and the ground not needed for approaches should be treated for planting both economically and attractively. It should be in charge of a competent man and looked after by the head gardener or horticulturist of the system.

Within recent years annual plants have been largely used for ornamentation at the station grounds by all the large companies, but at present there is a tendency to do away with all the annuals which perish with the season, and plant ornamental trees, shrubs and vines. Some of the officials of the road contend that many of the passengers only catch glimpses of the park, on fast trains running at a high rate of speed, and the shrubs have more of a pleasing effect on account of their higher and larger growth,

and then the cost of caring for the annuals is much more than **the** shrubs.

Among the various hardy shrubs used for planting on station grounds are hydrangea, Philadelphus grandiflora, weigelia, tamarix, cut leaved sumach, lonicera, barberries and spiraeas and a few more of the very attractive, hardy shrubs.

While in Minneapolis this summer I was very much pleased to see planted around the flagman's shanties at the street railway crossing a small area of annual plants. This was a very attractive sight while passing through the dusty, dirty railroad yards. It was a relief to see, now and then, a bright, attractive spot to break the dull monotony of the surroundings, such as cinders and gravel.

Railroad planting, approach to railway station at Ames.

Railroad managers are beginning to recognize the fact that no more effective advertising can be done than by replacing unsightly objects, such as are common along the system, by the planting of shrubbery and various ornamental plants.

The railroad gardens should be planted by competent gardeners who have a knowledge of trees and shrubs, and understand grouping, planting, etc., of the same. This may require a great outlay of money at the outset, but after once well established the cost of mantaining it will be small and it will remain beautiful and attractive for many years.

DENDRO CHEMISTRY.

J. B. Weems, Ames, Iowa.

The destruction of our forests for the purpose of private gain, with no consideration given to the future, is one of the ways by which the selfishness of man. presents to the coming generations problems of great importance an such as must be solved for the world's welfare. To care for and improve the condition of our forests and the development of a general interest in the planting of trees will result not only in wealth to our country, but the interests in the beautiful will be of inestimable benefit to the world.

The application of chemistry to this field of human industry is realized at once as a vast study. Dendro chemistry in its field touches almost every branch of chemistry. Beginning with the seed of trees, there are in this connection two interesting features of Dendro chemistry; the chemistry of germination and the value of the nuts for food. The nut has been regarded as a relish and little attention has been given to it as a food product. We have imported nuts from other countries and given little or no attention to the home grown product. Nuts have been used for desserts and in other ways that overtax the digestive system, thus resulting in a general opinion that they are indigestible. With care in thorough mastication and if eaten at the proper time, there is no doubt that our common nuts may prove to be a valuable addition to our palatable foods. In this connection it may be of interest to compare the composition* of some of our common nuts with other foods.

AMOUNTS OF NUTRIENTS FURNISHED FOR TEN CENTS IN NUTS AT ORDINARY PRICES.

NUTS AS PURCHASED.	Price per pound.	Weight of kernel.	TEN CENTS WILL PAY FOR				Total fuel calculated.
			NUTRIENTS.				
			Total.	Protein.	Fats.	Carbo-hydrates.	
	Cents.	Lbs.	Lbs.	Lbs.	Lbs.	Lbs.	Calories.
Almonds	15	.23	.21	.05	.12	.04	675
Brazil nuts.	12	.42	.38	.07	.28	.03	1370
Filberts	15	.32	.30	·05	.21	.04	1055
Pecans	15	.33	.32	.04	.23	.05	1140
Hickorynuts†	9	.42	.40	.07	.28	.05	1405
Walnuts	15	.28	.27	.05	.18	.04	925
Chestnuts‡	8.4	1.00	.62	.07	.08	.47	1840
Peanuts§	7.3	1.01	.89	.28	.42	.19	2645
Peanut‖	14.6	.50	.44	.14	.21	.09	1320
Wheat flour	3.00		2.88	.43	.04	2.41	5450

*Maine Experiment Station Bulletin 54, p. 91.

† At 10 cts. per quart, 488 grams.

‡ At 5 cts. per quart, 270 grams.

§ At 5 cts. per quart, 22 pounds per bushel.

‖ At 10 cts. per quart.

These results will be of value when we compare them with other pro-ducts such as the breakfast foods, as for example:

AMOUNTS OF NUTRIENTS FURNISHED FOR TEN CENTS IN CEREAL FOODS AT ORDINARY PRICES.

KIND OF CEREAL.	Price per pound.	TEN CENTS WILL PAY FOR					Heat of combustion.
		NUTRIENTS.					
		Total food material.	Total.	Protein.	Fat.	Carbo-dydrates.	
	Cents.	Lbs.	Lbs.	Lbs.	Lbs.	Lbs.	Calories.
Quaker rolled white oats.	6.3	1.59	1.41	.25	.13	1.03	3117
Cream of wheat....................	8.8	1.14	1.01	.15	.01	.85	2023
Granose biscuit....	18.6	.54	.48	.07	.01	.40	973
Granose flakes	22.4	.45	39	.05		.34	794
Shredded whole wheat	15.0	67	60	.08	.01	51	1213
Grape nuts	14.6	69	64	.09	.01	54	1300
Ralston health barley food	6.9	1.45	1 27	.06	.01	1.10	2529
Force......................	16.5	.66	.60	.09	.01	.51	1201

2. Maine Exp. Sta. Bul. 83, p. 138.

The results show that some of the common nuts furnish nutritive material as reasonable in price as many of the well advertised breakfast foods. The chestnut can no doubt be used in preparing special dishes and its use extended in many ways. Attention should be not only given to the production of the various varieties of nuts but we should learn how to use them to the best advantage.

The seed of the forest tree when pressed into the soil sends down its rootlet to collect the plant food and moisture. At the same time it sends up its tiny leaves to meet the sunlight. The plant food brought up by the root is combined with the material taken from the air and the tree grows. As the years go by the tree becomes larger, sends its roots down deeper in the soil, and spreads its thousands of leaves to collect the material from the atmosphere. The different varieties of trees each have their characteristics which they have elaborated from the plant food in a common soil and from a common atmosphere. The leaf of a tree is a small part of nature's laboratory, taking from the invisible gases what is needed for its purpose. The atmosphere is a mixture of gases consisting of

78.40 parts nitrogen.
20.94 " oxygen.
.63 " argon.
.03 " carbon dioxide.
————
100.00

The leaves of the tree take from the atmosphere the carbon dioxide and with the water brought by the roots change it to products which ultimately become part of the tree. In producing this change the carbon dioxide is returned to the atmosphere. The mutual dependence of plant and animals is seen in this relation, the animal using products of vegetable world in order to exist, and in existing uses such products to produce heat and to increase the body growth. In using these substances carbon dioxide is given off from the lungs of the animal and becomes a part of the atmosphere. When wood or coal is burned the same product is produced. Everywhere where vegetable matter is being used for food, fuel or similar purposes there is being added constantly large quantities of carbon dioxide to that already present in the air. The trees and plants make use of this product to produce material of value to man. When wood is used for fuel an ash remains consisting largely of the plant food that the roots have brought for the use of the tree. The chemical composition of some of the different woods and their ashes may be shown by the following results:

ASH CONSTITUENTS OF DIFFERENT WOODS.

KIND.	AIR-DRY WOOD CONTAINS				THE ASH CONTAINS			
	Water.	Ash.	Phosphoric acid.	Potash.	Phosphoric acid.	Potash.	Lime.	Magnesia.
Ash, wood	10.00	0.32	0.012	0.149	3.53	46.04	23.57	0.60
Chestnut, bark	10.00	3.51	0.114	0.278	3.25	7.93	47.02	0.01
Chestnut, wood	10.00	0.16	0.911	0.029	6.76	18.10	49.18	2.11
Dogwood, bark	10.00	9.87	0.140	0.341	1.42	3.46	49.20	1.40
Dogwood, wood	10.00	0.68	0.057	0.190	8.51	23.04	28.93	6.80
Hickory, bark	10.00	3.97	0.061	0.141	1.54	3.56	46.82	2 59
Hickory, wood	10.00	0.48	0.058	0.138	11.97	28·60	37.94	10.04
Magnolia, bark	10.00	2.98	0.095	0.192	5.31	11.87	23.64	4.89
Magnolia, wood	10.00	0.36	0.032	0.071	8.75	19.54	38.94	8.05
Maple, bark	10.00	9.49	0.421	1.197	4.44	12.61	37.91	3.25
Oak leaves, mixed	......	4.70	......	......	3.35	3.74	29.03	..
Oak post, bark	10.00	12.10	0.116	0.249	0.96	2.06	52.04	0.65
Oak post, wood	10.00	0.77	0.070	0.169	9.00	21.92	46.39	6.88
Oak, red, bark	10.00	8.29	0.103	0.179	1.63	2.84	50.51	1.81
Oak, red, wood	10.00	0.57	0.060	0.140	10.55	24 66	48.26	5.38
Oak, white, bark	10.00	5.95	0.074	0.125	1.24	2.10	52.73	1.62
Oak, white, wood	10.00	0.26	0.025	0.106	9.48	42 16	29.85	3.43
Pine burr	......	1.09	.	......	3.31	6.92	10.30	..
Pine, Georgia, bark	10.00	0.37	0 013	0.024	1.99	3.56	34.14	2.45
Pine, Georgia, wood	10.00	0.33	0.012	0 050	3.82	15.35	53 24	6.25
Pine, old field, bark	10.00	1.94	0.095	0.077	4 88	3.96	27.95	3.10
Pine, old field, wood	10.00	0.18	0.007	0.008	4.11	3.85	67.73	6.54
Pine, straw, mixed	......	1.65	.	......	4.28	2.08	14.47	..
Pine, yellow, wood	10 00	0.23	0.010	0 045	4.18	19.70	65.53	3.20
Pine, black, wood	10.00	0.21	0.009	0.080	4.33	14.30	58.98	0.50
Sycamore, wood	10.00	0.99	0.121	0.230	12.23	23.17	31.62	0.62

In addition to the above results the analysis of ashes from other sources may be useful.

COMPOSITION OF COMMERCIAL FERTILIZING MATERIAL.

KIND.	Moisture.	Nitrogen.	Potash.	Phosphoric acid.	Lime.	Magnesia.	Sulphuric acid.	Chlorine.
Ashes (anthracite coal)	......	......	0.10	0.10	......	......	......	
Ashes (bituminous coal)	......	......	0.40	0.40	......	......	......	
Ashes (lime-kiln)	15.45	......	1.20	1.14	48.50	2 60	......	
Ashes (wood, leached)	30.22	......	1.27	1.51	28.08	2.66	0.14	
Ashes (wood, unleached)	12.50	......	5.25	1.70	34.00	3.40	......	
Cotton-hull ashes	7.80	......	22.75	8.85	9.60	10.75	......	
Seaweed ashes	1.47	......	0 92	0.30	6.06	4.37	2.98	6.60

The value of the ash from wood may be calculated by taking the commercial values of the potash of 5 cents per pound and of phosphoric acid of 4 cents per pound. The nitrogen, the element of plant food which has the greatest value, does not form part of the ash but escapes as a gas when the wood is used for fuel purposes.

PRODUCTS OF THE FOREST.

Some interesting chemical processees are those known as destructive distillation, paper making, the manufacture of varnishes, etc. The old time process of charcoal burning where great masses of wood were covered with earth and allowed to slowly burn to charcoal, has given place to the more modern method of destructive distillation. The object in this process is not only to produce charcoal but to save the volatile products and separate them so that these substances are made to yield a revenue to the manufacturers. The products produced from wood are charcoal, tar, crude acetic acid, wood alcohol and gas.

Wood tar is used in many cases as a preservative for wood, especially that known as Stockholm tar. Wood tar creosote is prepared from wood tar and is used in place of coal tar creosote for preserving railroad ties. The purified product is used in medicine as an antiseptic.

Wood alcohol is also a product from the distillation of wood and is used in varnishes, the preparation of aniline colors and as a cheap substitute for common alcohol in lamps. Another product is acetone which is used quite extensively in commerce. Acetic acid and the acetates are also produced from the wood when it is subjected to distillation.

In the production of the best varities of paper it is necessary to use the best grades of cellulose fibres such as come from cotton and linen rags, but for the largest production of the common variety of paper, the wood of the forest furnishes the material. The daily newspaper could not exist if it were not for the paper produced from the pulp of wood.

The production of turpentine and the varnishes is another great industry which may be included under dendro chemistry. The vast pine forest of the south and west are sending out great quantities of turpentin and rosin, to other parts of the country and it is only a question of time before they are exhausted. Already chemistry has been used in the preparation of various products from the distillation of the roots of trees which have been used for lumber.

It was claimed that a tree from which turpentine and rosin had been obtained was of less value for use as lumber and that its composition was different from that of the normal tree. Chemistry and engineering tests have shown that this is not true but that the chemical composition of materials from both sources that of the normal tree and when the tree has been tapped for turpentine and rosin, are the same and this is also true for the material in its strength for general use.

Another important work for dendro chemistry is that related to the bark of trees used for tanning purposes. Already a department for this work has been established in connection with the bureaus of forestry and chemistry at Washington, and the first work undertaken relates to the study of the chemical composition of the wood and bark of the chestnut oak, red oak, black oak, etc., the western hemlock and other trees being included also.

The production of wood for fuel purposes is still another important product of the forest. Coal is used to a larger extent for this purpose than wood, yet wood has many advantages. It kindles quicker and is cleaner. As coke is produced from coal, charcoal may be produced from wood. To show the effect of heat on wood the following may be of interest;

TEMPERATURE.	C.	H.	O.	Ash.	CHARACTER OF PRODUCT.
150° C.=302° F..........	47.51%	6.12%	46.29%	0 18	Imperfectly carbonized.
200° C.=392° F..........	51.82	3 99	43.96	0.23	
270° C.=518° F..........	70.45	4.64	24.19	0.85	Brown charcoal.
350° C.=662° F	76 64	4.14	18 44	0.61	
440° C.=824° F	81.64	1.96	15.24	1 16	
945° C.=1733° F	81.97	2.30	14.15	1.60	Black charcoal.
1045° C.=1913° F	88.14	1.41	9.26	1.20	
1775° C.=3227° F	96.52	0.62	0.94	1.94	

Wood in a dry condition contains 50 per cent of carbon, 6 per cent of hydrogen, 42 per cent of oxygen, .1 per cent of nitrogen and 1 per cent of ash, and has a calorific value of about 3,000 calories while black charcoal has a value of 8,000 calories. When we compare the composition and calorific value of the products of the forest with the various varieties of coals we realize the value of wood for fuel purposes, as may be seen by the following results:

CLASS OF COAL.	C.	H.	O.	CALORIES.
Dry coal burning with a long flame	75.80%	5.5-45	19.5-15	8,250
Caking coals with lone flame (gas coals)...........	80.85	5.8-5	14.2-10	8,650
Caking coals proper, forge coal, coking coal......	84.89	5 5-5	11.5-5	9,050
Caking coals with short flame	88 91	5.5-45	6.5-5.5	9,450
Anthracitic or lean coals burning with short flame	90.93	4.5-4	5.5-3	9,250

While wood will furnish only about one-third the heat that can be obtained from anthracite coal, its cost in many localities is a favorable consideration. Black charcoal, however, compares favorably pound for pound as a heat producer.

As the attention given to the application of science to the problems connected with forestry increases, the greater will be the demand upon dendro chemistry for aid in the work. The products of the forest used in commerce will be subjected to adulteration more and more. Turpentine will be found to contain substances which have been added to increase the profit of the producer. The gums will consist largely, if not entirely of cheaper substances and these will be represented as the natural products. Adulteration of the products of the forest will be possible in many ways and to protect these products will be an important work or dendro chemistry.

The study of the physiological processes of the growth of the tree will offer a splendid opportunity for research and the results will not only add to our knowledge but will be of practical value.

This elm is 7½ feet in diameter. Its branches spread a distance of 280 feet. This tree stands in the yard of the Geo. Simpson home, Knoxville, Iowa.

The production of new substances from the waste of many of the present processes will increase the value and add to the productiveness of our forest products. As our knowledge of the chemical processes connected with the forest reaches a larger sphere, the tree will mean more to us. One will not look upon a tree as the means of obtaining so much cord wood or so many feet of lumber. The commercial value will be considered only a part of the value of the tree. The work of the tree as it aids to prepare oxygen from the expired air of animals and its relation to the atmosphere in general will be regarded as important as its value for producing technical products. On the whole mankind will be the better in every way for viewing the products of nature from many sides. It will be a part of man's education in order that he may be capable of viewing nature from many sides, and the product will be a many sided man useful in every way as growth is made to meet the demands made upon him.

THE FARM WOOD LOT.

E. R. Hodson.

The amount of timbered land in the state of Iowa is given as thirteen per cent in a recent report of the United States geological survey. Of this area a large amount, in its present condition is almost worthless as timber land. Iowa is pre-eminently a prairie state. The timber area is of minor importance both in extent and quality. Despite this fact, however, there is some fair timber in the state. In the eastern part and extending westward along the rivers are some fine bodies of native hardwoods. Reproduction readily replaces the old trees, especially is this the case since settlement has restricted the prairie fires which formerly ravaged the country and drove all the tree growth to the banks of the streams, in some cases wiping it out completely. These fires coupled with a small rainfall did much to give the main part of the state the present treeless aspect.

The forest is practically hard wood. There is an occasional red cedar, scattered groups of white pine in northeastern and eastern Iowa, and a small group in Hardin county. With these exceptions we may say that the forest is exclusively a hardwood forest.

In comparing the hardwoods with those east of the Mississippi river we find some important trees missing. The beech, chestnut and yellow birch are left out. Our birches—the paper, cherry and red birch are small and hardly ever reach a large size.

The oaks are the most valuable of the native timber. White oaks head the list, then comes black walnut, hard maple, the hickories, etc.

White oak and hard maple make their best growth in different situations; white oak on upland slopes and ridges; hard maple on bottom land, although hard maple will grow on moist slopes and should be encouraged to grow there as the rich alluvial bottoms are too valuable for tree growth. Black walnut grows best in the bottoms also, but as it demands primarily a rich soil, it grows well on rich slopes. Red oak is a tree of the uplands, like the white oak, but demanding a moister situation. Honey locust and white elm are found on low lands. The remaining species such as red maple, hackberry, bur oak, sycamore, willow and cottonwood all prefer low ground. Post oak, white walnut, black oak, prefer the upland slopes and ridges, while the hickories seem to do well in either situation.

Another important consideration is the light demanding or shade enduring capacities of the various species, especially when coupled with varying rapidities of growth in a mixed forest. A great deal of care is necessary to avoid crowding out desirable light demanding species by rapid growing shade enduring ones with their heavy foliage. As the soil of the forest must have more or less protection, a large number of heavy foliaged trees are necessary, and if they are slower growing than the light demanding species, which it is desired to foster, the best interests will be conserved. On the other hand if the shade enduring species are valuable in themselves, the matter will take care of itself.

The kind of seed a tree bears has a most important influence on its ability to hold its own and to widen its territory. The light seed of the cottonwood, aspen, maple, etc., are carried by the wind long distances and wherever there is a chance for those trees to grow, their seed is there in readiness. The trees that bear edible fruit have their seeds carried by birds, as the black cherry and red cedar; but nut bearing trees seem to be sadly lacking in means of dissemination. It is true that their seeds are carried by squirrels, but only to be stored up somewhere and eaten. Those that get a chance to germinate must do so in the immediate vicinity of the parent tree. This fact must be rememberer in treating an Iowa wood lot for a future supply, for the heavy seeded trees, as the oaks, hickories and walnuts, are very valuable.

The timbered land is very unequally distributed in the state, the best timber being in the eastern part. It reaches out toward the west by way of the rivers and does not thrive any great distances from them. It also tends to become stunted and scrubby as it goes westward and is unfit for many of the uses to which that grown in the eastern part is put, although it is all the more valuable for firewood, fence posts and such uses because of its scarcity. A wood lot even here will repay careful treatment. Bur oak does well on the low soil of the western part. It never reaches the size it does in the eastern part, but is a valuable tree and one it pays to favor.

Taking a bird's eye view of the distribution we find the eastern border of the state well covered with timber, with small prairies in between the streams. As we go west the timber is confined more and more closely to the streams and in general decreases in size and density, which very plainly shows the close relation to rainfall.

Now as to the cutting of this small area of native timber, I have not the figures to show how much has been cut. It is the greater portion, however, and very little of that which is once cut is allowed to go back to timber as it would naturally do in most cases, first by coppice and then by seedlings. Blue-grass comes in and never surrenders its hold. The small amount of timber is being wiped out at a rapid rate. Farming, and especially the live stock industry, is the most important in Iowa. Timber was stripped off the rich alluvial bottoms because the land was valuable for farming. The lumber, firewood, etc., were incidental, the main object being to clear the land and raise corn, wheat and other crops. The slopes and uplands were cleared for the same purpose. When not fertile enough for farming purposes they still served admirably for pasture land, blue-grass coming in and making a fine turf. So it was—cut down the trees, let the grass in and make better pasture. And so well does blue-grass hold its own that when pastured closely not many trees succeed in getting back; yet if left alone such places would again be covered with trees.

In this way the timber has been treated in the past, either clean cut or else the most valuable kinds and individuals have been cut without any regard for the future supply. The vigorous, thrifty young polewood was cut; the dead, faulty and mature trees were left. The first class could be gotten out more easily and found a readier sale, thus paying the expense of getting the main object accompished, which was to clear the land for cultivation or for pasture. It naturally followed that there was a great deal of waste with this method. Timber was cut, rolled into heaps and burned. Some was rolled into streams or piled up in out of the way places and left to rot. As much as possible was cut and used, the remainder destroyed in order to clear the land in a short time. Of course no thought was taken of reproduction. It was not wanted.

Thus we find the timber at the present time driven to the pasture lands. There it has not been treated so roughly. The greater part that has been cut has been used. It was not necessary here to remove every tree as in the land intended for cultivation. It is only the trees selected that has worked against the best results. In every case the young, thrifty polewood was taken as it was more easily worked and found a ready market, the object being to thin out the timber and get the ground grassed over. Preservation or a future supply was not thought of.

So we find the timber scattered over the pasture lands; here and there a strip on a steep hillside or ravine which has not been culled so severely. The remainder is rather scattered and of poor quality for all the old faulty trees and those of the least desirable species are left. The old trees of the desirable species are valuable in one respect, they furnish seed trees. No matter how gnarled and windshaken, they serve this purpose well.

It is from this kind of a forest that our future wood lots are to be made. Little scattered groups of timber in the natural condition, larger areas of culled trees and, where not pastured too heavily, a fair reproduction. Unfortunately in many cases the inferior species predominate in this reproduction. The inferior species are like weeds; they grow and spread very rapidly when they have a chance.

This is the condition of the timber at present. The question arises how can it be improved and conserved. Does scientific forestry give any

40

aid which is practical in such a case? Can we apply its teachings so that we gain the good without being led astray by theory?

In the first place timber should be cut with the idea of preserving it. To use timber without destroying the power of producing a future supply is the leading principle of forestry. Some immediate gain must be sacrificed in order to do this. It is very true that to cut the most desirable and best timber will bring in the most money for the time, but it will result in an almost worthless tract of timber. With proper treatment the same amount of money may be obtained in the long run and the timber not injured.

Let us consider some of the methods forestry proposes in handling a tract of timber so that it can be used to the best advantage with the idea of perpetuating and improving it.

There are three pretty well defined methods of cutting:

1. The strip method.
2. The selection method.
3. The group method.

In the strip method a narrow strip is cut through the woods, the width of the strip is usually about the height of the trees. It is to be covered over with natural reproduction and when this is safely accomplished another narrow strip is clean cut by the side of the first, and so on until the whole tract has been cut over.

One can readily see that some skill and forethought is necessary here to secure the best results. For instance, the strip should not run up and down a steep hill as when the protecting cover is removed the rains will wash and deteriorate the soil. The cutting should be made the first winter after the seed year of the species it is desired to favor in the wood lot. The width of the strip should be adapted to the species desired. If it has a heavy seed like the hickories, the strip should not be so wide as when a light seeded tree is desired, like the ash or cottonwood. Then, too, the width must bear a close relation to general conditions of growth, such as moisture, light and suitableness of the desirable trees for the climate if the strip is to be satisfactorily covered by young growth.

The selection method is simply cutting out a single tree here and there over the tract. The mature trees are taken and care is exercised to get the openings stocked with valuable species.

The group method is similar to the strip method except that the openings are usually circular and much smaller. It differs from the selection method in that instead of a single tree a group of trees is taken out. As in the other methods the desirable trees must be fostered by the size of the opening and the proximity of seed trees. It has a great advantage over the strip method in its greater adapability.

In brief these are the principal methods of cutting timber according to approved forestry management. But before any of these can be put in practice the timber must be cleared up and put in good healthy condition. In short, what is known in forestry as an improvement cutting must be made. The first thing is to clean out all the dead trees and down timber. Then the next step must be taken more carefully; the crooked, faulty, broken topped and otherwise unsound mature trees are to be cut out. But here several considerations come in. It may be necessary to save some of them for seed trees. It may open up too much ground to the light, let in the rain to wash and deteriorate the soil. So it may be necessary to save imperfect trees for a time for the cover they afford. But let the owner be on the watch and when possible cut them out. Take the seed trees of the undesirable species first; then all the young trees which cannot grow into good timber. Last the unsound trees of the most desirable species, always keeping in mind that it is injurious to open the forest cover too much at one time.

Proceeding in this manner with a little care the owner can have in a few years a thrifty and valuable wood lot. We will have a dense stand of the most desirable species in suitable situations with sufficient reproduction to keep it stocked. All that is necessary is to know a few facts about the requirements of trees and their growth in mixture, to apply that knowledged intelligently and to exercise along with it some good common sense.

Now comes the question of cutting the timber in such a manner so as to conserve the wood lot, to use it without destroying it. Of the three methods outlined above the writer is very strongly in favor of the selection method for Iowa conditions. It is in keeping with the small wood lots and the use to which they are put to make the smallest cuttings possible. The selection method exposes the smallest areas. It permits the greatest freedom in selecting trees and it supplies timber in small quantities as it is needed.

The first reason is an important one. Timber in Iowa is handicapped to some extent and is apt to be not any too dense, therefore, a single tree removed in a place, in most cases, opens up wide enough area. Wood lots have been and will be, although it is against their best interests, to some extent pastured. This with the small rainfall will tend to keep them open and will lessen the chances of a large cut over area being stocked satisfactorily. Second, the greater flexibility of the method in a small wood lot; a mature tree here and there can be taken, the neighboring trees left for further growth. Lastly, a wood lot is used frequently; a small quantity is taken at a time. On that score alone the selection method is the best all around. Firewood will be the most important item that the wood lot will be called on to supply. This must be supplied annually and occasion can be taken to get rid of any faulty and unsound trees. Fence posts will come next and will demand a better class of timber. The mature and unsound trees can be used for that purpose. Part of an unsound tree is certain to be fit for posts and other rough building material for farm use; the remainder can be worked into firewood.

In regard to the kind of trees that are valuable, the oaks head the list. White oak is the most valuable oak, then bur oak, post oak, red oak and black oak. Black walnut is probably the most valuable tree after the white oak, but is found in very small quantities. Next in order comes hard maple, the hickories, white ash, black cherry and black locust.

The oaks are light demanding but will endure some shade. Black walnut is light demanding; hard maple and the hickories are shade enduring; white ash, black cherry and black locust are light demanding.

On the uplands and slopes, the oaks, white oak, black cherry and black locust form the first story and the hickories underneath form the second. On the bottom lands bur oak, black walnut and hackberry will form the first story; hard maple, the second. Other less valuable native trees may be tolerated for a time for the sake of ground cover, and some for the sake of their wood where it is impossible to get the better kinds to grow. These may be black oak, the elms, soft maples, cottonwood, etc.

One of the most important things to a forester is the soil cover. He wishes to maintain an unbroken leaf canopy. Failing in this he allows undergrowth and reproduction to protect the soil. No stock should be allowed in the wood lot. They trample out the reproduction and do immense harm to the undergrowth. If any stock is allowed in at all, only a very small number should be. The wood lot should not be treated as a pasture, for if grass begins to come in it is a sign that the forest is not in good condition. The soil is deteriorating for grass does not afford the protection that trees or undergrowth does; and grass and weeds use a great deal of water, much more than they conserve in the forest.

Trees should be grown as closely together as possible when young in order to make them grow in height and to clear themselves of the lower limbs. For these reasons it is well to have a light demanding species followed by a shade enduring species of slower growth. The light demanding species will be forced to grow in height as well as the shade enduring one. When the proper height is reached, growth in thickness is desired. Then it is time to thin out and allow the crowns of those remaining to enlarge which immediately causes rapid diameter growth; thus more volume is grown in fewer trees and is more valuable. By such methods the skillful forester can direct the growth of the trees as he wills, first getting the desirable species in proper mixtures and then handling them in such a manner as to concentrate the most volume in the fewest trees.

The most suitable place for the wood lot is on the roughest and poorest land on the farm. Trees do not demand very rich soil for a fair growth, although most of them do better in rich soil. There are poor places on many farms which can be turned into wood lots with profit. Besides this, many places need protection from erosion. A covering of trees is an admirable protection. Erosion does not do the damage that it does in other places. Take the Southern Appalachians, for instance. There the slopes are very steep and the rainfall heavy, and in a great many cut over areas the soil is washed away down to the rocks. Of course such an effect would hardly occur on the moderate slopes of Iowa, but it is well to protect the hillsides when such a cheap and convenient means is at hand. Besides furnishing a ready supply of wood for the various uses of the farm, the products sold, such as fence posts, cord wood, railroad ties, piling and lumber, will bring quite a small sum. Wood of all kinds is constantly growing scarce and a ready supply of it will not come amiss in the future.

The United States bureau of forestry has made an offer of expert advice on the treatment of wood lots, which is well worthy the attention of those who wish the best advice that careful study and wide experience can give, at a nominal expense. The agreement to be entered into is as follows:

WOOD LOT AGREEMENT.

WASHINGTON, D. C., September 1, 1898.

The Department of Agiculture of the United States and John Doe, of Doeville, county of Bell, state of Pennsylvania, mutually agree together as follows:

1. The Department of Agriculture, in pursuance of investigations in forestry, and in order to disseminate a knowledge of improved ways of handling forest lands, shall, after personal study on the ground by its agent or agents, prepare a plan for harvesting the forest crop and reproducing the forest on the land of the said John Doe, situated and described as follows: 100 acres, more or less, of second growth hardwood forest land, in the town of Doeville, county of Bell, state of Pennsylvania, on the farm known commonly as the Old Doe Place, and in the northwest portion of the same.

2. The said plan shall be prepared for the purpose of promoting and increasing the present value and usefulness of the said land to its owner, and to perpetuate and improve the forest upon it.

3. Upon completion of the said plan and its acceptance by the said John Doe, the Department of Agriculture shall supervise the execution thereof, so far as may be necessary.

4. The Department of Agriculture shall render all services under this agreement wholly without charge to the said John Doe, nor shall it participate in any degree in the receipts and expenses arising from the said land, except to defray the pay and expenses of its agent or agents.

5. The Department of Agriculture shall have the right to publish and distribute the said plan and its results for the information or farmers and others whom it may concern.

6. This agreement may be dissolved by either party upon ten days' notice given to the other.

(Signed.) ....

....

If the working plan is accepted when completed a signed acceptance is made of the same. The agreement is very loose, as one readily sees, and it offers the greatest freedom possible.

The requests for working plans are taken up in regular order by the bureau of forestry, with this exception; if it is thought that a working plan in a locality would be especially instructive for the general public, that plan will be considered out of its regular order.

For an example of a working plan the reader is referred to the article in which the above agreement was published, an article entitled "Work of the Division of Forestry for the Farmer," by Gifford Pinchot, in the Yearbook of the United States department of agriculture, 1898, also reprinted by the bureau of forestry. The plan was made for a New Jersey owner by Henry S. Graves, now director of the Yale school of forestry. It will give a good general idea of the nature of such a plan, but in order to be of particular value the plan must be made after careful study on the spot, as an inspection of this plan will show. A plan made for New Jersey would not answer in all its details for a wood lot in Iowa.

Where there is no native timber, resort may be had to planting. This planting may be placed under three heads; planting with home consumption, for shelter, and for market. Under the first head comes the wood lot. For a quick and temporary supply of firewood, willow, the soft maples, cottonwood, etc., may be planted. In among these may be planted hardy catalpa, black walnut and black locust. For shelter, red cedar, Norway spruce and Austrian pine answer the purpose well.

For market probably the best are the following: Black walnut, hardy catalpa and black locust.

Black walnut is valuable for fence posts and lumber but its greatest value is for furniture. It has a high price in the market and the supply is very limited. In places in the south where it was formerly abundant they are now digging up stumps and using old fence rails for furniture material. An acre or even a half acre of black walnut would be most valuable in twenty-five or thirty years. There is no chance of the market being supplied with something else for the value of black walnut lies in its rich color and beautiful finish which is peculiar to itself and can be supplied by nothing but black walnut. Almost all, practically all the native supply must come from planted groves. The price will continue to go up until there is an adequate supply; scarcity will only enhance its value in the eyes of furniture buyers. Here is a chance for a pretty safe investment for the future. The tree grows fairly rapidly and is quite free from fungus or insect attacks. It does not cost much to plant a half acre and have five or six hundred trees for market in twenty-five years. The seed should be planted with some cheaper tree for a nurse, say red maple. They should be planted four feet apart each way, every alternate tree being a red maple. That will be 2,722 trees to the acre or 1,361 black walnuts. The red maple will force the walnut to grow in height rapidly, which will produce long, clean boles. When the maple has served its purpose it may be cut out for firewood.

Catalpa is valuable for fence posts, railroad ties and telegraph poles. Black locust makes excellent and durable fence posts in a short time.

For a full discussion of the possibilities of planting on the western plains and prairies the reader is referred to an article entitled "Forest Extension in the Middle West," by W. L. Hall, published in the Yearbook of the Department of Agriculture for 1900; also reprinted by the bureau of forestry. Other articles of interest are "The Practice of Forestry by Private Owners," by Henry S. Graves, reprinted from the Yearbook 1899 United States Department of Agriculture by the bureau of forestry, and "Forestry for Farmers," by B. E. Fernow, reprinted by the bureau of forestry from the Yearbook United States Department of Agriculture for 1894.

EVERGREENS FOR WINDBREAKS.

A. T. Irwin, Ames, Iowa.

The planting of evergreens, like other enterprises, is likely to be viewed in its pioneer stages primarily from the material rather than from the esthetic. The most impotant subject under the former heading is the one of planting for shelter belts, etc. In evergreen planting, as in other operations of the early settler, immediate results are of prime consideration, hence even in evergreen planting we have what may be termed the "popular stage" of development; that is, the use of evergreens which are hardy and effective but above all, of rapid growth, something that will give early returns. Probably the trees which fulfill these requirements best are the Scotch pine and Norway spruce. This, no doubt, accounts for their extensive use throughout the northwest, and for this purpose they have answered admirably. It should be remembered, however, that these evergreens as with other rapid growing trees such as the cottonwoods, soft maples, etc., the wood is not durable, and early results are always obtained at the expense of longevity.

In Iowa we are now past the pioneer stage and the point I desire to emphasize is that with this new era of permanent improvement and better buildings, better fences, better homes, we should also make it a point to plant species of evergreens which are longer lived and more enduring. As a good example of this class we may mention the Austrian pine. Though of slower growth than the Scotch, the indications are that its life period is fully double that of the latter. On the Iowa State college campus are to be found many species of the Scotch and Austrian pines which were planted in the early seventies. Each summer for the past four or five years we have been compelled to remove a number of specimens of the Scotch and the remaining ones give evidence of decay. The Austrian, however, with few exceptions, are thrifty and yet in their prime.

Among our native pines of this long lived class we would name the bull pine (*Pinus ponderosa*, variety *scopulorum*). From the limited planting so far many of the species give good evidence of being a strong, hardy, long lived tree, and adapted even where the climatic conditions are severe. Its scarcity in the nursery probably precludes its more extensive use at present.

A third species, and a monarch of them all in some respects, is the white pine. It is somewhat exacting and requires a soil which is neither too dry nor too wet. In severe locations it sometimes proves tender in the first three or four years of its growth. For the first ten years after planting its growth is slow, but after this age the annual growth is very heavy and the tree is also more hardy. To secure protection for the first few years, and also to combine early results with permanency, windbreaks of the Scotch pine and the White or with some of the other species named, make an ideal combination. In many sections of our state the belts of Scotch pine have reached their maturity, and in renewing them let us not fail to build a more permanent and enduring foundation.

PART XI.

SOME PAPERS READ BEFORE FARMERS' INSTITUTES OF IOWA.

THE PURPOSE OF THE FARMERS' INSTITUTE.

Chas. E. Hearst before Black Hawk County Farmers' Institute.

My intimate acquaintance with the farmers' institute of this county for the last few years has led me to select this subject as a text from which to deduct the good that may be accomplished by the yearly gatherings, to find and point out, if possible, wherein they do good and wherein we do not derive the greatest benefits from mingling together for the few days each year that is occupied by the session.

This is a day of organization.

The smallest industries to the giant corporation are each day uniting their forces to obtain results that they could not obtain in their separate organization. They unite to form great trusts and syndicates that, if need be, stand ready to brow beat and coerce a smaller dispenser of the same wares.

It is a day when the people of the nation are putting forth every effort to obtain the best and most from what they are engaged in, our railroads are expending enormous sums to straighten a small curve or lower a grade whereby a very few minutes may be saved in carrying their passengers and express, in delivering our mail and transporting our freight. To the casual observer the results do not seem commensurate to the expenditures, but they must "get there" and they will "get there" at any cost. Our ocean steamers that transport our cargoes and mail from one country to another, are endeavoring all the time to so unite their forces that nothing can stand in their way. The nations of the world did not dare to dream one hundred years ago that the time would ever come when a vessel could cross the Atlantic ocean in five or six days.

Our great manufactories are adding new machinery to their works, are forming combines by which they are able to turn out the greatest number of articles at the least expense.

This enormous enterprise which has been under discussion much of late among our law makers—the Panama canal enterprise. What does it mean?

Our great coal trusts—the tin and steel industries and numerous other gigantic enterprises—what do they all mean? They mean that we are living fast.

Going at a tremenduous pace, and if we would keep abreast of the times we must use every means in our reach to attain the things we are setting out to accomplish..

And so we come together today to join our hands and hearts in endeavoring to unite in perfect harmony the greatest enterprise, the largest enterprise, ᴜᴦᴇ largest combination, the most invulnerable trust that the sun ever shone upon—the American farmer.

I do not use the word trust here in its technical sense. I *do* mean that our interests are one, our aims are one, and we must strike to accomplish the same results—that of making the most out of the powers and oppor tunities given us.

It is not possible for us all to attend an agricultural college. Our positions in life demand that we stay where we are; our conditions necessitate our staying where we are and the necessities of the world demand our every effort as a duty to provide them the wherewith to subsist. It is then that we see the absolute necessity of making the most of what we have at hand to better our condition. The Farmers Institute affords us an opportunity that to get the most out of should be attended, should be participated in, should be taken home and practiced—it is here we get our ideas together and vie with one another in the best methods to be applied, the proper management of what we have in our care and the realization of the fact that we are here for business and not for play.

In telling a successful retired farmer friend of mine that I had gleaned a few new ideas from the farm papers, said, "Yes, I was always a great hand to read the papers, but I think I got more good from just going to my different neighbors and seeing how they did, learning what they knew, and then going home and profiting by what I had seen and heard, both in their successes and their failures. Just so it is with our Institute. We come here to gain by our neighbors' experiences, and where is there a better place than right here among ourselves to impart this knowledge? But we go farther. We are enabled by the co-operation of the farmers and their trust, or better say, the trust of these men in the farmers—to have among us men who *have* had the agricultural college training, the experimental training backed up by this great farming country, to give us the results of their life time of study and research in our lines, which we cannot with our limited time and means accomplish. They have made it a business to find out by actual experience the best manner of care and the best and cheapest feeds and conditions to make milk, to make beef, and to utilize the products we, by our co-operation with nature produce—to the very best advantage.

It cost money to find this. It costs time and labor and well can we afford to employ these men and make these experiments and get from them what we could not get from any other source. Not only have we here men who have learned how to feed, but men who have toiled in the field with soils and seeds and secured for us results we hardly thought possible —that of the improvement of our yields of grain and corn and the quality of the same. In even changing the composition of grains so that by careful selection and breeding we may be able to raise corn that will make a more nearly perfect feed in itself. This is not time spent idly. This means success to those who are willing to accept and cultivate this knowledge and then go home and apply it. And again this is not all. We have here as fine a company of business men as can be gathered together. To be one of them is a pleasure and to know them adds to a man's estimate of himself in being one of them.

The social feature of this meeting with one another is greatly to be desired. In *all*, How can a man afford to miss a meeting of this character?

It is conceded by all that it is a good thing for a man to be up before this meeting and tell his experiences. It helps him in a line he has very little opportunity to be disciplined in—that of thinking on his feet, of being able to put forth the best there is in him at a time when he most needs it. It is hard for a sensitive person to stand before an audience and be perfectly comfortable, and a farmer's business calls him less frequently than any of the professions to such experiences, and it is right that he should become as easy as possible while in such a position. For is it not from among our ranks that the men of the world—I mean *men*—men that are men in the fullest sense—morally, mentally and physically, come from? Look over the best men of our age, the professional and business men. Who are they and from whence did they hail? They are farmers' sons and spent the greater part of their childhood and youth on their father's farm.

We grow while we are assembled here together, and it is right and well that we should thus learn to teach and be taught.

On the other hand, what are the benefits that escape us? In every organization the burden of carrying forward the work of that body is almost invariably left to a very few. The others help by their absence. This may be too true of the institute work, a few leaders have to carry the burden of making it go, or else it is only half done. One of the great faults is the fact that so often those placed upon the program fail to respond and thus disarrange and sometimes have a subject seriously crippled for lack of a few hours' preparation. Even though one feels he cannot give a subject the justice it should receive, he should give it time and thought enough to open it for those following in the discussion.

The way in which we derive the least amount of good from these meetings is when we go home and continue in our old mistakes, and do not heed the things we have heard and should have learned. It very often happens that those interesting themselves in institute work are really not the ones most in need of instruction.

Might it not be an improvement for us to provide lecturers in the line of domestic economy for the benefit of the women? If it is profitable for us to meet and exchange our experiences might it not be pleasant and profitable for them to have a few hours of instruction along this line, being provided with an expert, if you please, to render whatever assistance is possible and make it a pleasing feature of our institute. If this would be a source of enjoyment for the women it would certainly be a pleasure for the men to provide means for just such opportunities. For there is none whom we would rather please than those who make the home and give the cheer.

Home! What a world of meaning that word implies! What in the world is nearer and dearer than the home. It is to the homes of the land that we must look for the strength of the nation. Therefore we should strive to make the home what it should be—not just a place to go to when convenient, but a place from which we cannot keep away. A place where peace and harmony prevail; a place where amid the cares and turmoils of this world we can go and find rest, comfort and contentment.

Then let us make the most of these days of social and business intercourse and enter into the full enjoyment and profit of the occasion, and inspire one another by our presence, our advice, and our experiences, to make the most of the things at hand.

THE BREEDING AND MANAGEMENT OF THE FARM HORSE.

T. M. Wilkinson, before the Calhoun County Farmers' Institute.

The farm is the nursery of the horse. Here it is that the horse spends his colthood days, if not his entire life. How to make the production of this class of the domestic animals more profitable is a problem that confronts the farmer at the present time. How to increase the profits and reduce the chances of loss are the questions the farmer and breeder are trying to solve. The first cause of loss is in the selection of the brood mare. There are but very few farmers, if they own a choice cow, sow or ewe that will sell that female for the common market price. Not a man present could be induced to sell such a female, even if offered a premium, but how is it with the mare. If a farmer raises a colt that developes into a mare of exceptional merit, or if he happens to buy such a colt or mare and some shrewd dealer comes along and offers a slight advance over what common horses are ordinarily worth and which may not be more than half her value on the market. We will venture to say that forty-nine men out of fifty will take the dealer's money. Then when the time comes to select the brood mare for the production of the farm and market horse, if they have a decrepit old mare that is no possible use for anything else they propose making her a matron, even though they have reason to believe they are wasting their time. If they fail then the stallion is to blame. Or maybe the farmer has a balky mare or one so vicious that she is unsafe to work and so notorious that she cannot be traded off or sold. This animal is selected for the brood mare, regardless of future results. If the colt inherits these vices, as the chances are it will, the farmer suffers a loss. If you do not own a good brood mare buy one or else don't try to raise colts.

When the farmer comes to select a stallion, as a rule he does not take into consideration the defects of his mare. Nor does he take into consideration the good qualities or defects of the stallion. Generally, one of three things decides his choice—the size of the stallion, the size of the fees, or the size of the owner in the estimation of the owner of the mare. In this country where the farmers have been educated to the idea that draft blood is the whole thing in breeding horses, the majority will select something big. regardless of the size or quality of their mare and expect to secure a high class draft horse and are disappointed if they do not succeed. Others again will patronize no horse unless the fees are cheap and they are another class who don't see any money in growing horses. Other farmers have been laboring for years breeding up their stock and while they have secured size they have made bad selections and their stock lacks quality, hence this farmer is disgusted with the draft horse because they lack action, style, endurance and it takes an enormous amount to keep this class of horse so he proposes to make a change, instead of selecting a large, compact, easy kept draft stallion, they select some light, cheap, cross roads stallion of mixed breeding to mate with his draft bred mares and the chances are there is disappointment again. We have observed that the men who make a success of growing horses are the men who put brains into the business. They judiciously select some type of the horse they think they are adapted to grow. They select the best mares of this type their money will buy. A man had better own but one high class brood mare, whether she be draft, coach, trotting, saddle or thoroughbred, than a whole barn yard full of mixed breeds, sizes and inferior quality, having selected the type and mare, the net step is the selection of the stallion. It is best to select a stallion of known reputation as then you can see his colts. By observing the class of mares and kind of colts produced you can draw conclusions how he will mate with your mare. It is time the farmer began to realize that he must abandon the production of the common general purpose horse. This is the class of horse that brings the least money to the farmer of any except the broncho. He is strictly a horse of no particular type. The farmer with a light mare, weighing from 800 lbs. to 1200 or 1400 lbs. carrying a strong infusion of Morgan trotting or thoroughbred blood imagines that mating her with a large draft stallion he will secure a general purpose horse. He often claims that such a horse suits him, and he is the one to be suited, but when he comes to sell the dealer will find fault with his ideal general purpose horse and offer but a small price. The farmers horse lacks weight, muscular development, style and finish and is neither draft, coacher or a road horse. While had he mated these same mares with a good sized coach or trotting bred stallion they would have a general purpose horse with plenty of style, finish and endurance, and when they come to make a sale they have a horse that will have a definite market and realize the farmer good prices. At the present time, buyers are scouring the country looking for horses of this type in size from 15½ hands to 17 hands and weighing from 1100 to 1350 pounds, with good style, action and finish and they are paying good prices. Of course the farmer may not receive more than $125 to $200 for this style of horse but after he is educated to be a high stepper he commands good prices, while the market is constantly glutted with the ordinary general purpose horse. While we are a great admirer of the large draft horse and the demand for this class of horse is of the best, some choice specimens command the high figure of five to six hundred dollars each, yet there are some drawbacks to their production. One is the lack of vitality and endurance. Importers and producers of the best strains of European draft stock concede this, and admit that they are not so strong in these points as the lighter American breeds. It is seldom one sees a grade draft horse that is of any use after reaching eighteen or twenty years, while it is a fact, that in communities where the lighter American breeds predominate one often sees horses ranging from twenty to thirty years of age doing active service. It is no uncommon thing for dealers to buy trotting or Morgan bred stallions or geldings twelve to sixteen years old, teach them the high stepping art and sell them for seven to nine years old, and the horse will look it, while the draft horse when he passes twelve years of age generally shows age very fast. The farmer wishing to grow a general purpose horse from his light mare should if he has light mares patronize either the American trotter or the coach stallion and thus secure a colt with a definite purpose. If the farmer has draft mares of large size then by all means patronize the best stallion within reach. The best of any type is none too good and a person will raise enough cheap stock trying to produce the best. It is to be regretted that most of the best draft mares were sold out of the country during the recent hard times and this section never possessed many trotting or coach bred mares so at present the majority of the brood mares are an inferior lot. Many farmers have said to me during the past year that in a couple years horses will be as cheap as ever, not worth raising. Let me submit some figures. Jan. 1, 1899, the census reports 16,000,000 head of horses; Jan. 1, 1901, the government reports show 11,000,000. Do you grasp the meaning of this? In two years this country has used all the increase and 5,000,000 head of the original stock. In 1899 there was only 21 yearling colts assessed for taxation in Union township, one of the best townships in this county. In 1901 there was but 41 head of yearlings returned for taxation. Does that indicate a surplus in the near future. The government officers whose duty it is furnish horses for the army made a tour recently of the states and territories known as the range country and they report the ranges practically cleaned up. So the farmer need have no fear of a break in prices for some time unless the country suffers from a financial panic. But to return to our subject. Having selected our brood mare or mares and mated them with a proper sire the next is the care of the mare to foaling time. Give the mare good care, good feed and moderate work. By moderate work we do not mean the heavy end of all the heavy team work, for then she is apt to be strained, the embryo foal lost, a good brood mare spoiled and the owner of the stallion loses his fees. And right here let me say if the breeder was as particular about living up to his part of a breeding contract as the stallion owner is to execute his part of it this business would be more satisfactory. When it comes near to foaling time the mare should be given a roomy stall if she is due to foal early in the season, and at nights especially, and give her a reasonable amount of attention. If not due to foal until warm weather comes on, turn out into a near-by pasture, but not where the swine are or you may loose both mare and colt and if you work the mare don't leave her tied up with the other horses or you may have cause to swear the foal came dead when you are called on to settle your bill with the owner of the stallion. Give the mare reasonable attention so as to give her some assistance should she need it. After foaling give a reasonable time for the mare to recover before sending away to pasture or putting to work. It is a decided advantage to both dam and foal to give them a small feed of grain twice a day even in pasture. No difference how good the sire and dam or how well bred, the colt is always better for a strong case of grain bin. During the colt's early life it is necessary to guard it against accident as far as possible. The barbed wire has been one of the chief causes of these. We venture the assertion there has been enough money lost the past six or eight years, in horses alone, from barbed to replace every fence in Calhoun county with a safe four foot web fence. We are hoping the day will come when barbed wire will not be known on the farm except when woven into a safe web fence. As soon as the colt reaches two years of age and not later than three years his harness education should begin. Now even if you have a quiet, easy going colt don't break it, to use a common expression, by hitching it with a slow, poky old horse, to a wagon and then whoop and yell and try to scare it into going and if the colt gets scared and runs or sulks and won't go, lambast it with a rawhide and just teach it enough so you can herd it across a field. ·A good plan is to harness it up and let stand in the stable for a day or two. Then fasten hames so no part will come loose and turn into the barn lot for a week. Then hitch it to a cart or wagon and tie to side of a barn or corn crib or other suitable place and let stand for an hour or two. After a couple or three lessons of this kind the colt is ready for his first driving lesson. For the first six months the colt should be taught to walk and walk fast. If you wish to teach a colt to walk four or five miles per hour the first six months of his education is the time to teach it. It can be taught to trot any time. During the rush of spring work be careful in feeding. See that the collar and harness fit well so the colt does not become chaffed and sore, and learn some disagreeable trick from this cause. Keep the colt thrifty and in good spirits and one great help to do this is, turning the horses out an hour or two every evening where they can get a good bite of grass as grass is nature's best tonic. Keep the colt growing and thrifty and we believe the farmer will have no reason to complain that it does not pay to raise horses. Remember that when you grow a colt that you are not the only one to please but you must figure on the future buyer as well and work with a definite object in view.   ,

---

THE POLLED ANGUS BREED OF CATTLE.

Wm. Miller, before Buena Vista County Farmers' Institute.

The question is asked why I prefer Polled Angus cattle to Polled Durham, Short-horn and Hereford breeds. Endeavoring to answer this question, will state a few pertinent facts, leaving my hearers each to draw his own conclusions. To begin with I am a breeder of Angus cattle, by accident rather than choice, being a Short-horn man by heredity, and early and perhaps intense association with the breeds and breeders. Also having intimating acquaintance with the Hereford men and cattle, particularly in their native country, importing some very good ones to this country. However, this connection was temporary. But when I was compelled to cut the Short-horn tie, to say it caused a pang of sorrow is putting it mildly, but am trying to comfort myself with what are sometimes termed the "black-skinned beauties," and whether in my situation the loss or gain is the greater I will leave you to determine. I am really content. A great deal could and should be said in this connection, but to suit a paper of this kind, at this time, will only touch briefly on the main points.

Great Britain has given to this country all our really valuable breeds of animals, excepting, perhaps, the nigger and the mule, and had we had no others no loss would be felt, but considerable disappointment avoided. It seems to be the generally accepted fact that we have the three distinct breed. And what their promoters are trying to do is not revealed to me, farmer, in what is called the corn belt region of this country, in which a kind Providence has placed us. I need hardly name them, but will just give you them in priority as introduced to this country on their great mission, as our domestic and export beef trade shows. Nearly 100 years in advance of any other came the noble Short-horn, to begin the struggle for better beef and higher civilization, against the scrub steer and the scrub farmer. Then came the Hereford, followed closely by the Angus. As far as I have seen and understand, the cattle called Polled Durham are not as yet at any rate, entitled to the distinction of a breed, certainly not a pure breed. And what their promoters are trying to do is not revealed to me. unless it is to have something uncommon, enjoying a free field for—well, I will not say what.

Surely the loss of the horn even if it becomes hereditary, will not make up for the loss of valuable flesh which is certain to become hereditary.

If you eliminate the waxy horn, mild eye and roan, mossy skin, you eliminate the quality that has made the Short-horn so justly and world-wide famous. This was tried partly by the red craze. A great deal of character is shown and I believe held in the horn of a Short-horn so much so that by my experience I find that the matured bull will not sire so good calves after as before he was dehorned. And if you dehorn the breed either by the introduction of inferior Polled blood or individual breeding animals by the saw, you are not a friend but a Delilah shearing Sampson of his locks. "Sampson! Sampson! The Phillistines are upon thee, Sampson." Barnum masquerading in kilt and plaid! But we will lay the Polled Durham by with the white willow, the Bohemian oat and the "gold brick" and proceed to consider the three beef breeds claiming our attention in this country. In order to do so effectively we must acquaint ourselves with the conditions and influences under which each has been moulded, soil, climate and general environment that produce these breeds. Knowing these particulars it will be easier for us to determine which will best suit our conditions and requirements here. Beginning in the south leads us to the country drained and watered by the tributaries of the crystal Severn, Hereford and Salop. Here we quote from a work published by John Speed in 1627 on England, Wales and Scotland, in which he says of Herefordshire:

"The climate is most healthful and the soil so fertile for corn and cattle that no place in England yieldeth more or better conditions."

So it was then, so it is now the garden spot of England and an ideal home for man and beast. Sloping to the western ocean it is fanned by moist and gentle breezes from the gulf stream, making its climate almost continual spring and summer. Standing as I have on the ruins of Ludlow castle, looking toward the south and west, taking in the valleys of the Lug, the Wye and the Teme, you have a landscape before you that cannot be equaled for rural richness and beauty. The harmony is so complete that it is hard to tell what to admire the most, the rich yellow grain fields, the soft green pastures, the clear ripping trout streams or the finest of England's spreading oaks, altogether a scene that neither brush nor words can describe and one wonders is it real or an angelic sketch of Eden before the fall. Surely it is a blending of heaven and earth inspiring the prayer of the honest old plowman, "O, Lord, if there is nae room for me up there let me bide at the Meadows and fish in the Teme." This is the cradle of the Hereford cattle, where Benjamin Tompkins in 1742 tended their infancy, giving direction to their color and form, supplemented by the Hewers and succeeded by Elder John Price, who with great care and skill brought them down to the early masters of the passing generation, many of whom I have met, and no wonder that such artists from such material and opportunity should mould forms so perfect as by care and selection in mating they have done. Here we have a breed of cattle fitted exactly for that country and also for the London market. A country that will hold against all comers. But on that island they have not spread. I never saw one in Scotland and they remain almost unknown in Ireland. But the shrewd and enterprising American noticed and appreciated their quality and large numbers in late years have been brought to this country, including many of the finest individuals of the breed. Along with the cattle come some of their best herdsmen. Many of the best falling into the hands of the rich, liberal and broad-minded men, many of their sterling qualities will be preserved, although breeding here under such changed conditions necessarily the original type will also change. Their field of usefulness seems to be the southwest. This is not a country of great distances but of considerable diversity of climate and soil. Going north from Hereford two or three degrees we come nearly to the center of the island, north and south, the valleys of Tees and Weare, Darlington, Yarm and Durham surrounded by a rich agricultural country, particularly adapted to the growth of turips, oats and the cultivated grasses as well as permanent pastures by the river sides, "holmes" as they are called, where the grass will fatten as well as in any part of England. The climate here is not as fine as farther south, sloping as it does to the east. Here originated the Short-horn. Here is the birth place of the brothers Colling, Bates, Mason and Booth. Here, too, are their graves.

On market days at neighboring towns they met and discussed the merits and defects of their different animals. Here was first heard the names of Hubback, Favorite, Comet and the Duke of Northumberland.

Names now as familiar almost as sacred as to the Short-horn man as the name of Washington to the American patriot. The breed originating in narrow limits soon spread over the whole island and still claims Ireland as its own and the utmost ends of the earth seem to be its limit, its mission the elevation of the human race, the cow being the barometer indicating the altitude of the civilization. Nations can be estimated by the number and quality of their domestic animals, also communities and individuals. A farmer with thin scrub cattle is a thin scrub man with soul in proportion. The cow and her owner must have a relative level. Give a scrub man a good cow, one of three things must happen. The cow will elevate the man or the man will starve and degrade the cow, or it may be a compromise.

But I must take the train and go north, the land of hill and heather. Aberdeen and the Angus country lying on the northeast part of the island, draining to the Northern ocean and receiving its wind and gales. It has been said by a close observer that "the Lord made England and England made the Englishman," but "that the Lord made a Scotchman and a Scotchman made Scotland," certainly if He did not make it the Scotchman has exhausted every possibility in its improvement, impelled by necessity, a clear case of "root hog or die," and he rooted. Every effort seemed to bring fresh energy. With a will and judgment a way was found, resulting in these people originating a brand of beef called the "Prime Scot" that tops the London market every week, year in and year out. A hundred or even fifty years ago these people could not put beef on the London market at all. The distance was too great to drive on foot, had they started fat it would have been driven off before they got there. Their surplus cattle were then sold to the southern grazer and feeder and by them put on the market, but when steam navigation began a boat was run weekly between Aberdeen and London. Later followed the railroad and regular trains. This marks the beginning of real improvement in agriculture and stock raising in that country. Draining, making fences with the stone that lay on the surface, erecting buildings for shelter and introducing the Swedish turnip (where it is now grown in its greatest perfection), extending the cultivation of oats that for straw has no feeding equal. It was also found that the cultivated grasses known to the island would grow there and thrive and although the winter day was short and almost sunless, the summer day was long with moisture and warmth sufficient to mature these crops to a degree of excellence. As commercial fertilizers were considerably used and all farm manures scrupulously saved and applied to the land, fertility increased. McDonald and Angus historian claims great antiquity for his breed, saying that Caesar stood, I think it was on one of the Grampian hills and I suppose with a field glass, saw to the northward some cattle or animals that from his description is taken to be the ancestors of the Aberdeen Angus cattle of today, but I think it is unnecessary for us to go farther back than the generation of Hugh Watson of Heillor and Wm. McCombie of Tillyfour, who from among the cattle of this country by selection and care made such wonderful improvement to meet changed conditions. No doubt good cattle well adapted to requirements existed long before this time. But as there was no regular market

41

or concerted action of any kind, the cattle remained without fixed character, varying in different localities. The country of Watson had the Angus "Doddie," that of McCombie the Buchan Humlie, both mostly hornless and mostly black and much of the same character not being widely separated by distance or environment.

The hornless and black character was preserved and intensified but the main object was to produce an animal that would consume the product of the farm and make the best return on the London market, "rent payers" as they were called, as their breeders were all on rented farms. These men thought this could be best done by selection from the native cattle, but others having the same object in view had seen the Short-horns in the Tees valley and Barclay of Ury, Hay of Shethin and others established herds of this breed in Aberdeen, laying the foundation of what is now termed the Scotch Short-horn. From these herds Cruickshank probably drew his inspiration and certainly a deal of material that has made Sillyton so famous. The bulls of these herds were all used in this country as well as others brought in and from that cross on, the cattle of the country became very popular, the bullocks aiding in no small degree in establishing the claim of "Prime Scots" on the London market and how much if any of this blood was taken in to build up the superior qualities of the modern Aberdeen Angus, we do not know—neither have we any reason to care. A uniform type is surely fixed, not only among themselves but when crossed on other breeds they produce this uniformity of excellence as well as appearance with wonderful certainty. Until 1878 this breed was little known outside of their own locality and not at all in this country. when at the world's fair in Paris McCombie surprised the world by making a clean sweep against every known beef breed of cattle as there exhibited, numbering against him 170 head. This brought them into notice abroad and a few years later some large and valuable importations were made to this country, being closely followed by others. Fortunately these importers were men of considerable means and good ones were brought, as by this time their qualities were becoming known and it took money to move them. Their career in this country is too well known to justify reciting here. To recount their fat stock prizes would amount to all the prizes that have been offered within the last 15 or 20 years in Britain and America, as over 75 per cent have been taken by them. And still it goes on. This year in Chicago all championships were taken and 8 out of 9 principal prizes. This week it was Shamrock in Chicago and next week the most perfect specimen of beef animal skill has yet produced Lyia of Glamis at Smithfield (London), where this show season all the championships and 9 per cent of the prizes fell to the pure bred Angus, where their crosses in every instance stood second or "reserve number," as it is called there. But why repeat, as it is now taken as a matter of course—so much so that in the anguish of spirit Mr. Mitchell, who guides the destinies of Choice Goods, Ruberta and Cicely, exclaims as we quote here from the *Twentieth Century Farmer* dated Feb. 4, 1903: "The day of 1800 and 2,000- pound three-year-old steers has long since given way to the tidy yearling, familiar to us as 'baby beef,' and when the Short-horns are able to land the championships in steer classes and car lots at

the great International Exposition it must of necessity be with animals
of identically the same type as that of their most formidable adversaries."
No doubt this is true, but Mr. Mitchell, if imitation is good and necessary
would not the real thing be better, for there is nothing so like a good Angus
as a good "Doddie?" I prefer the Angus because their breeding here is
carried on under similar conditions and with the same object under which
and for which the breed was originally evolved. Consequently after generations of breeding here the offspring fully retain the valuable qualities
of their imported ancestors.

Two causes lead to peculiar sales here, namely: Dispersions of established herds and surplus stock caused by rapid natural increase. Men
buy at these sales because they want the cattle and want them as low in
price as honorable and pair competition will allow. The female passing
through the ring for the first and last time on to their new homes where
their female produce is kept to increase the herd, the bulls sold to neighboring farmers to cross on grade cows, raising steers and heifers that at
from twenty to thirty months old top the market as "Angus," that being
the Chicago name for " Prime Scots." For the last fourteen years in unbroken succession this breed has topped the Chicago Christmas market.
This business will last as long as corn or grass is grown in the northwest
and men eat beef, prefering the best as it is proportionately alike profitable to the breeder and the feeder, to the butcher and the consumer. No,
you buy at my sale today and I will buy at yours next week and so on. I
know cows, yes many, originall good, now with a few wrinkles on the
horn, but no live calf to credit (had no time for maternal duties), but who
can repeat the colonel's good jokes without looking at a book. The Angus
sales in 1903 were opened at Chicago January 6th and 7th by the disper-
sion of the Redwood Falls, Minn., herd of Tyson & Company, made necessary by the death of one of the two partners when the estate had to be
closed out. Old and young, bull and heifer, 76 in number, averaged $347.
This herd had never been shown at a fair so far as I know, certainly not
at a leading fair. Tyson & Co. had never bought an animal at a public sale
and rarely attended one. I was not at the sale but from the published report was astonished to find the name of every buyer completely unknown
to me, showing plainly, if such were needed, that the foundation of their
popularity rests on the farming community. He who owns the cattle upon
a thousand hills, has been graciously pleased so far to shield our chosen
breed from the "boomer" and the "scalper." The boom being more fatal
to the cow than the tuberculosis, hollow horn and worm in the tail all
rolled together, and at this time of prosperity more to be dreaded. We
fear that something smelling very like this terrible scourge has made its
appearance in a spot among us, but hope the authorities (common sense)
will stamp it out by quarantine until all is purged and purified just as
the proper authorities with the bubonic plague on the Pacific coast. Another reason for the faith and hope that is in me then I am done. If we
have to walk through the vale of tears it is less dreary to march with the
victorious. The Angus men say they have let their cattle hitherto do the
"tooting." But now they are going to get brass band and yellow chariot.
I don't care for the band but have my eye on the wagon in which they
say will be many seats.

BUYING STEERS FOR THE FEED LOT.

A. L. Ames, before the Black Hawk County Farmers' Institute.

The best method of buying steers for the feed lot is a problem never solved, and is always new and of vital interest to the feeder. The old adage, "An article well bought is half sold," was never better illustrated. When? How? Where? What kind? What weight and what price? are questions that should be thoroughly settled in the mind of the prospective buyer. I wish to call attention to a few necessary and important points to be observed before attempting to secure the cattle.

In this age of change and if you will progress, when the tendency of every industrial department is toward combination and centralization, in this land where labor rules and where unions are more powerful than law, religion or right, where the successful man in every business department devotes his whole energy and thinking being to the perfection of some one idea and to prove to the world its value, the farmer, feeder and stock man is expected to take his place.

In order then to buy well a drove of cattle for the feed lot he must know something more than cattle. There must be long, hard hours of study over the industrial problems of the day. The reason why he feeds being his desire to sell beef at a profit, it becomes necessary for him to study the future prospect of the market. He must be well posted on the number of cattle relative to other like periods that are going "on feed" at the time he expects to start his. He must know to a certainty the power or feeding value of the feed he is to use and its cost per hundredweight when ready for the cattle. He must also be reasonably sure of the pounds gain to be made during the feeding period by the used of this feed. He will then know just exactly what he can take per hundredweight for his cattle and not lose on the investment. He also has the advantage of knowing at all stages of the feeding period the actual cost of the cattle up to date, and can take advantage of a profit should the proper inducement present itself. To all of these questions and many others should the feeder give his best thought and study before deciding to feed.

It would be impossible in one article to speak of all the different methods or combination of circumstances that must inevitably arise and can only be settled by one person and he the originator of the plan. I will therefore confine myself to a few general principles that I have found useful in buying all kinds of cattle but more particularly those to be used for the "dry lot" or placed immediately on full feed.

The first and most important point to be decided by the buyer is the class of cattle to buy. This question should be settled at home before any attempt is made to find or purchase any cattle whatever. Only those of the same class, age, weight and breeding should be fed in the same yard. A mixed drove of big and little, rough and smooth, well bred and scrubs, do not feed so well nor sell as well as though they were all of the same kind Having fully determined this point do not allow your judgment to be overruled by what the other man is doing. A good axiom to follow is to "Buy when the other man wants to sell." You can then get your money's worth. The kind or class you buy will depend largely upon your surroundings and the time of year but you will certainly take those which in your judgment will make you the most money. In order to determine this we find four factors, three of which are known: the cost price, the feed bill and the average gain per day or ratio between feed and gain. The fourth member of the equation is more uncertain and at times very difficult to control, namely the selling price. If this were known the solution would be easy but as many of us can testify, such is not the case.

In the selling market are four well defined grades of beef cattle: the choice, good, medium and poor. In one of these four market divisions the feeder must place his finished product and his profit or loss be estimated from the price obtained. This being true it will be well to examine these divisions a little as a help toward selecting your feeders.

In the division of choice cattle you will find only the very best bred cattle. Those as good or better than registered stock and always a selected bunch and fed to a finish. They must be prime in every way—in breeding, style, finish, flesh, fat, form and weight. Cattle that occupy this exalted place on the market are as a rule bred and fed by the same individual and pushed from calfhood up and so need not be considered at this time. In the next two divisions come the bulk of the cattle sold, the principal difference being a matter of flesh and finish, the medium cattle covering a wider range and not dressing out quite so large a per cent when slaughtered. In the poor column a feeder should never be found for they are invariably money losers. A person can hardly be called a feeder unless he can make a medium fat steer out of a poor stocker.

We find then the large majority of feed yard cattle are sold on the market for what are known as useful cattle and to make these cattle with the last possible expense is the business of the feeder.

It is impossible to say just *where* to buy your feeders, for if any one place were known to be the best we would all try to be there at once. There is however a growing tendency among buyers to use the market centers for this purpose, and on the whole it is a good plan with many points in favor. You can get what you want and just when you want it. Have more to select from and therefore an evener bunch of cattle. It takes less time and may not cost any more. There are drawbacks to this method as well, and not every man can be sure of getting just what he was looking for the first time he tries. A word of caution may not be out of place.

Cattle will look different confined in a close pen than at home in a large yard or open field. There is more danger of overlooking some physical weakness in the short time you have made up your mind to buy or not to buy.

You may not have the right valuation of the cattle you are looking at. A countryman is often known by his impetuosity. Don't be in a hurry. You have more time than money at your disposal just now. The cattle may be in no condition to buy at all for the reason of an extra fill. You can supply matter at home cheaper than you can pay for it there. Sixty pounds of water make a very material difference in the gains you make during the feeding period.

If you do not feel entirely competent to buy for yourself go to some reliable commission firm to help you select the cattle, to pay for them and see they are properly loaded on cars. Nine times out of ten it will be money well spent. If you are buying in the country the same points are to be observed but it will be necessary to use more care in order to secure cattle of the same class. I would say then buy the kind of cattle you need as cheaply as possible and *never* buy water. Throw out all undesirable steers such as weak legs, backs, lungs, lump jaws. Buy only those with good backs, head, legs and digestion and it will be your fault if he does not fatten.

WHAT THE SCOTT COUNTY LIVE STOCK IS ENTITLED TO.

A. P. Arp, before Scott County Farmers' Institute.

It would have been better if this subject had been cattle instead of live stock, as I am going to confine my remarks entirely to cattle. Some are entitled to more to eat and a different ration but that is not the class that I am going to deal with. I am going to deal with that class that constitutes the majority of Scott county's cattle. They eat more than they are entitled to because they don't pay for what they eat. But they are not to blame. They are doing the best they can. They are putting on beef with the same speed and putting it on in the same places that their ancestors did. And that is all any man has any right to expect. These cattle are all right to raise yoke oxen or material for Spanish bull fights which is just what the Spaniards raised them for and they are the breeders of the foundation of practically all the scrub cattle in the country The only difference between the scrub cattle of today and one hundred years ago is that those of today have been mixed and crossed back and forth with grades and an occasional pure bred of all the different breeds of cattle on the face of the earth. Now it is an undisputable fact that we have more of these cattle than we should have. In fact we should not have any.

Now before trying to prescribe a cure for these conditions let us first look for some of the causes. The foundation of these causes is that the owners of these cattle do not take enough interest in their stock to study the different breeds and their characteristics. But simply feed them and take care of them and when they get too many sell for what they can get. Then when they want a new herd header buy the one that is closest by and easiest got. Some will go a long way to get a cheap one regardless of the breed, shape, size, color or anything else. Now the great question is why do some farmers handle and mate their cattle in such a careless way. There are only a few sources through which the average farmer gets his education. The principal one is through what he reads. And right here is where a big part of his carelessness comes. Now just stop and think, what does the average farmer read? You will say that he lives on a mail route and gets his daily paper every day. Now I do not want to be understood as being opposed to mail routes and daily papers but I do want to say that in the hands of the average and especially the young farmer the daily paper is about the worst thing he can get hold of. If all the agricultural news and useful information to the farmer that is published in the average daily papers for one year could be squeezed out you would not get enough to drown a cow louse in. But on the other hand you will find everything that has a tendency to draw the farmer's attention away from what he should read and study. They will give you an account of all the robberies, murders, suicides and hold-ups from Maine to California and if some lawyer or politician should get sick or die you will see his picture and they will give you an account of his life and actually make it appear as though he really was the only man that we had any use for. But if the greatest breeder of improved stock on earth should get sick, die, be born, get married or anything else happen to him you would never find it out through the daily papers. And if he should die they would never tell you whether we had had any use for him or not, when the truth of it is that the breeders of improved stock have done more to enhance the value of this country than any other class of people. You must all admit that here I am laboring under extreme disadvantages for the reason that the class of farmers that is here present are really not the class that require such talking to. But it is that class that is at home today, chopping wood or hauling barley that we really want to get at, but we cannot reach them. They are at home with the mistaken idea that our institute is a humbug and that if there is anything going on that they should know the daily papers will tell them about it. I presume there are reporters here to pick out a word here and there and make it as short as they dare and still have the honor of reporting the institute. Then they will publish no agricultural information until our next institute.

I am not here to tell you how to keep boys on a farm but I do want to say that if you have a boy or several of them and want them to be good farmers I would advise you to have your daily papers stopped and in place of them have your name put on the experiment station bulletin mailing list and subscribe for the *Breeders Gazette* and one or two good farm papers. Then instead of reading of the rascality going on, instead of reading the dirty side of our country, read the clean, progressive and industrious side and study and learn how to breed, feed and take care of stock. And I will guarantee that the scrub cattle that do not pay for what they eat, that are seen on so many farms in Scott county will soon be replaced by better bred and more profitable cattle.

Now it is impossible for us all to have pure bred cattle, but it is not impossible for us all to have high grade well bred cattle. We can get them by using pure bred sires. But you will say that we cannot all have pure bred sires for the reason that some do not have the money to pay for one and besides there are not enough of them for us all. As for those that do not have the money to pay for one, they need him all the more. The more he is in debt the more important it is that he should have one. I do not know of an investment or improvement that a farmer can make that will bring him better returns than the use of a good pure bred sire. It is almost impossible to lay too much stress on the sire. He is always 50 per cent of the herd. If you have one or two inferior cows it is only their calves that are affected but with an inferior sire the whole calf crop must suffer. Then as for there not being enough for us all to get one that is undoubtedly true and will be so for a long time to come. But we could make more and better use of those we have got. In the first place we could use them longer than is generally done and out of every ten go to the slaughter house just when their usefulness for breeding purposes be-gins. Then there should also be more company sires. It would often be less trouble and expense to take your cows to a neighbor than to have a sire of your own breaking fences and getting in with your neighbors' cattle and with your own young heifers that you do not yet want bred. There are a few cases in Scott county that our secretary asked me to speak about. In these cases farmers have invested in improved stock and did not re-ceive the benefit that they had expected. These cases all have about the same cause and require the same cure. The people get excited and think that by buying one or two pure bred sires they will in four or five years have a whole yard full of high grade cows and eight or ten pure bred heifers. When they get their first sire, which is always a calf about six months old, they put him to work as fast as they can. Then when their first crop of calves comes they all have the color and marking of their daddy and their owner is simply delighted and when they are about six months or a year old it would be a dangerous thing for any one to tell the owner that the breed he had selected was not the right one. This is about the time when the excitement is at its fever heat and they can not wait for their calves to mature but they want to raise three-fourths and they will get their second sire which in turn is also a six months calf. Then they mate their immature heifers with this immature calf. Then when these calves that are sired by a calf have calves from a calf they have three-fourths bred calves that will always be calves and when they find it out they get disgusted with the breed and say it is too small and peaked or fine boned or something and they try some other color with exactly the same result. Do not expect to raise big, strong cows from calves. You never see a breeder try to do it. Their herd headers are always from three to twelve or fourteen years old and their cows are kept as long as they will breed and often five or six years after they have quit breeding which accounts for the lean, poor looking cows that you often see in a breeder's herd.

Now to conclude, I want to say that the cattle of Scott county are en-titled to at least three things that the majoriy do not get. First, that their owners study and learn how to feed, breed and take care of them. Then second, I say that every animal of the bovine family in Scott county is entitled to be sired by a good pure bred or high grade male. And third, that the cows that have the honor of having such a sire are entitled to be mated to a sire of the same breed so that they will have a chance to do for their offspring what nature intended them to.

THE COW PASTURE.

J. J. Taylor, before the Winnebago County Farmers' Institute.

In keeping stock on the farm there is no one thing of more importance than the pasture. Cows will give more milk, young cattle will grow
faster and give us better returns for the expense than any other feed. I
will not undertake to tell what constitute the best pastures. The most I
want to do is to set the farmers to thinking, to take notice of their own
pastures and that of their neighbors. When riding through the country,
notice the condition of pastures in general. Some will be low, wet and
marshy, with nothing but coarse grass; others with part dry land eaten
so close there seems to be nothing left, and then there is the upland pasture that is covered with weeds, so much so, that grass will not grow to
any extent. Now how long would it take a man with a pair of shears to
clip off enough grass for a cow a day in some of these pastures? Is it
any wonder that cows do not give much milk? This is too common, right
in June when there should be a surplus to help out later in the season. Did
any of you ever have the cows get out some night and get in the garden,
or where there was plenty of feed, and see what an increase there was in
the flow of milk? Now, that is just the condition our pastures should be
in all summer, having an abundance of good feed and then you would see
what a profit there would be in cows. When the pasture is not eaten close
there is a great deal more feed grows on that same land. Take a pasture
that has more feed for a year or two than the stock could eat and we can
keep more stock on that same land, and have plenty of feed, than we can
when it is eaten close every year.

I believe the best and also the cheapest way to rid the pasture, as well
as the rest of the farm, of weeds, is to keep a few sheep. They will do more
and also do it better than to have an extra man. The care is not great to
fence a farm sheep tight. Two extra wires, that is a five-wire fence, put
up in good shape and kept tight, will be all right to keep sheep. And right
here is where so many fail in keeping their cattle in the pasture. They
let the wires get slack so cattle crowd through, and soon you have crawlers
that a fence will not keep. Never have slack wires and you'll never have
crawlers, unless you buy of your neighbor who never fixes his fence until
the cattle have learned the trick.

I think we have men here that can tell us what grasses are best for the
different pastures. If we must use the low lands for pasture, get rid of
the surplus water and seed with some suitable grass; then it is all right;
it makes a good, permanent pasture. But with good, tilable land I think
we get better returns with a rotation, besides I think the chances are better
for keeping the stock healthy by turning the land over every few years
and changing the pastures to other parts of the farm. I know this is so
with sheep and I do not see why it should not be with other stock. The
great trouble seems to be, that any land not suitable for anything else is
put in pasture and also as little land as possible. But this will never do
if we are to make any profit on the cow. There must be good feed and
plenty of it. We have some low land in our pasture that is well seeded

with blue grass and white clover, which the stock do not eat when there is plenty of feed on the dryer ground, but in the fall, after it freezes, they will eat there until it is gone or covered with snow. So by having a surplus through the summer it is not wasted, but only kept for winter use.

THE HOG.

W. S. Farquhar, before Page County Farmers' Institute.

The great antiquity of the hog is fixed from the fact that several fossil species have been found in deluvial deposits of Europe and allied species in India. His native country was Europe, Asia and Africa. The utility of the hog as an article of food is in great measure owing to the remarkable fecundity of the animal, it being capable of reproduction at about one year of age and producing from eight to twelve and even more at a birth twice every year. Hence it would look as though the supply would always be equal to the demand. Vauban has estimated the product of a single sow with only six at a time in ten generations to be about six million five hundred thousand, of which he deducts five hundred thousand on account of accidental death, but his sows must have lived longer than they do now and he must not have been troubled much with hog cholera.

The filthy habits of the hog are due in great measure to its domestication. The *wild* hog is cleanly and selects its food chiefly from vegetable substances. The hog has the propensity to wallow in the mire chiefly to protect itself from insects and flies to which its thin covered skin exposes it. The wild hog is in this respect no more filthy than the elephant, the rhinocerous, or the hippotamus.

No animals displays the changes arising from domestication more than the hog as may be seen by contrasting the large, lean, savage, long legged wild boar leading dogs and horses and men a long and weary chase with the small domestic, plump, short legged, well bred hog of today, scarcely able to get to his feed or from one side of his pen to the other. The wild hog is a native of the Eastern Hemisphere, including Britain, from which the Berkshires were developed. In America, Australia and the Polynesian group the hog was unknown originally in a natural condition but having been turned out everywhere by the early navigators who discovered the coasts and islands of the Pacific he has propogated his species so rapidly that he is everywhere abundant, either in a state of confinement or a state of nature. During the middle ages the wild boar abounded in England and France and in England he was protected by the game laws during the tenth and eleventh centuries. Hunting the wild hog in the old world used to be one of the great sports of the times and it is said that the flesh of the wild hog was much superior to that of the domestic animal of today. It was a singular fact, however, that the flesh of the boar was superior to that of the sow, while in the domestic animal the flesh of the boar is unfit for food after they attain any age. While boar hunting was in its palmy days, a particular dog was cultivated for the sport which was of great value and it is said that the full grown, wild hog could give an Arab courser or a fox hound an equal chase for twenty or thirty minutes, after which generally he showed signs of hostility and often inflicted serious wounds to his pursuers.

So great was the fecundity of swine in Virginian forests that in eighteen years after the founding of Jamestown by the English and introduction of swine by them, the inhabitants were compelled to palisade the town to keep them out and history tells us that for some years after it seemed to be a question whether the white man, the Indian or the swine were going to take possession of the new world.

The breeding and management of swine is *one of*, if not *the* most important agricultural interests of the great west and to be successful none but the best breeds should be allowed on the farm.

The fecundity of swine leaves no excuse for holding to a bad breed of swine. A good male hog of any breed can be bought so reasonable that no one can afford to raise anything but the best of its kind. There is no class of farm stock that pays better as between indifferent and good breeds than hogs and the wonder is that in some sections of the country farmers still cling to a breed of grunters that will always greet you with a snort and a boh-o-o and which no filling can fill fully, a match for the average dog, always ready to eat anything that falls in their way, even to a half grown kid, but which when wanted for meat are nowhere to be found.

There is no class of stock that will respond to good general care and management better than the hog. We see men today that seem to have a fascination for nice horses or for feeding cattle, men who will throw all their thought and energies to producing these kinds of stock which is all right in its place but how few farmers get down to their best on a drove of hogs. When we consider the origin of the hog of today in his natural state when it took him from two to five years to develop, when his destructive habits made him a menace to the community in which he dwelt and made him cost more than he was worth when he was developed, and you did not know whether it would be you or your neighbor that would get him at last and compare him with the hog of today in all his ease and comfort, and development, we may well say, "Behold what man hath wrought." I have often said, and I think facts justify the assertion, that there is no industry in the great west that interests so many men and helps to make so many homes as the hog of today. I feel that there is no branch of western farming if gone into intelligently and persistently that will yield a quicker, a surer or a larger return than the raising of good hogs. There are many products of the farm that cannot be utilized by swine and one cannot keep up the fertility of a large farm with hogs alone, yet the fact remains that when you sell your hogs the balance is almost always on the right side of the ledger while in the case of cattle one has to hunt for some one else to help him to let loose, and when he does let go he wonders what it was that hit him, and in regard to the breeding of swine it is as in almost anything else, nothing else beats a good start and

I think many of us fail right here. I think that in order to get a good start in a drove of pigs and to do one's best much depends on the treatment and feed of the sows before the pigs are born and even the management of the sows before they are bred. I think in order to get large litters the sows should not be too fat and should be gaining in flesh at time of breeding and that sows should be fed food such as oats, bran and oil meal or some of the other by-products in order to keep pigs of good bone, which I think is one of the things hardest to keep up to the standard of hog raising. Then another critical time in the pig's life is the first two or three weeks after birth. We get anxious and feed the sow too heavy and too rich food which is often an injury to the sow and detrimental to the pigs, thereby often ruining what, under proper treatment, would have made good hogs. I know that some men will think that this is all nonsense but I am sure it makes lots of difference what is fed to our breeding animals before they give birth to their young. Have any of you ever noticed a bunch of fall calves that were dropped in September or October. If so you will have noticed that they almost always are of more than ordinary size and always have extra large bone and muscle, the reason being that the foetus was developed when the mother had nature's food for her to eat.

The hog has a reputation which it does not deserve, namely of peculiar filthiness of habits but there are none of our farm animals that will if possible keep their bed so scrupulously clean. The too common filthiness of the pig pen is rather the fault of the owner than of the occupant and a dry and clean sleeping place is of great importance in the keeping of hogs. Neither is the hog the stupid animal he is generally given credit with being. There is no animal that if he gets where he ought not to be and is pushed, can better remember where he got in or out than the hog. As with other branches of live stock you cannot starve profit into a hog. As in other things it holds true that what costs little brings little in return. I am not here to argue whether he should have all the grain he could eat from the start or should be raised largely on grass for the first six months of his life. I think that depends somewhat, but there are others here to take up this phase of the subject but he should have plenty or some kind of food from the time he begins to eat *for himself*. Another requisite for a good crop of pigs is sunshine and warmth, two things conspicuous by their absence this last year, but warm weather does not generally come until about a certain time of the year and men looking over their last year's crop of pigs generally conclude that the early ones did best and often breed too soon, bringing their pigs too early, entailing loss that they blame on the weather.

But in the development of the hog all has not been a bed of roses. With his early maturity, his fattening qualities, and his docility came disease, sickness and death, and often when we have had our calculations made as to what we would do with our hog money, and we were struck with the cholera we were made to quote the words of the poet, "Things are not what they seem."

Another thought here. Is there any connection between the scarcity of corn and the high price of feed last year and the present healthful condition of the hogs of the west today or is it due to other natural causes, I will leave this with you to decide.

But the hog with all his civilization, education and refinement still retains some of his natural characteristics. It is true that in his domestic state, we will call him lazy, and hear men speaking of a man when he is drunk and say that he is as drunk as a hog but that is not just, nor is it complimentary *to the hog I mean*, for there is no civilized hog but would have more sense than to get into such a condition.

There are several allusions to swine in the Bible, one of which was by Solomon when he compared a jewel in a swine's snout to a woman without discretion, and Solomon had a good deal of experience with women and I expect he knew what he was talking about. And again in the days of our Saviour here on earth we have an account of Him casting the devils out of two men and allowing them to enter into the swine, nor are the men all dead upon whom a similar miracle would be a great blessing to mankind. Neither are the swine all drowned in the sea that are affected in a similar way and I fear that it will take several crosses to eliminate this one of his prominent characteristics, but we have the promise that in the latter days Satan shall be bound and perhaps then the hog as well as man will get relief and will be more easily governed. And *yet* the hog with his indomitable disposition to have his own way and many other characteristics found in the heart of man is truly the western farmer's best domestic friend. Truly great is the American hog.

THE POLAND-CHINA HOG.

Wm. Hester, before the Dallas County Farmers' Institute.

The Poland-China hog is an American. He cannot boast of an ancestry coming down from the old world, or of centuries of conquest and victory. True, the component parts of which the breed is composed came from the ends of the earth, but as a distinct breed, he is an American.

No only is he an American, but he is a product of the west and adapted to western ideas and western conditions. The broad prairies and fertile valleys of the middle and western states are his native habitat, and our bursting corn cribs and rich clover pastures are congenial to his taste, and conducive to his happiness. Moreover, the Poland-China hog is a modern production, the result of modern thought, the outgrowth of modern needs —or, briefly stated, up-to-date. Assuming that most of you are as familiar as I am with the origin and history of the breed, I will not dwell on these, but pass on to a discussion of the merits and demerits of these well-known and popular swine.

Something like a half century ago, some prominent farmers and breeders of Ohio, then the center of pork production, becoming dissatisfied with existing breeds with a view to producing a breed adapted to the corn belt. There is some controversy as to the breeds used for this purpose, but it seems to be established that the Poland and big boned China entered into to make up the new breed, hence the name adopted later when the various breeders organized into a record company.

It is doubtful if any of the several men instrumental in the founding of this new breed had any conception of the wonderful results that would grow out of the movement. Truly, they "builded broader than they knew." The big spotted breed soon became popular in Ohio, and spreading to the other states westward soon became the leading variety throughout the corn belt, driving out and superseding other and older breeds. The original Poland-China hog, however, was not the Poland-China of today. The earlier specimens of the breed were large and coarse, with long, deep bodies, coarse heads and large, drooping ears. They were spotted black and white with occasional splashes of sandy. They could be fed to very heavy weights, and were well adapted to the then prevailing custom of feeding, being usually fattened at a year and a half old. But American push and energy demanded a hog of quicker growth, and early maturity. The custom of feeding until 18 months old gave place to the method of pushing from start to finish, and finishing at 9 or 10 months. It was here the breeders' skill became apparent in transforming the coarse, ungainly type of an early day to the smooth, symmetrical type of today, the smoothest, most symmetrical, easiest feeding and most profitable hog on the face of the earth. It is claimed by some that this fining process has been overdone; that size and vigor have been sacrificed for fancy points. It may be that in many instances this is true, and, from the almost universal demand for size and bone, I believe the limit has been reached, and perhaps in many cases, passed, and the breeder who would promote the best interests of the breed, and incidentally find a ready sale for his product, should give due attention to size, if a little less to style, finish, etc. Another objection that is sometimes urged against the breed is want of fecundity, and we hear advocates of other breeds boasting of large litters— 12, 15 and 18 pigs at a litter. But who wants a sow to have 18 pigs? I do not; nor 15, nor 12. It is more than a sow has any business with; more than she can properly nourish with ordinary care, and with the best of care there is likely to be several unprofitable runts, or a whole litter stunted. The sow that will uniformly produce six to nine strong, healthy pigs, and suckle them properly, is the true money maker. Taking Volume 2807, American Record, and taking 100 pedigrees entirely at random, and noting number of litter in each, I find on footing up an average of eight pigs to the litter which is, I think, a sufficient answer to the objections under consideration.

The growth of the Poland-China hog in public favor, considering the short time it has been before the public, is unparalled. From an humble beginning in a few counties in Ohio, it has rapidly spread over the western states, the great corn and pork producing states, driving out and superseding other breeds, until now perhaps fully two-thirds of the hogs marketed from these states are more or less pure Poland-China blood.

From a small beginning also, the breeding of registered stock has grown to gigantic proportions. Four large record companies are doing business in the western states, representing thousands of registered animals. Among the great sires that have been instrumental in bringing the breed up to its present popularity, have been "Old U. S. 779" by "World Beater," "Tom Corwin 2d" by "Star of the West," "Success 1999" by "Tom Corwin 2d," "Adam and King Butler" by "Victor Black U. S.," "One Price," "Free Trade," the "Tecumsehs," the "Wilkes Family," and so on, while some of the great dams have been "Bess Stebbins," "Corn Shellingbarger," "Lady Duffield," "Butler Girl," "White Face," "Courtney," "Early Rose," "Lady U. S." and many others. "Tom Corwin 2d" and "Old Black U. S.," each a giant in his day, had much to do in reducing the size and increasing the symmetry of the Poland-China. Both were small, or medium, in size, compact and dark in color. The "Wilkes," the "Tecumsehs," and the "Mediums," are of common origin, and are much the same in general characteristics. They are usually of large, growthy type combined in general characteristics. They are usually of large growthy type combined with plenty of style and finish, quick, easy feeders, smooth coated, good color— in fact, combining about all the good qualities that have made the breed famous. But to make a long story short, I claim for the Poland-China hog, that they are the most popuar, the most profitable, the nearest perfect of all the many breeds of swine; that they are bred by more breeders, fed by more feeders, and have sold for higher prices, than any other hog; that they are easy feeders, good mothers, of quiet disposition, and adapted to the rigor of our climate; that they excel in the show ring, in the breeding pen, and in the fed lot; that as a breed they combine more good qualities, and present fewer defects, than any other breed; that they are an artist's dream, a lady's favorite, and a mortgage lifter. May their shadows never grow less.

ECONOMICAL PRODUCTION OF PORK.

Geo. V. Fowler, before Black Hawk County Farmers' Institute.

That is to say, make use of the pig some one named him the great mortgage lifter, while our Irish friends call him "The gintleman that pays the rint") as to get the greatest possible gain in growth and weight at the least cost, chances of disease considered.

I seems to me there is a mistake in assigning this subject to me, for it is of vast importance, especially to the people of this vicinity, the most productive section of the state which produces the most corn, beef and pork, according to its area, of any state in the Union. And it is only because of the gratitude I feel on account of being located in so highly a favored section that I consent to make an effort to assist in promoting this product.

As to this subject we are now to consider, would say it is all included in the statement of Hon. D. M. McPherson when he says, "Furnish to every animal perfect comfort and a balanced ration." Indeed, I doubt whether an animal can have perfect comfort without the balanced ration, so I would say, "Furnish to the swine family, which are the most economical meat producers of all animals, a balanced ration." This being settled, each shall use his utmost efforts to secure this ration at lowest possible cost, whether purchased off the farm for cash, or indirectly on the farm with the equivalent of cash. The method will differ to some extent according to the individual as to his knowledge of the contents of the different feeds and the conditions under which he can produce or purchase the same.

Some one says how are we to know what a balanced ration is. Well, we all know nature makes no mistakes, so we will commence with milk— whole milk, which surely is a balanced ration for the young pig, which we find to contain the following nutrients water 87.5, protein 3.2, carbohydrates 5, fat 3.6. Now, the ratio is what most concerns us, which is to be found by multiplying the fat by 2½, add to the carbohydrates and divide by the protein, which in this case gives us 1 to 4.4 which is the ratio of whole milk. As skim milk and whey are among the products, many think they must have for pigs. We will figure a ration from these products.

First, skim milk with a ratio of 1 to 1.9 and oats 1 to 6.5, we will add the two ratios and divide by 2 which we find to be 1 to 4.2 using 10 pounds oats to 100 pounds milk.

Now, if the feeders wish to use whey instead, which has a ratio of 1 to 6.6, he may use oil meal, which has a ratio of 1 to 1.5, and middlings. which has a ratio of 1 to 4.7. Adding these three ratios and dividing by 3 you have a ratio of 1 to 4.2, same as the skim milk ration. In this case 6 pounds each oil meal and middlings would be used to 100 pounds of whey. Whey and oats are practically the same, were it not for the bulk skim milk and whey could be used half and half and make the balance. In this case middlings alone added would make a balance.

But another party says I have neither skim milk nor whey. Well, we are sorry for him but still he can use one-half wheat, rye, oats or barley, and the other half, the "better half," should be oil meal, gluten soy bean, or cow pea. So each of these mixtures will give practically whole milk.

The above ration should be widened as the pig grows older until the last stage of fattening should be about the ratio of 1 pound oats, barley, wheat or rye to 2 pounds of corn. Blue grass in the latter case would balance the corn.

On our own farm we use a system of pasture with peas, rape, oats and rye. Mr. McPherson says young clover and peas have practically the same value per 100 pounds as whole milk and to them may be added as pasture rape, alfalfa, soy bean and cow pea, each being a fine balance with corn. So it will be seen it is comparatively cheap to balance the ration while on pasture.

The rule followed by Mr. McPherson and others of our Canadian friends (who are as good feeders as I have ever met) is to feed 1 pound of corn to every 60 pounds the hogs weigh and have found this to give best results. However, do not feed corn to speak of even while on pasture till they weigh about 60 pounds. In this way the pig himself gathers the most valuable part of the ration, viz., the protein part, and at the same time fertility left where most needed, which in most cases is worth the rent of the land thus used.

Now, to balance in winter we have found sorghum very economical and last winter, a year ago, had 27 brood sows which we fed in this way, and as sorghum is wider or richer in carbohydrates, we then looked for some feed narrow or rich in protein, so we took gluten meal, which I believe for most purposes to be most satisfactory. This we used, giving 2 pounds each per day with one-half bundle sorghum, and they came through in good shape having good success with each one of them and saved 150 fine pigs, although they came in March.

This winter we wintered 40 in the same way and first one so far farrowed yesterday, giving us 15 fine strong pigs. We have four fields about four acres each on which we pasture the hogs, one a clover pasture which we do not wish to plow at all, but can from this open into each of the others at will. We now have two of these in rye, which we expect to pasture until June 1st, when will plow and drill in 6 pounds of Dwarf Essex rape to the acre and cultivate same as corn. We had double rows 7 inches apart. This will be ready to pasture in about five weeks and when we take the hogs off the rye we turn them on the third field which we sowed to rape, peas and oats as early in spring as we could, and turned on to when 5 inches high, then sow again the last of August. It is well to keep them off the rape in wet weather.

It is well to note with this system of pasture that the candidate for the packing house is enabled to spend a large part of his short life in the open air and gather at will from one-third to one-half of his sustenance which makes a balanced ration and under such conditions our Canadian friends believe we will lose all opportunity to learn anything by experience at least of the ravages of the so-called hog cholera.

THE HOG.

W. W. Burns, before the Iowa County Farmers' Institute.

Mr. Chairman, Ladies and Gentlemen: The subject assigned to me is one of much importance to every farmer. There are a great many possibilities and many probabilities in the hog business today.

The hog is the poor man's friend. He is often and justly called the mortgage lifter. He is at first small and weak as compared with many other domestic animals. They will increase or decrease faster than the larger domestic animals. The hog with careful attention and care is the renter's rent payer—is the debtor's debt payer—the mortgagor's mortgage lifter—the farmer's true and valued friend and the up-to-date breeder's delight. He will respond quickly to good care, will make money quickly and fast if of the proper type and given the proper care.

42

We have several good and useful breeds of hogs, and it is your duty and privilege to study the breeding and characteristics of the different breeds and decide which as a breed would suit you and your surroundings the best, always buying or picking on the best individuals for breeding purposes. Do not in any case sell the largest and best ones because they will bring a little more money at the present time. But retain them in your herd and try to improve every year. Use the same judgment in all Kinds of live stock. Use the best that you can get. The good money as we often term it is not made in raising the average or under the average. either crops or live stock of any kind. But the best money is made in raising more than the average of everything. I raise the Poland-China hogs. Why? Because I believe they suit me and my customers better than any other breed. They are good feeders, quick maturers, easy keepers, good mothers, plenty of size, generally good color and prize winners in the hottest of swine shows. I will give brief description of what I would call a good Poland-China sow.

Commencing with the head it should be short and wide, cheeks full, jaws broad, forehead high and wide, wide between the eyes, face slightly dished and surface even and regular; eyes, large, prominent, bright, clear and free from wrinkles or much fat around them; ears, thin, soft, silky, tips pointing forward and slightly outward and under full control of animal and should be of the same size and shape; neck, wide, deep, short, and nicely arched; shoulders, broad, deep and full, and carrying width from top to bottom; chest, large, wide, deep, roomy, with plenty of room for the vital organs with a good girth around heart, wide between fore legs which should be six inches apart in a full grown hog; back and loin should be broad, slightly arched carrying same width from shoulders to ham, surface even and free from lumps, broad on top indicating a well sprung rib; sides, full, smooth, firm and deep, carrying size from shoulder to ham; ribs, long, strong and well sprung at top and bottom; underline, wide, straight and full, and as low at flank as at bottom of the chest; flank, full and out even with the surrounding portion of body; hams, broad, full, long and wide, lower part should be full and well covered with flesh; legs, large, firm, straight, well set apart and squarely under the body, well muscled and wide above knee and hock, capable of holding up more than its own weight, pastern, short; feet, firm, short, tough and free from defects; tail, well set on, smooth, tapering, and carried in a nice curl; coat, fine, straight, smooth; color, black, white in face or on lower jaw, white on feet and lower part of each leg, also bunch of tail; size, should be of good size for age, two years or over should weigh 500 lbs., at 18 months about 350 to 400 lbs., 12 months 300 lbs., 6 months about 150 lbs; action and style, should be easy, quick and graceful and attractive; condition, healthy, skin clear, soft and mellow to the touch; disposition, quiet, gentle and easily handled.

Now as I have tried to describe a good hog I will try to tell you a few things about raising them. As I told you pick out the best you have always selecting pigs from large, even litters. Try to get large sows and a little fancier male. Use well matured animals at all times. Do not have breeding hogs too fat but after they are mated you may profitably increase their weight slowly up till farrowing time. Keep corn away from them as much as possible at this period. Feed as much green feed as you possibly can at all times. Feed slops made from middlings, shorts, poor grade flour and brān meal, plenty of oats green and soaked and it is well to scatter some loose over the pasture in winter and keep them busy and give plenty of exercise. Oats, barley and rye ground together make a good feed for brood sows. Pumpkins are fine for brood sows this time of the years. Feed regular and in a good, clean place have plenty of pure fresh water handy at all times for the hogs to drink. Keep salt and ashes mixed and in a handy place so the hogs will have free access to it at all times. Do not feed all the different kinds of medicine that people tell you that are good for hogs. Some will kill. Keep your hogs healthy by proper feeding, plenty of exercise, keeping their pens well cleaned and disinfected. Keep the lice down if possible. Do not allow your hogs to sleep in a draught of wind. Do not allow diseased hogs on the place. Keep the hogs on clover, blue grass or rape pastures as long as you can. Feed a balanced ration and plenty of bone and muscle forming food. Get one or more good farm journals, read and study the experience of others and tell your experience. If any one here would like to take the best hog journal that I know any thing about I would cite you to *The American Swine Herd*, published at Chicago. It is a monthly journal, comes full of hog news and can be had in clubs for 25 cents per year. There are several good hog papers and any of them can be had at a reasonable price.

We should be careful not to keep too many brood sows in one place. It is better to have them in several places for their health. Keep track of farrowing time and be willing to set up nights if needed. Get sow used to her farrowing place by shutting her in it for about ten days or two weeks beforehand. Have her gentle and quiet and avoid all noise possible. Be ready to give aid if needed or take the pigs to the house if needed. Feed sparingly for a few days but of the same feed as sow has been used to. Do not feed for at least twelve hours and then feed sparingly at first, gradually increasing but always feed intelligently and regularly. Remember that 40 per cent of all pigs farrowed die before they reach the markets. This is why the hog business is uncertain. What we should do is to study preventives. It is much easier to prevent than to cure. The axe is the best, surest and cheapest cure for a great many diseases. Too many hate to use it. Our lesson is, study preventives and if you do prevent you will not need a remedy for cure. I had the disease once in my herd but I am sure it was by not having hogs in the proper condition to guard off the disease when they came in contact with the disease or when the disease was brought to the herd. I believe the diseases are brought on by improper care, improper feeding, poor places to sleep, one kind of food and not a variety of feeds, lack of plenty of fresh water, kept in a small, muddy pen where exercise would be impossible for them. In-breed has its effect on bringing on disease. The use of small and immature breeding stock, a radical change from one kind of feed to another and the feeding of all kinds of medicine that some people tell you will cure and keep your herd in first-class condition. I believe it will pay any good, up-to-date farmer to always buy a recorded male or at least one that can be recorded and then you can keep track of your breeding and avoid using a pig of the same family as the one you just used.

Hoping that what I have written will furnish some thoughts for discussion, I very much regret that I cannot be present with you and help discuss the subject.

THE SILO ON THE DAIRY FARM.

H. C. Carpenter, before Black Hawk County Farmers' Institute.

Mr. President, Ladies and Gentlemen: Silo experience in the United States now covers about twenty-five years, and so far as the economy and advantages of feeding it are concerned, there appears to be a strong conviction that good silage is a superior and cheap food. After eight years of practical experience with ensilage, I have no hesitation in saying that no dairy farmer in the state can afford to be without a silo. Even on the so-called "natural grass farm," a moderate use or ensilage will prove beneficial. Now, if this is true and I am sure that time will demonstrate that it is, then the more rapidly farmers adopt the system, the better.

More actual food material can be produced from an acre of corn than from any other of our common farm crops. Land capable of producing two tons of hay will, as a rule, produce twenty tons of ensilage having at least 25 per cent of dry matter, or actual food material; 40,000 lbs. of ensilage equals 10,000 lbs. of dry matter, 2 tons of hay equals 3,000 lbs. of dry matter. It is safe to say, therefore, that three times as much substance may be produced from a given area of corn as from a like area of grass. Then green food is especially favorable to the production of milk.

The succulent pasture grass in May and June is without an equal as a milk producing food. Mangels and other roots, when fed in combination with other fodder, are known to have a very beneficial effect, and with ensilage the same has been observed. The writer in Bulletin No. 11 of the New Hampshire Experiment station says: "There are those who say that a pound of digestible matter in one substance, is as good as a pound in any and all other substances, and that succulence adds nothing to the value of food." This I do not regard as proven by practice. In this bulletin it was shown that 100 lbs. of digestible matter in a ration made up of skim milk and corn meal was equal to 146.6 lbs. of digestible matter in ration chemically identical but made up of corn meal and middlings. Practically there can be no doubt that a pound of food material in the skim milk ration was superior to a pound in the mixed grain ration, and I believe this was due largely to the favorable condition in which the digestive and assimilative organs were kept by the skim milk ration. This being true, I see no reason why pasture grass, roots, or ensilage may not be likewise more valuable than dried fodder. In fact, I am convinced that foods containing a large per cent of water keep the system in such tone that it is able to make better use of the food digested.

The physiological condition of the animal may be such that this digested matter may in one case be utilized to far better advantage than in the other. The problem then, is not one of efficiency of food so much as efficiency of machine and it is this animal efficiency which succulent or watery food increases. Conveniences and cheapness of storing is a point in favor of the silo. A corn crop having been produced, must in some way be preserved for winter feeding. Stooking the entire crop as soon as the ears are well glazed, and allowing it to dry for a month or more, husking the ears, mowing away the stalks, shelling and grinding on the farm, or taking to and from the mill and expense of grinding, all bear too heavily on the farmer. To reduce the cost of production is the great problem in agricultural progress, and it must be done by reducing the amount of human labor which enters into farm products. A system of stooking corn in large stooks and leaving them on the field until wanted for feeding purposes, has been and is practiced to some extent; it saves labor, but wastes the crop and is inconvenien in many ways. Curing the crop and storing is practically impossible on a large scale, since the amount of water to be dried out is very great, and the weather frequently unfavorabe; in a small way it may be practical, but the disadvantages more than offset the advantages. The silo, while not an ideal storage vault, does combine *more good points* and less bad ones than any method yet devised, for the following reasons:

The farmer who has a silo is about as independent of the weather as any man can be. Heavy rain, it is true, will prevent the storage of ensilage, but aside from that nothing interrupts this kind of harvesting; light rains and showers, while making the work disagreeable, does not put a stop to it, and when once in the silo, all danger of imperfect curing which so often injures the crop harvested in the old way, is past. The season is practically lengthened from two to three weeks, since it is not desirable to have the corn for the silo much past the dent stage, hence a variety may be planted for this purpose which stands no show of ripening even one year in ten, and later varieties of corn are of larger growth and produce more actual food per acre.

This gain is very important in our state. Again, if from unfavorable weather in May, planting is delayed, as already stated, until the first days of June, there is very little risk connected with the crop for the silo, where a crop for husking would be almost certain to be cut off by the fall frosts. The early date at which the land is cleared makes it possible to seed to rye or other winter grain. The cost of harvesting provided the crop is planted within reasonable distance of the silo, is reduced to a low point. Our silo was filled the past season in 11 days, including chores which involved milking 27 cows, caring for 10 horses and 50 hogs. Probably not ten days of actual labor was expended with four men and a boy ten years old to drive corn wagon and three teams. Capacity 150 tons; cost of filling about 75 cents per ton.

I wish to give you the testimony of Jas. M. Turner, of the great Springdale Farm. He says: "I am keeping 300 cows for dairy purposes, besides my herd of Herefords and Short-horns, and every animal was given during the past winter, two rations per diem of silage, amounting generally to about 45 pounds per head, with a noon ration of hay or oat straw, and I have never seen a dairy produce more milk, or cattle in general come out at the end of the season in finer shape that did ours. The silage was also fed daily awice to a large flock of Shropshire sheep as well as to the standard bred trotting horses, the Clydesdales, and the Shetland ponies. I wintered in this way nearly 200 head of horses, consisting of brood mares, colts, and fillies, and I am safe in saying that we have never done as well with our stock of all kinds under any other system of feeding. Our flockmaster was somewhat anxious until after the lambs dropped, but now that he has saved 196 lambs for 122 ewes, his face is wreathed in smiles and he gives the ensilage system the strongest endorsement."

He says: "We gathered last season all the way from twenty to thirty tons of ensilage per acre, the quantity varying with the various conditions of the soil. Until the advent of the silo, farmers and stockmen in this vicinity were about discouraged with the outlook for live stock, but now we believe we can successfully compete with the great ranchman whose stock is carried on the public domain and who are called upon to contribute nothing toward the support of the highways, schools, churches, and other evidences of civilization. I believe a cow can be maintained all the year round on each and every acre that a farm contains by a judicious system of soiling and ensilage, so that farmers occupying 80 acres of land can keep 75 or 80 cows quite as well as they are now maintaining twenty."

This strong testimony for silage copied from the *Breeders' Gazette*, should have weight with every farmer who care to produce all possible from an acre of land.

Another strong testimony for the silo is that of Oatman Bros. of Dundee, Ill. Ten years ago when the Oatman "boys" purchased the farm it was considered the poorest in that section of the state. The previous owner had been trying to keep thirty cows and himself on the 200 acres of land and had made a failure. The cattle were starved and the farmer bankrupt when these progressive young business men took hold of the property. They are now the owners of one of the best farms in the country. They said in relating their experience: "We determined to make an experiment and built our first silo. It was a success though rather a primitive affair. The cattle ate the ensilage and their condition greatly improved. The next year we built another silo and increased our herd of cattle. That has been going on every year until now we have on that farm 250 head of live stock including 220 milch cows. This is on the 200 acres where the former owner starved thirty cows almost to death and gave up, only when forced to the wall. Every year the value of the soil increases. The manure from 220 cows is sufficient to more than restore the land. We have only 50 acres of pasture for all our cows and are selling our hay to neighboring farmers; some of our milk is sent to Chicago, and the rest is used in our factories. The farm yielded a gross revenue last year of over $16,000. I would not take a check for $12,000 for the net profit." That is the result of the adoption of the silo and ensilage system. The Oatman Bros. claim that they made their land pay a net income of $60 per acre the year these statements were published.

Among the great farmers of Kane county, Ill., who have successfully introduced the system may be mentioned Mark Dunham (now deceased), the proprietor of the largest stock farm in the world. Mr. Dunham is a man that makes few mistakes, and elaborate series of experiments has convinced him that the silo is the greatest invention in the world for a stock raiser. During the winter this article appeared in *Hoard's Dairyman*. Mark Dunham's barns at Wayne, Ill., contained nearly a thousand horses whose feed consisted largely of ensilage. He says: "The food agrees with, and is relished by the horses, and I propose to greatly increase the capacity of my silos."

Mr. Tillson, in Norfolk county, Ontario, spares no time or money to perfect his ensilage, 1,000 tons of which is put in silo every year.

In a late issue of the *Rural New Yorker*, John Gould says: "The confession of C. E. Chapman, that all roads for the economical feeding of cattle, especially cows, ends at the silo, is valuable reading for those who have been waiting for years to see the outcome of the silo "fad" and have tried everything they could hear of as a substitute for ensilage, to abandon each in turn and in so doing put far more labor into the venture than would build and fill a silo. As compared with the roots the Ohio station found that 100 pounds of good ensilage was worth more than twice its weight in beets or roots, and that while ensilage was a sustaining food, roots were little better than an appetizer.

I have endeavored to compile a long array of testimony in this paper from reliable men and successful feeders, with the additional testimony of several experiment stations, where experiments have been extended over a term of years, which should be most convincing. In a personal discussion of this subject, some have said to me, "I am only waiting to be convinced that the silo is an advantage and I shall have one." If there are any other doubting Thomases here today, I ask them to consider the testimony of the prominent men of whom I have spoken. "We have fed our herd of 100 Jerseys on ensilage morning and night, with hay at noon, for five years, and each year we find the result more and more encouraging. We find that with one-half the quantity of grain we used to feed with hay, if fed with ensilage gives us two per cent more cream and a better flow or milk." This from John Mayer, Mahwah, N. Y.

Prof. Alvord, Secretary of the Dairy Division in the Department of Agriculture of Washington, D. C., found in a test made at Houghton farm, that a greater per cent of the fats of the milk were converted into butter when the cows were fed on grain and corn ensilage than when fed hay and grain. Prof. W. A. Woll, Wisconsin, found that 12.6 per cent more of the fat was churned out from the mixed milk of two cows when fed on ensilage than when they received corn fodder.

Don't say you cannot afford to build a silo. It is just the opposite. You cannot afford to do without one. Don't waste money on a stone or cement silo; a wooden one is better. Don't subscribe to the doctrine that ensilage is too watery to be good for anything.

Remember that pasture grass in June has more water in it than ensilage. Plant a variety of corn that will perfect the kernels and ear well. You can double the supply of fodder by adopting this system, and more fodder means more milk and more milk more cash.

CORN GROUND.

A. C. Garner, before Ida County Farmers' Institute.

Mr. President, Ladies and Gentlemen: I feel a little timid in regard to introducing this question. Now regarding the listing of corn, I haven't much to say about that. To those who think of adopting this, will say that my experience has not been very good in this line—it seems to me unprofitable. It is certainly the right thing in a clay soil, where the soil for corn is not very good. Corn demands large cultivation. There never was a time in the history of corn raisers when there were so many inducements for corn cultivation. Among those most important is the high price of corn, and the growing demand of corn. Then we should cultivate to the best of our ability, that the land would produce as much as possible, considering its high price. Fifteen years ago, our intention was not so much as to how much corn we could produce on an acre, but the number of acres we could cover. Then we had plenty of land. Today we have not the land, and it is to our interest to make the best out of the fewest acres.

There are two ways to do this—fertilization and cultivation. Yet there are certain conditions of the soil when fertilization is not successful, when the best fertilization has produced the least corn. The important question is how to cultivate and fertilize so we can succeed in a dry season with soil that is very susceptible to cultivation. We must prepare our soil today to meet the requirements of what we plant. I speak of our soil of being susceptible.

There are two kinds of corn which may be cultivated. One kind produces a tall, slim plant. The other is a strong stock. The former grows to be strong after a time.

To cultivate thoroughly we must cultivate in such a manner as to have the soil retain its moisture. We have soil in which the capillary process is profitable. Furthermore, to promote the production of corn, it is a good idea to pulverize the soil to preserve the moisture. Some farmers cultivate their land with a view to preserve the moisture at the top and others a great deal deeper.

I would advise that the land be prepared before the corn is even planted. In this, cultivate to preserve the moisture. Some farmers cultivate their lands with a view to preserve the moisture from the top. I would advise that the land be prepared before the corn is even planted. In this cultivate to preserve the moisture. A wet season doesn't make much difference.

After the corn is up, do not depend too largely on the weeder, though it is a good machine. In my experience two plows and once over with the weeder does well. The principal object of the corn raisers of today is to get as many bushels of corn to the acre as possible. The sixty and eighty dollar land must do more work. After the grain is in the ground use the weeder once, also level cultivation later in the season. In the cultivation of corn the disc is used by many.

GRASSES FOR CALHOUN COUNTY.

Thos. Parsons, before the Calhoun County Farmers' Institute.

It has been said that, "He that produces two blades of grass where only one has been grown is a public benefactor." The object of these discussions is to try to bring about the greater result. Your program committee has placed me upon this subject. I accept with reluctance, as I believe I have been more successful in some other lines of production, than in the formation of pastures and meadow lands. It is not altogether what we know or what we may tell you that will bring about the desired result, as every tiller of the soil must by observation and study, coupled with the practical application of his knowledge, bring about the improvement desired. We do not expect to instruct you as perhaps every one present has given this subject more thought and observation than myself. My remarks may not be practical and be directly in opposition to your experience in the matter, yet if I can drop one word which will cause you to do more thinking and investigating on this subject what I may say will not be in vain.

I have heard it said that Calhoun county is not adapted to grass and pasture. It was also said a few years ago that "this county never had and never would produce a paying crop of corn," and yet it is now recognized as one of the first not only of Iowa but of the world in the production of this cereal. It seems that a soil and climate that produces every other product of its latitude in such abundance must be adapted to the growth of grass and pasture, and perhaps when the same attention is bestowed upon them their production will be beyond expectations. The reason of the comparative neglect of the tame grasses until recently is because nature has furnished a substitute in the wild grasses without labor or care on the part of man. These wild grasses are now a thing of the past, and farmers must hereafter depend upon their own resources for its supply. With us now, it is one of the questions of the day, How to make our pastures and meadows profitable upon high priced land? This has been done in less favored localities than this county and we believe it will be done here also.

All grasses should be sown with two objects in view, excepting on land which is unfit for general farming, and they are: the building up of the soil, and to make the crop a paying one, while it occupies the land.

To attain both objects it will be necessary to make the grass crop one in rotation. In making it a rotation crop, the kinds of grass seed to be sown is very limited. We can only use those kinds that will occupy the land the first year and produce a paying crop the second. And any grass that will take a number of years to be established must be rejected. We only know of two kinds that will fill the requirements and they are the clovers and timothy. We recommend in nearly every case the combining of the two grasses as much greater crop can be produced by their union than can be raised by sowing them separate. And we think the soil can be built up more rapidly by occupying every available space with rootlets which will be produced in greater numbers by the two grasses combined than by sowing them separate. The raising of corn enables us to have one of the most perfect seed beds for the sowing of grass seed. The corn field that has been thoroughly plowed and cultivated the previous years is sufficiently mellow, not lumpy and without open spaces to dry out as is the case with newly-plowed fields. Land in this condition will retain moisture with the elements they require for their growth. The dry stalks left on the ground from the previous year's crop will also be a benefit to the newly-sown seed. The stalks will not act as a mulch but will protect the tender grass shoots from the damage caused by strong, sweeping winds. The time and manner of sowing the seed is very important, and we think to get the best results clover and timothy should be sown at different times and covered at different depths. Our plan would be to sow the clover some time in March and let it lay until the ground thaws out. As early as possible after thawing we would sow the nurse crop, disking or cultivating it in, which would also cover the clover to a sufficient depth. One would then sow the timothy and complete the work by covering with the harrow. The reason for advocating this method is because if both kinds of seed are sown at the same time they will both be covered to the same depth. As clover requires a greater depth than timothy to properly germinate, it follows that if we cultivate the clover to the proper depth, it will place the timothy too deep, thereby weakening or destroying the life of the seed. We do not think it is practical to sow grass seed without a nurse crop, as it would entail a loss of the use of the land for one year. Sometimes the young grass is smothered or dried up by its removal but perhaps all we can do in this matter is to take all possible precaution in selecting the kinds of grain sown. Barley or the early varieties of oats seem to be the best for this purpose. It seems that the earlier the nurse crop can be removed the less danger of the young grass being killed by the fierce heat of summer. Recently flax has been advocated as a nurse crop in some quarters but in this country it has so many disadvantages it seems that it is not worth considering in this relation.

It is a mistaken idea that we can sow grass seed in any manner and get the best results. It is the most difficult crop to get an even distribution, and no crop will show the way the work is done more plainly. To sow the seed properly it must be clean, and the seeder used should have the most perfect mechanical apparatus. Perhaps no tool on the farm is required to work with greater nicety. If we were to give one reason above all others why some meadows have failed to give the best results after properly seeding we would say over pasturing, perhaps this is a wrong statement as any pasturing is detrimental to the hay crop. There may be some soils and climates where meadow lands may be pastured without injury, but in this county to bring them to their highest development both in production and building up the fertility of the soil, we would say that stock should not be allowed to pasture.

After cutting the hay crop there will grow a short, heavy aftermath. If this is allowed to remain it will strengthen the grass plant and form a mulch which is a protection from the rigors of winter. Allow this to be removed by the pasturing or stock the plant will be weakened and subjected to exposure without protection. This alone will materially affect the outcome of the hay crop, but the evil results do not end with this reduction. The grass plant builds up the land principally by the filling of the soil with fibres and roots, which in turn decay, forming a mold upon which later crops feed. If the plant is weakened in any manner the roots will also suffer and if the soil is not thoroughly filled with these roots, the fertility of the soil will suffer in the same ratio.

In many of our pastures there is much room for improvement. In this county and perhaps all others of the state we can see them from a waste of weeds and bare land up to those that are a joy to the eye of their possessor. The worst pastures that we see are those that are supposed to be permanent and are located upon land which is thought to be unfit for cultivation. On most of these lands much can be done to make them more productive. Channels can be made to draw off the surplus water. Kinds of grass can be sown adapted to the character of different soils, and by keeping stock off at certain seasons of the year, the grass plant can be strengthened and made more productive. On lands that are overflowed or under water in any other way for long periods, we do not think they can be used profitably until some way is devised to drain them. On all other lands we should have a good stand of thrifty grass. This can only be done by care and proper selection of seed sown. On lands that are suitable for blue grass no better selection could be made, but it should be sown with timothy so that a quick pasture can be secured until the blue grass is firmly established. Those that have tried alsike clover recommend it for land that is not too subject to overflow. But this grass requires extra attention to start, as it must be mowed at least twice in the summer to keep other grasses from shading it. Red top may not be as desirable for pasture as other kinds, but there is much land now going to waste which might be utilized and partly reclaimed by its use. Some pastures which have been good when first seeded down, seem to have lost their grass producing qualities. We can offer no remedy except where possible to plow them up and reseed them. This would be a radical measure and entail loss where the land is unfit for the production of other crops. We would like to have the renovation of old pastures discussed by some person who has had experience along this line. Land has now become too valuable to run the risk of failure by slip-shod methods. There will always be seasons when it will not produce a full crop. The object of every farmer should be to put his crops in such condition that they will withstand the extremes of different seasons in the best possible manner. No part of the work should be too small to enlist his attention, as the success or failure of his ventures often depends upon the manner in which the little things are performed.

There is much written and said about the production of grass, and it is well that we should obtain information from every possible source. But it is not always advisable to discard our own ideas and plans for others. We often see others successful along certain lines and when we attempt to pattern after them failure is the result. We believe that success in raising grass and pasture is best attained by having a matured plan of our own which can be modified by studying the ideas and works of others and by our own experiences. The time has come that more labor must be expended in the production of a crop than when land was less valuable. High priced land has come to stay and we must adapt ourselves to these conditions. A paying return for the value of land, labor and money expended in the production of a grass crop can only be had by the closest study and attention to the small details and to see that every foot of land contributes its share to the aggregate of the crop. I am aware that upon no question is there a greater diversity of opinion. I submit this paper as an introduction to the subject and leave the question for the gentlemen who are to follow.

AGRICULTURAL PROBLEMS FOR THE FUTURE.

George F. Coburn, before the Farmers' Institute, Washta, Cherokee, County.

When one looks back a quarter of a century and compares the condition of Iowa farmers with the present conditions and then draws a picture of the conditions that will exist in twenty-five years hence, it is very doubtfult to my mind if one could color the picture too highly. If any one were to remind you now of one-half of the century that is gone and foretell one-half of our present century to come he would be regarded as a dangerous man and rickety and it would be used against him in the next campaign no matter on what ticket he ran. The fact is that not many realize the rate at which the world is traveling. Time is so noiseless that it wakens very few. The Rip Van Winkles are as numerous as the Smiths and Joneses. While we are yet shaking hands with the events of yesterday Genius taps us on the shoulder and introduces a stranger and we exclaim what imposter is this? With an increase of 15,000 of people every decade the question is asked, Where are they going? What will they do? One thing sure—there is no room for the rising generation of the rural districts in the cities and towns and if they go there they seldom ever acquire a *competency*. If upon the other hand they would stay on the farm and *farm* the *farm* (for there is a vast difference between staying on the farm and farming a farm). By doing this they are sure to obtain a competency for old age. Another problem for Iowa farmers to solve is, the difference between farming a *farm* and staying on a farm. Webster tells us that farming is the practice of tilling land, but farming in western Iowa I would say consists of tilling land and raising stock and poultry and one who does this is a busy man. He has a place for everything and everything in its place and when one passes by one of these farms he is struck by the tidy appearance and skillful manner in which he finds everything arranged.

Farming·is a business, just as much so as the manufacturing of goods and selling them. The underlying principles are alike, the general methods are alike, the causes of success or failure are the same—the same things which take most attention in any factory business are exactly the things needed for successful farming. These are: knowledge of what the market wants and when it wants it; selling produce where there is the most demand and the least supply; the art of dicreasing the cost of production; of finding out just what the cost of production is and the study of market conditions to decide what we can and cannot profitably raise. It is unnecessary for me to draw a picture of what staying on a farm consists in because I do not suppose there are any of this class of farmers in this part of Iowa. There is another item that comes up as we look at the future— the price of farm land in Iowa. Many of you here today have the price of land at five dollars per acre and some of you have undoubtedly seen it for much less. With the present, value of farm land in this vicinity ranging from fifty to one hundred dollars per acre the question is asked, is this an actual or a fictitious value. It is an actual value to be sure. While I do not believe the farm land will advance as much in the next five years as it has in the past five years, yet there is a future for Iowa that we know not of. To be sure the present value cannot be sustained if land owners all rent their land, but I believe the time is not far distant when every farmer in Iowa who owns a farm will make his home on the farm, thereby bearing his part of the burden of society in the locality that is entitled to it above all others. Just think of a farmer from fifty to sixty years of age leaving his home on the farm and moving to town to spend the rest of his natural days in indolence. It is a matter of fact that men are all well and strong from fifty to seventy years are at their best. Their judgment is ripe, they have an extensive line of experience and they have long since learned not to make the same mistake twice. The free delivery of mail in the rural districts of Iowa will have a tendency to keep the older class of farmers on their farms and the rural telephone lines will do even more. Still there is *another* advantage awaiting your welcome. The interurban railroad (we have every reason to believe that in the next decade). All of the principal thoroughfares of Iowa will have a road of this character, thus enabling us to transport our products much cheaper and more conveniently than by present methods. Emerson declared a little while before he died, "We think civilization near its meridian, but we are yet only at the cock crowing and morning star." The future will verify Emerson.

WINTERING BEES OUT OF DOORS.

J. C. Bergen, before Humboldt County Farmers' Institute.

In order to successfully winter bees, you must love the little bee and enjoy caring for them, as we always have better success when we work in the spirit of love for the work, or the object itself.

To winter bees successfully do not take all of their stores from them in the fall and expect them to gather sufficient to keep them alive through the winter after frost comes. One who cares for his bees in this way will find that many of them have ceased their gentle hum for they will have all died long before the robins come in the spring.

I was asked to write a paper on wintering bees out of doors. I suppose one could write of as many ways as there are apiarists, and every one is perhaps partial to his own plan and is more or less successful with it in their vicinity.

About the first of September we remove all surplus honey, either comb or extracted; then after this is cared for we go through each colony and inspect the amount of honey and bees in the brood chamber. If we find a colony with more bees than we think is necessary to winter well (as we do not want too many bees to go into winter quarters with and would prefer a colony that covers six frames full rather than one that covers eight frames). We change places with all weaker ones, to the stand of stronger and in that way even them up as to the number of bees in each colony. We then feed all colonies that need it, and you will find most all need it.

We find it more profitable to take honey away from them and then feed sugar syrup. The profit comes from two sources. We feed from ten to fifteen pounds of granulated sugar with the same weight of water, making a total of sugar and water fed to each colony twenty to thirty pounds at a cost of from fifty to seventy-five cents per colony for their winter feed bill. Now this same amount in honey would only buy four to six sections of honey and all beekeepers know that that amount of honey or even two or three times that, would not keep the colony through the winter. You would hardly dare begin on less than twenty sections of honey or even two or three times that, would not keep the colony through the winter. You would hardly dare begin on less than twenty sections of honey to winter a colony, and that at twelve and a half cents per section, which is an average price in this vicinity would make the cost two dollars and fifty cents for winter stores per colony. Then again the bees winter better, there are fewer dead bees in hive in spring and the colony is stronger in bees than those wintered on all honey.

After feeding is through contract the entrance with blocks, to about three inches long by three inches wide. We then pack the supper, first using the Miller device or tops from peach baskets. We like the last better as they are higher, placing two of the tops side by side they cover the ten frame hives nicely and give about one inch bee space above brood frames, we then put on a thick layer of woolen covering. We then fill the balance of the supper with old newspapers, layed in nicely to fit into all corners, but do not press down too tightly. These dry papers absorb all the moisture from the bees below, and bees are always dry and nice when opened in spring, then put the top of the hive on and you are ready for the outside covering.

This we make from light boxes, taking the boxes apart and making them into an outside hive six inches larger than the hive we wish to cover, and two inches higher in the rear than in front. This is to cause the water to run off rapidly, so as not to stand on the top and soak through to the packing below. Then we line the box with from four to six thickness of old dry papers and fill the space with excelsior or dry leaves packed in fairly tight. In this way the bees are kept warm and dry during coldest winter weather, and will come out in spring in fine condition. If the spring should be cold and backward it will be necessary to feed about one-fourth to one-half what you feed in the fall, and your bees will breed up and be in fine condition when the honey crops begins to come in, which is about the 5th to 10th of June in this vicinity. I believe this takes the bee through the winter and this is as far as I had them to deal with in this paper.

With the coming honey crop, comes something that worries more bee-keepers the most of all else. That is what we call the swarming fever. Now the best method we have tried is to cut the caps from drone brood, cutting the head of the young drone off with the cap. If they are scattered through the comb so as to be hard to decap, split the cell to the bottom, and thus kill the drone, and whenever we find a queen cell in this operation we cut it out, and invert the frame in the hive and you will not be bothered any more with that hive for ten or twelve days if at all.

When you desire to increase by swarming, clip the queen's wing (we clip all queens). We clip the left wing for a queen that was hatched in the odd year and the right for those hatched in the even year, and thus we can keep some track of their ages. When the bees swarm we only have to go to the hive and pick up our queen and place a new hive in the place of the old one and move the parent colony to a new stand and this gives you a good, strong working force in the new hive, as all the field bees will return to the old place, and find a new empty hive will work with more vigor than ever before.

After the bees have returned from the swarm let the captured queen loose on the running board in front of the hive and she will run in and be received gladly by the bees in their new home. In managing a swarm thus one can get nearly as much honey in this way as if they had not swarmed, with this method one can double their stock each year and still get a good crop of honey, as the parent colony will raise a queen from cells that were started before the swarm came off, and be a good, strong colony to go into winter quarters as there will be no after swarming when this method is used.

NURSERY STOCK, HOW TO BUY IT.

R. M. C. Rohlfs, before the Scott County Farmers' Institute.

It has been my good mission for the past two winter seasons to sell nursery stock, consequently have some experience along that line. I say good mission because I believe an honest nursery agent or nurseryman to be one of the best missionaries to the (so-called) civilized world. But today as our secretary has put it, I am to assume the role of discussing nursery stock from a buyer's standpoint.

Of nursery stock we have a great many varieties and classes. As to varieties I shall, with probably a few exceptions, leave them undisturbed turning my pointers chiefly to the grades and classes.

Most of our trees as put upon the market, are two and three years old, with an occasional lot of one-year-old whips and four-year-old scrubs. Remember the nurseryman has also to contend with the perplexities, of not being able to make a first-class tree out of every graft planted, just as well as the fancy stock breeder has at times on hand, stock of his own raising, which might well do as a living advertisement for some of our large meat canning establishments. What the nurseryman likes to raise is as large a tree with as good and plenty of roots as he can in three years. What most buyers like to buy is a tree just a little larger than the nurseryman has or can raise in three years, without once giving a single thought to the size of the roots. To hear some men buy trees would seem to a blind, although not deaf, person as though the conversation tended towards buying fence posts or telephone poles. Now why not be reasonable and upon investigation find that a small tree has more roots in proportion to its top than a large one. And surely roots are what you want, because a tree without roots or even with poor roots such as you can find by the dozen through the country is indeed a poor investment. The roots to a tree are what a foundation is to a house. The top can grow and be trimmed, but the roots are out of man's reach. Upon them depends the future, the longevity, the ability to reward the planter with bountiful fruit, and further its capability to resist our summer's heat and our winter's cold.

Ninety-nine per cent of our, during the winter of 1898-99, damaged trees were hurt at the root. But why you may well ask? Quite natural. Most of our old orchards and a number of the young ones were planted with eastern trees. Eastern trees are raised by methods of propagation entirely different from our own western methods. Of course entirely suitable to their climate and conditions but not at all to ours. Their trees are raised by means of budding on whole seedling roots, while our western trees are mostly grafted on piece roots, using a long scion, which finally takes root, thereby giving us a tree on its own roots. In other words a Ben Davis tree on Ben Davis roots, etc. By their methods they get nearly as large a tree in one year as we do in two years, consequently their trees at three years old will take the cake for size and beauty when those fence post or telephone men come along. Alas! but have they not forgotten something? Will their trees on seedling roots stand such winters as Dakota sent down four years ago? For an answer go to our old orchards and see, as I have done during the past summer, trees apparently sound, topple over at the first strong wind, with trunk and branches solid and sometimes even having leaves and half matured fruit—but without roots. Such is the doom of the trees from the east and even those gotten here without consideration for the roots.

Although I have a great respect for the eastern people, nevertheless some of the worst frauds ever perpetrated on our Iowa people were done by Ohio men. To charge one dollar each for grape vines, the fruit of which was claimed to be seedless, or ten dollars a dozen for vines which were to grow grapes containing in each berry only one seed—such are a few examples of their work. Take a step nearer home, if you please, to Illinois. There find a man who is advertising and has even copyrighted the very name (to forbid wholesale propagation) of a pear which he claims to be entirely "blight proof" and which he sells at two dollars a tree, the fruit of which, according to the investigations of some of our most experienced western pear growers is nothing but that "old timer" the Birkert.

For my taste a tree five feet high, healthy and thrifty, with a good set of roots, is more to my satisfaction than larger in height. But varieties differ in growth. You mustn't expect as large a Willow Twig or a Duchess of Oldenburg tree as of most varieties. In this case you have to contend with a smaller or an older tree. This is one of the reasons why the Willow Twig can so seldom be had true to name in the nurseries. On my grounds in the nursery row, at one year old ,it is a measly, scrubby and I almost dare say lousy product of Dame Nature. So don't wonder if your Willow Twig trees will bear Wealthy apples or Whitney crabs if you persist in a large tree. For the home orchard three-year-old trees are best, although commercial orchardists usually buy heavy two-year-olds. One-year-old grape vines and asparagus plants give best satisfaction. They make better vineyards and asparagus beds in time than older plants and the one year seemingly lost is quite made up for by the perfection of the work.

Quite often the people are taken in by the following Some Dick, Tom or Harry comes along, from where, God alone knows, with his fancy picture book of varieties of fruits of all descriptions, sizes and colors, suitable to all climates, soils and sites. Varieties that surely were originated in cold Russia; trees having fruit buds almost before planting, so are sure to bear early; the fruit is to keep as our best keepers, with quality and beauty for which Webster's book has no word of definition. Usually these varieties have a name which mortals never heard nor will they ever hear them again after the agent has gone. At times the arrangement is like this: Dicky raises the trees, Tommy sells them and promises to plant, care for and replace free of charge all that die, and lastly if the poor sucker won't bite otherwise, he guarantees them to bear in from three to five years. When planting time comes, the trees come, but not Tommy; instead comes Harry who knows nothing of the arrangement made by the agent. As to the planting, replacing and guaranteeing it most likely disappeared with the agent. In connection, did you ever think seriously as

43

to what a guarantee really meant? Does not our law require it to be in writing, in order to be valid? Did you ever see a nursery agent give a guarantee in black upon white, to make trees bear at a certain age? You may but to me it would be a great curiosity. But it seems as though the multitudes are very anxious to fulfill that prophecy of P. T. Barnum. A better way would be to patronize home trade. Go to your local nurseryman and trust him with your order and plantings at a reasonable price. He is just as ready to serve you as the stranger from a distance and in case your trees die or fail for any fault of his, then you have some one to go to with your lamentations. But where could you find Dick, Tom or Harry who probably canvass a certain territory once in ten years or even less.

I have so far spoken chiefly of the deviltry of the nursery agent together with the genuineness of the nursery stock, so it now remains in justice to the patron, to stretch forth his saintly side. Patrons of a nursery may be classified, for want of better terms, into three classes, namely: careful, careless and every-year buyers. The careful buyer know what he wants, looks to what he gets, plants with a purpose and for the future, and generally has success and is a satisfied customer. The careless man buys cheap stock, wherever he can get it, plants without a purpose in view, and roars when stock does not all grow. The every-year buyer is the nurseryman's best customer. He buys a little every year—mostly novelties. His chief aim is to get something new. He does not believe in "letting well enough alone." Has no definite place where to plant, but generally finds room in the old orchard which grandfather laid out, or in the lot where the sows and young pigs usually take their early spring sunning. After he has planted the trees (so to speak at least) they are left and forgotten until if by chance they may be spared to begin to bear. Of course Our genial customer has trusted his memory with names and locations of varieties and is *sure* to remember them all. Oh! but should he happen to forget, and get the exact location of the Ben Davis and the Grimes Golden turned around in his mind. Ah! that rascal nurseryman who sold me Ben Davis trees and they bear yellow apples! Upon further investigation after having eaten of the genuine Grimes Golden he proceeds to sample the real Ben Davis, but with an oath throws it to the hogs, crawls through yonder fence, makes a bee line for the good neighbor's turnip patch, pulls one of the largest, peels it and eats away. And he chews his juicy vegetable, he turns his head towards the Ben Davis tree, with a look of defiance, he smacking his lips, exclaims, "How delicious!" Such is the career of the Ben Davis, the business apple, made to look well and sell well but not to taste well. Why not plant something better? Plant the Jonathan! Its fruit is delicious to the taste, fragrant to the smell and beautiful to the sight while on the market after once better known it will surpass all others in demand and price. It will bring money into your pocket and health into your body, while it will make your children's lips rosy as the cherry and their lids sparkle as the dew drops, and renew the all too soon faded blushes on your wife's cheeks.

In conclusion: Get good, honest trees with plenty of good and hardy roots as near home as possible. Your home nurseryman will be glad to receive your order and will do better by you than those from a distance. Buy a thrifty medium sized tree rather than a stunted or an overgrown large one. The nurseryman and the planter must work hand in hand. Remember "in union there is strength" and when the nurseryman and planter join hands and work in union they are both bound to succeed. Every honest tree that a nurseryman sells is an honor to his name, while every honest tree the planter plants is a living monument to his memory.

FRUIT RAISING.

W. O. Mitchell, before the Adams County Farmers' Institute.

In 1896 the writer had about twenty acres of rough land near Cornning worth probably about $40 per acre. Partly for profit but more for experiment than anything else, he decided to plant a portion of it to fruit trees. The first year he broke up about six acres and put out fifty peach trees of different varieties, 100 plums of different varieties, 500 Early Richmond cherries, 200 Mount Morancey cherries, 40 Jonathan and 35 Grimes Golden apples. The ground was planted to corn and a fair crop raised. The trees did well with the exception of the Early Richmond cherries all of which leaved out and then died. This I attributed to two causes, first, imperfect trees which had not been properly cared for after having been taken from the ground and second, the lateness of the season when they were transplanted, which was about May 1st. I think that cherry trees should be set out as soon as the frost is out of the ground in the spring and ground dry enough to work.

The next year the party of whom I bought the cherry trees replaced the Early Richmond but sent me a mixed lot of rather inferior trees. I also put out 400 Wragg cherries, 75 pears of different varieties and about 50 more plums. Each year I replanted what died, blew down or were destroyed by gophers, borers or other causes. Then came the hard winter of 1898, when all my peaches were killed almost to the roots and many entirely destroyed. Many of the plums, a few cherries, some pears and apples were also killed. I again replanted and have had no trouble with winter killing since. In 1901 we had a good crop of peaches. All the trees old enough bear heavily, some of them several bushels each, which sold readily at $1.50 to $2.00 per bushel. I think the Alexander, Bokara No. 3 and the Elhuta the best and I know of no more promising fruit than the peach in this locality on a limited scale. The plums do fairly well but unless used for a chicken yard or regularly sprayed the fruit is inferior and unprofitable. The pears are thrifty and of late healthy. For the first year or two they were subject to blight. They have bloomed heavily but bear only a few pears. I think, however, they are worth experimenting with on a small scale. The cherries are just beginning to bear. The

Wragg have borne two or three fair crops. They are a late cherry, heavy and early bearers but only medium fruit and ripen unevenly. The large Mount Morancey is a fine cherry—large, juicy and not strong, not so early nor profuse a bearer but the best market cherry I know of for this locality. The Early Richmond is a profuse bearer but short lived. The apples have borne no fruit as yet and have caused me more trouble from borers and other causes than any of the other trees. I have cultivated the orchard every year and consider that the use of the ground has paid all expenses of cultivation, planting and replating, and more too. From this on I do not expect to plant crops among the trees but do expect to keep up cultivation and shall probably use a disk for general cultivation. Now as to the last and profits. I have about 1400 trees all told and they have cost me about $150, making a total of land and trees of $1,150. I have used and sold in the last three years fruit worth probably $200 and the land is now well worth $2,500 or a profit of $1,550. The twenty acres of land without the orchard would probably sell for $1,200, which would leave me as an increase on the orchard alone of $1,300. I believe if any farmer will select five to ten acres of good, well drained land and plant it to an orchard and then cultivate, replant and care for it that it will not only be a source of profit but that it would keep many a family on the old homestead when they were too old to work on the farm. By the time a man has cultivated, pruned and cared for an orchard for ten years he becomes so attached to it that town would have few attractions for him and he would not care to turn it over to the tender mercies of the average tenant, or his own son for that matter, and I further believe that a good five-acre orchard will increase the value of almost any quarter section of Adams county land from $1,000 to $2,000 in value.

The orchard should be fenced by itself and have the fence pig tight at the bottom. Pigs and fowls will not injure an orchard and are of great benefit in destroying the wormy and injured fruit which drops from the trees.

HORTICULTURE.

F. C. Reese, before Adams County Institute.

The subject assigned me is "Horticulture," but as this subject is too broad to be covered by a single paper, and as I have not been confined to any particular branch of horticulture I have chosen for my subject, "The Evergreen, Its Propagation and Growth." I will try and not take up too much of your time in the discussion of this subject, as I believe you will derive more benefit in taking up the time in open discussions upon the various subjects to come before this meeting.

God in His goodness has given us many kinds of useful and beautiful trees for our comfort, but what has He given us more beautiful than the evergreen. They are adapted to every climate, from the sunny south to the Dakotas on the north, where the thermometer runs from 30 to 50 degrees below zero. The question is often asked, Could we do without the evergreen? I would answer no; and if this be true we should consider the propagation and care of same.

We must commence at the beginning—that is, the seed. I would like to say right here that this is a peculiar branch of the nursery business, in which few nursery men even care to engage and so is left to a few men who make a specialty along this line. I would not advise the ordinary farmer to attempt in the growing of this beautiful tree from the seed. Still if you desire to do so I will give you a few brief directions. First of all secure good seeds; make your beds in width of four feet and any desired length owing to the quantity of seed you wish to plant. In preparing your seed bed make the ground very rich and well pulverized, then sow the seed soon after being gathered in the fall, so they will lay about one-fourth of an inch apart, core with sifted sand to a depth of one-fourth inch and cover the whole with a light layer of leaves protect the beds with lath frames raised about six inches from the ground. It is well to sprinkle the beds with water sufficient to keep the sand moist, pull out all the weeds as soon as they appear and never let them get two or three inches high. Seedlings from these beds are transplanted at two years old and at this time any one can grow them successfully by using good judgment in the planting of the young trees. It is not necessary for me to enumerate the various kinds of evergreens, and will name only a few which make the quickest growth. These are the Norway Spruce, Scotch and White Pine, while the Cedar is not far behind and is one of the very best for shelter belts. If we could look upon the evergreens high up on the mountains and see them growing out of the rocks where scarcely any other vegetation can grow, then we would wonder why so many of us fail in growing this beautiful tree here in our rich and productive soil. It is simply this: the average farmer does not take the necessary care of the young tree, supposing they will stand as much sun and wind to their roots as the maple or willow, and when thus exposed you had just as well consign them to the brush pile.

SOME NOXIOUS WEEDS AND HOW TO DESTROY THEM.

F. O. Harrington, before the Iowa County Farmers' Institute.

During the year just passed, which was remarkable for its extremes of rainfall, the weeds became more conspicuous than usual. This should naturally awaken interest in the subject of the destruction of weeds among those who till the soil. For the complete destruction of a noxious plant the production of seed must be prevented, which in the case of annuals is sufficient, but in the case of biennials or perennials the root stock must be killed. This is very simple with many kinds, and in no case impracticable, and so it might seem at first thought, that with the best ways of destruction being known, one might reasonably hope for complete eradication. But still in the case of weeds that have become abundant and wide spread, the conditions in which many of them occur are such that we, as the farming community, can only regard their complete extermination as beyond the limit of probability, if not of possibility. It might be said that if taken when they commence it would not be difficult to eradicate them. For an instance, if the farmer on whose land the first Russian thistle grew in 1873 had known the evil character of the plant, and had spent a few hours to kill them in his flax field, it might easily have been destroyed in this county and millions of dollars and years of labor saved. This emphasizes the need that each land owner should be on the watch for new plants and learn their character if possible, before they become established and become an aggressive invasion on his domains.

There is another point that we as farmers should carefully bear in mind, which is, that if we do not interest ourselves and strongly support and enforce our laws for the extermination of weeds, those laws will be of little avail, in fact become but a dead letter on our statute books.

That we can ever expect the complete eradication of all weeds on our farm I do not even hope or claim, but if this suggestion can approach so near that point as to prevent very material damage without requiring too great extra labor in conducting our farm operations, this would be my ideal condition for a farm so far as weeds are concerned. But as you all know there are all gradations from this condition to that of the farm so very weedy that a profitable crop cannot be raised upon it; that is to say, that to raise a good crop upon it requires so great an amount of expense and labor that it creases to be a profitable crop. A large portion of our weeds here are annuals and may be brought under subjection by preventing seedage, but the seed of many of these retain their vitality many years, and when once plentiful in the soil they keep germinating from year to year when by the shifting of the soil by the various ways of soil preparation for crops they are brought under the proper conditions of plant growth. Instances of this delayed germination you are all familiar with as in the case of such weeds as the cocklebur and in the clovers, etc. None of these seeds will germinate to any great extent more than six inches deep. Some of the most troublesome annuals we have to contend with are cockleburs, velvet button, the various forms of smartweed and foxtail or pigeon grass in cultivated lands, and in meadows and pastures the rag weed, dog fennel, horse weed or colt tail and two new ones that are rapidly coming to the front as obnoxious weeds, are the prickly lettuce and squirrel tail or wild barley, *Hordemn pumatim.* The latter is not troublesome in cultivated fields, but the prickly lettuce is doubtless going to be troublesome in the fields and in the pastures, the garden and the orchards, in fact everywhere, even clover at its best cannot smother it. It is a very recent arrival here though it has been in the United States (Massachusetts) since late in the 60's. As giving you a slight idea of its powers of propagation a single average plant has been estimated to bear 8,000 seeds, which have wings capable of carrying them with the aid of the winds, long distances, and I want to impress it upon your minds that these seeds do not have to be kiln dried like our seed corn to grow. The squirrel tail is most troublesome in pastures and meadows and its most serious fault lies in its injury to stock from its sharp ahus or beards, which are exceedingly sharp and being recurved causes them to tenaciously adhere to the inner surfaces of animals' mouths causing often very serious sores and sometimes death. Mowing at proper times is efficient with both these plants but once cutting will not usually be enough because all do not reach the right stage at once.

Of the biennials such as burdock and bull thistles that store up nourishment and a heavy roots system the first year, but no seed stalk, and sending up that seed stock the second year, produce their seed and then die will in most cases live three years or more, if by mowing they are prevented from sending with their seed stock. In fact such cutting usually induce them to branch out at the bone and send out several stalks instead of one. I have often laughed quietly to myself when I noticed men using a scythe on their burdock patches. Cutting the roots below the crown is the proper remedy for this class of plants and my experience has been that a tile spade was about the best implement for the purpose, and will accomplish it quite rapidly with a proper degree of energy at the back of it as a moving power. All of the ordinary thistles are readily removed in this way, likewise burdock. mullein, etc., none of which should be allowed to seed in any place on the farm or upon the highways adjacent. One biennial plant that is camparatively a new comer but a very troublesome neighbor is the narrow leaved dock. While not troublesome in the cultivated lands it is likely to be very troublesome in pastures, meadows, waste lands, etc. Persistent mowing is the most feasable method of controlling them.

Like the annuals and biennials, the perennial weeds reproduce themselves from seed and therefore should not be allowed to seed, but here we have a class of weeds that have the inherent ability to reproduce and multiply, more or less abundantly without seed, after once being established, and to destroy them the underground portions must be destroyed. The most common and troublesome weeds of this class we have had to contend with here, have been the wild morning glory, and crab grass or quack grass. The last is not troublesome so far in our fields where a regular rotation is followed, though I believe they have trouble with it in some of the eastern states in that way. I find it most pernicious in waste corners and in orchards not cultivated, etc. The former is troublesome whereever found. If abundant it is bad even in meadows of good timothy and clover, and are especially bad in small grain, tangling it all up, decreasing the yield materially, and making bad work with reaping and binding.

Thorough cultivation accompanied with judicious use of the hoe, both long continued will finally master them. I believe but am not sure that sheep would destroy them if allowed the privilege of access to them during the growing season.

But a far more alarming and dangerous foe than these—aye than all others—the bane of our eastern states and Canada, the ubiquitous Canada thistle, is octupus-like, placing a tentacle here, another there and still another yonder, in an insidious and quiet way, but some day we may waken from our lethargy to find ourselves within the grasp of a resistless,

relentless destroyer, that shall throttle our energies and make mock of
our puny strength, until we drift—drift rudderless and helpless upon the
shoreless sea of grim despair, or of limitless night. Pleasant future to
face, isn't it; but beware, my friends, it is not all a phantasma of a dis-
ordered mind. There is more stern reality in it than many of you are
able at the present time to comprehend, and especially those of you who
have not formed intimate acquaintance with the grim monarch. The Canada thistle is bad—yea more than bad—upon the thin soils of the east,
what will it be upon the rich, deep, alluvial soils of Iowa. Some of you,
my friends may think I am sounding a false alarm, an alarm where danger is not imminent. You are wrong. I was never more in earnest. The
danger is imminent, decidedly, for within four miles of where Williamsburg perches upon its hills, are several patches of that accursed weed, that
are thriving with a vigor and a vim that simply takes one's breath, figura-
tively speaking. And what will you do about it. Supinely wait for the
"other fellow" to do something, or instead of waiting Macawber-like for
"something to turn up," will *you* wake up to the fact that it is *your* duty,
and *yours* and *yours* to guard in every available way against the approach
of so treacherous an enemy. Let me tell you one way of doing your duty
toward the material interests of our great commonwealth of Iowa. Turn
with me to Sec. 5024 of the Code of Iowa, 1897, which reads:

"If any person or corporation, after having been notified in writing
of the presence of Canada thistles on any lands owned or occupied by such
person or corporation, or if any road supervisor after having been notified in writing of the presence of any such thistles on the road under his
jurisdiction, shall permit such thistles or any part thereof to blossom or
mature, such person, corporation, or road supervisor shall be guilty of a
misdemeanor and shall be punished by a fine not exceeding one hundred dollars, or imprisonment in the county jail not more than thirty days."

There is another section which also refers to this question. Sec. 1562:

"The road supervisors when notified in writing that any Canada
thistles, or any other variety of thistles are growing upon any lands, or
lots within his district, vacant or owned by non-residents, the owner, agent
or lessee of which is unknown, shall cause the same to be destroyed, and
make return in writing to the board of supervisors of his county, with a
bill for his expenses or charges therefor, which in no case shall exceed
two dollars per day for such services, which shall be audited and allowed
by said board and paid from the county fund. And the amount so paid
shall be entered up and levied against the lands or lots on which thistles
have been destroyed, and collected by the county treasurer the same as
other taxes, and returned to the county fund." Now I want to know whose
duty it is to set this machinery in motion. The law is silent in this, but
the inference cannot be doubted, that it is the duty of every citizen to con
stitute himself a watchful guardian, and an active one as well when there
is cause for action. It would be a false ideal of friendship toward one's
neighbor to remain silent when that neighbor, through ignorance or a
worse reason failed in caring for his pet thistles. It is a practical question
for us all as to the remedies to apply for the complete extinguishment of

this hydro-headed monster. I must confess to a considerable degree of ignorance on the subject and not have a printed line on the subject by others as authority, but "In a multitude of counsel there is safety," so we will proceed to compare notes for we have doubtless some among us who have had long acquaintance. Personally, my experience with it has been limited. Although born in central New York where the thistle was all too plentiful, I came westward to "grow up with the country" at an age in which weeds were among the least of my troubles. My experience and acquaintance with this vile pest began a few years ago, perhaps a dozen, in about this manner. I had a few acres upon which I had been growing the black locust trees, and concluding that I had grown them long enough. I cut all clean and burned the rubbish. I sent to Chicago for a quantity of special mixture of grass seeds that when grown should constitute a permanent pasture and produce fresh feed at all hours from the earliest blue bird's call in spring till the next winter's snows buried all. Blue grass, red top, rye grass, sheep's fescue meadow foxtail, sweet vernal grass, Bermuda grass, crested dog's tail, and probably a few others that I do not now recall, all of course to be thoroughly recleaned seed. This seed was sown in March over the cleared tract which had very little of any kind of grass over it having been too much shaded. The sequel proved that these people had been very generous in this mixture and had included more varieties of seed than they had agreed upon, among which was a considerable amount of seed of the sheep sorrel, also Canadian thistle, as well as several other kinds of the thistle family. I turned sheep into this lot after a few weeks, and they cleared up for good the locust grove. One day in midsummer four or five years later in crossing the patch I noticed a patch of thistles perhaps thirty by fifty feet in area that at once attracted my attention and interest, as well as suspicion. Upon taking sample stalks to my father he immediately pronounced them Canada thistle. Examination showed three or four other patches of much less extent on the lot. I proceeded at once on a raid of extermination. I cut each plant about an inch below the surface putting a small amount of salt upon each cut root stem. The sheep were not otherwise salted at that period, and naturally made life a burden for any tiny head of thistle peeping out. This was continued every few days while the growing season lasted. There were a very few tiny, weak plants came up the next season but a repetition of the salting process two or three times closed the deal on the Canada thistle on Evergreen Farm. Where one has sheep I believe the treatment I used would be as effective and as cheaply applied as any other, unles the area be very limited so we might smother them.

I think I would make two general propositions—that is to say, follow one or the other of two principles. First, cut two or three inches deep, put on the cut root stalks, salt, coal oil or strong acids, any of which will destroy the root for some distance from the point of contact. Probably carbolic acid would be the most effective cheap application. You may buy it for 50 cents per gallon. Of course this system must be frequently applied and thoroughly carried out. The other line of work would be starvation of the plant by preventing any development of green leaves or other parts above ground. You may accomplish this by covering the plants so densely and heavily with some kind of mulch as manure, straw in various conditions, or any other refuse or any coarse material, but the coarser it is the thicker it must be to shut out the air and heat, thus absolutely preventing growth. This same process of starvation may be accomplished by thorough, persistent cultivation in fields, which also makes a good opening for "the man with the hoe" in connection with the cultivators. No slop-shop haphazard work here. It will not answer to do this for a month or so, and when you get busy putting up hay, etc., forget about your thistle patch. It must be as regularly and thoroughly done as the milking of your cows, though not quite so often. The vital principle operative here in all these ways, is that a plant cannot grow without leaves. A plant derives the greater portion of its food from the soil in the shape of ignorganic materials held in solution by what we term the sop of the plant. This sop ascending upward through the cell structure of the plant to the leaves, and by them through a process of evaporation and elaboration become associated with or changed into organized compounds similar to starch and sugar celulose, etc., and then used in the repair and growth of every part by deposits to each, leaves, stem and roots to their uttermost significance.

Thus we may see how largely the growth of roots and roots only but the entire structure is determined by the amount, health and vigor of the leaf system and its consequent ability to supply this elaborated food in sufficient quantities. Deprive a plant of this leaf structure, starvation begins, make this deprivation continuous and death by starvation inevitably follows. Of course we all know there is a vast difference in the inherent, organic vitality of the different plants, but it is simply a question of degree, and the Canada thistle must succomb when its uttermost degree is reached as well as others, but you must expect a stubborn resistance until that limit is reached.

NEW MACHINERY.

Henry Wallace, before the Fremont County Farmers' Institute.

It isn't always best for the small farmer to buy every new machine that comes along. The farmer on forty or eighty acres must go slow. His capital is small and his investments must be made on a corresponding scale. But there are some new machines which most farmers can buy with profit.

DISK PLOWS.

The profits of corn growing are pocketed by the man who produces at the least cost. There has been a great improvement in plows in recent years. I well remember the old long-nosed plow with the long handles. Now and then it would strike a boulder and one handle would take you under the fifth rib, and for a little while you wouldn't know whether you were dead or alive.

The greatest improvement that has been made in plows is the invention of the disk plow. Last spring the Hancock disk plow was tested on our farms near Des Moines. It was on cornstalk ground and the ground was in fine condition. A machine was used for measuring the actual force used in pulling the plows. The average force registered on common riding plows turning a sixteen-inch furrow was 585 pounds. The disk turned two thirteen-inch furrows, or a total of about twenty-four inches, with a pull of only 500 pounds. The disk plow did one-half more work with less power.

I have a farm south of town that has a piece of land on it what you would call "gumbo." The disk plow stirred five acres a day as easily as the ordinary plow stirred three acres. The lightness of the draft was marvelous. The disk plow does not cut a square furrow. The center is about an inch lower than the sides.

In order to understand why the disk plow pulls so much easier than the ordinary kind it is necessary to know where the tug comes in. In a series of plow tests made at Cornell university ten or fifteen years ago it was found that 35 per cent of the force necessary to pull a plow is used to overcome the friction of the land side and mold board. This is largely avoided in the disk plow, which has neither land side nor mold board. Only 10 per cent of the force is used in pulverizing the ground and 7 per cent in pushing the plow through the ground and dislodging the soil particles. The disk plow does not push its way through, but has a rolling motion like a circular saw. The difference in the way they cut is the same difference you will find in pressing a knife down on a piece of beefsteak and drawing it across in the ordinary way.

If the mold board of a plow is very sloping the ground is pulverized but very little, being simply turned over. The disks of a disk plow push against the ground at a very steep angle and the scrapers also help in the pulverizing process. We plow mainly for the purpose of pulverizing the soil, which the disk plow does much more thoroughly than any other. It will not work in sod or wet ground. The price is about $55, I believe.

CLOD CRUSHERS.

When I was speaking at institutes down in southern Illinois, near Carlinville, what they call "Egypt Land," I found they were using a kind of roller that I am convinced is a splendid implement. I am not a friend of the ordinary roller because it requires so much sense to use it right that it is apt to do more harm than good in the hands of the average farmer. Hard clods are not crushed, but simply pressed into the ground. By compressing the surface of the soil the moisture can come to the surface and pass off by evaporation.

This new roller or clod crusher is built on an entirely different principle. The work is done by a number of steel disks about twenty inches in diameter and three inches thick in the center and sloping to a thin edge. These disks are set very close together and work independent of each other. The pressure is down below the surface and clods are cut and, ground between these wedge-shaped disks. I believe this is the same tool used by H. C. Campbell in his system of soil culture. He calls it a "sub-surface packer," because it packs the subsoil; yet it leaves the surface loose and thus prevents evaporation of moisture.

My men always harrow what they have plowed before they unhitch at noon or night. A neighbor does not follow this plan, and last spring when he had finished plowing a forty-acre field he found it was so cloddy the harrow made little impression on it. He didn't see how he was going to get it in shape to plant, but borrowed our clod crusher and soon had the field ready for the planter.

He said he didn't know what he would have done if it hadn't been for that new fangled machine, the use of which he said was worth $5♦ to him. It enabled him to cover his mistake. It is the only kind of a roller I would have on the place.

WEEDERS.

The Hallock weeder is the poorest kind of a tool for a poor farmer. It is a good tool for a good farmer, but it must be used with lots of judgment.

One of my farms was one of the worst and weediest farms you ever saw when I bought it. There was a velvet weed wherever there was room for one to grow and then cockleburs in between. The cornfield was green with velvet weeds before the corn was up, but with the weeder everyone was killed. The Hallock weeder will knock velvet weeds every time, but it won't knock cockleburs, because they are too low down and strongly rooted.

You can't use a weeder unless you get your seedbed thoroughly prepared. The ground must be very fine and loose and you must use the weeder just before the weeds get in the dew of their youth, just as they are a-bornin'.

A weeder will not work when the ground is wet. Start it after the planter and keep it going whenever the ground is dry. You will have to stop when the corn is coming up, but after it gets about three inches high go into the field after the corn dries off in the morning and you can kill weeds by the million, and do it so easy, too. Don't pay any attention to the corn at all. It will be dragged down, but it will raise up again all right.

Thirty acres a day can be gone over with a weeder. Last spring part of our corn was laid by with a weeder and it stood the dry weather better than any of the rest. With a disk plow, disk roller and Hallock weeder corn can be produced at 6 cents a bushel ready to harvest.

SIDE DELIVERY HAY RAKES.

One of these machines is an admirable substitute for a tedder. I wouldn't buy a tedder and an ordinary hay rake, but a side delivery hay rake, especially if I was going to use a hay loader. It kicks the hay out to one side, making a continuous windrow. Two swaths can be thrown over on the net swath and then the two on the other side thrown back on it, making five swaths in a windrow.

MANURE SPREADERS.

On my farm in Adair county I have about 125 cattle, thirty horses and 300 sheep. They make a great deal of manure and it is a big job to haul it out. I got a manure spreader to tempt my man to get out the manure on our land. The spreader makes it cover more ground by thoroughly there is a supreme satisfaction in setting the machinery in gear and seeing it work. If there were some way to get it on as easy as off men would pay for the privilege of hauling out manure.

The manure spreader saves nearly half the labor and does a better job than it is possible to do with a fork. We usually put too much manure on our land. The spreader makes it cover more ground by thoroughly pulverizing it and spreading it on evenly all over.

HOME SURROUNDINGS.

C. W. Lau, before the Scott County Institute.

We are told again and again by persons who are in a position to know, that Scott county as compared with other counties, presents an appearance of substantial wealth and prosperity. It is studded with farms well worked and well managed, large buildings well repaired and under paint, an air of thrift and economy pervading the whole which reflects credit upon the individual farmer. However true this may be, there is lack of attention in one particular place and that is the immediate surroundings of the dwelling house. While he may bestow great care on his live stock, his grain and his fences, while he may furnish the interior with all modern requirements and luxuries, viz., furnace heating, acetylene gas light, piano, books, telephone, etc., yet the immediate outside as a rule presents a most God forsaken appearance, decidedly not in keeping with the interior, and out of harmony with the balance of the farm.

Weeds have unrestricted liberty to grow as far up to the door as they can; so have dogs, cats, chickens, ducks and other nuisances. This botanical and zoological display is offset by a liberal sprinkling of empty fruit cans, tin pans, broken crockery, slop buckets and ash heaps. And this promiscuous accumulation constitutes the sum total of what might be called "landscape gardening in the country."

If there is any part of the farms or yards which would show to the best advantage for attention received, it is that part surrounding the home. And if the average farmer is industrious and well-to-do as he unquestionably is, he is least of all to be excused for tolerating such a state of affairs around a place where he has asked his wife to live and labor with a sweet and unruffled disposition and children to grow up to manhood and womanhood with lofty ideas and appreciations of the beautiful.

Although shiftlessness and slum conditions are unavoidable in the crowded cities, there is no earthly excuse for allowing them around your country home where without and within conditions should be congenial with nothing to mar or disturb the domestic happiness, and where the growing mind of childhood can absorb from its surroundings the very best impressions for a pure and noble character.

City people are heavily taxed and will go a great way to enjoy park conditions. They seek for healthful recreation, for physical as well as mental invigoration and benefit, but the farmer with ample opportunity, better facilities, and very little sacrifice, ridicules the idea of a lawn because "it don't pay" or "I haint got no time."

As far as finding time is concerned, you will find that the farmers who have well kept places are the busiest of their class, and if they have any time to fool away they certainly could not do it more profitably than by putting their lawn in trim. There are other and disastrous ways of fooling away time. I have been repeatedly asked if it paid to have so large a place with trees and shrubs, if potatoes or corn might not have been a better investment.

The man who calculates the value of an ornamental garden merely by what it yields in dollars and cents, is to be pitied rather than criticised; pitied because he is poor amidst wealth; because he is calloused and dead to nature's grandest creation unfolded in beautiful flowers, shrubs and trees.

To me, my large garden has been and is yet a vast field for study and observation. It is a natural laboratory where I toil with increasing pleasure. Here I have a fountain yielding joys and pleasures so keen as not to be measured with sordid dollars and cents. I doubt whether those of you who seek pleasures in other avenues of life, are finding them better, cheaper or healthier than I am having them at my very door, saying nothing of the money value that trees add to a farm.

My garden with its attractive groups and retreats, the results of many years' care and nursing, is for me a place of refuge when world-weary and heartisck to get recreation, get strength and inspiration to meet the arduous tasks which fall to the lot of the average farmer. In short it is my heaven on earth.

Byron says: "The cumbersome pomp of Saxon pride, accords not with a free born soul, that loves the mountains craggy sides, and seeks the rocks where billows roll." So would I say, I care not for commercial strife, for the pursuit of the almighty dollar. I care not for the noise, the din and contaminations of city life; I care not for the shams and hypocracies of so-called society, or the scramble for social or political distinctions. With disgust and loathing I turn from these to undefiled nature, seek rapture in her idyllic abodes, commune with the silent muses, be at peace with myself and the world at large. Yes, it has paid me well and will pay everyone to have nice surroundings. You will receive pleasure that you may now be unconscious of. You will be all the more proud of your home if it is beautiful, and without wishing to pose as an example, I do believe that a man is more respected, will be in better standing with his family and the community for showing high ideals and appreciation of the beautiful. He will be a better patriot to his country for he will defend that home with

Buildings at "Quietdale," home of H J. Hess, near Waterloo Iowa.

its pleasant associations at a great sacrifice. For the defense of an attractive home he would willingly transform from a horticulturist into a soldier.

For the benefit of our children it pays to make home beautiful without as well as within. Blessed is he who cherishes the memory of a grand old homestead with its pleasant associations and endearments, on which were spent childhood's happy days. Although children will appear unappreciative of home attractions, yet there will come a day when thrown upon their own resources for a living, fighting the battles of life in a cold and unresponsive world, and when awakened to a fuller realization to all that is good and noble, they will recall with grateful remembrance not only the attractions of the old home, but hold in sacred regard the moral precepts and teachings of those who made home attractive for their sake. And as full grown men and women we can hear them repeat, "What father used to tell us," and "How mother used to do." Yes it will pay you a thousand fold if not for your own enjoyment then for those whom you shelter and provide for, to make home not a barren, disagreeable place, but an attractive abode.

Nor does it cost much money or labor to add attractions to a place. Be it ever so humble or unpretentious you do not have to be such plungers in horticulture as my brother or myself. You do not have to be such a horticultural crank as I am, and yet with a little attention and outlay you can give tidiness and ornamentation to a home. The amateur landscape gardener should imitate nature in his ground plat and carefully avoid planting in circles and rows, except in case of roads and lanes, for nature abhors symmetry and angles. Lawn plantings should be in groups and clumps, in such manner to open views near and distant and produce surprising effects, by way of contrast and color. We have purple, silver. golden and the various tinges of green colors to accomplish this. All suckering shrubs and trees, as well as soft maples, seed bearing box elders. and cotton woods are not suitable for lawn planting. However valuable a tree or shrub may be in the right place, it may become a nuisance in the wrong place. Above all we should plant a variety and not share the experience of many farmers of today whose maple trees are all dying at the same time, leaving the place treeless just when it ought to be in its prime. There is every chance of making a bungling job of your first planting unless you are an experienced landscape gardener, which none of you are, and rather than master the difficulties of this branch of horticulture, it would pay to engage a professional to assist and advise in laying out a new place, thus starting right and avoiding serious mistakes. Some eastern firms will furnish plans if you give them an order for trees. Henry Wieses' place here has been worked on that order and proved very satisfactory. For a durable, lasting shade tree, that does not obstruct the view, and improved with age, and is suitable for planting around the house, is pre-eminently the high growing elm tree. The different oaks should have a conspicuous place in lawn ornamentation. If in addition to ornamental trees and shrubs in number and kinds as circumstances allow, you have a good lawn kept short by smaller boys, and studded here and there with a few flowers to give color, the problem of home surroundings will be settled.

The extent of a lawn should be limited to your ability and interest to take care of it. Do not overreach yourself with a large, ill kept garden, when a smaller one might have been kept in better shape. You will have a thousand things to contend with. Rabbits, mice, sunscald, blight, borers and caterpillars; things seen and things unseen, will drive you out of the business in short order if you are a half-hearted horticulturist with a big lot of trees on your hands. The spring following the hard winter of '90 and '91, I hauled out two big wagon loads of dead trees of every description. It was the saddest cremation I ever attended, to see the pets of my lawn, objects of many years' care, go up in smoke and ashes. But the final triumphs and success in this as in all undertakings will enable us to forget its attending failures and disappointments, and today I realize the fulfillment of my boyhood dreams of being the proud possesser of every tree and shrub adapted to this climate.

WHAT FARMERS SHOULD READ.

Mrs. John Carson, before the Winnebago County Farmers' Institute.

Not the least among the privileges and delight of a farmer's life is the leisure for reading. The opportunity of holding fellowship with noted men and women through books and papers. Our city and town friends may well envy us this boon of leisure to one's self and family for reading. After the evening work is finished and all gather around the lamp in winter, on or the porch or in a hammock in summer the interruption is the exception, not the rule as in town or business life. One can actually lose himself in the perusal of some good book, can travel all over the world by means of descriptive essays; and make friends of the greatest men and women in the world through a sympathetic following of their thoughts. Man instinctively grows to be like those with whom he constantly associates. In the line of books, and reading matter, there is no reason why farmers and farmers' wives should not choose the very best there is in the world—consequently they may have for associates the best people in the world, and grow to be themselves like those, and with whom they are constantly thinking.

One is never alone, with a good book at hand and there can be no thought of loneliness in connection with farms on the mail routes, where fresh reading matter is at hand each day. A public library is a blessing to any community, and even if it be ten miles away, a book can be kept two weeks; and all go to town on business oftener than that.

Those receiving the mail, early in the day, on the mail routes, have the advantage in this way—they can all look over the daily papers at noon time, or in the intervals of leisure, and still have the evening left for the periodical, while if the mail is not brought in until night, it is a temptation to some to spend the entire evening, with the papers. There is a great deal in our daily papers, not worth reading, much less studying. One must cultivate the habit of glancing over the headings and gleaning here and there the wheat, leaving the chaff. It was Bacon who said, "Some books are to be tasted, others to be swallowed, some few to be chewed and digested." This is especially applicable to our newspapers—most of it is to be merely tasted. We do want to know of course the progress of the war in Venezuela, how the coal commission is coming on, the movements of the political parties, market reports, etc. But that fearful suicide, and the detailed record of a divorce suit and countless other things too numerous to mention, we cannot afford to spend our valuable time upon any more than we can afford to spend our hard earned dollars on tawdry jewelry instead of comforts. Few of us think of doing the latter. Why then should we do the former? In the periodicals such as McClures, The Cosmopolitans, Ladies' Home Journal, Scribners' and Harpers' one finds articles of great value—food for thought, a mental stimulus. There are so many things which we need to know; we are discouraged some times at the vast funds of knowledge that we can barely touch.

Some farmers' families club together, taking several magazines and exchanging so all can have the benefit. One family, however, I have in mind never economizes in this matter; but five or more magazines and as many papers are found in that home. By the way I can't think of anything more attractive than that parlor—a cheerful fire, plenty of easy chairs and a table literally covered with interesting and instructive reading matter.

I never can resist treating myself to at least one or two glimpses into a freshly cut magazine. Some articles in our farm journals are not practical. They are theories written by some one who does not know as much about actual farming, feeding and stock raising as the farmer himself. Therefore we can't afford to spend much time with them. Occasionally, however, one finds an exceptionally good article and derives sufficient benefit therefrom to more than pay his subscription price.

But let us so plan our reading as to have some time for periodicals, good biographies and stories like "Eben Holden" and "She Sky Pilot." All farmers enjoy Hamlin Garland's stories, especially Iowa farmers. His descriptions are true to life and some of his scenes are taken from Iowa. His picture of threshing time in "Main Traveled Roads" is especially good. The reader will seem to hear the whir and noise of the threshing machine; and see the men seated at dinner around a long table passing jokes with their coffee. The descriptions of western scenery found in the "Sky Pilot" by Ralph Conner are beautiful. One can imagine himself right there in the grand canyon. In "Eben Holden" farmers cannot fail to be interested. An ideal farmer's home is presented to us and in that story as also in "David Harum" the horse trade is well written up.

Then of course in our reading we must not forget that best of all books, the Bible. Some one may possibly say that he is too tired at night to read. Then, my friend, you have been working too hard. You are not making your life all it ought to be, when you so abuse your physical make-up, by overwork, that the mental part refuses to take its share in natural food and consequent growth. Another says he never has any time

44

for reading. Let me read you what Col. Woods says to farmers. All stock men know of Col. Woods. "Mr. Farmer, let me advise you. I speak from experience. I have endured poverty, hard times and calamities unnecessary to mention here. I have seen the time that a copper cent seemed more valuable to me and I would guard it with more care than I would today a five-pound chunk of gold. I say, let me advise you to halt in your mad race for gold and take a little time for reading, recreation and enjoyment. You have only one life to live, and when you die, you will stay dead a long time. I was fifty years old before I thought I could afford a vacation, but I made a mistake. I can see it now. Go slower and live longer and you will take just as much cash with you when you die."

Possibly some of us don't care for reading. If so let me urge you to encourage your children to read. Have the magazines in the home for their benefit. In so many homes, sometimes before the evening work is all done, we find the boys with their horses already saddled to go to town to spend the evening and sometimes part of the night at the village stores listening to and participating in all sorts of village gossip. Let us educate our children for something better than this; so that the next generation of farmers may rank high in ability, thought and life.

We will not educate them to leave the farm, but to love the farm—to make farm life the best of all lives and the vocation of farming superior to what it now is, and thus truly a desirable vocation. The time is past when people feel sorry for the farmer. A drive out through any of the townships, with their fine barns and commodious even elegant homes, with all modern conveniences will convince anyone he is wasting his sympathy when he pities the farmer.

Of all classes of people a farmer needs a liberal education—because the pursuit of farming covers such a wide range—biology, the care of the animals he has around him—botany, horticulture, chemistry and meteorology. He must know the use of machinery, hence a knowledge of mechanics. He buys and sells and needs also to understand finance. How useful, how indispensable is a knowledge of all these to the successful farmer! People used to think, no need of a farmer's son going farther than the district school (unless he meant to be a professional man of some sort) and to claim that education made a boy dissatisfied with farm life. But now from the present advanced standpoint of the farmer in the light which the progress of the last century has thrown around us, with our free mail delivery and our telephones bringing us into touch with the great world around us, we feel and know that those ideas were wrong. The more thorough an education the child has, the broader his life view— the happier he is because he sees more in nature and greater possibilities in his work and he is contented. He is able to reason intelligently from cause to effect (very necessary on a farm) and will be able to make a grand success in his life; to exert an uplifting influence in all questions of the day, civic and politic. Let us read then with these ends in view, to keep abreast of the times and to be able to lead our children ever to higher and nobler fields of life.

Since writing this paper I have heard for the first time of a "Farmers' Reading Course." It is under the auspices of the United States Department of Agriculture. A description of it may be found in "Farmers' Bulletin No. 109." Pennsylvania was the first state to adopt it. Michigan followed, then New Hampshire, Connecticut, New York, West Virginia and South Dakota. The work was set on foot by the agricultural colleges and experiment stations. The supervision and direction of the work has been largely in their hands. The work is conducted on the Chautauqua plan. The college lays out certain courses of agricultural reading on such subjects as soils and crops, live stock feeding and breeding, dairying, fruit culture, gardening, farm economics, domestic economy and other like topics, selects sets of books for reading, provides for superintending the work and makes arrangements for supplying readers with book, examination questions, etc. The reading course is designed to bring to the farmer in his own home the opportunity of taking under college directions a course of reading on subjects especially pertaining to his work. Then, where a number of farmers in the same community are reading the course they can organize themselves into a farmers' club and meet occasionally to exchange ideas. I think Iowa had better follow the lead of South Dakota.

INFLUENCE OF FARM LIFE.

Mrs. W. T. Goodman, before Page County Farmers' Institute.

Why are so many of our great men and women from the farms? First we as a nation wish men to manage the affairs of state, and generals to lead our armies that are physically, as well as mentally strong; and all know that no labor is so conducive to health as that found in the tilling of the fields. The prosperous farmer is judicious, broad minded and careful when, how and what he sows, that we may reap an abundant harvest; and a good statesman will always be on the alert to strike when the iron is hot. It has been at the knee of some dear old country mother that our most devout and saintly pastors first felt called upon to do God's work. From where springs our sympathy and tenderness? How they blend in that word love in the country home. Does sympathy and science clash? No, not if the true man stands behind the surgeon's knife. There is something almost divinely brave and tender in the great physician, who can increase suffering, if need be to have life, all the while ready with watchful eye to give that sympathy so needed when both body and heart fail; our best skilled physicians came from the farm homes. In the city a mothers' time is spent in clubs and entertaining her guests; her children are left to the care of hired help, while in the country home the mother ministers to her child's needs. Think what an advantage the one mother has over the other in leading those children into paths of honor and right. Children here with us while they are tender and flexible; we can bend them as a twig. Mothers, none in the world have such an interest in your child as you have; if of everything else in this world you make a success, and your boy or girl goes astray, your life has been a failure; for while looking after the temporal things of this life you have allowed the treasure (the soul of your child), intrusted to you, to be lost, the foundation of their whole life depends upon you; then those that have had the foundation of their lives laid by any one but that loving mother cannot have a stone whereon to build; and of course will not fill so well any public office. Lincoln said, "All that I am or ever expect to be I owe to my mother," and that mother was a country mother. The way to teach our children was given us by Christ. We were told to lead them by our own example, and how can we do that if we have them not under our watchful care. Teach your children that if they would be great and good men and women, to be true to themselves, stand by their own character; and be sure their calling in life in a good one; then think, plan, work and live for it, throw into it their whole mind, strength, heart and soul; then no matter what their work is, if it be the planting of a nation, or a patch of potatoes, they will do it with honor to themselves; and be able to fill with credit any position to which they may be called. How many brave men were called from the plow to silence the angry tumult in the Civil War? Washington could wield alike sickle and sword. Our heroes are not men that have been raised in the lap of luxury; but are men whom necessity has compelled to spend many long days in the scorching rays of the sun; it is by darkness and storm that heroism gains its greatest developments, then it kindles the black clouds into a blaze of glory. Now we would ask what makes the great man? I would answer physical bodies, moral and religious character—and all these are gathered from the farm.

ARE WE, AS FARMERS, MAKING THE PROGRESS THAT WE SHOULD?

Mrs. Blake Cole, before the Mitchell County Farmers' Institute.

A short time ago your program committee man interviewed me and requested that a paper be prepared for this institute on the subject, "Are We Improving?" He made no explanation as to whether that we, he and I as individuals, or we of Mitchell county, we Iowans, or whether it should include all the nations and peoples of this great terrestrial ball.

Then there are such varied opinions as to what improving is. The great, tall, stalwart woodsman would tell of his physical conquests and his son would have advanced only as he could outdo his fathers, with the ax or in the fight.

With the scholar, mind is paramount and intellectual progress alone is improving.

Then there is moral progress, religious progress, financial progress, political progress, social progress and so on *adinfinitum*.

Hence you see, my original subject is a very broad one as well as one of exceedingly great importance, for upon an affirmative answer being a truthful one, depends much of our weal and woe, our success or non-success and not of ours only, but of our posterity as well. Progression or retrogression is the universal law.

Fifty years ago, Mitchell county was uninhabited. Its broad prairies stretched out in all their grandeur. The eye could look for miles and miles and see nothing but grass, grass with now and then a tow-head to break the monotony. But the cry went up in the east—go west, young man, go west. Leave your rocks and stumps and go out and inhabit the beautiful. Brave men and brave women too, heard the cry and came with stout hearts and willing hands. At first they settled near the streams as timber for fuel and water were necessities. On their $1.25 per acre land, little log houses sprang up. A yoke of oxen and a cow often constituted a man's personal property. Many came with even less than that. Market one hundred miles away, no roads, no bridges, no fences. They had none of the modern machinery; they sowed broadcast by hand; they mowed with the scythe, they harvested with the cradle. They plodded along, doing the best they could on their meager incomes while they subdued the tough but fertile soil. Long days, hard toil, poor rations, thin clothing, small incomes—these were their portion. All honor to these veteran pioneers; they laid the foundation, firm and strong and sure upon which we are building. I trust that none of the present or future generation will ever feel the least inclination to belittle their labors, or fail to reverently honor such of the noble fathers of Mitchell county as are yet among us.

They solved the problems of life as they came to them. When some twenty-five years ago they realized that land could deteriorate in fertility and that wheat was an uncertain crop, they cast about to find some other means by which they could provide life's necessities and liquidate indebtedness. They hit upon the cow and fortunate for them and for you and me as well, that she came to their rescue. It was a long step up the ladder of prosperity.

But we soon tired of the rows of long shelves in the cellar filled with six-quart pans of cream-covered milk, all of which must be skimmed, the cream ripened and then churned by hand after pail upon pail of water had been carried down and up those tiresome cellar steps to reduce the temperature of said cream. The very thought of the labor is appalling to the farmer's wife of today and who sees only so much milk and cream as are necessary for the family consumption, the rest of it having passed through the farm separator and found its way directly to the milk tank or to the calves and pigs.

The creamery—what a boon it has been to the busy wife and mother. In this line Mitchell county is proud of her improvement over old fashioned methods. I wonder if there is a creamery in the state that puts out more butter than Osage Co-operative, and at less expense per pound. We think not, at least it has wrought wonders. But we are not at the top. A dozen years ago our butter sold for Western Extra—it sells for that today.

With all our modern improvements and opportunities for enlightenment in handling milk and cream, our grade should have advanced one point at least, and why should we not climb to the top?

Formerly, any bovine was in demand and little thought was given to quality, but gradually, there came about a change. Men of pluck, energy and foresight, having unbounded faith in the future of the cattle industry, secured a few head of what was then high blooded cattle.

It was an object lesson and for years worked marvels. Iowa's experiment station was glad to procure some of Mitchell county's blood. At the World's Fair, nine years ago, the first prize for Short-horn cow was given to Mitchell county. Could we win a like prize at St. Louis a year hence? Nay, verily. Most truly do I dislike to admit it and (should there be any townsmen or strangers among us, I hope they will charitably close their ears) but the fact remains—we are not abreast of the times in either our cattle or horse industry. Fellow farmers, I ask you as you travel over Mitchell county, can you truthfully say there has been one iota of improvement in the past ten years? Rather have we not gone backward and I wish you might all answer audibly in the negative.   ,

"New occasions teach new duties,
    Time makes ancient good uncouth,
  They must upward still and onward
    Who would keep abreast of truth."

The improvements made in the herds of the leading breeds of cattle in the past few years is something marvelous. More particularly is this true in the western hemisphere. It has been a sure and steady growth. Few started as did Jamison whose first purchase consisted of 129 Herefords to which the following spring, he added forty-five more. Sotham's record-breaking herd was built up by the life work and thought of its owner.

And how have the Black Polls come to the front, $9,100 with one exception, the highest price paid in recent years for one black animal, was received by Judy at his late sale in which were twenty-four head averaging $1,276.05.

Then the Short-horn, the farmers' favorite, the dual purpose cow (may her tribe increase) will take no back seat. Many breeders, patient, painstaking and practical, have enlisted to do her honor. Robbins began at the bottom round of the ladder and his life has been spent bringing his herd to its present high standard. He paid $85 for Ruberta's mother— money will not buy Ruberta. Casey has shunned fad and fashion and labored for merit only. Then we have Ward of Iowa, with his St. Valentine, and Westrope who has probably done more than any other one man to build up the cattle interests of the state. A proud day it was for him when at his dispersion sale twenty-nine pure Scotch struck an average of $820 and Sweet Violet sold for $3,705. The Scottish breeder, Wm. Marr, hesitated long before he consented to send a cow to our International, fearing western breeders would not appreciate her worth. But when the auctioneer's hammer dropped and she was declared sold to W. C. Edwards for $6,000, he was converted. Western breeders did recognize the merit and were willing to pay the price for it.

At the fat stock show a year ago, the Angus were in the lead—this year the Herefords. Next year we look for the Short-horns to have their innings. Sickness and death prevented the load prepared by Henry Browner from being exhibited. They were sold six weeks later, then overripe, and lacked but three-tenths of one per cent of dressing equal net to gross with the prize load of Herefords which were taken at their best. Capable cattle buyers at the yards thought this load would have been a very close competition for the prize. At the Edinburg exhibit the Short-horn cows averaged 1,760 pounds, and the largest one weighed 2,280. Hundreds of cows supply that city with milk and the Short-horns are considered the most profitable, for they not only make good milkers but their large well rounded carcasses sell well for beef.

Better blood is the demand of the times. An Idaho rancher wrote asking a Hereford man the price of seven of his animals. On getting a reply he wrote back: "Can't afford; 'twould take forty-five of my cattle to buy them; pure bloods are for the rich." "Get some pure bloods and you'll soon be rich was the retort."

Now we cannot all own Dale, whose symmetry it is said is perfected by a silver plate in his back; we cannot all be Robbins and take in two years, $12,000 in prizes; we may not be able to pay $9,100 for a single Doddie Polled Angus, but Mitchell county has a number of farmers who can afford and ought to have $1,000 in a single animal. Who will be the first to give us an up-to-date herd of cattle, that in a few years will put us on a par with any county in the state?

The outlook for horse industry is brightening. Praise, gratitude and honor should be bestowed upon the enterprising, far-sighted farmers, who are risking from $2,000 to $3,000 in a single horse. May they reap the profit they so richly deserve. It is said "he who makes two blades of grass grow where only one grew formerly is a benefactor of mankind." How much more truly may this be said of him who doubles or quadruples the value of any of our domestic animals. And that is not impossible— sometimes it seems as if it will be a necessity.

One problem that confront us today is our high priced land. When farm sells at from $50 to $90 per acre we cannot farm as did our fathers on their ten shilling land. Plans must be laid so as to get all possible out of each acre yet leave it no less productive. Our yields per acre are increasing but our average is still entirely too low. In this line as in many others we are being helped and encouraged by our experiment station. They do have variety and they get yields. Our station produced seventy-four bushels of barley per acre, three times the average for the state. Their wheat also yielded thrice the state's average.

There is so much in the know how. I have been told that probably the fattest steer in Chicago last December, was a grade Short-horn from Iowa and that ninety days before the show, his owner was offered $600 for him. He was fat but not symmetrically fat. The finishing had been improperly done. The feeder didn't know how. Hence the animal was not entered. To give us the know how is the aim of our stations. They are continually sending out valuable reports and statistics. They try new varieties and we get the benefit. They tell us how to raise calves on skim milk, and yet not have skim milk calves—how to fatten the steer and the hog—in fact they are continually giving us the benefit of everything in the line of progressive agriculture.

A few years ago, Ames was looked upon as an inferior school—today she is second to none. The names of her president and professors are familiar to all who read agricultural papers. Her reputation is national. Her two weeks' course in grain and stock judging the past winter was commented on far and near. Over four hundred men of all ages, and from all over the state and many from outside the state as well, assembled each morning at six o'clock and studied until nine thirty in the afternoon, with only intermissions for meals. All seemed anxious to learn, from the gray haired farmer, whose education was obtained mainly in the rugged school of experience to the younger and more polished graduates of our best schools and colleges and universities. Never before did a like class have such an opportunity for up-to-date work. Proud of our agricultural college? Words cannot express it.

> Lives there a man with soul so dead
> Who never to himself hath said,
> "This is our own loved Iowa's school?"

Do our boys practice what they learn? Some do and some do not. I am intimately acquainted with a young man who is attending one of these agricultural colleges. Last summer he spent his summer vacation at home. Could you have visited him, you would have seen a few acres of speltz, a little rape, a patch of bromus, part of an acre of mangles and various other varieties with which he was experimenting. In fly time you would have seen him going among the Short-horns applying a mixture that served to give the animals relief from their enemies. He did their welding. All his father's discarded saws were filed and put in order. A year ago, he paid his own expenses to fat stock show—this year, he was requested to go at station's expense to care for the cattle. In buying stock he is ever urging his father to get better. Progress is one of the many things taught at these valuable schools.

But I must hasten and dwell for a moment upon our own district schools. The little white—not red—school house, still stands on the hill, but how much more beautiful and attractive than twenty or thirty years ago. Not so well filled as formerly but so much better equipped, with their pictures, libraries and organs.

I look with dread and dismal forebodings upon any attempt to disenthrone these inspirers of our youth, these promoters of our peace, these guardians of our liberty. Do not statistics show that the majority of our best and ablest men started their school lives in these same little country schools? Is not one of the great objects for living in the country that our children may not mingle in great masses where there is sure to be much of impurity and depravity? Is not childhood better off in the small country home where the teacher can know and mother each individual.? Do the town people begrudge us our good records that they harp in our ears, township schools for our little ones? We are told it will be cheaper. Does not the average farmer pay his taxes as willingly and honestly as anyone though they are no light burden? I might speak of the winters with their deep snows and impossible roads. I might speak of the bitterly cold days when you would not think of sending your children a half dozen miles or more to school. I might speak of the spring break-up when the roughness of the highways would be death to a delicate child. I might go on indefinitely, but I refrain. We have no fight against town schools; we glory in those of our state and in the work they are doing. As our children advance in years and knowledge, we seek their services and gladly pay their prices. But in regard to our country schools we would that our legislators and educators would cease their murmurings. We ask, we beg, we implore them to permit us to retain the school house on the hill, the church in the valley. They have done much toward giving to Iowa the lowest percentage of illiteracy in the nation. Their work is not yet finished—we trust it is only just begun.

Mitchell county farmers making progress? Is there one that doubts it? Each year sees the price of land mount a little higher—his farm home a little larger and more beautiful, his outbuildings more numerous and modern, the yields of his grain a little larger, the sales of his stock a little greater and statistics show that mortgages are being paid off more rapidly than in the days of the cheap land.

We are abundantly supplied with machinery of modern invention. The corn binder a few years ago was unknown. Last fall Mitchell county put into shock hundreds of acres of corn and thereby saved for herself thousands of dollars. The cutter, planter and digger have greatly increased our potato average, and the crop is a profitable one.

But yields of grain must be still farther increased—all fodder must be used—the amount of forage per acre must be doubled—all scrub stock must go, even the mongrel poultry we will have none of. We must come to know that the best is none too good for our Iowa soil.

The comforts of life receive due consideration. Few are without a surry or carriage or both. The homes are tastily and elaborately furnished. Books and periodicals are abundant. Telegraphs and telephones do his bidding. Two rural mail routes are now in operation and it is reported that three more will start with the beginning of next month. Life's necessities, comforts, yea many of its luxuries, are ours. As if to keep pace with all the rest, the very clime has modified and improved, and delightful winters are now our portion.

One other thought and I am done. It is this: Commercial, financial, even intellectual progress counts for little unless accompanied by true moral worth. In regard to our improvement or lack of improvement in this line, the last census is silent—no statistics are compiled and so, farmers of Mitchell county, I come to you asking, are we making moral progress? Is there an upward tendency? Are we more temperate? Are honesty and honor abroad in the land? Is there any danger of our ideals becoming commercialized? What of the home influences? Do they tend toward piety and reverence?

We live in Iowa, the banner agricultural and live stock state of the union. Iowa, small in illiteracy, great in political prestige. Iowa, with her newspapers, schools and colleges. Iowa, blest of generous heaven, may the life of the Mitchell county farmer but add to her laurels. May his ideals be lofty, his purposes noble. In the midst of so much complexity of life may he still retain simplicity and purity. May charity in thought and word be his. May he be upright, honest, honorable. May he build character, pure, steadfast and undefiled. May time show that worldly prosperity shall not be undoing but rather shall be a power in his hands for the hastening of the time when love is law and all men shall brothers be.

ENTERTAINING ON THE FARM.

Mrs. Belle Miller-Dunn, before the Page County Farmers' Institute.

The essence of good entertainment is the spirit in which we entertain. Our own happiness is so interwoven with the happiness of others that we cannot seek our own highest interests without being mindful of the welfare of others. No matter how humble a person may be, if they regard us enough to enter our home they have honored us and are worthy of our cordial hospitality. I know it is natural to be unresponsive and unsympathetic towards some and there are times when we are not in the mood for entertaining; but let us rise above self and we will not forget our ailments and trials in becoming engrossed with the welfare of others.

Entertaining is a grand school for studying human nature. As the honey bee sips nectar from the flower, so may we absorb knowledge and develop latent possibilities from social intercourse with our visitors. Entertaining does not consist in vieing with one another in the display of costly tables and fine dwellings. I have been in finely furnished homes where the very atmosphere seemed to freeze me because of the stiffness and formality of the family. Then I have been in homes where wealth and luxury had no part, yet the warmth and sunshine that seemed to radiate from the hostess more than compensated for the poor surroundings. While attending college my roommate and I once took dinner with one of her friends. It was in a humble cottage and the meal consisted simply of bread, butter and coffee. The bread was faultless, the butter gilt-edged and the coffee of the best. The hospitality of the genial hostess gave us a keen appetite for the simple, home-made food, which tasted extra good beside the oleo butter and baker's bread we had been used to at collge. What need was there for apologies?

Harriet Beecher Stowe has said, "There would be more obedience to the apostolic injunction, 'Be not forgetful to entertain strangers,' if it could be gotten into the heads of well meaning people what it is that strangers want." What do you yourself want when you are away from home among strangers? Is it not the warmth of the fireside and the sight of people who take an interest in you? And had you rather not dine with an old friend on simple cold mutton offered with a warm heart than to go to a splendid ceremonious dinner party where people have no real sympathy for you? Well, set it down in your book that other people are like you and that the art of entertaining is really the art of caring for people. If you have a warm heart, congenial tastes and a real interest in your acquaintances don't hesitate to invite them even though you have no fine dinner set and the plates you have are sadly chipped at the edges. Remember, you can give love, good will and sympathy, in which there is more real enjoyment than in Haviland china and sterling silver.

An error to be avoided is preparing such a superabundance of eatables for guests that we are so exhausted we cannot display our social qualities, besides endangering the digestion of our company. However, don't go to the other extreme of serving merely cut blass and silverware. There is a medium course to follow. Don't attempt to prepare anything for which you have never tried the recipe but have everything well cooked and well seasoned.

So many suggestions are given in the papers for parties and receptions that it seems hardly worth while for me to give any, though perhaps I should. Have a few simple games in which everyone may take part. Memory tests are an incentive for us to be more studious. One is to arrange articles to suggest the titles of books. Thus tooth-picks, small pieces of paper and a lampwick suggest "Pickwick Papers." A picture of a soldier placed beneath a couple of small flags suggests "Under Two Flags."

The conundrum idea never grows stale. At one reception I attended the guests were required to give each a conundrum before being served with refreshments. At another a prize was given to the one giving the best newspaper joke.

As to refreshments, there is generally plenty of milk and eggs on the farm and there is nothing nicer than ice cream and cake either winter or summer. Peach or pineable sherbet is nice for a change. Just cake and coffee is very suitable and easily prepared. If something more elaborate is desired a little chicken salad with a sprig of parsley may be served first, or bread and butter sandwiches cut into fancy shapes.

Children should be entertained in a room where all the bric-a-brac has been removed. Then they will not be under restraint for fear of breaking something and can have a jolly good time playing "Color," "Fruit Basket" or "Magic Music." If any of the family are musicians they can be of great help at a children's party. The refreshments should be very simple and easily prepared. Animal crackers are just the thing to pass around first. Square soda crackers with nut icing or two with butter and jam between are very nice served with iced milk to drink. And don't forget that children always enjoy apples, even if they have plenty at home.

The average young lady on the farm has been drilled in the culinary art and she not only helps her mother in the ordinary cooking but is chief cook when her mother has company. When the guests are the daughter's the thoughtful mother will allow her time to entertain them. The majority of young ladies in this age are so accomplished that they can sing, play or recite and thus be of great help in entertaining company, whether it be their own or their mother's.

In closing, I will say, let us remember to give our guests the best of ourselves and of our homes. No one can do more, no matter what their facilities for entertaining are.

READING AND ITS EFFECT UPON CHARACTER.

Elmer E. Norris, before the Ringgold County Farmers' Institute.

You will all agree with me that reading is a very important study but as to the class of reading you will probably differ. Reading is the basis of all educational advancement; yet it may be a deadly enemy to intellectual progress. Don't think that because your boy or girl can call words rapidly or that they have read many books that they are good readers. They may not have read at all for reading includes more than calling words or going through books. The definition that reading is pronouncing or perusing written or printed words falls far short of my idea of reading. Oral reading is sounding thought and mute reading is getting thought and anything short of that does not come up to my idea. The greatest enemy to intellectual development is too much (so-called) reading and not enough thought or study. The causes are many. Among them are daily papers; cheapness of papers and books of light character, written to pass the time away, to entertain the reader and not for reflection; failure of teachers to give proper time and to bring out the thought in every reading lesson. It is not the amount of words gone over but the amount of thought developed in going over the words that count in intellectual life.

Good training in reading includes ideas, thoughts, as well as the mechanical. Under language: words, sentences, general expression, reading, writing, pronunciation; under principals, thought, action, manhood, womanhood, citizenship, character.

In teaching reading (and I take it that all parents are teachers of reading) I want to make some observations:

1. Observe grace and ease of position.
2. Observe a natural and conversational tone.
3. Observe the cultivation of a good voice.
4. Observe the sentiments of the selection read.
5. Observe the meaning of words.
6. Observe the greatest amount of information from the first reading; then you should secure a ready recognition of words.

Secure clear and distinct articulation, proper breathing, natural inflection and expression, a reproduction of the thought, quickness of eye and ear, a desire for reading, good literature, proper picture reading.

To get the best results from reading in our country homes, we should have a program and devote a certain time—say four hours per week in winter—to systematic reading, with some fixed purpose in view. If it is a standard novel, and no other should enter your home, read it carefully, take up its leading parts and discuss it with the family. It will aid your memory and at least give you a wholesome thing to talk about. If you take up the classics, and you should three or four each winter, they are very helpful and you can get them very cheaply—English classics as low as 5 or 10 cents. I am not a book agent but I will gladly give any one a list of either the novels or the classics that I would recommend you to read.

Allow me to argue for a short time the value of a literary education, rather than the scientific to furnish the equipment our children need for active service in the cause of humanity. There is no other preparation in our schools so valuable as the study of our great authors. I know there is a prevalent idea that literature is not strengthening but to consider it thoughtfully proves the contrary. Shakespear's training, like all the great writers of ancient or modern times, was wholly literary rather than scientific. Caesar knew nothing of science. Milton was indebted to Homer, Spencer and Shakespeare. The greatest statesman of England, Wm. E. Gladstone, was a man of letters; Bismarck a graduate of two classic universities; Wm. M. Evarts, the foremost lawyer of America, a Yale classic graduate. Did not the pen of Moses shape the Hebrew civilization? In Greek and Roman life was not the Iliad the most potent factor, and is not our modern civilization but the outgrowth of the Book or Books. He who wrote the Preamble of our Constitution, "We, the people," etc., and 118 of the 350 men who sat in the Continental Congress were classic graduates. He who ably wrote and who grandly defended by his mortal utterances the Declaration of Independence and 28 of the 56 signers who hurled this charter in to the teeth of the British lion making the republic possible and bequeathing to us and our posterity the blessings of liberty, were classical graduates.

The proper study of literature corrects wrong tendencies. It does not give radical changes but always tending forward and so accomplishes its purpose.

To get the best results in literary work in our public schools, we should have a place for it on the program and in our course of study and devote as much time as to any other subject—not bring it up some Friday afternoon as though of no great importance. The child should be taught that right expression is as important as the multiplication table. Emerson says: "We send our children to school thinking that the teacher, the studies educate them. But in reality it is their companions, the shop windows, the streets.' Now if true I know of nothing better to counteract this street education than to make pure wholesome literature his companion. It should be presented so prominently and attractively that the child will learn to recognize its value and to love it.

"Twinkle, twinkle, little star,
How I wonder what you are.
Up above the world so high,
Like a diamond in the sky."

This is a quotation that most every child has heard and can repeat and really what child has not been made better and his thoughts of things made higher and brighter by those words.

There should be two objects in view in reading: intellectually, morally and indirectly physically. But how can reading give these practical requisites. I answer it can. It does and even more. It is in short that which distinguishes the classic from the average scholar. It brings a person in contact with the best minds of the past and present. You listen to the voice of learning that has been accumulating during the ages; you live in a higher atmosphere and under purer laws. The pen that is chrystalizing the beautiful thoughts of the present will be on the printed page tomorrow. The admonitions of the poet and sage come to us through reading.

We may not know the complete worth of Dante, but who has not paused when he read, "He who enters here leaves all hope behind." Literature gives us the key that will unlock the hidden treasures of the authors and the books will open the temple of learning that contains the priceless treasure. It will open the word palaces of the language that holds the thought imprisoned within their lettered walls. It will open the vestibule doors to the marbled halls of history. It will open the delicate casket of the flower and the leaf and reveal to the mind the secret thoughts that were imprisoned there at creation's morn. It will open the stone vaulted libraries of the rocks and the hills and bring to light the biography of the earth writen without hands upon the marble and the clay. It will open the mind and heart to that wisdom which the noblest of prophets and poets say cannot be gotten for gold; neither shall silver be weighed as the price thereof.

Holmes says: "One story intellects, two story interrects, three story interrects, with sky light. All fact collectors who have no aim beyond their facts are one story men. Two story men compare reason, generalize, using the labors of the fact collectors, as well as their own. Three story men idealize, imagine, predict; their best illumination comes from above through the sky light."

I have partly spoken in regard to its intellectual advantages but what of the physical. Right thoughts give right actions and right actions become habits and correct habits are conducive to proper physical development. Again we should use the gems of literature in quotation. An apt quotation is as good as an original remark, says one. Shakespeare gives us a lesson on opportunity in Julius Caesar.

"There is a tide in the affairs of men
Which taken at the Flood leads on to Fortune
Omitted all the voyage of their life
Is bound in shallows and in miseries."

And how we are spurned up to study and reading by hearing the words, "He that was taught only by himself has a fool for a master;" "they that will not be counseled cannot be helped;" in short, we hear of Chaucer in "Truth is the highest thing a man may keep;" of Spencer, "Knowledge is power;" from Milton, "Accuse not nature; she has done her part. Do thou but thine;" from Dryden, "Men are but children of a larger growth;" from Pope, "To err is human, but to forgive divine." We hear Goldsmith in the "Deserted Village." We hear the songs of Burns in "Honest Poverty," and from Cowper in the good old hymn, "God moves in a mysterious way His wonders to perform; He plants His footsteps on the sea and rides upon the storm." While Burk tells us, "To read without digestion." Moore gives us Irish songs of "Evening Bells;" and Keats says that "A thing of beauty is a joy forever." Mrs. Browning tells us, "That a happy life means prudent compromise." Geo. Elliott tells us, "That our deeds determine us as much as we determine our deeds." And our own country's illustrious authors we become acquainted with—Edwards and Drake and Franklin and Jefferson. We hear from Bryant, Longfellow and Poe. We talk with Lowell and Holmes and Saxe and Read. We read, "The Dirge for a Soldier" from Baker and "The Song of the Camp," from Taylor. One sweet and solemn thought comes from Phoeba and the "May verses" come from Alice. We hear of Holland and Harts and Miller; or Irving and Prescott and Bancroft and Motley. Webster makes us patriotic by telling us, "Liberty and union, now and forever more, one and inseparable." Everett points us to the rising sun. Whipple tells us that "Books are the lighthouses erected in the great sea of time." Then Sims finishes our list by saying that our distinctions do not lie in the places which we occupy but in the grace and dignity with which we fill them, and now at last literature serves as a great moral influence, while beautiful thoughts seem to be "wasted on the desert." They are not but the impressions they form, ever an unseen guide that whatever may come he must follow. West says, "That a kiss from my mother made me a painter," and if a kiss would so encourage the boy, how much more a beautiful sentence affect the delicate mind. But this is only exemplifying the truth—

"That as a man thinketh so is he; yet I doubt not through the ages, one increasing purpose runs and the thoughts of men are widened with the process of the sons."

THE FARM BOY AND GIRL'S RELIGIOUS TRAINING.

Julia Balt, before Fremont County Institute.

In ancient Sparta the training of children was confined to severe physical discipline. The frail ones were left in some mountain glen to die, while the sturdy ones were drilled in all sorts of athletics. They were also taught to steal, but if caught in the act were flogged unmercifully for their awkwardness. Under this system Sparta produced a fine race of warriors, but lack of moral fortitude defeated the benefits of physical strength. It is not enough to study the laws of hygiene and plan the food, clothing and exercise for the little ones.

If every farm child had the soul of a poet he might gain much spiritual truth from his surroundings. From the violet he might learn a lesson of humility, and from the songs of birds one of thankfulness and good cheer. But the truth is, we haven't many poets among our farm boys and girls, and the sturdy lad who follows the plow sees little in the broad fields save the posibility of grain.

When should the religious training of a child begin? When the tiny toddler approaches the fire you quickly warn him of his danger and soon by sad experience he learns that you were wiser than he and spoke the truth. In similar ways his confidence increases in you day by day until he becomes a veritable interrogation point. Just now is your golden opportunity, for he will accept that which in after years—when bitter experiences have filled his mind with doubt and perplexity—he may reject.

A little boy once told me of being sent on an errand, and while gone he met a horse which frightened him very much. "But," said he, "I just asked God to take care of me, and I got home all right." Though scarcely more than a baby, this little boy is older in Christian experience than many a man. If his mother succeeds in training him so he retains the faith of his childhood his life will be crowned with success.

Parents have reason to rejoice in the good morals taught in our public schools, but this cannot take the place of home training. Nor can a Sunday school teacher who is a comparative stranger do in half an hour what the parents should perform in a week's time at home.

On the farm home life may be what it cannot be in the city, with its many interruptions and temptations. Country children may see few shows and sometimes wince under the title of "back number," but I would rather one of my brothers should blow out the gas than become hardened in sin.

Miss Mulock beautifully describes the direct teaching of Bible truth when she pictures to us John Halifax with his wife and children gathered around him on Sunday afternoon reading to them the Holy Book. This may seem old-fashioned, but so is mother-love and many more of the best things in life. Good books may be a power for good in any home, and they are within the reach of all. Nowhere is good literature more appreciated than on the farm.

The moral value of good music can hardly be overestimated. Among the first things boys are taught in reform schools is to sing. Happy the family where all join together in singing at least once a week. The harmony of feeling will make up for any discord in sound.

The best of home influences cannot supplant the work of the church. Example in this, as in everything else, is all important. Only a few years and you will be beyond your children's call, but by your example you are preparing for them a legacy which will always remain with them. Do not decide every Sunday morning whether or not you will go to church,

but decide once for all that you will go whenever you can and you generally can. I have often wondered what the farm boy is thinking of as he
goes back and forth across the field all day long. Surely there is nothing
better for him to think of than the sermon he has heard on Sunday, or the
Christian Endeavor and Sunday school lessons.

Fathers and mothers, do not neglect the highest interests of your
children, for whom you are living and toiling. What doth it profit if your
clover fields are fragrant with an abundant crop and your stock brings
the highest market price if you have not provided for the eternal welfare
of your children?

MUTUAL INSURANCE.

M. Z. Bailey, before the Ringgold County Farmers' Institute.

Mutual insurance has passed the experimental stage. During the
thirty-seven years that the farmers' mutuals have been in existence, there
has been a gradual growth and development of these companies until now
we find 137 such companies doing business in the state. They have millions of dollars of insurance written and hundreds of millions behind them
in the best farmers of Iowa.

Thirty-seven years ago the state grange of Iowa organized the first
farm mutual company in the state. It comprised two townships in Johnson county. Starting with $10,000 written it now has $500,000 or one-
half million. That little company is a monument to the old state grange,
that will stand for years. It has saved the patrons over fifty per cent of
what it would have cost them to have carried insurance in a stock company, and it is a monument that we farmers can well afford to pattern after.

When the farm mutual was first organized, its promoters were paying to the stock companies 5½ and 6 per cent for combined insurance. At
first the mutuals were made light of, but as they developed strength the
stock companies began to cut on their rates, first from 6 to 5 per cent, then
from 4 to 3½ and finally down to 2½ per cent. But the 2½ rate was too
near the danger point. It was too small to allow the agents and officers
their usual large salaries. A convention was called by the stock companies and rates placed at two per cent for fire and lightning insurance
and three per cent for combined insurance. This made four mills on the
dollar for fire and lightning and six mills for the combined insurance,
payment in advance or your note at six per cent, making five mills every
year. The farm mutuals have averaged 2½ per cent yearly, making a
difference of one-half mill in favor of the latter.

Our county mutual has been in existence seventeen years, with nearly
all of the charter members still living. Starting with fifty thousand dollars written it now has nearly one million, or more accurately, $920,700.
Economy has had a great part in making our record cheap insurance; not
by litigation and trying to beat our patrons out of their losses, but by the

45

careful management of the association by its officers, our secretary and directors settling all claims and losses promptly and satisfactorily to the insured and to the association. Our county mutual in the last year paid out in losses $2,036 with a two-mill levy, and has 350 in the treasury, and in the seventeen years we have been running it has cost us an average of 2 1-5 mills on the dollar or just one-half of what it would cost in any stock company in the state of Iowa.

At no time in the history of the association has our state mutual windstorm and cyclone association occupied such a commanding position of usefulness and strength as at present. We have broken all previous records in amount of risks written, losses paid and amount of assessment levied. We have demonstrated our reliability and our ability to pay our losses, both great and small with a promptness not exceeded by any other company on earth. The amount of losses paid this year ($151,700) is more than the paid up capital stock of any Iowa company, yet we hear it argued that capital stock is necessary for the stability of the company. Thirty days after our assessment was made we had every dollar paid and a cash balance in the treasury of $45,000, and this too in one of the most disastrous years Iowa ever experienced. In the face of all these facts, I have no doubt some stock company agents will tell you that this association could not pay a loss of a few thousand dollars.

The town mutual dwelling house association more than holds good with our farm mutuals for cheap insurance. In the ten years it has been running it has paid less than a one mill levy or $7.5 on one thousand, for five years, which makes it the cheapest and safest insurance of any company in the state. In the ten years they have paid in losses $60,000, and now have $23,000,000 written, putting it in the front rank of any fire company in the state. You may howl about trusts and combines and pools and boards of trade, but the man that insures in a stock company is helping one of the largest combines along there is in the United States today. They take more money from the people according to the money invested than any other combination there is in the state of Iowa. And yet with all these facts before the people we still have lots of them helping the trusts along. Gentlemen, if you will give me the commission you are giving to these stock companies for five years, I will be the richest man in Ringgold county, or if you will come to me and let me write your insurance in the farm or town mutual, you can save that money for yourself and be your own company, and by so doing you help your fellow man as well as yourself which we all owe to one another as neighbors and friends.

ORNAMENTAL AND FOREST TREES FOR PROTECTION.

W. H. Lewis, before the Madison County Farmers' Institute.

Ladies and Gentlemen of the Madison County Farmers Institute: The subject, "Ornamental and Forest Trees for Protection," has been assigned me for such consideration as I may be able to give it.

In the haste which the very limited time for making arrangements for this institute compelled, the labor of making such preparation falling upon those—perhaps I had best say upon one—whose time was fully occupied by duties that could not be laid aside or postponed, and the whole matter new, resort was had as the only assistance that was available, to a list of topics that had been used at some farmers' institute previously held in this state. Like some other ready made articles it does not seem to fit my ideas very well and consequently my remarks may not fit the topic.

I shall expect that my views on this subject will agree with those of very few, if indeed of any of you—not because I propose to present improper or unreasonable views of the topic, nor because I assume to a superior or complete knowledge of the subject, but because you have each of you, your own personality and your own views, and those personalities and views differ with mine. If the expression by me of views not agreeing with your views and opinions, impels you to express your views on the subject, I shall think I have achieved a success.

Wisdom—valuable knowledge on any subject—is not acquired by unhesitatingly and unthinkingly accepting every statement which a speaker may make, even if that speaker is supposed to have superior knowledge of the topic a view which is specifically disclaimed in this case. An ostrich catches and swallows everything thrown to it—food, stones, or iron alike. An Iowa squirrel rapidly picks up every nut he comes to, but sitting at the door of his house, he carefully examines each one, in cases of doubt weighs it with each paw, and if he lays it away in his store for winter, it is because he knows it to be a good one. One of the homely philosophers of our time has said, "It is better to only know a few things than to know a great many things that are not so."

The topic seems to be limited to the protective feature of the value of trees. Protection seems at this time to be an absorbing topic of consideration with the men in the public eye, so I had best, in sympathy with the tendency of the times speak on protection. If we could get some way to protect our corn crop from the injurious winds, it would save for us a vast sum of money; indeed I am confident that wind is the cause of more injury to our corn than any other thing. Hot winds at tasselling time prevent proper fertilization and strong winds at filling and ripening time loosen the roots and make light, chaffy grain, and winds at other times work much harm to the growing crop.

Quite a variety of trees have been used for shelter, or as the term in common use has it—for windbreaks. The change that has come over this prairie region by reason of tree planting is very great. Forty years ago the settlers who had homes on the open prairies had planted cottonwood trees. Their rapid growth soon made the settler's grove a land mark by which the traveler was guided on his way. The rapid growth of the white willow, and the more potent consideration that money could be made in selling it caused many willows to be planted. The soft maple was native, and people soon found it was easily grown, and many maples were planted. These two trees, the white willow and the soft maple, have been of untold benefit to this prairie region. They have mitigated the rigor of the climate very materially. The relentless sweep of the arctic winds have been checked, the rate of evaporation has been reduced, the extremes of temperature have been lessened, the total rainfall increased and in general this region has been made a more agreeable place for those who live in it.

Since the general planting of the willows and maples a few men have tried other trees. Scattered here and there over the country are shelter belts and groves of evergreen trees. These have their merits and demerits. Comparing the two, the maple and the willow may be said to have the fault of occupying much space, their roots spread widely and monopolize the supply of moisture and the elements of fertility over a wide strip or land. They possess the good qualities of great height to intercept much of the sweeping wind, and good health, adaptability to this location, cheapness and rapid growth.

The evergreens have the advantages of their persistent foliage, making the same shelter during the entire year and a much less demand on the moisture and fertility of the soil in which they stand, and much less spread of roots thus occupying much less land and making it possible to grow good crops much nearer the row of trees than can be done with the maples or the willows. As objections, they are of less height, and some of them have tops diminishing in width as they ascend, not filling all the space or stopping all the wind. Some of them are of full width at their tops and are not liable to this objection. I feel free to speak on this matter as I am not in this branch of business, and I will say from a knowledge based on considerable experience that a shelter of Scotch pine is the best and the cheapest shelter a farmer can plant. Fewer trees are needed, its root system is deep so as to endure the extremes of our climate, and many desirable plants can be grown under their shelter than elsewhere. If a farmer will plant a single row of good trees of Scotch pine, setting them not closer than sixteen feet and I think wider would be better, give them good care for time enough that they become well established, and then treat them with prudent neglect, he will in a few years have a shelter that no one could buy of him.

Shelter belts occupy much land, and I think I have an example of an extreme use of them, having three belts on the length of a forty-acre tract and yet leaving one-fourth of the tract unprotected. They are on high priced land and occupy much of it, but I am fully convinced that year by year the product of the remaining part of that tract of land with the shelter belts upon it, is greater than would be the product of the entire tract without them.

There are other uses of trees both for ornament and protection, especially in the vicinity of our dwellings, but time will not allow of speaking of them now. The use of trees for protection—any kind rather than none —the best if you can get them—is one of the matters that no farmer can afford to neglect. The time is at hand when the absence of such protection will detract from the selling value of a farm, and make it more difficult to sell, as much as any other condition connected with it. If you have not already done so, plant a shelter at once.

PART XII.

REPORTS OF COUNTY AND DISTRICT SOCIETIES.

ADAIR COUNTY.

S. Y. Cornell.

Fair held September 9, 10, 11 and 12 at Greenfield. The exhibits in all departments were numerous and of excellent quality. A good list of attractions was secured and the meeting was favored with a week of fine weather. The attendance was not large, however.

Adair county crops were of an average yield but considerably damaged by rain. Corn was below an average yield because of the wet. Late planted fields failed to mature, making a large amount of light corn.

The surface of Adair county is rolling, thereby freeing this section from much damage because of excessive rains, which would do great damage on more level lands. The soil is rich and very productive, being well suited to the growing of grass, corn and all small grains and vegetables.

The price of farm lands has advanced rapidly during the past year and farms are now selling at $45 to $80 per acre. Many sales are reported at these figures.

The county is well supplied with stock of all kinds.

ADAMS COUNTY.

J. M. Devore.

The ground never worked better than it did last spring and those who took advantage of the early season secured the beter cropst both in quality and quantity. Wheat and oats sown early were good, while late sown oats were light and of a poorer quality. The excessive rains of harvest time made it impossible to save a great deal of the grain without its coloring.

Corn was a heavy crop, one of the largest since 1880. Pastures were good all season.

All stock did well last season. There was little disease of any kind to speak of. Not a case of hog cholera has been reported in this county for the past six months. Cattle are also doing exceptionally well.

ALLAMAKEE COUNTY.

E. E. Beeman.

Fair held at Waukon, September 2, 3, 4 and 5, 1902.

The fair was a success financially and otherwise. The showing of cattle and swine was not large, but the exhibit of horses and sheep was good. In all other departments the exhibits were numerous, the total number being 1,087.

Crops in this section were poor the past season as compared with former years. Hail greatly damaged the crops after they were nicely started in the spring. The great amount of moisture and rain during the summer also retarded the growing and ripening of crops. The early frost caught fully ninety per cent of the corn crop, that much not being fit to crib at all.

The interest in pure bred stock is increasing in this county. Short-Horns have the lead among cattle, and Poland Chinas with the swine.

Allamakee county is well supplied with creameries but has no cheese factories, though I am of the opinion that they would pay well.

AUDUBON COUNTY.

John Weighton.

Fair held at Audubon, September 2, 3, 4 and 5, 1902. The attendance was all that could be desired. On account of rain the fair was declared off for the last day.

The exhibits in all departments were good, excepting that of cattle. Nearly all swine exhibited changed hands before being taken from the grounds.

The society offered a special premium for the best exhibit of corn from the crop of 1902, which brought out a magnificent display. Many ears were immature because of the wet season, nevertheless a good showing was made.

Small grain was good in yield but poor in quality. It was greatly damaged during the summer by the heavy rains. The corn crop was the largest probably in twenty years, though much of it was soft. The merchantable portion was reduced at least twenty-five per cent.

Horses and cattle are on the increase. Swine not so numerous as in other years.

Land has increased in value the past year from twenty-five to thirty per cent. It is now selling from $60 to $150 per acre.

BENTON COUNTY.

J. E. Marietta.

Fair held September 2, 3, 4 and 5, 1902, at Vinton.

The early dates were an unfavorable experiment, coming too soon for the agricultural products of the county. Later dates will be chosen for 1903. The fair was very successful nevertheless, far beyond the most sanguine expectations of the management. The exhibition of live stock and poultry was exceptionally large. The showing in the field and orchard department would do credit to a state fair. The floral display was also very fine.

All farm lands are rapidly advancing in price, selling now at $80 to $100 per acre. The soil of the county is a black loam. The surface is gently rolling. Much natural timber is found along the Cedar river, besides there are many belts of natural timber in the county.

Benton county now exceeds all other in the packing of sweet corn. The Vinton and Iowa Packing company last season packed 9,000,000 cans of sweet corn. They also doubled the packing of pumpkin, beans and tomatoes. The farmer realizes $5 per ton for his sweet corn besides having the fodder for feed.

BLACK HAWK COUNTY.

B. L. Manwell.

The annual fair of the La Porte City association was held in that city September 23 to 26 inclusive. Very unfavorable weather greeted the fair, nevertheless the showing in all departments was good, that of the floral hall being the finest in the history of this society. The cattle departments were all well filled, the Polled Angus and Duroc Jerseys capturing the championship awards in their respective departments. All kinds of live stock is in good condition to go into the winter.

Corn was killed by frost at least three weeks before being fully matured. Oats, barley and hay were a good crop but badly damaged by the wet weather.

Much real estate is changing hands at $60 to $100 per acre.

BOONE COUNTY.

A. J. Gardner.

Fair held at Ogden September 11, 12 and 13, 1902. The fair was very successful so far as exhibits went, though it was less so financially. The exhibit of stock was better than for several years past.

Last spring being very favorable for planting, a large acreage was put under cultivation, and early prospects were for a large yield. However, the excessive rains of the summer did great damage to small grains, much of the low lands being flooded and the crops entirely destroyed. Corn also suffered greatly. The early acreage was the largest in several years and under favorable conditions would have made the largest yield ever known. As it was the yield was about thirty bushels per acre. The greater portion was soft. The oat crop ran about thirty bushels per acre and of a poor quality. Potatoes yielded well though those of early planting rotted considerably.

Farm lands have advanced considerably the past year and are now selling at $75 to $90 per acre.

BUCHANAN COUNTY.

A. H. Farwell.

Fair held at Independence, September 30, October 1, 2 and 3, 1902. Good weather prevailed and the gate receipts were the second largest in the history of the present society.

Exhibits were satisfactory in all departments, fully up to the average of former years. A noticeable feature was the large increase in the number and improvement in the quality of the sheep exhibit. Our farmers are beginning to realize that no other kind of stock will bring as good returns with so little labor, and on a considerable number of the farms of the county are found small but well graded flocks of sheep.

The corn crop of the county, much of it planted late and its growth and maturity delayed by wet, cool weather, was much below the average in quanity and quality. Our best informed farmers estimated that the feeding value of the crop was not above twenty-five per cent of the average for the past ten years.

The oat crop was almost a total loss. The quality, poor at best, was further damaged by the wet weather which prevailed at harvesting time and interfered with cutting, stacking and threshing.

An unusally large crop of hay was secured, somewhat damaged by wet weather, but in a fairly good condition.

BUENA VISTA COUNTY.

C. E. Cameron.

Fair held August 19, 20, 21 and 22, 1902 at Alta.

The fair was one of the most successful in the history of the society, both from a financial and exhibition point of view, the attendance being from 4,000 to 12,000 daily, and the display in every department larger than in any previous year. Considering the year the weather was excellent, having rain only on the first day sufficiently to interfere with the program. The field of speed horses was smaller than in some previous years, but made up in quality what it lacked in quantity and the racing was excellent.

The past season was a very unfavorable one for the farmers. In common with nearly all portions of the state, the extremely wet season interfered with the maturing of grain and all crops were light. There was but little corn in this county that was not injured by frosts on account of the backwardness of the season. Oats would have been a fair crop except for wet weather during harvest and the same will apply to all small grain. For this reason small grain did not yield fifty per cent of a crop. The potato crop was very short on account of rotting.

Horses and cattle of all kinds are being raised at a profit and the breeds are being rapidly improved. Hogs are plentiful and show very little sickness. There has been an increased interest in sheep raising the past year and we believe this industry will receive more attention from our farmers in the future. Poultry is about an average in numbers and shows a continued improvement in quality. The exhibits as the fair in stock exceeded all previous years both in number and quality, and has set a high standard for future years.

The increase in the value of land has been over twenty-five per cent. Land is now selling from $75 to $90 per acre and in one case reached as high as $150. The demand for good farms is unprecedented and they will still further advance the coming year.

BUTLER COUNTY.

G. E. Burrough.

Fair held at Allison, September 1 to 4, 1902.

The fair, everything considered, was a success.

The corn crop of the county averaged about sixty per cent of the average yield. Oats were a fair yield but damaged by the rains making them a poor quality. Potatoes in dry ground were a large yield, but in wet ground rotted badly. Hay was a big crop.

Farm lands have advanced in price at least $25 per acre the past year and now are selling at $75 to $100 per acre.

CASS COUNTY.

S. W. W. Straight.

Fair held at Atlantic, September 8, 9, 10 and 11, 1902.

The fair was a success in every way except financially. Outside of the sheep department the showing in all departments was good.

There was a large acreage of corn planted last spring. Early planted corn matured well, but bulk of crop was poor owing to the wet weather. Grains of all kinds were damaged by the rains. Potatoes yielded well if early planted. Late potatoes did not do nearly so well. Fruit was of a poorer yield and quality than usual.

Stock of all kinds doing well and in good demand. A great deal of blooded stock is being raised.

Lands have advanced in price to a great extent, good farms, well located, selling at $80 to $100 per acre.

CEDAR COUNTY.

H. Piatt.

The annual exhibition of the Tipton Fair association was held in that city September 2, 3, 4and 5, 1902, and was favored with good weather and large attendance. The association suffered considerable loss during the summer on account of a heavy wind which blew down several of the buildings on the grounds.

The principal feature of the exhibit was that of cattle, which was one of the best ever seen at the fair. Messrs. Clarence McClellan of Clarence, Iowa, and M. F. Bunker of Tipton, divided honors in the Short-Horn classes. There was a good showing made in the horse department while the swine and sheep pens were also well filled. Floral hall was full to overflowing and the horticultural department presented a fine appearance, especially in its display of apples.

The crop conditions of the county were, because of wet weather, below the average, taken as a whole. Little wheat is raised in the county yet the crop was good both in yield and quality. Oats were poor, while barley was a good yield but stained. The hay crop was heavy and vegetables good while the apple crop was the best in years.

No better agricultural section can be found in the state than Cedar county and land is selling readily at from $75 to $100 per acre while several sales at $125 have been recorded. These were for farms lying near the city however. Tipton, the county seat, is a live and wideawake town of 2,500 population.

CEDAR COUNTY.

A. F. Fairchild.

Fair held at Mechanicsville, September 16 to 19, 1902. The gate receipts were very small owing to wet weather, otherwise the meeting was very successful. The exhibits in all departments were quite numerous and of a good quality.

The yield of oats was rather poor, yielding about thirty bushels per acre. All crops with the exception of wheat, rye and barley were good.

Land has been selling at $85 to $105 per acre. The soil of Cedar county is a deep black loam and very productive.

CHEROKEE COUNTY.

F. E. Paine.

Fair held at Marcus, September 9, 10 and 11, 1902.

The fair was very successful notwithstanding the weather was cold and rainy. The showing in all departments was good, especially so in the live stock. The exhibit of swine was the largest ever seen here.

Owing to the heavy rains of the harvest season, the small grains in the western part of the county was considerably damaged. An early frost nipped the greater part of the late corn.

Our cattle breeders are branching out in the better grades of cattle, some going so far as to import them from Europe. The prevailing grades of cattle are the Polled Angus, Hereford and Short-Horns.

Farm lands have advanced and are now selling at $75 to $100 per acre.

CHICKASAW COUNTY.

C. H. Bander.

The showing of cattle at the fair was very good. That of swine while not so large as last year was creditable. The same was true in the sheep department.

The season of 1902 was entirely too wet for good crops. The corn did not mature before being caught by the frost.

CLAYTON COUNTY.

Henry Luehsen, Jr.

The annual exhibition of the Clayton County Society was held at National, August 19 to 22. The interest taken and entries made in all departments showed a marked improvement over former years. Though the fair was held a little early and the season somewhat backward still we had one of the most successful ever held in the county.

The cattle exhibit was fully up to the average while that of horses was a little below that of other years. Still many fine animals were shown. Many swine are produced in Clayton county and this department at the fair was filled. An improvement was noticeable in the sheep exhibit, one of the features being a herd of Angora goats.

Very little wheat and rye are raised in this section but the crop of both was up to the average. Oats were damaged somewhat by the rains. The yield was from thirty to forty bushels per acre. Corn was a three-fourths crops. The early frost did some damage, only about twenty-five per cent being far enough advanced to escape.

The potato and apple crop were the best raised in years. Small fruits were about a half crop.

CLINTON COUNTY.

C. L. Root.

Fair held September 9 to 11, 1902, at Lyons.

The exhibition was fairly successful in way of exhibits and attendance. On Wednesday the attendance reached 10,000 persons. The vegetable department was filled with the largest display in the history of the fair. There was also an excellent display of grains and corn.

The small grains turned out well last season in Clinton county. Hay was an abundant crop and corn a fair yield. There was considerable soft corn, however.

Many farms are changing hands at $90 to $110 per acre, an advance of $10 to $20 per acre over 1901.

CLINTON COUNTY.

L. D. Winnie.

Fair held September 16, 17, 18 and 19, 1902 at DeWitt. The exhibition was successful both in exhibits and financially.

The crops of the county were good. Oats were slightly damaged by the wet season. Corn was a large yield and generally escaped the frost. Stock of all kinds is in a healthy condition.

Land is high in price, good farms selling at $80 to $100 per acre.

DALLAS COUNTY.

H. H. Crenshaw.

Fair held at Adel, September 17 to 22, 1902.

Crops in Dallas county averaged better last season than the season before. Oats averaged forty bushels per acre, and corn though slightly damaged by frost yielded fifty bushels. Potatoes and apples were also good.

The soil of Dallas county is adapted to all kinds of farming. It is rich and productive. Land is $10 per acre higher than in 1901 and is selling at $70 to $100 per acre for choice farms.

DAVIS COUNTY.

J. C. Brouhard.

Fair held September 9 to 12, 1902 at Bloomfield.

The meeting was one of the most successful ever held by this society. The exhibits in all departments were numerous and of a good quality. Those of the agricultural department were much the largest ever shown in the county. The showing of cattle and swine was also large, that of horses being about an average.

Small grains yielded fairly well and would have been of a good quality had it not been for the excessive rains of the summer. The yield of corn was the largest of years, and the quality fair. Hay was a good crop and the seed a fair yield. Small fruit did not mature well because of the drouth of early spring. Peaches were a total failure.

DELAWARE COUNTY.

James Bishop.

Fair held September 16 to 19, 1902, at Manchester.

The quality of the agricultural and horicultural exhibits shown at the annual fair was excellent. The number of animals in the live stock departments were not numerous but were of good grades.

Small grain though of fair yield was of poor quality, being more or less colored and of light weight. Late corn was nearly all soft as frost did a great deal of damage to all fields both early and late plantings. Hay was a good crop so far as yield went but was damaged by the rains during the time of cutting. Potatoes yielded well but many were rotten. Fruit of all kinds was abundant.

DES MOINES COUNTY.

C. M. Garman.

The Des Moines county fair was held August 5, 6, 7 and 8, at Burlington. It was quite successful though not equal to the meeting of last year owing to the unfavorable weather. The attendance was cut down considerably by the bad conditions of the roads which kept many country people at home.

Crops as a whole were fairly good, though hay and small grains were damaged by the rains of harvest time. Corn was not injured by the frost and yielded well.

The display in all departments of the fair were exceedingly good.

FAYETTE COUNTY.

Fair held September 2 to 5, 1902, at West Union.

The fair was quite successful, the attendance being good. That of Thursday being the largest for years. The exhibits were all large, that of cattle and swine being especially fine both in quality and numbers.

Crops were very uneven the past season. A large crop of hay was gathered, although some of it was badly damaged by the rains. The growth of small grains was rank, causing it to lodge badly and therefore cutting down somewhat the yield. Potatoes yielded well but rotted quite badly. Corn was uneven in yield. Many fields were badly damaged by the frost. The yield was not over half an average crop.

Fayette is a grand stock county. Creameries are numerous and profitable. Stock of all kinds is in a flourishing condition.

Lands have steadily advanced in prices and are now selling at $50 to $100 per acre.

FAYETTE COUNTY.

L. C. Kuney.

The Arlington District Fair was held at Arlington, August 19 to 22, and despite the extremely disagreeable weather the entries in all departments were large and the attendance good.

Corn was very good considering the season, being two-thirds of a yield. Oats threshed out much better than last year but were of much poorer quality. Hay was a good yield and excellent quality. Potatoes were good in sections of the county. In the localities having a sandy soil the crop was much better than where the soil is a loam. In the latter sections they rotted considerably.

No horses were shown at the fair because of the disagreeable weather, and a few cattle. A great many horses are being raised in the county, however.

Farm lands of Fayette county are advancing and are now selling at $55 to $100 per acre. The soil is mostly a black loam.

FRANKLIN COUNTY.

R. E. McCrillis.

Fair held September 9 to 11, 1902, at Hampton.

The meeting was fairly successful.

Corn, the principal crop of this section, was about fifty per cent of an average yield in the county last season. Oats rather a poor yield and damaged by rain. Potatoes were about a three-fourths yield. Fruit of all kinds did well.

Much fine stock is raised in this section.

Land is not changing hands to any great extent. Prices range from $75 to $200 per acre. This is for farms near town, while those a few miles out sell for $60 to $80 per acre.

GRUNDY COUNTY.

J. W. Pipperman.

The annual fair of the Grundy County Agricultural Society was held at Grundy Center, September 9, 10 and 11, 1902. The meeting was a financial success. The weather with the exception of the last day, was perfect, bringing out large crowds of people. Had the same kind of weather prevailed on the third and last day of the meeting the attendance would have broken all previous records.

The entries in all departments with the one exception of swine were below the average in numbers.

Crops of the county were below the average. Much grain was damaged while in the shock, by the heavy rains which made it impossible to thresh. The yield of oats was thirty bushels to the acre and of poor quality. The early frosts caught the corn before it was matured, it being very backward because of the excessive rains of the late summer. The yield was fair but with many soft ears. Potatoes were fairly good.

Grundy county is exclusively a farming section, the soil being a black loam and from one to three feet in depth. Land is selling as high as $112 per acre.

GUTHRIE COUNTY

A. H. Grisell.

The crop season of 1902 in this locality was one of unusual conditions. The fields were in the finest possible condition for early sowing and planting. Wheat and oats were sown in good season. The cool dry weather of April and the early part of May prevented early or rapid germination and growth. Later in the season these crops made fine growth and gave promise of a large yield. There was a large planting of early potatoes and a large yield of tLe early planted crop. Corn was generally planted in good season, and was never planted with the ground in better condition. The latter part of May and the early part of June were unusually favorable for its cultivation and the crop gave abundant promise. Pasturage started late but through the summer and down to the present it has been unusually abundant. The meadows promised a large yield.

The fruit trees except peaches were laden with bloom. The summer and fall varieties of apples produced a large crop, the fruit being unusually large and of fine quality. Plums produced well. Some rotted on the trees before ripening, but the crop was large. Melons and grapes were of poor quality owing to the long continued wet cool weather through their maturing period.

The six months including April and September furnished unusually heavy rain fall. The signal service under the charge of W. F. Brann reports the rainfall for the six months as follows: April, .90 inches; May, 3.30 inches; June, 6.99 inches; July, 9.27 inches; August, 7.21 inches; September, 5.49 inches; a total for the six months of 34.88 inches. The three months of the hay and grain harvest furnishing 24.17 inches, upwards of two feet of water. These unusual floods worked great damage and loss to the hay and small grain crops. That period being not only unusually wet but also abnormally cool prevented the early maturity of the corn crop which suffered on the low lands serious damage from the frosts of September 12 and 13.

46

The winter wheat gave a large yield of fine quality of grain where it was stacked before the heavy rains after it was cut. Oats and spring wheat suffered material loss in the shock as well as in the field before it was cut. The wet condition of the ground precluding the cutting of the crop in the sloughy portions of the fields. The yield of oats we would estimate, however, at an average of thirty bushels per acre. Corn was a large yield in bulk but much of it was light in weight. Average, thirty-five bushels per acre. The apple crop was of fine quality—fall apples were low in price, but hand picked winter fruit of good quality as Jonathans, Ben Davis, Grimes' Golden, etc., are selling at $1 a bushel. Late potatoes are poor in quality. Too wet and soggy and are rotting in the ground. Cattle are unusually abundant in this county.

The week the fair was held, was one of storms and rains, and reduced the receipts about one-half. Owing to the wet condition of the track the races were eliminated. All premiums were paid in full and the society had a balance of a couple of hundred dollars in the treasury.

HANCOCK COUNTY.

John Hammill.

Fair held September 16 to 18, 1902, at Britt.

The exhibits of stock at the fair were the largest ever on the grounds. Many fine herds of cattle and swine were on exhibition. The other exhibits were about the average with those of other years.

The excessive rains of the summer greatly damaged crops of all kinds in Hancock county in 1902. The yield was in all cases below the average. The low lands of the county suffered more than other lands.

The condition of all stock in this section is healthy. The dairy interest is receiving a great deal of attention and is proving very profitable.

HARDIN COUNTY.

C. E. Greef.

Fair held at Eldora, August 19, 20 and 21, 1902.

The Hardin county fair, like scores of others in the state, experienced a disagreeable spell of weather, which had the effect of keeping hundreds away. The last two days of the meeting, however, saw about the usual crowds. The prospects were for the most successful fair ever held on the grounds and such success would have been fully realized had it not been for the unfavorable conditions of the weather.

An exceptionally good showing was made in the live stock departments and the same was true in some of the others. A magnificent display of apples were to be seen. The showing of corn was poor, many farmers complaining that the fair was held too early in the season to make a good showing of corn possible. It was the opinion of the management that the grades of stock were not improving as they should in this section and consequently premiums were offered only on blooded animals. As a consequence the exhibit was somewhat cut down, but the grades shown were better than ordinarily.

Hardin county crops were exceptionally good and farm values have advanced at least fifteen per cent during the past twelve months. Land is selling at $50 to $125 per acre.

HARRISON COUNTY.

W. H. Withrow.

Fair held October 7, 8 and 9, 1902, at Missouri Valley.

The weather during this week was very favorable and the exhibits quite numerous though not so much so as they would have been had the fair been held on the dates first selected. But the fair was postponed from September on account of the rains. The quality of all exhibits was good.

The acreage of crops in the county last season was greater than of former years. Early planted corn yielded fully as well or better than the season before. All small grain was somewhat damaged by the rains.

In the cattle and horse departments at the fair the number of exhibits was below what it ought to have been but the grades of those animals shown were good.

The soil of this county is adapted to the raising of corn especially, though all grains do well. Sugar beets are raised to some extent.

Land values have advanced during the past three years. The prices at present vary from $20 for the poorest land to $100 per acre for the best. What is considered farming land is held at $65, being about a raise of $10 over former prices.

HENRY COUNTY.

C. M. Clark.

Fair held August 12 to 15, 1902, at Mt. Pleasant.

The entries were numerous in nearly all departments, the cattle show being the best in years. Many fine herds were shown, the same herds also showing at the state fair. The show in horses, swine and sheep was also good. The display was very fine though it was not up to former years. The kitchen and pantry display was exceptionally fine. That of fruit was not large.

Small grain was greatly damaged because of the rains of harvest time. The corn crop was good.

Farm lands are selling at $35 to $125 per acre and steadily advancing in price.

HENRY COUNTY.

Theo. Russell.

Fair held August 19 to 22, 1902, at Winfield.

Considerable damage was done to the building on the fair grounds by a storm which occurred during the early summer. The amount of damage done amounted to at least $1,000. While rain cut down the gate receipts somewhat, still the fair was very good. The exhibits compared favorably with those of other years. The showing of cattle was exceptionally good. The agricultural exhibit was also very good.

The crop conditions in this county last season were fair. Small grain a fair yield but damaged on account of the rains. Corn also an average yield.

HUMBOLDT COUNTY.

E. K. Winne.

Fair held September 2 to 5, 1902, at Humboldt.

The weather during the week of the fair, with the exception of one pleasant day, was very disagreeable. The attendance on the one pleasant day, however, exceeded that of any other one day in the history of the organization. The farm products were plentiful and well displayed. The horse and cattle departments were will filled and also made a fine showing.

Of crops, small grain was generally a good yield and quality. Corn was also good, yielding about fifty bushels per acre.

Land is selling at $60 to $100 per acre according to location and improvements.

IOWA COUNTY.

F. C. Rock.

Fair was held September 9, 10, 11 and 12, 1902, at Williamsburg.

All departments were well filled with fine exhibits, the attendance was good and the fair a success. The live stock exhibit was especially fine and great interest was manifested in this department. The vegetable and fruit departments, and also the floral hall were all well filled.

Farm values in this section have advanced at least twenty-five per cent the past year, and are now selling at $75 to $100 per acre.

IOWA COUNTY.

E. L. Morse.

Fair held September 2 to 4, 1902, at Marengo.

Rain interfered with the attendance, though the displays in all departments were very good. The showing of cattle surpassed any we have had for several years, both in number and grades. Hogs and sheep were also plentiful and included many fine animals. The display of farm products was not large owing to the unfavorableness of the season for maturity.

Generally speaking the crops in this county were below the average, resulting from the unfavorable weather. Small grains yielded well but were damaged by the rains. Corn was backward and a great deal of it was soft because of the frost. Better stock is being raised in the county than heretofore. Land is selling at $60 to $100 per acre, an advance of $10 an acre over other years.

IOWA COUNTY.

J. F. Schulte.

The annual fair of the Victor District Agricultural Society was held at Victor, August 27, 28 and 29, 1902, with a good attendance but expenses were higher than ordinary on account of the wet weather. All classes were well filled with the exception of poultry and the sharpest competition existed in all departments. Especially true was this in the horse and cattle classes.

Because of the wet season the crops of the county were not of the best either in yield or quality. Here as elswhere the rain did great damage to grain in the shock and to hay that has been cut but not gathered.

A great many head of live stock are raised in the county and in the immediate vicinity of Victor are several fine herd of Short-Horns, Angus and Herefords. Few sheep are raised in this section.

Farm lands are selling at $45 to $85 per acre.

JACKSON COUNTY.

Adam Ringlep.

Fair held September 2 to 4, 1902, at Maquoketa.

The fair was one of the most successful ever held in this county, though the weather was somewhat unfavorable. The showing of cattle at the fair was very good, though the exhibit of swine and sheep was not up to the average of other years.

This section requires very moist weather and the past season was therefore favorable for good crops. Small grain yielded an average crop and corn went from forty to sixty bushels per acre. The season was very favorable for seeding and timothy and clover did exceptionally well. The finest apple crop of years was harvested.

Farm lands are selling at good prices.

JASPER COUNTY.

C. W. Campbell.

Fair held September 8th to 11th, at Newton.

It was the forty-eighth annual exhibition held by the society and was the most successful fair yet held. The weather was fine and attendance large. The exhibit of farm products was fine, especially fruit. The showing in the live stock departments was never better. One of the special features was the grand parade of all premium winners.

Small grains were of a fair yield though damaged by the rains. Hay was a good crop as was corn. Some fields of small grain were completely destroyed by the wet weather.

Farm lands are from $6 to $8 higher than in 1901, and are selling at $75 to $125. The county is well supplied with coal, water and railroad facilities.

JEFFERSON COUNTY.

Jno. R. McElderry.

The twenty-seventh fair of the Jefferson Agricultural Society was held at Fairfield, September 9, 10 and 11, and was a financial success. The number of exhibits in the swine, sheep and poultry departments were a little short of those of former years while the showing in the art hall and line of farm machinery was never better.

Small grains were badly damaged by the rains of harvest time. Many fields were not harvested because of the soft condition of the ground, it being impossible to operate a binder. Wheat is only raised in a small way and was a poor crop. Corn yielded well.

The soil of this section is very rich and the county is well supplied with water, coal and timber. Fairfield, the county seat, is an up-to-date town and a great horse market. Prevailing prices for horses have been good and there has been a great increase in their production. The celebrated Parson's college is located at Fairfield, and though recently destroyed by fire will be rebuilt on a larger scale than before. The city has a fine public library, fine churches and schools and the principal streets are being paved.

JOHNSON COUNTY.

Bruce Moore.

Fair held September 2 to 5, 1902, at Iowa City.

The fair was a success in every way and a record breaker generally. The gate receipts were the largest ever known. All barns and pens of the live stock department were well filled. The exhibit of grains was rather small owing to the wet season.

Crops were generally of good yield though the wet weather of harvest time somewhat damaged them. Corn was a great crop though a little of it was soft. This is the staple crop of the county. Much fine live stock is being produced in the county and farmers and breeders are taking more interest in the improvement of the grades of their animals.

Lands are higher than last year and are selling at $60 to $100 per acre.

JONES COUNTY.

W. G. Eilers.

The corn yield was short and the quality poor because of the heavy rains and early frosts. The oat crop was fair but continuous rain did it some damage. Hay crop good but also damaged somewhat by rain.

JONES COUNTY.

E. R. Moore.

Fair held at Anamosa, August 25 to 29, 1902, and was a grand success in every particular. The attendance was the largest in the history of the association. Crops in the county were very good. Except in the very low land corn was more than an average crop. Oats were a good yield and in most places a good quality.

The exhibit of stock at the fair was not up to the standard owing to the fact that it rained all day Monday, the day the farmers bring in their stock, the roads being almost impassable for loads. Stock is on the increase in all kinds.

Land in Jones county is selling as high as $100 per acre.

KEOKUK COUNTY.

George A. Poff.

Fair held August 19 to 22, 1902, at What Cheer.

Though it rained three out of the four days on which the fair was held, nevertheless, the attendance was good and the exhibits up to the average.

The yield of corn was good, though much on the low lands was soft. The acreage was large. The yield of small grains was about the average of other years, that of hay being very heavy. Much excellent stock is to be found in this section as is evident from the number of fine animals that were shown at the annual fair last fall. Farmers are taking a deep interest in the improvement of their herds.

Land is selling at $65 to $90 per acre according to improvements.

KOSSUTH COUNTY.

T. H. Wadsworth.

Fair held September 2, to 5, 1902, at Algona.

The fair of 1902 was fairly successful both in attendance and number and quality of the exhibits.

The crops of the county all yielded well but were more or less damaged because of the excessive rains of the summer. The crops generally do not compare favorable with those of other years.

A great many creameries are to be found in Kossuth county and all are well patronized by the farmers. Much fine stock is also to be found in this section.

The prevailing prices of land are $60 to $70 being from $10 to $15 per acre higher than in 1901.

LEE COUNTY.

E. P. Armkencht.

Fair held at Donnellson, August 27 to 29, 1902.

The weather was good and the attendance large, making a financial success of the fair.

Crops in the county were all that could be desired last year in quantity, but owing to the rains, the oats, wheat and rye were not of first-class quality. The crop of timothy seed was a record breaker, the average yield being from six to eight bushels per acre. Nearly 100 cars of the seed were marketed in the county at a price of $1.50 per bushel. There is a noticeable change for the better in the grade of live stock of all kinds in this section, and breeders are paying more attention to the improvement of the grades of their stock than heretofore.

. LEE COUNTY.

John Walljasper.

Fair held August 19 to 22, 1902, at West Point.

The exhibits in nearly all departments were large and of the very best, the average, but the wet weather marred the exhibition so far as attendance was concerned.

Corn was an immense crop. Wheat and oats were also good in yield and quality. While all crops were damaged some by the rains, still they are an average crop. The health of all live stock is good. Much fine stock is being raised in this section.

LINN COUNTY.

E. F. Knickerbocker.

The Prairie Valley fair was held at Fairfax, August 12, 13, 14 and 15, 1902, but owing to the rainy weather the fair was a partial success.

The exhibits in nearly all departments were large and of the very best, especially all articles in the fine arts, fancy department, pantry stores, fruits and vegetables.

The flower display was by far ahead of any exhibit of the kind ever seen at our fair.

The exhibit of horses was not as large as in some former years but the animals shown were fully up to the standard and ahead of most exhibits of this kind.

The cattle display was unusually small, but the best animals of the herds at Iowa City, Mt. Vernon, Norway and this place were on exhibition.

Cattle in this vicinity are in better condition than usual, but feeders are scarce.

The exhibit of swine was about an average of former years.

Corn was more than an average yield but of poor quality.

The incessant rain of the season kept corn growing until it frosted, and the result was a great amount of soft corn.

The oats crop would have been far superior to what it was but most oats was sown late which made a late harvest. The yield being about thirty bushels per acre but of poor quality and badly colored.

Wheat and barley very poor in both quality and quantity with a very light acreage.

Timothy and clover were the two best crops the farmers raised this season as conditions seemed to be especially favorable for them.

There is quite an interest manifested by the farmers of this section in planting of fruit. In a few years from now there will be a number of commercial orchards in this vicinity while small fruit is being raised in great abundance, and a canning factory is badly needed at this place.

LOUISA COUNTY.

R. S. Johnson.

The Columbus Junction District fair held at Columbus Junction, September 17, 18 and 19. enjoyed a week of very favorable weather. The meeting was a complete success, fully paying out. The exhibit of live stock was as large as was ever shown here and the grades were all good.

While the attendance fell off somewhat from that of former years, yet the management was pleased with the result of the meeting. Over $2,000 was paid out in premiums alone.

The acreage of corn and oats in the county last year was larger than that of the season before. All small grains were damaged by the rains and while most of it was threshed it was all of a low grade. The hay crop was very large, though somewhat damaged by over ripening.

Although the season was excessively wet the corn made a satisfactory growth and very little was drowned out. Its ripening was retarded, however, and it was consequently caught by the frosts of September. Pastures were good all season and the growth of fall pastures was exceptionally heavy.

Land ranges in price from $40 to $60 per acre for medium and up to $80 for the best. All land is at least $10 per acre higher than last year.

MADISON COUNTY.

T. J. Hudson.

The Madison County Fair, held at Winterset, August 19 to 27, 1902, was sadly marred by rain which kept many people away.

There was a fair showing of live stock, Mr. T. M. Scott showing an exceptionally fine herd of Polled Angus. There was also a very good showing of draft horses.

Rain interfered with the harvesting of small grains, especially oats. Corn was a good yield and of fair quality.

MAHASKA COUNTY.

John W. Irwin.

Fair held September 16-18, 1902, at New Sharon.

The weather during the week of the fair was rainy most of the time, thereby keeping many away. However, the exhibition was a success, all features of the program being given and the premiums paid in full.

Corn was a fair crop, through some failed to mature because of the continuous rains. Yield about sixty bushels per acre. Oats were a heavy crop but greatly damaged by the wet. Yield of barley and rye light. All other crops yielded fairly well. Stock of all kinds is in a healthy condition.

MARSHALL COUNTY.

Benjamin Richards.

Fair held September 23 to 26, 1902, at Rhodes.

It was a very rainy week during which the fair was held. The last day was the only pleasant one and as a consequence the only day on which there was a good attendance.

Crops in the county were poor. The land in this section is more rough and rolling than in some counties, the crops as a consequence not being so badly drowned out as is some sections. The weather being so wet, however, that small grain was badly colored and of light weight. Oats went from fifteen to thirty-five bushels and wheat did not average over eight bushels per acre. Corn yielded on an average of fifty bushels. The frosts of the 12th and 13th of September did not catch over fifteen per cent of the crop. There is much thoroughbred stock in this section. Our fair had a magnificent display of cattle and stock of all kinds.

Good land is selling at $75 per acre and some pieces as high as $100, which is fully $20 per acre higher than a year ago.

MILLS COUNTY.

I. J. Swain.

Fair held September 2, 3 and 4, at Malvern. The weather during the week was ideal and attendance larger than usual. The people of the county appeared to take more interest in the annual fair than ever before.

Horses, swine and poultry were shown in large numbers and were all of excellent quality. The cattle department was somewhat neglected, though there were some very fine animals shown.

The agricultural department was filled to overflowing.

Crops of all kinds were good, exceptionally so the corn, which gave a big yield. This crop went from forty to fifty bushels per acre. Some fields were slightly damaged by the frost.

MITCHELL COUNTY.

W. H. H. Gable.

Fair held at Osage, August 26, 27 and 28, 1902.

The meeting was fairly well attended and the exhibits very good considering the early date of the fair and the immaturity of the crops. The showing made in the live stock department was very good. The number and quality of the exhibits in the fruit and floral departments were exceptionally fine.

Crops in Mitchell county the past season were good nothwithstanding the long and heavy rains of the summer. Corn was slightly injured by an early frost, but upon the whole was an average crop.

This county can boast of many fine animals, both horses and cattle. The recent high prices of horses has brought into the county many well bred animals.

The prices of farm lands are steadily advancing.

MONTGOMERY COUNTY.

D. B. Gunn.

Fair held August 19 to 22, 1902, at Red Oak.

The fair met with a downpour of rain which had the effect of lessening attendance and receipts. The showing in the cattle department was the best in fifteen years and the showing in the swine department was also fine. The horse exhibit was hardly up to the average.

Montgomery county last year was, we believe, up to an average so far as agricultural conditions were concerned. Small grains, except on flooded lands, were of a good yield and quality. Some few pieces of corn was damaged by the frost, still the crop as a whole was very good. Hay was a fair yield and potatoes extra good. Pastures were never better than last summer and fall.

MUSCATINE COUNTY.

W. H. Shipman.

Fair held at West Liberty, August 19 to 22, 1902.

The attendance and receipts of the fair were both good, and had the rain not interfered with the meeting early in the week it would have been the banner year.

The exhibits were all good. While some of the grains and farm and garden products were slightly below the average, the whole was very good. We had a good showing in the beef herds in the cattle departments but the exhibit of dairy stock was light. Swine and sheep departments were both well filled. There was an extra good showing of draft horses, and a fair showing in the road classes.

Corn was a light crop and considerable of it soft. The prospect in July was never better, but the crop was kept from maturing by the rains of the summer. Small grains would have yielded well had it not been for the wet weather which interfered with thrashing.

A great deal of attention is paid to stock raising, and a great deal of pure bred stuff is produced.

MUSCATINE COUNTY.

E. R. King.

The excessive rains of the summer did a great amount of damage to small grain in shock, causing it to sprout and rot. That which was well stacked was little damaged. Straw ranges all the way from good to worthless.

The yield of small grains as reported from the different sections was about as follows: Spring wheat, eighteen bushels per acre; winter wheat, thirty-six bushels; oats, forty bushels. Corn yielded about fifty bushels per acre, with twenty per cent of the corn soft. There was an increase of five per cent in the acreage of corn last year over that of the year before, and a corresponding decrease in the acreage of hay land. The latter crop went a ton and a half to the acre and the second crop one half ton. Early potatoes yielded 100 bushels per acre while late ones yielded about one-half that.

Muscatine county land is selling at $100 to $117 per acre, and rents at $3.50 to $4.25. The county has ten county telephone lines and many rural routes.

O'BRIEN COUNTY.

J. C. Briggs.

Fair held at Sutherland, September 3, 4 and 5.

The attendance was not so large as usual. The exhibits were good with the exception of grain.

The wet weather of summer greatly damaged small grains. Frost caught the corn, thereby causing a great deal of soft ears. The yield was good however.

The soil of O'Brien county is a black loam, and adapted to all kinds of farming.

Farm lands are selling at $60 to $90 per acre.

O'BRIEN COUNTY.

E. L. Richards.

Fair held at Sheldon, August 27, 28 and 29, 1902.

While the success of the meeting was very gratifying, it would have been still more so had the weather been pleasant. One hundred and twenty-three head of cattle were shown as were 156 head of swine. There was also a good showing of horses and sheep.

I believe I am safe in saying that the yield of crops was not more than fifty per cent of that of 1901. The extreme wet weather of the summer was very damaging to grains of all kinds and corn instead of ripening continued to grow until checked by the heavy frosts.

PAGE COUNTY.

C. E. Young.

Fair held at Shenandoah, August 12 to 15, 1902.

The fair was a success in exhibits, attendance and financially. The exhibits in most departments were better than those of the year before.

The corn yield in Page county last fall was good, and wheat, oats and hay were really better than were expected. Owing to the great amount of wet weather early in the season the small fruit crop was small, but apples were plentiful.

The soil of Page county is a rich black loam and very productive. Farm lands are selling at a good figure.

PALO ALTO COUNTY.

P. V. Hand.

Fair held at Emmetsburg, August 19 to 22, 1902.

The fair did well both in exhibits and financially. The showing of cattle was the best ever made in this county at a fair. The swine, sheep and poultry departments were also well filled, and the quality of animals and fowls good. Because of the early dates of the fair, agricultural products were not as well represented as they would have been had the dates been later. However, the showing was very creditable.

The yield of oats and barley was good; that of barley being about thirty-five to forty bushels per acre, and for oats forty-five to fifty bushels. Corn promised to be a good crop but the continued wet weather prevented its ripening and as a consequence it was caught by the frost. Potatoes yielded well and were of a good quality.

POCAHONTAS COUNTY.

J. P. Mullen.

The Big Four District Fair was held at Fonda, August 26, 27, 28 and 29, 1902. The exhibition was a success in every particular. More horses and cattle were shown than ever before and great interest was shown by every one in these departmnts. The exhibits in all other departments were especially fine.

The yield of crops for 1902 was somewhat below the average.

POTTAWATTAMIE COUNTY.

John Fletcher.

Fair held at Avoca, September 16, 17, 18 and 19, 1902.

The exhibit of live stock of all kinds was much larger and of better quality than ever before. The exhibit of cattle is worthy of special mention, for it is doubtful if ever a finer lot of animals were shown in this county. The swine exhibit was nearly twice as large as in previous years.

Throughout the county the crops were abundant. The small grains were not up to the average in quality, owing to the excessive rains of the summer, but the yield was large. Corn yielded well but was of light weight owing to the severe frost of early September.

POWESHEIK COUNTY.

James Nowak.

Fair was held at Malcom, August 19, 20, 21 and 22. The weather for a week previous to the fair was a continual down pour of rain. During the fair the roads were consequently impassible or nearly so, and this together with the fact that many farmers were behind with their farm work, had the effect of keeping many away. Rival attractions on the same dates at nearby places also had the effect of keeping down our attendance below the average.

Our display of farm products was good excepting corn, which was not yet matured. There was a fine display of fruits of all kinds. The showing of fancy work and pantry stores, a special feature, was the display of school work.

Live stock of all kands was shown in large numbers and the grades were excellent.

The wet weather damaged small grains to a considerable extent. Oats were only a half crop and of poor qualtiy. Potatoes yielded abundantly though there was complaint of rot. Apples were a good crop. There were no peaches and few grapes. The hay crop was large and pastures were in good condition the whole season.

Corn was a good yield excepting on the low lands. About twenty per cent of the crop was soft.

Land in Powesheik county has rapidly increased in value the past year. Improved farms are selling at $60 to $100 per acre, an increase of ten to fifteen per cent over last year.

POWESHEIK COUNTY.

J. E. Van Evera.

Fair was held at Grinnell, September 2, 3, 4 and 5. The weather was rather unpromising to start with but on Thursday the third day of the fair the weather had cleared and gave us a perfect day, with the largest crowds ever in attendance.

The exhibits were of a high order.

Three large herds of cattle were entered, besides a number of individual entries.

Vegetable were fine, also a nice display of pantry stores. The ladies of Grinnell pride themselves especially upon their fancy work, of which there was an elegant display.

The season was unfavorable for the farmer; continuous rains making it difficult to harvest the hay crop which was large.

The oat crop also suffered greatly from the same cause, the average yield however, was from twenty-five to thirty-five bushels.

The corn of which there was an unusually large acreage, gave promise of an enormous crop, but the wet weather and an early frost did considerable damage, leaving it unevenly matured.

RINGGOLD COUNTY.

Thos. Campbell.

Fair held September 2 to 4, at Mt. Ayr.

The attendance at the fair exceeded our most sanguine expectations and the receipts at the gates were therefore large. We had a fine showing of all kinds of stock. The agricultural exhibits were all very creditable.

Corn went from thirty to sixty bushels per acre and oats a fair yield but damaged by the rains.

Farm lands are selling at prices ranging from $35 to $65 per acre.

SIOUX COUNTY.

H. Slikkerveer.

Fair held September 17 to 19, 1902, at Orange City.

The wet weather interfered with the financial success of the fair, though the exhibits in the live stock departments were good. Those in the department of farm products were not up to the average.

Crops were below the average in 1902, corn being damaged by the frost. Hay was a good crop. Oats went about forty bushels to the acre, while barley went twenty and wheat about twelve bushels.

Much fine thoroughbred stock is raised in Sioux county.

Sioux county is one of the banner counties in the state and its soil is exceptionally fertile and productive.

SIOUX COUNTY.

James Walpole.

Crops in this section were about an average, especially oats and hay. The same is true of wheat. Potatoes were a big crop.

There are at least 1,500 head of recorded cattle in this county, and farmers and breeders are taking great interest in the industry.

The prevailing price of land is from $70 to $100 per acre. These prices are from $10 to $15 above those of a year ago.

STORY COUNTY.

J. F. Martin.

Fair held at Nevada, August 19 to 22, 1902.

The fair was unsuccessful because of the heavy rains during the week it was held. The attendance was light and gate receipts likewise. We find it difficult to compete with the state fair which is but a few miles from Nevada.

Story county soil is low and flat, being what is known as black gumbo, very fertile and productive, but in wet seasons it suffers worse than the lands containing more clay and sand.

Corn was a light yield going from twenty-five to thirty bushels to the acre. That is of merchantable corn. Oats on the higher ground yielded from fifty to sixty bushels, those on the flat lands being poor. Hay was an abundant crop.

Farm lands are selling at $85 to $90 per acre.

TAMA COUNTY.

A. G. Smith.

Fair held at Toledo, September 23 to 26, 1902.

Rain sadly marred the success of the fair as only Thursday and Friday were at all pleasant. However, on these days a fair attendance was had and the races and amusements pulled off. The entries in all departments were rather light on account of the rain. Still the showing in all departments was very creditable considering the circumstances.

Crops were damaged a great deal by the rains, especially the small grains. Corn also suffered from the frost.

TAYLOR COUNTY.

W. F. Evans.

Fair held September 16, 17, 18 and 19, 1902, at Bedford.

The exhibits in all departments were lessened to some extent because of the rains. This is more true of the farm products than of the live stock shown. Many horses were on exhibition and made as fine a showing as we ever had. The showing of cattle, while not large, was very creditable. The exhibits in the farm and garden lines and also fruit were all good, many fine samples being shown.

The wet season played havoc with the small grains and hay crop. Many fields were not harvested, it being impossible to run a mower or reaper over the ground it being so soft. Corn was very weedy on account of the wet. The fields could not be properly cultivated.

Farm lands have been on a boom the past year, prices ranging from $60 to $100 and fully fifteen per cent higher than last year.

VAN BUREN COUNTY.

E. O. Syphers.

Fair held August 26 to 29, 1902, at Milton.

The exhibits though not so numerous as in former years were of an excellent quality. The conflicting of our dates with those of the fair in Lee county were responsible for the cutting down of the exhibits.

Crops of all descriptions were good in Van Buren county in 1902. The fruit with the exception of peaches, was the finest ever grown here. Corn was good, some pieces yielding as high as 100 bushels per acre.

WAYNE COUNTY.

G. T. Wright.

The small grains were all more or less damaged by the heavy rains of the summer. A large amount of timothy and clover seed was never threshed because of the rains. Corn was never a larger yield. Much fine stock in the county and prices good. All in a healthy condition.

The prices of lands have advanced from twenty to thirty per cent and are now selling at $30 to $60 per acre with many farms changing hands.

WINNEBAGO COUNTY.

C. W. Good.

Fair held September 9 to 11, 1902, at Buffalo Center.

The fair was well attended and the exhibits in all departments were numerous and of a good quality.

Corn and oats are the principal crops raised in this section. The yield of the latter was good but they were considerably damaged by the wet weather of harvest time. The yield was about forty bushels per acre. Corn was a great deal of it soft and yielded about forty bushels per acre. Frost visited this county first about September 11.

Land is selling at $50 to $60 per arce, being about $8 or $10 per acre above the prices of 1901.

WINNESHEIK COUNTY.

H. L. Coffeen.

Fair held August 26 to 29, at Decorah.

The attendace was fair and the weather very fine The live stock exhibits were below the average, while the showing made in the agricultural and floral departments was excellent.

Wheat in this section yielded from fifteen to twenty-five bushels per acre and was of good quality. Oats were nearly up to the average yield and quality. Barley and rye about the same as oats. There was a very large crop of hay but was badly damaged by the rains. Potatoes yielded well. Corn was a fair yield and fairly good quality. Live stock is all in good condition.

Prices of land are fully ten per cent higher than last year and farms are selling at $70 to $100 per acre. Some of the rougher land is changing hands at $25 to $50.

WORTH COUNTY.

Bert Hamilton.

Fair held September 17 to 19, 1902, at Northwood.·

The exhibition was one of the most successful held in Worth county for years. The attendance was large and the exhibits numerous. There is more of a determination among the farmers of the county to make it "their fair." Grain, fruit and vegetables made up the principal exhibits and these departments were well filled. There was also a fine showing of live stock.

While crops in Worth county last season were large, but there was a great deal of damaged grain because of the excessive rains.

Creameries are proving very profitable to the farmers of this county and all are well patronized. Nearly all are run on the co-operative plan. Farm lands have steadily advanced in price and are selling at $40 to $85 per acre. Many farmers are disposing of their farms here and investing in the cheaper lands of the northwest.

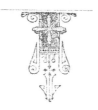

FINANCIAL STATEMENT OF COUNTY AND DISTRICT FAIRS, 1902.

COUNTY OR DISTRICT	RECEIPTS				DISBURSEMENTS					
	Balance on hand December 1, 1901.	Receipts for 1902.	Overdrafts for 1902.	Total receipts for 1902.	Expenses for 1902.	Speed premiums paid for 1902.	Premiums paid for 1902.	Balance on hand November 1, 1902.	Total disbursements for 1902.	Indebtedness for 1902.
Adair	662.03	2,821.20	338.21	3,159.41	1,482.76	1,036.75	619.90	108.84	3,159.41	.60
Adams	26.71	4,091.30		4,753.33	2,775.10	1,181.29	688.10	29.37	4,753.33	2,822.00
Allamakee	472.66	3,131.06		3,157.77	2,107.65	545.75	475.00	318.00	3,157.77	700.00
Audubon		2,773.66	214.08	3,246.32	1,343.47	914.00	670.85	54.44	3,246.32	1,200.00
Benton		2,922.03	255.01	2,922.03	1,565.94	561.00	740.65		2,922.03	1,600.00
Black Hawk—LaPorte City district		1,946.05		2,160.13	738.43	855.45	546.25		2,160.13	266.43
Boone	284.16	1,551.67		1,806.68	760.38	740.00	306.31		1,806.68	4,000.00
Buchanan		2,444.29		2,728.45	1,279.46	174.00	547.75	727.24	2,728.45	
Buena Vista	53.70	5,318.95		5,318.95	1,936.23	2,270.00	904.00	208.67	5,318.95	.60
Butler		1,811.49		1,865.19	750.00	712.00	316.85	121.34	1,865.19	
Cass	129.73	3,100.85		3,100.85	1,203.66	1,103.75	777.15	16.29	3,100.85	
Cedar—Mechanicsville district	67.87	1,154.60	698.33	1,952.66	699.16	750.00	503.50		1,952.66	500.00
Cedar—Tipton district	18.50	2,765.55	307.63	3,201.05	1,666.32	541.50	993.23		3,201.05	567.63
Cherokee		1,670.00		1,688.50	650.00	300.00	527.00	211.50	1,688.50	2,396.00
Chickasaw—Big ... district		2,012.75		2,012.75	717.22	595.00	658.75	41.78	2,012.75	4,000.00
Clayton	204.70	2,104.98	391.77	2,496.75	1,405.55	482.50	608.70		2,496.75	
Clinton—Clinton district		6,377.70		6,582.40	3,006.01	2,025.00	933.66	617.73	6,582.40	
Clinton				4,154.93	2,184.66	708.00	1,178.50	83.77	4,154.93	
Dallas		2,250.00	130.50	2,390.50	730.00	750.00	900.90		2,390.50	510.00
Davis		3,430.35		3,430.35	1,628.45	810.00	990.90	1.00	3,430.35	50.00
Delaware	275.09	2,021.39	13.52	2,310.00	1,128.89	563.00	618.20		2,310.00	2,200.00
Des Moines	484.78	4,708.45		5,193.23	1,750.00	2,230.00	754.75	438.48	5,193.23	
Fayette		3,920.80	102.95	4,023.75	2,420.75	820.00	783.00		4,023.75	2,000.00
Fayette—Arlington district	120.36	710.36	189.90	900.26	566.26	187.25	146.75		900.26	
Franklin	58.39	3,053.42		3,173.78	1,169.62	1,225.00	550.77	228.39	3,173.78	1,350.00
...ay	8.59	1,808.17		1,956.58	760.35	511.75	426.05	258.41	1,956.58	580.00
Guthrie		1,880.94		1,899.53	705.00	235.00	636.88	262.65	1,899.53	1,200.00
Hancock	39.29	2,056.25		2,056.25	425.00	1,075.00	3.00	43.25	2,056.25	1,300.00
Hardin	227.92	5,531.10		5,570.39	2,251.43	2,337.00	676.40	305.56	5,570.39	600.00
Harrison	809.14	1,083.40		1,911.32	774.00	543.32	498.50	107.30	1,911.32	250.00
Henry	10.80	9,059.43		9,868.59	2,996.63	2,100.00	1,125.70	3,646.26	9,868.59	
Henry—Eastern Iowa district	41.36	2,182.03	570.85	2,763.68	1,364.28	467.90	981.50		2,763.68	50.85
Humb...		1,576.79	187.89	1,806.04	784.94	590.00	431.10		1,806.04	620.00
Iowa—Victor district		2,367.60	190.40	2,558.00	1,064.90	990.00	503.10		2,558.00	375.60

Iowa		2,453.65		342.32	63.00	1,148.13	2,453.65		2,380.50	
Iowa—Williamsburg district	1, 0.00	2,725.88	188.28	537.60	815.00	1,185.00	2,725.88	73.15	2,725.88	400.08
Jackson	35.00	4,745.43	545.95	876.10	B5.00	3,288.38	4,745.43		4,385.75	261.44
Jasper	60.00	6,741.46	459.99	1,007.13	913.50	4,360.84	6,741.46		6,480.02	17.71
Jefferson		2,097.21	203.06	716.75	455.00	717.40	2,097.21	155.16	2,079.50	129.84
Johnson	2,400.00	4,707.50		1,106.25	1,910.00	1,691.25	4,707.50	76.93	4,422.50	
Jones	0.00	6,188.29		955.86	2,288.00	2,944.43	6,188.29		4,111.36	
Jones—Anamosa district	2,900.00	6,832.33	143.53	544.90		4,546.40	6,832.33		6,593.14	230.19
Keokuk—What Cheer	76.93	3,257.35	82.35	657.50	97.50	908.50	3,257.35		3,257.35	
Kossuth		1,96.20	402.48	517.75	1, 69.00	520.97	96.20		1,916.80	9.40
Lee—West Point district		1,738.24		301.16	485.00	950.05	1,738.24		1,738.24	
Lee	1,700.00	2,561.02		506.75	487.03	750.63	2,561.02		2,256.48	304.54
Linn—Prairie Valley district	1,600.00	2,902.95	728.64	585.95	575.00	816.16	2,902.95	117.52	3,111.25	145.05
Lonisa—Columbus Junction district	1,575.00	7,368.22	26.79	1,944.25	88.00	1,887.46	88.22		2,125.55	242.67
Madison	1,505.00	2,155.34	291.51	409.60	3,275.00	455.36	2,155.34		2,155.31	
Mahaska—New Sharon district	2,200.00	1,132.00	90.38	115.00	1,200.00	368.60	1,132.08	50.50	1,119.55	12.53
Mahaska	500.00	1,132.08	8.48	40.60		600.00	50.00			
Marion—Lake Prairie district	1,050.00	3,520.00	195.00	300.00	1, 65.00	1,375.30	3,520.00	306.08	3,520.00	
Marshall—Eden district		1,991.81	50.16	433.70	132.65	695.77	1,991.81		1,186.08	806.13
Mills	150.00	1,133.02		437.25		1,475.23	1,133.02		1,015.50	
Mitchell		2,548.22	319.14	508.35	185.10	556.66	88.22		218.50	329.72
Montgomery		2,902.95	1.08	397.35	00.00	249.45	65.09		1,955.09	
Muscatine—Union district	919.00	1,955.09		528.50	1,125.00	958.63	1,881.30	50.50	832.45	
Muscatine—Wilton district	2,150.00	3,881.30	86.67	1,271.10	65.00	871.05	2,193.35	206.08	3,881.30	
O'Brien—Sheldon district	400.00	2,193.35		1,422.30	80.00	1,734.67	5,513.14		1,707.27	691.83
O'Brien	396.08	5,513.14	0.92	757.55		1,200.00	88.40	248.75	2,579.85	1.28
Page—Shenandoah district	2,500.00	2,828.00		628.60	1, 35.00	433.60	642.29		1,656.85	1,357.69
Palo Alto	450.00	6,642.29	1,037.75	606.80	97.50	3,642.74	65.85		1,244.00	
Pocahontas		1,656.85	84.25	201.50	1,575.75	1,180.33	476.23		425.75	50.48
Pottawattamie	900.00	476.23	44.95	675.20	25.00	1,590.00	702.22		3,484.73	217.49
Poweshiek—Central at Malcom	900.00	3,702.22	196.67	640.55	1, 00.00	1,295.81	48.04		3,356.21	
Poweshiek—Central at Grinnell	1,100.00	4,048.04	84.23	768.00	1,072.44	1,229.46	65.53		2,965.25	
Ringgold		2,905.53	87.84	516.75	497.00	1,235.85	68.05		2,668.05	
Sioux—Rock Valley district	3,950.00	2,668.05		935.20		1,107.70	442.80	692.55	1,750.15	
Sioux	1,700.00	1,342.80	4.88	310.00	1, 35.00	657.17	1,342.80		1,312.15	30.65
Story	1,024.00	2,670.49	182.13	414.50	26.25	981.54	670.49		2,670.49	
Tama	500.00	2,494.20		455.33	1,051.40		94.20	230.16	244.04	
Taylor	2,200.00	1,764.63		408.70	96.50	1,159.00	1,764.63		1,648.07	115.96
Van Buren—Milton district	450.00	1,623.29	12.38	756.88	150.00	845.37	1,623.29		1,612.69	10.00
Warren		3,441.73	105.28	290.50	50.00	677.51	3,441.73		3,441.73	
Wayne—Lineville district	1,100.00	1,391.00	869.56	788.41	750.00	1,663.76	1,391.00	24.00	1,366.40	
Winnebago—Buffalo Center district	6,500.00	1,316.02		396.00	400.00	625.00	1,316.02	65.79	1,131.78	118.45
Winneshiek	1,500.00	3,234.67	834.94	204.90	536.25	574.87	3,234.67		2,817.62	447.05
Worth	1,400.00	1,074.28	28.62	448.23	325.75	1,651.55	1,074.28		1,074.28	
Wright	700.00	1,715.05		348.95	100.00	596.71	1,715.05	179.75	1,595.30	
				541.65	302.00	871.40				
Total	**$81,138.06**	**$245,105.43**	**$15,747.16**	**$49,078.38**	**$75,376.51**	**$104,908.35**	**$245,105.43**	**$5,978.98**	**$229,142.29**	**$9,984.16**

PART XIII.

FARM, CROP AND LIVE STOCK STATISTICS.

The tables herein given are compiled from volumes 5 and 6 of the United States census report for 1890, except as otherwise noted.

TWENTY-FIVE-BILLION DOLLAR INDUSTRY.

Breeders' Gazette.

A bulletin recently issued by the Census Bureau at Washington contains figures which give American agriculture at June 30, 1900, an aspect of vast commercial importance. At that time 5,739,657 farms were being operated. These were valued at $16,673,694,247, of which amount $3,560,-198,191, or over 21 per cent, represented the value of buildings and $13,-114,492,056, or over 78 per cent, represented the value of lands and improvements other than buildings. The value of live stock for that year is placed at $3,073,050,041 and farm machinery and implements at $761,261,-550, making a total value of farm property amounting to $20,514,001,848. Farms averaged 146 acres in size and 49 per cent of the farm land is reported as improved. The total acreage for the entire country was 941,201,546. Texas leads with the greatest number of farms, 352,190, and also with the highest acreage, 125,807,017, though only 17 per cent of the farm land in that state was improved. Missouri ranks second in the number of farms. Iowa leads the list in the percentage of improved land. Illinois follows. Ohio comes next followed by Indiana. Illinois occupies the first position in the matter of the total value of farm lands, the figures being $2,004,316,-897. Iowa is second. Live stock lands are put down at a value of $7,505,-284,273, or more than 36 per cent of the whole. The total value of farm products for 1899 is given at $4,739,118,752, of which amount $1,718,990,-221 was for animal products and the products of live stock, poultry and bees. Irrigators in the arid states and territories increased from 1889 to 1899 from 52,584 to 102,919, or 95 per cent, and the number of acres irrigated increased from 3,564,415 to 7,263,273, or 103 per cent.

Marvelous improvement in agricultural conditions throughout the country according to these figures may be read between the lines, and still Secretary of Agriculture James Wilson himself in a recent address on "The New Agriculture" said: "We have not yet begun. It is a new subject; so new, in fact, that its possibilities cannot be comprehended."

HOLDINGS OF CATTLE.

Breeders' Gazette.

Some interesting statisitcs may be culled from the completed census of cattle taken by the United States government for June 1, 1900. By grouping the various states and territories into divisions according to the conditions under which cattle are usually kept we have practically four different cuts of the country—the corn belt where most of the feeding for market is done, the range country where the cattle run out all year round, the south and far east north of Maryland. Taking the census figures and arranging the holdings according to numbers in these divisions we get the following tables.

CORN BELT.

State.	No. cattle owned
Iowa	5,367,630
Kansas	4,491,078
Nebraska	3,176,243
Illinois	3,104,010
Missouri	2,978,589
Wisconsin	2,314,105
Ohio	2,053,313
Minnesota	1,871,325
Indiana	1,684,478
Michigan	1,376,408
Total	28,417,179

RANGE.

Texas	9,428,196
Oklahoma Territory	1,709,752
South Dakota	1,528,486
Indian Territory	1,499,364
California	1,444,624
Colorado	1,433,318
New Mexico	991,859
Montana	968,387
Arizona	742,635
Oregon	700,303
Total	20,446,924

THE SOUTH.

Kentucky	1,083,248
Tennessee	912,183
Georgia	899,491
Arkansas	894,535
Mississippi	873,356
Virginia	825,512
Alabama	799,734
Florida	751,261
Louisiana	670,295
Total	8,349,397

THE EAST.

New York	2,596,389
Pennsylvania	1,896,847
Vermont	501,940
Maine	338,847
Massachusetts	285,792
New Jersey	239,948
New Hampshire	226,792
Connecticut	217,058
Delaware	54,180
Rhode Island	36,034
Total	6,393,863

The foregoing furnishes the totals for the ten leading constituted divisions in each of the four sections into which we divided the country. It will be seen that the ten states called the corn belt contain the most cattle. Few will think that there are more cattle in these ten commonwealths first named than there are in the entire range country, but there are. To show this we add to the total given in the range cut 2,832,057 head representing all the cattle owned in Idaho, Nevada, North Dakota, Utah, Washington and Wyoming and we reach a grand sum of 23,278,981 for the ranges, as against 28,417,179 for the corn states. To complete the count and show the strength of the four divisions made we must add to the figures given for the south 1,242,062 head for Maryland, North Carolina and South Carolina and still farther 1,462 for the District of Columbia and we obtain a grand southern total of 9,592,921. The east as divided off has only its ten states with 6,393,863 head.

Allowance must be farther made for the cattle listed by the Federal Government for Alaska and Hawaii ,but the figures for these two territorial possession of Uncle Sam do not concern us. The corn belt leads thus:

The corn belt, ten states	28,417,179
The range, sixteen states and territories	23,278,891
The south, thirteen states and District of Columbia	9,592,921
The east, ten states	6,393,863

Few would have believed that the corn belt holds such a great lead over the ranges, but there are the census figures for purposes of comparison. Texas is far and away the greatest owner of cattle, but the unexpectedly small totals for the states in which the northwestern range lands lie tell eloquently why it is that the men from the north must annually journey to the Lone Star state to buy steers wherewith to turn their grass into money. The rank taken by Oklahoma and the Indian Territory will occasion surprise and also the prominent position enjoyed by South Dakota. But the cattle are in the corn country, according to the figures.

LIVE STOCK RECEIVED, SHIPPED, AND SLAUGHTERED IN CHICAGO, ILL.: 1870 TO 1900.*

Breeders' Gazette

YEARS	HOGS Received	HOGS Shipped	HOGS Slaughtered	CATTLE Received	CATTLE Shipped	CATTLE Slaughtered	SHEEP Received	SHEEP Shipped	SHEEP Slaughtered
1870	1,693,158	924,453	768,705	532,964	391,709	141,255	349,853	116,711	233,142
1871	2,380,083	1,162,298	1,217,797	543,050	401,927	141,123	315,053	135,084	179,969
1872	3,252,623	1,835,594	1,417,029	684,075	510,025	174,050	310,211	145,016	165,195
1873	4,437,750	2,197,557	2,240,193	761,428	574,181	187,247	291,734	115,235	176,499
1874	4,258,379	2,330,361	1,928,018	843,966	622,929	221,037	333,655	180,555	153,100
1875	3,912,110	1,582,643	2,329,467	920,843	696,534	224,309	418,948	243,604	175,344
1876	4,190,006	1,131,635	3,058,371	1,096,745	797,724	299,021	364,005	195,925	168,170
1877	4,025,970	951,221	3,074,749	1,033,151	703,402	329,749	310,240	155,354	154,886
1878	6,339,654	1,286,906	5,072,748	1,083,068	699,108	383,960	310,423	156,727	153,693
1879	6,448,330	1,692,361	4,755,969	1,215,732	726,908	488,829	325,119	159,266	165,853
1880	7,059,355	1,394,990	5,664,365	1,382,477	886,614	495,863	335,810	156,518	179,292
1881	6,474,844	1,289,679	5,185,165	1,498,550	938,712	559,838	493,624	253,980	239,694
1882	5,817,504	1,747,722	4,069,782	1,582,530	921,009	661,521	628,887	314,200	314,687
1883	5,640,625	1,319,392	4,321,233	1,878,944	966,758	912,186	749,917	374,463	375,454
1884	5,351,967	1,392,615	3,959,352	1,817,697	791,884	1,025,813	801,630	290,352	511,278
1885	6,937,535	1,797,446	5,140,089	1,905,518	744,088	1,161,425	1,008,798	260,277	742,178
1886	6,718,761	2,090,784	4,627,977	1,963,900	704,675	1,239,225	1,008,799	266,612	915,708
1887	5,470,852	1,812,001	3,658,851	2,382,008	791,483	1,590,525	1,360,862	445,694	913,773
1888	4,921,712	1,751,829	3,169,883	2,611,543	968,385	1,643,158	1,515,014	601,241	1,121,151
1889	4,998,520	1,786,659	4,211,887	3,023,281	1,259,971	1,763,310	1,832,469	711,315	1,252,813
1890	7,663,828	1,985,700	5,678,128	3,484,280	1,260,809	2,223,971	2,182,067	929,854	1,465,332
1891	8,600,805	2,962,514	5,638,291	3,250,359	1,066,294	2,184,005	2,153,537	688,205	1,661,711
1892	7,714,435	2,928,145	4,788,290	3,571,796	1,121,675	2,450,121	2,145,079	483,308	2,588,309
1893	6,051,278	2,149,410	3,907,868	3,133,406	900,738	2,233,223	3,031,174	442,805	2,766,227
1894	7,483,228	2,465,058	5,018,170	2,588,558	950,183	2,023,625	3,099,625	333,398	2,932,063
1895	7,885,283	3,100,613	5,784,670	2,974,363	785,092	1,803,461	3,406,739	474,646	3,029,416
1896	7,659,472	1,896,312	5,763,160	2,600,476	818,326	1,782,150	3,590,655	561,239	2,908,530
1897	8,363,724	1,629,984	6,733,740	2,554,924	843,392	1,711,532	3,606,640	638,110	3,046,014
1898	9,166,095	1,340,544	7,825,551	2,480,897	805,642	1,615,255	3,589,439	513,425	3,295,841
1899	8,721,325	1,689,439	7,032,086	2,514,436	811,874	1,702,562	3,682,832	386,991	3,061,631
1900	8,695,097	1,452,183	7,243,914	2,729,046	934,649	1,794,397	3,548,885	487,254	

* Compiled from data furnished by Cincinnati Price Current.

LIVE STOCK RECEIVED, SHIPPED, AND SLAUGHTERED IN ST. LOUIS, MISSOURI: 1868 TO 1900.*

Breeders' Gazette.

YEARS.	HOGS.			CATTLE.			SHEEP.		
	Received.	Shipped.	Slaughtered.	Received.	Shipped.	Slaughtered.	Received.	Shipped.	Slaughtered.
1868	301,560	16,277	285,283	115,352	37,277	78,075	79,315	6,415	72,900
1869	344,848	39,076	305,772	124,565	59,887	64,698	96,626	12,416	84,210
1870	310,850	17,156	293,694	201,422	129,748	71,674	94,477	11,649	82,828
1871	633,570	113,913	519,457	199,527	130,018	69,509	118,899	37,465	81,434
1872	759,076	188,700	570,376	263,404	164,870	98,534	115,904	29,540	86,984
1873	973,512	224,873	748,639	279,678	180,602	99,016	86,434	18,902	67,532
1874	1,126,586	453,710	672,876	380,925	226,678	134,247	114,913	35,577	79,336
1875	628,569	126,729	501,840	335,742	216,701	119,041	125,679	37,784	87,895
1876	877,160	232,876	644,284	349,043	220,430	128,613	157,831	67,886	89,945
1877	896,319	314,287	582,032	411,909	251,566	160,403	200,502	87,569	112,933
1878	451,634	528,627	923,007	406,235	261,723	144,512	168,045	74,433	93,662
1879	1,762,724	686,099	1,076,625	420,654	228,870	194,399	182,648	88,083	94,565
1880	1,840,684	770,709	1,069,915	424,720	228,255	195,841	205,989	93,522	112,447
1881	1,672,153	889,909	782,244	503,862	298,082	210,770	334,425	170,395	164,031
1882	846,228	264,584	581,644	443,169	188,486	254,683	443,120	245,071	198,049
1883	1,151,725	609,388	542,397	405,090	249,523	155,567	398,612	217,370	181,242
1884	1,474,475	678,874	795,601	450,717	315,433	135,284	380,822	248,545	132,277
1885	1,455,535	789,487	666,048	386,320	233,249	153,071	362,858	233,391	129,467
1886	1,264,471	520,362	744,109	377,550	212,958	164,592	328,985	202,728	126,257
1887	1,052,240	324,735	727,505	464,828	277,406	187,422	417,425	297,018	130,407
1888	929,230	294,989	634,361	546,875	336,206	210,669	456,669	316,676	189,993
1889	1,120,980	420,980	700,000	508,190	297,879	210,311	388,495	255,375	103,120
1890	1,359,791	665,471	694,320	639,014	361,705	277,309	358,496	251,728	106,768
1891	1,360,569	704,378	676,191	779,449	464,794	314,655	402,989	277,886	125,103
1892	1,310,311	715,969	594,342	801,811	465,328	336,483	376,922	248,085	128,887
1893	1,105,108	575,846	529,262	903,257	473,996	429,291	397,725	231,476	166,249
1894	1,489,856	642,699	847,157	773,571	281,260	492,311	359,895	90,526	269,369
1895	1,440,342	605,480	834,862	851,225	272,856	578,419	510,660	119,148	391,512
1896	1,997,895	885,462	1,112,433	965,613	350,036	605,577	632,872	254,602	378,270
1897	2,085,283	887,895	1,227,388	960,763	386,127	594,636	660,380	212,243	448,137
1898	2,136,328	573,516	1,562,812	795,611	254,619	540,992	477,091	127,184	349,907
1899	2,147,144	578,067	1,569,077	766,082	224,177	541,855	432,566	97,722	334,844
1900	2,156,972	513,561	1,643,411	795,810	207,998	587,802	434,133	65,199	368,934

* Compiled from data furnished by Cincinnati Price Current.

LIVE STOCK RECEIVED, SHIPPED, AND SLAUGHTERED IN KANSAS CITY, MISSOURI, 1875 TO 1900.*

Breeders' Gazette.

YEARS.	HOGS.			CATTLE.			SHEEP.		
	Received.	Shipped.	Slaughtered.	Received.	Shipped.	Slaughtered.	Received.	Shipped.	Slaughtered.
1875	63,350	15,790	47,560	174,754	126,262	48,492	25,327	17,742	7,585
1876	153,777	26,964	127,513	183,378	120,340	63,038	55,045	22,460	32,585
1877	192,645	15,973	176,072	215,768	126,570	89,198	42,190	28,329	13,881
1878	427,777	91,671	336,106	175,344	131,761	43,583	36,700	30,483	6,217
1879	588,908	208,851	380,057	211,415	155,831	55,584	61,684	47,782	13,902
1880	676,477	152,920	523,557	244,709	194,421	50,288	50,611	36,285	14,326
1881	1,014,304	195,524	818,780	285,863	223,989	61,874	79,924	61,078	18,846
1882	963,036	191,325	771,711	434,671	359,012	80,659	80,724	52,632	28,072
1883	379,401	313,879	1,065,522	400,780	387,598	73,182	119,665	61,977	57,688
1884	1,723,586	590,133	1,133,453	533,526	443,001	90,525	237,964	105,973	131,991
1885	2,358,718	801,182	1,557,556	500,827	402,381	104,246	221,901	115,755	106,046
1886	2,364,484	538,005	1,726,479	490,971	370,350	120,621	172,959	83,234	89,425
1887	2,423,262	524,492	1,898,770	669,224	483,372	185,852	209,956	103,128	106,830
1888	2,008,964	413,937	1,595,047	1,056,086	682,622	373,464	351,050	169,932	181,118
1889	2,073,910	331,434	1,742,476	1,220,343	744,510	475,833	370,772	174,851	195,921
1890	2,865,171	558,227	2,306,944	1,472,229	923,552	548,677	535,869	336,207	199,662
1891	2,599,109	605,457	1,993,652	1,270,917	739,093	531,824	386,760	178,271	208,489
1892	2,397,477	591,623	1,805,854	1,479,073	810,010	669,68	438,208	219,230	219,038
1893	2,948,373	520,694	1,427,679	1,690,807	761,876	899,131	569,517	196,892	372,625
1894	2,547,077	436,804	2,050,273	1,689,193	764,592	924,601	589,555	196,061	393,494
1895	2,457,697	286,340	2,171,357	1,613,464	719,704	883,750	864,713	287,294	577,419
1896	2,605,575	341,689	2,263,876	1,714,532	819,799	884,733	983,126	303,693	689,433
1897	3,350,796	263,841	3,086,955	1,817,526	875,756	941,770	1,134,236	306,356	827,880
1898	3,672,909	373,219	3,29,690	1,757,964	851,188	906,778	980,303	330,865	649,438
1899	2,959,073	257,718	2,701,355	1,912,019	919,573	902,448	953,241	308,403	644,888
1900	3,094,39	223,963	2,870,176	1,969,718	853,303	1,116,415	860,449	216,272	644,177

* Compiled from data furnished by   Nati Price Current.

LIVESTOCK STATISTICS.

CATTLE IN IOWA BY COUNTIES JUNE 1, 1900.

COUNTIES	Calves under one year	Steers 1 and under 2 years	Steers 2 and under 3 years	Steers 3 years and over	Bulls 1 year and over	Heifers 1 and under 2 years	Dairy cows 2 years and over	Other cows 2 years and over	Total number and value of cattle in Iowa	Horses all ages	Mules all ages	Asses and burros, all ages
Tal value	$14,413,585	$17,655,451	$23,624,389	$9,510,610	$4,408,021	$12,242,609	$46,349,012	$14,315,225	$142,518,902	$77,720,577	$3,586,761	$150,768
Tal No. in state	1,290,279	730,681	603,745	173,016	98,154	502,076	1,423,648	461,081	5,367,630	1,362,573	55,747	1,832
Adair	15,445	9,623	8,830	2,393	1,136	7,508	16,620	6,627	68,182	15,299	839	8
Adams	12,019	7,309	7,542	2,189	785	5,833	11,538	6,647	53,812	12,640	963	23
Allamakee	13,069	5,735	1,828	111	892	5,458	15,633	2,790	45,516	10,912	62	1
Appanoose	9,800	7,043	5,684	3,320	687	5,364	11,187	4,924	48,069	12,120	794	16
Audubon	12,648	6,885	5,627	1,440	933	5,779	13,147	4,395	51,164	11,922	787	18
Benton	18,639	7,711	5,237	2,080	1,253	8,516	19,090	6,735	74,353	19,395	413	6
Black Hawk	16,416	6,641	5,079	1,075	1,143	6,737	21,931	6,116	62,208	14,491	195	3
Boone	13,312	3,704	4,614	1,135	899	6,067	15,809	3,108	51,585	15,317	498	6
Bremer	13,486	7,805	1,043	274	1,134	5,967	22,314	1,946	49,868	11,406	66	1
Buchanan	16,575	6,979	4,722	1,516	1,125	7,387	22,068	2,388	63,476	15,459	267	10
Buena Vista	14,887	6,584	7,269	1,846	1,057	6,409	15,981	4,506	60,994	12,454	302	52
Butler	15,516	7,113	3,713	1,362	1,261	6,822	15,219	2,388	57,554	14,232	148	5
Calhoun	12,789	6,390	4,60	2,148	940	6,178	4,246	4,170	50,746	13,942	445	3
Carroll	15,907	9,676	4,720	2,349	1,128	6,518	15,184	4,835	59,031	14,111	471	20
Cass	13,776	9,770	10,213	3,357	1,156	6,789	11,105	8,563	64,645	15,650	1,155	6
Cedar	15,983	9,646	7,880	1,836	1,056	7,382	13,982	8,083	65,882	16,590	1,170	49
Cerro Gordo	12,854	9,770	7,139	1,821	771	5,858	14,730	2,056	53,179	12,606	130	4
Cherokee	13,247	1,646	10,489	2,184	880	5,639	10,559	7,334	60,977	13,151	222	1
Chickasaw	4,794	5,485	2,110	355	665	4,748	19,522	2,565	32,010	12,268	76	1
Clarke	9,184	7,655	5,513	2,269	1,052	5,038	11,508	3,760	51,378	11,308	471	8
Clay	12,262	6,203	6,867	2,046	744	7,802	12,942	4,824	42,862	11,436	140	1
Clayton	18,829	10,391	2,362	316	1,474	7,808	24,974	2,750	51,308	16,261	178	13
Clinton	19,296	10,821	11,345	2,897	1,319	7,537	21,660	4,005	64,770	17,854	201	1
Crawford	17,606	8,822	12,375	3,389	1,326	6,325	14,623	8,327	78,651	16,299	835	1
Dallas	12,884	5,997	8,653	3,619	836	4,681	13,524	5,229	75,954	15,635	754	5
Davis	9,231	5,368	4,469	2,202	647	5,730	11,654	3,774	41,426	13,190	535	11
Decatur	10,790	5,997	4,798	2,999	797	7,691	11,453	7,147	48,711	13,852	596	11
Delaware	17,613	6,519	2,960	1,173	1,431	7,691	25,971	2,679	65,037	14,270	197	18
Des Moines	7,059	4,484	4,754	1,376	443	3,253	8,881	3,031	31,781	10,622	395	11

Dickinson	6,853	3,949	1,970	623	470	3,5?3	6,800	3,831	28,009	6,775	124	1
Dubuque	14,680	7,409	4,345	917	1,266	6,685	20,780	3,821	59,903	12,964	195	4
Emmet	6,196	4,40	4,088	983	470	2,841	7,915	3,215	28,838	7,181	203	4
Fayette	21,988	9,380	4,153	540	1,483	8,995	27,612	3,403	80,554	17,925	200	3
Floyd	12,430	4,788	2,190	781	870	5,039	14,819	1,402	42,317	13,657	77	6
Franklin	13,628	9,096	7,884	2,065	1,273	5,951	14,913	3,156	57,866	13,008	175	63
Fremont	13,620	5,498	9,281	3,474	401	3,870	6,523	4,542	42,003	12,526	174	7
Kae	14,455	7,154	5,985	1,803	875	5,864	13,916	4,224	54,427	16,000	313	—
Grundy	14,696	8,182	5,965	1,393	1,123	5,894	15,933	7,165	56,359	12,818	302	5
Guthrie	11,522	8,815	7,012	1,855	961	7,050	14,194	1,752	61,509	15,251	636	6
Hamilton	14,602	7,812	6,090	1,530	1,091	6,098	18,335	3,393	57,342	14,284	429	6
Hancock	13,157	8,713	6,300	988	786	4,890	12,630	3,481	46,208	11,059	189	7
Hardin	6,948	7,453	5,880	1,201	1,130	6,604	18,639	5,924	58,470	13,912	817	34
Harrison	12,296	8,065	8,146	4,355	873	6,052	17,932	3,740	60,513	16,272	1,188	7
Henry	10,476	5,581	4,870	3,157	314	3,475	11,961	2,094	38,238	14,028	621	3
Howard	9,695	5,222	2,202	682	866	5,118	14,984	2,181	43,883	9,676	77	2
Humboldt	9,695	9,625	4,371	784	695	4,183	12,191	4,286	40,698	9,793	202	2
Ida	15,438	9,094	7,996	2,286	676	5,242	8,994	9,096	48,800	15,400	537	17
Iowa	17,099	9,021	6,764	603	1,164	7,894	14,976	8,237	66,533	14,449	1,024	139
Jackson	8,340	10,163	5,837	3,317	1,244	7,763	19,108	8,237	65,297	12,069	219	13
Jasper	8,913	10,988	11,663	1,189	1,353	8,239	16,297	12,813	74,106	12,101	1,098	5
Jefferson	8,340	10,207	4,954	1,283	570	4,156	10,277	2,445	37,928	17,583	989	8
Johnson	17,494	8,657	5,851	1,580	1,244	8,452	23,416	12,813	66,706	15,087	892	7
Jones	18,435	7,615	7,850	1,251	1,304	4,432	11,928	3,765	72,518	19,104	412	12
Keokuk	9,074	8,343	5,553	1,102	953	7,801	25,297	2,045	53,765	19,181	835	3
Kossuth	18,928	4,840	6,364	737	1,409	4,140	10,757	3,651	70,706	12,485	332	68
Lee	9,074	10,373	3,141	1,331	599	8,790	24,826	4,130	36,519	20,071	690	6
Linn	6,447	4,251	7,134	988	1,259	3,163	7,002	2,602	76,771	7,514	521	6
Louisa	6,447	5,486	4,641	1,745	446	3,957	10,829	2,132	30,480	11,154	459	10
Lucas	6,447	4,467	4,298	1,248	630	3,741	8,900	2,270	41,111	11,104	544	1
Lyon	8,495	8,514	3,188	2,042	657	5,509	11,987	4,717	33,036	14,624	199	9
Madison	13,038	6,906	7,588	2,644	9.2	5,900	13,378	6,141	60,407	14,360	784	x
Mahaska	12,140	7,448	6,643	2,511	853	6,317	11,078	6,614	52,794	17,050	929	10
Marion	11,253	8,352	6,543	1,335	692	4,442	14,227	6,550	51,566	16,524	915	18
Marshall	14,961	6,857	5,362	1,610	1,122	4,718	6,423	1,772	58,290	11,152	357	16
Mills	9,130	5,691	9,094	373	60	4,972	13,703	7,723	44,706	10,243	1,194	4
Mitchell	12,096	9,110	3,254	882	815	4,603	9,808	6,751	42,427	14,985	96	10
Monona	10,896	5,022	10,343	2,917	700	5,304	10,653	6,075	56,354	10,223	1,245	7
Monroe	8,699	8,981	4,445	917	572	4,058	8,957	4,311	35,014	11,611	533	9
Montgomery	11,046	5,474	8,917	1,756	821	5,259	9,133	2,050	50,463	12,020	701	8
Muscatine	9,679	6,347	6,245	667	674	6,057	11,885	6,389	38,985	12,962	507	1
O'Brien	11,652	9,591	6,135	1,081	937	4,488	11,900	8,311	48,207	7,696	209	2
Osceola	12,620	11,076	1,111	248	430	4,974	17,688	3,671	20,449	16,381	128	72
Page	11,804	8,047	9,336	2,471	859	6,202	14,802	3,637	57,423	11,013	1,550	4
Palo Alto	15,614	3,702	8,047	1,669	826	4,488	15,369	—	45,678	18,510	111	8
Plymouth	12,849	7,539	8,506	3,035	1,253	6,823	14,930	9,432	65,741	13,012	591	43
Pocahontas	12,242	7,405	4,892	1,869	923	9,349	19,107	6,542	56,094	17,542	353	62
Polk	19,980	13,531	17,422	4,621	783	7,923	14,825	—	51,581	24,362	1,012	284
Poweshiek	15,122	9,375	8,227	5,719	1,225	—	—	—	69,959	17,588	810	—

LIVE STOCK—Continued.

CATTLE IN IOWA BY COUNTIES JUNE 1, 1900.

COUNTIES.	Calves under one year.	Steers 1 and under 2 years.	Steers 2 and under 3 years.	Steers 3 years and over.	Bulls 1 year and over.	Heifers 1 and under 2 years.	Dairy cows 2 years and over.	Other cows 2 years and over.	Total number and value of cattle in Iowa.	Horses all ages.	Mules all ages.	Asses and burros, all ages.
Ringgold	13,018	8,607	8,878	5,748	857	6,470	13,789	6,172	63,539	14,616	1,167	55
Sac	16,329	10,957	9,111	1,403	1,134	6,082	14,410	7,954	69,380	14,083	552	3
Scott	11,576	5,463	3,264	294	1,073	5,100	15,501	2,777	45,048	12,592	510	9
Shelby	16,658	8,904	8,425	1,593	1,270	7,556	14,155	8,604	68,065	15,385	857	12
Sioux	14,312	8,900	6,905	618	1,076	6,115	13,204	5,028	56,618	15,889	490	45
Story	14,632	6,772	3,826	511	1,089	5,923	17,280	3,174	53,207	16,733	597	5
Tama	17,092	11,701	11,132	1,971	1,349	8,664	16,406	7,690	88,005	17,728	485	114
Taylor	12,716	6,913	8,019	1,998	905	9,081	13,706	6,629	59,913	16,900	1,072	33
Union	11,148	6,992	6,925	1,569	802	5,770	13,463	4,557	51,226	12,102	503	1
Van Buren	8,653	4,283	4,194	2,147	569	4,163	9,903	4,023	38,670	12,299	528	48
Wapello	8,426	7,624	2,955	510	528	4,756	10,275	2,671	33,811	11,599	1,108	24
Warren	12,426	7,040	7,407	2,080	845	5,975	13,122	6,408	55,947	16,989	803	28
Washington	12,327	6,251	6,969	1,349	907	5,973	11,841	5,831	52,237	16,813	885	18
Wayne	12,225	7,852	7,210	2,853	1,012	6,736	11,615	2,103	52,905	15,530	1,071	25
Webster	14,278	4,082	4,553	805	1,078	6,403	17,030	3,552	54,556	15,838	494	5
Winnebago	9,480	6,588	1,685	575	705	4,074	11,009	1,097	33,517	7,576	77	2
Winneshiek	18,550	9,211	2,225	277	1,455	4,290	22,662	2,000	61,047	15,329	70	28
Woodbury	13,990	4,154	10,867	3,418	850	7,290	13,825	7,692	66,159	20,611	1,039	1
Worth	10,108	7,676	1,996	299	838	6,306	12,999	1,205	35,712	8,248	63	5
Wright	12,345		5,648	1,657	907	4,143	14,853	2,563	50,984	12,727	316	
Sac and Fox Res	10				1	1	8	11	81	123		

STATISTICS OF SHEEP, SWINE, GOATS, POULTRY AND EGGS IN IOWA.

COUNTIES	Sheep, all ages	Swine, all ages	Goats, all ages	Chickens, including Guinea fowls (Fowls 3 mo. old and over June 1, 1900)	Turkeys	Geese	Ducks	Value of all poultry, June 1, 1900	Value of poultry raised in 1899	Dozens of eggs produced in 1899
Total value in state	$3,056,142	$43,764,176	$146,708					$6,535,464	$9,491,819	$10,016,707
Total number in state	1,056,718	9,723,791	41,468	18,907,673	424,300	223,612	487,752			99,621,920
Adair	14,043	115,895	241	172,457	5,061	2,400	5,654	67,449	107,454	1,020,930
Adams	18,506	97,274	25	158,097	2,315	1,719	4,953	59,426	75,297	1,015,970
Allamakee	7,133	87,835	76	183,730	3,455	1,605	1,684	54,615	65,932	974,800
Appanoose	9,510	41,557	42	183,446	6,905	2,893	2,761	67,502	105,807	927,220
Audubon	2,961	99,494	321	140,256	3,438	2,634	5,083	50,852	77,292	854,740
Benton	7,675	150,583	285	225,051	2,914	3,142	5,730	78,745	123,803	1,208,670
Black Hawk	7,103	121,176	28	155,041	4,011	1,760	4,984	65,854	84,927	922,780
Boone	3,714	95,702	266	250,435	3,807	1,408	5,983	65,157	96,861	1,307,300
Bremer	3,980	82,709	311	173,304	5,254	1,999	4,735	86,157	76,533	732,650
Buchanan	11,312	107,892	84	216,887	5,752	1,939	5,491	58,825	111,890	1,085,610
Buena Vista	5,984	96,223	5	158,959	3,287	1,763	4,875	46,534	82,724	797,150
Butler	8,563	99,421	146	214,997	4,440	2,185	5,324	75,033	95,382	1,108,700
Calhoun	5,961	83,802	217	185,956	6,713	1,845	6,066	75,808	119,259	909,660
Carroll	3,331	117,255	135	230,519	5,593	3,296	5,347	65,748	90,980	1,048,240
Cass	14,371	109,221	416	161,100	2,966	1,566	4,145	70,354	85,555	1,171,530
Cedar	18,473	148,646	107	189,436	2,475	2,385	4,084	60,349	112,482	1,023,700
Cerro Gordo	18,170	77,924	2	164,660	6,078	2,374	5,111	66,313	95,900	919,370
Cherokee	4,419	112,401	386	180,767	756	2,351	5,409	61,745	64,623	1,027,770
Chickasaw	6,923	73,750	282	135,870	4,541	2,651	4,534	47,365	82,048	901,320
Clarke	8,493	59,537	334	135,094	4,598	1,885	4,529	54,964	61,202	756,540
Clay	15,017	60,659	252	155,512	6,074	1,099	4,672	50,738	84,568	677,610
Clayton	14,443	112,360	946	286,467	5,466	4,141	7,675	90,295	132,123	1,710,150
Clinton	5,375	162,183	313	223,865	2,678	4,045	7,389	72,675	108,122	1,117,330
Crawford	2,017	188,508	115	247,624	6,948	4,317	5,888	78,754	95,977	1,200,220
Dallas	6,336	114,300	2,157	230,287	4,491	2,003	2,810	82,670	99,609	1,028,210
Davis	44,921	51,527	589	170,180	5,339	3,862	3,461	64,867	126,640	920,160
Decatur	15,710	59,028	500	167,415	4,621	2,564	3,160	70,476	94,016	1,015,328
Delaware	10,740	156,453	105	175,991	5,329	3,160	3,898	60,601	80,212	970,850
Des Moines	5,227	61,453	24	190,413	2,570	1,427	4,015	63,483	90,495	1,068,210

STATISTICS OF SHEEP, SWINE, GOATS POULTRY AND EGGS IN IOWA.—CONTINUED.

COUNTIES.	SHEEP, all ages.	SWINE, all ages.	GOATS, all ages.	Fowls 3 mo. old and over June 1, 1900. Chickens, including Guinea fowls.	Turkeys.	Geese.	Ducks.	Value of all poultry, June 1, 1900.	Value of poultry raised in 1899.	Dozens of eggs produced in 1899.
Dickinson	9,783	19,134	9	72,443	4,083	62	2,963	25,322	44,228	387,960
Dubuque	9,592	125,596	160	200,883	3,886	4,101	2,978	64,242	94,769	939,710
Emmet	6,636	30,838	96	79,199	4,205	852	2,598	24,653	50,275	374,290
Fayette	6,619	119,475	139	208,094	6,018	2,436	5,765	86,751	125,745	1,315,690
Floyd	13,825	67,777	68	188,599	4,557	1,805	3,961	64,282	82,734	1,005,690
Franklin	12,865	101,878	126	198,507	5,651	1,569	6,048	65,023	84,137	869,140
Fremont	1,613	71,747	220	146,355	2,548	1,186	4,141	60,314	87,043	852,620
Greene	4,810	82,103	255	250,976	7,708	1,554	4,530	79,189	130,547	1,126,790
Grundy	5,237	100,518	45	157,496	2,218	1,487	4,766	53,464	77,654	850,800
Guthrie	10,558	96,355	923	169,903	5,553	1,605	5,521	67,742	118,238	1,033,590
Hamilton	4,657	86,133	89	217,287	6,569	1,240	5,414	70,823	104,834	866,490
Hancock	3,684	60,500	76	145,057	5,025	1,818	11,252	48,350	73,664	774,770
Hardin	10,808	119,584	251	234,471	8,078	2,915	4,985	73,335	121,591	1,525,190
Harrison	2,620	129,128	1,282	233,704	1,958	1,397	3,131	81,486	100,837	1,529,150
Henry	24,135	72,426	222	227,028	4,714	1,639	3,420	81,222	108,269	677,410
Howard	12,407	56,312	97	133,927	4,284	2,123	4,320	42,503	63,795	559,820
Humboldt	6,552	64,361	28	125,223	4,842	1,076	3,899	41,015	65,110	793,650
Ida	2,725	109,948						39,033	51,758	
Iowa	12,068	133,704	87	128,550	1,019	1,903	6,158	74,501	109,097	1,067,540
Jackson	8,707	122,783	961	207,160	1,074	1,158	4,165	72,201	165,298	1,014,930
Jasper	24,271	163,967	2,925	208,000	4,286	2,528	7,112	94,464	153,900	1,408,980
Jefferson	16,666	71,075	1,316	235,273	5,490	3,270	2,940	66,420	93,320	884,540
Johnson	18,706	134,927	249	272,443	4,087	2,541	5,748	98,442	133,139	1,238,920
Jones	8,020	134,252	484	169,411	4,253	1,891	4,098	61,974	98,251	826,620
Keokuk	11,895	114,469	351	263,964	3,820	3,063	5,299	96,234	134,283	1,413,730
Kossuth	8,678	102,721	50	223,418	11,132	3,172	11,539	84,259	130,057	1,205,320
Lee	22,084	42,682	221	205,752	3,393	3,434	3,856	67,121	93,013	1,283,940
Linn	10,614	143,380	686	130,688	6,063	3,159	7,648	95,507	165,266	1,427,810
Louisa	6,137	74,069	173	144,715	3,434	1,762	3,292	45,411	68,025	646,880
Lucas	20,296	56,117	444	116,829	4,113	2,417	3,199	60,571	77,496	705,090
Lyon	4,166	83,781	46	204,150	862	2,149	9,644	45,231	48,700	674,660
Madison	13,938	114,797	3,704	254,888	5,339	7,434	6,135	82,446	120,168	1,368,940
Mahaska	27,452	113,402	355	262,519	3,906	2,808	5,673	92,791	136,052	1,598,480
Marion	26,618	102,303	230	262,519	2,165	3,628	5,555	101,139	109,871	1,497,640

Marshall	910,490	100,907	61,386	4,434	2,904	2,423	167,527	878	104,276	14,739
Mills	672,170	81,124	48,986	3,191	1,223	1,957	98,681	116	91,678	2,065
Mitchell	759,380	62,234	49,903	2,904	1,389	4,114	151,986	69	62,889	10,743
Monona	905,050	74,077	57,786	2,089	1,349	1,529	166,394	82	101,984	532
Monroe	865,870	77,388	49,059	2,798	1,819	4,954	116,167	272	44,299	7,422
Montgomery	733,380	71,492	60,567	3,854	1,025	1,810	162,740	253	111,603	4,677
Muscatine	818,700	80,567	46,284	4,818	1,528	3,212	142,006	56	77,402	4,381
O'Brien	901,330	69,263	49,642	2,608	2,140	1,077	180,083	80	104,011	18,298
Osceola	485,860	43,536	34,204	2,608	1,169	2,375	106,472	11	40,122	8,856
Page	1,111,420	101,804	75,138	3,332	2,211	3,059	198,274	532	120,574	13,599
Palo Alto	600,690	82,100	49,200	5,287	1,642	6,949	147,555	28	55,573	6,241
Plymouth	1,129,830	90,189	73,240	6,383	3,810	390	258,684	354	135,823	3,729
Pocahontas	892,330	109,343	56,833	7,109	2,409	9,705	190,235	142	78,003	6,706
Polk	1,311,580	152,604	98,257	8,019	1,782	5,479	233,596	2,374	94,986	4,688
Pottawattamie	1,733,670	139,018	115,047	5,950	3,395	3,053	315,233	1,463	198,565	7,955
Poweshiek	1,037,230	112,854	68,389	3,739	2,271	4,565	184,831	303	147,859	17,081
Ringgold	974,790	124,949	69,070	6,146	2,677	4,650	170,962	859	84,190	13,754
Sac	1,067,300	97,659	63,425	5,495	2,434	3,520	192,651	92	117,803	9,508
Scott	909,190	107,315	65,535	5,441	2,234	3,149	200,337	144	107,905	3,587
Shelby	920,230	92,895	60,332	4,948	1,753	2,889	177,083	64	142,643	5,685
Sioux	1,144,180	64,099	63,228	4,414	2,140	730	229,929	70	150,243	7,839
Story	1,375,420	124,946	86,623	4,414	531	6,287	267,044	614	92,699	8,589
Tama	1,107,240	107,709	78,981	7,222	4,366	4,206	246,875	866	145,185	13,320
Taylor	1,139,170	109,897	73,549	4,843	2,737	3,831	184,823	957	111,693	11,555
Union	826,340	70,316	51,768	3,426	1,625	2,299	131,329	462	62,348	11,917
Van Buren	1,037,450	121,127	71,225	3,002	1,419	4,747	180,044	536	47,875	53,521
Wapello	896,040	93,398	62,463	2,378	2,328	2,321	160,426	107	65,465	17,891
Warren	1,086,670	112,505	77,883	5,069	2,162	4,324	183,452	1,476	106,405	12,178
Washington	1,526,530	124,046	89,010	4,551	1,953	4,705	264,378	371	139,702	7,122
Wayne	801,830	111,499	63,324	3,792	3,851	7,745	162,807	1,718	63,003	10,275
Webster	1,041,060	102,567	71,649	4,896	1,840	6,982	232,682	188	94,331	4,553
Winnebago	548,950	22,621	38,917	6,167	1,094	211	121,108	22	37,722	3,896
Winneshiek	1,508,920	85,412	73,625	3,179	2,844	6,255	208,524	163	117,286	13,518
Worth	1,244,190	91,975	77,313	6,677	2,202	734	223,415	119	124,502	4,562
Wright	599,110	56,212	39,241	2,834	1,027	4,889	125,962	75	30,917	8,473
Sac and Fox reservation	702,870	89,929	55,458	5,088	1,693	7,335	164,816	181	81,461	7,050
	1,590	240	195	17	3	100	539		90	

TOTAL NUMBER OF SPECIFIED DOMESTIC ANIMALS IN INCLOSURES, NOT ON FARMS OR RANGES, JUNE 1, 1900, IN IOWA.

CATTLE.	Calves under one year.	9,015
	Steers one and under two years.	2,824
	Steers two and under three years.	2,891
	Steers three years and over.	3,142
	Bulls one year and over.	337
	Heifers one year and under two years.	3,313
	Dairy cows two years and over.	56,028
	Other cows two years and over.	1,151
	Horses all ages.	154,775
	Mules all ages.	5,238
	Asses and burros all ages.	503
SHEEP.	Lambs under one year.	980
	Ewes one year and over.	1,564
	Rams and wethers one year and over.	313
SWINE.	Swine all ages.	128,138
GOATS.	Goats all ages.	807

NUMBER AND ACREAGE OF FARMS AND VALUE OF SPECIFIED CLASSES OF FARM PROPERTY, JUNE 1, 1900, BY COUNTIES.

COUNTIES.	NUMBER OF FARMS.		ACRES IN FARMS.		VALUE OF FARM PROPERTY.			
	Total.	With building.	Total.	Improved.	Land and improvements except the buildings.	Buildings.	Implements and machinery.	Live stock.
The State	228,622	220,626	34,574,337	29,897,552	$1,256,751,980	$240,802,810	$57,900,660	$278,830,096
Adair	2,387	2,295	360,224	331,570	10,868,310	1,965,700	503,840	2,414,436
Adams	1,949	1,843	273,042	249,130	9,662,040	1,628,760	418,450	3,903,761
Allamakee	2,308	2,333	383,324	223,256	8,389,430	1,284,640	627,670	2,110,408
Appanoose	2,526	422	325,147	265,492	8,111,620	1,653,450	373,280	2,321,730
Audubon	1,988	1,901	282,456	272,197	9,814,950	1,630,500	474,110	2,650,485
Benton	2,774	2,691	458,801	403,859	20,788,190	2,906,730	799,280	3,896,565
Black Hawk	2,257	2,177	349,930	318,102	14,943,470	3,354,200	675,210	3,067,935
Boone	2,670	2,597	349,194	307,338	13,481,850	2,495,200	632,200	2,656,709
Bremer	2,004	1,957	275,501	247,494	10,389,470	3,084,690	624,200	2,255,818
Buchanan	2,447	2,380	357,516	320,901	12,852,520	2,755,840	646,880	3,014,781
Buena Vista	1,955	1,919	360,231	338,925	13,001,470	2,306,120	562,610	2,796,760
Butler	1,304	1,231	360,578	323,179	14,145,360	571,020	641,120	841,148
Calhoun	1,134	1,092	382,873	345,079	13,248,880	992,560	534,120	496,244
Carroll	2,175	2,150	356,987	346,597	13,676,400	2,327,550	602,630	2,875,297
Cass	2,395	2,255	354,644	388,357	13,725,420	2,385,780	602,070	3,610,416
Cedar	2,291	2,245	348,056	313,257	16,824,370	3,627,460	649,060	3,658,147
Cerro Gordo	1,908	1,907	353,188	314,078	13,272,230	2,384,700	640,230	2,610,465
Cherokee	1,839	1,839	354,643	323,883	13,341,580	2,298,410	573,840	3,051,784
Chickasaw	2,197	2,128	311,208	255,930	11,594,740	2,330,060	599,290	2,251,826
Clarke	1,714	1,663	259,491	197,318	7,131,900	1,248,960	318,790	2,183,388
Clay	1,684	1,604	344,960	324,815	11,440,140	1,750,250	524,780	2,413,062
Clayton	3,318	3,264	489,892	314,776	13,826,980	3,965,540	808,390	3,217,318
Clinton	2,786	2,719	423,251	383,562	19,623,090	4,285,110	822,230	3,959,715
Crawford	2,649	2,564	449,956	416,917	15,286,790	3,049,900	759,560	3,988,215
Dallas	2,607	2,522	359,280	307,221	14,124,010	2,505,300	566,000	3,279,689
Davis	2,553	2,473	318,392	246,558	7,762,460	1,724,020	399,310	2,260,854
Decatur	2,508	2,412	326,078	235,657	8,637,330	1,076,120	402,600	417,731
Delaware	2,241	2,199	355,619	292,986	14,607,900	3,123,380	754,600	3,038,823

NUMBER AND ACREAGE, ETC.,—CONTINUED.

COUNTIES	NUMBER OF FARMS		ACRES IN FARMS		VALUE OF FARM PROPERTY			
	Total	With buildings	Total	Improved	Land and improvements except the buildings	Buildings	Implements and machinery	Live stock
Des Mos	2,189	2,104	260,572	186,832	9,875,800	2,475,230	490,030	1,989,403
Dickinson	995	936	221,970	198,812	6,243,020	970,260	329,660	1,143,256
Dubuque	2,485	2,442	307,203	259,735	13,931,410	3,336,240	779,250	2,894,809
Emmet	1,156	999	236,580	209,877	6,859,570	379,200	312,020	1,341,214
Fayette	3,261	3,1?9	445,118	356,848	15,210,420	756,290	828,120	3,562,448
Floyd	2,054	1,976	303,843	278,541	11,533,320	2,384,020	614,370	2,201,362
Franklin	1,874	1,815	362,601	326,411	13,873,480	2,025,880	500	2,723,713
Fremont	2,394	2,245	328,958	295,577	12,791,750	1,996,800	420,290	2,646,021
Greene	2,314	2,260	366,125	329,617	13,018,450	2,188,710	584,070	2,819,654
Guthrie	1,783	1,738	316,912	304,421	15,614,830	2,387,520	615,590	2,751,280
Hamilton	2,492	2,?87	357,076	304,646	11,201,840	2,025,720	512,750	3,046,133
Hancock	2,245	2,195	364,042	328,308	13,245,110	2,384,880	585,720	2,704,918
Hardin	1,703	1,660	349,342	3?2,088	11,367,060	1,735,180	565,060	2,063,541
Harrison	2,294	2,245	351,046	305,871	13,272,250	2,471,260	604,990	1,852,577
Henry	3,294	3,003	422,749	322,303	12,580,850	2,481,820	655,470	3,374,820
Howard	1,708	1,671	271,588	215,464	10,728,740	2,506,750	461,980	2,372,?28
Humboldt	1,478	1,438	291,263	257,938	9,?00,850	1,971,910	507,630	1,987,949
Ida	1,493	1,460	274,613	258,1?6	10,101,640	1,746,790	468,160	1,974,374
Iowa	2,454	1,318	270,415	260,556	10,740,830	1,933,970	538,590	2,597,118
Jackson	2,637	2,574	388,779	312,378	11,905,350	2,828,300	616,280	3,463,023
Jasper	3,320	2,196	394,420	271,742	18,995,090	3,067,650	656,930	3,101,633
Jefferson	2,206	2,135	464,105	425,393	9,042,520	3,344,060	778,600	4,447,620
Johnson	2,712	2,661	288,189	211,089	15,328,830	2,247,510	445,610	2,247,468
Jones	2,373	2,319	385,770	319,284	14,761,750	3,789,670	748,320	3,693,848
Keokuk	2,927	2,839	354,699	289,431	13,550,100	3,081,6?0	598,930	3,484,931
Kossuth	2,807	2,731	361,544	300,975	17,923,910	2,724,690	664,590	3,340,985
Lee	2,549	2,450	537,147	539,818	9,539,660	2,880,460	947,420	3,289,751
Linn	3,567	3,453	312,852	216,794	19,207,170	2,441,880	453,130	1,986,872
Louisa	1,619	1,580	482,888	351,998	8,812,240	4,254,110	819,790	1,848,881
Lucas	1,892	1,817	237,872	182,032	7,296,300	1,770,590	352,660	1,791,864
Lyon	1,619	1,518	263,674	198,724	11,590,090	1,318,340	334,550	2,127,340
Madison	2,600	2,505	354,218	271,717	11,373,450	2,206,850	517,980	3,325,282

Mahaska	3,320,208	683,130	8,073,970	14,835,900	307,823	353,250	3,082	3,202
Marion	3,122,870	460,680	2,104,720	12,043,240	292,560	351,163	2,729	914
Marshall	3,132,011	700,740	993,000	15,403,970	334,372	360,232	2,334	2,400
Mills	2,‘83,799	441,020	2,083,310	11,492,560	241,455	272,815	1,851	2,016
Mitchell	2,083,5‘4	550,550	2,181,900	12,321,630	257,107	288,600	1,665	1,718
M...	2,977,524	566,500	1,851,220	12,084,550	305,664	386,780	2,374	2,491
Monroe	1,839,749	384,850	1,363,820	7,758,140	1.1,110	262,296	1,883	1,987
...mery	2,799,733	470,850	1,976,010	12,045,490	252,009	272,067	1,883	1,940
Muscatine	2,197,576	492,710	2,604,270	11,342,880	219,652	284,121	1,909	1,976
O'Brien	2,618,240	633,950	2,171,510	13,754,540	343,008	390,025	1,791	1,815
...ola	1,096,678	400,770	1,123,000	8,011,380	230,099	246,875	1,047	1,088
Page	3,446,301	579,370	60,300	14,902,640	311,445	385,132	2,649	2,643
Palo Alto	1,982,055	442,310	1,421,810	19,372,930	326,854	342,509	1,661	1,661
Plymouth	3,425,044	877,200	1,425,490	19,338,570	439,765	541,907	2,642	2,643
Pocahontas	2,653,0.5	589,880	2,246,070	11,938,110	344,243	365,455	1,938	2,005
Polk	35,246	689,040	3,272,560	18,799,790	326,789	370,252	3,023	3,171
...ate	5,414,155	1,0.7,670	4,440,710	24,223,790	523,790	599,930	3,954	4,289
Poweshiek	3,998,124	682,730	2,824,640	14,983,600	338,773	366,620	2,245	2,322
Ringgold	3,215,154	414,870	1,683,320	9,877,970	295,581	340,111	2,249	2,326
Sac	2,189,585	633,120	2,590,680	13,892,900	354,151	364,232	1,962	1,999
Scott	2,489,635	750,200	3,973,940	14,987,980	354,739	278,945	2,307	2,347
Shelby	3,626,677	661,610	2,418,480	13,813,760	350,733	371,873	2,285	2,387
Sioux	3,094,98	757,980	2,675,470	18,553,110	452,031	476,621	2,322	2,451
...ry	?,839,454	653,280	2,627,300	15,780,830	329,866	356,654	2,326	2,436
...or	3,895,081	802,290	2,070,700	18,403,280	3.1,068	438,596	2,632	2,725
Union	3,244,361	448,500	1,593,830	18,381,040	294,010	935,002	2,487	2,581
Van Buren	2,517,181	395,850	2,052,030	8,622,540	212,705	268,513	1,742	1,823
W...	2,280,911	414,380	1,965,530	8,079,130	210,723	300,111	2,192	2,242
Warren	2,141,102	404,310	1,951,710	9,282,280	205,849	262,459	2,237	2,311
W...	3,306,985	468,390	2,932,440	11,951,710	287,010	283,783	2,833	2,923
Wayne	3,348,190	617,770	1,891,240	14,662,740	293,219	344,695	2,404	2,511
Webster	2,732,306	462,590	2,643,920	9,826,640	298,910	332,7.2	2,189	2,564
Winnebago	2,733,918	758,620	1,294,890	15,556,930	360,558	429,975	?,?70	1,512
Winneshiek	1,397,096	367,910	3,623,140	7,643,020	207,969	239,085	1,470	2,960
...y	2,941,0.6	731,980	2,878,120	16,297,170	338,358	423,227	2,902	8,231
W...	1,703,887	809,110	1,662,570	8,9.9,130	443,681	522,737	3,073	1,485
Wright	1,472,731	436,570	2,048,830	13,221,370	233,292	249,081	1,452	1,878
Sac and Fox Reservation	2,521,948	613,460	4,310	31,450	390,951	366,371	1,818	
	7,540	8,380			789	881	18	28

NUMBER AND AVERAGE AREA OF FARMS, SUMMARY—1850 TO 1900—AN

SUMMARY 1850 T

	TOTAL NUMBER OF FARMS.						AVERAGE AREA OF FARMS IN ACRES.						
1900.	1900.[1]	1890.[2]	1880.[2]	1870.[2]	1860.	1850.	1900.	1900.[1]	1890.[2]	1880.[3]	1870.[2]	1860.	1850.
228,622	227,723	201,903	185,351	116,292	61,163	14,805	151.2	151.8	151.0	133.5	133.6		

[1] Not including farms with an area under three acres, which reported a gross income of less thai $500.00 in 1889.

[2] Not including farms with an area under three acres, which reported the sale of products of les than $500 00 in the census year.

VALUE AND AVERAGE VALUE OF FARM-LAND WITH IMPROVE-

IN

			TOTAL VALUE.			
1900.	1890.	1880.	1870.[1]	1870[2]	1860.	1850.
1,497,554,790	857,581,022	567,430,227	392,662,441	314,129,953	119,899,547	16,657,567

[1] Currency values, as reported by enumerators.

[2] Values in gold, one-fifth less than currency values.

NUMBER OF FARMS OF SPECIFIED TENURES, WITH PERCENTAGES, 1900 IN IOWA.

ARMS OPERATED BY OWNERS.			FARMS OPERATED BY CASH TENANTS.			FARMS OPERATED BY SHARE T'N'T'S.			PERCENT OF FARMS OPERATED BY—								
									OWNERS.			CASH TENANTS.			SHARE TENANTS.		
1900.	1890.	1880.	1900.	1890.	1880	1900.	1890.	1880.	1900.	1890.	1880.	1900.	1890.	1880.	1900.	1890.	1880.
35,234	31,780	35,753	65.1	71.9	76.2	19.5	12.4	4.5	15 4	15.7	19.3						

MENTS INCLUDING BUILDINGS, SUMMARY 1850 TO 1900 IOWA.

AVECAGE VALUE PER FARM.							AVERAGE VALUE ACRE OF FARM LAND.						
1900.	1890.	1880.	1870.	1860.	1860.	1850.	1900.	1890.	1880.	1870.	1870.	1860.	1850.
6,550	4,247	3,061	3,377	2,701	1,960	1,125	43.31	28.13	22.92	25 26	20.21	11.91	6.09

NUMBER OF FARMS OF SPECIFIED AREAS IN ACRES, SUMMARY 1880 TO 1900, IN IOWA.

	UNDER 3.[1]			UNDER 10.			10 AND UNDER 20.			20 AND UNDER 50.			50 AND UNDER 100.			100 AND UNDER 500.			500 AND UNDER 100.			1000 AND OVER.		
	1900.[2]	1900.[3]	1880.[4]	1900.[2]	1900.[3]	1900.[4]	1880.[4]	1900.	1890.	1880.	1900.	1890.	1880.	1900.	1890.	1880.	1900.[5]	1890.	1880.	1900.	1890.	1880.		
	975	76	122	5,731	4,882	2,921	2,185	5,917	3,280	3,334	27,475	18,418	23,488	49,605	53,345	58,519	142,676	121,003	95,169	2,818	3,158	2,298	340	428	364

[1] Not separately reported in 1890, but included with farms under ten acres.

[2] Including all farms of less than three acres that continuously require the labor of one individual.

[3] Including only those that reported a gross income of $500.00 or over in 1899.

[4] Including only those that reported the sale of products of $500 or over in the census year.

[5] Reported in 1900 under three heads, 100 under 174, 175 and 259, and 260 and under 499.

INDEX.

---

(755)

PART III. REPORT OF IOWA WEATHER AND GROP SERVICE.

PART IV. IOWA STATE COLLEGE OF AGRICULTURE AND MECHANIC ARTS.

PART V. IOWA IMPROVED STOCK BREEDERS' ASSOCIATION.

PART VI. FARM CROPS AND LIVE STOCK.

A—THE SILO.

PART VII. PROCEEDINGS OF THE IOWA SWINE BREEDERS' ASSOCIATION.

PART VIII. EXTRACTS FROM THE REPORT OF THE STATE DAIRY COMMISSIONER.

PART IX. TWENTY-SIXTH ANNUAL REPORT OF THE IOWA STATE DAIRY ASSOCIATION.

PART X. PROCEEDINGS OF THE IOWA PARK AND FORESTRY ASSOCIATION.

49

PART XI. SOME PAPERS READ BEFORE FARMERS' INSTITUTES IN IOWA.

PART XIII. FARM, CROP AND LIVE STOCK STATISTICS.

CPSIA information can be obtained
at www.ICGtesting.com
Printed in the USA
BVHW08*1150170918
527708BV00009B/293/P